A History of Money
From Ancient Times to the Present Day

A History of Money

From Ancient Times to the Present Day

GLYN DAVIES

Published in co-operation with
Julian Hodge Bank Limited

UNIVERSITY OF WALES PRESS
CARDIFF
1994

© Glyn Davies, 1994

First edition, 1994
Reprinted, 1995
Paperback edition, with revisions and Postcript, 1996

British Library Cataloguing in Publication Data

A catalogue record for this book is available from the British Library

ISBN 0-7083-1351-5

Cover design by Design Principle, Cardiff

Cover images: Manilla, tally sticks, dollar and whale's tooth courtesy of Design Principle; 'Owl' of Athens and cowrie shell with permission of the Ancient Art and Architecture Collection; Tribute Penny with permission of B. Wilson/Ancient Art and Architecture Collection; Barclaycard with permission of Barclays Bank plc; commemorative two pound coin to celebrate three hundred years of the Bank of England with permission of the Royal Mint; five million mark banknote from the period of high inflation in Germany with permission of Mary Evans Picture Library.

Typeset in Wales at the University of Wales Press, Cardiff
Printed and bound in England by Bookcraft, Midsomer Norton, Avon

Foreword

From earliest times money in some form or another has been central to organized living. Increasingly it shapes foreign and economic policies of all governments. It is synonymous with power and it shapes history in every generation.

Professor Glyn Davies, Economic Adviser to the Julian Hodge Bank Ltd, and sometime Chief Economic Adviser to the Secretary of State for Wales, and then to the Bank of Wales, is an ideal person to write the history of money itself. In his fifteen years as Sir Julian Hodge Professor of Banking and Finance at the University of Wales Institute of Science and Technology, Glyn Davies earned worldwide recognition as one of the United Kingdom's front line economists. Both the CBI and various Select Committees of the House of Commons have sought his help.

For over two decades there has been a unique partnership between Wales's financial wizard, Sir Julian Hodge, and Professor Glyn Davies. The genius of Sir Julian is matched by his intuitive caution in matters financial: it is therefore a high tribute to Professor Glyn Davies that for two decades he has been Sir Julian Hodge's trusted Economic Adviser.

This book is a masterpiece of scholarly research which economists and bankers will find invaluable. Professor Glyn Davies enjoys a rare gift in being able to present the most complicated issues in clear and simple terms.

I declare my personal interest in this book because I have proved the quality of Professor Glyn's work both when I served as Secretary of State for Wales and when I was Chairman of the Bank of Wales.

George Tonypandy
The Right Honourable Viscount Tonypandy PC, DCL,
House of Lords, Westminster
1 March 1994

Contents

Acknowledgements

First and foremost I wish to thank Sir Julian Hodge for his unfailing support and generous encouragement. For a quarter of a century I have been fortunate in being able to observe at close quarters Sir Julian's genius for making money – and for making money do good. As an economist I have particularly enjoyed the opportunities provided by such experiences to analyse how far abstract theories stand up in comparison with the practical tests of the market place.

To Viscount Tonypandy I extend my heartfelt gratitude for his typically kind and prompt response in writing the Foreword in his unique, incisive style.

The academic sources on which I have drawn are widely spread over time and space and include, for the more recent decades, colleagues and former students. Only to a small degree can such debts be indicated in the bibliography. To the many librarians who have made essential material easily and pleasantly available to me I am glad to record my thanks, especially to Ken Roberts of the University of Wales Library, Cardiff and to my eldest son Roy Davies of Exeter University Library.

The staff of the Royal Mint and scores of practising bankers, building society executives, accountants and civil servants who have generously given of their time to discuss matters of financial interest similarly deserve my gratitude, not least Mr Eric Hammonds of Julian Hodge Bank Ltd who was most helpful when the manuscript was in its final stages preparatory to publication.

My warm thanks go to Ned Thomas, Director of the University of Wales Press, and to his staff, including especially the Senior Editor, Susan Jenkins, who have worked most expeditiously and with commendable skill and zeal on my behalf. Despite such enthusiastic professional assistance any errors remaining are my own.

Finally, the long-suffering and devoted support of my wife, Anna Margrethe, is beyond praise.

Preface to the First Edition

In our technological age too many agree with Henry Ford's blunt dictum that history is bunk, though he was far from thinking that money was bunk. This ambivalent attitude remains prevalent today in the general approach to economic and financial studies, so that whereas there is a superabundance of books on present-day monetary and financial problems, politics and theories, it is my contention first that monetary histories are far too scarce and secondly that those which do exist tend in the main to be far too narrow in scope or period.

Because of the difficulties of conducting 'experiments' in the ordinary business of economic life, at the centre of which is money, it is most fortunate that history not only generously provides us with a potentially plentiful proxy laboratory, a guidebook of more or less relevant alternatives, but also enables us to satisfy a natural curiosity about the key role played by money, one of the oldest and most widespread of human institutions. Around the next corner there may be lying in wait apparently quite novel monetary problems which in all probability bear a basic similarity to those that have already been tackled with varying degrees of success or failure in other times and places. Yet despite the antiquity and ubiquity of money its proper management and control have eluded the rulers of most modern states partly because they have ignored the wide-ranging lessons of the past or have taken too blinkered and narrow a view of money.

Economists, and especially monetarists, tend to overestimate the purely economic, narrow and technical functions of money and have placed insufficient emphasis on its wider social, institutional and psychological aspects. However, as is shown in this study, money originated very largely from non-economic causes: from tribute as well as from trade, from blood-money and bride-money as well as from barter, from ceremonial and religious rites as well as from commerce, from ostentatious ornamentation as well as from acting as the common drudge between economic men. Even in modern circumstances money still yields powerfully important psychic returns (such as an individual's social rank and standing or a nation's position in the GNP league table), while the eagerness to save or to spend is a fickle, moody, contagious, psychological characteristic, not fully captured in the economist's statistics on velocity of circulation. Thus money, more than ever in our monetarist era, needs to be widely interpreted to include discussion not only of currency and banking, but also savings banks, building societies, hire purchase finance companies and the fiscal framework on those not infrequent occasions when fiscal policy conflicts with or complements the operation of monetary policy. In this regard it is demonstrated that even in medieval and earlier periods these wider aspects were of considerably greater importance than is conventionally believed. There are therefore many advantages which can only be obtained by tracing monetary and financial history with a broad brush over the whole period of its long and convoluted development, where primitive and modern moneys have overlapped for centuries and where the logical and chronological progressions have rarely followed strictly parallel paths.

Anyone who attempts to cover such a wide range inevitably lays him- or herself open to criticisms similar to those inescapably faced by map-makers in attempting to portray the whole or a major part of the globe on a flat surface. If the directions are right the sizes of the various countries become grossly disproportional; attempts at equal areas beget other distortions in shape or direction; while the currently politically correct Peters projection looks like nothing on earth. Similar criticisms relate to the selection of historical material from the vast mass currently available. What some experts would regard as vitally important features may have been glossed over or omitted, while other aspects which they might consider trivial have been given undue attention. Selection from such a vast menu is bound to be arbitrary, depending on the personal taste of the author. Furthermore any claim to complete neutrality and unbiased objectivity is similarly bound to be untenable. Every list of sins of commission or omission would vary, especially among economists . . . six economists, at least half a dozen opinions.

A further point: where one is dealing with a narrower, more manageable period or area it is all the more possible (and highly fashionable) to construct a sophisticated model or theory closely fitting the subject under scrutiny. Conversely, only the most loose-fitting (but none the less useful) garment could possibly cover the variety of models comprising such a wide range as is examined in this book. One such simple theory does, however, emerge: the quality–quantity pendulum; although it must be borne in mind that its repetitional swings become discernible only where a long period of time is taken into consideration.

The first three chapters look at primitive and ancient money and at the origins of coined money and its development up to the fall of Rome. The next two chapters look at the unique disappearance and re-emergence of coined money in medieval Britain, followed by the great expansion of trade and finance in Britain and Europe from around 1485 to 1650. We then trace the development of British money and banking to its dominant position in the gold standard system that eventually broke down in the period from 1914 to 1931, thereafter analysing the monetary controversies during the rest of the twentieth century including the implications of entry into the European Monetary System. The monetary development of the USA (in chapter 9) provides a considerable contrast, moving from wampum to world power in less that two centuries. Only a few of the salient features of money and banking in parts of continental Europe and Japan are sketched in chapter 10 but with some emphasis being given to the closer relationships seen in those countries between financial and industrial companies and the consequences that this might have for a faster rate of economic growth than has occurred elsewhere. Chapter 11 deals with pre- and post-colonial monetary systems, the rise of indigenous banking in the Third World and the vast problems of international indebtedness. Chapter 12 summarizes progress towards a possible universal free market in money.

Henry Ford, the father of mass production, unconsciously gave the world a powerful push towards the goal of global finance where eventually the colour of everyone's money will be the same. Fortunately, that blissful day has not quite yet dawned.

Preface to the Paperback Edition

The demand for the original hardback and its reprint has been such as to justify publishing a paperback version. This new edition enables me to draw attention in the Postscript to a few of the more significant developments since the book was first published in 1994 and to comment briefly on one or two earlier matters where recent events tempt a backward glance.

I am again greatly indebted to the University of Wales Press, especially to Richard Houdmont, Commercial Manager, and Liz Powell, Editor, for their enthusiastic assistance.

February 1996

1

The Nature and Origins of Money and Barter

The importance of money

Perhaps the most common claim with regard to the importance of money in our everyday life is the morally neutral if comically exaggerated claim that 'money makes the world go round'. Equally exaggerated but showing a deeper insight is the biblical warning that 'the love of money is the root of all evil', neatly transformed by George Bernard Shaw into the fear that it is rather the lack of money which is the root of all evil. However, whether it is the love or conversely the lack of money which is potentially sinful, the purpose of the statement in either case is to underline the overwhelming personal and moral significance of money to society in a way that gives a broader and deeper insight into its importance than simply stressing its basically economic aspects, as when we say that 'money makes the world go round'. Consequently whether we are speaking of money in simple, so-called primitive communities or in much more advanced, complex and sophisticated societies, it is not enough merely to examine the narrow economic aspects of money in order to grasp its true meaning. To analyse the significance of money it must be broadly studied in the context of the particular society concerned. It is a matter for the heart as well as for the head: feelings are reasons, too.

Money has always been associated in varying degrees of closeness with religion, partly interpreted in modern times as the psychology of habits and attitudes, hopes, fears and expectations. Thus the taboos which circumscribe spending in primitive societies are basically not unlike the stock market bears which similarly reduce expenditures through changing subjective assessments of values and incomes, so that the true interpretation of what money means to people requires the sympathetic understanding of the less obvious motivations as much as, if not more than, the narrow abstract calculations of the computer. To concentrate attention narrowly on 'the pound in your pocket' is to devalue the all-pervading significance of money.

Personal attitudes to money vary from the disdain of a small minority to the total preoccupation of a similarly small minority at the other extreme. The first group paradoxically includes a few of the very rich and of the very poor. Sectors of both are unconsciously united in belittling its significance: the rich man either because he delegates such mundane matters to his servants or because the fruits of compound interest exceed his appetite, however large; the poor man because he makes a virtue out of his dire necessity and learns to live as best he can with the very little money that comes his way, so that his practical realism makes his enforced self-denial appear almost saintly. He limits his ambition to his purse, present and future, so that his accepted way of life limits his demand for money rather than, as with most of us, the other way round. At the other extreme, preoccupation with money becomes an end in itself rather than the means of achieving other goals in life.

Virtue and poverty, however, are not necessarily any more closely related than are riches and immorality. Thus Boswell quotes Samuel Johnson:

> When I was a very poor fellow I was a great arguer for the advantages of poverty . . . but in a civilised society personal merit will not serve you so much as money will. Sir, you may make the experiment. Go into the street, and give one man a lecture on morality, and another a shilling, and see which will respect you most . . . Ceteris paribus, he who is rich in a civilised society, must be happier than he who is poor. (Boswell 1791, 52–3)

Johnson's commonsense approach to the human significance of money not only rings as true today as it did two centuries ago, but may be mirrored in the statements and actions of much earlier civilizations.

The minority who find it possible to exhibit a Spartan disdain for money has always been exceptionally small and in modern times has declined to negligible proportions, since the very few people concerned are surrounded by the vast majority for whom money plays a role of growing importance. Even those who as individuals might choose to belittle money find themselves constrained at the very least to take into account the habits, views and attitudes of everyone else. In short, no free man can afford the luxury of ignoring money, a universal fact which explains why Spartan arrogance was achieved at the cost of an iron discipline that contrasted with the freedom of citizens of other states more liberal with money. This underlying principle of freedom of choice which is conferred on those with money became explicitly part of the strong foundations of classical economic theory in the nineteenth century, expounded most clearly in the works of Alfred Marshall, as 'the sovereignty of the consumer', a concept which despite all the qualifications which modify it today, nevertheless still exerts its considerable force through the mechanism of money.

Sovereignty of monetary policy

This essential linkage between money, free consumer choice and political liberty is the central and powerful theme of Milton Friedman's brand of monetarism consistently proclaimed for at least two decades, from his *Capitalism and Freedom* (1962) to what he has called his 'personal statement', *Free to Choose*, published in 1980. An even longer crusade championing the essential liberalism of money-based allocative systems was waged by Friedrich Hayek, from his *Road to Serfdom* in 1944 to his *Economic Freedom* of 1991.

Yet for a generation before Friedman, the eminent Cambridge economist Joan Robinson called into question the conventional basis of consumer sovereignty in her pioneering work on *Imperfect Competition* (1933). Indeed she doubted 'the validity of the whole supply-and-demand-curve analysis' (p.327). Many years later, with perhaps too humble and pessimistic an assessment of the tremendous influence of her writing, she felt forced to lament: 'All this had no effect. Perfect competition, supply and demand, consumer's sovereignty and marginal products still reign supreme in orthodox teaching. Let us hope that a new generation of students, after forty years, will find in this book what I intended to mean by it' (1963, xi).

By the mid-1970s it became obvious that, as in the inter-war period, the fundamental beliefs of economic theory were again being challenged, and nowhere was this probing deeper or more urgent than with regard to monetary economics. Mass unemployment had pushed Keynes towards a general theory which, when widely accepted, helped to bring full employment, surely the richest reward that can ever be laid to the credit (if admittedly only in part) of the economist's theorizing. But persistent inflation posed questions which Keynesians failed to answer satisfactorily, while the return of mass unemployment combined with still higher inflation finally destroyed the Keynesian consensus, and allowed the monetarists to capture the minds of our political masters.

Nevertheless, Joan Robinson's view is quite true in that the modifications of classical value theory (now being painfully and patchily refurbished by the New Classical School) were as nothing compared with the surging revolutions in monetary theories which have occurred since the 1930s, mainly taking the form of a forty years' war between Keynesians and monetarists, until the latter ultimately achieved control over practical policies in much of the western world by the end of the 1970s, despite the continuing strong dissent of the now conventional Keynesian economists. Whereas the man in the street knows nothing of the economics of imperfect competition or the theory of contestable markets, he feels himself equipped and more than willing to take sides in the great monetarist debates of the day. Without being dogmatic about this, it is unlikely that in any previous age monetary affairs and monetary theories have ever captured so vast an army of debaters, professional and amateur, as exists in today's perplexing world of uncertainty, inflation, unemployment, stagnation and recession. Can the control of money, one wonders, be the sovereign remedy for all these ills?

Never before has monetary policy openly and avowedly occupied so central a role in government policy as from the 1980s with the 'Thatcherite experiment' in Britain and the 'Reaganomics' of the United States. Needless to say, if monetary policy finally reigns supreme in the two countries of the world which have together dominated economic theory and international trade and finance over the last two centuries this fact is bound to have an enormous influence on current financial thought and practice throughout the world. If money is now of such preponderant importance in the North it cannot fail also to exert its powerful sway over the dependent economies and 'independent' central banks of the developing countries of the South. This tendency is of course strongly reinforced by the growing burden of sovereign debt, i.e. debts mainly owed or guaranteed by governments and government agencies in countries like Mexico, Brazil, Argentina, Poland, Romania, Nigeria, India and South Korea, and to private and public banks and agencies in the West. The unprecedented scale of this long-term debt, coupled with the vast short-term flows of petro-dollars and Euro-currencies, is in part reflection and in part cause of the worldwide inflationary pressures, again of unprecedented degree, which have raised public concern about the subject of money to its present pinnacle. There are far more people using much more money, interdependently involved in a greater complex of debts and credits than ever before in human history. However, despite man's growing mastery of science and technology, he has so far been unable to master money, at any rate with any acceptable degree of success, and to the extent that he has succeeded, the irrecoverable costs in terms of mass unemployment and lost output would seem to outweigh the benefits.

If money were merely a tangible technical device so that its supply could be closely defined and clearly delimited, then the problem of how to master and control it would easily be amenable to man's highly developed technical ingenuity. In the same way, if inflation had simply a single cause – government – and money supply came simply from the same single source, then mechanistic controls might well work. However, although government is powerful on both sides of the equation it is only one among many complex factors. Among these neglected factors, according to H. C. Lindgren, in a rare book on the psychology of money, 'the psychological factor that continually eludes the analysts and planners is the mood of the public' (1980, 54).

Furthermore, technology in solving technical problems often creates yet more intractable social and psychological problems, which is why, according to Dr Bronowski, 'there has been a deep change in the temper of science in the last twenty years: the focus of attention has shifted from the physical to the life sciences' and 'as a result science is drawn more and more to the study of individuality' (Bronowski 1973). It is ironic that just when physical scientists are seeing the value of a more humanistic approach, economics, and particularly monetary economics, has become less so by attempting to become more 'scientific', mechanistic and measurable.

Unprecedented inflation of population

There is an additional factor, 'real' as opposed to 'financial', which helps to explain the sustained strength of worldwide inflationary forces and yet remains unmentioned in most modern works on money and inflation, viz. the pressure of a rapidly expanding world population on finite resources – virtually a silent explosion so far as monetarist literature is concerned. Thus nowhere in Friedman's powerful, popular and influential book *Free to Choose* is there even any mention of the population problem, nor the slightest hint that the inflation on which he is acknowledged to be the world's greatest expert might in any way be caused by the rapidly rising potential and real demands of the thousands of millions born into the world since he began his researches. Further treatment of these matters must await their appropriate place in later chapters, but since the size and distribution of this tremendous growth of population is crucial to an understanding of why the study of money is currently of unprecedented importance, a few introductory comments appear to be essential. One neglected reason why monetary policy may appear to be so attractively powerful in the richer North and West is precisely because there population pressures are least. In contrast, whereas monetary policy is of special importance in the poor developing countries of the South and East, its scope and powers are considerably reduced because this is where population pressures are greatest. Too many people are chasing too few goods.

The currently fashionable monetarist explanations of inflation fail, then, to take into account the rapid rise in real pressure on resources stemming from the population explosion. This forces communities to react by creating, by means of various devices easily learned from the West, the moneys required to help to accommodate such pressures. The enormous size of these increases since 1945 is such that millions of relatively rich have added their effective demand to the frustrated potential demands of the thousands of millions more who have remained abysmally poor. The trend of demand increases year by year causing relatively greater scarcities of primary resources and also of manufactured goods and services such as consumer durables, health care and education. The vastly increased competition for such goods and services helps to give an upward twist to the inflationary spiral despite the periodic changes in the terms of trade for certain primary products. World population has ultimately increased, in some ways as Malthus predicted nearly two hundred years ago, at a pace exceeding productivity, since productivity is at or near its lowest in those areas where population growth is at or near its greatest.

It took man a million years or so, until about 1825, to reach a total population of 1,000 million, but only about one hundred years to add another 1,000 million and only some fifty years, from 1925 to 1975 to double that total to 4,000 million, by which time the population was already increasing by 75 million annually. In the generation from 1975 to the year 2000, according to a consensus of opinion among experts in Britain, USA and the United Nations Organization, world population will increase by 55 per cent or 2,261 million to a total of 6,351 million and will then be increasing by around 100 million annually, so that, if currently projected growth rates continue, world population may reach 10,000 million by around the year 2030, well within the life expectancy of persons now reaching adult years in the western world.

The whole world has now broken the link with commodity money which once acted as a brake on inflation. The less developed countries are even less able than the industrialized countries to avoid the mismanagement of money, so that in their attempts to create monetary claims, including borrowing, to compete for resources which are tending to grow ever scarcer relatively to demand, runaway inflation with rates of up to 100 per cent or more per annum are not uncommon. Added to these unprecedented monetary problems over 90 per cent of the projected increase in population to the end of the century will take place in these poor and less developed countries, which by their very nature find it more difficult than their richer, industrialized neighbours to stem the full tide of inflation. Intensifying this trend is the increasing urbanization of previously predominantly rural communities, with the greater emphasis on money incomes that is the inevitable concomitant of such migration. A few telling examples must suffice, taking the population in 1960 and the projections for the year 2000 in parenthesis based on UN estimates and medium projections: Calcutta 5.5 m (19.7 m); Mexico City 4.9 m (31.6 m); Bombay 4.1 m (19.1 m); Cairo 3.7 m (16.4 m); Jakarta 2.7 m (16.9 m); Seoul 2.4 m (18.7 m); Delhi 2.3 m (13.2 m); Manila 2.2 m (12.7 m); Tehran 1.9 m (13.8 m), and Karachi 1.8 m (15.9 m). These ten towns alone will increase from a total of 31.5 m to 178 m. (*Global 2000* 1982, 242). This gives a new twist to William Cowper's claim: 'God made the country and man made the town.'

The young age composition of such vastly expanding populations increases mobility, the acceptance of change and the political pressures for change, including the desire to have at least some share in the rising standards of living of the richer countries, of which, through rapidly improved communications, they are becoming increasingly conscious. This international extension of the 'Duesenberry effect' (Duesenberry 1967), viz. that the patterns of consumption of the next highest social class are deemed most desirable, again helps to create increased expenditure pressures throughout the developing world and particularly in those populous pockets of relatively rich areas which exist almost cheek by jowl among the urban poor. Duesenberry also makes the important point that 'the larger the rate of growth of population the larger the average propensity to consume' (Duesenberry 1958, 265). Confronted with the magnitude of the problem of world poverty, western man may feel uncomfortable, individually helpless and perplexed by the merits of 'aid versus trade'. There is an imbalance in awareness as between North and South, and whereas it would be a caricature to say 'They ask for bread, and we give them . . . *Dallas*', nevertheless the three-quarters of the world's people in the hungry south are increasingly aware of how the other quarter lives. This caricature is not unlike Picasso's definition of art as a 'lie which helps us to see the truth'. Be that as it may, the expenditure patterns of society throughout the world are becoming westernized, breaking down indigenous social patterns and so leading to modern habits which, unfortunately, tend to encourage inflationary monetary systems. Thus, the worldwide expansion of money has been partly caused by, but has far exceeded, the vast expansion of population.

Although the question of whether the world is approaching the limits of growth may cause a growing number of fortunate men in modern affluent societies to cast doubt on the need for greater economic growth, nevertheless there is no question that economic growth affords the only means whereby approximately half the world's population – its women – can escape from the daily drudgery that has brutalized life for millions throughout time. The appalling persistence of poverty and what it means for families and especially mothers is brought out (insofar as these matters can ever meaningly be described in words) by the Brandt Report in 1980 which gives the estimate of the United Nations Children's Fund that in 1978 more than twelve million children under five years of age died of hunger (Brandt 1980, 16). UNICEF's estimate for 1979, the 'Year of the Child', rose to seventeen million. It may be an eminently debatable point as to whether man without money is like Hobbes's famous picture of man without government: 'No arts; no letters; no society; and which is worst of all, continual fear and danger of violent death; and the life of man, solitary, poor, nasty, brutish, and short' (Hobbes 1651, chapter 13). However, there can be no such doubt as to the direct ameliorative influence of economic growth on the standard of living of the female half of the human race, growing numbers of whom, at long last, are beginning to enjoy a diffusion of welfare that helps to raise, patchily and hesitatingly, the quality of family life over a large part of the world.

Increasingly wealth, i.e. additions to capital stock, mostly takes place through a rise in incomes and expenditures, which necessarily leads to an increased use of money. Therefore an increasing proportion as well as an increasing amount of trading in the rapidly growing less developed countries of the world is now based on abstract developments of money, and far less than formerly on barter and more primitive forms of money. Thus the individual finds release from irksome restraint and is able to exercise greater freedom of choice as a necessary corollary of the monetization of the economies of the less developed countries. In the aggregate, however, hundreds of millions of people, though still poor, have moved out of what were still largely subsistence economies into market economies where money naturally plays a bigger role. The speed of political, social, economic and financial change (partly but by no means entirely because of technological development) is telescoping what were previously secular trends in the West into mere decades. This is particularly so with regard to the dramatic change from primitive to modern money. Before turning to look at barter and what is still for us today the important but generally neglected subject of primitive moneys we may therefore conclude our preliminary assessment of the importance of modern money by stating that there are good reasons for believing that money means much more today to many more people throughout the world than it has ever meant before in human history.

Barter: as old as the hills

The history of barter is as old, indeed in some respects very much older, than the recorded history of man himself. The direct exchange of services and resources for mutual advantage is intrinsic to the symbiotic relationships between plants, insects and animals, so that it should not be surprising that barter in some form or other is as old as man himself. What at first sight is perhaps more surprising is that such a primeval form of direct exchange should persist right up to the present day and still show itself vigorously, if exceptionally, in so many guises particularly in large-scale international deals between the eastern bloc and the West. However, barter is crudely robust and adaptable, characteristics which help to explain both its longevity and its ubiquity. Thus when the inherent advantages of barter in certain circumstances are carefully considered, then its coexistence with more advanced and convenient forms of exchange is more easily appreciated and should occasion no surprise. Foremost among these advantages is the concrete reality of such exchanges: no one parts with value in return for mere paper or token promises, but rather only in due return for worthwhile goods or services. In an inflationary age where international indexing and the legal enforcement of contracts are either in their infancy or of very shaky construction, this primary advantage of barter may more than compensate for its cumbersome awkwardness.

Throughout by far the greater part of man's development, barter necessarily constituted the sole means of exchanging goods and services. It follows from this that the historical development of money and finance from relatively ancient times onwards – the substance of our study – overlaps only to a small degree the study of barter as a whole. Consequently we know more about barter's complementary coexistence with money than we do about barter in those long, dark, moneyless ages of prehistory, and thus we tend to derive our knowledge of barter from the remaining shrinking moneyless communities of more modern times. It is principally from these latter backward communities rather than from the mainstream of human progress that most accounts of barter have been taken to provide the basic examples typically occurring in modern textbooks on money. Little wonder then that these have tended not only to overstress the disadvantages of barter but have also tended to base the rise of money on the misleadingly narrow and mistaken view of the alleged disadvantages of barter to the exclusion of other factors, most of which were of very much greater importance than the alleged shortcomings of barter. Barter has, undeservedly, been given a bad name in conventional economic writing, and its alleged crudities have been much exaggerated.

As the extent and complexity of trade increased so the various systems of barter naturally grew to accommodate these increasing demands, until the demands of trade exceeded the scope of barter, however improved or complex. One of the more important improvements over the simplest forms of early barter was first the tendency to select one or two particular items in preference to others so that the preferred barter items became partly accepted because of their qualities in acting as media of exchange although, of course, they still could be used for their primary purposes of directly satisfying the wants of the traders concerned. Commodities were chosen as preferred barter items for a number of reasons – some because they were conveniently and easily stored, some because they had high value densities and were easily portable, some because they were more durable (or less perishable). The more of these qualities the preferred item showed, the higher the degree of preference in exchange. Perhaps the most valuable step forward in the barter system was made when established markets were set up at convenient locations. Very often such markets had been established long before the advent of money but were, of course, strengthened and confirmed as money came into greater use – money which in many cases had long come into existence for reasons other than trading. In process of time money was seen to offer considerable advantages over barter and very gradually took over a larger and larger role while the use of barter correspondingly diminished until eventually barter simply re-emerged in special circumstances, usually when the money system, which was less robust than barter, broke down. Such circumstances continue to show themselves from time to time and persist to this day. In some few instances communities appear to have gone straight from barter to modern money. However, in most instances the logical sequence (barter, barter plus primitive money, primitive money, primitive plus modern money, then modern money almost exclusively) has also been the actual path followed, but with occasional reversions to previous systems.

Persistence of gift exchange

One of the more interesting forms of early barter was gift exchange, which within the family partook more of gift than exchange but beyond that, as for example between different tribes was much more in the nature of exchange than of gift. Silent or dumb barter took place where direct and possibly dangerous contact was deliberately avoided by the participants. An amount of a particular commodity would be left in a convenient spot frequented by the other party to the exchange, who would take the goods proffered and leave what they considered a fair equivalent in exchange. If, however, after obvious examination, these were not considered sufficient they would remain untaken until the amount originally offered had been increased. In this way the barter system, despite being silent was nevertheless an effective and competitive form of hard bargaining.

Competitive gift exchange probably reached its most aggressive heights in the ritualized barter ceremonies among North American Indians, whence it is generally known from the Chinook name for the practice, as 'potlatch'. This was far more than merely commercial exchange but was a complex mixture of a wide range of both public and private gatherings, the latter involving initiation into tribal secret societies and the former partaking of a number of cultural activities in which public speaking, drama and elaborate dances were essential features. The potlatch was a sort of masonic rite, eisteddfod, Highland games, religious gathering, dance festival and market fair all rolled into one. The cultural and the commercial interchanges were part of an integrated whole. However it is clear that one of the main purposes of these exchange ceremonies was to validate the social ranking of the leading participants. A person's prestige depended largely on his power to influence others through the impressive size of the gifts offered, and, since the debts carried interest, the 'giver' rose in the eyes of the community to be an envied creditor, indeed a person of considerable standing. So much time and energy, so much rivalry and envy, coupled with a certain amount of understandable drunkenness and, for reasons about to be explained, of wasteful and deliberate destruction also, accompanied these proceedings that the Canadian federal government was eventually forced to ban the custom. It did this first by the Indian Act of 1876, but its ineffectiveness led to further amendments and a comprehensive new enactment some fifty-one years later. Although the potlatch system was fairly widespread over North America and varied from tribe to tribe, the experiences of the Kwakiutl Indians of the coastal regions of British Columbia may be taken as typical. A recently taped autobiography of James Sewid, chief councillor of the largest Kwakiutl village in the 1970s, contains vivid first-hand descriptions of potlatch ceremonies during the period of their final flourishes (Spradley 1972). According to Sewid, awareness of rank dominated his tribal society, and the major institution for assuming, maintaining and increasing social status was the potlatch, of which there were local, regional and tribal varieties in ascending order. After much feasting and many speeches the public donations were ostentatiously distributed. A person would fail to attain any social standing without a really lavish distribution, and in the extreme cases chiefs would demonstrate their wealth and prestige by publicly destroying some of their possessions so as to demonstrate that they had more than they needed. Increasing trade with European immigrants in the 1920s at first considerably raised the material standards of the Kwakiutl and increased the number and wanton waste of the potlatches, so much so that the federal government felt compelled to react strongly.

The Revised Statutes of Canada 1927, clause 140, stipulated that 'Every Indian or other person who engages in any Indian festival, dance or other ceremony of which the giving away or paying or giving back of money, goods or articles of any sort forms a part . . . is guilty of an offence and is liable on summary conviction to imprisonment for a term not exceeding six months and not less than two months.' Sewid himself, as a boy, saw his relatives sent to prison for participating in the proscribed potlatches. In Sewid's experience, these potlatch ceremonies would last for several days, and the competitive presents would include not only such traditional items as clothing, blankets, furs and canoes, but also copper shields and such twentieth-century luxuries as sewing machines, pedal and motor cycles and motor boats. After reaching their high point in the mid-1920s the age-old potlatch ceremonials gradually died away – the combined result of the new legislation, its stronger enforcement and, probably of still greater influence, the cultural penetration of Indian villages by teachers and entrepreneurs. It is rather ironic that by the time the clauses of the 1927 Act prohibiting potlatches were finally repealed in 1951, these age-old ceremonies were already on their last legs and to all intents and purposes ceased to exist by the end of the 1960s. Modern money and European cultures had however taken nearly three centuries to conquer this form of tribal barter in North America.

Having persisted for many hundreds of years this elaborate system of barter, more social than economic, at first easily absorbed the various kinds of money brought in by the European conquerors, but after a final flourish in the inter-war period, rather suddenly slumped.

Unfortunately, in trying to suppress the less desirable aspects of the potlatch, its good features were also weakened. The replacement of one kind of exchange by another, or of one kind of money by another, often has severe and unforeseen social consequences. In the case of a number of Indian tribes the conflict of culture was particularly harsh and the ending of the potlatch removed some of the most powerful work incentives from the younger section of the communities.

One cannot leave the subject of competitive gift exchange without a brief reference to the most celebrated of all such encounters, namely that between the Queen of Sheba and Solomon in or about the year 950 BC. Extravagant ostentation, the attempt to outdo each other in the splendour of the exchanges, and above all, the obligations of reciprocity were just as typical in this celebrated encounter, though at a fittingly princely level, as with the more mundane types of barter in other parts of the world. The social and political overtones were just as inseparably integral parts of the process of commercial exchanges in the case of the Queen of Sheba as with the Kwakiutl Indians, even though it would be harder to imagine a greater contrast in cultures.

Money: barter's disputed paternity

One of the most influential writers on money in the second half of the nineteenth century was William Stanley Jevons (1835–82). His theoretical approach was enriched by five years' practical experience as assayer in the Sydney Mint in Australia at a time when money for most people meant coins above all else. He begins his book on *Money and the Mechanism of Exchange* (1875) by giving two illustrations of the drawbacks of barter, and it was largely his great influence which helped to condition conventional economic thought for a century regarding the inconvenience of barter. He first relates how Mlle Zélie, a French opera singer, in the course of a world tour gave a concert in the Society Islands and for her fee received one-third of the proceeds. Her share consisted of three pigs, twenty-three turkeys, forty-four chickens, five thousand coconuts and considerable quantities of bananas, lemons and oranges. Unfortunately the opera singer could consume only a small part of this total and (instead of declaring the public feast which she might well have done had she been versed in local custom) found it necessary before she left to feed the pigs and poultry with the fruit. Thus a handsome fee which was equivalent to some four thousand pre-1870 francs was wastefully squandered. Jevons's second account concerns the famous naturalist A. R. Wallace who, when on his expeditions in the Malay Archipelago between 1854 and 1862 (during which he originated his celebrated theory of natural selection) though generally surfeited with food, found that in some of the islands where there was no currency mealtimes were preceded by long periods of hard bargaining, and if the commodities bartered by Wallace were not wanted then he and his party simply had to go without their dinner. Jevons's readers, after having vicariously suffered the absurd frustrations of Mlle Zélie and Dr Wallace, were more than willing to accept uncritically, as have generations of economists and their students subsequently, the devastating criticisms which Jevons made of barter, without making sufficient allowance for the fact that those particular barter systems, however well suited for the indigenous uses of that particular society, had not been developed to conduct international trade between the Théâtre Lyrique in Paris and the Society Islanders, nor was it designed to further the no doubt interesting theories of explorers like Wallace. Obviously, whilst one should not take such inappropriate examples as in any way typical, nevertheless they show up in a glaringly strong light, as Jevons intended – even if in an exaggerated and unfair manner – the disadvantages appertaining to barter.

By far the most authoritative writer on barter and primitive moneys in the twentieth century was Dr Paul Einzig, to whose stimulating and comprehensive account of *Primitive Money in its Ethnological, Historical and Economic Aspects* (1966) this writer is greatly indebted, as should be all those who write on these fascinating subjects. Unfortunately most writers on money seem studiously to have avoided Einzig's most valuable and almost unique contribution, possibly because his lucid, readable style belies the quality, erudition and creativity of his work, and possibly also because his sharp attacks on conventional economists' treatment of barter were driven home with unerring aim. As he demonstrates:

> There is an essential difference between the negative approach used by many generations of economists who attributed the origin of money to the intolerable inconvenience of barter that forced the community to adopt a reform, and the positive approach suggested here, according to which the method of exchange was improved upon before the old method became intolerable and before an impelling need for the reforms had arisen . . . The picture drawn by economists about the inconvenience of barter in primitive communities is grossly exaggerated. It would seem that the assumption that money necessarily arose from the realisation of the inconveniences of barter, popular as it is among economists, needs careful re-examination. (Einzig, 1966, 346, 353)

One must not of course overplay the adaptability of barter, otherwise money would never have so largely supplanted it. The most obvious and important drawback of barter is that concerned with the absence of a generalized or common standard of values, i.e. the price systems available with money. Problems of accounting multiply enormously as wealth and the varieties of exchangeable goods increase, so that whereas the accounting problems in simple societies may be surmountable, the foundations of modern society would crumble without money. Admittedly the emergence of a few preferred barter items as steps towards more generalized common measures of value managed to extend the life of barter systems, but by the nature of the accountancy problem, barter on a large scale became computationally impossible once a quite moderate standard of living had been achieved and, despite the growing importance of barter in special circumstances in the last four or five decades, modern societies could not exist without monetary systems. A second inherent disadvantage of barter is that stemming from its very directness, namely the double coincidence of wants required to complete an exchange of goods or services. In pure barter if the owner of an orchard, having a surplus of apples, required boots he would need to find not simply a cobbler but a cobbler who wanted to purchase apples; and even then there remained the problem of determining the 'rate of exchange' as between apples and boots. In the same way for each transaction involving other exchanges, separate and not immediately discernible exchange rates would have to be negotiated for every pair of transactions.

In very simple societies exchanging just a few commodities the absence of a common standard of values is no great problem. Thus trading in three commodities gives rise at any one time to only three exchange rates and four commodities to six possible rates. But five commodities require ten exchange rates, six require fifteen and ten require forty-five. Obviously the drawbacks of barter quickly become exposed with any increase in the number and variety of commodities being traded. As the numbers of commodities increase the numbers of combinations become astronomical. With a hundred commodities nearly 5,000 separate exchange rates (actually 4,950) would be necessary in a theoretical barter system, while nearly half a million (actually 499,500) would be required to support bilateral trading for 1,000 commodities.[1] Consequently, despite the undoubted 'revival' of bartering in recent years this must remain very much an exception to the rule of money as the basis of trade. Even in final consumption there are many thousands of different goods purchased daily, as any glance at

[1] The formula for the number of combinations is $C^n_r = n!/[(n-r)!r!]$ where n is the number of commodities and r = bilateral groups of 2.

the serried ranks of supermarket shelves will immediately convey – but these represent only the final stage in the complex network of intermediate wholesale dealing and the multiple earlier processes in the productive chain. Retail trade, massive as it is in modern societies, is simply the tip of the iceberg of essentially money-based exchanges: a perusal of trade catalogues should convince any doubter.

What money has done for the exchange of commodities, the computer promises to do at least partially for information retrieval and the exchange of ideas – and not before time. To give but one example from a relatively narrow and specialized field of human knowledge, *Chemical Abstracts* for the year 1982 gives 457,789 references. Perhaps nothing provides a more enlightening snapshot of the essence of money than the ability it gives us to compare at a glance the relative values of any of the hundreds of thousands of goods and services in which we as individuals, families or larger groups may be interested, and to do so at minimal costs. Of course there are still very many national varieties of money where prices are less certain, more volatile, where bilateral restrictions are not uncommon and where the costs of exchange are far from being negligible. The *Financial Times* publishes every week tables giving the world value of the pound and of the dollar, listing over 200 different national currencies. If these were each of equal importance then foreign exchange would involve arbitrage between some 20,000 different combinations. Luckily, as with 'preferred barter items', a few leading currencies, notably sterling throughout the nineteenth and early twentieth century, plus the American dollar and more recently the German mark, the ecu and the Japanese yen, have provided the basis of a common measure of international monetary values. Every time a preferred commodity or a leading currency acts as a focus for a cluster of other commodities or currencies, so the progressive principle of the law of combinations works in reverse and thus greatly reduces the possible number of combinations. Internally money reduces all these to a single common standard, just as would the single world money system that reformers have dreamed about for generations in the past – and probably for generations to come also. Even so, the world's major banks have been forced to install the most modern electronic computational and communications equipment to handle their foreign exchanges: a costly and speculative, but essential and generally quite profitable business.

Traditional condemnation of the time-wasting 'higgling of the market' (to use Alfred Marshall's phrase) which was inevitably associated with much African and Asian barter, even up to the middle of the present century, might well indicate a lack of awareness among critics of the fact that the enjoyable, enthusiastic and argumentative process of prolonged bargaining was very much the prime object of the exercise – the actual exchange being something of an anticlimax, essential but not nearly as enjoyable as the preliminaries. What the European saw as waste the African saw as a pleasant social custom. However, given the spread of western modes of life the wasteful aspects of barter become more insupportable and unnecessarily curtail not only the size and efficiency of markets but also act as a brake on raising the living standards of the communities concerned. Specialization, as Adam Smith rightly emphasized, is limited by the extent of the market, and so is the mass production upon which the enviable standards of living of modern communities depend. However, the size of the market is itself crucially dependent upon the parallel development of money. Thus just as continued reliance on barter would have condemned mankind to eternal poverty, so today our lack of mastery of money is in large part the cause of widespread relative poverty and mass unemployment, while the enormous waste of potential output forgone is lost for ever.

Among other disadvantages of barter are the costs of storing value when these are all of necessity concrete objects rather than, for example, an abstract bank deposit which can be increased relatively costlessly and can whenever required be changed back into any marketable object. Besides, a bank deposit earns interest, whereas, to reverse Aristotle's famous attack on usury, most barter is barren. Services, by their nature cannot be stored, so that bartering for future services, necessarily involving an agreement to pay specific commodities or other specific services in exchange, weakens even the supposed normal superiority of current barter, namely its ability to enable direct and exactly measurable comparisons to be made between the items being exchanged. In the absence of money, or given the limited range of monetary uses in certain ancient civilizations, it is little wonder the completion of large-scale and long-term contracts was usually based on slavery. Thus the building of the Great Pyramid of Ghiza, the work of 100,000 men, and a logistical problem commensurate with its immense size, was made possible at that time only by the existence of slavery (even though these slaves enjoyed higher standards of living than others). This is not to deny that some relics of bartering for services still exist in the tied cottages, brewery-owned public houses and company perquisites or 'perks' today. However despite the drawbacks in our use of money, particularly the recurrence of enormously wasteful recessions, caused partly by instabilities inherent in money itself, it is plain from these few revealing contrasts with money, that barter inevitably carries with it far greater intrinsic disadvantages. Thus barter's stubborn survival into modern times and its occasional flourishes do not mean that it can play other than a comparatively very minor role in the complex interactions of our economic life as a whole.

In the uncrowded, predominantly agricultural communities which preceded modern times, it was possible to carry on a fairly considerable amount of trade and to enjoy a reasonably high standard of living since subsistence farming occupied such a large role, even when barter was the main method of exchange. However, this should not lead us to conclude that barter and a similarly extensive trade or a comparable standard of living would be possible in any major area of the modern world. Attention has already been drawn to the overpopulated areas of urban squalor in less developed countries, so that, despite the fact that agriculture is still the major occupation in most developing countries, the economies of such countries can no longer rely on a mixture of subsistence farming plus barter but are inescapably dependent upon their modern monetary systems, however inflationary. Their recent involvement with bartering in their international trade with the more advanced countries should therefore be seen in true perspective, as special cases arising from current pressures and not in any sense a return to the old pre-monetary methods of barter. For most people most of the time the economic clock cannot be turned back.

Modern barter and countertrading

Having thus differentiated between modern barter where the participants are fully conversant with advanced monetary systems and early barter where such knowledge was either rudimentary or non-existent, we may now turn to examine a few of the more salient examples of modern barter and to explain the reasons for this surprising regression. The many recurrent and the few persistent examples of barter in modern communities are most commonly though not exclusively associated with monetary crises, especially runaway inflation, which at its most socially devastating climax destroys the existing monetary system completely. Thus in the classic and well-documented case of the German inflation of 1923 the 'butter' standard emerged as a more reliable common measure of value than the mark. Towards the end of the Second World War and immediately after, much of retail trade in continental Europe was based on cigarettes – virtually a Goldflake or a Lucky Strike standard, which also formed a welcome addition to the real pay of the invading soldiers. A most interesting and detailed account of the cigarette currency as seen from inside a German prisoner of war camp was published by R. A. Radford (1945, 189–201).

Such inflationary conditions were widespread from western Europe through China to Japan at this time, but the world record for an inflationary currency belongs to Hungary. Its note circulation grew from 12,000 million pengö in 1944 to 36 million million in 1945. In 1946 it reached 1,000 million times the 1945 total until at its maximum it came to a figure containing twenty-seven digits. Its largest denomination banknote issued in 1946, was for 100 million 'bilpengos', which since the bil is equivalent to a trillion pengos, was actually for 100 quintillion pengos or P.100,000,000,000,000,000,000. This astronomical sum was in fact worth at most only about £1 sterling. Little wonder that in such circumstances the monetary system temporarily destroyed itself and people were forced to revert to barter, at least for use as a medium of exchange even if they continued to use their currency as a unit of account, though even here for the shortest possible space of time, until confidence in the new unit of currency, the forint, had been established.

The breakdown in multilateral trading in the Second World War was mended only slowly and painfully in the following decade. In the mean time, as Trued and Mikesell (1955) show, bilateral trade agreements, most of which included some form or other of barter, became very common. In fact, these authors concluded that some 588 such bilateral agreements had been arranged between 1945 and the end of 1954. Many of these involved strange exchanges of basic commodities and sophisticated engineering products, such as that arranged by Sir Stafford Cripps whereby Russian grain was purchased in return for Rolls Royce Nene jet engines (which were returned with interest over Korea). However, these awkward methods of securing international trade were first thought to be due simply to the inevitable disruption of the war and would fade away completely in time as the normal channels of peacetime trade were reopened. From the end of the 1950s to the 1970s this faith was justified, and it therefore occasioned some surprise when new forms of barter and 'countertrading' began to grow again in the 1970s and persisted strongly into the 1980s.

By 1970 a new growth in international barter was already becoming obvious, with the London Chamber of Commerce having noted some 450 such deals during the course of the previous year, a rate about twenty times the pre-war average. Already there were some forty companies in the City of London actively engaged in international barter. The Financial Times (11 May 1970), reporting on this new growth in barter, commented that 'We have moved on from the days in which beads were offered for mirrors to ones in which heavily flavoured Balkan tobacco is offered for power stations and when apples are offered for irrigation.' The same article reported that a conference on barter, arranged by the London Chamber of Commerce was heavily oversubscribed, with more than 300 representatives present, including clearing and merchant bankers, members of the Board of Trade and, of course, academics.

Most of the countries then involved in barter – the eastern bloc, Iran, Algeria, Brazil and so on – continued to figure prominently a decade or so later. Thus the *Morgan Guarantee Survey* of October 1978 reported yet 'A New Upsurge' in barter and countertrade, 'an ancient custom that suddenly is enjoying new popularity'. The largest of the deals described was a $20 billion barter agreement between Occidental Petroleum and the Soviet Union. In a similar spirit, Pepsico arranged a counter-purchase agreement with USSR selling Pepsi-Cola concentrate to Russia in return for the exclusive right to import Soviet vodka. Levi Strauss licensed trouser production in Hungary to be paid for by exports to the rest of Europe, while International Harvester gave Poland the design and technology to build its tractors in return for a proportion of such production. 'Iran, short of hard cash but swimming in oil', said the same source, 'barters to the tune of $4 billion to $5 billion a year, ladling out oil for everything from German steel plants and British missiles to American port facilities and Japanese desalinization units.' It was estimated that some 25 per cent of East–West trade involved some degree of barter, with the proportion expected to rise to around 40 per cent in the course of the 1980s. Algeria, India, Iraq and a number of South American countries again figured prominently in these projections. Five years later the international interest in barter was still strong, as evidenced by the influential papers presented at a conference, 'International Barter – To Trade or Countertrade' held at the World Trade Centre, New York, in September 1983, dealing with the barter of agricultural commodities, of metals and raw materials, of the special role of trading houses assisting large western companies to trade with the less developed countries, and so on.

Among the many reasons for this rebirth of barter are first the fact that external trade from communist countries is normally 'planned' bilaterally, and therefore lends itself more naturally to various forms of barter than does multilateral, freer, trading. This is of course why the General Agreement on Tariffs and Trade sets its face sternly against bartering arrangements. Secondly, the international trading scene has been repeatedly disrupted by the various vertical rises in the price of crude oil since it first quadrupled in 1973. Thirdly the relative fall in the terms of trade for the non-oil Third World countries caused them greatly to increase their borrowing from European and American governments and banks, a proportion of this being in 'tied' form, and thus, as with eastern bloc trade, becoming more susceptible to bilateral bargaining. Fourthly the rise in the world inflationary tide, together with the monetarist response in the main trading nations, caused international rates of interest to rise to unprecedented levels and so raised the repayment levels of borrowing countries to heights that could not readily be met by the methods of normal trading. In this respect the recrudescence of barter is simply a reflection of what has become to be known since the early 1980s as the 'sovereign debt' problem facing the dozen or so largest international debtor countries, including especially Mexico, Brazil and Argentina, but also Poland, India and Korea. The fifth and fundamental cause (though these various causes are interactive and cumulative rather than separate) is the breakdown in the stability of international rates of exchange following the virtual ending of the fixed-rate Bretton Woods system after 1971. With even the dollar under pressure there was no readily acceptable stable monetary unit useful for the longer-term contracts required for the capital goods especially desired by the developing countries. In such circumstances the direct exchange of specific goods or services for other such goods or services, assisted by all the various modern financial facilities, seemed in certain special cases such as those just indicated, to be preferable either to losing custom entirely or to becoming dependent solely on abstract claims to paper moneys of very uncertain future value.

Modern retail barter

Most of the examples of modern barter given so far refer to wholesale trading or large-scale international projects. Barter however continues to show itself in the retail trade and small-scale level, not only in such self-evident examples as the swapping of schoolboy treasures but also in much more elaborate and organized ways. Of particular importance in this connection is *Exchange and Mart*, an advertising medium which has been published in Britain every Thursday since 1868. Jevons himself noticed it in its earliest years and was obviously puzzled that any such publication, partly dependent on serving such a long obsolete purpose as barter, should appear to have any use to anyone. He refers to *Exchange and Mart* as 'a curious attempt to revive the practice of barter' and quoted examples of advertisers offering some old coins and a bicycle in exchange for a concertina, and a variety of old songs for a copy of *Middlemarch*. 'We must assume', concluded Jevons, 'that the offers are sometimes accepted, and that the printing press can bring about, in some degree, the double coincidence necessary to an act of barter.' He would no doubt be surprised that the publication has lasted for well over a century and that on average each issue contains around 10,000 classified advertisements. However, well over 95 per cent of these are not barter items, though sufficient remain to testify to its original purpose. A few examples must suffice: 'Exchange land for car, 2½ acres freehold land, Dorset, for low mileage 280 SL Mercedes Benz', 'Lady's Rolex 8363/8, exchange computer, word processor, etc.'; 'Council exchange, three bedroomed house, Coventry, for same Cornwall', obviously a very good swap for the advertiser; but then, possibly remembering the imperative pressures of double coincidence, he adds, 'all areas considered' (*Exchange and Mart*, 30 June 1983). The example of council house exchanging is a good reminder of what happens in a constrained situation where the normal market forces cannot freely operate. In these circumstances barter offers a way out.

A further reason for the re-emergence of barter in recent years may be seen as a by-product of the so-called 'black or informal economy'. According to Adrian Smith 'the informal economy can be seen as one of the main trends in economic evolution today, going with the continuous shrinkage in terms of employment and value added, of the production of goods and the corresponding growth of recorded employment in the service sector' (Adrian Smith 1981). A contributory factor was tax evasion. Smith estimated that the informal economy represented about 3 per cent of the economy of the USA, between 2 and 7½ per cent of that of UK, 10 per cent for France and as much as 15 per cent for Italy, though by the very nature of the 'hidden' economy such estimates could be hardly more than partly informed guesses. With regard to the importance of changes in employment in recent years the present writer has pointed out that 'In little over a decade from 1971 Britain has lost almost two million jobs from manufacturing – a devastating change; while almost as significant has been the good news of a gain of around one-and-three-quarter million jobs in services . . . a sort of industrial revolution in reverse' (Davies and Evans 1983). Such a massive switch has provided a wealth of opportunity for informal economic activities. Although only a very small proportion of the hidden economy would involve barter, the point to bear in mind is that, though small, it seems to be growing vigorously. We may conclude therefore by saying that although modern man cannot live by barter alone, it may still make life more bearable for a minority of hard-pressed traders and heavily taxed citizens in certain circumstances.

Primitive money: definitions and early development

Perhaps the simplest, most straightforward and, for historical purposes certainly, the most useful definition of primitive money is that given by P. Grierson, Professor of Numismatics at Cambridge, viz., 'all money that is not coin or, like modern paper money, a derivative of coin' (1977, 14). Even this definition however fails to allow for the ancient rather sophisticated banking systems that preceded the earliest coins by a thousand years or more. Nevertheless, with that single exception, it serves well for distinguishing in a general way between primitive and more advanced money, whether ancient or modern, and in its clarity and simplicity is perhaps preferable to the almost equally broad but rather more involved definition suggested by Einzig, as 'A unit or object conforming to a reasonable degree to some standard of uniformity, which is employed for reckoning or for making a large proportion of the payments customary in the community concerned, and which is accepted in payment largely with the intention of employing it for making payments' (1966, 317).

On one thing the experts on primitive money all agree, and this vital agreement transcends their minor differences. Their common belief backed up by the overwhelming tangible evidence of actual types of primitive moneys from all over the world and from the archaeological, literary and linguistic evidence of the ancient world, is that barter was not the main factor in the origins and earliest developments of money. The contrast with Jevons, with his predecessors going back to Aristotle, and with his followers who include the mainstream of conventional economists, is clear-cut. Typical of the latter approach is that of Geoffrey Crowther, formerly editor of *The Economist*, who, in his *Outline of Money*, begins with a chapter entitled the 'Invention of money' and insists that money 'undoubtedly was an invention; it needed the conscious reasoning power of Man to make the step from simple barter to money-accounting' (Crowther 1940, 15). It was possibly such gross oversimplifications that caused Paul Samuelson, in an article on 'Classical and neo-classical monetary theory' to contrast 'Harriet Martineau. who made fairy tales out of economics' with those 'modern economists who make economics out of fairytales' (see Clower 1969, 184).

The most common non-economic forces which gave rise to primitive money may be grouped together thus: bride-money and blood-money; ornamental and ceremonial; religious and political. Objects originally accepted for one purpose were often found to be useful for other non-economic purposes, just as they later, because of their growing acceptability, began to be used for general trading also. We face considerable difficulty in trying to span the chronological gap which separates us from a true understanding of the attitudes of ancient man towards religious, social and economic life, and similarly with regard to the cultural gap which separates us from existing or recent primitive societies. In both ancient and modern primitive societies human values and attitudes were such that religion permeated almost the whole of everyday life and could not as easily be separated from political, social and economic life in the way that comes readily to us with our tendency for facile categorization. To us the categories may seem sensible and justified and no doubt they help us to appreciate the role of money (or of other such institutions) when we relate them to methods of thought and social, religious, political and economic systems with which we are familiar. But there are limits to our ability to force ancient or recent primitive fashions into modern moulds. In particular, primitive moneys originating from one source or for one use came to be used for similar kinds of payments elsewhere spreading gradually without necessarily becoming generalized. For example, moneys first used for ceremonial purposes, because of their prestigious role were frequently ornamental also, these purposes being mutually reinforcing. Mrs A. Hingston Quiggin, in her readable and well-illustrated survey of *Primitive Money* gives a number of examples 'to show how an object can be at the same time currency or money, a religious symbol or a mere ornament' (Quiggin 1949, 2). However, the penalty of widening the functions of primitive moneys from their original rather narrow group of roles lay in weakening their force in their main function. It was a matter of balancing the formidable powers of money in one narrow group of, say, religious and ceremonial roles against the greater usefulness which followed from extending the currency of the money at the cost of losing part of its original religious or ceremonial associations.

Because of this conflict a division arose (though it had long been latent) between the experts on primitive economies as to whether or not to exclude the whole body of relatively narrowly functioning primitive objects from being called 'money' at all (see G. Dalton 1967). Some would argue that unless such objects can be seen to have performed a fairly wide variety of functions they should not really be classed even as primitive money. This view seems to be far too narrow and rules out much of the long evolutionary story of monetary development. For money did not spring suddenly into full and general use in any community, and primitive man commonly used a number of different kinds of money for different purposes, some of which are almost certainly older than others. Even today we have not arrived at universal money, nor even universal banking, and just as we buy houses by going to see a building society and insurance through the insurance agent coming to see us, so primitive men saw different moneys being naturally confined to different groups of uses. The origins of these were quite varied, and although we emphasize that many of the most important of these origins were non-commercial, they established concepts, attitudes and ideas which conditioned the growth in the use of a huge variety of different kinds of 'money' in ancient and modern primitive communities.

Loving and fighting are the oldest, most exciting (and usually separate) of man's activities, so that it is perfectly natural to find that payments associated with both are among the earliest forms of money. Thus 'Wergeld', a Germanic word for the compensation or fine demanded for killing a man, was almost universally present in ancient as in modern primitive societies. Our word to 'pay' is derived from the Latin 'pacare', meaning originally to pacify, appease or make peace with – through the appropriate unit of value customarily acceptable to both parties involved. Similarly payments to compensate the head of a family for the loss of a daughter's services became the origin of 'bride-price' or 'bride-wealth'. The pattern of payment for human services was sometimes broadened to include the purchase or sale of slaves, who for centuries acted as 'walking cheque-books'. Although there may be room to doubt the extent of the direct connections between the compensatory payments of wergeld and bride-wealth, a number of social anthropologists argue, with many supportive examples, that they were closely related both in the nature and scale of payments. Thus Grierson cites among a number of similar examples the custom of the Yurok Indians of California where wergeld was identical with bride-price. He admits, however, that such identities are not evident everywhere: one could hardly expect it.

Over the course of time, paying for injuring, killing, marrying and enslaving became elaborated into different values according to the customs of the community concerned, with the tribal chief or head of state intervening either to accept the payments or to lay down the law as to what was or was not acceptable compensation. Tribute or taxation, ransoms, bribery and various forms of protection payments such as those which we later came to know as 'Danegeld', were all various means by which the early state became involved in the extension of the geographical area of the peaceful enforcement of law and hence confirmed the greater role for the monetary payments that such a peace made possible. As we approach the medieval period these laws, specifying the amount and types of indemnities, were encoded. Such codes, extending from the Celtic laws of Ireland and Wales eastward through those of Germanic and Scandinavian tribes to central Russia, exhibit basic similarities and, in contrast with the ancient Mosaic laws which demanded an eye for an eye and a tooth for a tooth, they provided peacemaking monetary alternatives. The role of the state in thus spreading the use of money has been stressed by generations of economists, but by none more than G. F. Knapp.

Knapp's *State Theory of Money* considerably influenced Keynes, through whose efforts the work was translated into English. Knapp was nothing if not forthright: 'Money is a creature of law . . . the numismatist usually knows nothing of currency, for he has only to deal with its dead body' (1924, 1). This view of the role of the state as the sole creator and guarantor of money, although useful as a corrective to the metallistic theories current at the end of the nineteenth century, nevertheless carries the state theory of money to an absurd extreme, a criticism of which the author himself appears to be aware since in his preface he defends himself with the plea that 'a theory must be pushed to extremes or it is valueless' – surely a most dangerously dogmatic assertion. The main point at issue, however, is simply this, that right from the inception of money, from ancient down to modern times, the state has a powerful, though not omnipotent, role to play in the development of money. Yet neither ancient money nor, despite Sir Stafford Cripps's view to the contrary, even the Bank of England, is a mere creature of the state.

Knapp's pre-monetarist emphasis on the fundamental role of the state in the creation of money does at least consistently reflect the tendency of German economists in the late nineteenth and early twentieth centuries to extol the power of the state. Modern monetarists such as Friedman however, strongly uphold the supremacy of the market and at the same time seek, inconsistently, to minimize the role of the state – except in monetary matters: an exception which fits ill with their basic philosophy. Whatever barriers the state – or academics – may erect within which to confine money, money has an innate ability demonstrated not only during recent decades but by thousands of years of history to jump over them. Experts on primitive and modern money disagree where to draw the line between money and quasi-money precisely because it is in the nature of money to make any such clear distinction impossible to uphold for any length of time. Money is so useful – in other words, it performs so many functions – that it always attracts substitutes: and the narrower its confining lines are drawn, the higher the premium there is on developing passable substitutes.

Economic origins and functions

Having emphasized the non-economic origins of money to the extent required to counteract the traditional strongly entrenched viewpoint, we may now more briefly examine its economic or commercial origins, since these require, at this stage, little elaboration. Money has many origins – not just one – precisely because it can perform many functions in similar ways and similar functions in many ways. As an institution, money is almost infinitely adaptable. This helps to explain the wide variety of origins and the vast multitude of different kinds of objects used as primitive money. These include: amber, beads, cowries, drums, eggs, feathers, gongs, hoes, ivory, jade, kettles, leather, mats, nails, oxen, pigs, quartz, rice, salt, thimbles, umiaks, vodka, wampum, yarns and zappozats, which are decorated axes – to name but a minute proportion of the enormous variety of primitive moneys; and none of this alphabetical list includes modern examples like gold, silver or copper coinage nor any of the 230 or so units of paper currency.

Table 1.1 Functions of money

Specific functions (mostly micro-economic)
1 Unit of account (abstract)
2 Common measure of value (abstract)
3 Medium of exchange (concrete)
4 Means of payment (concrete)
5 Standard for deferred payments (abstract)
6 Store of value (concrete)

General functions (mostly macro-economic and abstract)
7 Liquid asset
8 Framework of the market allocative system (prices)
9 A causative factor in the economy
10 Controller of the economy

Because it appeared that, at some time or place, almost anything has acted as money, this misled some writers, including especially the French economist, Turgot, to conclude that anything can in actual practice act as money. One must admit that in any logical (not chronological) list of monetary functions, such as that suggested in table 1.1, that of acting as a unit of account would normally come first. It follows from the fact that money originated in a variety of different ways that there is little purpose in the insistence shown by a number of monetary economists in analysing which are the supposed primary or original and which are the supposed secondary or derived functions (see Goldfield and Chandler 1981). What is now the prime or main function in a particular community or country may not have been the first or original function in time, while what may well have been a secondary or derived function in one place may have been in some other region the original which itself gave rise to a related secondary function. Here again there is exhibited a tendency among certain economists to compare what appears in today's conditions to be the logical order with the actual complex chronological development of money over its long and convoluted history. The logical listing of functions in the table therefore implies no priority in either time or importance, for those which may be both first and foremost reflect only their particular time and place.

Turning back now to the first function listed, it is easy to see that, since an accounting or reckoning unit is of course abstract, it has in theory no physical constraints. Theoretically one could easily make up any word and apply this as an accounting record. As a matter of fact in recent years the European monetary authorities co-operated in producing just such a unit – and called it the European 'unit of account', later becoming the Ecu. There is an essential connection but not necessarily an identity between counting and measuring money.

Thus cowries, coins and cattle were (and are) usually counted, whereas grain, gold and silver were usually weighed: hence come not only our words for 'spend', 'expenditure', etc., from the Latin 'expendere' but also originally 'pound', as being a defined weight of silver. But acting as a unit of account is only one of money's functions and although anything picked at random, whether abstract or concrete, admittedly could act as such a unit – and if a sensible choice, might do so admirably – this would not necessarily mean that it could perform satisfactorily any or all of money's many other functions. Although acting as a unit of account or as a common measure of value – which are two ways of looking at the same concept – are both abstractions, it added greatly to the convenience of money if the normally concrete media of exchange and/or the means of payment carried the same names as, or were at least consistently related to, money's two abstract qualities of accounting and measuring. By that is meant that, for example, one's bank balance is kept in pounds (including subdivisions), that prices are quoted in pounds, that one is paid in pounds, and that one pays others for purchases or services also in pounds. But for around half the long monetary history of the £ sterling in Britain this was not the case: there was no such *thing* as a pound; it existed only as a unit of account. There are numerous similar examples.

As well as the specific functions of money listed in table 1.1 there are also a number of more general functions. All these various functions and the changing relationships between them will form the main subject of the remainder of our study, stemming from cowries to Euro-currencies. However a few further important aspects of money, not captured in the given categories, need to be at least hinted at in this introductory chapter, namely first the dynamic quicksilver nature of money – or to vary the analogy, its chameleon-like adaptability. Money designed for one specific function will easily take on other jobs and come up smiling. Old money very readily functions in new ways and new money in old ways: money is eminently fungible.

Let us come now to the little matter of definition: what, after all is money? The form in which the question is put tends to indicate that the proper place for a definitive definition, as it were, is at the end rather than near the beginning of our study; but the dictates of custom would suggest the need at least for this preliminary definition: *Money is anything that is widely used for making payments and accounting for debts and credits.*

The quality-to-quantity pendulum: a metatheory of money

Money is the mechanism by which markets are most perfectly cleared, whereby the forces of demand and supply continually and competitively fight themselves out towards the draw known as equilibrium. As we have just seen with regard to barter, no other mechanism is nearly as good as money in this function of sending early and appropriate signals to buyers and sellers through price changes, so helping smoothly to remove excess balances of demand or supply. Markets are, however, rarely perfect, and in practice even money cannot remove all the uncertainty surrounding them. There are three fundamental reasons for market uncertainty. First, the full information and correct interpretation necessary for perfect balance are costly; secondly, the aggregate flow of goods and services which form the counterpart to the total quantity of money changes over time in volume and trading velocity; and thirdly and most importantly money is by its very nature dynamically unstable in volume and velocity, in quantity and quality.

We shall see as our history of money unfolds that there is an unceasing conflict between the interests of debtors, who seek to enlarge the *quantity* of money and who seek busily to find acceptable substitutes, and the interests of creditors, who seek to maintain or increase the value of money by limiting its supply, by refusing substitutes or accepting them with great reluctance, and generally trying in all sorts of ways to safeguard the *quality* of money. Although most consumers and producers are at some stage both debtors and creditors it is their net power that influences the value of money. What is most interesting in historical perspective is to analyse the long-term pendulum movements between the net forces of debtors, which cause the pendulum to swing excessively towards depreciating the value of money, and the net forces of creditors which act strongly the other way to raise the unit value of money or at least to moderate the degree of depreciation. While the historical record will confirm popular condemnation of the inflationary evils of an excessive quantity of money, it will also point to the more hidden but equally baneful effects when excessive emphasis on quality has severely restricted the growth of the economy.

Although monetary stability may be to the long-term advantage of the majority, there are always strong minorities who tip the net balance of power and who wish to increase or decrease the value of money. They thus help to push the pendulum into a state of almost perpetual motion. During all periods of history the debtors are generally much poorer and always much more numerous than the normally more powerful and less numerous creditors, even though by definition the total of debts and credits is the same. In this context it is the distribution which matters, while it should be remembered that debtors can and often do include the most powerful of politicians and the most ambitious of entrepreneurs. For long periods of history the most important net debtor has been the single monarch or the composite state, each possessed with a varying degree of sovereign power to determine the supply of money, though never with complete control over the acceptability of money substitutes. Not surprisingly when the state becomes a net debtor the pendulum tends to widen its oscillations.

An indebted monarch or government is usually able not only to reduce the real burden of its own debt, but can as a bonus consciously or unconsciously court popularity with the indebted masses by allowing the net pressures of indebtedness to increase the supply of money or the acceptance of substitutes and so lift some of the heavy burden of debt from the shoulders of the poor masses – and from many up-and-coming entrepreneurs. There is therefore a secular tendency for money to depreciate in value, a tendency halted or partially reversed whenever net creditors, such as large landowners, rich moneylenders and well-established bankers, are in the ascendancy or can bring their usually powerful influence to bear upon governments.

Corresponding therefore to our simple preliminary definition of money we have a simple theoretical framework for assessing changes in the value of money, namely the 'pendulum theory' or more fully, the 'oscillating debtor–quantity/creditor–quality theory'. At any given time, especially after drastic changes have taken place in monetary affairs, a whole host of theories may arise in attempts to explain the existing value of money. Given a wider historical perspective these temporary theories, whatever they are called, group themselves with little distortion into either debtor–quantity or creditor–quality theories. The pendulum theory brings these two apparently contradictory and divergent sets of theories together into a symbiotic union. It indicates why these temporary theories, like certain aspects of money itself, tend to rather extreme oscillations, and helps to explain why such opposite theories tend to follow each other in repeated alternations over the centuries, interspersed with the occasional long period of comparative stability.

The pendulum theory is therefore of particular relevance to the long perspectives of monetary history and yet may shine some light on current financial controversy, for it is within the vectors of that wider theory that the shorter-term, fashionable 'temporary' theories appropriate to the particular period in question play out their powerful but inevitably limited roles. In this sense the pendulum theory acts as a metatheory of money, i.e. a more general theory comprising sets of more limited, partial theories, which latter spring out of the special circumstances of their time. The enveloping pendulum or metatheory also explains why the usual theories of money, despite being so confidently held at one time, tend to change so drastically and diametrically (and therefore so puzzlingly to the uninitiated) to an equally accepted but opposite theory within the time span appropriate to historical investigation. The longer view given by the pendulum theory may also help to correct the dangerous 'short-termism' present in much current financial theory and practice.

The most recent, and therefore perhaps the most obvious, example of the workings of the pendulum theory can be seen in the enormous swing from almost universal acceptance in theory and policy of the broadly based but temporary 'liquidity theory of money' held by the Keynesians to the now fashionable, widely based acceptance in theory and still more in practice of the very narrowly based monetarist theories of Milton Friedman and his followers. Another recent example of the age-old principle of the pendulum may be seen in the much discussed tendency of the external values of currencies to 'overshoot' their equilibrium values in the foreign exchange markets once they became free to move away from their fixed-rate anchors. The extreme volatility of rates of interest in the post-war period points to a third instance of the pendulum in vigorous 'overkill' action.

In the chronology of oscillation, quality comes first; for if whatever is intended to act as money is not desired strongly enough to be held for that purpose, it will fail to be selected long enough to be imitated. Once the selection is confirmed by general acceptance then, sooner or later, depending on the society in question, quality faces competition from an increased quantity of substitutes. Monetary imitation is the most effective form of flattery. As quantity increases so quality generally falls, and if the process is speeded up, the currency may become completely discredited and useless, requiring replacement by a new monetary form which emphasizes its special quality; hence the periodic currency reforms which punctuate monetary history, followed by eventual backsliding.

It follows from the pendulum theory that the nearer the money supply is kept to its equilibrium position, the more moderate will be the policy measures, such as variations in the official rate of interest, required to re-establish equilibrium. Conversely, a wide swing away from equilibrium will require such strong counteracting policy measures, such as very large changes in interest rates, that dangerous 'overshooting' or 'overkill' will commonly result. A monetary stitch in time saves nine.

Finally it is of the utmost significance to realize that because the monetary pendulum is rarely motionless at the point of perfect balance between the conflicting interests of creditors and debtors, so money itself is rarely 'neutral' in its effects upon the real economy and upon the fortunes of different sections of the community, for all sections are involved all the time in their daily lives. This feature further enhances the importance of money in economic, social and political history.

2

From Primitive and Ancient Money to the Invention of Coinage, 3000–600 BC

Pre-metallic money

If economics, defined briefly, is the *logic of limited resource usage*, money is the main method by which that logic is put to work. In commonsense terms, therefore, economics is very largely concerned with how to make the most of one's money, since the allocation of resources and changes in the valuation of assets necessarily involve accountancy and payment systems based on money, although the degree to which such allocations are left to the freedom of the market, and therefore the demands which are made upon the efficiency of the monetary system, will vary from place to place and age to age. It is important, however, to realize that the close relationship between the development of money and its efficient use in the allocation of resources is complex and convoluted. In particular the logical and chronological developments are not exactly parallel. Thus, as has already been noted, one would logically expect all pre-metallic monies to be associated exclusively with primitive communities, and similarly all metallic money to be associated exclusively with more advanced societies. But this is far from being the case, and the logical order differs significantly from the chronological. Thus the development of banking in Britain followed a thousand years behind the introduction and widespread use of coinage. To us this seems both a natural and a logical process of development and we may at first find it difficult to believe that that process could be reversed. But banking in Babylon preceded the 'invention' of coinage by a similarly long period. Again, we find firms in Birmingham in the first decades of the twentieth century still manufacturing metallic bracelets for use as primitive forms of money among certain Nigerian tribes, in preference to the coinage systems which were readily available for their use and which the state authorities had been trying to enforce with little success for many years.

When we come to look at many of the earliest types of coins, we shall see that these were produced as direct imitations of those primitive types of currency with which the communities concerned had long been familiar. Primitive moneys may be recent, banking may be ancient. Consequently in seeking to combine as far as is possible the chronological with the logical stages of financial development, their sometimes strongly conflicting currents should always be borne in mind. Even in our own days, innovation and progress are not necessarily synonymous terms: apparently it has always been thus. Therefore, in presenting the mainstream of development we should not remain unaware of the counterforces which occasionally run strongly in the opposite direction, nor ignore the fact that the mainstream may itself flow in sluggish meanders back upon itself and thus reverse some of the progress formerly made. In tracing the advance from primitive cowries to early coinage we must therefore necessarily be diverted into a study of early banking, a sophisticated and promising development which was first helped and then hindered by the rise of coinage systems.

Since, according to Toynbee's *Study of History*, over 650 separate primitive societies – most of which were still in existence in the twentieth century – have been categorized by social anthropologists, and since most of these have used one or more forms of primitive money, it follows that the subject of primitive money is of vast proportions (Toynbee 1960, chapter 3). Moreover despite the debt that present students owe to scholars like Einzig, he believed the subject to be still 'largely a *terra incognita*', and emphasized that practically every chapter of the ethnological and historical sections of his book could and should be expanded into a full-size volume (1966, 518). Unfortunately, despite the appeal and importance of this fascinating subject, only a handful of primitive moneys can be touched on in this study, and these few are chosen in order to illustrate the timeless relevance of the subject. However, the total populations using primitive money throughout time have been very small compared with the many millions in the vast populations of civilized, coin-using communities. While the allocation of space in studies of the historical development of money must inevitably be somewhat arbitrary, the present writer would strongly commend Einzig's view that monetary economists should take much more interest in examining primitive money to compensate for their previous neglect, and that our understanding of modern money would be significantly improved were this wise advice followed.

The ubiquitous cowrie

Of the many hundreds of objects that have been used as primitive moneys we begin with the cowrie because of all forms of money, including even the precious metals, the cowrie was current over a far greater space and for a far greater length of time than any other. The cowrie is the ovoid shell of a mollusc widely spread over the shallower regions of the Indian and Pacific Oceans. It comes in various types, colours and sizes, from about the size of the end joint of the little finger up to about the size of a fist. The most prolific single source was the Maldive Islands whence for hundreds of years whole shiploads were distributed around the shores of Oceania, Africa, the Middle and Far East, their values rising as they became scarcer farther from their point of origin. Quite apart from their religious and obvious ornamental qualities, the cowries are durable, easily cleaned and counted, and defy imitation or counterfeiting. For many people over large parts of the world, at one time or other they have appeared as an ideal form of money. Modern moneys found the cowrie a formidable rival, especially for items of small value. An interesting example of their modern use was described to the writer by one of his Nigerian students, who as a small boy regularly collected the smaller cowries which tended to be lost during the hustle and bustle of the open Ibo fair days. If he managed to collect between six and eight of these, he could purchase something useful to eat or play with. This personal illustration is also a powerful reminder of the speed of change in financial matters in developing countries, for the student concerned, Dr G. O. Nwankwo, later became the first professor of banking and finance at the University of Lagos and an executive director of the Central Bank of Nigeria and chairman of one of the country's largest commercial banks, in which capacities he has represented his country abroad at OPEC and similar conferences – from cowries to petro-currencies in the course of a single career.

Across the other side of Central Africa, when cowries were first introduced into Uganda towards the end of the eighteenth century, two cowries in the most remote regions were known to have been sufficient to purchase a woman; by 1860 it required one thousand cowries for such a purchase. As trade grew and cowries became more plentiful they naturally depreciated further, but were still officially accepted for payment of taxes until the beginning of the twentieth century. It was only with the penetration of the country by the Uganda Railway that coins gradually took over from cowries, and only then for medium- and large-sized transactions. By the 1920s literally thousands of tons of cowries had been brought into Africa, not only from the Maldives but from other areas as they became progressively even more devalued elsewhere, and in so doing accelerated the depreciation of the cowrie in the internal regions of Africa also. However, in East as in West Africa it took until the middle of the twentieth century before the cowries virtually disappeared from circulation for the smallest purchases, especially in the remotest districts. Their attractiveness plus their immense circulation and prolonged popularity have caused them not only to coexist with modern types of moneys, but from time to time the cowrie has pushed debased coinage from official acceptance in a strange reversal of Gresham's Law. Many such examples have been recorded in the long history of Chinese currency, for in this as in many other aspects of civilization the Chinese offer the longest sequence of authentically recorded development. So important a role did the cowrie play as money in ancient China that its pictograph was adopted in their written language for 'money' (See Cribb, in M. J. Price 1980, 296).

Fijian whales' teeth and Yap stones

In contrast to the vast range of the cowrie two much more geographically limited types of money are the sperm whale's tooth or 'tambua' of the Fijian group of islands, and the peculiar stone currency of the island of Yap. The ceremonial origins of the former are demonstrated by its continued use as part of the ritual of welcome to visiting royalty, as on the occasion of the visit of Queen Elizabeth and the Duke of Edinburgh in 1982. Official receptions are still unthinkable without such a formal presentation of a whale's tooth, representing as it does, deep-rooted Fijian cultural traditions. As well as their uses in official ceremonials, whales' teeth were also used as bride-money, with a symbolic meaning similar to that of our engagement ring. Much prestige was derived from the ownership of whales' teeth, which were constantly oiled and polished and, in earlier days, considered to be far preferable even to gold. Thus when a chest of gold coins was captured aboard a trading brig off one of the Fijian islands in the mid-nineteenth century the finders put them to a novel use. They literally threw them away playing 'ducks and drakes', for which purpose one supposes that they were absolutely ideal, although few westerners, however rich, could vouch personally for this novel function of modern money, or imagine a more happily disdainful treatment of these westernized 'barbaric relics'. One of the young Fijians among the party that had played with the plundered gold coins became in later life a government official, shortly after Fiji became a British Crown Colony in 1874, and was still reluctant to accept payment in sterling silver or even gold sovereigns. He requested to be paid instead in the traditional whales' teeth since with these he could demonstrate his prestige and authority much more convincingly than with mere modern money, which, although then of full intrinsic value, yet lacked the sacred attributes so conspicuously associated with the 'tambua'. The customs associated with tambua were first described in detail in Captain James Cook's *Journal* of his voyages through the Fijian and Tongan islands in 1774. To the Pacific islanders the term possesses a positive significance suggesting a sacred sense of proper or fit usage, as well as the negative form to which we have become accustomed to limit the term 'taboo'. Thus although the monetary functions performed by the tambua might be rather weak at one end of the spectrum they compensated by vigorously performing a number of ceremonial and religious functions at the other end of the wide spectrum of monetary custom and usage.

The peculiar stone currency of Yap, a cluster of ten small islands in the Caroline group of the central Pacific, was still being used as money as recently as the mid-1960s. The stones known as 'fei' were quarried from Palau, some 260 miles away, or from the even more distant Guam, and were shaped into discs varying from saucer-sized to veritable millstones, the larger specimens having holes in the centre through which poles could be pushed to help transport them. Despite centuries of at first sporadic and later more permanent trade contracts with the Portuguese, Spanish, German, British, Japanese and Americans, the stone currency retained and even increased its value, particularly as a store of wealth. It seems highly appropriate that James Callaghan, who a few decades later was destined to become Chancellor of the Exchequer and Prime Minister, was informed that these stones were still internally important when he visited the Yap islands in 1945 when serving in the Royal Navy; though the American dollar was already current for most purchases involving external trade. When Mr Callaghan became Chancellor of the Exchequer from 1964 to 1967, he was automatically also Master of the Mint and therefore ultimately responsible for the new coins issued by the Mint to a number of Pacific Islands, where primitive currencies had still been in use thirty years earlier. The completed triumph of coinage over indigenous primitive monies in the islands of the Pacific and Indian Oceans may be illustrated by noting that the Royal Mint at Llantrisant produced in the financial year 1981/2 coins for fifty-seven countries overseas, including the Maldive Islands – the home of the cowrie – Fiji, Tonga, Tuvalu, Kiribati, Papua and the Seychelles; though not Yap, whose dollars were minted in USA (Royal Mint, Annual Report 1982, 11).

The largest of the stone discs now in Yap include two fully 20 ft in diameter, which remained in the mid-1950s at the bottom of Tomil harbour where they had accidentally sunk. They had been quarried under the direction of a certain Captain O'Keefe, an American-Irish sea captain who, shortly after becoming shipwrecked in Yap in December 1871, set himself up as the largest trader in that part of the Pacific and 'ruled' as 'His Majesty O'Keefe' until his death in the great typhoon of 1901. Also used as subsidiary currency to 'fei' were shell necklaces, individual pearl shells, mats and ginger. But it was the stones which were 'the be-all and end-all of the Yap islander. They are not only money, they are badges of rank and prestige, and they also have religious and ceremonial significance' (Klingman and Green 1952, 45). Though of limited use as currency they were nevertheless without doubt by far the most acceptable form of money to the Yap islanders. In contrast to the Fijians who have had to use legal measures for strictly limiting the export of their precious stock of whales' teeth, the Yapee administration has relied mainly on the penalties of very high prices to limit those foreign purchasers, such as curators of museums, who have in recent years been seeking to acquire specimens of one of the world's most peculiar forms of primitive money. One of the largest of such stones stands proudly but somewhat eccentrically in the courtyard of the Bank of Canada in Ottawa. The tambua and the fei have both been criticized as not quite deserving to be called money because of certain limitations in their usage; but such criticisms ignore the compensating functions beyond the materialistic range of modern money.

Wampum: the favourite American-Indian money

One of the long-lasting difficulties of the early colonists of North America was how to establish a generally acceptable monetary system. The chronic shortage of coin caused them to jump from one expedient to another. Thus in 1715 the authorities in North Carolina declared that as many as seventeen commodities including maize and wheat were legal tender. Strangely enough, there already appeared to be a much commoner and more generally acceptable currency when it came to dealing directly with the indigenous communities, namely, strings of (mainly) white beads. In course of time these beads were also generally accepted among the colonists themselves. 'Peag' is the Indian word for a string of beads and 'wampum' meant 'white', the most common colour of their money, hence the full title of their famous currency 'wampumpeag' is usually abbreviated to 'wampum'. The earliest account of this widespread Indian currency was given by Jacques

Cartier in 1535, who noted an unusual additional function, its usefulness in stopping nose-bleeding, a curative property which his exploratory party tested and confirmed. This is a quaint reversal of the better-known nasal connotations of money, namely 'to pay through the nose', which telling phrase stems from the disconcerting habit of the Danes in Ireland, who in the ninth century slit the noses of those unable or unwilling to pay the Danish poll tax. One of the most detailed of the early accounts of the development of wampum as currency was that given by Roger Williams, a Welsh missionary who after graduating from Cambridge in 1627 emigrated to Boston in 1631 and made a comprehensive study of the languages and customs of a number of the Indian tribes of north-eastern America.

Wampum was made out of the shells of the clam (Venus Mercenaria) and other similar bivalves which were most plentiful in the estuarine rivers of the north-east of America and Canada. Naturally wampum was most commonly used in what are now the coastal states from New Brunswick and Nova Scotia in the north to Florida and Louisiana in the south; but wampum spread inland also and was used by certain tribes right across the continent. The powerful Iroquois amassed large quantities by way of tribute, though they lived far from the original source of wampum. The shells are mostly white but with a smaller deep purple rim. The scarcer 'black' or blue-black wampum was usually traded at double the price of the white. The average individual piece of wampum was thus a cylindrical bead about half an inch or so long and between an eighth and a quarter inch in diameter, with a hole drilled lengthwise for stringing; but other shapes and sizes were not uncommon. Even the genuine highest-quality wampum became depreciated over time in quality as well as through increased quantity. For normal currency purposes the wampum strings were either about 18 in. or 6ft long and were therefore usually reckoned in cubits and fathoms, but on occasions singly or in feet; they were eminently divisible. Some tribes, such as the Narragansetts, specialized in manufacturing wampum, but their original stone-age craftsmanship was swamped when the spread of steel drills enabled unskilled workers, including the colonists themselves, to increase the supply a hundredfold. Thus that tribe lost its partial monopoly. Even before this massive devaluation brought about mostly through greatly increased quantities but partly also through poorer quality, the exchange value of wampum fell with the decline in the value of beaverskins. Roger Williams found it difficult to explain this relationship to Indian traders who saw the value of their wampum halved in a few years, and saw this as deliberate cheating by the white traders. Of course it is always a temptation to personalize the laws of supply and demand behind which the authorities, however constituted, are always prone to hide their own failings.

As an indication of the essential role wampum played in early colonial days even among the white settlers, it was made legal tender in a number of the original thirteen American colonies. In 1637 Massachusetts declared white wampum legal tender at six beads a penny and black at three a penny, but only for sums up to one shilling. Apparently this experiment succeeded, for the legal tender limit was *raised* to £2 in 1643, a substantial amount for those days and far exceeding the real value of our coinage limits today. Although wampum ceased to be legal tender in the New England states in 1661, it still remained a popular currency in parts of North America for nearly 200 years subsequently, although the blanket and the beaverskin were strong competitors among the Indians of Canada. In 1644 Peter Stuyvesant, the director general of New Netherland, raised a loan via a merchant in Albany of between 5,000 and 6,000 guilders *in wampum* in order to pay the labourers' wages for the fort he was building in New York (Myers 1970, 3). Around 1760 demand in New England still remained strong enough to justify starting a wampum factory, opened in New Jersey by J. W. Campbell, where an expert worker could produce up to 20 ft of wampum a day. This factory remained in production for a hundred years. Thereafter, although retaining its ornamental attributes, particularly for belts, bracelets and necklaces, wampum generally faded away for currency purposes, and modern coinage almost completely replaced it even for small change by the last quarter of the nineteenth century. However, the belts were still used in competitive exchanges well into the present century, and even now help to sustain the growing tourist trade.

Wampum's monetary death therefore resembled its birth, for its use as money undoubtedly came about as an extension of its desirability for ornamentation. Indeed there is a considerable degree of doubt about the extent to which wampum was actually used as currency before the arrival of the colonists, but again, its possible weakness in this regard was compensated by taking into account its psychic functions. However, both before and after it acquired its additional uses as a medium of exchange and a means of payment it functioned strongly as a store of value. The step from the European coinages of their homelands to the use of primitive beads was thus more of a sidestep than a sign of backwardness. In the meantime, while Americans and Canadians were sorting out their own monetary systems, they found the humble strings of beads a most desirable and durable bridge to more modern forms of money, performing quite well for a considerable period all the functions of a modern money, from accounting and acting as a means of payment – or 'shelling out' – to providing usefully compact and durable stores of value. Although the American example of a more advanced economy incorporating and adapting primitive money is the best known, it is far from being an isolated case. The same process occurred in many other instances, including the ancient civilizations of Egypt and China, and even showed itself to such an absurd degree in nineteenth-century England that Charles Dickens felt constrained to pour his powerful contempt on British official insistence on using primitive wooden forms of money right into the modern era.

Cattle: man's first working-capital asset

Just as the cowrie played a major part in primitive money from the point of view especially of being a medium of exchange, so cattle have occupied a central role in the long evolution of money as units of account. Cattle – a vague term variously meaning cows, buffalo, goats, sheep and camels, and usually but not always excluding horses – historically precede the use of grain as money for the simple reason that the taming of animals preceded agriculture. Despite their age-long use as money, some authorities on primitive money would contend that cattle cannot be properly considered as money because, being such a 'heavy' or expensive unit of account and standard of value, they were not very suited to performing the other more mobile functions of being a good means of payment and medium of exchange, which apparently demanded something much smaller than, say, a cow. But if the 'pound' sterling was clearly accepted as money for hundreds of years during which it had no physical existence and despite being a 'heavy' currency, cattle, which at least do have a very substantial physical presence, may with even greater justifiability be called money, provided only that they are of course used for monetary purposes, as they indubitably were, with sheep, goats and hides being used, among other objects, as subsidiary 'coinage' where emphasis was required on the mobile monetary functions.

As we have stressed, it is quite wrong to consider the various functions of money to be separated by unclimbable barriers. In particular one should not confuse the abstract concept of an ox as a unit of account or standard of value, which is its essential but not its only monetary function, with its admittedly cumbersome concrete physical form. Once that is realized (a position quickly reached by primitive man if not yet by all economists or anthropologists), the inclusion of cattle as money is easily accepted, in practice and logic. Smaller animals or more convenient physical objects – so many sheep and goats for a cow or camel, so many chickens for a sheep or goat, and so on – can easily supplement the apparent but unreal problem of having a heavy accounting unit, just as the old pound was divided into 20 shillings, 240 pennies and 960 farthings. In any case it has been the common custom among primitive communities to have more than one money medium, each one necessarily being linked with the particular unit of account. Until well into the present century horses were the main monetary unit of the Kirghiz of the Russian steppes, and formed their main store of value, though sheep were used as subsidiaries, with lambskins being used as small change. To exclude one of the world's longest-lasting and one of its most uniform financial accounting units from being money just because it was better at performing some functions than others would be as unjustified as excluding cowries or wampum because, being individually of small value, their monetary functions were performed less well for large as compared with smaller amounts. Just as cowries and wampum could be aggregated in bucketfuls, basketfuls or stringfuls to overcome the apparent disadvantages of their small size, so over many millennia it has been easy to think up and apply in practice subsidiaries for bovine currencies without having to resort to imaginary slaughter whenever the equivalent of a pound of flesh was required in exchange.

Cattle used as money were of course counted by head so that, for monetary purposes at least, quantity has generally though not invariably been more important than quality. The preference for quantity over quality is well illustrated in this account of Negley Farson's contacts with the Wakamba, a Kenyan pastoral tribe, just before the Second World War. Much more recent reports indicate that the attitude displayed by the Wakamba has not materially altered. An agricultural expert had been trying to persuade the tribal chiefs not to keep their old and diseased cattle. In reply one of the Wakamba answered: 'Listen, here are two pound notes. One is old and wrinkled and ready to tear; this one is new. But they are both worth a pound. Well, it's the same with cows' (Farson 1940, 264).

The same regard to cattle is shared by the Masai and, with regard to goats, by the Kikuyu among whom Jomo Kenyatta, the 'father of modern Kenya' was himself reared. The common unfortunate ecological result of this economic characteristic has been a marked tendency towards overgrazing which from time to time has turned grasslands into desert, and which explains why in recent times the introduction of modern money has been stressed by state authorities for soil conservation as well as for other more obvious economic purposes. Attempts to change farming practices to control erosion appear doomed to delay if not failure. Thus in 1938 the economist A. E. G. Robinson stressed the need 'to change the attitude of the native towards his domestic animals that they become not tokens of wealth or a form of currency but a source of income'. The *Global 2000* report projects a world increase in cattle of 200 million between 1976 and the end of this century and points out that in the twelve years between 1955 and 1976 Africa's sheep and goat population increased by over 66 million (*Global 2000* 1982, 232–5). Attention has already been drawn, in the case of the Indian tribes of Canada, to the deleterious results of replacing the old with a new money system: here one may see the dangerous effects, given the increased pressure of human and animal populations on limited resources, of maintaining one of the oldest monetary systems in the world. In 1983 the new Brandt Commission re-emphasized 'the need to halt and reverse these processes of ecological degradation, which now assume emergency proportions' and estimated the cost of doing so as 'well over $25 billion by the end of the century' (p. 126). In certain instances, particularly when cattle were used for sacrifices, the quality – 'without spot or blemish' – was important, and in a number of such cases the religious usages of cattle probably preceded their adoption for more general monetary purposes. But there need be no incompatibility in the argument as to the relative merits of quality as opposed to quantity – good or bad, the essence of the argument is that they were in either case money. Furthermore, they were movable, an immense advantage, forming man's earliest working capital and the linguistic origin not only of our 'pecuniary' from the Latin 'pecus' or cattle, but also our terms 'capital' and 'chattels'. Similarly the Welsh 'da' as an adjective means 'good', and as a noun, both 'cattle' and 'goods'.

Although these examples of the cultural, ecological and economic relationships of the monetary use of cattle are taken mostly from the modern world, similar problems of overstocking and resalinization, even if on a much smaller scale, occurred in the ancient world also, particularly in Mesopotamia and along the North African coastal area. The latter, once in large part the granary of the Roman empire and more recently feeder of the empty imperial dreams of Mussolini, is now, despite its vestigial wells which slaked the thirst of the Eighth Army, simply a northern extension of the Sahara. The use of cattle as visible and useful evidence of wealth and its superiority as a form of money for many centuries in various communities around the world combine to explain why it has not always been very easy to substitute modern money in place of cattle in primitive pastoral communities. The other staple food used as money, namely grain, will be considered shortly in the context of the monetary development of ancient Egypt. We turn first, however, to the essential preliminary stage on the road to coined money; the use of metals as money.

Pre-coinage metallic money

To primitive man emerging from the Stone Age, any metal was precious: the distinction between base and precious metals became of significance only after his skill as a metallurgist had improved and supplies of various metals had increased sufficiently to reflect their relative abundance or scarcity. Thus copper, bronze, gold, silver and electrum were known and used before iron, while aluminium, the most common metal in the earth's crust, became available for use only in the nineteenth century. It was first named by Humphrey Davy in 1809, first isolated by Hans Christian Oersted in 1825, introduced to the public as one of the special attractions of the Paris Exhibition of 1855, while its ranking as a precious metal was confirmed by Napoleon III, who temporarily laid aside his gold plate to eat off aluminium on state occasions. Within a relatively short period of time millions of soldiers in the two World Wars were also eating off aluminium plate without considering it in any way luxurious, while for a number of years in the immediate post-Second World War period certain European countries resorted to the use of aluminium coins. This was, however, considered to be very much an emergency and far inferior to the more normal use of the heavier metals, of copper, brass, etc. to which they promptly returned, aluminium being considered no longer fit for even the humblest tokens.

The eagerness with which metals were accepted by late Stone-Age man and their growing indispensability once he had become accustomed to them together form the key explanation as to their ready transformation into use as money. Indeed the word for 'silver' and 'money' has remained the same from prehistoric to modern times in a number of languages, e.g. French 'argent' and Welsh 'arian'. The metals therefore formed a strong and wide bridge from primitive to modern or coined money. There is no need at this point to dwell on their ornamental attributes, which obviously helped enormously in making and maintaining their almost universal acceptability, but it is perhaps more appropriate to note here how often the metals began to be used symbolically in imitation of and as a more valuable extension of the age-old primitive moneys. The Chinese at the end of the Stone Age began for instance to manufacture both bronze and copper 'cowries';

and these dumpy imitations, which must have represented very high values at least when they were first introduced, are considered by some numismatists to be among the earliest examples of quasi-coinage, although this depends on how strictly one defines the term.

The transition from specific usage as tools to symbolic and more general usage as media of exchange and units of account may also be seen in a range of metallic objects made of copper, bronze and iron, such as axes, spears, knives, swords, hoes and spades. Swords and spears were obviously treasured possessions, replicas of which could conveniently be reduced in size as they lost their purpose and became used as money. A number of writers have commented on Julius Caesar's castigation of the ancient Britons for still using crudely made iron sword-blades as currency when more civilized Europeans had long used coins; but, as Einzig points out, the Greeks themselves had earlier been using iron spits or nails as money at a time when they could hardly have been derided by Romans as being backward (1966, 235) Spade, hoe and knife money is best looked at below in the section on Chinese coinage as being logically inseparable from any discussion of the 'invention' of coinage. Meanwhile a brief examination of the non-representational monetary use of pre-coinage metal may be in order.

As well as representational or symbolic money, metals have long been used more simply and directly as money, sometimes just as unmarked lumps of various shapes and sizes but more often in the form of rods, wire coils and rings, anklets, bracelets and necklaces, that is in forms which were intended especially to facilitate their acceptance as money. A particularly interesting example of this wide-ranging group of metallic moneys is to be seen in the 'manilla' currencies of West Africa. The manilla is a metal anklet, bracelet or front section of a necklace, depending on its size and curvature, usually of copper or brass, long used in parts of West Africa, particularly in Nigeria, for money which could be conveniently and ornamentally carried on the person. Its linguistic and actual derivations are in considerable doubt. Its claimed linguistic origins range from being possibly derived from Spanish or Portuguese 'little hand' (from Latin 'manus') to a most unlikely combination of Phoenician and Irish. Claims as to the actual physical origins of the manilla are, with varying probability, ascribed to either ancient Phoenician trading links between Tyre and Sidon with West Africa, or spring from the attractiveness of the bolts, clamps and other such metal devices salvaged from the ships of early Portuguese explorers wrecked on the Guinea coast in the fifteenth century. It is a recorded fact that in the short period 1504–7 just one trading station alone along the Guinea coast imported 287,813 manillas from Portugal.

The Irish connection stems from the more than superficial resemblance between current manillas and ancient Celtic torque ornaments found in Ireland. These various explanations as to the origin of manillas are not mutually exclusive. We know that the ancient Phoenician traders exported considerable quantities of open-ended bracelets to their distant trading centres including Ireland and West Africa.

Although attempts had been made as early as 1902 to suppress the manilla, attempts which were repeated by the West African Currency Board after its formation in 1912, the United Africa Company still found it necessary to trade in manillas in the immediate post-Second World War period. Eventually, after a long struggle they were officially withdrawn from circulation in 1949, and a little later this recent triumph of modern bureaucracy over primitive money was celebrated by the issue of special postage stamps. The tribes who, like the Ibo, stubbornly preferred cowries and manillas to coins, are eloquent examples of the persistence of their need for psychic satisfactions, in this case religious and ornamental gratification, to be combined with the more purely economic aspects of money, a combination lost by having to rely exclusively on the narrower range of functions performed by coins. Though mass-produced and imported like minted coins, manillas and similar objects were nevertheless felt to be far more adapted to the needs of primitive societies than were coins. The manillas were virtually a modern metallic money integrated into primitive societies to such a degree that they performed the functions usually associated exclusively with primitive moneys.

The normal process of monetary development was of course just the reverse, being a series of occasionally interrupted improvements which cumulatively transform primitive communities through increasing recourse to metals for all sorts of uses including money, into more advanced economies, diffusing higher standards of living and more sophisticated monetary and trading systems over wider and wider areas and involving vastly greater populations. Money and civilization usually marched onward together, and, occasionally, declined together. Once it had become available, the increased preference for metallic money is easily appreciated, for as Jevons has convincingly demonstrated, it possessed, in the pre-electronic era, to a higher degree than any other material, the essential qualities of a good money, namely, cognizability, utility, portability, divisibility, indestructibility, stability of value, and homogeneity (Jevons 1910, 31).

Although Jevons arranged these in a different order of priority, we have already seen that what may be a correctly interpreted order for one society may be quite misleading in another. Certainly with regard to the development of coinage, cognizability would be placed among the first ranks rather than in the last position to which Jevons relegated it. The pace of financial bargaining was enormously speeded up when recognized pieces of metal could be simply counted than when metals had to be weighed, as was the case in all pre-coinage days in all primitive societies and even for long periods in the earlier stages of civilized communities. Admittedly the ancient world of the Near East managed to carry out an extensive system of trading based very largely on metallic currencies exchanged by weight without any knowledge of coining. But that extensive degree of trading was possible only because they had already 'invented' an effective system of banking.

Money and banking in Mesopotamia

Man may not have originated in the traditional site of the Garden of Eden, to the east of the Holy Land, but more possibly in the Rift Valley of Africa. Nevertheless, it may well be that myth and science can more easily be reconciled in recognizing the probability that the world's first civilization grew up in the warm, fertile, alluvial plains between the Euphrates and the Tigris some seven thousand years ago and spread gradually to neighbouring regions. It is equally probable that this traditional Eden saw the first use of money, while over three thousand years ago the world's first bankers were living in Babylon. Toynbee isolates some twenty-one different 'civilizations' but, since fifteen of these were directly or indirectly derived from earlier examples, he narrows the separately developed into six: the Sumerian, Egyptian, Minoan, Chinese, Mayan and Andean. Of these only the Incas of the Andes had managed to achieve a high degree of civilization without the use of money, though paradoxically they possessed a superabundance of what has generally been regarded as by far the best material for money – gold and silver.

As was explained in chapter 1, the greater the stratification of society and the more efficiently meticulous the planning system, the less necessary it is for people to use money. This may account for the fact that whereas the Spanish conquistadores found that the more liberally governed Mexicans regularly used gold dust (kept in transparent quills) and cocoa-beans (kept for large payments in bags of 24,000) as money, in contrast the more rigidly hierarchical Incas had no such money: an exception proved by an iron rule. The origin of money in China occurred quite independently of that elsewhere, but the relatively closer proximity of the Sumerian, Egyptian and Minoan civilizations may still raise some doubt as to the degree to which they were ignorant of each other's monetary affairs, particularly since strong trading links are known to have been established in quite early times.

The upsurge of interest in archaeology in recent years, combined with the application of scientific methods such as dendro-chronology and radiocarbon testing generally increased the confidence with which historians of ancient times can establish the age of some of the past data by which they trace the rise of civilization. Even with all these modern aids however, there remain legitimate doubts concerning how to interpret even the most cast-iron of facts. As Joan Oates disarmingly concedes, 'Any study of Babylonian civilisation is, and will remain, an amalgam of near-truths, misunderstandings and ignorance, but this can be said of more periods of history than most historians would admit' (1979, 197). However, so far as monetary studies are concerned we are at least favoured by the exceptional durability of the precious metals and, in the case of the Middle East, by the almost equal durability of the innumerable clay writing tablets which form a vast reservoir of usable information. Yet behaviour leaves no fossils, and even where detailed written texts exist, their discovery by its very nature is apt to be random. Of course there are exceptions, for when records are written in tablets of stone, whether these are the biblical ten commandments or the more numerous laws of Hammurabi, we may assume, from the form and material in which they were written, that they were considered to be of great importance in contemporary life, and our historical treatment should take notice of such facts.

'Money,' said Keynes in his *Treatise*,

> like certain other essential elements in civilisation, is a far more ancient institution than we were taught to believe some few years ago. Its origins are lost in the mists when the ice was melting, and may well stretch back into the paradisaic intervals in human history of the inter-glacial periods, when the weather was delightful and the mind free to be fertile of new ideas – in the Islands of the Hesperides or Atlantis or some Eden of Central Asia. (1930, 1, 13)

It was from this lost Eden that money and banking, as well as writing and our duodecimal methods of counting time, space – and money – originated. If one were to speculate as to how writing first appeared one might dreamingly imagine that romantic necessity or poetic inspiration were the causes rather than the prosaic need to record debts and credits, which in historical reality turns out to have been the source.

Thus handwriting from its very beginnings was closely associated with, and improved in parallel with, the keeping of accounts. The earliest Sumerian numerical accounts consisted of a stroke for units and a simple circular depression for tens. The economic origins of writing are unequivocally confirmed by expert archaeologists. Thus Dr Oates asserts that 'Writing was invented in Mesopotamia as a method of book-keeping. The earliest known texts are lists of livestock and agricultural equipment. These come from the city of Uruk c.3,100 BC' Further to emphasize its mundane, economic character the same authority adds that 'the invention of writing represented at first merely a technical advance in economic administration' (Oates 1979, 15, 25). Neighbouring tribes such as the Akkadians borrowed the Sumerian system of handwriting and gradually this picture-writing or pictographic script developed into various cuneiform standards that lasted for three thousand years, and especially for certain economic documents, well into the first century AD. Numerous records exist in this script describing the activities of a number of banking houses and of prosperous merchants in Babylon and Nippur after the region became part of the Persian empire (Oates 1979, 136).

The royal palaces and especially the temples were the centre of Babylonian economic and administrative as well as of political and religious life (these elements were not as compartmentalized as we have made them). Security for deposits was more easily assured in the temples and royal palaces than in private houses, and so it was natural enough that the first banking operations were carried out by royal and temple officials. Grain was the main form of deposit at first, but in the process of time other deposits were commonly taken: other crops, fruit, cattle and agricultural implements, leading eventually and most importantly to deposits of the precious metals. Receipts testifying to these deposits gradually led to transfers to the order not only of the depositors but also to a third party. 'This was the way in which loan business originated and reached a high stage of development in Babylonian civilisation' (Orsingher 1964, 1). In the course of time private houses also began to carry on such deposit business and probably grew to be of greater importance internally than was the case in contemporary Egypt. The banking operations of the temple and palace-based banks preceded coinage by well over a thousand years, and so did private banking houses by some hundreds of years: notably the reverse of later European monetary development.

Literally hundreds of thousands of cuneiform blocks have been unearthed by archaeologists in the various city sites along the Tigris and Euphrates, many of which were deposit receipts and monetary contracts, confirming the existence of simple banking operations as everyday affairs, common and widespread throughout Babylonia. The Code of Hammurabi, law-giver of Babylon, who ruled from about 1792 to 1750 BC,[1] gives us categorical evidence, available for our inspection in the shape of inscriptions on a block of solid diorite standing over 7 ft high now in the Paris Louvre, showing that by this period 'Bank operations by temples and great landowners had become so numerous and so important' that it was thought 'necessary to lay down standard rules of procedure' (Orsingher, 1964, viii).

The oldest Babylonian private banking firms still remain anonymous, but by the seventh century BC the 'Grandsons of Egibi' emerged into recorded fame. Their headquarters were in the city of Babylon, whence they carried out a very wide variety of business activities combined with their banking. They acted as pawnbrokers – and in case anyone objects that this is hardly banking, perhaps one should be reminded that the original charter of the Bank of England empowered it to act as a pawnbroker. The House of Egibi also gave loans against securities, and accepted a wide range of deposits. 'Customers could have current accounts with them and could withdraw the whole or parts of certain deposits with cheques . . . The ships of the firm were used in trade expeditions exactly like those of the royal and temple households. Speculation and investment for secure income were combined in the business pattern of this bank' (Heichelheim, 1958, I, 72). After having flourished for some hundreds of years this bank seems to fade from the scene some time during the fifth century BC.

A similar but younger banking firm of which we have records is that of the Sons of Maraschu, which operated from the town of Nippur. As well as carrying on the same kind of banking functions as the Grandsons of Egibi, they specialized in what we would call renting and leasing arrangements. They administered, as agents or tax farmers, the royal and larger private estates; they rented out fish-ponds, financed and constructed irrigation canals and charged fees to farmers within their water networks; and they even had a partial monopoly on the sale and distribution of beer. They also acted as jewellers and goldsmiths. Thus it is not surprising that in Babylon the use of precious metals, and later coinage, became much more generally accepted than was the case in Egypt and, because they had a less rigid and more 'mixed' economy, the peculiar kind of state giro system based on grain did not reach so high a pitch of development in Babylon as it did in the Egypt of the Ptolemies; to which account we now turn.

---

[1] The dates suggested by Orsingher, 1728–1686, are probably too late; but as Dr Oates warns: 'Chronological systems currently in use give a range of 200 years for the accession of Hammurabi' (see Oates 1979, 24).

Girobanking in Egypt

Nowhere has grain achieved such a high degree of monetary use as in ancient Egypt. Although copper, gold and silver were long used as units of account, there is some doubt as to the extent they were also used as media of exchange, particularly for the majority of the population, when the allocation or rationing of resources was based on a strict form of feudalism which restricted the need to use money. Despite the existence of metallic money, it was grain which formed the most extensively used monetary medium, particularly for accounting purposes, even after the Greeks had introduced coinage. The origin of transfer payments to order developed naturally by stages, arising from the centralization of grain harvest in state warehouses in both Babylon and Egypt. Written orders for the withdrawal of separate lots of grain by owners whose crops had been deposited there for safety and convenience, or which had been compulsorily deposited to the credit of the king, soon became used as a more general method of payment for debts to other persons, the tax gatherers, priests or traders. Despite the other forms of money, such as copper rings which had been in use from time to time and from place to place, there was an impressive permanency and generality about the use of grain as money, especially for large payments, in ancient Egypt. This system of warehouse banking reached its highest peak of excellence and geographical extent in the Egyptian empire of the Ptolemies, (323–30 BC). Private banks and royal banks using money in the form of coins and precious metals had by then long been known and existed side by side with the grain banks, but the former banks were used chiefly in connection with the trade of the richer merchants and particularly for external trade. Obviously, anything in strong demand by the state, the value and condition of which were carefully measured and guaranteed by a well-trained, and largely Greek, bureaucracy, became almost universally accepted in payment of debt. Long-established private merchant banks were almost entirely foreign and dominated in particular by the Greeks.

There was a wide gap between this smoothly working system and the monetary habits of the native Egyptian population. The native Egyptian's reluctance to accept metallic money probably suited the Ptolemies' economic strategy very well. They seemed to be forever short of the precious metals which were indispensable for foreign purchases and especially for external military expenditures, for which purpose they were forced to drain Egypt internally of its precious metals (very much as the internal gold coinage of Europe disappeared to meet the demands of the First World War). Yet the Ptolemies wished to stimulate economic activity within Egypt and were fully aware that this would require more rather than less money. If they were short of monetary metal, which not only appeared too precious to be used widely for internal monetary use, but which in any case was not very popular with the natives, there was of course an abundance of grain – and grain had for centuries possessed a quasi-monetary character in Egypt. If the Greek expertise in banking could be adapted by the Egyptian bureaucracy to the peculiar preferences and habits of the indigenous population, then the Ptolemies would have the best of both worlds. This they did. Thus it was partly in order to economize on internal coinage that much greater use was made internally of grain for monetary purposes: and this meant a much fuller development of the system of warehouse banking and grain transfers than had ever been previously achieved anywhere. Consequently, although some rudimentary elements of a giro system of payment had developed much earlier in Babylon and Greece than in Ptolemaic Egypt, undoubtedly the honour for the first full and efficient operation of that most important financial innovation that enabled a nationwide circulation and transfer of credit belongs to the Egypt of the Ptolemies.

We have seen that most of the external and some of the internal trade of Egypt was carried on with the aid of Greek and other foreign bankers. It was with their aid that the Ptolemies transformed a scattered local warehouse deposit system into a fully integrated state giro of such a high standard of efficiency and sophistication as to be almost beyond credence by modern man, who too readily assumes that the use of grain as money must necessarily imply a primitive economic system. It is perhaps for this reason that Preisigke, one of the most authoritative writers on banking developments in the ancient world, in his *Giro System in Hellenistic Egypt* (1910) emphasizes its modernistic aspects. Rostovtzeff, another eminent Egyptologist, in his monumental study of *The Social and Economic History of the Hellenistic World* (1941) gives conclusive evidence that by means of the grain banks, the banking habit had been greatly extended in Egypt: 'The accounts of the bank are especially interesting because they show how popular recourse to the banks became with the people of Egypt . . . the system of paying one's debts through the bank had the additional advantage of officially recording the transactions and thus providing important evidence in case of litigation', and of course greatly assisted the state in matters of economic and fiscal control.

Rostovtzeff explains in considerable detail the accounting system of the private and royal grain banks, in order to make it crystal clear that 'the payments were effected by transfer from one account to another without money passing' (1941, 1285). Double-entry bookeeping had of course not yet appeared, but a system of debit and credit entries and credit transfers was recorded by varying the case endings of the names involved, credit entries being naturally enough in the genitive or possessive case and debit entries in the dative case. As already stated, Rostovtzeff found it necessary to mention 'this detail in the bank procedure, familiar in modern times, because many eminent scholars have thought it improbable that such transfers were made in ancient times' (1941, 1285). The numerous scattered government granaries were transformed by the Ptolemies into a network of corn banks with what amounted to a central bank in Alexandria, where the main accounts from all the state granary banks were recorded. The separate crops of grain harvested by the farmers were not separately earmarked, but amalgamated into general deposits, except that the harvests for separate years, and therefore of different qualities, were stored in separate compartments (Preisigke 1910, 69).

Seed corn, the capital base both of the economy and of the banking system, was directly under the control of the state by means of an official appropriately termed the *Oeconomus*, whose duty it was to see that seed corn would not be used for any other purpose. Vagaries of the weather, though on occasions disastrous, were of course much less of a hazard in the Nile Delta than with us: so that inflation or deflation could to some extent be controlled and the monetary scarcity of one year be compensated by the bounty of the next. Thus the giro system in Egypt had come about because of the need to economize on coins and the precious metals, by the need to supplement the existing private banks with a state bank system, and above all by the desire to spread the banking habit throughout the community. It also gave to the rulers a closer control over the economy for fiscal purposes, while providing a general stimulus for trade more widespread than had previously been possible, particularly among the poorer classes. In the new economic organization of the Ptolemies 'two systems were . . . blended, so as to form one well-balanced and smoothly working whole: the immemorial practice of Egypt and the methods of the Greek State and the Greek private household' (Rostovtzeff 1941, 1286). Grain may have been primitive money – but the world's first giro system transformed it into an efficient medium of payments partaking of many of the most desirable features of modern money.

The precise nature and extent of banking activity in the ancient world is likely to remain an uncertain matter, about which it would be unwise to be too dogmatic. Heichelheim has listed a number of distinct banking services such as deposit banking, 'foreign exchange', giro, secured and unsecured lending not only internally but also externally, and is satisfied that 'almost all these forms of banking business existed already as early as the third millennium BC . . . we have unmistakably clear records of such transactions between Babylonians, Assyrians and other nations of Asia Minor' (1958, II, 134). He goes on to show that 'incasso' or the taking in and paying out of money on behalf of customers' orders was part of the normal economic activity of the royal and temple store houses, to a more marked degree in Egypt than even in Babylon.

> We can see what a great part this banking system must have played over the whole of this vast country, and how detailed was its organisation, by the number of its branches and employees and by the daily records and accounts kept of the capital invested in them, so that these may well compare with the greatest banks of the nineteenth and twentieth centuries AD. (Heichelheim, 1958, III, 122)

To what extent, one wonders, are such comparisons between ancient and modern times valid?

Coin and cash in early China

Chinese civilization has enjoyed the longest history and has, at least until the present century, directly involved far more people than any other. Yet for a number of reasons it is very largely ignored by western writers,[2] partly from a contagious ignorance, but mainly because our modern western civilization has been largely derived from Roman and Greek sources which in their turn learned much from Mesopotamia and Egypt but nothing directly from China itself; from which, with a very few notable exceptions, the West was cut off until the geographical discoveries of the sixteenth and later centuries. Consequently the debt which western money owes to Chinese development is small (with the possible exception of the banknote), since the route to modern money follows the general course of Hellenistic and Romanized western civilization. Nevertheless while obviously being unable to do justice in the space of a few pages to such a vast subject, there are a few salient features of Chinese monetary development which repay even the most cursory examination.

We have already noted how metal cowries, of bronze or copper, were cast in China as symbols of objects already long accepted as money. A

[2] Thus Lord Clark's *Civilisation* (1969), the text of the successful television series, completely ignores China.

similar process took place with regard to spades, hoes and adzes (variants of the most common tools) and also of knives. The common characteristic of all these metallic moneys was not only that they were cast but that they were almost invariably composed of base metals. Another important aspect of most of the popular Chinese moneys was that they had holes in them, either at one end, as with the cowrie and knife currency, or in the centre, as obviously with ring-money and, later, the conventional coin currencies. The holes which were mostly square, but not uncommonly circular, served two main purposes. First, in the process of manufacture, a rod would be inserted through a number of coins which could then have their rough edges filed or be otherwise finished in a group of fifty or more coins together. Secondly, when in use, they could be strung together in large quantities for convenience of carriage and of trading. This leads us to another vital feature of Chinese coins namely that because they were made of base metals they had a low value density, and therefore it was all the more necessary to handle them in very considerable quantities even for items of relatively moderate value.

In contrast to the development of coinage in and around the Mediterranean where the precious metals held the most important role, China concentrated almost exclusively on base metals for coinage, with important consequences for the differential development of money in the eastern and western worlds. In China, too, the state played a dominant role in coinage, and although there were hundreds of mints, the state insisted on central control and uniformity of standards. A further consequence of the base-metal composition was the ease with which such coins could be imitated and counterfeited. The raw material costs were low, the method of manufacture was simple and the superficial inscriptions easy to apply. Consequently imitation was endemic particularly at the periphery of the authorities' power. Because coins were confined to base metals the precious metals generally had to be used for all large purchases and had to be weighed in the primitive fashion even in modern times rather than counted, as with coins. Consequently, although China was easily the first to introduce 'coins', the possibilities which they offered were not as fully exploited as in the western world, where, once invented, their development went ahead much more quickly.

The question of when coins were 'invented' depends very largely on one's definition of a coin, and one must concede that a definition which might suit the numismatist, who might legitimately be rather more concerned with technical considerations than the economist, might not quite suit the latter who is, or should be, much more concerned with function than with form or technique. Functionally speaking, the early spade, hoe and knife currencies were 'coins'; they were state-authenticated, more or less identical, and guaranteed symbols of value, accepted by tale not by weight, with their authorization clearly indicated by the inscriptions they carried. Although the experts differ as to the earliest dates to be ascribed to these tool-coins, they probably were in general use at the end of the second millennium BC, while round coins were, according to recent research, at least roughly contemporaneous with those of the eastern Mediterranean, though earlier writers would date Chinese round coins very much earlier, in the twelfth century BC.[3] Part of the difficulty in being as precise in dating Chinese coins compared with others is the fact that Chinese emperors would not allow their names or heads to appears on their coins, so that sequential series are difficult to establish. One may summarize the difference between Chinese and western coinage by saying that, as in so many other aspects of civilization, China had a long lead; but in the case of coinage this lead was quickly overtaken when, quite independently, a different type of coinage was invented elsewhere, using superior techniques and precious metals, which were much better for most monetary functions.

Ever since the Portuguese opened the sea route to China round the Cape of Good Hope the typical, small, base-metal coins of China have been known as *cash*, an extension geographically and linguistically of the Tamil word for such money. This cash was virtually the same as that circulating in ancient China: numismatically speaking, time had stood still. The enormous difference in values between the large gold coins favoured in the rest of the world for larger payments and the small stringed 'cash', typically consisting of a thousand coins, may be seen by the average ratio between them of a thousand to one. Thus although China can boast a 'coinage' of unbroken continuity going back almost three thousand years, this longevity rested on a rigid conservatism which confined coins to act only as the small change of the economy, a position similar to that occupied by coins in our own society today where precious metal coins, for currency purposes, have disappeared.

It is a remarkable fact that China did not issue any substantial precious metal coinage, and then only in silver, until 1890, and even then the minting of traditional cash continued until 1912 (Cribb 1979, 184). The arrested, or at least limited, development of coinage in China was however in large part responsible for stimulating the growth of a powerful substitute for money – the banknote in modern form – some

---

[3] Contrast J. H. S. Lockhart *Collection of Chinese Copper Coins* (1907) with J. Cribb 'The Far East' in *Coins* ed. M. J. Price (1980).

five hundred years before similar developments took place in Europe. Conversely the greater value-to-weight ratio of the superior western coinage probably inhibited the development of the banknote in Europe; a classic historical example of good money being an enemy of the best. It is appropriate now to consider the origin and early development of this superior form of coinage.

Coinage and the change from primitive to modern economies

Although one cannot draw a clear line separating the untidily overlapping types of 'primitive economies' from more modernistic types, one can certainly affirm that in no instance has this momentous process of change been more exhaustively studied than in the case of early Greek history. One might add also that the rapid development, if not quite the original invention, of coinage of a modern type appears to have been an essential, if possibly almost accidental, catalyst in the astonishing development of Greek civilization. Both *economics* and *numismatics*, linguistically and more generally speaking, come from the Greek, originally meaning *household management* and *custom* or *currency* respectively, though both these terms naturally had rather different connotations then than now.

We have earlier seen numismatics described, by Knapp, as the 'dead body' of the dismal science. Nothing could be further from the truth. There must be something about money which generally stirs the blood and occasionally the mind, for in recent years the 'science' of numismatics has been in the sort of uproar that has long distinguished the protagonists of the various schools of monetary economists. It was, most appropriately, the matter of how to interpret the history of the classical Greeks, probably the most exciting but possibly also the most bellicose of people, that became the occasion for open verbal warfare between the various schools of thought. Was the Greek economy 'modern' or was it 'primitive'? In principle the conflict was not confined to Greece, for it covered the general interface between primitive and modern societies; but it became focused more sharply on the Greek economy in general and Greek coinage in particular than has been the case elsewhere.

Does the introduction of coinage mark a watershed in human progress, or is it simply a minor technical improvement in political accountancy and in methods of exchange? Is the invention of money not only accidental but also incidental, not only to the development of Greek civilization in particular but also to other civilizations? What were the causes of this invention, or in other words what were the origins of coinage? In particular it is important to realize that current debates among historians regarding the degree to which non-economic factors, mainly political, as opposed to economic factors, mainly trade, were responsible for the introduction of *coinage* are precisely the same kind of debates which arose in the past and still arise as to the origins of primitive *money*. Indeed, in the form 'how is money created today' this perennial argument still proceeds. It is in the nature of money to give rise to these polarized attitudes, and it is this that gives an added dimension to the intrinsically interesting history of the origins of coinage.

This problem of the degree of modernity of Greece and especially of its 'economy' (as a sort of theoretical average of the distinctly different city-states) thus brought into sharp relief the misleading oversimplifications of the early school of mainly German economic historians such as Hildebrand, Bücher and Beloch, who saw the past in terms of a logically neat economic model consisting of a few definite stages through which each civilization had inevitably to pass. Given this model, or some variant modified to suit the purpose in hand, it became customary to make a wide and apparently meaningful series of heroic comparisons between different civilizations at the same 'stage' of development, with the division between primitive and modern being marked by the rise of a money economy. Greek development, for example, from the seventh to fifth centuries BC could thus be seen to correspond closely in its nature and almost even in the speed of its growth with that of modern Europe during the course of the fourteenth to sixteenth centuries inclusive. The very extremes to which these views were pressed inevitably created a strong reaction, also led appropriately by German writers such as the sociologist Max Weber and especially the economic historian Johannes Hasebroek, who emphasized the differences rather than the similarities between ancient Greece and modern Europe. Hasebroek demonstrated how elementary were Greek industrial techniques, how limited in scale and nature was their trade, and above all he showed the fundamental errors of attributing modern concepts of national economic policy, such as mercantilism, money markets or labour markets to the city-states of ancient Greece (Hasebroek 1928).

Certainly the Greeks liked to display a distinctly different, even apparently hostile, attitude towards trade and commerce from that which exists today. Partly because of their slaves but perhaps also because of their nature, they publicly pretended to disdain business affairs. As in all pre-industrial societies agriculture was the main occupation and landownership the basis of society. In general, trading was the business of foreigners, the 'metics' who were not normally allowed to own land or receive the privilege of citizenship. Most manufacturing (with a few notable exceptions which have been overemphasized by the modernists) was on a very small scale, hardly more than cottage industry or handicraft activity carried on either in the open or in small workshops. Given these attitudes, it would clearly be wrong to assume that the city-states pursued consistent 'economic' policies, whether 'mercantilist' or 'free-trade' such as those appropriate to seventeenth- or nineteenth-century Europe. Nevertheless when due allowance has been made for the typically small-scale and locally confined nature of most Greek business, economic activities were crucially important to their development, and their monetary innovations were essential stimulants in this process. An authoritative assessment by Antony Andrewes, professor of ancient history at Oxford, gives the following balanced picture: 'Commerce and industry in ancient Greece were exceedingly important, but the individual operations were on a very small scale.' He also warned that 'although it is salutary to insist that the standard categories of nineteenth-century economics are not applicable, the reaction may go too far, eliminating the effect of trade on Greek history altogether (Andrewes 1967, 119, 145).

Nevertheless the primitivist view, magisterially reaffirmed by Moses Finley, professor of ancient history at Cambridge (1975), and his numerous disciples, continues to claim considerable support, despite the accumulation of more recent 'modernistic' evidence, such as that provided for example by Austin, Vidal-Naquet and Oswyn Murray. The last, after examining the degree to which foreign trade and early coinage were mutual stimulants, concluded: 'I am not convinced that trade plays as little part in the early use of coinage as most modern scholars (i.e. the primitivists) believe' (Murray 1980, 225). Although the balance of argument is thus beginning to veer away from the primitivists, one of the important permanent benefits of their scholarship has been to demonstrate conclusively that in general the 'economy' was inseparable from the body politic and in particular that the drive which pushed the Greeks into predominance as coin-makers came very largely from non-economic motives and not simply from commercial considerations.

Whereas earlier modernistic writers confined their attention too narrowly to the economic factors which gave rise to coinage and overemphasized the degree to which the 'economy' of Greece could be compared with that of modern countries, most recent writers have taken note of these other important features affecting Greek monetary history. Thus Austin and Vidal-Naquet give as much prominence to the politics as to the economics of money: 'In the history of Greek cities coinage was always first and foremost a civic emblem. To strike coins with the badge of the city was to proclaim one's political independence' (Austin and Vidal-Naquet, 1977, 57). One might perhaps add, despite the warnings of the primitivists, that this political badge of independence conferred by striking their own coins is not dissimilar in concept to the fashion of newly independent ex-colonial states, most of them with a recent history of primitive money, insisting on setting up their own central banks in this century in an attempt to proclaim to the world both their political and their economic independence. Had the ex-colonialist officials been more conversant with the history of primitive and ancient money they would have welcomed and modified rather than have impotently resisted such changes.

Although the primitivists may well be blamed for their overcautious refusal to make or condone what others would see as useful and indeed essential intertemporal generalizations, they have at least correctly insisted on the important part played by non-commercial considerations in the origins and growth of coinage. Thus, although they themselves might hesitate to do so, the implied comparisons with the non-economic aspects of primitive and even modern moneys still need to be more explicitly, clearly, consistently and emphatically repeated.

The invention of coinage in Lydia and Ionian Greece

Turning now to the question as to how, when and where non-Chinese coinage was first 'invented', it should be made clear that the innovative road was a long one, involving many intermediate stages though the final stages took less time than had previously been thought. Whereas the production of roughly similar metal ingots, so long as these gave no authentic indication of their weight or purity, can be definitely excluded, yet, when their weight and purity became authenticated to such a degree that they were accepted fairly generally without having of necessity to be weighed, then we may take this as being the first step towards coinage – but still a long way from the final product. Such a preliminary stage was reached in Cappadocia, where the state guarantee, probably both of the weight and purity of her silver ingots, helped their acceptance as money; a position reached as early as between about 2250 and 2150 BC. As the rather cumbersome ingots gradually became conveniently smaller, they were fashioned into a number of different forms of more standardized monetary objects, such as bars, which in their turn were reduced to rods, spits and elongated nails.

The most obvious and direct route to coinage was however through the improvement in quality and authority of the kind of large silver blobs or 'dumps' such as those in use in Knossos in the second millennium. These Minoan pre-coins were however not very uniform and required either a state seal or a punched impression to help their still hesitant circulation. However such metal quasi-coins gradually became more plentiful in Greece, including the Greek islands and the eastern Mediterranean, during the first half of the first millennium BC, during which the final stages in the inventive process took place quite rapidly. In retrospect we can see that this invention meant that a new monetary era had definitely begun, of a form and nature that by today has penetrated virtually the whole world, and even ousted, in the latter part of the nineteenth century, its ancient Chinese rival.

Both Lydia and the mainland portion of Ionia, the birthplace and nursery respectively of coinage, formed parts of what is now Turkey, Lydia lying along its southern and Ionia along its south-western coasts. Though separated by 400 miles of mountainous terrain they were fairly close neighbours by sea. During the seventh century BC their rulers became united by marriage, and Lydia, under its mythical Midas, its semi-legendary Gyges and their equally but verifiably rich and restless successors, aggressively sought to exert sovereignty over the Greek city-states of mainland Ionia and some of the Greek islands. Croesus succeeded in annexing Phrygia until he in turn was conquered by the Persians in 546 BC.

It was during this period that the final stages in the inventive process of modern-type coinage were completed, although the actual steps in this process remain matters of active debate among the experts. Both Lydia and Ionia had a hand in these developments but with priority going definitely but narrowly (more narrowly, it now seems as the result of recent research, than was formerly believed) to Lydia. The rivers of this region rush down from the mountains and then, typified by the River Maiandros, silt up as they 'meander' over their plains. It was from 'panning' in these rivers that the Lydians and Ionians derived their special type of light-yellow precious metal, a natural amalgam of gold and silver, which the Lydians probably fashioned into the world's first struck or hammered coins. According to Greek legend the rich deposits of the Pactolus river near Sardis, the Lydian capital, were the result of Midas' bathing in its torrents to wash away his dangerously embarrassing golden touch which had even turned his food into gold. This Lydian metal was called 'electrum' because of its amber-like appearance (it was the electro-magnetic attraction of amber that was the common test for distinguishing precious amber from worthless beads). As the Lydians' metallurgical skill improved, they learned how to separate the gold from the silver and so from both separate and mixed ore-sources, began issuing separate gold and silver coins. Croesus in the mid-sixth century BC is thus credited with the first bimetallic coinage, the manufacture of which began thereafter to be still further improved.

At the beginning of the seventh century BC it would be stretching the imagination to call the early Lydian dumps of electrum 'coins': well before the century closed they can be clearly recognized as coins. At first the bean-shaped dumps (possibly reminiscent of cowries), were heavy, cumbersome, irregular in size and unstamped. They were then punch-marked on one side and rather lightly inscribed on the other. Such inscriptions were at first hardly more than scratches, and probably meant more as a guarantee of purity rather than of weight, although as they became more regular in form and weight the official authentication was taken to guarantee both purity and weight. All these stages were quickly carried through until, some time in the second half of the seventh century, they had undoubtedly become coins, rounded, stamped with fairly deep indentations on both sides, one of which would portray the lion's head, symbol of the ruling Mermnad dynasty of Lydia.

It was not unusual for some of the earlier coins to carry a number of punch-marks, made it is thought by well-known merchants some distance from the Lydian city-states as a local reassurance regarding the quality of the money. With due allowance for the difference in cultures, the concept of such stamping was not unlike the 'acceptance' of bills of exchange by merchant bankers in modern times to increase their currency and liquidity. The Lydians were great traders, as were the Ionians. Indeed Greek traders had considerable influence in Lydia and on their way of life and of making a living for themselves; that is because what we would call their 'economies' were basically similar. It is little wonder therefore that the Lydian idea of coinage was so readily taken up by Ionia and passed quickly westwards over the other Greek islands to mainland Greece. It was this rapid series of improvements in the quality of coinage that enables us to credit Lydia, and shortly thereafter Ionia, as being the true first inventors of coins, numismatically speaking; even if from the wider, economic point of view, where greater emphasis must be given to function rather than to form, the Chinese quasi-coins have a longer history. In quality, range of functions and influence over the rest of the world, however, the Lydian–Greek coinage has undoubted priority.

The chronology of Lydian and early Greek coinage has undergone a thorough revision in the last few decades, the result of which has been not only to establish a new general consensus but also to bring forward, closer to today, by a century or more the timing of the various stages which had previously been accepted, though with growing reluctance. Thus Milne in his influential *Greek Coinage* published in 1931, thought that 'there can be little doubt that before 700 the Ionians possessed a plentiful and systemized coinage', and considered it 'reasonable to suppose that the first coins [in Greece itself] were struck about or soon after 750 BC' (1931, 7, 16). It is an occupational hazard of archaeologists in general and numismatists in particular to be at the mercy of the latest pick, spade or metal-detector, and as further evidence of Greek coinage accumulated so the doubts about the previously accepted dating multiplied. The economic history of money, even in its simplest and most concrete form of coinage, is still not an exact study, despite its recent scientific accoutrements. What has led, however, to the current strongly held agreement was a particularly important series of findings in 1951 under the ruins of the temple of Artemis (whom the Romans later called Diana) which we know was built around 600 BC at Ephesus, perhaps the most important centre of the ancient Ionian mainland.

The whole series of changes, from unstamped dumps, dumps punched on one side only, and so on to proper double-struck coins with the lion head device, badge of the royal house of Lydia, were found together in this important hoard, which included not only some ninety-two electrum coins but also a vast quantity of jewellery and precious metal statuettes, some three thousand items in all. Among the many results derived from this crucial find and corroborated by others are that the first true coins date from around 640 to 630 BC. Thus the literary tradition derived from Herodotus and Aristotle, which gave the old conventional date of 687 BC for the earliest Lydian semi-coins, is nearer the mark than was previously supposed. Herodotus remarked most disparagingly on the gross commercialism of the Lydians, for not only were they the first to coin money, but they also sold their daughters into prostitution and were the first people to open permanent retail shops – the latter said in the same vein as Napoleon's castigation of the English as a nation of shopkeepers. The Artemisian find clearly confirms the literary tradition of Lydian precedence in coinage since the Lydian coins show all the earlier stages, whereas the Greek coins, being all proper coins, are consequently confidently considered to be derived from and direct copies of the Lydian finished product. The other early Greek coinages have therefore been revised downwards. Thus instead of the '750 BC' suggested by Milne for the coinage of Aegina we now read

595 BC, with the Athenian around 575 BC and the Corinthian around 570 BC. This change in chronology accelerates the speed of change and the degree of success achieved by Greek money in the relatively short period of a few centuries following the Lydian invention of proper coins. This perceptive recent eulogy captures the spirit of this achievement: 'The extraordinary characteristic of Greek coinage is the speed with which it developed from the primitive level . . . to become a perfect, if minor, art-form. By 550 BC the techniques were still primitive . . . The fifth century saw the minting of the most beautiful coins ever made' (Porteous 1980). The important researches of Porteous, M. J. Price (1980) and E. S. G. Robinson (1956) have done much to clarify the previously misty chronology of early coinage.

Since the time of this mainly Greek invention the financial history of the world has undergone a series of revolutionary changes around the central, relatively unchanging core of coinage; for subsequently, to most people most of the time, money has simply meant coins. In the western world for two thousand years since coinage was invented, the relationship between bullion and coinage has been the foundation of private and public finance. Until recent times coins have continuously been the main, though never the only, monetary medium; and although there have been units of account for which no coins existed, these units of account always stood in a known and definite relationship to the existing coins. Money has always meant more than simply coins; but it was coins that thereafter in the main constituted money and also provided a simple and therefore universally understood and accepted base and reference point for all other financial accounting devices and exchanging media. It is this central characteristic of coinage which illuminates the hidden importance of its discovery, for, through the Greeks, the Lydians have given the Midas touch to economic history. Subsequently economic history without coin-centred money is largely meaningless. We have now to trace the steps by which this exciting essentially Greek concept of money has spread far and wide, east to the Indus, west to Spain, south to Upper Egypt and, finally the route of most direct interest to us, northerly into western Europe and Britain, thence to be re-exported worldwide.

The Development of Greek and Roman Money, 600 BC–AD 410

The widening circulation of coins

From its birthplace in Lydia and Ionia the knowledge and use of coins spread rapidly east into the Persian empire and west through the rest of the Ionian and Aegean islands to mainland Greece, and then to its western colonies, especially Sicily. It also spread northward to Macedonia, Thrace and the Black Sea, but it was only partially, reluctantly and belatedly accepted in Egypt. Mainland Italy also was at first rather slow in accepting the Greek financial innovations, in contrast to the speed with which they were adopted by Sicily. Apart from these two limited exceptions of mainland Italy and Lower Egypt, the use of coinage spread rapidly around the countries bordering the central and eastern Mediterranean and over the widespread and growing Persian empire through Mesopotamia into India. There is some doubt whether India had itself by this time developed an embryo coinage system quite independently of that in China or Lydia. Whether or not it had itself independently 'invented' coinage, the increasingly close contacts between India and the Near East soon meant in practice that Indian coinage became an adaptation of the Lydian/Greek invention via first the Persian and later the Macedonian empire. For those reasons the direct influence of any alleged indigenous Indian invention of coinage was small compared with the overwhelmingly greater importance of the indubitably independent inventions of coinage in China to the east and even more, the Lydian–Greek developments to the west. The rapid eastward spread of coins from Lydia was not so much because of Lydian traders going east but rather a case of the spoils of war through the Persians moving quickly west. As we have seen, Croesus was himself captured in 546 BC during the westward drive of the Persian armies, a drive that was to continue across the Greek islands and the Bosporus, and so gravely threaten the rise of Greek civilization to its zenith, to what in some ways has been the finest hour in the history of man. The birth and rapid growth of coinage played a significant part in this story: how significant is still a matter of exciting dispute.

As it happened there was a basic distinction between the development of coinage east and west of Ionia. To the Greeks, coins were to be minted almost exclusively in silver, with other metals, including gold being of no great importance. On the other hand, the Persians and others to the east of Ionia, showed a very strong and continuing preference, like the Lydians themselves from whom they directly derived their views, for gold. Silver was a subsidiary. In effect the bimetallic influence of Croesus, with gold being paramount, continued in the Persian empire. An interesting administrative division gradually developed, which meant that the minting of gold coins was the jealously guarded sole right of the Persian emperor, whereas silver coinage, being very much a subsidiary, was from time to time delegated to the satraps and minor rulers of the Persian kingdom. The period from the middle of the sixth century BC to the death of Alexander in 323 BC saw the world's first great intermixing of eastern and western cultures, a process inescapably involving fundamental changes in the nature and extent of money and banking.

The choice of which metal to use for this powerful new economic and political tool depended on a mixture of changing factors, among which initially the availability of the raw materials was obviously the most important. The availability of ores could not however be divorced from increasing metallurgical skills and also the availability of labour, preferably cheap labour, to mine, process and transport the ores. Long before coins were invented, the monetary role of the precious metals made them eagerly coveted, an elemental desirability which was greatly increased as the political importance of coinage began to be more fully appreciated, particularly when the minting of coins and their more or less enforced distribution added a new dimension to the political and military rivalry of that warlike age. In coinage as in other matters the Greek city-states strove desperately for predominance, as did their arch-rivals the Persian emperors. Among the earliest and most popular of Persian coinages were the series known as 'archers' because on the obverse they depicted the emperor armed with spear, bow and arrows. The pre-Danish, Danegeld mentality of the Persian kings is captured in their threatening boast, 'I will conquer Greece with my archers'; a vivid illustration of contemporary views concerning the political power of coinage, to buy allies and to buy off potential enemies.

Conquest, taxes, tribute, offerings to the temples and to the gods, gift exchange and finally trade; all these were methods of gaining precious metals in amounts sufficient to establish and maintain mints. As with the origins of money itself the economic cause of the spread in the use of coinage was therefore only one, and at first probably only a relatively minor one, of the many causes of the rise of rival coinage systems and of the spread of coinage over the civilized world. In course of time the influence of trade as a factor leading to the flow of specie and coin grew to be much more significant, even if some of the more extreme 'primitivist' historians still like to denigrate the economic factors in the rise and spread of coinage.

Laurion silver and Athenian coinage

If we match up the factors favourable to minting with the actual situation existing in Greece during the sixth to fourth centuries BC we may readily see the reasons for the rise of Athens in particular to financial prominence, its splendid coinage mostly reflecting but at least partially assisting its rise to fame. We have already seen how the natural deposits of electrum helped to give rise to Lydian and Ionian currencies, and how those states soon learned to separate the gold from the silver. Freely occurring silver deposits of any size were rare in Europe, being known only in Tartessus in Spain and in the Alps. Before the sixth century pure silver was known to occur only in two quite small mines in Greece and one in Macedonia, and consequently the ratio of silver to gold was much more favourable to silver than was the case after the Greeks learned how their new sources could be exploited. In ancient Egypt silver had in fact actually been more valuable than gold. The changing relationships between gold and silver have bedevilled monetary history from the beginning of time right up to the bimetallist controversies in USA and Europe towards the end of the nineteenth century.

At first the potentially plentiful supplies of silver were technically inseparable from their argentiferous lead ores and therefore could not be exploited. Luckily for the Greeks, necessity appeared to mother the invention of new processes, enabling them to unlock vast reserves of silver on their own doorsteps. 'It is very probable that technological improvements resulted in the increased exploitation in silver-bearing lead ores in mining areas such as Laurion near Athens and in Macedonia and the Greek Islands; and this new availability of silver led to the striking of coinage throughout Greek lands' (M. J. Price 1980, 27). The close connections between coinage and economic development is indicated by Professor Michell who believed that 'It was no accident that the invention of metal coinage was made in the seventh century when industry and commerce were fast advancing', (1957, 313), and he might have added, the necessary technical skills kept pace with this growth.

Cheap labour meant slaves, mostly working in domestic service and on the land but also used in 'manufacturing' and especially employed in great concentrations in the mining industry. The real cost of slaves, that is their annualized capital costs plus their operational costs, had to be balanced against the value of their output. Of course the jargon of equating real marginal costs with the value of marginal output, or of reckoning sunk capital costs against the realizable sales value of the human capital involved – all this would have been as nonsensically unintelligible in those terms in ancient Greece as it is Greek to the majority of small-scale bosses today. But there can be little doubt that such economic factors inescapably determined the real 'surplus' or 'profits' available to the employer in ancient Greece as in modern small-scale industrial or mining activity. Despite the aristocratic denigration of manual labour there was a limit to which slaves could be used as substitutes for voluntary paid labour by the Greeks themselves: 'and so the great majority of the Greeks both in classical and Hellenistic times worked just as hard as anybody else in any time or country' (Michell 1957, 15). Socrates' father was a mason, Demosthenes' father a manufacturer of armour, while Aristotle married the daughter of a banker, Hermias (who was crucified by the Persians). Among the majority of artisans in the Athenian Assembly were blacksmiths, carpenters, farmers, fullers, merchants, shoemakers and shopkeepers: after all had not Solon at the beginning of the sixth century decreed that all fathers should teach their sons a craft? As Michell shows, the prejudice against manual labour was a comparatively late development in Greece, though once established, it persisted through Hellenistic into Roman times. St Paul, free-born, highly educated, a citizen of no mean city, was still, as a tent-maker, very sensitive about this strong prejudice: 'We labour, working with our hands, being reviled' (1 Corinthians 4.12). It is also commonplace but none the less true to observe that Plato's *Republic* was essentially based on an economic interpretation of history, which at least reflected the importance to contemporary classical Greek society of being able to enjoy the leisure necessary for a cultured life mainly because the necessities of life were adequately secured through an abundant supply of cheap labour. Furthermore, in other city-states the majority of the citizens were probably artisans, as Plato showed regarding Athens. Consequently the aristocratic disdain of labour should not be taken by 'primitivist' academics at face value as a means of devaluing the economic forces fashioning everyday Greek life. Greek citizens could afford to be, or could pretend to be, dismissive about the bases of their economy: we need not confirm their claims.

Although some of the more Marxist modernists have grossly exaggerated the number of slaves in Greece, they certainly played a major role in the dirty, heavy and dangerous task of mining for the precious metals. Aegina, one of the first of the western Greek islands to produce its own coins, was once held to employ 470,000 slaves – on a rocky and mountainous island with a total area of about 35 square miles! Much more reliable are modern estimates that the silver mines of Laurion, which supplied Athens with its raw material, employed in periods of its most intensive working, some 30,000 slaves. This large aggregate labour force, predominantly of slaves led by 'metics' but mostly owned by Greeks, was exploited by means of the city-state authorities, who granted leases to Athenian citizens who employed their own gangs of slaves, thus combining large-scale development with small-scale management, the same kind of approach which the Greeks used so successfully in the construction of their imposing public buildings.

The Laurion mines some twenty-five miles south of Athens derived their name from the 'laurai' or horizontal adits or alleys driven into the hillsides. When these horizontal 'drifts' were worked out deeper mining became necessary. The ore was chiefly galena, a lead sulphide, and yielded a rich reward of between 30 to 300 ounces of silver per ton. One of the first Athenian rulers to recognize the importance of these mines was the tyrant, Peisistratus, and the 'owls' first coined by him in 546 BC, and stamped with the Athenian emblem which gave them their name, became famous throughout the ancient world. A particularly rich seam was struck around 490 BC, part of the proceeds of which were saved by the Athenians, after powerful persuasion by Themistocles, and used to build the fleet that destroyed the Persians under Xerxes at the battle of Salamis in 480 BC. Thus was Greek civilization saved from being strangled on the eve of its greatest triumphs. Themistocles' wisdom enabled the Athenians to conquer the Persians with their 'owls'. Most of the great battles of history, however overwhelmingly victorious for one side at the end of the day, are at some time during their course, 'the nearest run thing you ever saw in your life' – as Wellington said of Waterloo. Who would dare say (even among the 'primitivists') that it was not the economic wealth of Athens and the wise investment of her silver that enabled the Greek soldiers and fleet to be trained and supplied well enough to carry the day?

A further indication of the extent and importance of the Laurion mines to Athens may be seen from the fact that well over 2,000 shafts were sunk, the deepest being 386 ft, with the main shafts up to 6 ft in diameter, and with each leading to numerous small branch galleries of about 2 ft square, along which the miners – and probably their children as in nineteenth-century British coalmines – crawled as they extended their workings. We have looked briefly at Athens alone since it was the most important of Greek cities. To a lesser degree the same kind of developments took place in a large number of other city-states such as Aegina and Corinth, with the exception, as already noted, of Sparta, which stubbornly clung to its iron bars. Given such facts, it is difficult to agree to the minimization of the economic basis of Greek life which is the tendency of the more extreme 'primitivists'.

Greek and metic private bankers

Coins had thus become the foundation of the Greek financial system. To what extent and in what manner did it influence the development of banking? Given the enormous energy devoted to coinage it should come as no surprise to learn that Greek banking was largely fashioned to supplement coinage, and not largely to supplant it, as in our modern age. Nor was it a complete substitute for coinage as was necessarily the case in ancient Sumeria and partially and deliberately the case in Ptolemaic Egypt. Until the Banking Act 1979 it was the common practice in Britain to deride the lack of a proper definition of banking by referring to legal cases which defined a banker as someone carrying on the business of banking, and banking as a business carried on by a banker! If the line between deposit-takers and recognized banks remains *functionally* unclear even today after the passing of that Act, one should not, therefore, expect to be able precisely to define the nature and functions of banks and bankers in ancient Greece, despite 'primitivist' claims that it is inappropriate to talk of modern-type banking, investment or capital 'markets' in those early days. It is, however, as easy to point to similarities as it is to contrasts, with the similarities being especially significant if, as already noted in manufacturing and mining, the smaller scale of Greek activity is borne in mind. Despite the primitivists it is more than probable that the goldsmith-bankers of seventeenth-century London, who also came to banking through specializing in exchanging foreign coinages, would readily recognize the Athenian bankers as their close relatives, while even the nineteenth-century private merchant bankers would probably not feel too far from home.

One of the important by-products of Greek prejudice against manual labour and against the everyday boredom of business life was to leave the field wide open to enterprising 'metics' or foreign residents, many of whom were to become particularly prominent in banking. The first banker of whom we have records is Pythius, a merchant banker who operated throughout western Asia Minor at the beginning of the fifth century BC and was purported to have become a multimillionaire. The earliest banker in Greece proper was Philostephanus of Corinth, who prospered early in the first half of the fifth century. Among his many important customers was the far-sighted Themistocles, who deposited the considerable sum of seventy talents in Philostephanus' bank. Among the earliest and most important bankers in Athens were the citizens Antisthenes and Archestratus who built up their banking business in the second half of the fifth century BC. They appear to have worked in close partnership and jointly employed a promising slave, Pasion, who rose to eclipse his former masters and became the most wealthy and famous of all Greek bankers, gaining in the process not only his freedom but also Athenian citizenship. Pasion began his banking career in 394 BC and retired in 371 BC, having amassed one of the largest private fortunes known in classical Greece. In addition to his more customary banking business Pasion directed the largest shield factory in Greece, at Athens, where around 200 slaves were employed. He owned his own ships, farms and a number of houses in Attica. He also conducted an embryo hire-purchase or at least hiring business, lending for a lucrative fee domestic articles such as clothes, blankets, silver bowls and so forth. In turn, among his employees was the slave Phormio to whom Pasion granted his freedom. We learn that Phormio likewise set up in banking business on his own. He married Pasion's widow shortly after the death of Pasion, and also grew to be enormously rich.

Among rich moneylenders who might not quite be ranked as full bankers were the partners Nicobulus and Euergus who financed slave-owners taking leases for working the Laurion silver mines. Among other Greek bankers of whose names we have record are Aristolochus (who became bankrupt), Dyonysodorus, Heracleides (who also became bankrupt), Lycon, Mnesibulus, Parmenon and Sumathes, the latter at least remarkable for his honesty. These lesser but named bankers stand halfway in status and function between the famous houses like Pasion and Phormio, who conducted a wide variety of mostly large-scale merchant banking business, and the much more numerous but anonymous moneylenders and money exchangers, whose activities were such a common and essential feature of everyday Greek life. These minor bankers and money-changers would normally conduct their business in or around the temples or other public buildings, setting up their trapezium-shaped tables (which usually carried a series of lines and squares for assisting calculations), from which the Greek bankers, the 'trapezitai', derived their name, much as our name for 'bank' comes from the Italian 'banca' for bench or 'counter'. The continued close association of money-changing with banking is probably best known to us through the episode of Christ's overturning of such tables in the Temple of Jerusalem (Matthew 21.12).

Money-changing was the earliest and remained the commonest form of banking activity, especially at the retail level, and was an essential aspect of trading because of the great variety of different types and qualities of coinage and the prevalence of imitation and counterfeiting which have always appeared to be inseparably associated with coinage. Some of the largest bankers like Pasion himself were so successfully immersed in 'wholesale' banking that they diverted this less prestigious side of retail money-changing to smaller bankers. One of the most important and well-recorded kinds of lending business carried out not only by bankers but sometimes by other rich persons willing to take a risk, was 'bottomry' or lending to finance the carriage of freight by ships. Its high risks were recognized by allowing considerably higher than average rates of interest. 'Undoubtedly, of all banking and loan business', says Michell, 'the most general and at the same time most lucrative and hazardous were the loans made to merchants and shipmasters for furtherance of commercial ventures in overseas trade,' (1957, 345). Reference has already been made to lending for leasing mining activities, especially in the Laurion mines, but this kind of financial assistance was more widely spread in financing farming and the construction gangs working on public buildings.

As for deposits, although the particular banking customs varied, like the coinage, from city to city, these were mostly either current or deposit accounts, with the latter including (as still to a much lesser degree with modern banks) valuables of all kinds, such as jewellery and bullion as well as cash. Contrary to modern practice, no interest was paid on such cash deposits, whereas interest was paid on current accounts. The probable reason for this reversal of modern banking habits was that whereas valuables including cash were kept intact in 'safe' deposits, we know that it was the current accounts which the Greek bankers relied upon for their lending business, for, as Demosthenes – who was heavily involved in legal issues for bankers and their clients – remarked, any banker whose lending was based solely on his own capital was headed for bankruptcy. Current accounts, then, provided the major sources of money for lending, and since they paid interest, such lending had to reflect these costs plus the risks attached. Most lending was secured, and the various legal systems of the city-states laid down what could or could not be accepted as security for loans. Among securities accepted for such loans were copper, silver, gold and even slaves. Armour or farming instruments were sometimes among objects not allowed to be used for purposes of borrowing, the security and sustenance of the city-state obviously came before private profit.

Recorded rates of interest varied between the exceptionally low rates of just over 6 per cent, to what Demosthenes considered a normal and fair 10 per cent for run-of-the-mill business, to between 20 and 30 per cent for such risky business as lending for shipping, although in the calculations regarding marine lending it is difficult to disentangle the interest from the insurance elements of the recorded contracts. In general, the Greek city-states did not lay down maximum rates for usury. In any case the records of Greek banking are only the tip of the iceberg, for much of Greek business was informal and spontaneous, based mostly on the private banker employing the minimum of written accounts, in sharp contrast to the situation in contemporary Egypt or, to a lesser degree, in Rome despite the fact that it was mostly Greek bankers who taught Rome and the rest of the world what banking meant, at any rate after the advent of the coin.

The Attic money standard

Despite the leadership of Athens which enabled her to spread the sphere of influence of her coinage system – the Attic silver standard – over a large part of the western Mediterranean and occasionally beyond, there were always large numbers of rival coinage systems and quite a few complicated standards of financial accounting in use at any one time, creating a persistently powerful and widespread demand for 'bankers' who could find their way through the money maze. This wasteful duplication of multiple coinage systems was a probably inevitable result of the vigorous particularism that gave life and meaning to the Greek city-state. Few of these rival states, however, had the advantages in size, political power and prestige – and as the largest entrepot of Greece, in trade and commerce – that Athens could boast. Above all they lacked access to such an abundant source of silver as that enjoyed by Athens. Consequently the most commonly accepted among a large number of coinage systems was that of Athens. Since pre-coinage moneys had to be weighed it was a natural development for first the abstract accounting systems and then the complete coinages to be related to such weights, the basic unit of which throughout the Greek-speaking world was the 'drachma' or 'handful' of grain, though the precise weight taken to represent this varied considerably, for example from less than 3 grams in Corinth to more than 6 grams in Aegina.

Taking the silver drachma as the main, central, standard monetary unit, one moved down to the less valuable and proportionally lighter sub-unit, the obol, six of which made one drachma. The obol itself had an earlier pre-coinage existence as the pointed 'spit' or elongated nail, and six of these constituted a customary handful similar to that of the even earlier grain-based measures. Below the obol came the *chalkous*, in normal times the smallest monetary unit, and made, as its name implied, of copper, just like our use of 'coppers' for small change. Eight *chalkoi* – usually – made one obol. Moving above the central unit of the drachma, and ignoring for the moment the stater and other multiples of the drachma, we come first to the mina, roughly a pound in weight, equivalent to one hundred drachmae, and finally the talent, equivalent to sixty minae. If we bear in mind the necessary caution that this widely used system was only one among many we may build up the following lists of Attic coins and weights:

Units of account and coins
(a)   8 copper *chalkoi* = 1 silver obol
(b)   6 obols = 1 silver drachma
(c)   2 drachmae = 1 silver stater

Units of account and weight only
(d)   100 drachmae (or 50 staters) = 1 mina
(e)   60 minae (or 6,000 drachmae) = 1 talent

Both the mina and the native Greek talent were derived from the Babylonian sexagesimal system and throughout Greece, Asia Minor and much of the Near East the basic unit of money was the stater meaning literally 'balancer' or 'weigher'. In the west and mainland Greece it was initially the two-drachma coin, the didrachm which became the standard, while a number of eastern city-states preferred their own three-drachma staters. It was however the Athenian double-stater, the four-drachma or tetradrachm, with the owl on one side and head of the goddess Athena on the other, which eventually became the ancient world's most popular coin by far and therefore in practice the most common standard or stater by which other coins were weighed and judged. Thus the term 'stater' referred in various places, depending on local mint preferences, to two, three or four drachmae when coined in silver, though electrum and gold staters, worth between twenty-four to thirty silver drachmae were not uncommon in eastern Greece where they had to compete closely with the golden Persian 'daric' coins. Bearing in mind the caution that 'standards' were not universal, the eastern Greek standard, as befitted its geographical location, kept more strictly to the sexagesimal system, as follows:-

Units of account and coins
(a) 12 copper *chalkoi* = 1 silver obol
(b) 6 obols = 1 silver drachma
(c) 3 drachmae = 1 silver stater

Units of account and of weight only
(d) 60 staters = 1 mina
(e) 60 minae = 1 talent

When copper became used as money in ancient Greece a copper sheet of around 60 lb in weight, roughly as much as the average man could conveniently carry, became the common concrete equivalent of the 'talent'. A strong man could of course carry more, hence the symbolic significance of talent. Neither the talent nor the mina appeared in coin form but were, like the pound sterling throughout the Middle Ages, simply units of account. Coinage covered an enormously wide value range from the equivalent of twenty-four or twenty-five drachmae for a gold coin at the top of the range to small base-metal coins or silver bits of coins like fish-scales or even smaller almost pin-head-size silver coins at the bottom of the range. The famous Athenian silver 'owls' usually in one-, two-, and four- (and more rarely in eight-, ten- and twelve-) drachma pieces, became by far the most widely used coins in the ancient world, lasting for nearly 600 years, until the supply dwindled after the exhaustion, given existing techniques, of the Laurion mines in 25 BC. Their basically unchanged design and unadulterated quality gave rise to countless but intrinsically unflattering imitations throughout the Mediterranean and Middle East.

Although values initially fell as coins became commoner, most Greek cities, and particularly Athens itself, were determined to maintain the quality and reputation of their coinage. Two obols were the day's pay of a labourer, while the architect of the Erechtheum temple on the Acropolis earned about three times as much, a drachma a day. As a rough but useful guide as to the value of such coins, the average day's pay for a manual worker in Great Britain in 1982 was over £27, while a first-rate consultant architect (not necessarily of the quality of those that built the Parthenon) would expect to earn at least £200 a day, worth in today's inflated currency some 25,000 drachmae.

The development of the subsidiary coinage system was therefore of much greater importance than we might at first think, and not until these smaller coins were minted did the new invention play its full part in the everyday life of ancient Greece. Furthermore the high values of the precious-metal coins provided a commensurately greater temptation for counterfeiters, and at the same time speaks much for the pride of the cities in maintaining their standards which they enforced by strong penal codes. Hikesias, the father of Diogenes, the famous philosopher, escaped rather lightly when he was merely banished for adulterating the silver coinage. Thus the Attic system ranging from subsidiary coinages of low value for the everyday use of ordinary people through the medium values of silver coinages for a wide range of local and overseas trade, to high-value gold coinages used mostly outside Greece together formed the indispensably strong basis for trade, banking and political finance. So well known were the Attic and eastern standards that they could fairly easily, with the aid of the ubiquitous bankers, be adapted to fit the Persian and other mainly gold-based systems.

With such a welter of coinages plus a variety of different standards one may easily appreciate the need for exchange bankers and the strong desire for a more widespread uniform standard. All the city-states agreed on the need for uniformity – provided that it was either their own or that of their current ally that was chosen to be the standard. In 456 BC Athens forced Aegina to take Athenian 'owls' and to cease minting her own 'turtle' coinage. In 449 BC Athens in furtherance of still greater uniformity issued an edict ordering all 'foreign' coins to be handed in to the Athenian mint and compelling all her allies to use the Attic standard of weights, measures and money. However as Athenian power declined, so the former subject city-states reissued their own currencies – and what was much worse, when Sparta in 407 BC cut Athens off from her silver mines at Laurion and released around 20,000 slaves from the mines, Athens herself was faced with a grave shortage of coins. Faced with this emergency she minted 84,000 golden drachmae from the statue of Nike, or Victory, and other treasures which adorned the Acropolis.

When the coin shortage got even worse in 406 and 405 BC she issued bronze coins with a thin plating of silver – with the result that the good coins tended to disappear, which made the shortage even worse. This infamous situation was made the occasion of what is probably the world's first statement of Gresham's Law, that bad money drives out good. In Aristophanes' comedy, *The Frogs*, produced in 405 BC the author wrote: 'I have often noticed that there are good and honest citizens in Athens who are as old gold to new money. The ancient coins are excellent . . . well struck and give a pure ring; everywhere they obtain currency, both in Greece and in strange lands; yet we make no use of them and prefer those bad copper pieces quite recently issued and so wretchedly struck' (Aristophanes 1912). The base coins were demonetized in 393 BC and Athens regained her reputation for fine coinage. Her civic pride was completely healed when the citizens, in 380 BC voted the money to rebuild their golden treasures in the temples of the Acropolis, a feat which took them until 330 BC to complete. However, her drive for greater financial uniformity had to await the more powerful armies of Alexander and Rome.

Banking in Delos

Athens' predominance in political and cultural affairs and, to a large extent, therefore in trade, coinage and banking, was continuously being challenged. Among its many rivals for leadership in banking the island of Delos may claim a special place. Delos rose to prominence during the late third and early second centuries BC. Its importance in banking history can hardly be exaggerated. As a barren offshore island, its people had to live off their wits and make the most of the island's two great assets – its magnificent harbour and the famous temple of Apollo. Around these its trading and financial activities grew to support a large and very cosmopolitan city of some 30,000 inhabitants, developing first as a centre of Aegean and later of Mediterranean commerce and banking and one of the principal clearing houses of the ancient world. It was an entrepot for the Macedonian trade in timber, pitch, tar and silver, the best place for the slave trade and the main western depot for eagerly sought oriental wares brought along the ancient caravan routes from Arabia, India and even China.

We have well-documented continuous accounts as kept by its magistrates, recording its main banking and trading activities for over 400 years. Its economy was typical of that prevailing in the other temples which stood in close connection with the city but was probably the best of its type and one of the most enduring. Whereas in its earliest days 'banking in the Athens of Pasion was carried on exclusively in cash: deposit contracts, Giro transfers and receipts in writing do not appear to have been known at this period', by the time the Bank of Delos was in operation 'it was particularly interesting that transactions in cash were replaced by real credit receipts and payments made on simple instructions, with accounts kept for each client' (Orsingher 1964, 4). Some indication of the public wealth of the city authorities and the close involvement of the state with its bank is given by the substantial savings in cash form, in two public treasuries or chests, kept for greater protection within the temple of Apollo itself. The different purposes for which these reserves were kept were indicated on the sealed jars kept separately within either the 'public' or the 'sacred' chest. Some of these turned out to be very long-term savings, for the seals of one series with over 48,000 drachmae remained unbroken for about twenty years, from 188 to 169 BC.

The direct interest of Delos to us stems from its being both a historical and geographical link in the wider and more flexible development of banking business. It connected the early Greeks with the later Hellenistic and Roman banking eras and it provided the bridge which joined Italian traders and bankers of the West with those of the eastern Mediterranean and beyond. The Italian merchants who were attracted first for purely trading purposes became domiciled and rose to prominence as citizens of Delos, eventually taking over from the Greeks and becoming the most important bankers in the city, maintaining the closest links with the main centres of the rising Roman empire. The early Greek colonies in Sicily and southern Italy were replicas of Corinth and Delos; and we have seen how Roman citizens became increasingly important as merchants and bankers in Delos and over the Aegean islands. Their activities spread in similar fashion throughout the central and western Mediterranean, gradually extending into the interior of Gaul and Spain. For political reasons Rome destroyed Carthage and Corinth, the main commercial rivals of Delos, and in contrast until well into the first century BC strongly supported the economy of Delos, strengthening its position as one of the chief free ports of the Mediterranean. Consequently, it was a most natural outcome that the Bank of Delos became the model most closely and consciously imitated by the banks of Rome. In matters of culture and commerce, the Hellenistic and Roman empires merged into each other with mixed results, some baneful and some beneficial as we shall now see, at least so far as their financial and commercial aspects are concerned.

Macedonian money and hegemony

The greatest military exploits in history were naturally not without their important economic and financial causes and consequences, even if those were clearly of a second order. Even so they should not be neglected, for the economic and financial effects linger on far beyond the more flamboyantly obvious political results. We have seen how the enormously wealthy Persian inheritors of the Babylonian and Assyrian empires had twice, in 490 and 480 BC, threatened the independence of Athens and therefore of all the other Greek city-states, and how the ready wealth of Athens was a not unimportant factor in defeating the Persians abroad. We shall now see how finance and, especially, readily minted coinage, played no small part in defeating the Persians in the centre of their own empire.

The mainland route from Asia to Greece lay through Thrace and Macedon, kingdoms of such minor importance that they were simply bought off by the Persian 'archers'. However, this situation changed with the accession of Philip II in 360 BC. Philip formed one kingdom out of a number of previously warring tribes and used their unity as the basic strength of his growing economic and military power, so that well before the end of his reign he became the acknowledged leader of all the Greek states, despite the hostility of Demosthenes' verbal attacks – his vitriolic *Philippics*. During Philip's reign the agricultural basis of Macedon was greatly improved by vast schemes of irrigation, land drainage and flood control. As Alexander reminded his people shortly after he became king on the assassination of his father in 336 BC: 'My father took you over as nomads and paupers, wearing sheepskins, pasturing a few sheep on the mountains . . . he made you inhabitants of cities and brought good order, law and customs into your lives.' With better irrigation and drainage and with the canalization of sections of its more important rivers the agricultural output of the rich alluvial plains, far larger than those available to the Greeks farther south, provided the basis for building up the new towns and increasing their professional armies. Philip was therefore as well supplied with grain as the Greeks and far better supplied with cattle and with the horses which were to form his élite cavalry. Robin Lane Fox, who adds his biography of Alexander to the thousand others, repeats a common view that the martial superiority of the Macedonians was in part due to their generous meat diets. Napoleon was obviously not the first to note that an army marches on its stomach: 'Macedon's more frequent diet of meat may not be irrelevant to her toughness on the battlefield' (1973, 28). By raiding his neighbours, Philip could add substantially to the produce of his own pastures – one such raid alone reaped a harvest of 20,000 mares. From such a vast wealth of horses, Alexander could take his pick, for his twelfth birthday, of his Bucephalus which was to carry him for fifteen years and many thousands of miles. As an integral part of Philip's policy of Hellenization a considerable number of prominent

Greeks were invited to Macedon, including Aristotle who acted as tutor to Alexander for three years of his youth, from thirteen to sixteen.

It was, however, the substantial economic improvements that provided the essential foundation for the growth of Macedonian political power and enabled Philip to succeed in maintaining the allegiance of most of the Greek city-states and overcome even the persuasive influence of Demosthenes on the Athenians. Under Philip, the Greek centre of gravity moved from what Socrates had denigrated as the 'frog-ponds' of the south to the wider vistas of the north; a vital first step in preparation for the vast continental empire that was shortly to be opened up to Macedonian and Greek arms and Greek culture. Greece's strategic geographical position at the crossroads of three continents was about to be used to full advantage.

Towards the end of his reign Philip began issuing his golden stater depicting his victory in the chariot race at the Olympic games of 356 BC on one side and the head of Zeus on the other. These coins, and their inevitable imitations, all advertising his power and influence, spread far and wide, particularly among the Celtic tribes of central and north-western Europe, and even crossed the Channel, where they were among the earliest-dated coins to have been found in Britain. Philip's numerous coins were important for a number of reasons, quite apart from their obvious role in improving the media of exchange and accounting. By widely demonstrating his achievements in the Olympics they confirmed his social and therefore also his political acceptance as leader of the Greek nation; Greeks could no longer dismiss the Macedonians as rough and rude barbarians. To many who used the coins, the head of Zeus was mistakenly interpreted as that of Philip himself, and so prepared the way for the issue of coinage to become more fully accepted as the personal right of the king, a process carried to fulfilment by Alexander and his followers in the late Hellenistic kingdoms. Also, as already indicated, his coins 'were to have a dramatic influence on the Celtic coinages of Europe' (M. J. Price 1980, 41). Furthermore Philip appears deliberately to have minted far more coins than were currently justified by the needs of trade or of his armies, probably to act as readily available financial reserves to support the anti-Persian campaign for which he was actively preparing in the period immediately preceding his assassination. 'Alexander had need', says Professor N. G. L. Hammond, 'of a prolific and stable coinage' and 'the considerable stock of gold philippeioi and silver tetradrachms served part of his needs in 336 and 335 BC' (1981, 156).

The financial consequences of Alexander the Great

When Alexander succeeded to the throne in 336 BC he thus had at his disposal all the necessary material resources – the armies, allies, supplies and reserves of coinages and so on – that Philip's unfinished task required. Alexander himself, then barely twenty, was soon to display a leadership and inspiration unrivalled in history, which in the remarkably short space of less than a decade, established a vast Hellenistic sphere of influence of two million square miles, stretching from Gibraltar to the Punjab. The armies which achieved those results were paid in cash, and since they were well fed, expensively trained, highly paid and well supported by ancillaries, a rich and ready supply of coinage became a prerequisite of Macedonian imperialistic ambitions. Macedon was fortunate therefore in having rich mineral resources of iron, copper, silver and gold, all of which, being the personal property of the king, could be used directly by him in ways which made them more effective than when ownership was divided among a large number of city-states. The payment of his troops was similarly his personal responsibility, and thus, given his explicit political ambitions, the financial groundwork for the conquest and occupation of the Persian empire by Macedonian troops and mercenaries was being single-mindedly, deliberately prepared. Initially this was bound to be a costly business, with the costs being met very largely from Macedonian and Greek resources: only later on did the enormous booty captured by the army more than pay its costs. Some indication of the size of these costs may be gleaned from the following facts.

The cavalry, the élite in Alexander's highly skilled army, were paid on average two drachmae a day, an infantryman one drachma and an ordinary mercenary, two-thirds of a drachma, or twice the pay of a labourer. In addition, basic rations were probably supplied free. By the time this army was fully engaged in Asia Minor the total cost was around twenty talents a day, that is some half a ton of silver, or 120,000 drachmae (N. G. L. Hammond 1981, 155ff.). Thus by a combination of foresight, luck and conquest Alexander was not only easily able to afford such enormous and initially 'unproductive' expenditure but very quickly took control over coins, bullion and other essential resources in quantities far beyond the dreams of either his father or his followers.

Once Alexander had established himself in Asia Minor the drain on Macedonian finance was first halted and then reversed, for the victorious army, with little cost to itself in lives or equipment, had little need of replenishment from its home base. Not only could it live off the country but all the many mints with their stores of bullion were taken over en route, and issued as many coins as Alexander required. After the capture of the Persian emperor's family at the Battle of Issus in 333 BC, Darius began to negotiate terms for peace. At the siege of Tyre, he offered Alexander 10,000 talents as ransom plus his daughter's hand in marriage and all the lands to the west of the Euphrates. 'I would accept,' said his senior general, Parmenio, 'were I Alexander.' 'I too,' said Alexander, 'were I Parmenio.' Alexander's demand for 'all Asia' was soon granted including *all* the wealth of the Persian kingdoms. The capture of Damascus brought him 2,600 talents in coin alone, and there were similar if smaller amounts from a score of other mints. The reverse flow of coinage to Europe, quite apart from the demands of trade, may be illustrated by the 3,000 talents which Alexander is known to have sent to Antipater in Macedon in 331 BC, a considerable sum, but merely one of the first in a veritable flood of coinage, easily spared from his rapidly growing fortune in coin and bullion. A similar sum of 3,000 talents was also given by Alexander that year to Menes who deputized for him after he left Syria. The captured treasury at Susa contained an incredible amount of bullion including 50,000 talents of silver. When the dying Darius was finally captured in 330 BC a further 7,000 talents were taken.

In addition, Darius' central mint at Babylon was taken over and new currencies, designed by Alexander's moneyers, poured from what was the most prolific mint in the Persian empire, second only to that at Amphipolis, the chief mint of Macedon. However there were a large number of other substantial mints, such as those at Ecbatana, Sardis, Miletus, Aradus, Sidea, Sydon, Citium and Egyptian Alexandria, to name only the more important, which together far surpassed the previous total Greek and Macedonian output. Furthermore, because of the demands not only of his army, but also of his engineers, scientists, explorers, retainers and the whole auxiliary forces accompanying his campaigns – which Alexander saw as being much more of a civilizing, Hellenizing mission than simply military conquest – the mints became highly active, coining temple and royal treasures which otherwise would not have entered circulation. Thus not only was the supply of money, and of intrinsically full-bodied money, vastly increased, so too was its velocity of circulation.

The methods by which a large proportion of this immense coinage was distributed further guaranteed its rapid velocity and wide dispersal. After all, his soldiers were to a considerable extent mercenaries, themselves children of mercenaries, and with their Asian and Eurasian wives, providers of the next generation of mercenaries. Over seventy towns, new or extended, were established by Alexander, at least twenty-one of them named after him – and one after his horse – from Egypt to 'Alexandria Eschate' or 'the farthest', north-east of Samarkand. Young families and new towns meant high spending; and even single soldiers are not on average noted for parsimony. The rigid discipline maintained throughout Alexander's forces prevented personal looting, and therefore made his soldiers dependent on their generous salaries. These were frequently handsomely enhanced by large bounties to the soldiers themselves and to the families of the fallen. After the capture of Susa, Alexander distributed bounties ranging from 600 drachmae for his Macedonian cavalrymen to 50 drachmae for the ordinary mercenary. Generous gratuities were paid to men who through age or sickness, had become unfit for further service. They were either sent home with their gratuities or allowed to settle locally. Thus '1,000 over-age Macedonians garrisoned the citadel of Susa' (N. G. L. Hammond 1981, 164). In mid-323 BC, at the treasure-base of Ecbatana Alexander distributed a total bounty of 2,000 talents to those Greek troops who, after faithful service, had decided to return home to Greece. Professor Hammond has also shown how Alexander's care for his troops extended even to assuming responsibility for their debts to civilians, and he had his accountants pay off such debts amounting to some 2,000 talents. He also gave wedding presents to some 10,000 of his soldiers who married at Susa. His troops were obviously big spenders – or as the modern economist might say, they had a high marginal propensity to consume. A large multiplier thus intensified the effect of the high velocity of circulation.

The accidents of geology and the chances of war combined with the preferences not only of those who had authority over minting but also their many unofficial competitors, who issued imitations or counterfeits, to make the various metallic ratios a bothersome, hit-or-miss affair. Whatever the ratio that was finally chosen – and as soon as coins were made the choice was inevitable – the initially established ratio was bound to come under pressure. These pressures were considerably lightened if one metal alone was given official preference for coinage. In that case all the other metals had, by reason of their being ignored for official coinage, to bear the brunt of fluctuating values. It was more difficult to juggle with two or even more so with three metals; hence the tendency through time for the cheaper metals to become merely tokens, and for bimetallist currencies to lose their originally chosen relationships. In a way, it was fortunate for the Greeks, who needed to build up public acceptance for their innovation, that they had such an abundance of silver and so little of their own gold, so that silver, the best metal, numismatically speaking, became also the best for their own economic and political purposes. Therefore, except for emergencies, they ignored gold for coinage and let others, such as Croesus and the Persians who absorbed his kingdom, wrestle with bimetallism.

It is believed that the Persians, who learned of coinage from Lydia, also took over its bimetal ratio, but in any case the Persians soon established and enforced throughout their domains a ratio of 13⅓:1, i.e. forty units of silver were equal to three units in weight of gold. The values of their coins were consistently issued at this ratio of 40:3. They could not of course enforce this ratio outside their kingdoms, so that the ubiquitous Greek trapezitai were kept busy and wealthy exploiting divergences, and in the process, like any such arbitrage, reducing the widest margins to differences which traders could tolerate. Even so the mainland Greeks would usually expect to purchase one unit of gold with only twelve units of silver, and this acted as a barrier to the penetration of Persian gold 'darics' (named after Darius I who first issued them as early as about 500 BC) into western Greece, so that the monometallist silver monopolies which Aegina, Corinth and Athens operated in their own regions were not really threatened by foreign, golden intrusions.

Such cosy relationships broke down however when huge deposits, not only of silver, but also of gold, were opened up by Philip in Thrace and Macedon. In Philip's earlier years he had used the Thracian and not the Attic standard for his silver, and for the less important gold issues used the Attic standard. However, as his vast precious metal resources were more fully exploited, the gold/silver ratios had to be re-established. In order to safeguard and develop the new gold finds at Mount Pangaeus near Crenides, the 'town of fountains', which Philip rebuilt and renamed Philippi, he set up a new mint to help in producing his new golden *Philippeioi* from around 356 BC. It is an indication of the greater relative supply of gold to silver that, toward the end of his reign, Philip was issuing his silver and gold coinage at a 10:1 ratio. There were other precious mineral deposits in his enlarged kingdom, but Mount Pangaeus alone yielded 1,000 talents of gold and silver a year. As we have seen, these mineral reserves helped political and economic power to move north from Greece to Macedon in the second half of the fourth century. Philip and Alexander (who continued minting posthumous *Philippeioi*, just as his followers continued issuing posthumous 'Alexanders') naturally took full advantage of these god-given riches and put their existing mints into continuous operation at Pella, the capital, at Philippi, Damastium, and above all at Amphipolis. Alexander also opened a new mint in 330 BC at Sicyon in the

Peloponnese. The mint at Amphipolis, in the eighteen years between 346 and 328 BC produced a vast total of thirteen million silver tetradrachms plus a considerable but unknown amount of gold coins. All this activity in the Macedonian homeland was in addition to the continued and vastly increased output of the existing mints in Greece, Asia Minor, Syria, Egypt, Mesopotamia and indeed throughout the Hellenistic world. Thus, in Professor Hammond's words, 'we may realize the stupendous increase in coined money, expenditure and employment which Alexander brought about in Europe alone, quite apart from the economic revolution in Asia' (1981, 258).

Alexander could not be bothered with trying to maintain, as his father had done, an Attic standard in gold and a Thracian for silver. Instead he insisted on employing the Attic standard only, not just in Macedon, but, so far as was practicable, throughout his new empire. Alexander did however follow Philip's custom rather than the Persian ratio in his bimetallist (though mostly silver) coinage system. Despite the long-established and widespread acceptance of the Persian 13⅓:1 ratio Alexander must have seen this for what it was – an awkward and complicated relationship which inhibited the quick and ready growth of trade which he was determined to promote. For he was a man with a mission, in a hurry to integrate the best of Asian, African and European civilization under the undoubted supremacy of that of the Greeks.

Coinage was at the heart of communication, hence nothing should inhibit its wider, more common and ready acceptance. And so Alexander cut through the knotty problem of bimetallic ratios as he did with the fabled knot at Gordion. Ten to one, that was the sensible, practical, straightforward ratio to adopt: let slaves and metics quibble over minor fractions. In any case Alexander had the reserves of either gold or silver to apply wherever the divergences were too marked, so as to remedy a shortage of either one or the other. His armies abroad, wherever they were, accepted the Attic standard and the Alexandrian ratio, and this was sufficient guarantee for a wider general acceptance of these simple and beneficial reforms which enabled coinage, as part and parcel of the Greek way of life, to penetrate far and wide at a speed which otherwise might have taken centuries.

While it would be cynical in the extreme to attempt to measure the significance of Alexander simply in terms of his economic and financial achievements, nevertheless in recognizing that these alone were so substantial and far-reaching, one cannot fail to marvel at this additional if restricted view of his many-sided genius. (Whether cynical or not, Marxist historians might feel constrained to attempt such an impossibly one-sided assessment.) Coins were by far the best propaganda weapon available for advertising Greek, Roman or any other civilization in the days before mechanical printing was invented. We have seen how Philip's representation of Zeus as king of the Olympian gods became commonly associated with the king himself. This trend became much more marked in the case of the coins issued by Alexander and his Hellenistic rulers, for the head of Heracles (Hercules) which appeared on these coins probably intentionally bore a remarkable resemblance to the idealized portrait of Alexander. After all, it was generally believed, possibly even by Alexander himself, that he was descended from Heracles. The Lydians had begun by issuing coins portraying their kings, but the vastly more important output of coins in mainland and more democratic Greece had avoided such pretensions. Philip and Alexander carried the original Lydian concept of monarchical badges forward into all parts of the ancient world, and, via the Celts and Romans, into western Europe and Britain. After Alexander the power to coin money became more obviously, though not exclusively, a jealously guarded sovereign power, the first to be assumed by any conquering army (just as British Military Authority money accompanied the army in the Second World War). On this note we may conclude our account of the financial consequences of Alexander by taking the year 197 BC, when the Roman general Quinctius Flaminius defeated Philip V at the battle of Cynocephalae, as marking the end of Macedonian hegemony. Thereafter the once mighty Macedon became a mere vassal of Rome, and the Greek city-states reverted to their disunited particularism. However in the eastern Selucid and Egyptian Ptolemaic empires the Hellenistic influences continued, though on a declining trend, for many generations. Needless to say Flaminius commemorated his victory by minting gold staters bearing his own image – the first representation of a living person to appear on Roman coins. The Greeks, who taught the world the meaning of coined money, found the Romans, though slow starters, the most persuasively powerful imitators.

Money and the rise of Rome

The abstract legendary and linguistic influence of Rome on our basic monetary terms and standards complements the enormous historic importance of her actual coins. The tribes of Latins and Etruscans had emerged as neighbours by the time Rome was founded, traditionally in 753 BC, on the site of the lowest bridgeable point of the Tiber, Italy's only really navigable river. On the Capitol, one of the famous seven hills, the early Romans built a temple to Jupiter and, naturally enough, the temple became the most secure place for keeping reserves of money in whatever forms were then common, some of which will be examined shortly. When, according to legend, the Gauls overran most of Rome in 390 BC, the cackling of the geese around the temple on the Capitol alerted the defenders against what would otherwise have been a surprise attack, and so saved them from defeat. In return the Romans built a shrine to Moneta, the goddess of warning, or of advice. It is from Moneta that we derive both 'money' and 'mint'. Among many other Latin influences on our terms related to coinage are 'copper', 'brass' and '£. s. d.' as well as the terms 'pecuniary' and 'expenditure' already described. The copper deposits of Cyprus were worked up in considerable quantities in Italy by the early days of Roman expansion, so that the island gave its name to the product. The skilled metallurgists of Brindisi (Brundisium) in southern Italy who combined the copper with other metals similarly gave their name to 'bronze'.

It has been well said that 'the final legacy of the Hellenistic world to the Roman Empire was an extensive bronze coinage . . . the Roman army was paid in bronze until the middle of the second century BC' (Burnett 1980). The 'libra' became our '£', the French 'livre' and the modern Italian 'lira'. That 'd' should mean 'penny' is not immediately obvious, but came from one of the most famous Roman silver coins, the 'denarius', and this origin has been acknowledged for two thousand years, until the new penny or 'p' finally replaced it in 1970. The abbreviation 's' is still a little more complicated. Linguistically and originally a 'schilling' simply meant a piece cut off a ring or bar of precious metal. But the Romans produced a number of coins more valuable than the denarius among which were the 'sestertius' and the 'solidus'. The 'solidus', officially issued in a limited number of Roman mints, meant that it was of 'solid' or pure gold or silver, in contrast to the 'mancus' or 'manqué' coinages which were impure, substandard or imitations. It is generally accepted that among the many different types, the 'solidus', worth one-twentieth of a pound of silver and equivalent to a dozen pennies, became engrafted in the Anglo-Saxon and Norman mind with the original primitive meaning of 'shilling' to form the middle of the famous old £.s.d. notation.

The Romans were rather late in adopting the types of well-struck coinages which the Greeks had developed and had demonstrated so clearly on their very doorsteps in their colonies in Sicily and southern Italy. Syracuse, Catania, Taormina in Sicily; Rhegium, Croton and Tarentum on the southern coast of Italy; Massilia (Marseilles) and other Greek colonies – all these used and produced a variety of constantly improved coinages, as did Carthage, with which Rome was in conflict. The inferior quality of the Romans' early coinage fittingly reflected their as yet undeveloped state, economically and politically. Heavy and cumbrous currency bars, the *aes signatum*, were still in common use in Rome in 275 BC, and although some crude cast silver coins may have been issued there as early as 300 BC, silver coins did not receive a wide circulation until the middle of the third century BC. For lower denominations the most common early Roman coin was the *aes grave*, a heavy bronze coin that was also cast rather than struck. The traditional date of 269 BC is confirmed authoritatively by Mattingly for Rome's first regular struck silver coinage (Mattingly 1960).

As in Greece, a large number of Roman towns issued their own currencies, at least until the ending of the Carthaginian wars with the final defeat of Hannibal at the battle of Zama in 202 BC. Since the payment of troops was the most urgent (but not the only) cause for minting, these wars led to an immense increase in coinage all around the western basin of the Mediterranean and Carthaginian north Africa. Even so, the vast quantities of bronze and silver coins were insufficient to meet the demands of war, and an emergency short-lived issue of gold coins was made. It appears that for a short time Rome may have altogether run out of money, and was forced to exist on credit alone. Furthermore towards the later stages of the war the quality of coinage, both in purity and weight, was noticeably reduced. After the end of the Punic Wars as a result of the unsatisfactory state of the coinage a thorough reform of currency had to be undertaken, another early example of the pendular swing between quality and quantity.

This was made easier by centralizing the minting of silver in Rome itself from which a new uniform silver coinage of denarii was issued with quinarii and sestertii as useful subdivisions. Provincial town mints were demoted by being allowed to issue bronze coins only. Although this debasement was merely a minor matter compared with what was to reach almost astronomical proportions in the age of Diocletian, nevertheless it was an indication that the Romans did not quite possess the integrity of the Greeks when it came to maintaining the values of silver. Rome needed to coin vast quantities of silver to maintain her growing armies. However, after these emergency debasements the quality of the reformed silver coinage was generally maintained for over two hundred years. To support just one legion cost Rome around 1,500,000 denarii a year, so that the main reason for the regular annual issue of silver denarii was simply to pay the army. In addition the vast population of Rome, which multiplied to a peak of about a million, became increasingly dependent on doles of free corn and other gratuities. The famous public buildings of Rome were similarly paid for by minting the necessary coinage, though some work was free.

The temptation towards debasement though in the main held at bay for a couple of centuries in Rome itself, was strongly felt in those peripheral areas which retained their rights of coinage. Thus in the later Hellenistic empire the Ptolemaic regime in 53 BC fell prey to temptation by issuing grossly debased coinage. In this case it was not so much the direct effects of war but rather the huge bribes that Ptolemy XII paid to regain his throne that brought about a debasement that became a permanent feature of Egyptian currency in the period of the Roman empire. As an example of the financial importance to Rome of the tribute from subject tribes, the Carthaginians, after their defeat, agreed in 201 BC to pay to Rome fifty annual instalments which came in all to 10,000 talents. A vast total of slave labour, continually reinforced by captured soldiers, was employed not only in agriculture but also in the various mines within the Roman empire to supply her needs for iron for military and general purposes; and for copper, silver and gold for coinage purposes, these latter purposes also being initially determined by the requirements of the armies. Over 100,000 slaves were taken from Gaul alone to work in Italy, while large numbers were retained in Gaul to work in her mines. The output of iron from the Montagne Noire region alone is estimated at some thousands of tons per year during the latter part of the first century AD. These mines also produced considerable quantities of lead, silver and copper. Even greater supplies of silver came from Spain, especially from its famous Rio Tinto area where recent archaeological digs have revealed the vast extent of Roman workings (G. D. B. Jones 1980, 146ff.).

Roman currency circulated not only over its own vast domains but also was found beyond the imperial boundaries. Britain, for example, though outside the empire until the conquest of a large part of the country by Claudius in AD 40, had already become familiar with Roman coins and especially with Celtic coinages of Roman type for at least a century earlier. When Julius Caesar made his two raids in 55 and 54 BC a number of Celtic tribes in southern and eastern Britain were already producing coins from their independent mints and these, together with Roman coins, circulated alongside the crude sword-blade currencies that Caesar disdained. Julius Caesar was no longer content to adorn his coins with ancestral heads but preferred to portray his own likeness. Indeed, nowhere has the propaganda value of coins been used to greater effect than in Rome. Brutus, following Caesar, not only had his own profile on the obverse, but advertised on the reverse the gruesome events which led to his brief rule: a cap of freedom flanked by two daggers. Nero, as actor and fiddler, faithfully reflected his ego in his coinage, while the official adoption of Christianity by Constantine, when, in

Grant's vivid phrase, 'Galilee conquered Rome', began the long series of crosses that remain on British coins to this day, e.g. the Llantrisant mint mark on the £1 coin.

Despite the slogan SPQR (*Senatus Populusque Romanus*), which paid lip-service to the authority of the Senate, in actual fact the issue, design and amount of coinage became the personal prerogative of the Roman emperors themselves. For over 500 years the coins of Rome publicly portrayed the events, hopes, ambitions, lives and lies, of its rulers. The enormous but previously neglected importance of such coinage as a historical record, is powerfully captured by Professor Grant's stimulating account of *Roman History from Coins* (1968). Grant clearly demonstrates that 'we need to study the coinage as well as the literature before we can attempt a political history of the Romans'; and the same applies with equal if not greater force with regard to its economic history. So enthusiastic is Grant's assessment of the propaganda value of such money that he even goes as far as saying that, in certain cases at least, 'the primary function of the coins is to record the messages which the emperor and his advisers desired to commend to the populations of the empire' (Grant 1968, 17, 69). If this particular aspect were generalized it would surely portray an exaggerated view and one that the economist must dispute. Yet it does illustrate with typical clarity the tremendous interest aroused by coins in ancient times, even in the most advanced peoples.

Coins were clearly far more than merely media of exchange. But then one of the constant themes that emerge from this study of money, whether in primitive, archaic or modern times, is just that: money is always much more than simply a method of exchanging goods and services. Thus economists who ignore the non-economic aspects of money are as guilty as those numismatists and 'primitivists' who minimize its economic bases. In fairness to Professor Grant, it must be added that despite the views given in the quotations above, he provides many telling examples of the widespread distribution of Roman coins as a result of trade in such articles as amber, ivory, silk, incense and pepper, and refers to Mortimer Wheeler's vivid description of these as 'the five main-springs of Roman long-range trade' (Grant 1968, 85). Similarly, he shows that the 'local' issues of coinage cannot be dismissed as of local consequence only or of narrowly limited circulation, but in contrast were commonly widely dispersed by the needs of trade.

Given the dominance of coinage, what role was then left for banking? In sum one might say that although coins overshadowed banks in monetary importance, the rise of Rome and the vast size of its economy gave considerable scope for the development of banking also, although banks remain of secondary importance throughout the whole period of the Roman empire. In no way was there a sense that coinage was a necessary preliminary to the development of banking. Our modern experience of this kind of 'inevitability' must not lead us to look for parallels where they patently do not exist. We know, and are still learning, an immense amount about Roman coinage, because of the huge reservoir of hundreds of thousands of such coins still existing in private collections and museums. In comparison our knowledge of Roman banking and credit is minimal. Coins are durable; paper is perishable, so that though much nearer in time, the Roman bankers have provided us with much less concrete evidence of their activities than is given by the far older Babylonian bankers with their abundance of financial accounts recorded as it happened for all time in tablets of clay. Admittedly, coinage was dominant in Rome; but its dominance over banking may well have been exaggerated by its greater durability. Keith Hopkins, an expert on Roman trade, neatly summarized the situation thus: 'We know almost nothing of credit in the Roman world; that does not mean that credit played a negligible role, but rather that we cannot estimate its importance' (1980, 106).

However, despite the advanced development of private banking, partly in conscious imitation of that of the Greeks and the Egyptians, no centralized state giro system developed in the Roman empire to compare with that which had been the case in Egypt. The Romans either failed or did not attempt to establish a unified state banking system, despite evidence that Roman statesmen were well aware of the advantages that Egypt had gained from its giro and from its royal state banking system. 'It is interesting', says Rostovtzeff, 'that the idea of a central state bank survived', and had it received more support it might well have become 'a credit institution for the whole of the Roman Empire' (Rostovtzeff 1941, 1288). Rome and Constantinople became the main inheritors of the banking wisdom of the ancient world, which by means of the Roman conquest had become 'knitted together into one economic unit by the establishment of lasting and uninterrupted social and economic relations between the united West and the equally united East' (Rostovtzeff 1941, 109). However the Babylonians had developed their banking to a sophisticated degree, since their banks had also to carry out the monetary functions of coinage, because they lived long before that invention. The Ptolemaic Egyptians segregated their limited coinage system from their state banking system. The Romans, however, preferred coins for the many kinds of services which both ancient (and modern) banks normally provided. Nevertheless Rome's banks very quickly outgrew their early confinement to the Capitol, and soon spread their tables and booths along the sides of the Forum.

During the second century BC these booths were replaced by a fine basilica where, according to Breasted,

> the new wealthy class met to transact financial business and large companies were formed for the collection of taxes and for taking government contracts to build roads and bridges or to erect public buildings. Shares in such companies were daily sold, and a business like that of a modern stock exchange developed in the Forum. (1920, 630)

This possibly extreme 'modernistic' view is confirmed in part, though not on the whole, when account is taken both of the immense size of private fortunes which large numbers of the richest Roman citizens had amassed and which required daily recourse to bankers, and of the extent to which the 'publicans' or the tax-farming estate agents, so often linked with sinners in the Bible, directly carried out banking functions. Thus a recent, and on balance 'primitivist', authority on the Roman economy shows that 'the scale of the largest private fortunes at Rome was extremely high' and gave examples of two such fortunate men who were worth around 400 million sesterces, or in real terms between three-quarters and one and a half million metric tons of wheat. He then compares this with the largest private fortunes in mid-sixteenth- and mid-seventeenth-century England, which at a real value of between 21,000 and 42,000 tons would appear to make the wealthiest Romans some thirty or forty times richer than their English counterparts (Duncan-Jones 1982, 4–5).

Roman bankers knew their place: and Roman banks, despite their growing importance were supplementary to the dominant mints. By controlling the mints personally, the emperors saw no need to stimulate banking: a state system of banking failed to appear and private banking remained functionally inferior to coinage. Thus the Greeks, although they were not strictly speaking the inventors of money or of banking, had developed both sides of money, the anonymous and the written, to a high pitch of efficiency. However, because the invention of coinage enabled the financial aspects of political and economic life to make such considerable advances and be so adaptable, there was no pressure to improve banking practices to anything like the same degree. With us today, coinage is very much a minor monetary matter (though not as unimportant as is dismissively implied by its almost total neglect by most modern economists), while banking because of its general excellence is paramount. In the Roman empire the situation was almost exactly the reverse.

Roman finance, Augustus to Aurelian, 14 BC–AD 275

Although the history of the Roman republic and empire, west and east, spans some twenty-two centuries, from 753 BC to AD 1453, the important section, so far as our financial study is concerned, comprises barely a third of that immense period, from around 300 BC to the fall of the western empire early in the fifth century AD. The great expansionary stage was almost completed in or shortly after the Augustan age (say by AD 138, if we include the conquests of Trajan and Hadrian, though some later emperors added considerable new territories). Rome seems thereafter to have adopted a defensive policy of containment. As the contemporary Roman historian Appian described it: 'Possessing the best part of the earth and sea the emperors reject rule over poverty-stricken and profitless tribes of barbarians.' Therein lies the heart of the matter so far as the financial watershed in Roman history is concerned. Once expansion over the richer lands ceased to yield its customary handsome rewards the Roman empire found itself inevitably thrown more and more upon the further utilization of its existing resources. In a macro-economic sense, diminishing returns began to exhibit their universal and, at first, hidden consequences.

In political and military terms, 'by giving up the task of expansion she can be said to have sown the seeds of her own destruction, by those she had failed to conquer', the eager barbarians on her borders (Mann 1979, 183). In coinage terms, that is in the fundamental economic terms of those days, expansion meant a flood of precious metals, with slaves to work the mines, in addition to the tribute exacted, which was customarily also paid largely in the precious metals. Thus in addition to the 14,000 talents extorted from Carthage in the first and second Punic Wars (10,000, as noted above, after the second war), Sidon paid Rome 15,000 talents between 189 and 177 BC, Greece and Macedon paid some 12,000 talents between 201 and 167 BC, while Spain paid over 3,300 talents in the ten years following the Roman conquest in 206 BC, besides giving up her enormously more valuable gold and silver mines, which like all such mines became the property of the Roman state, and later, the personal property of the emperor. Even so, as we have seen, occasionally the influx of new bullion supplies failed to keep pace with demand. These occasions changed from being the exception into being the rule from the end of the second century AD onward.

During one of Rome's greatest periods of expansion, between 157 BC and about 50 BC the active circulation of Roman coinage, mostly silver, multiplied by ten times, but this was accompanied by an increased amount and geographical extent of trading which, with other factors, such as the holding of greater cash reserves in the expanding cash-based banks and in the Roman treasury, held back the inflation which would otherwise have followed such a flood of new money. As Keith Hopkins has perceptively observed: 'The steep rise in money supply had little impact on prices because of the substantial rise in the volume of trade in an expanded area and partly because money percolated into a myriad of transactions which had previously been embedded in the subsistence economy' (1980, 110). However, all these factors began cumulatively to work the other way as soon as the era of expansion was over, culminating in rampant inflation, rigid rationing, a substantial return to payments in kind rather than in money, gross debasement of the coinage, and inevitably in the West, the end of empire itself.

Since coinage was the direct responsibility of the central authorities, with gold and silver coins being the direct, personal responsibility of the emperor, any financial pressures on them were immediately reflected in their coinage – mostly, in the later stages of the empire, by progressive debasement. The debasement occurred initially in the bronze coinages, which virtually became tokens, and then affected mainly silver, which had become by far the most important metal for coinage. Gold remained as far as was possible, undebased or suffered to a far smaller degree than did the silver and bronze coinages. The Romans were as proud of the high quality of their aureus and, at least after Constantine, their gold solidus, as Athens had been of its silver 'owls', and with almost as good reason. As Mattingly has demonstrated, 'a gold coinage was clearly necessary for the Empire, both for the sake of prestige and for the practical necessity of dealing with the expanding trade and rising prices' (1960, 121).

Augustus (30 BC to AD 14) carried out a thorough reform of the coinage system, issuing a new gold aureus at 42 to the pound weight, and a half-sized gold quinareus at 84 to the pound as well as a large silver denarius, also at 84 to the pound, with 25 denarii being worth 1 aureus or 100 sesterces. Both gold and silver coins were practically pure. In addition, there was a less carefully produced subsidiary coinage of both brass and copper, e.g. a one-ounce brass sestertius and a copper as and quarter as. Financial accounting, both public and private, was carried out in terms of the denarius and the sestertius, which was one-quarter of a denarius. In the long-lived Augustan system, the gold aureus and the silver denarius were the main, standard coins of the Roman bimetallist system which, by and large, functioned effectively for two centuries. Augustus also laid the basis of a new taxation system which similarly endured, but with increasing strain, for almost as long. It was not until the flood of foreign tribute was exhausted that the state's financial inadequacies necessitated drastic changes in fiscal policy. Taxes were unchanged for generations if not for centuries. Augustus had however managed to establish three new taxes: first, a 1 per cent general sales tax; secondly the *tributum soli*, which was a 1 per cent tax on the assessed value of land; and thirdly the *tributum capitis*, a flat-rate poll tax on 'adults' aged from 12 or 14 to 65.

With occasional adjustments, supplemented by frequent recourse to requisitioning, these remained adequate until the increased pace of inflation from the middle of the third century AD caused a complete breakdown in Rome's financial affairs. Eventually Diocletian managed to find a temporary and partial solution to the problem. Nero (AD 54–68) reduced the gold weight of the aureus to one-forty-fifth of a pound and also began the process of debasing the denarius by moderately and therefore unobtrusively reducing its silver content to 90 per cent. Thereafter, despite a few desperate attempts to restore the Augustan standard, debasement became gradually the accepted method by which emperors sought to make ends meet. Even so, the degree of inflation remained moderate until the latter half of the third century AD. The contrast between the relatively mild inflation based on a relatively sound and successful bimetallist currency during the first two centuries AD and the chaotic monetary conditions of the two following centuries is most marked, and together they highlight the importance of the reign of Diocletian and his immediate precursors and followers as a watershed between these widely different eras.

Public finances, crumbling under the mounting weight of welfare payments and subsidies, appear to have been the Achilles' heel of ancient, as perhaps of modern, civilizations. Themistocles was not immortal, and the Athenians could not rely on always having someone to persuade them to save their money from immediate consumption. 'It is perfectly clear,' says Professor Michell, 'that the chance of currying favour with the irresponsible masses by offering them the means of plundering the rich was in Greece, as it is today, the best policy for the demagogues' (1957, 393). There can be little doubt, too, that it was these financial pressures, to which such generous subsidies added their considerable weight, that 'should in fact be branded as, in all probability, the real cause of the destruction of the noblest of all states known to history' (Andreades 1933, 363). As with Greek public finance, so later was it in Rome.

Only the superior administrative and legal systems of the Romans plus the fiscal innovations of Diocletian delayed the inevitable decay for so long, for the scale of demands made on the public purse was far higher in Rome than in Greece. The richer Romans were also able to avoid high taxation more easily than was the case in Greece, and as we have seen, the differences between rich and poor were also far greater in Rome. Taxes were constantly inadequate, and difficulties with such increasingly inadequate, belatedly adjusted, visible taxes made Rome rely all the more on the easy, ready-to-hand, hidden taxation in the form of currency debasement. Short-lived, fitful reforms failed to reverse the secular downward slide.

The financial pressures through the wearing out of coins, shipwrecks, drains of money in exchange for the luxuries of the east, gifts to German barbarians, the growth in urban populations, the decline in the output and perhaps also in the physical productivity of agriculture, the working out of the richest mines, and above all the 'bread and circuses' policies deemed essential to keep minimum standards of orderly city life, all these worked together cumulatively to tempt imperial Rome into perpetual debasement, interspersed with occasional reforms which were soon doomed to failure. As well as supplying free or cheap bread and wine, imperial 'liberalities' or 'congiaria' in the form of cash doles were distributed from time to time, notably by Trajan (AD 98–117) and even more so by Hadrian (117–138) and his successors. What emperor and citizens had originally seen as a rare privilege had become a customary expectation from the beginning of the second century AD. They 'constituted a serious burden on the exchequer and contributed their share towards State bankruptcy' (Mattingly 1960, 149).

Even when the urban poor in Rome alone (the population of which was a million or more) were provided with food in kind, most of this was necessarily imported, and, though some was requisitioned, much of it was purchased with cash. Rome needed to import at least 150,000 tons of grain every year, most of the imports coming from North Africa. The children of the poor received 'alimenta', bread rations or the equivalent for their support. As many as 200,000 persons in Rome itself, without counting similar subsidization known to be common elsewhere, received distributions of wheat free of charge. When to these burdens is added the immense cost of a large army and a growing bureaucracy (even if the numbers of the latter were in fact small in relation to the huge populations they administered), one can easily see how the strains on the public budget grew to breaking point, all the more so when these strains were channelled unequally on to the coinage system. After Augustus' reform of the monetary and fiscal system at the beginning of the first century, the silver coinage remained pure, or nearly so, for the rest of that century. By AD 250, however, the silver content of the coins was down to 40 per cent.

Thereafter the pace of inflation and of debasement rapidly

accelerated, and by AD 270 the silver content had fallen to 4 per cent or less. Since there was obviously no general index of prices with which to measure the force of inflation, we are thrown back on using prices of important commodities such as wheat, pork and slaves plus the wealth of information contained in Diocletian's famous 'Edict of Prices'. While the decline in output was a partial cause in the phenomenal rise of wheat prices, there can be no doubt that monetary inflation was by far the more important. A recent expert quantification of the pace of inflation summarizes the position thus:

> Overall, the evidence suggests that prices in the mid-third century were about three times the level of first-century prices but that mid-Diocletianic prices were 50–70 times more than those of the first century. This argues relatively slow price-change up to the time of Gallienus, followed by very rapid price increases from about 260 onwards. (Duncan-Jones 1982, 375)

Gallienus' relatively short reign (260–8) marked the climax of physical debasement, with the so-called 'silver' denarius containing only about 4 per cent silver. In addition his mints produced a flood of copper 'billons' hardly more than flakes of metal impressed on one side only. Such grossly inferior coinage was refused by the banks. The limits of that form of debasement, which had begun moderately with Nero 200 hundred years earlier, had been reached. As long as coins of reasonable quality had to be produced, so long was inflation, given the practical absence of credit inflation in the cash-based Graeco-Roman system, limited by the slow and laborious process of hand-produced coinage. Gallienus threw any pretence of quality to the winds, but his temporary success in securing funds soon led to a marked increase in the pace of inflation and a temporary breakdown of the banking system.

The next emperor of note in this connection was Aurelian (270–5) who, faced with the chaotic condition of the coinage following Gallienus, was forced to carry out a most peculiar 'reform' of the coinage. He issued two new coins, the main issue marked 'XX.I', the precise meaning of which remains a matter of dispute among numismatists. The economic importance of Aurelian's coinage however comes from the fact that he retariffed or revalued the coinage to fit the current rapidly increased level of prices. In general he raised the nominal value of his coins by 2½ times the previous value of similar coins. In this way the Roman state (or any other state) could keep one jump ahead of the inflation inevitably caused thereby. This new principle of coinage revaluation released the brake upon inflation previously exerted by the limited means of hand-struck minting, for this new and subtle form of 'debasement' masquerading as 'reform' could be applied at a stroke to the whole of the existing as well as to the currently produced coinage. Aurelian had invented a method of inflationary finance which continued to be used by hard-pressed emperors for over one hundred years and is one of the main reasons for the contrasting types of inflation in the first and second main periods in the financial history of imperial Rome. Inflation took off; and money-based trade came to a virtual standstill. Though Aurelian was murdered in 275, such remained the position facing Diocletian when he became emperor in AD 284.

Modern believers in the disinflationary magic of a gold currency, whether followers of Jacques Rueff or the pro-gold lobby of the US Congress, should note that Aurelian proved conclusively that a 'reformed' currency is perfectly compatible with an increase rather than a decrease in inflation. Those who, erroneously, hold that an increase in the metallic quality of money is either a necessary or a sufficient step to remove inflation, would probably be as puzzled over Aurelian's financial adventures as was that most famous historian of the *Decline and Fall of the Roman Empire*, Gibbon himself. While it would appear to be irrefutable that the vast tributes which Aurelian brought to Rome from his eastern conquest (discounting the 15,000 lbs weight of gold that he donated to Rome's temple of the Sun) formed the main source of the issues of reformed coinages from his mints, Gibbon was puzzled as to why the issue of new coins should have led to an insurrection led by the moneyers themselves. Gibbon quotes a private letter from Aurelian: 'The workmen of the mint, at the instigation of Felicissimus, a slave to whom I had intrusted an employment in the finances, have risen in rebellion. They are at length suppressed, but seven thousand of my soldiers have been slain in the contest.' Rarely can a reform of the coinage have been so costly in real terms – nor as it turned out in long-term inflationary costs either. However, Gibbon, who obviously considered Aurelian to have been a misjudged monarch, plaintively reminds us that 'the years abandoned to public disorders exceeded the months allotted to the martial reign of Aurelian, [so] we must confess that a few short intervals of peace were insufficient for the arduous work of reformation'. Given the inflationary consequences of Gibbon's favourite, one wonders at his conclusion that 'since the foundation of Rome no general had more nobly deserved a triumph than Aurelian' (1788, I, 300–2). However as far as the Roman economy was concerned Aurelian's contribution was more of a disaster than a triumph. It was largely because of the nature of his 'reform' that the rate of inflation was enabled to rise far above what had previously been possible, even by the irresponsible Gallienus. After Aurelian, for two centuries inflation became rampant throughout the Roman empire.

Diocletian and the world's first budget, 284–305

In the short space of four decades (244–84), between the assassination of Gordian and the accession of Diocletian inclusive, Rome had endured no less than fifty-seven emperors. The state was in a complete mess, administratively, economically and financially. The strong rule of Diocletian, (284–305), followed fairly shortly thereafter by the equally strong Constantine (306–37, if we date the beginning of his power in the West from the time he was declared emperor by his own troops in York), recreated sufficient order and stability in government and, in a peculiar fashion, in finance also, to enable the empire to endure more or less intact for a further century. The logistical foundation of the army and of the administration was made secure through Diocletian's rationing and budgetary system, while Constantine succeeded in supplying the richer citizens as well as the two main spending units, the army and administration, with a pure and adequate supply of gold coins. Thus rampant inflation in prices, accommodated by and generated by a flood of inferior coinage proceeded apace, afflicting the majority of the relatively poor, while the rich and powerful found a way of avoiding the disadvantages of the runaway inflation. It was Diocletian who first taught Rome how to live with such inflation, and the success of his new system was confirmed and strengthened still further by Constantine. In retrospect there can be no doubt that together they saved the empire in the West until the fifth century, while Constantine set the basis for maintaining the strong financial influence of Constantinople on the coinage of the shrinking eastern sections of the empire until the middle of the fifteenth century. The political, economic and financial chaos of the third quarter of the third century was replaced by an enduring two-tier system, whereby the persistent inflation was overcome in those key sectors where governmental finance and administration were concerned, even if over the unshielded sectors of the economy inflation continued unabated.

The weaknesses of the empire from 260 to 284 were so grave that only a complete reformation stood any chance of success. Diocletian's prescribed cure was comprehensively planned. After an initial period of detailed and painstaking assessment of the political and economic facts his ideas were then rigorously pushed through to their logical conclusions. His comprehensive, and well-integrated package of reform was based on the following five features: first, a reformed currency;

secondly, a prices and incomes policy; thirdly, a demographic and economic census coupled with an annual budget; fourthly, a systematic adoption of taxation and payment in kind; and finally – a feature without which all other aspects would have failed – an administrative reconstruction of the army, civil service and regional government. Although these five features may be separated for analysis, the success or failure of each directly affected the other features. Together they made an integrated policy which developed gradually into a formula for successful and stable government.

Diocletian's main efforts in currency reform took place in AD 295. He realized that confidence in coinage (i.e. in money) had been almost completely lost despite Valerian's short-lived 'reforms'. He therefore struck five new coins: a full-weight, pure gold aureus, at sixty to the pound weight, and an almost pure silver coin at ninety-six to the pound. In addition there were three coins, covering large, medium and small sizes, all made of silvered bronze. In retrospect it is clear (from letters and declarations made by Diocletian) that he expected his currency reforms to eradicate or at least to slow down the rapid inflation which had been eroding the basis of economic life throughout the Roman empire. After all, his coinage system was very similar in quality to that of Nero: but in contrast prices under Diocletian remained a hundred times higher than in Nero's reign. To Diocletian's surprise, anger, and consternation, however, prices continued their upward surge. The momentum of price rises, built up to an accelerated degree during the previous forty years and supported by a flood of poor quality coinage, was far too strong to be halted simply by minting a supply of new coins which in total was small in relation to the vast supply already in the hands of the people. Not that, in themselves, the new coins were inconsiderable in amount, for, as Mattingly shows, 'it is highly probable that Diocletian's eastern victories placed large new stocks of gold and silver at his disposal' (1960, 250). This was another example of the integrated nature of his policies. Nevertheless, for a number of years the selective process inevitable whenever good and bad coins circulate together had been at work, whereby the good coins were retained, or parted with only when absolutely necessary, as in particular, for the payment of taxes, while the velocity of circulation of the bad coins used as far as possible everywhere else, was speeded up. No doubt, Diocletian's new coins received this same selective treatment. Diocletian was therefore driven to attempt to impose direct controls on all prices.

The Edict of Prices of 301 is among the most important economic documents – or rather, series of documents – of the Roman empire.

Although issued 1,700 years ago, we are still in the process of discovering more information about this famous edict. In 1970 an earthquake at Aezani in central Turkey, in destroying a mosque, gave easier access to previously existing buildings in and around that site, which included some of the best-preserved Roman ruins in Turkey. Amid the ruins of the modern mosque, the medieval Christian church and the ancient temple of Zeus, which occupied the same general site, were found Roman coins of the fourth century and also a fairly comprehensive and very well-preserved copy of Diocletian's Price Edict, comprising 8½ of the original fourteen sections. The uncovered coins also cleared up another archaeological mystery, namely the precise appearance of the statue of Zeus after which the vast marble temple was named – another example of the more general historical evidence provided by coinage. It is perhaps appropriate that our knowledge of the worst inflationary period of the ancient world should thus accidentally come to light at a time of the most widespread inflation yet suffered in the modern world. Even so our knowledge of the edict is still not complete despite fragments having been found in over thirty different cities; and though these are mostly in the eastern half of the empire, there is no doubt that the code of prices was to apply equally throughout the whole empire. Indeed one of the criticisms subsequently levied against the code, and a reason for its failure, is that it made no allowance for regional differences in prices, when such differences were very considerable.

It is of some importance to realize that the edict was in effect both a *prices* and *incomes* policy, for as well as giving the official prices for an incredibly long list of goods, the edict also gave the rates for services and personal wages and salaries, for slaves, agricultural labourers, public workers, from architects to stonemasons, the various grades of the civil service and the ranks of the army – all these were clearly stipulated in very considerable detail. Although this mass of detail was based on painstaking and laborious study, the edict nevertheless represented official wishful thinking – the prices that were listed were thought fair and reasonable at the time (AD 301) but were not the market prices that actually obtained. Indeed there is little doubt that 'profiteers' were singled out for blame, for naturally in such inflationary conditions, they flourished at the expense of honest traders. However the fact that inflation was not caused by profiteers soon became obvious, for there is considerable evidence not only that goods were driven off the market when traders held on to their stock rather than exchange at the official prices, which were too low to enable them to earn a living, but that the prices at which trading was actually carried out were in fact far higher than those stipulated in the edict.

The maximum prices for goods and services laid down in the edict are, in retrospect, extremely important in giving a picture of the *relative* values of goods and services, even if the actual prices given were rather low at the time they were issued and even if they were very soon overtaken in practice. Richard Duncan Jones gives a number of examples to show how the inflation of prices continued despite Diocletian's reform of the currency and despite his Edict on Prices. Thus a papyrus of 335 shows wheat prices sixty-three times higher than listed in the edict. Given the very limited success of his monetary policy and also of his prices and incomes policy, Diocletian was driven to rely very much more on isolating the more important sectors of the economy from the harmful and unreliable influences of the market.

The third aspect of his policy was, as noted, to produce an annual budget on the basis of a complete economic and demographic census of the empire – a sort of Roman Domesday Book, but a much more thorough and advanced survey than that of King William, for Norman England was far more primitive than ancient Rome. Nevertheless the comparison brings out the flavour of the detailed researches which underlay the most famous of all Diocletian's innovations – the world's first budget. We have already noted that the sound Augustan system of taxation allowed room, whenever the state's revenue fell short of its expenditure, for supplementing its revenue by various means. Nero and others had tried confiscating the property of rich citizens after serving trumped up charges against them. However the main method of supplementation was simply by the emperor or Senate authorizing the prefect or general concerned to requisition whatever was necessary for his purpose, for example for paying for public works or for supplying arms or uniforms for the army.

Until the time of Diocletian such requisitioning was done on a piecemeal basis, as and when necessary. It was a wasteful process, for very often the central authorities in Rome or elsewhere would not be in a position to relieve the shortages existing in one place with a surplus existing – but unknown to the central authorities – elsewhere, since it was natural for those in charge of resources, whether the civil service or the army, to keep quiet about their surpluses and to complain loudly of their deficits. Furthermore there was no foreknowledge of the likely balances of surplus or deficit since planning and requisitioning were both carried out independently and on an uncoordinated time basis. Diocletian changed all that. His census gave him a view of the reasonable output of the various regions in relation to the needs of the army and civil service and of the public works required in that region. As far as possible each region was to supply its own needs, though few could be self-sufficient, while special allowances were made for large towns like Rome which could obviously never attain such a balance. Each September the civil and military administrators had to submit their estimated revenues and expenditures (in real as well as in monetary terms, as we shall note below) to the emperor. The central authorities could then, by comparing one regional set of accounts with the other, see where savings could be made by offsetting estimated surpluses with estimated deficits. September was the obvious month on which to base the annual budget, since knowledge of the year's harvest would first become available then, and after all agriculture was by far the most important sector of the economy, so that fluctuations in agricultural output had a preponderant importance in the total budget. Keynes once remarked – significantly in connection with unbalanced budgets – that there was nothing sacred in the time it took the earth to go around the sun: but to Diocletian and subsequently to most societies throughout time, the dominance of agriculture has inevitably caused most accounts, whether public or private, to be based on the results of the annual harvest. It was Diocletian's genius which first recognized the importance of bringing the affairs of state into line with the regular order of the universe.

Diocletian's fiscal policy would not have been successful without the fourth arm of policy, namely the implementation of a system of receipts and payments in kind rather than simply in money. The instability of money prices and the habit of hoarding good coins meant on the one hand that the supply of good money was insufficient to pay the increasing taxes necessary to the Diocletianic system, and on the other hand that allocations from central to local authorities, if based on money alone, would have been far too unreliable and in general inefficient. This would have led inescapably to an unworkable increase in requisitioning in the old, sporadic uncoordinated and highly wasteful fashion. Consequently the regularization of requisitioning based on a rigid rationing of resources became a vital feature of Diocletian's reform. Taxes need not be paid in gold (though some continued to be): they would be accepted in kind, and taxpayers were encouraged or forced to make their payments in kind. Similarly allocations were distributed largely in kind. In this way the vital services of the army and civil service were secured, for on these rested the whole of the economic and political structure of the empire. In this way the most important sectors of the economy, from the official viewpoint at least, were safeguarded from the rigours of inflation. This did not mean the end of a market economy – far from it: but it did mean that over a large part of the economy where the civil service and army had direct influence, money became mainly used for accounting purposes rather than also as a medium of exchange and a means of payment of wages, taxes etc. Of course the release of coinage from these official duties in a significant part of the economy, mostly wholesale or large-scale in nature, actually increased the supplies of money available for spending in the still largely uncontrolled part of the economy, which was mostly but not solely, retail. It is little to be wondered at then, that despite the economic stability attained by Diocletian's system of budgeting and direct rationing, prices continued their vigorous inflationary progress unabated – or if anything, at an enhanced pace. The other side of the coin is that although, in the circumstances obtaining under Diocletian, an annual budget had to be combined with rationing, under different circumstances, for example once a sufficiently plentiful supply of reliable coinage had become available, the budget could function with greater financial freedom – a position approached by Constantine and later emperors, at least until weaknesses elsewhere wrecked the whole system.

The fifth and final feature of Diocletian's integrated policy requiring some attention is that concerning his general administrative reforms of the army, civil service and provincial government. It was the peace and security provided by these reforms that was basic to the recovery of trade and the functioning of the rest of Diocletian's reforms. First, the size of the army was considerably increased, and its structure reorganized. Morale was improved when the requisitioning system was regularized, which guaranteed the soldiers in real terms their standard of living and, importantly, the differentials which had been squeezed in the inflationary vices of the previous half-century. In order to carry out his detailed census and his rationing and budgetary policies it was essential for Diocletian also to increase the size of the civil service: according to some estimates its size was almost doubled in the twenty-one years before his abdication. Certainly complaints about the burden of taxes and the new methods laid down for payment increased considerably during his reign and for many years subsequently. As far as the reform of regional government is concerned, one of the previous difficulties was the great variation in the size, wealth and output of the various regions, some of which were far too large for efficient administration, particularly given the degree of detailed assessments required in the new fiscal system which Diocletian's civil and military services were introducing. Consequently Diocletian reorganized regional government, almost doubling the number of provinces, and subdividing Italy itself into provinces. In order to reduce the wanton destruction suffered in the peripheral areas from barbarian attacks

Diocletian relocated the army in strategic positions in the frontier areas. Security, trade, fiscal and administrative reform thus went hand in hand. Perhaps only in the two related features of his currency reform and his prices and incomes policy did Diocletian fail, or at least gain only partial and temporary success – but these very failures caused him to reinforce the undoubtedly strong and lasting successes achieved by his administrative improvements and, above all, by the fiscal reforms for which he is mainly, and with justice, remembered. Diocletian became one of the very few emperors ever to abdicate voluntarily when in 305 he retired to farm and build a palace in Spalato (Split). It is said that when pressed by Galerius to return to rule rather than merely 'to grow cabbages' Diocletian replied: 'Obviously, he hasn't seen my cabbages.' Inflation always enhances land values and places cabbages and kings into healthy perspective.

Finance from Constantine to the Fall of Rome

Shortly following Diocletian's abdication in 305 Constantine took over an initially disputed control of much of the western empire in 306, and eventually established his authority throughout the empire after extensive and successful campaigns in Thrace, Byzantium and Egypt. The first effect of these campaigns was to extend the twenty-one years of relative stability achieved by Diocletian for a further thirty-one years. It was during his long reign that Christianity, from having been a persecuted minority religion for nearly three hundred years, was made the official faith in 313. One might at first think that his eastern conquests and his conversion were not of much relevance to financial developments, but a little reflection will show that in fact both these events, together with the encouragement to trade given by the long years of peace and stable government, were directly related to the success of his financial and economic policies.

Just like Diocletian, Constantine's first major decision in the financial field was to reform the currency – or at least the higher-value coinage. The small copper and grossly debased silver currency, by that time known disparagingly as *pecunia*, appeared to have degenerated beyond recall; but good-quality silver and pure gold coinage, known respectively as *argentum* and *aureum* still commanded sufficient public loyalty to be worth rescuing. Early in Constantine's reign he issued a coin that is in some ways the most famous single coin in history – the gold solidus, which was to be produced, at a rate of 72 to the pound weight, for some seven hundred years. No other coin has remained pure and unchanged in weight for anything like so long a period, for when

Rome fell it continued to be issued from the Byzantine capital, which had been rebuilt in Roman splendour by Constantine. The choice of 72 solidi to the pound gave convenient subdivisions, of a gold semissis worth half a solidus, and a gold tremissis worth one-third of a solidus. Some experts, such as Blunt and Jones state that the solidus was 'not in the full sense of the word a coin'. They argue this because it was primarily issued for the convenience of the imperial treasury, and also because its value in terms of non-gold subsidiary coinage was not fixed but fluctuated from day to day as the inflation of the subsidiary coinage proceeded at a fast but erratic pace. This argument appears however to do less than full justice to the solidus. It was the other coins that in effect were not coins in the full sense since the public had lost a great deal of faith in them and yet had to make use of them, in the absence of good-quality, small-value coins. That these exchanged with that supreme coin, the solidus, at a fluctuating rate is not to be wondered at; nor is the fact that the banks and money-changers would quote their varying exchange rates for the solidus, day by day. In recent years we have become used to the 'floating' pound, which is no less a pound by reason of the fluctuations in its value as against other currencies. If one thinks of the vast Roman empire as having horizontal divisions between its main and its subsidiary currencies (instead of the vertical divisions between countries which give rise to the floating exchange rates today) then the acceptance of the solidus as a coin in every sense of the word is more readily seen. The purity of the solidus was maintained by the state's insistence on full-weight coins in payment of taxes, even though it equally insisted on enforcing acceptance without weighing for the private sector – an order with which the private sector complied all the more easily because from Constantine's day onward, the imperial issues were kept meticulously up to full weight and purity.

Supplies and precious metals in sufficient quantity to meet the demands of the state and those of trade came from a number of sources. First the eastern conquests of Constantine yielded a profitable surplus of tribute. Secondly Constantine established a number of new taxes payable strictly in gold or silver. Thirdly his agents operated compulsory purchase orders at reasonable but fixed prices for gold. Fourthly what was the most important source of all came as a direct result of the official conversion to Christianity, which allowed Constantine to confiscate the enormous treasures amassed over the centuries in the numerous pagan temples throughout the empire. The result of this religious revolution was far greater but in some ways similar to the financial effects of the dissolution of the monasteries in sixteenth-century England. Indeed given this massive new gold source, the three new types of gold coins began to become so plentiful as to make it possible for the state to begin to relax the strict rationing inflicted by Diocletian as more and more of the economy became serviced by coinage of good quality. Diocletian's gold coinage had been rather too small to have a lasting effect. Armed with the gold of the pagan temples, Constantine succeeded where Diocletian had failed. Although, like Diocletian, Constantine also issued a reformed silver currency, his degree of success in silver fell considerably short compared with his famous solidi. The *pecunia* of debased copper and silver-washed copper still existed in considerable volume.

Consequently despite the high quality of coins at the top of the range, inflation was far from cured. In effect, the very considerable supply of new good money, supplemented rather than supplanted the existing supply and so in a perverse way added to the inflationary pressures during and after Constantine's reign. In this connection it is important to note that the imperial mints, both during and after Constantine, continued to issue vast quantities of the old, grossly debased coins. Diocletian's edict stipulated that a pound of gold was worth 50,000 denarii. By 307 gold was worth 100,000 denarii; by 324 it was worth 300,000. In some parts of the empire the inflation was even more astronomical. In these circumstances the prestige and the value of the solidus continued to soar. Possibly the record rate of exchange between the debased denarii and the solidus is the figure of 30 million to one reached in mid-fourth-century Egypt, at which reckoning, and discounting the premium attached to the coin, a pound of gold was worth 2,120,000,000 denarii. Thus inflation had brought the once proud silver denarius to dust.

Given the fact that the influential sections of the community – the emperor, landowning senators, the civil service and army – could be content with their appreciating land and gold currency holdings, the empire struggled on. But the mass of the population, despite the degree to which they were saved by their direct dependence on agriculture, could not escape the disadvantages of inflation; and though the pace of inflation was considerably reduced in the last quarter of the fourth century and the beginning of the fifth, the damage had been done. Thus the barbarian pressures were more easily able to achieve increasing success. Economically it matters little whether we date the end of the western empire with the fall of Rome to the Visigoths in 410 or extend it to 476 when the last Roman emperor, Romulus Augustulus was deposed in favour of Odoacer the Barbarian. Of course, Constantinople continued in some form for a further millennium, and, for most of that long period, so did the solidus; a rather empty if glittering symbol of the old imperial Rome.

The nature of Graeco-Roman monetary expansion

From a few city-states in the north-east corner of the Mediterranean, Greek and Roman monetary systems spread to cover almost the whole of the non-Chinese civilized world. Contrary to the situation in our modern world where the advanced economies comprise only a quarter of the world's total population, it is probable that it was the most civilized regions of the world that were not only the most prosperous but also the most populous in the ancient world. In other words the new monetary systems had a greater significance than might at first be supposed in terms of the total numbers of people directly influenced. It was the simple, concrete, anonymous nature of the new invention of coinage which assisted its ready assimilation into the economic life of millions of new users in the expanding Hellenistic and Roman empires. For the first time in history 'money' mainly meant 'coins': all the more so since in Graeco-Roman times coins performed not merely their modern function of supplying the small change of retail trade, but covered in addition almost all the range of payments now performed by banknotes and cheques. Coins followed – indeed accompanied – the sword; payment for troops and for their large armies of camp-followers was generally the *initial* cause of minting. Only the best was good enough for an all-conquering army, and what was good enough for the army, even if at first accepted through compulsion, was soon universally accepted by everyone with alacrity. Although armies could always take, or 'requisition', whatever they wanted, payment in good coinage was a better way of getting eager co-operation. Consequently trade and, with it, coinage, as the most convenient and most readily acceptable method of financing trade, expanded in step with the armies of Alexander and Julius Caesar.

If the spread of Greek, Macedonian, Hellenistic and Roman money had had to depend solely on trade, the process would have been far slower and far more limited in extent: it was military conquest which forced the pace and extent of change. That is not to say, however, that trade was unimportant in causing the adoption of Greek and Roman monetary systems based on coinage: on the contrary, trade expanded enormously as all roads and a large proportion of shipping, led to Athens, Pella or especially Rome. Priority in causation may well have been military conquest, and the maintenance of the army and of the administration was always of considerable importance in the total economy: but once the sword had initiated a novel or an expanded need for coinage, commercial trade took over, added substantially to the military needs and so became confirmed in its generally preponderant role. Despite the fact that the state, mainly through having to support a large army and administrative machine, always loomed large in the economic life of Hellenistic and Roman civilization, nevertheless the market economy and the price system furnished the basis of a largely private-enterprise system, with a high degree of specialization of labour, dependent on an intricate network of trading in everyday requirements as well as in luxuries, on a scale extensive enough to guarantee that the large urban populations were adequately fed and clothed, while enabling considerable numbers of its richer citizens to enjoy a most enviable standard of living, at a level which few would be able to attain until relatively recent times. It is not a question therefore of *either* the army *or* trade being responsible for the establishment and maintenance of the new monetary systems based on coinage. Both had their interconnected roles to play, with the sword leading the way. Without the security established by the sword, seen especially in the four long centuries of the 'Pax Romana', trade would not have been able to have basked in the peace and goodwill necessary for its unprecedented growth and extent. Coinage enormously facilitated and clearly symbolized the degree of imperial success in war and peace, in conquest and trade.

Since the new money was the product of the sword the pace of monetary expansion was naturally greatest during the last few decades of the fourth century BC when the pace of Hellenistic advance was at its height. As we have seen, the Persians learned about coinage when they captured the Lydian King Croesus. Their attempts to conquer Greece were thwarted when Athens, Sparta, Corinth and the rest managed to turn from fighting each other to fighting the common enemy. Philip II's financial, economic and military preparations to advance against Persia helped Alexander towards his astonishing successes which led to the most rapid extension of any single monetary system in world history. As we have seen, the expansion was more than simply geographical, for vast treasuries of precious metals which had previously been unavailable for monetary uses were coined for immediate use for military and more general economic purposes. Although the easternmost sections of Alexander's empire were lost by the time its Hellenistic remains were consolidated within the Roman empire, Julius Caesar and his followers extended the uniform Graeco-Roman monetary system over all of Gaul and most of Britain, though here the sword followed and more strongly confirmed various imitative coinage systems which had already to some extent been built up partly by trade and partly by aggression by a number of warring Celtic tribes. Thus in the thousand years between 600 BC and AD 400 the whole of the civilized world had become accustomed to coinage as the basis of its monetary systems. At one time or other, between 1,500 and 2,000 mints were busy turning out the coins required in the non-Chinese and non-Indian areas of the civilized world.

However, when the impetus of growth gave way to the stagnation of defence the nature of monetary expansion gradually began to change also, from real growth to spurious, inflationary expansion. The Roman desire for disciplined uniformity, though long successful, eventually succumbed to the conflicting need to delegate administrative and military decision-making (and therefore coin-making) to a number of provincial regions and to the peripheral areas where fighting to defend the vast imperial boundaries was endemic. Many mints producing from a limited number of official imperial dies enabled uniformity to coexist with decentralization, though with increasing difficulty. Currently, expert numismatists have been unable to decide in a significant number of instances whether the coinage dies in a number of provincial centres were truly 'official' or just very good imitations, undiscovered or possibly condoned by the local administration who would often gain power, prestige and of course literally money thereby. Numismatically the problem of official versus unofficial dies is a matter of considerable importance, although from the economic point of view the real concern is the degree of acceptability of the coins. The very fact of imitation indicated that the demand for money locally exceeded the official supply, a gap which the counterfeiter exploited directly for his own interest and indirectly and more importantly for influencing the economy as a whole; for good if trade was otherwise being inhibited, for evil if the increased unofficial supply simply fed an existing general inflationary oversupply of money. The better the imitation, the wider was the actual or potential extent of the currency of the counterfeit coinage. Furthermore, as official debasement proceeded apace, so the metallic costs and the workmanship costs of counterfeiting were reduced, encouraging the unofficial supply to be more readily expanded and so multiplying the force of the officially-induced inflation.

Although the Romans had frequently reduced the size of gold coins, i.e. increased the number coined from a given weight and moreover tried to pass off the reduced weights at their former values, they generally avoided debasing their gold in the sense of alloying gold with less precious metals; and from Constantine onwards they re-established the purity and stability of their gold coinage. They reserved mixed-metal debasement for their silver coins, reducing many to mere silver-washed bronze or copper coins, with the thinnest of silver coatings. However, an economy cannot live by gold alone. The destruction through debasement and inflation of the monetary media in which most retail trade was necessarily conducted, and which involved by far the greatest number of transactions for by far the greatest number of the people, progressively weakened the economic basis of the Roman empire. Thus although it was the barbarian invasions that brought about the fall of the empire, the main underlying cause was the chronic economic and financial chaos suffered in the fifth century, the product of excessive, unproductive expenditure on defence and welfare. European unity disintegrated as and when its uniform currency disappeared, never again to be re-established not even by the Holy Roman Empire – which, as Voltaire remarked, was neither holy, nor Roman, nor an empire. Significantly, at the end of the twentieth century a single currency is being seen as the essential ingredient in European unity.

As for Britain, from being part of a vast empire with a currency of relatively high quality produced from a limited number of carefully controlled mints, she became isolated and undefended from about the year 410 onward. With the Romans went their peace, their order, their language and their coinage. But elsewhere as the Dark Ages began to cast their deepening shadows, the memories lingered on. Each warring tribe and city-state attempted to combine defence or conquest with the universally understood symbol of power and trade, its own coinage. Painfully, from the disintegrated remnants of imperial power and finance, new tribal, and eventually, national currencies were to emerge involving not only former Romanized but also 'barbarian' or primitive tribes. Subsequent to the Graeco-Roman extension of coinage the most important, simple, single test of whether an economy is 'primitive' or 'civilized' lies in whether or not it uses coins.

After the end of the Roman empire in the West, the primitive, newly emerging peripheral kingdoms had first to learn or relearn how to coin. Then, 1,000 years later – and at least 3,000 years later than the advanced banking system of Babylon – they had once again to learn for themselves the significance of banking, being ignorant of the earlier foreign models. This time the further development of banking in a more advanced monetary system was not impeded by the supremacy of coinage, and in process of time coinage began to occupy a place of progressively diminishing importance. In the very long mean time the penny and the pound, as coin and unit of account respectively, became the main focus of financial concern for the rulers of medieval and early modern Britain.

4

The Penny and the Pound in Medieval European Money, 410–1485

Early Celtic coinage

Before tracing the rise of the penny and the pound sterling it is convenient to look briefly at the development of early Celtic coinage, a generally neglected subject the importance of which has been overshadowed by the money of imperial Rome. Peripheral in every sense of the word to the Graeco-Roman coinage system were the many mainly imitative coins produced by the Celtic tribes along the northern and western borders of the Roman empire. The coins of the Celts had been in existence for a century or more before their lands, extending from Finisterre in Spain, through Gaul and southern Britain, to the Elbe in Germany, became incorporated in the Roman empire. This area of north-western Europe experienced three coinage phases between the middle of the second century BC and the seventh century AD. First came two centuries or so of recognizably indigenous coins based mainly on the Macedonian coins of Philip II and Alexander and later those of the Romans. Secondly, the middle period lasted some 400–500 years, when the greater part of the regions concerned was conquered by Rome, when Roman coinage was predominant and when the previous indigenous, and usually inferior, coinage was discontinued. In effect, the periphery was pushed several hundred miles north. In the new, more distant peripheral regions some indigenous Celtic coinage was still produced, though far less distinctively Celtic, being hardly more than copies of the dominant Roman coins which circulated in their own kingdoms as well as within the vast empire to the south. Thirdly there came a period of 300–400 years following the break-up of the Roman empire in the West when new types of coinage patchily re-emerged in the previously Celtic countries which meanwhile suffered the shocks of barbarian invasions. It was during this latter phase, after Britain had endured two completely coinless centuries, that the early English penny eventually made its appearance. In contrast to the headlong decline in the quality of coined money in the disintegrating Roman empire of the West, coins of the highest quality continued to be produced uninterruptedly in parts of the eastern empire based on Constantinople for over seven centuries. In north-west Europe the barbarian invasions led to a marked reduction in the quality and in the quantity of coined money, with Britain's economy as an interesting extreme case being reduced to a prolonged period of barter.

Traditional historians have tended to overlook the role played by Celtic coinage in the early history of British money. Since Celtic coinage was to a considerable extent simply crude imitations of that of Macedon and Rome, why should it claim our attention? However, as D. F. Allen has emphasized, firstly, 'it is in Britain that all the streams of western Celtic coinage converge' so that much of Celtic monetary development is seen in concentrated form in Britain. Secondly, 'no other surviving Celtic remains illustrate more vividly the life and thoughts of our insufferably quarrelsome but superbly imaginative forebears' (1980 25, 41). Surely these are sufficiently telling reasons for examining briefly the involved, incomplete and often confusing history of Celtic coinage. There are two other reasons, one negative, one positive, but both equally compelling. The negative reason is perhaps most easily captured in the simple question: what other evidence is there? It so happens that there is a marked paucity of written evidence, and what exists is of doubtful reliability. On the other hand literally hundreds of thousands of Celtic coins have been found, mostly on the Continent, where hoards of up to 40,000 coins have been discovered. In a number of instances we have learned of the existence of certain rulers only through their representation on their coins (though some are spurious). Although the evidence presented by coins is copious, it may nevertheless be confusing in that forgeries, imitations and migration may make it impossible to fix the place of minting and the region of currency with any precision. Similarly with dating: unlike our coins, dates were not generally indicated on early coinages. For instance the first date on English coins did not appear until 1548 in the reign of Edward VI, and with the Roman numerals MDXLVIII.

The copious and concrete evidence of coins is therefore not always either as obvious or as exact as might first be supposed. The interpretation of the plentiful and durable evidence given by coins is therefore a difficult matter, involving painstaking work over many

years. Fortunately British and other numismatists involved in the study
of early northern European coinage 'have reached a very high standard
in their identification of individual coins and in the scientific analysis of
coin hoards'(Thompson 1956, 15). Unfortunately, in contrast with the
propaganda that was such a revealing feature of Roman currencies,
many of the Celtic and early English coins were sparing in their
inscriptions, so that they do not yield as much information as that
customarily provided by Roman coins.

The most plentiful of the earliest Celtic coins in north-western
Europe and the earliest found in Britain were of pure gold, being direct
imitations of the gold stater of Philip II of Macedon, with the head of
Apollo on the obverse and Philip riding his chariot on the reverse. It
may well be that some trading connections, e.g. with the early
Phoenicians, may have brought southern Britain into sporadic contact
with the eastern Mediterranean. But the spread of knowledge of such
coinage is more generally held to be the result of migration and in
particular of the use of Celtic mercenaries by Philip and Alexander.
Given the high value of gold coinage, the military influence in
originating the spread of such coinage was therefore almost as
important in Celtic as in Graeco-Roman financial history. In the same
way that the aggressive military ambitions of the Macedonian, Persian
and Roman armies were largely responsible for multiplying their coins,
so also did such wars stimulate coin production by their 'barbarian'
enemies. As Daphne Nash, an expert on Celtic coinage, has recently
confirmed: 'In every area, wars with Rome provoked unusually high
levels of coin production to pay for armies and associated expenses'
(1980, 77). Britain was probably the last of the major Celtic areas of
northern Europe to begin to mint, and was the last to maintain
independent minting before being overwhelmed by Rome. The last of
what may be strictly called 'Celtic coinage', as distinct from later coins
produced in still largely Celtic-speaking countries, thus came to an end
by the middle of the first century AD.

The earliest date given for Philip's stater in England in Seaby's
standard catalogue is 125 BC. Thereafter independent minting
continued until AD 61 (Seaby and Purvey 1982, 1). As well as gold, silver,
bronze and 'potin' were also coined by the Celts. As their confidence
grew, so did the independence of their designs, which no longer were
simply imitative. The Celts were a pastoral people, so the horse is a
strongly favoured design. As Celtic town life developed, so the quantity
of their coinage increased very considerably, particularly of alloyed
silver, bronze and copper–tin alloys, showing that trade was growing
and becoming the main purpose for coining. At the same time the

quality of the gold and silver coinage, in weight and purity, declined with the increased output. The Celtic love of hunting is also given prominence in the boar designs favoured by the Iceni of East Anglia, and as farmers they also gave tribute to the fertility of East Anglia by prominently depicting ears of wheat, similar to that on modern French coins.

The Iceni in East Anglia, the Cantii of Kent, the Atrebates of Hampshire, Surrey and Sussex, and the Dobunni of the Midlands and south-west were the most prolific coin-makers of Celtic Britain between about 75 BC and AD 61. In the latter year, after the Iceni's revolt under Queen Boadicea had sacked London and Colchester, killing some 70,000 Romans, Celtic independence, and with it Celtic coinage, over most of southern Britain was extinguished when Roman authority was restored. Thereafter England became absorbed into the Roman monetary sphere. From time to time, usurping kings marked their ambitions in the usual way by issuing their own coins, and the rarity of such occasions is indicated by the enormously inflated prices quoted in Seaby's catalogues. Thus whereas the catalogued price, in 1982, of a good Celtic copy of a Philippian gold stater, was £500 and an Iceni boar-head or horse coin fetched only £45, the gold and silver coins of the usurping kings commanded far higher prices. The gold aureus of Victorinus (268–70) was priced between £3,500 and £10,000; a Carausius (287–93), who minted his gold in London, would fetch between £7,500 and £17,500; while the gold solidus of Magnus Maximus (383–8) was priced at between £2,750 and £8,000.

Whereas the numismatist and, even more, the ordinary coin collector, may invest great significance in rarity, the economist must express far more interest in the mundane, common and everyday coinage. Of particular interest in this connection are the 'potin' currencies that became of especial importance on the Continent, but also spread to southern England in Celtic times. The composition of the 'potin' coins varied with tribe and locality, but their basic similarities derived from, first their cheap method of manufacture, secondly their 'token' nature, thirdly their small size and fourthly, related to all three previous aspects, their purpose in meeting the ordinary needs of small-value trade. Various combinations of copper and tin, probably dependent on the cheapness and availability of the raw materials, formed the most common metals used for this currency, which was very plentiful in Gaul before it was conquered by Julius Caesar. Potin coins continued in circulation into the first century AD. They were also common in Kent and circulated at least until AD 43.

Instead of being struck or hammered, as were the dearer coins in silver and gold, the potin coins were cast. They may first have been cast individually, but to meet the growing demand for this popular form of everyday money, a method of casting in fairly long strips was developed. Since their intrinsic value was low in comparison even with the debased and imperfect struck coins of gold and silver and their alloys, it is probable that they circulated as tokens, accepted for trade at a higher value than their metallic worth. No great skill was required in their manufacture and it is quite possible that the ubiquitous Celtic smiths were therefore able fairly easily to supply local demands to supplement the official issues. Although Roman coinage displaced the Celtic varieties, the small 'minissimi' coins produced towards the end of the Roman occupation of the Celtic lands served a somewhat similar purpose to the earlier 'potin' coins.

Money in the Dark Ages: its disappearance and re-emergence

When the Romans arrived in Britain they found a Celtic-speaking country, as were the majority of its peasants when they left – or left Britain to its own fate – in 410. Even before that date Germanic mercenaries had been imported by the Roman authorities into Britain in fairly large numbers. Gradually thereafter the Roman language, the relatively new Christian religion and Roman coinage ceased to influence the life of the people. In practice the pace of the attenuation of Roman influence varied with the raids, invasions and settlements of the Angles, Jutes, Saxons and Friesians. The *Anglo-Saxon Chronicle* gives the traditional date of 449 for the first landing in Kent by the brothers Hengist and Horsa. At any rate it is clear that from about that time the number of the invaders' settlements grew, spreading from the south-east over most of England during the following century, changing the whole country from Romano-British to Anglo-Saxon, from Christian to pagan, from relatively urbanized to a pattern of deserted towns and rural settlements, and from a thoroughly monetized economy based on a uniform coinage system, to a backward economy where coins first became scarce and then, with surprising speed, disappeared completely from circulation.

The disruption accompanying the decline and fall of the Roman empire was nowhere more marked than in Britain, where the term 'the Dark Ages' therefore carries special significance. Given the increased insecurity of life and the disruption of trade and social contacts, the burial of treasures for reasons of safekeeping was a natural and common reaction. There was a remarkable increase in the hoarding of coins in the late fourth and early fifth centuries up to around 440. The fact that these cluster in the south-west 'suggests that the accumulation and burial of these hoards should be a Romano-British phenomenon' – a sort of retreating frontier attesting the advance of the early Anglo-Saxon armies (C. E. King 1981, 11). Whereas on the Continent Roman influence on language, laws and coinage continued to exert a weakening but still pervasive influence, the break between island Britain and Roman civilization was far more complete and the disruption through wars and invading settlers much more marked. Britain reverted, suddenly in some areas and fairly quickly everywhere, to a more primitive, less urbanized, moneyless economy. This most significant and rare example of a virtual reversion to barter for as long as around 200 years by a country which had known, used and produced coins for nearly 500 years remained a matter of dispute among the experts for many years. However, the authoritative, painstaking and monumental researches of experts like Professors Spufford, Grierson and Blackburn, among others, have removed any lingering doubts about the total collapse of coinage and currency in Britain and the contrast this showed with the situation just across the English Channel.

Thus Professor Spufford emphasized the fact that after the Roman army left 'no further coin entered Britain and within a generation, by about 435 AD, coin ceased to be used there as a medium of exchange. Not for 200 years . . . were coins again used in Britain as money' (1988, 9). Similarly Grierson and Blackburn state that 'Britain was the only province of the Roman Empire where the barbarian invaders brought a complete end to coin production and monetary circulation for almost two centuries' (Grierson and Blackburn 1986, 156). The Continent managed to maintain a degree of continuity in customs and coinage. The contrasting discontinuity in Britain meant that not until the seventh and eighth centuries (despite a false dawn in the sixth century) did she relearn how to use and make coined money, and then only in painfully slow stages. Thus the monetary use of either existing or imported coins probably ceased in the generation following 430, while only in the generation preceding 630 did Britain, and then mainly in the south-east, begin slowly to accustom itself once more to the gold coins imported from across the Channel.

The Canterbury, Sutton Hoo and Crondall finds

In examining the origins of the 'penny' we must first look at when coins of any kind were first minted in Anglo-Saxon England, and then tackle the question of which type of indigenous coin might first legitimately be called a penny. English indigenous 'coinage' had a possibly abortive birth in Canterbury in the last few decades of the sixth century, although only in recent years has the nature of the birth or abortion become clear. The traditional origin of English coined 'money-like objects' is said to begin in about 561, after the marriage of the Christian Merovingian Princess Bertha with Prince Aethelbert, who became king of Kent in 590. Bishop Liudard, who came with Bertha to Canterbury, minted a number of gold 'coins' shortly thereafter. However, when these Canterbury 'coins' were critically examined it appears that they were more in the nature of medallions, including a necklace of 'coins', more for ornament than for use as currency. In 597, heartened by the welcome shown to the Christian religion in Kent, Pope Gregory the Great – allegedly stirred also by the sight of the young blond, blue-eyed English prisoners in Rome ('not Angles but Angels') – dispatched St Augustine to Canterbury. According to Sir John Craig, London, too, 'accepted a Bishop and gained a mint between 600 and 604' (1953, 4). Bishop Mellitus issued gold coins from the London mint from about 604 for a dozen years to 616.

Since Christianity and coinage had disappeared from England together it seemed highly appropriate and unsurprising that it became widely accepted that they also returned together. However, the researches of Professors Spufford and Grierson show these early mintings to be a false dawn. 'In the larger part of England coin did not circulate as money [even as late as] the eighth century, having spread very slowly from the south-east from around 630' (Spufford 1981, 41). It was from the gradual rebuilding of commercial and cultural contacts with France and Italy that Anglo-Merovingian types of coinage gradually began to circulate for commercial purposes in south-east England. According to J. D. A. Thompson, 'the presence of Merovingian and Byzantine gold pieces in various parts of the country points to a resumption of commercial intercourse with Europe long before 600 and to a widespread acceptance of the East Roman solidus and the Merovingian tremissis as a convenient trade-currency' (1956, xviii). In the light of more recent research Thompson's timing appears premature. Christianity, trade and coinage did, however, grow faster and earlier in the south and east of England than in the rest of the country and prepared the way for a more general acceptance of both the cross and the coin during the seventh and eighth centuries. Still later on in northern Europe the influence of Christian missionaries in persuading Nordic rulers to issue their own coined moneys is indisputable (Spufford 1988, 83).

The re-entry of coinage into England in the sixth and seventh centuries repeated in certain respects the pattern of its original entry some 600 years earlier. In both cases the original coinage was of gold, then of gold and silver alloys. In both cases it was natural that our nearest neighbours across the Channel should have been responsible for the circulation of coins which were the object of our initial indigenous imitations. In the first century BC it had been the Celtic Belgae, in the sixth and seventh centuries AD it was the Merovingian Gauls who first taught the inhabitants of south-east Britain how to use and mint coins. However, the Anglo-Saxons were not quite ready in the early seventh century for the full acceptance of either Christianity or coinage. Whatever limited issues may have come from the London mint in the first two decades of the seventh century soon ceased as the backsliding Londoners reverted to paganism after 616.

In unravelling the tangled threads of early English monetary history the following three factors have been found to be of critical importance. First the Sutton Hoo hoard found in a ceremonial burial ship near Woodbridge, Suffolk in 1938; secondly the Crondall hoard found at the village of that name in Hampshire as far back as 1828 but the subject of much recent research; and thirdly the patient researches of Grierson, Spufford, Blackburn, Kent, Oddy, Sutherland, Dolley and other experts on Anglo-Saxon coinage, which have enabled us to improve our interpretation and especially the dating of the coins found in these and other similar hoards. The Sutton Hoo ship, buried in about 620 to 625, contained no English coins. Most of the Crondall hoard of 101 gold coins, relating to the 630s and 640s – the precise date is still, as we shall see, in dispute – had, however, undoubtedly been minted in England. Of the original Crondall hoard, three have been lost. Of the remainder eighteen are Merovingian, nineteen are Anglo-Merovingian copies minted in England, fifty-two are Anglo-Saxon both in type and minting, three are blanks, while the other six are of mixed provenance. Despite the fact that some 1,200 Roman hoards have been uncovered in Britain, such as that at Beachy Head in 1973 which unearthed 5,540 Roman coins, early Anglo-Saxon coin finds are so rare that the positive evidence of the Crondall hoard remains of the utmost importance. Somewhere between 620 and 650, probably from about 630, a date confirmed by a number of other smaller finds, England had begun again to mint her own coins, now in moderately significant amounts for general circulation and for trade, and not simply for gifts or decoration.

Among the many rich treasures found in the Sutton Hoo ship was a bejewelled purse containing some thirty-seven gold Merovingian coins (plus three gold blanks). Unfortunately only one of these was readily identifiable by bearing the ruler's inscription, the Frankish King Theodebert (595–612). Tentatively the date of 650 became generally, but not universally, accepted as the burial date. However a number of numismatists, including Jean Lefaurie in France and Dr John Kent of the British Museum, doubted the authenticity of this date. Dr Kent and his assistant Dr Andrew Oddy, a physicist, carefully devised a method of dating Merovingian coinage which could be applied to the Sutton Hoo, Crondall and other finds, based on the fact that Merovingian gold coinage became progressively debased with silver during the seventh century. They very carefully tested the specific gravity of some 900 Merovingian coins, and by combining the results with base-reference coins, the dates of which were already established beyond doubt, derived a time-scale against which all other Merovingian currency could be assessed. As a result of this painstaking and scientifically based research, Dr Kent came to the firm conclusion that the mint date of the latest coin found in the Sutton Hoo ship was between 620 and 625 (see Brown 1978).

The economic and financial significance of the Sutton Hoo find should not be based narrowly or exclusively on its foreign coins, but rather the richness and widespread origins of its luxuries should also be taken into account. These would seem to indicate that by the first half of the seventh century Britain's trading links with the Continent had again become of significant proportions. Gold and silver ornaments of the finest craftsmanship, extending in geographical range from the Celtic west to the Byzantine east, are to be seen in the burial ship. Furthermore if a relatively unimportant and almost unknown East Anglian ruler (probably King Raedwald – but the matter is disputed by the experts) could command such wealth, fully comparable with that of any contemporary Germanic prince, then the early Anglo-Saxon standards of living, at least in and around the courts, were not nearly so crude as has often been assumed. F. M. Stenton considered the evidence of the Sutton Hoo find sufficiently clear on this point at least to conclude that it was 'in every way probable' that the eastern silver had come to England 'through trade rather than plunder' (1946, 52). The Sutton Hoo find therefore suggests that the rudimentary foundations of a trading, coin-using economy, though at first dependent on foreign coins, were being laid down in southern and eastern Britain early in the seventh century, while the Crondall find further confirms the progress made in trade and payments, using indigenous as well as foreign coin, as the century progressed. As to the relative importance of such trade as compared with tribute, gifts or other ways of stimulating the issue and exchange of coins in the Dark Ages, we are still very much in the dark. Some authorities, such as Grierson, insist that 'alternatives to trade were more important than trade itself' (Grierson 1979, 140). However, from the point of view of the development of a coin-using economy *both* trade and its alternatives, such as ransoms, tributes and payments to mercenaries, acted together as complementary and self-reinforcing inducements to extend the currency of coinage.

The somewhat negative evidence of the Sutton Hoo hoard stands in contrast to the positive evidence of the mixed Anglo-Merovingian coins of the Crondall hoard. Carried to its extreme, the Sutton Hoo evidence simply proves that there were no Anglo-Saxon coins in that purse: it does not prove that there were none anywhere else at the same time, although in the absence of other significant and undisputed finds, Dr Kent, like most other experts, considers that this is probably the case. He therefore attaches much more importance to the positive evidence of the Crondall hoard which points to the probabililty of a significant Anglo-Saxon gold coinage circulating from about 630 and continuing until about 675. This summary of the main schools of thought concerning the origins of English coinage demonstrates that the financial history of the Dark Ages is still very much a live issue. In 1980 Dr Kent reaffirmed that 'the first English coinage is known almost entirely from the Crondall hoard' which 'seems to date from the 630s' (p.129). This is earlier than the date given by Grierson and Blackburn. The view of the latter authorities is that 'not until the 630s and 640s was coin production sustained in England and it is this phase which is represented in the Crondall Hoard now dated to *c.*650 or a little earlier' (1986, 161). The gap between the various schools regarding the birth of English coinage has thus been narrowed from an unbridgeable seventy years to a now generally accepted couple of decades at the most.

The main denomination of the coins found in both the Sutton Hoo and Crondall finds consisted of what English numismatists have called the 'thrysma', derived from the tremissis or one-third of the gold solidus, and about one-sixth the weight of a modern English sovereign. Once the new gold thrysma had established itself its gold purity began to be reduced. We have seen how the gold content of the Merovingian coinage became progressively debased with silver from the early part of the seventh century onward – a pattern frequently repeated. The same process occurred at a later date but at a faster pace in England. Rapidly from about 675 onward the early English coinage was replaced by silver as the main metal. This marked an important step on the way to a wider circulation and to the adoption of the silver penny as the age-long trademark of English currency.

From sceattas and stycas to Offa's silver penny

Gold was too scarce and too precious a metal in England and France to be used as the basis of a rapidly expanding monetary system. As it happened, the rejection of gold in favour of silver was a most propitious development, for Britain, unlike Byzantium, lacked the considerable supplies of gold needed to maintain the output of coins in sufficient amounts to meet the increasing demands of government, Church and trade and in denominations low enough to be suitable for an extensive coverage of commercial interchange. Thus the original gold currency of Anglo-Saxon England lasted barely seventy years, for from about 675 the gold issues first became alloyed with silver and then early in the eighth century gave way almost completely to silver, supplemented for a time with a subsidiary coinage of brass or copper. Even so, the various rulers of the different regions of a still disunited England issued silver alloyed with inferior metals to the extent of up to 50 per cent or more for a century after 675 – and in Northumbria until 867, when Osbert was defeated by the Danes. Eventually a handsome penny of good-quality silver supplanted all other rivals in the kingdom of Kent in about 765 and was being extended all over England, except Northumbria, until the wholesale disruption caused by the Viking invasions and the settlements in the Danelaw interrupted the political and financial unification of England.

The most substantial issues of the first half of the seventh century have been – erroneously – known as 'sceat' or, in the plural, 'sceattas'. The term originally meant 'treasure', similar to the present German 'Schatz' and the even more similar Danish 'Skat'. Although it is, strictly speaking, an error to use a word which was purely a unit of account to refer to a specific coin, the habit has become so ingrained in modern scholarship that it would be rather too pedantic not to conform to the custom. For this reason the term 'penny' is not generally applied to the sceat currency but reserved for later issues of a distinctly different type of coinage. Compared both with the previous thinnish gold coins and the later pennies, the sceat was typically dumpy, thick and small in diameter rather like the modern short-lived decimalized halfpenny but twice as thick and of course very much cruder. As with the gold currency, sceats were issued not only by royal but also by a number of ecclesiastical mints, especially York and Canterbury.

The sceattas varied greatly in type and purity. As with the previous gold coinage, relatively few of the sceattas originally carried the name or head of the king. The designs became more thoroughly and confidently indigenous, and less like mere copies of Roman or

Merovingian coins. A most popular series were the 'porcupines' while others carried imaginary designs such as that known by numismatists as the 'fantastic animal'. Other common types of design consisted of 'whorls', 'wolves' and 'serpents'. The lettering of some of the early Anglo-Saxon coins was made in the Runic alphabet; some show mixed Roman and Runic writing while some later types copy Arabic designs, including at least one series with the script written backwards. The names of bishops rather than kings occur occasionally, while the importance of the officially appointed 'moneyer' is prominently displayed in name, abbreviation or other mark. The degree of debasement varied not only in time but geographically, with the northern half of the country generally having a higher proportion of debased silver and crude bronze or copper coins, although the London mint also produced heavily debased issues. The smallest of these debased sceattas, issued for a century or more in Northumbria, were termed 'stycas'. While the numismatists might possibly – and the collector certainly – decry the degree of debasement that produced these stycas, the economist welcomes them as evidence of the degree of penetration of coinage among the population and as clear proof of the increase of the coinage habit.

It was during this period, from the sixth to the ninth centuries, that the traditional seven kingdoms of England, the so-called heptarchy, of Kent, East Anglia, Essex, Sussex, Suffolk, Mercia and Northumbria, became forcibly merged under the overlordship of the kings of Mercia in the south and Northumbria in the north, the latter being itself the product of a previous merger between Deira and Bernicia. This process was inevitably accompanied by a much more uniform monetary system and a more obvious assumption of regal authority for coinage, with the suppression of the right of subsidiary authorities, whether regal or ecclesiastical, to coin money. The head and name of the king therefore began regularly to replace the previous anonymous and ecclesiastical issues, while the prominence given to the names of the moneyers and their mints was reduced, but, luckily for the numismatists, not eradicated.

The true silver penny, then, is quite distinct from its precursor, the sceat. In fact, to produce these fine new, broader, thinner coins capable of registering finer details, without damage, something that had not previously been possible in Anglo-Saxon coinage, required much more highly skilled minting techniques. This most significant change in Anglo-Saxon coinage took place during the reign of Offa (757–96), although the first of the pennies that he was to make famous, was not in fact produced by him. Offa, having secured his western flank by constructing the impressive Dyke along the Welsh border, enlarged his native kingdom of Mercia so that he eventually became overlord of much of western, central, southern and south-eastern England, including Kent. Just like many of the previous monetary innovations, the penny was based directly on the new 'denier' produced in Paris by Pepin the Short from 775 onwards, and adopted by his famous son, Charlemagne. The quality of the English product, however, soon became markedly superior to its continental counterparts. Once again, the first to imitate the new French coin were the still independent kings of Kent; first Heaberth in 765, followed by Ecgbert in 780. The first true English penny, though initially produced only in Kent, almost certainly at the Canterbury mint, thus dates from 765. However, it was Offa's conquest of Kent and his canny take-over of the three Kentish moneyers Eoba, Babba and Udd, whose skills had produced the first pennies, that enabled Offa so to increase the production of these magnificent coins that their fame soon spread all over northern Europe – even if Northumbria still stuck stubbornly to its sturdy sceattas and cheap stycas. Sir John Craig gives some telling examples of the popularity of Offa's penny:

> When Boguslav the Mighty founded the coinage of Poland, he copied English designs so literally that coins for the steppes of Volga and Don bore the names of Aethelred I, then king of England, and of a London minter. English pence were the first models of Denmark, Sweden and Norway; they were reproduced in the evanescent coinage of Dark-Age Ireland, and their imitation in the Low Countries and Lower Germany became a nuisance to England in more sophisticated times. (1953, 7)

From being merely the clumsy pupils, England's moneyers had now risen in prestige to become unconsciously but in effect the masters of minting in northern Europe. The penny came in with a bang. Consequently it seems much more appropriate to associate the true birth of the 'penny' with the precision and prestige of these new coins rather than to ascribe the term vaguely to an indefinite number of relatively unknown issues of 'sceats' produced a hundred or so years earlier by Penda, Ine and other relatively unimportant rulers. The term 'penny' had of course been used for a century before Offa. One of the earliest references occurs in the laws of Ine, king of the West Saxons from 688 until 726, when he resigned the cares of kingship to retire to Rome, rather as certain present-day rulers of less developed countries occasionally retire, whether voluntarily or not, to Bath, London or Paris. Penda, king of West Mercia (632–54), appointed his son Peada as prince of part of his realm. Pada, a Kentish moneyer, whose name is prominently impressed in Anglo-Saxon and in Runic characters on his coinage, may also have added to the folklore which attributes the term 'penny' to a particular person. Indeed it has been customary for a number of contemporary authorities to repeat the claim that the very word 'penny' is derived from Penda, just as the early Irish pennies were called 'Oiffings' after Offa. But the power and prestige of Offa and his coins were far greater than that of Penda. One may doubt whether Penda's influence could in reality account for the fact that variants of the term penny occur during this period in the languages spoken across almost all of north-western Europe, including Germany and Scandinavia. The widespread use of the term seems more likely to have come from a common element in producing all the numerous crude coinages emerging across northern Europe in the Dark Ages, namely the 'panning' of coins, when pouring the molten metal from crucibles into the 'pans' required either for casting or for the blanks of hammered coins.

The very wide linguistic use of the 'penny' thus probably corresponded more readily with its method of production than with the obscure personality of a West Mercian ruler. 'Penig', the old English word for penny, compares almost exactly with the Friesian and Dutch equivalents, and with the Danish word for money in general, which is still 'Penge'. This, like the German 'Pfanne', from which Pfennig is believed to stem, refers to the pans which were then essential for coining money ('Penge, from Old Danish "penninge", diminutive of "Pande" = a pan'). Whether the Penda or the panning theory is really the true linguistic origin is unlikely to be resolved to the complete satisfaction of the protagonists. It may well be that the two elements reinforced each other. In any case the progress of Anglo-Saxon coinage from the crudity of Penda's sceattas to the relative splendour of Offa's penny marked a revolution in our monetary history and established the penny as the only English coin (with relatively rare and unimportant exceptions) for 500 years subsequently. Money and penny thus became practically synonymous throughout most of the Middle Ages.

Offa greatly enlarged the quantity of money produced in his domains, and for this purpose increased the number of his moneyers from three to twenty-one. There were also another nine moneyers known to be producing coins elsewhere in England. Estimates of the total resulting 'money supply' vary considerably, even though, unlike today, all the experts agree on what should be included in the total figure. Before briefly examining the apparently eternally controversial question of the money supply we may pay tribute to the extraordinary vitality of Offa's experimentation and designs. He is the only English king to have issued a coin bearing the name and bust of his consort, Queen Cynethryth (a custom of some Roman emperors), and it was Offa who made the upside-down Arabic inscription on his golden 'dinar'. In the end, however, as we have seen, it was his own indigenous designs for his silver penny that became the model for others to copy (Blunt 1961). According to estimates by Dr D. M. Metcalf, the thirty moneyers at work in England in Offa's day used some 3,000 dies on some '30 tons' of silver to produce between '30 and 40 million' coins (Metcalf 1980). These probably excessive preliminary estimates were later reduced to allow for considerable recoining and for the heavier weight of the new pennies, which would reduce the required total of precious metal proportionately below 30 tons to perhaps 6 tons net, and also reduce the number of coins in question. A very much lower estimate, frankly admitted by Dr Grierson as simply the intelligent guesswork which even the best of such figures is bound to be, put the total of Offa's output as probably not exceeding a million, or at the utmost, two million, arguing that what really controlled the supply of money was the actual demand for it. Dr Grierson also expressed some doubt as to whether, outside Kent, London, East Anglia and southern England, the use of coinage was as yet very extensive (1979 chapters 15 and 16).

While there might thus be considerable room for argument as to the quantity, there could be none regarding the quality of Offa's coinage – and even with regard to the quantity there can at least be no gainsaying that it had shown a very considerable growth. Indeed, the essential point to grasp in this early contest in trying to quantify the supply of money, is not the differences between the estimates, but rather that, for the first time in Anglo-Saxon history, the quantities involved *millions* of new silver pennies rather than merely thousands or tens of thousands of 'sceats'. Each of these new pennies would command values much higher than we might at first assume. Offa was undoubtedly supplying the necessary currency on a most substantial scale, and thus laying the foundations of a money economy. Furthermore, unlike so many previous occasions, the substantial growth of the new currency was not at the expense of the quality of the coinage. In short, Offa's place in the development of our monetary economy has been aptly summarized by Sir Albert Feavearyear thus: 'The continuous history of the penny begins with the coins struck by Offa (and) the history of the English pound begins with the history of the English penny' (1963, 7). The ability that Offa had demonstrated, of rapidly increasing the quantity of coins of a superior standard, was soon to be repeated by later monarchs in minting the still larger quantities of money needed to arm themselves against the Vikings and in their vastly expensive attempts to buy them off.

The Vikings and Anglo-Saxon recoinage cycles, 789–978

Perhaps the most telling way to summarize the enormous impact of the Vikings on English monetary development is to state the simple fact that far more English coins have been found in Scandinavia than in England relating to the most active period of Viking raids. The first of these raids took place in 789, shortly before the death of Offa in the next year. The first raids, such as those on Portland in 789 and on Lindisfarne in 793, were small, isolated and sporadic affairs but thereafter they grew gradually in intensity and, beginning with the arrival of the 'Great Host' in East Anglia in 865, changed their nature to permanent invasion, immigration and settlement. As a result of this process of settlement the newly coalescing national state of England again became divided, into a roughly northern and north-eastern 'Danelaw', and a more or less independent kingdom of central, southern and south-western England. The two kingdoms lived in uneasy rivalry with each other until, after a new series of more vicious raids, a stronger national unity was achieved incorporating the whole of England, and for a short time much of Scandinavia, in the generation before the Norman Conquest. The reunification of England prior to its conquest by Gallicized 'Northmen' from the south, is inseparably connected with the story of its coinage, developments in the latter shedding considerable light on the course of the more or less continual armed conflict, or costly preparations for engaging in or avoiding such conflict, in the period between 789 and 1066.

Although no part of Britain remained immune from Viking invasions, whether directly from Scandinavia or indirectly from Ireland, Scotland or France, it was the kingdom of Wessex which first saved itself and then acted as the example to inspire a more widespread resistance without which all England would have been submerged by the Danish settlers. It is for this reason that Alfred is usually considered as one of the greatest of the long line of English monarchs. Effective defence was – and always seems to be – a most costly business, necessarily involving much increased minting of money. Given the mobility of the Danes on land as well as at sea, Alfred was faced with an immense problem. He first reorganized the system of occasional levies in order to keep an army reserve constantly in the field. The unfortified or poorly fortified townships which had previously provided the Danes with easy pickings were repaired or fortified for the first time so that outside the Danelaw there was built a ring of well-defended burghs which were regularly maintained and garrisoned. Alfred's donations to the Church, his generous sponsorship of artists and writers and his constant endeavours to improve educational standards, added to the greatness of his achievements – and to some extent to the demands for finance. There is good reason to believe, says Stenton, 'that the origin of the *burh* as a permanent feature of a national scheme of defence belongs to the reign of King Alfred' (1946, 289). In addition Alfred earned his title as 'father of the English fleet' by building a number of large ships to try to deny to the Danes their previous maritime supremacy.

The heavy financial burdens required to support his improved system of national defence on top of his other expenditures were very largely met by payments in kind. These were based on customary assessments of the ability of the locality to pay, according to the size and wealth of the community, based on land units, the smallest for such tax purposes being the 'hide'. In course of time the hides became consolidated into 'half-hundreds' and 'hundreds'. The exigencies of war could not be met by simply living off the land, but in addition put a premium on liquidity, so that as the conflicts with the Danes increased in intensity, so did the number and output of the mints. The same pressures led to increased coinages within the Danelaw also, with the London mint, for instance, alternatively active under both Saxon and Dane. The fact that the Danelaw generally adopted the penny as their unit of account and means of payment and very largely used the same mints that had previously produced the coins required in northern England made possible much commercial exchange in the peaceful intervals between armed conflict. However, as Professor Loyn has shown, the antiquated 'thrysmas' in Northumbria and the Scandinavian 'oras' in much of the Danelaw initially created 'some difficulty in achieving a satisfactory monetary standard in the new Anglo-Scandinavian world' (1977, 128). However, such difficulties were relatively short-lived as the English pennies issued to pay increasing tributes of Danegeld flooded the Danelaw.

Alfred began the process of increasing the number of mints to at least eight, most of these being within the protection of his newly fortified burghs, such as Exeter and Gloucester. In addition, the older mints at Winchester, Canterbury and London were pressed into more active service, producing, as well as the standard penny, for the first time in English history, the minting of a halfpenny. The latter custom died out after Edgar's reign despite the fact that there appeared to be an appreciable demand for halfpennies as being more convenient than the common practice of having to cut pennies in half. That such a demand existed would appear to have been proved by the many imitations of Alfred's halfpence produced primarily in the Danelaw where their unofficial minters would more easily escape punishment. Alfred also minted a number of heavy silver coins which, according to Dolley and Blunt, are 'without parallel in the coinage of Western Europe' (Dolley 1961, 77). These may have been intended as 'sixpences' or, possibly as papal payments; hence their having been dubbed 'offering pieces' by the numismatists.

Alfred's successors, including especially Athelstan and Edgar, found it necessary to increase the number of mints still further in order to supply the increasing demands for coinage for purposes of war, tribute and trade. Both Athelstan and Edgar made significant contributions to the development of English currency. By means, partly of conquest and partly of alliances, Athelstan (925–40) managed to make himself effective overlord of all England and of the greater part of Scotland. His achievements in this direction were rather overambitiously celebrated in a coin claiming himself as 'King of all Britain'. He increased the number of mints to thirty and continued the practice, which had now become more of a necessity than a convenience, of indicating the name of the mint as well as that of the moneyer. Obviously the increase in the number of mints carried with it a danger of loss of royal control unless this was expressly guarded against.

It was in order to make such control clear and explicit that Athelstan enacted the Statute of Greatley in 928 specifying a single national currency. Such a national currency had been approached from the days of Offa. Athelstan's conquests and his vision combined to enshrine the concept in law and to confirm the importance of coinage in the national system of taxes, trade and tribute. Thus England became the first of the major countries of Europe to attain a single national currency in post-Roman times. However the renewed incursions of the Danes postponed the uninterrupted establishment of this principle until 1066. Even so the achievement of a uniform national currency in England preceded that of France by more than 600 years, and of Germany and Italy by nearly 900 years: a factor perhaps in Britain's instinctive reluctance to embrace a single European currency today.

The uniformity declared as a policy objective by Athelstan was brought still nearer to reality by Edgar's thoroughgoing reforms. Edgar, 959–75, is generally known as the Pacific since he managed to preserve the peace unbroken for sixteen years – no mean achievement in the circumstances. In financial history he is best known for two related features: firstly for his reform of the nation's coinage, and secondly for setting the precedent for a more or less regular cycle of recoinage, both aspects being taken up more thoroughly by later rulers. The years of unaccustomed peace appeared to be highly convenient for making sure that the variety of silver pennies in circulation of slightly differing weights and considerably differing designs, should all be recalled and a new uniform currency reissued. For this purpose Edgar increased the number of mints by the year 973 to forty and, by carefully controlling the issue of dies and strictly regulating moneyers, assured a coinage of uniform type and standard. Having once achieved uniformity, he soon saw that it would be necessary to repeat the operation from time to time, and this for four main purposes: first to ensure that the quality of the coinage was maintained; secondly to enforce his express 'legal tender' order that 'no one was to refuse acceptance'; thirdly to benefit from the profits associated with reminting; and fourthly to assert the royal prerogative over minting and prevent unauthorized competition. It may well not have been Edgar's original intention in 973 to institute a regular six-year cycle of recoinage but in fact such a cycle ensued, becoming shortened to three years or less by a number of subsequent monarchs, who greedily milked its fiscal benefits to the utmost.

Danegeld and heregeld, 978–1066

Aethelred II's long and unhappy reign (978–1016) began inauspiciously with the murder of his half-brother Edward and the renewal of Danish invasions on a gradually increasing scale. His name, literally 'noble advice', went so ill with his character that he became known, with sick humour, as the Unready, from his stubborn refusal to take good counsel. He was not of course the first to attempt to buy off the Danes, but his reign marks the climax of this self-defeating policy. He already possessed an administrative and financial machine able to deliver promptly the vastly increasing tributes demanded. An instance of this took place in 991 when he paid over to the leader of the Danish invaders some 22,000 pounds of gold and silver, in addition to payments already made by local rulers. When it seemed as if peace might at last be possible, he ordered the massacre of all Danish men in England on St Brice's Day, 13 November 1002. Although his orders were only partially obeyed, their obvious effect was to strengthen Scandinavian determination to conquer all England.

To meet this threat Aethelred relied rather more on the power of his seventy-five mints than on his army or navy. Edgar's 'invention' of regular recoinages was now put into full effect by Aethelred who introduced seven changes of coinage type in his 38-year reign. When coupled with a not-too-obvious reduction in the weight of the penny this policy enabled the number of coins in circulation to be increased and yet be accepted internally at face value. At the same time 'by devaluing the penny in relation to its continental (bullion) rate, the government was able to discourage imports, encourage exports, improve the balance of trade and cause silver to flow into the country' (Dolley 1961, 154). With so many mints operating throughout the country no man outside the Danelaw had to travel more than about fifteen to twenty miles to find a mint to change his old for new coins. Simply to pay the Danegeld Aethelred had to coin nearly forty million pennies. Of some ninety known mints, as many as seventy-five were in use at the same time.

Since a considerable proportion of these coins naturally found their way to Denmark, Norway and Sweden, it might at first appear that England itself would have become practically drained of coins – but for a number of good reasons this was not so. The speed with which Danegeld was paid certainly meant that a proportion of the payments was almost certainly passed straight on after being collected by taxes without any recoinage being involved. Yet the total quantity of money remaining in circulation in England appears to have been just as large at the end of the period of most rapid Danegeld payments between 980 and 1014 as in the beginning, although no doubt there were considerable, if temporary, regional imbalances of surpluses and deficits from time to time. However, recent authoritative research confirms that 'in the long run virtually all the silver that went out of England as Danegeld was matched by similar quantities that had come in from overseas' (Metcalf 1980, 21). Despite the repeated and intermittent wars, trade was substantial, steadily increasing and, for reasons already indicated, favourable to Britain, allowing a considerable influx of silver from the Continent. European silver was in any case becoming more plentiful since a large new silver mine was opened at Rammelsberg in Germany's Harz Mountains. Its output became diffused by trade and mercenary payments all over northern Europe. According to Professor Sawyer 'the location of the main English mints is consistent with the hypothesis that the main economic activity lay in the east and that the silver came from abroad' (1978, 233). A vast recycling operation was thus taking place in northern Europe during the last half of the tenth and first half of the eleventh century, with tribute being the major component in the first period but with trade becoming increasingly important in the second. In 1012 Aethelred raised additional taxes payable in coinage and specifically earmarked for paying mercenaries to man a new fleet of ships and a larger army, its military purposes being clearly indicated in its description, the 'heregeld', literally 'army-debt'. This nationwide tax, 'yielding perhaps £5000–£6000, was a powerful means of drawing cash out of every village' (Metcalf 1980, 23). However, Aethelred's reign was effectively drawing to a close, since in 1013 he was forced to seek refuge in Normandy, where after further ineffectual battles and intrigues, he died in 1016. The concept of the heregeld did not however die with him but was put to more effective use by his successor.

Cnut (1016–1035) first paid off his vast invasion army and fleet, but maintained a standing army in England while he expanded his Scandinavian empire, the handy and prolific heregeld being again used for this purpose. Since the disbanding of the invasion force alone cost some twenty million pence, the mints were almost as active from time to time under Cnut as they had been under Aethelred. The pressures on the mints from the necessity of producing the vast coinages associated with repeated Danegeld and heregeld payments led to successive reductions in the average weight of the penny, from a high weight of 27 grains at the beginning of the tenth century to 18 grains in the early eleventh century. After the heregeld was (temporarily) abolished in 1051 the penny regained a weight of 21 grains. It was obviously increasingly difficult to maintain the customary high standard of the English penny during the first half of the eleventh century.

On his accession Cnut's declared intention was to rule the reunited England according to its customary laws, and he used the efficient existing embryo English civil service for this purpose. Later, in a letter from Rome to his English subjects, he claimed, 'I have never spared, nor will I ever spare, myself or my labour in taking care of the needs of my people' – a promise that he carried out to an extent such as to justify his appellation, 'the Great'. His similarity to Alfred may be seen in his encouragement of education, his generous endowment of churches, his draining of the fens, and his building of bridges. Trade expanded considerably under his 'free-trade empire' which extended over most of Ireland, Scotland, England and Scandinavia, and accounted for a rising proportion of the still growing demand for coinage. The more settled, peaceful conditions of his reign allowed a greater concentration of mint output in the seaports bordering the North Sea, so that over 50 per cent of the total coinage produced in England was minted in London, York and Lincoln. Numismatic evidence for this period is derived mainly from Scandinavia rather than from Britain, with the mint marks enabling us to assess, approximately at least, the rate of activity of the various mints. The information given by these Scandinavian hoards is of a mixture of English coins of various types usually found together with coins from France, Germany and Scandinavia. If the English coins found in these hoards had been merely the result of the massive Danegelds they would most probably not have been so varied but would have consisted more of long runs of uniform issues. The actual degree of variation and admixture is held by most authorities to indicate trade, rather than plunder or tribute, as the usual source of such hoards, even if the original cause of issue may admittedly have been tribute or plunder. Modern numismatic researches would therefore appear to confirm the views of those earlier historians like Sir Charles Oman and of later authorities like Professor Sawyer that trade flourished whenever peaceful opportunities occurred. Thus according to Oman 'the immense quantities of Cnut's silver pennies that survive bear witness to active trade . . . there is every sign that by the time his reign ended the whole land was in a very flourishing and satisfactory condition' (1910, 601).

The death of Cnut in 1035 saw the break-up of his empire and a new period of political and financial confusion. The 24-year rule of Edward the Confessor (1042–66) failed to restore the stability enjoyed under Cnut. Edward appeared to have instigated, or at least allowed, a rare case of debasement in 1048 when the normally pure, if sometimes lightweight, silver penny contained an admixture of zinc and copper. The moneyers were kept almost as busy as ever with seventy mints active and ten separate coin-types issued during his reign, again confirming that the six-year cycle of Edgar had been reduced for fiscal reasons to somewhat less than three years. His efficient administrators saw that his life's ambition, to build a new church at Westminster, was completed just before his death. The same efficient civil service then became busy issuing the new dies for the new coins, designed for Harold II, which were being produced by forty-five mints as he marched around the country during his brief reign, from his victory at Stamford Bridge to his defeat at Hastings. 'Perhaps nothing shows more eloquently than this the degree of efficiency which the royal administration had by now attained in its central control of the wide net-work of English mints' (Sutherland 1973, 39). The contrast with England's coinless economy of the Dark Ages could hardly be more complete.

The Norman Conquest and the Domesday Survey, 1066–1087

Traditionally the Battle of Hastings has rightly been seen as one of the great turning points of British history, although long familiarity with this old-fashioned view has recently bred a degree of critical contempt.

To all intents and purposes the millennium of invasions which had disrupted Britain before the Norman Conquest was now ended and, with just a few relatively minor exceptions, Britain thereafter has remained free of foreign invasions. Peace within the country was, however, very much more difficult to achieve. Rebellions, baronial and civil wars, minor skirmishes of all sorts remained sufficiently widespread to engender recurrent feelings of insecurity among the people for some 500–600 years after 1066. A price had to be paid for freedom from the perilous insecurities of war, whether external or internal, this price being the restrictive formalization of the system of land ownership, work, tithes and taxes known as feudalism. Although the Norman Conquest resulted in a strengthening of an already nascent feudalism in England, it did not originate it, for a number of its most distinctive elements had already been developing in the century or so before 1066. The Conquest did usher in a far more complete, a far more standardized system of feudalism, especially in a legalistic, political and administrative sense, than had previously existed in England and it did so at a considerably faster pace than would probably have taken place had Harold, rather than William, been the victor on 14 October.

To William it seemed of vital importance to the legality of his claim (to be the rightful ruler of England) to date his accession as having taken place on Friday 13 October, the day *before* victory. This apparently trivial point indicated the thoroughness of the Norman approach to legal matters. The Conquest provided the opportunity, seen by William also as an absolute necessity, of reinforcing his legal authority by insisting that all his vassals should formally retake their oaths of allegiance in the course of which their rights, feus and duties were more clearly and explicitly defined. The legal and administrative forms of feudalism were more advanced in Normandy than in contemporary England, and it was therefore natural that the influx of Norman rulers would bring with them their more ingrained and more explicitly legalized new attitudes and habits. Furthermore, after the Conquest – and more especially after William's devastating harrowing of the North following a series of rebellions between 1069 and 1071 – there was no danger of any revival of the division of England into two nations, the Anglo-Saxon and the Danelaw. The Norman Conquest therefore meant that England never again became divided geographically but was united in a far more common form of administration than had previously been the case – although the Norman system was in fact modified in various ways by the survival of Anglo-Danish institutions. Nevertheless there is considerable truth in the view that the Normans transformed England from a vague and still somewhat divided feudal society into an administratively integrated feudal system.

Whereas military and political changes can take place suddenly, and while administrations can also on occasions be modified relatively quickly, changes in the economic life of a nation are generally impossible to achieve except by a process of relatively slow evolution, particularly when, as was the case throughout the Middle Ages, the great mass of the people worked on the land. For them the Conquest appeared at first to be almost irrelevant, and continuity, rather than change, best sums up their situation. However, given the greater formalization of land ownership and of feudal duties, and also given the diffusion of coin-using habits, the impact of the new Norman system of administration gradually affected life in the rural areas as well as in the towns. Since coinage was such a personal prerogative of royalty, William had the undoubted power of bringing about, had he so wished, the kind of drastic changes in England that he had already made in Normandy, where the profits derived from his debasement of the coinage had helped to finance the invasion of England. However William saw the wisdom of taking the advice offered to him by his feudal council that he should resist the temptation of debasing his English coinage, especially when the finance sacrificed thereby was more than made up by the imposition of a new tax, in the usual form of a land tax, promised expressly to avoid debasement. Subsequently, throughout the Middle Ages the English monarchy maintained the quality of its silver coins to a far higher degree than was the case with most continental coinages, though whether this was the unmixed blessing it is often assumed to be will be debated later.

We are of course enormously indebted to William I for the most complete record of national wealth and national income undertaken by any country in the Middle Ages – the 'Description of England'. This was ordered by William and his Great Council at Gloucester, Christmas 1085. The whole of the comprehensively detailed survey was carried out with such thoroughgoing vigour that it was completed by the end of 1086. The summaries of these incredibly detailed statistics were collected in a few volumes (two major volumes plus a few regional summaries, e.g. for Exeter, Cambridge and Ely), which soon came to be known as Domesday (or Doomsday) Book, so called because there could be no appeal against such an authoritative, meticulously detailed and publicly corroborated, quantitative and qualitative survey. 'As the ordered description of a national economy it is unique among the records of the medieval world' (Stenton 1946, 648). With two unfortunate and major exceptions, namely the four northern counties of Northumberland, Durham, Cumberland and Westmorland, much of which had been devastated by William himself and therefore had little to contribute to his coffers, and the towns of London and Winchester, the wealth of which may already have been well known, information was collected from every county, town, hundred and village.

The investigation was conducted by commissioners, assisted by the king's representative or 'reeve' in every shire – the sheriff – together with juries selected locally. The survey was thus a combination of a legal, demographic and most importantly financial, fiscal and economic investigation whereby the position and numbers of the more important persons were described, and the output and taxable capacity of the kingdom were evaluated. Altogether some 283,242 persons were mentioned in the survey, which would give an estimated total population of between about 1,375,000 as a minimum and about 1,500,000 as a maximum. It counted all farm livestock (such as cattle, sheep, pigs, etc.), the acreage, potential and actual yield of the arable lands, the number and ownership of plough-teams, other 'capital' equipment such as productive woodlands, fish ponds, beehives and so on. 'Not a single hide, not one virgate of land, not even one ox, nor one cow, nor one pig,' says the *Anglo-Saxon Chronicle*, 'escaped notice in this survey.' In towns, which were already of considerable importance in Norman times, the smithies, bakeries, breweries, markets, fords, mills and royal mints, were all meticulously recorded. The yield from tolls, taxes and fines of various kinds were all carefully aggregated.

No other European state at that time possessed such a sound basis for fiscal and financial assessment (what today we would call 'budgeting'), or for supplying the means for reasonably efficient and equitable decisions regarding taxation, coinage and farm management, which were then the main ingredients of monarchical economic policy. The king could now know with a degree of certainty whether he was pressing too hard on some localities, the taxable capacity of which had fallen, or too lightly on others, the taxable capacity of which had risen. There are numerous examples of such adjustments, no doubt rough and ready but nevertheless significant, having been made on the basis of the Domesday evidence. Here again the Normans created a national system of taxation on the foundations of the various regional systems which had been previously developed by the Anglo-Saxons and Danes so that, as in coinage, England was probably the first post-Roman state in western Europe to develop a uniform nationwide fiscal system.

The king's finances were derived mainly from five sources: first, directly from the proceeds of his own estates, the 'Crown lands'; secondly, from regular customary and therefore normally fixed payments made by the shires and boroughs; thirdly, from the fines and other fluctuating profits resulting from the maintenance of justice; fourthly, the mostly arbitrary profits from issuing the king's dies and minting the king's coins; and fifthly, in order to meet exceptional expenditures, a general tax on land, the 'geld', of which, as we have seen, the Danegeld and heregeld were the most famous examples. It follows that the greater the yield of the first four sources, the fewer and the less heavy would be the exceptional gelds. Despite his improved administration, William himself found it necessary to levy five gelds during his 21-year reign. Because the gelds were usually very heavy and were paid in cash, they had a close relationship with the demand for coinage. Furthermore it becomes clear that only an efficient tax-gathering system could guarantee that the quality of English coinage would be maintained – an early English example of how fiscal and monetary policies are necessarily interwoven.

Domesday Book gives a detailed picture of the basis on which the gelds were assessed. Although the details vary from region to region the most common basis for assessment was the 'hide'. Originally the hide comprised an amount of land which one team of eight oxen could manage to plough in a season, an amount which naturally varied as between hill and dale, light or heavy soils. Long before the Conquest the hide had become standardized at about 120 acres. One of the motives generally held to have given rise to the survey was to discover hidden 'hides' in order to give a clearer picture of taxable capacity and to reduce tax evasion. For tax farming purposes the hides in each 'hundred' were grouped into fives or tens, except that in the customary Danelaw regions the old 'wapentakes' were divided into districts, roughly comparable with the 'hundred', and further subdivided into blocks of a dozen or half-dozen hides. In fiscal affairs therefore the Domesday survey showed that the Normans continued to use the Anglo-Saxon and Danish customary dues and assessments and gradually modified them into a uniform national system. The output or yield of each locality investigated by the survey was given for the year of the Conquest and for the year of the survey, so that a picture of local growth or decline, and an aggregate, if vague, glimpse of what we might describe as 'national income growth' over a twenty-year period may be derived from the Domesday evidence. As well as those two base and reference dates, the income and output of a series of different intermediate dates, namely whenever the land concerned changed its feudal ownership, was also given. All in all, the actual and the potential revenue of the land available for the use of the king's government was, among a wealth of other details, provided for the first time in the history of Britain, a legacy available for use for two or three centuries by William's successors. Having thus standardized the fiscal system it was therefore all the more appropriate to standardize the monetary system also: a task easier said than done.

The pound sterling to 1272

So far as the penny, and therefore the pound also, were concerned the Norman Conquest spelt continuity rather than change, and stability rather than revolution. Apart from introducing a number of Norman moneyers, especially Otto the Goldsmith as chief moneyer and die master, no alterations of substance were made to English coinage during the reigns of the first two Williams (1066–1100), except that during the reign of William I the weights of the penny were if anything higher on average and less variable than were those issued in the generation before the Conquest. Some thirteen different coin types were issued, eight ascribed to William I and five to William II, thus indicating that the average pre-Conquest cycle of between two and three years between recoinages was being imitatively followed, a royal custom that, with some interruptions during the anarchy of Stephen and Matilda, was maintained until about a century after the Conquest, that is until the coinage reform and the ending of the regular series of short cycles brought about by Henry II in 1158. William I is known to have operated fifty-seven mints, details of over fifty of which are given in the Domesday survey. The survey shows how the privilege of minting was costly for the operators but lucrative for the king. As Sir John Craig shows, the average payment exacted by the king was £1 per annum for each moneyer, with an extra £1 payable every time the coin design was changed, that is, at least every three years (Craig 1953, 20). On average each mint town had three moneyers, but some had ten or more. William II similarly made use of fifty-eight mints, including a new mint at Totnes. In both reigns, given the average 31-month cycle, the mints were kept busy most of the time. It was obviously a lucrative business, dear to the heart of the monarch, and also to any counterfeiter.

The high quality established by William I and generally maintained by William II fell away drastically during the long reign of Henry I (1100–35), and even more so in the short 'reign', if it can be called that, of Stephen (1135–54). Henry I introduced fifteen new types in his 35-year reign, thereby reducing the coinage cycle from the previous level of thirty-one months to about twenty-eight. With the rare exception of one or two of these types they were of extremely poor quality and were therefore more easily clipped and copied. Most of Henry's coins were impure, light in weight and of execrable workmanship. Among the reasons given for this decline in quality are, first an influx of poor quality 'pennies' from the Continent which made it easier at first to accept lower-quality indigenous issues. Secondly, the death of Otto the Goldsmith removed from the scene the favourite, most strict and most widely travelled mint-master upon whom the first two Williams had relied in keeping not only the London but also the provincial mints up to scratch. Henry did, however, attempt two major reforms, though their beneficial results were short-lived. The first, in 1108, included plans for issuing halfpennies, but the inadequate cost allowance made to moneyers for producing two coins together equal in value to the age-old single penny coin inhibited their production. The issue flopped, and only one such coin appears extant in today's collections.

So impure was the current coin and so untrustworthy were the mints that it had become the widespread custom to cut a small snick into the coin in order to test whether it was genuine silver through and through or only silver-plated. This then led Henry to the ridiculous decision in 1112 to make an official snick extending to almost half the diameter of all his coins before they were issued, though this official idiocy was happily not carried into the subsequent revisions. By 1124 the quality of all the existing coins had again deteriorated so much that the *English Chronicle* tells of someone who managed to secure acceptance of only twelve of the nominal pound's worth of 240 coins that he took to market. Public confidence having been completely destroyed, the king looked for a public scapegoat. All the mint-masters in the kingdom, then numbering between 180 and 200, about the same number that operated in William the Conqueror's day, were summoned to the Assize of Winchester, on Christmas Day 1124, and a number of them – some accounts give a total, probably exaggerated, of ninety-four – were punished by having their right hands chopped off. (At least they were spared the stiffer penalties of being blinded or castrated or both, which were occasionally administered.) Even this drastic remedy produced only a temporary improvement, with the last three issues of Henry's reign being as bad as ever.

The bitter and destructive Civil War during 1138 to 1153 between the rival supporters of Stephen and Matilda made an already bad situation even worse. 'It was the only time in English history that the royal prerogative of coining money was set at nought by powerful barons' who issued their own currencies and so contributed to the downward slide in the general quality of the coinage (Thompson 1956, xxix). Whereas the blurred inscriptions of Henry's coinage had been the result of shoddy workmanship, in the case of a number of rival minters in the

Civil War the blurring was apparently intentional, to avoid identification and so escape punishment from the other side. Even some of
the better-quality coinage was deliberately and literally defaced when,
following a quarrel between Stephen and the pope, a number of mints
issued coins with two ugly, indented lines across Stephen's head. The
use of coins as propaganda in warfare was obviously not a lost art.

The breakdown in the usual channels of distribution of bullion to the
mints during the Civil War made local mints much more dependent on
local supplies and so stimulated production from the silver-lead mines
of the Mendips which supplied Bristol, Exeter, Gloucester and other
mints in the south-west. The Derby, Nottingham and Lincoln mints
were similarly supplied by the mines at Bakewell in the Peak District,
while silver and lead mines at Alston in Cumberland supplied the
Carlisle mint. The fact that speed of production during the wars was
more important than the degree of refinement of the ore played its part
in the drastic fall in the metallic purity of the coinage and in the poor
quality of the minting. The financial history of the first half of the
twelfth century exposed the myth of the superior administrative skills
of the Norman rulers and gave fresh and forceful evidence of the
insecurity of life in Anglo-Norman England and the dangerously
fissiparous proclivities of its barons. The efforts of the first two
Williams to unite the country and to maintain the quality of its coinage
seemed to have been all in vain. For the ordinary person in the many
regions of Britain afflicted by the 'harrowing of the North' and the
arbitrary terror of the barons during the Civil War the Norman
Conquest might have seemed more like a relapse into barbarism than a
step forward into a new, orderly, well-administered feudal system. Yet,
within a relatively few years, Henry II (1154–89) had restored the
prestige and unity of the kingdom, greatly strengthened its finances,
and raised the quality of its coinage in such a way as to render
unnecessary the costly revisionist cycles that had typified England's
financial history for over two centuries.

Henry's first task was to restore royal power by destroying the
unauthorized or 'adulterine' castles that had sprung up during the Civil
War, and similarly by closing down a number of the provincial mints
that had previously supported baronial independence. Because of his
quarrels with the Papacy, and especially with Thomas à Becket, a
number of ecclesiastical mints including those of Durham, Bury St
Edmunds and Canterbury ceased operating for a number of years. Each
time Henry closed down a provincial mint he strengthened the relative
and absolute importance of the London mint and hastened the process
of concentrating the bulk of money making within the Tower of

London. Furthermore by doing away with the triennial revision he had no need to reverse his policy of reducing the number of mints but could more easily manage to maintain a steadier output of coins from his smaller total number of mints, except on the two occasions when he carried out a general replacement of the whole currency, that is in 1158 and 1180, using some thirty and eleven mints respectively. Apart from those two occasions he usually managed with half a dozen mints, with London always being predominant. He further centralized his political and financial control of his English kingdom by reorganizing and strengthening the authority of his sheriffs in every county. His legal and financial reforms went hand in hand, assuring him of a more certain income, with fewer leakages than formerly, from the various fines, dues, customs, taxes and crown estate revenues, uninterrupted by civil strife. Little wonder that it was in this period that the first detailed description of the administration of the English Treasury, the *Dialogus de Scaccario*, and the first comprehensive treatise on English law, the *Tractacus de Legibus Regni Angliae*, were written.

As the first of the English branch of the Plantagenets, Henry's vast domains spread far beyond England, extending from the Pentland Firth in the north to the Pyrenees in the south. To safeguard his empire he needed an army available for continuous service. Rather than relying on the customary military services of forty days owed him annually by his tenants-in-chief with their retainers, he began insisting that these feudal services should be commuted into a cash payment or 'scutage' (from the Latin, 'scutum', a shield), a process as welcome to the barons as to Henry's finances. With the proceeds Henry was thus able to build up a more reliable and more mobile, permanent professional army of mercenaries, or 'soldiers' as they became known thereafter, from the 'solidus' or king's shilling that they earned.

Having restored order and set in train his political and legal reforms, Henry carried out a thorough reform of the coinage in 1158 to repair the damage done during the Civil War. This new coinage is known either as the 'cross and crosslets' from its design, or as the 'Tealby' issue from the hoard of nearly 6,000 such coins found at the Lincolnshire village of that name in 1807. (It is perhaps a commentary on official vandalism that over 5,000 coins from the Tealby find were melted down by the Royal Mint as scrap silver.) The name 'Henricus' remained unchanged on English coins for 121 years, that is until 1279, throughout the reigns not only of Henry II himself and Henry III but also those of John, Richard and the first seven years of Edward I: a classic case of what numismatists call 'immobilization'. In all that long period, there were only three distinctive changes of type: the 'Tealby', introduced as we have seen in 1158; the 'short cross' in 1180; and the 'long cross' in 1247. Apart from very minor details these issues would remain unchanged until the normal processes of wear and tear made a further general recall and reform necessary. This indicates how completely Henry II had broken with the old regular triennial revisionist tradition which was never reintroduced. Henry's fiscal reforms including the process of commutation of feudal dues, of which scutage was simply the most prominent example, made excessive reliance on seigniorage unnecessary. Henry's reform restored the prestige of English money, the quality of which was jealously safeguarded from any further major decline until the mid-sixteenth century. This was so unlike the situation on the Continent that the term 'the pound sterling' emerged into common usage with its well-known praiseworthy connotations.

The origin of the term 'the pound sterling' remained a puzzling and controversial matter to experts, at least until the authoritative and probably definitive treatment of the matter by Grierson in 1961 (see his 'Sterling' in Dolley 1961). He shows that although the earliest variant of the term goes back to 1078 in the form 'sterilensis', it was not until the thirteenth century that it appears as sterling, though 'starling' and 'easterling' also arise to confuse the issue. Both 'star' and 'starling' are plausibly suggested by those who see the origin arising from various designs of these found on early English coins. Less plausibly, some see the powerful 'Easterlings' (international merchants and money-changers) as parents of the term. It may be a misguided (but common) failing to seek a single explanation for matters concerned with money, which by its nature is inevitably among the most widely used of artefacts. Consequently the term 'sterling', like money itself, may in fact have a number of complementary origins. Grierson himself, despite the very powerful case he makes for his own interpretation, modestly admits room for doubt. Nevertheless he persuasively sees the origin in the strength and stability of sterling as given by the key Germanic root of 'ster', meaning 'strong' or 'stout', and the 'ling' as the corruption of a common monetary suffix. Hence 'sterling' would be the natural description for English money, which from the tenth century onward tended generally to be of higher quality than that of its continental neighbours, and therefore referred specifically to the penny coins weighing 22½ grains troy of silver at least pure to 925 parts in a thousand, 240 of which made the Tower pound weight or the pound sterling in value. It is also significant to note that the term 'pound sterling' was in common use throughout Europe in the Middle Ages, with all its connotations of solidity, stability and quality – long before the issue of a pound coin – when silver was almost the only metal used in British coinage and the penny was almost the only, and certainly the main, coin. Indeed, it is the minting of the gold sovereign by Henry VII which may be taken as a symbol of at least one of the many monetary developments which marked the end of the Middle Ages. So long as full-bodied gold and silver coins were issued in Britain, that is right up to the First World War, so long did the term 'the pound sterling' maintain its prestigious significance, that is for a period spanning well over 800 years, from 1078 to 1914.

Touchstones and trials of the Pyx

Edward I (1272–1307) kept to the 'Henricus' long-cross issues for the first seven years of his reign, by which time the state of the currency in general had deteriorated so much because of ordinary wear and tear that a general replacement was becoming overdue. Although the main purpose of extending the crosses on the long-cross type right to the perimeter of the coins had been in order to deter clipping, in this respect it had not been a great success. After 1275, when Edward forbade the Jews to exact usury, clipping increased and quality declined markedly. (The Jews were again blamed and suffered wholesale arrests in 1278 and expulsion in 1290.) Edward, however, did far more than simply issue a replacement coinage. He guaranteed for himself a place in the history of English money by the very thorough nature of his reforms of 1279 to 1281, particularly by introducing three new denominations: the halfpenny, the farthing, and the fourpenny-piece known as the 'groat' as well, of course, as the traditional penny. Instead of having to rely simply on a single denomination, there were henceforth four denominations bringing far greater flexibility and convenience to the monetary system. The increasing demand for low-denomination coinage – copiously confirmed by the persistence of the habit of cutting the penny in half or in quarters, at a time when a single penny was worth a full day's pay or would buy a sheep – had been resisted previously because, apart from the value of the metal, the cost of minting a farthing was practically the same as that for minting a penny. Edward overcame this difficulty partly by making over to the minters a greater allowance, in effect sharing his seigniorage, and partly by making the farthing slightly, but not noticeably, lighter in weight than strictly a quarter of the weight of the penny.

This was the first time the groat (from the French 'gros') had been issued in England and the first time 'Dei Gratia' appeared on English coinage, the larger size giving more room for such an inscription. Edward's reform marks the beginning of the regular and permanent

issues of the useful halfpenny and farthing, and although, as we have
seen, occasional issues of halfpennies had been made previously, these
all turned out to have been short-lived experiments. At the beginning of
the twelfth century King John (1199–1216) had produced a separate
design of pennies, halfpennies and farthings for Ireland, bearing his
own name, but these were not issued in England, where only the
Henricus short-cross type were issued. A similarly experimental but
abortive initial issue, this time of the first gold coins in medieval
Britain, appeared in 1257 when Henry III issued what he called a 'Gold
Penny'. This was part of a widespread new European fashion for gold
coins. Sicily and Italy, more closely under Byzantine and Arab influence,
started the fashion when gold coins were issued in Messina and Brindisi
in 1232; in Florence in 1252; and in Genoa in 1253. Of the three Italian
gold coins it was the Florentine variety, impressed with the town's floral
emblem, that coined a new name – the 'florin' – which became widely
imitated in Europe, significantly increasing the aggregate supply of
money.

Henry III's 'gold penny' was based on a simple 10:1 ratio of gold to
silver and, being twice the weight of the silver penny, therefore carried
an official value of twenty pence. However the issue failed, partly
because it was in fact undervalued but mainly because it was not
popular. There was insufficient demand to guarantee the widespread
acceptance of such a high-value coin in England. Not until almost a
century later was there a reissue of gold, this time by Edward III in
1343, and now called a gold 'florin'. This, at six shillings, turned out to
be overvalued, and was therefore replaced in 1346 by the gold 'Noble'
worth eighty pence, one-third of a pound or 6s. 8d. Considering the
contemporary victory of the English at Crécy, it was aptly named and
designed, with its large ship on the obverse being a tribute to English
sea power in general and the contemporary Battle of Sluys in particular.
This time the ratio of gold to silver was just about right – but the
stability of this ratio lasted only for a decade or so. These early
difficulties associated with the introduction of bimetallism into Britain
were to recur at irregular intervals throughout the succeeding centuries.

Gold coinage in the Middle Ages was, because of its high value, of
concern mainly to merchants, especially those engaged in foreign trade.
Yet anyone who had occasion to handle coins of silver or of gold in any
volume, whether merchants, traders, tax collectors, the king himself,
the royal treasury, or the sheriffs, required reliable devices for testing the
purity of what passed for currency. The people in general benefited
indirectly from this deep concern by merchants and administrators,
which acted to bring about periodic reforms of the currency back to the

official, legal standards. The two main methods used for testing purity were as follows: one rather rough and ready device for judging coins already in currency was the 'touchstone'; the other, as formal and meticulous as was technically possible in those times, was used for testing freshly minted coins, and became known as the Trial of the Pyx.

Touchstones were handy-sized pieces of fine-grained schist or opaque quartz, commonly red, yellow or brown, which had from antiquity been used for testing precious metals by drawing the metal object across the stone and examining the colour-trace left by the metal on the stone's smooth surface. Variations in colour corresponded with variations in the purity of the metal or its alloy. The resulting colour of any tested coin could be compared with that made by standard metals kept specially for test purposes. Although touchstones therefore enabled judgements to be made only subjectively and comparatively, nevertheless for most ordinary circumstances they served their purpose well. Certainly they readily exposed at least the grosser debasements which might otherwise easily pass the normal scrutiny of the market-place. As increasing use of gold coins became fashionable the need for touchstones grew considerably since the profits from debasement or adulteration, whether official or unofficial, were all the greater. In any cases of dispute it was natural for the contestants to turn to the experts – the goldsmiths – to decide the matter. In this way the Goldsmiths' Company of the City of London became, as early as 1248, and remains to this day, the official arbiter of the purity of British coinage. Before better techniques were introduced the London Goldsmiths regularly kept and issued twenty-four test gold pieces or 'touch-needles' for use in conjunction with touchstones, one for every twenty-four of the traditional gold carats, with similar test pieces for silver. They also were responsible for issuing test-plates of gold and silver to the nine regional hallmarking centres such as Birmingham, Edinburgh, Chester and Exeter. A number of public trials based on such test pieces grew up around all the regional mints; but the most formal, meticulous and strictest of all the monetary tests were those of the London mint – which by then had become by far the most important – known as the 'Trial of the Pyx'.

In this way a public jury of 'twelve discreet and lawful citizens of London with twelve skilful Goldsmiths' were, from the mid-thirteenth century onward, empowered to make a public testing of a sample of coins freshly issued or issued within a previously agreed time limit, by the Royal Mint. The earliest extant writ ordering such a public trial is that by Edward I, in 1282, another indication of his determination to maintain the quality of the currency. In 1982, to mark the 700th anniversary of the writ of Edward I, the Trial of the Pyx was attended by Queen Elizabeth II and the Chancellor of the Exchequer, Sir Geoffrey Howe. The 'pyx' derives its name from the box within which the coins were locked and so kept safe from being used or being tampered with until the day of their public trial. Whereas the simple touchstone method hardly damaged or marked the coin and was just concerned with a general indication of the composition of the metal, the trial by pyx was always far more thorough, investigating all aspects of the coinage, using the most up-to-date techniques available for testing the weight, design, diameter and purity of the coins, with a sufficient sample usually being melted down, to see that they complied with the strictest letter of the law. The pyx also indirectly encouraged the use of the most economical and least wasteful methods of turning precious metals into coinage, the allowable tolerances being continuously improved through time. The pyx thus helped the merchants to get the coins of the standards they liked, and the king to get full value in coins in return for the precious metals sent to the mint. The London Goldsmiths' Company and their jurymen were known to take their duties very seriously and so were a powerful factor in reinforcing the determination of most of the English kings during the Middle Ages to resist the general European slide towards debasement. Sound money was sound sense: that was the axiomatic and unquestioned assumption.

The Treasury and the tally

Any change in the quality of the currency was literally brought home to the royal treasury whenever taxes were collected, especially during the normal regular twice-a-year collections brought by the sheriffs to London. Because of this the sheriffs would have carried out their own preliminary selections throughout the previous six months, weeding out the more obviously inferior coins, fully conscious that a stricter scrutiny would face them at the court of the Exchequer. There was therefore a necessarily close connection between the minting of money and collecting it back in taxes. Minting and taxing were two sides of the same coin of royal prerogative, or, we would say, monetary and fiscal policies were inextricably interconnected. Such relationships in the Middle Ages were of course far more direct and therefore far more obvious than is the case today. In the period up to 1300 the royal treasury and the Royal Mint were literally together as part of the king's household. When the mint was moved to the Tower in 1300 it was because it needed larger premises and in any case it was still very close to the royal administrative centre. Our knowledge of these interconnections between the receipt and expenditure of royal moneys is known to us not only from the *Dialogus* which was written about 1176–9 to which reference has already been made, but also to the official collection of fiscal records known as the *Red and Black Books of the Exchequer*, compiled from the thirteenth century onward, and the Pipe Rolls of the Exchequer which extend from 1155 to 1833. The importance of this rich historical quarry is thus fairly summarized by Professor Elton: 'The history of the people of England, high and low though more the relatively high, is deposited in the materials arising from the efforts of her kings to finance their governments' (Elton 1969, 53).

The Treasury, or Exchequer, as it was more commonly called, was the first section of the royal household to be organized as a separate department of state clearly distinguishable from, though inevitably still very closely associated with, the management of the royal household. As early as the middle of the twelfth century its increasing workload caused it to become divided into two sections, one specializing in the receipt, storage and expenditure of cash and other payments, and the other into recording, registering and auditing the accounts. The first section, the Exchequer of Receipt, was also known as the Lower Exchequer, while the second section, the Exchequer of Account, was called the Upper Exchequer. For ease in reckoning and 'checking' the cash payments, the Exchequer tables, ten feet by five, were covered with a chequered cloth, either black lined with white, or green with red-lined squares, which custom gave its name not only to the institution but also subsequently to the 'cheque' or, as still in America, the 'check'. The Exchequer of Receipt made increasing use of an ancient form of providing evidence of payment by issuing 'tallies', and developed this system so much that the history of the Treasury is inseparately connected with that of the tally. Anthony Steel did not exaggerate in giving his expert opinion that 'English medieval finance was built upon the tally' (Steel, 1954, xxix).

From time immemorial, scored or notched wooden sticks have been used in many parts of the world for recording messages of various kinds, particularly payments. Wood was normally very readily available and therefore very cheap. Although easy to mark with the desired message or numbers, it was durable, and with reasonable care it was not easily damaged. Thus just as our word 'book' is probably derived from the 'beech' tree, so the piece of wood customarily used as a receipt was called a 'tally', from the Latin 'talea', meaning a stick or a slip of wood, and still retaining its monetary significance in the Welsh 'talu', meaning 'to pay'. This derivation seems more probable than the alternatively suggested derivation from the French 'tailler', to cut, which supposed the method of scoring to explain its origin – though here again this usage may have reinforced the acceptance of the term. In days before paper became cheap enough for everyday use, when literacy was low and numeracy limited, the use of special, simplified forms of wooden records was universally popular. Consequently it was perfectly natural for the Exchequer to adopt and adapt this well-known practice. Nowhere in the world, however, did the use of the notched stick or 'tally' develop to such an extent, or persist in official circles so long, as in Britain, even after the arrival of modern banking methods and cheap paper had long rendered them redundant (see Robert 1952 and below, p. 663).

At first the tally was used by the Exchequer in just the same way as in private business affairs, that is simply as a receipt. Our detailed knowledge of the ways in which the tallies were used again comes mainly from the *Dialogus de Scaccario*, written by Richard Fitznigel, whose family exercised a powerful influence over the king's business throughout the twelfth century, beginning with Roger of Caen, who was made bishop of Salisbury by Henry I in 1102, and became known as 'the principal architect of Anglo-Norman administration' – praise of the highest order. His nephew Nigel became bishop of Ely in 1133, and it was his son, Richard, who wrote the *Dialogus*, the first treatise on any government department in England, based on some forty years' experience as Treasurer of the Exchequer, from about 1156 or 1160 to 1198. For this long, effective and faithful service he was made bishop of London in 1189, an office which he held concurrently with that of Treasurer (Chrimes 1966, 50–65). From the example of this single family, entrenched in the new civil service, we can see how Church, state and finance were almost inseparably interconnected, a fact that also helps to explain how the kings' business was usually carried through with zeal and efficiency even during the sovereigns' considerable periods of absence on crusades or other wars abroad.

From Fitznigel's detailed account we know that the tally was commonly of hazel, about 8 or 9 in. long, although those representing very large amounts of money would need to be correspondingly larger, for the larger the sum, the larger the amount of wood removed in the cutting process. According to the *Dialogus*, £1,000 (a very substantial but not quite a rare amount) was represented by cutting a straight indented notch the width of a man's hand (i.e. 4 in.) at the far end of the tally; £100 was a curved notch as wide as a man's thumb (i.e. 1 in.). An amount very commonly represented was the score or £20, which was made by cutting a V-shape, the mouth of which would just take the little finger. The groove for £1 would just take a ripe barley-corn; that for one shilling was just recognizably a narrow groove; a penny was simply a straight saw-cut, a halfpenny merely a punched hole. Everybody, whether or not he could read or write was aware of the standard values. When the tax or other cash payment had been agreed the resulting tally was carefully cut long-ways into two so that the two parts would match or 'tally'. The larger part, retaining the uncut handle or 'stock' was kept by the creditor, while the smaller part, the 'foil' was kept by the debtor. From this practice most probably came our description for government or corporate 'stock' and for the 'counterfoil'.

The tendency throughout the Middle Ages towards commuting payments in kind to cash payments had the unfortunate result – for the Crown – of fixing such returns at the levels determined at the beginning of that period. Consequently, even in normal peacetime periods, the customary royal revenues were insufficient. Additional taxes, such as 'aids' and 'subsidies', grew from being special levies for helping to pay for wars, ransoms and so on, to become part and parcel of the annual fiscal requirements. By the middle of the thirteenth century the usual tax-gathering system, according to Fitznigel, took the following fashion. Half the taxes assessed for each region for the previous year were collected during the first quarter by the sheriff, who carried the proceeds to be paid in to the Exchequer of Receipt at Westminster at Eastertime. There the careful counting, checking and tallying processes were then completed and the audited results recorded in the Upper Exchequer. During the next six months the rest of the taxes would be collected and, if necessary, new assessments made. This adjusted half would then again be taken to Westminster, the final proceedings being completed in the Upper Exchequer, and the final tallies registered, at or around Michaelmas.

The true economic significance of the Exchequer tally soon grew to be far more important, however, than being simply a straightforward record of tax-collecting and receipt-giving. At a time when usury was strictly forbidden and subject to the direst penalties the tally became not only one of the main vehicles for circumventing such prohibition, but a method of raising loans and extending credit, of acting as a wooden bill of exchange, and a sort of dividend coupon for royal debt. It helped to develop an embryo money market in London involving the discounting of tallies, the negotiability of which led to an enlarged total of credit based upon a growing foundation of Exchequer debt. In the last century or so of the Middle Ages, when the demand for money was rapidly outgrowing the European supply of silver and gold, the tally became used in ways which effectively increased the money supply beyond the limits of minting.

The first stage in this process was the 'assignment', by which a debt owed to the king, shown physically by the tally stock held in the Exchequer, could be used by the king to pay someone else, by transferring to this third person the tally stock. Thus the king's creditor could then collect payment from the king's original debtor. Alternatively this new creditor might decide to hold the tally to pay his share of taxes required in a subsequent tax season. His decision of which alternative to choose (or any similar variant) would depend on the relative convenience and costs of the proceedings. What soon became clear from as early as the twelfth century onward, was that 'the exchequer of receipt was tending to become more and more of a clearing-house for writs and tallies of assignment and less and less the scene of cash transactions' (Steel 1954, xxx). The resulting economy in the use of coinage and the relief of pressures on minting were again of obvious importance.

A similar economy in the use of cash was made in the development of the 'tallia dividenda' or, more simply, 'dividenda', which were initially given to tradesmen who supplied goods to the royal court, the 'dividenda' being redeemable at the Exchequer, just as in the later, more open system of dividend payments on government stock or bonds. Similar net collections and net distributions of tallies were made by sheriffs in aggregating the shire payments into larger amounts, often with physically larger tallies, which again cut down on the amount of purely cash transactions. A considerable increase in the flow of tallies, and therefore a corresponding increase in credit, occurred when royalty began habitually to issue tallies in anticipation of tax receipts, a system commonly engrafted on to that of tallies of assignment. Owners of exchequer tallies in, say, Bristol might have to travel to York or further to collect their due payment – unless, that is, they could find someone who, for a suitable discount on its nominal value, would purchase the tally-stock from the holder. A similar process would result in order to avoid having to wait until the Exchequer received its anticipated taxes. In this way, by arbitrating between varying spatial and time preferences, a system of discounting tallies arose, especially in London, operated in a number of recorded instances by officials working in the Exchequer, who knew the best way to work the system, and who could give the best guarantees at the most reasonable discounts relative to the risks involved. In this way too the sin of usury could safely be avoided.

There were other ways around usury by means of the tally. One such method, particularly associated with cash payments into the Exchequer in anticipation of taxes, was to record in the rolls and to issue as a tally an amount greater, commonly by some 25 per cent, than the cash actually paid in. Although by the very nature of this procedure there could be no written or other very obvious method to incriminate its users, a number of expert historians have uncovered sufficient clues to suggest that such practices were not uncommon. Since the originally agreed date of redemption of such tallies was often delayed and sometimes uncertain, another avenue opened up for the discounter of these wooden bills of exchange. When the costs of discount were taken into account the true rate of interest generally became much less than the hidden allowance of 25 per cent or so initially granted.

However indispensable the tally may have been to the financial system of the Middle Ages one could in strict logic hardly see the need for it in later centuries. Here again, however, the logical and the chronological, the expected and the actual, the apparently sensible and the concretely historical, progress of events did not march hand in hand. Far from dying out towards the end of the fifteenth century, the tally went on growing from strength to strength, reaching its highest importance in the generation which gave rise to the Bank of England at the end of the seventeenth century and managing anachronistically to persist right down to 1834 – developments which will be traced accordingly in later chapters. It has already been shown how the humble tally in the Middle Ages developed from being a simple receipt to a fairly complex and sophisticated financial medium, providing elasticity in the money supply unobtainable if the path of grossly debasing the coinage were to be avoided, as was the case in England. The tally also stimulated the hesitant, partially hidden rise in London of an embryo money and capital market, where 'interest' was paid on the basis of the repayment of fictitiously swollen loans. The increased negotiability of tallies enabled rich individuals to raise larger loans for the Crown and for other merchants. The tally, that medieval maid of all monetary labours, possessed an engaging modesty that hid from legal scrutiny a growing public involvement in usurious affairs. The struggle to maintain the traditional Christian prohibition on usury began to clash with the desires of a richer society to reward productive savings, and with the even more urgent imperatives of the Crown to meet its increasing expenses in peace and war, though these tensions did not reach breaking point until much later. The tally was the main, though not of course the only internal device for concealing usury. In external trade Jews and foreign merchants (as we shall see below and in the next chapter) were to provide not only lessons in avoiding usury but also, more generally, the means by which British monetary practices were very considerably influenced during the later Middle Ages. These early developments were in principle not unlike those occurring today in the

Arab oil-producing countries, where Muslim teaching with regard to usury comes into conflict with the strong financial forces represented in the enormous increases in the flow of petro-currencies, at a time when the major banks and treasuries of the world are generally unconstrained by the laws of usury.

The Crusades: financial and fiscal effects

The main external influences on English economic, monetary and fiscal development in this period came not only from the usual causes – war and trade – but from wars conducted at unprecedented distances and also from the considerable growth of trade in the exotic new products associated with those distant lands. Although the Crusades lasted, intermittently, from 1095 to the mid-fifteenth century, it was during the twelfth and thirteenth centuries that their main direct influences were felt in England; with the so-called Hundred Years War with France, from 1338 to 1453, subsequently taking the centre of the stage. Currently fashionable arguments between historians as to whether the Crusades should be widely or narrowly interpreted in terms of their geographical extent are almost irrelevant from the point of view of their direct effects on English financial history, except that the costs of conducting wars such a long way from home as the eastern Mediterranean were considerably greater than sending and equipping an army of the same size for conflicts in western Europe (Riley-Smith 1982, 48–9). Payment for supplies, equipment, allies, ransoms and so on, from time to time required vast resources of cash and the means of safely and quickly transferring such money. These new needs gave rise to financial intermediaries such as the Knights of the Temple and the Hospitallers who began to perform important semi-banking functions such as those which were already being developed to a fairly advanced level in some of the Italian city-states and in the famous fairs of medieval France. These customs were later carried by Italian 'Lombards', other foreign merchants, and by the Knights Templar and Hospitallers, to London. Such activities were greatly extended in volume and value by the Crusades. Ships which carried armies to the eastern Mediterranean could and did offer cheap facilities for return cargoes, and thus increased two-way trade across the Mediterranean. Carpets, rugs, fruits, drugs, jewellery, glass, perfumes, finely tempered steel, new kinds of machine, and above all new knowledge of mathematics, navigation, architecture and medicine together constituted a most valuable variety of visible and invisible imports from the east, and led to secular pressures towards recurring deficits in the balance of trade of the Crusading countries.

The most immediately visible impact of the Crusades was, however, in capital transfers and in the heavy forced loans and taxes raised to finance them. All the same we must guard ourselves against the temptation to assume that, because modern wars are highly inflationary, then so also were those of the Middle Ages. This was far from necessarily being so, since the heavily increased demand for certain materials and services was roughly compensated by a corresponding external drain of gold and silver to 'service' the campaigns and to pay for the new luxuries from the East. The drain of real resources in the form of the export of knights and their retainers and camp followers together with their armour, horses, equipment, and their transport by ship, was generally roughly matched by the drain of cash and bullion, leaving the internal macro-equation between money and goods roughly the same. Prices were far from being completely stable of course, yet in view of the extent of movement of armies and goods, a surprising degree of stability was nevertheless maintained by the very nature of the physical basis of medieval money.

The importance of foreign exchange in the development of European financial institutions can hardly be exaggerated particularly since most of the earliest recognizable 'banks' of modern times arose, first in Italy and France and then in the Low Countries, mainly out of their involvement in foreign exchange. Such bankers had their agents in almost all the important financial centres, e.g. Rome, Venice, Genoa and Florence in Italy; at Troyes, Rouen, Lyons and Paris in France; at Valladolid and Seville in Spain; at Bruges and Antwerp in the Low Countries – as well as in London. Their financial involvement in London – just like England's involvement in the Crusades – was, however, at a lower level. It is significant that the early banks of modern Europe developed first in Italy and France out of their massive involvement in foreign exchange based largely on bills of exchange, whereas when some centuries later indigenous banking developed in London it arose primarily as a by-product of the activities of goldsmiths in handling gold and silver in the form of both bullion and coins. As in many other economic matters England relied mainly on foreigners to conduct most of its early foreign exchange and other quasi-banking activities, and leaned heavily on the specialized services provided by the two main orders of international chivalry, the Knights Hospitallers and the Knights of the Temple. The Order of the Knights of the Hospital of St John of Jerusalem – to give its resoundingly full title – was first formed in Jerusalem shortly after the city's conquest by the Christians in 1099, to carry out its task of caring for the casualties of the Crusades. Although the establishment of hospitals and the provision of medical care has remained of importance to the order right up to the present (in the form of the well-known St John Ambulance brigades) its commercial, military and financial activities, sometimes in conjunction with, but more often in competition with, the rival Templars, grew to overshadow its more charitable functions. The Order of the Knights of the Temple at Jerusalem – the Templars – was formed in Jerusalem in 1120 and grew in similar fashion to become a formidable economic and political force around the Mediterranean shores and in western Europe.

These two orders of knights had their own ships, kept their own private armies, depots and storehouses, and occupied strong-points and castles at a number of strategically placed ports and inland towns, from Spain to Syria and from England to Egypt. They could therefore easily arrange the safe custody and delivery of valuable goods, specie and coins, and often save the necessity of moving such specie and coins by bilateral and sometimes trilateral offsetting transfers. They also themselves owned considerable financial resources which they increased as a result of accepting vast deposits from kings and merchants, which they were then able to lend out to creditworthy borrowers, the interest element in such dealings normally being hidden by the nature of the transactions either in foreign exchange or as bills of exchange or, frequently, as both. Among a large number of princely gifts made to the two orders were the vast estates bequeathed by Alfonso I, king of Aragon, and the less valuable but still impressive estates granted to them in England by Stephen. They were even granted powers to mint their own coins, as for instance did the Hospitallers for many years from their bastion at Rhodes. They therefore were able to carry out the whole range of merchant banking activities relevant to the increasing demands of commerce and politics in the thirteenth and fourteenth centuries. Their long-standing and manifold contacts with the Muslim world in war and peace enabled them to act as a bridge by which the learning of the East enlightened the economic and social life of the West. It can hardly be a matter of mere coincidence that the first two fulling mills (water mills for 'fulling' wool to remove its excess oil) were both owned by and built on estates belonging to the Templars – in 1185 at Newsham in Yorkshire and at Barton in the Cotswolds, the latter known to have been actually built by the Templars themselves. The windmill, probably originating in Persia, had already spread to China and over much of the Middle East by the time of the Crusades and gradually spread its wings in Europe from this time onward. The crusading orders therefore seem to have played their part in bringing about what Professor Carus-Wilson has called 'an industrial revolution of the thirteenth century . . . due to scientific discoveries and changes in technique' (Carus-Wilson 1954, 41). 'Primitivists' might justifiably object to this premature use of the term 'industrial revolution', but they cannot deny the commercial and financial revolutions that accompanied and facilitated such industrial innovations. (For an authoritative modern survey of 'The Place of Money in the Commercial Revolution of the Thirteenth Century' see Spufford, 1988, chapter 11, 240–66).

Although the Crusades were not responsible for the origins of the bourgeoning financial centres of western Europe, they can at the very least be credited with greatly encouraging their growth by adding to the variety and volume of goods traded, and also in assisting the advancement of their financial techniques, especially in their widespread use of the modern type of bill of exchange. Our knowledge of the origins of the modern bill of exchange is rather vague, and despite some allusions to their use by the Arabs in the eighth century and by the Jews in the tenth century, there appears to be no concrete evidence of their use before the period of the Crusades. The growth in the use of bills of exchange was therefore coincident with, but never exclusively confined to, the rapid expansion in the transfers of the large amounts of capital required to finance the Crusades. Although a very considerable number of merchant bankers were involved in such transfers – at a time when most merchants were forced to act partly as bankers, and most bankers were similarly involved in wholesale trading – the two main intermediaries, so far as their direct involvement with the Crusades was concerned, were the Knights Templar and the Hospitallers.

According to Einzig, the first known foreign exchange contract was issued in Genoa in 1156 to enable two brothers who had borrowed 115 Genoese pounds to reimburse the bank agents in Constantinople, to which their business was taking them, the sum of 460 bezants one month after their arrival. Such examples grew fairly rapidly in the following century, especially when the profits from time differences in bills involving foreign exchange were seen as not infringing canon laws against usury. The Church itself used the same system. In 1317 'the Papal Chamber concluded with the banking houses Bardi and Peruzzi a contract covering a period of twelve months, during which the Papal Nuncio in England was to pay over to their London branches the proceeds of the Papal collections for remittance to Avignon', such contracts being renewed year after year (Einzig 1970, 68). The examples given refer to real transfers from one country to another; but partly to escape from the penalties of usury and partly to tap credit which would otherwise not have been made available, large amounts of 'fictitious' bills were issued which either were simply domestic deals masquerading as foreign or simply dealing in credit without real goods or services being involved. In this way again the constraints of a limited supply of gold and silver money were being overcome by the extension of paper credit, just as in the more backward use of wooden tallies for such purposes in England.

Although the financial results of the Crusades were far-reaching it was their fiscal effects in the form of urgent, heavy and repeated calls for cash through new aids, subsidies, tithes and other taxes, which appeared of most obvious concern to contemporaries in England. When the generous but weak Stephen was succeeded by the strong, rich but parsimonious Henry II (1154–89), the scene was set for an epic struggle between Henry in England, the Templars and Hospitallers who acted as his bankers in Jerusalem, and the Crusading armies in the Holy Land, who were fed on promises but denied access to Henry's funds. Henry first raised a special tax to support the Crusades in 1166, followed by such lavish payments to the Templars and Hospitallers from 1172 onward that he came to be considered – by the critical Gerald of Wales (among others) – as the 'chief support of the Holy Land'. In 1185 Henry levied a new 'crusading tax' at sixpence in the pound on all movable property and 1 per cent on all incomes whether from land or any other source, a heavy burden repeated in the following two years. In 1187 Henry's eastern account, therefore, securely maintained in the strongholds of the Templars and Hospitallers where it was as safe as if it were still held in the London Exchequer, amounted to the huge sum of 30,000 marks or approximately 20,000 pounds of silver. As Dr Mayer has shown, 'all the evidence points to Henry accumulating money in the East without permitting anyone to spend it', at least until after the disastrous battle of Hattin in 1187 (Mayer 1982, 724). Thus the explanation for the fall of much of the Holy Land to Saladin is not due to the 'damsel in distress' theory, namely the traditional story of the Crusaders' armies being diverted to aid the 'Lady of Tiberias', wife of Raymond III, Count of Tripoli, but rather the miserly restrictions placed by Henry on the use of his vast hoard of money, in an eventually vain attempt to have his cake and to eat it. Money, not chivalry, lay behind the fall of Jerusalem; money in apparent abundance but in reality frozen in the bank vaults of the Templars and Hospitallers.

The shock of the fall of Jerusalem stirred Henry to unfreeze his eastern deposits, to raise yet more taxes, and finally at long last to 'take the cross' himself (i.e. to fight personally in the Crusades). The 'Saladin Tithe' of 1188 extended the new source of taxation inaugurated in 1185, namely the taxation of personal property, and also speeded up the assessment system by demanding that each person should make his own personal assessment and that such assessments should be verifiable by persons in the locality who could vouch for their veracity. These examples of local accountability boomeranged against the royal prerogative in later years from its tendency to strengthen the customary right for greater public discussion of taxation by the king's council, a forerunner of Parliament's scrutiny of royal taxation. The principle of 'no new kinds of taxation without some more explicit form of representation' thus has a long, long history, stretching back well into the Middle Ages.

The outcry against the heavy burden of the Saladin tithe was far from being the end of the matter, for when the more adventurous Richard I (1189–99) succeeded his father, England's money problems multiplied. Richard's policy (reminiscent of that of the Thatcher government's 'privatization' of publicly-owned assets in the 1980s) was to put up as much as possible for sale in order quickly to supplement the taxes, liberally granting patents and charters to persons, guilds and towns, in return for cash with which to buy allies, ships, armies and munitions. He also raised ten thousand marks (or about £6,666) from the king of the Scots by releasing him from the vassalage he had previously been forced to promise. Thus armed, Richard embarked on the Third Crusade in 1190. His quarrels with Leopold, Duke of Austria, led on his return to his capture in Vienna, and his sale to Emperor Henry VI, who imprisoned Richard at a secret location. The delightful legend of his discovery – at Durrenstein Castle – when Blondel, his personal troubadour, played Richard's favourite tune, and so eventually received his royal master's response in song – has subsequently reinforced the many bright tales of medieval chivalry; but at the time it turned out to be a most expensive adventure.

The piper's tune cost England a pretty penny. A colossal ransom of 150,000 marks, i.e. £100,000 or twenty-four million pennies, was demanded, a sum which far exceeded the whole of the average revenue of the kingdom. Nevertheless, a high proportion of the ransom was quickly raised and paid over before Richard's release. An aid of £1 on each knight's fee, together with a general 'income tax' of 25 per cent on rents and property, supplemented once more by further sales of royal offices and privileges and by generous gifts, sufficed to raise the required amount. Among the most generous of the gifts were the £2,000 given by the king of the Scots, and the proceeds from the whole of the year's wool clip by the Cistercian monks from their sheep-rich lands.

Little wonder that the eventual reaction to such heavy and repeated burdens showed itself in a number of constitutional developments around this time. Article XII among the sixty-three clauses of Magna Carta, which the barons forced John to sign on 15 June 1215, stated that 'no scutage or aid, except for ransom, for the knighting of the king's eldest son, or the marriage of his eldest daughter, should be raised without the consent of his Barons assembled in Great Council'. Despite frequent royal backsliding, Henry III (1216–72) was similarly forced to toe the line when his crusading adventures led him into debts that could not be easily redeemed through the revenues from ordinarily acceptable taxation. Immediately on taking the cross in 1250 Henry attempted on behalf of the pope to wrest Sicily from the control of the Hohenstaufens, but soon quarrelled with his sponsor when he attempted to crown his younger son Edmund king of Sicily. When Henry was threatened with excommunication and found himself virtually bankrupt at the same time, he appealed to his barons for financial assistance. The barons, however, agreed to grant an aid only upon certain conditions. They demanded the reforms suggested by a royal commission composed of twelve royal appointees and twelve representatives chosen by the barons themselves. Although the report of this commission to the King's Council or Parliament at Oxford in 1258 – the famous Provisions of Oxford – was annulled in 1266, the importance of the event, as with Magna Carta, derives from the repeated use of royal indebtedness to secure redress from a number of royal impositions. These baronial protests were no mere empty gestures, but, according to Professor Mitchell, an authority on medieval taxation, represented 'a revolutionary change. The barons on the great council refused to grant any further gracious aids that took the form of a tax on personal property', so that 'from 1237 to 1269 no such levy was taken' (Mitchell 1951, 102).

Increasing indebtedness forced the pace of commutation, increased the role of money and revealed how closely interconnected were the royal prerogatives of minting money and raising taxes. The king's power to profit from debasing the coinage was certainly held in check by the Council who also occasionally even managed to modify the form of taxation and to wrest some constitutional advantage in return. The fact that such (for those days) enormous sums of money could be raised so quickly gives concrete evidence of the greatly increased wealth and taxable capacity of the growing population during the commercial revolution of the long thirteenth century – to be followed by what appeared in glaring contrast to be the inspissated doom and gloom of the fourteenth.

The Black Death and the Hundred Years War

Although famine and pestilence had always afflicted previous ages, the virulence and persistence of the plagues of the fourteenth century stand out as the most malign in the history of mankind, and the Black Death (1348–50) as the first and worst of the whole of the recurring series, the most recent of which was that of 1665–6. The flea- and rat-borne bubonic plague had spread quickly from central Asia, arriving in Sicily in 1347 via a ship from the port of Kaffa, a Genoese colony in the Crimea, which had become infected when a besieging Turkestan army catapulted into the colony bodies which had just died of the plague. The plague reached Melcombe Regis near Weymouth in Dorset from Calais in August 1348, and by 1350 had spread throughout the British Isles to the north of Scotland. Few regions or classes escaped, the plague being no respecter of persons or provinces. Thus Joan, daughter of Edward III died at Bordeaux on the way to her anticipated wedding; and while there is some evidence of local variations, there was no pattern of marked differences between town and country. Although the numbers dying in each of the later plagues were less than in the first case of 1348–50, their influence in the fourteenth century on prolonging and intensifying the fall in population was probably even greater, since they affected the younger age groups with special severity and so contributed disproportionately to the fall in the birth rate. Plagues of some sort or other (and not simply bubonic plagues) became endemic with hardly a year passing without renewed outbreaks in some region or other and with really major plagues recorded in 1361, 1369, 1375, and 1379 followed by plagues of national proportions in 1400, 1413, 1434, 1439 and 1464. Plagues prevailed in sixty years in England between 1348 and 1593, and returned in a final major epidemic in 1665.

The cumulative result was that the population of England, which had risen to a peak of between four and five million in 1300, had fallen by 50 per cent or so by 1425, back to the kind of level obtaining in 1175. All such figures are approximate, for despite the two bench-mark statistics supplied by the Domesday survey of 1086 which mentioned, as we have noted previously, some 283,242 persons, and the Poll Tax returns of 1377, which gave the total number of those actually paying the tax as 1,386,196, the margins of error remain wide. There is some evidence that the population was already beginning to decline before the arrival of the Black Death in 1348 – a feature which would have been of minor importance had it not given rise to contention among historians who became tired of what they assumed to be a simplistic tendency to ascribe to the Black Death trends which to the careful historian were clearly visible before that calamity. Whereas many of these arguments are irrelevant to our main theme, some of them have a direct bearing on the development of money and prices in the fourteenth and fifteenth centuries.

The arguments among the experts about the influence of the plagues on money and prices are still very much alive. The overriding, unmistakable, traditional view needs to be emphasized that, whether or not the economic changes ascribed to the Black Death originated earlier, there can be little doubt as to the devastating results of the plagues in swamping all previous trends, obliterating some and enormously accelerating others. Furthermore, since the direct effects of the plagues were so appallingly all-embracing, it is bound to be somewhat distorting to narrow the focus, as we must, simply to deal with its economic and financial effects. There is much merit in the following conclusion given by Professor W. C. Robinson in an interesting discussion of this subject: 'The present trend to "revisionism" notwithstanding, the Black Death, wars, and other disruptions which wracked Europe for a century are still the best explanation of the sudden collapse of economic growth and population which seem to have occurred in the late Middle Ages . . .' and he reiterates the traditional, classical view that 'changes in the money supply were probably the most important single factor in the price changes which occurred in medieval and early modern times' (W. C. Robinson 1959, 76: see also Postan 1972; Gregg 1976; E. King 1979).

The nature of medieval markets, a severe shortage of labour, a drastic fall in output, an initially unchanged money stock and a fall in the velocity of money: these are the five factors which, working in variously weighted combinations, help to explain the influence of the plagues on the course of financial development in the fourteenth and fifteenth centuries. Medieval markets exhibited a curious and changing mixture of long-term price stability in some respects, together with extreme volatility of prices in other respects. Where feudal ties remained strong, customary monetary payments as well as payments in kind tended to remain stable, though obviously the market value of that part of the harvest received by knight, lord or bishop from his serfs, villeins or peasants would fluctuate considerably whether or not they were supplied in kind. Agriculture was still by far the dominant sector, and with levels of productivity low (except in the special case of wool) the supply available for the market was generally simply the volatile, weather-controlled surplus left over from meeting the needs of the local community. There is considerable evidence of relative 'overpopulation' up to the early fourteenth century, so that famine prices for foodstuffs recurred from time to time. Medieval markets were usually 'thin', that is, the volume of goods available at a particular price was very limited and so were stocks compared with the situation in more modern times. Transport was slow and transport costs, particularly for the bulky goods which predominated in an agricultural society, were heavy. Local shortages could not be readily or inexpensively relieved and neither could the impact of local surpluses be readily siphoned away to other areas so as to maintain price levels locally. Furthermore, on the physical production side, agricultural output could not be easily managed or brought easily into rapid relationship with changing demand. Unavoidable waste and high inelasticities of supply made for widely fluctuating prices despite all the inbuilt attempts of feudalism to impose some sort of order and stability over the power of the markets.

When upon this normal instability was imposed the key shortage of manpower occasioned by the plagues, then the way was opened for a long and bitter struggle for freer labour markets, marked not only by an inevitable upward trend in wages but by increased expectations of liberty and of the removal of the irksome personal bonds imposed by the feudal system. The 'land hunger' of the thirteenth century, even if it had been growing less serious in the first part of the fourteenth century, was now suddenly replaced by an unmanageable surplus of land, as around one-third of the labour force died in 1348–9. Far higher death rates occurred in certain regions so that the resulting disruption to customary work programmes resulted in a massive fall in total output.

Most prices quickly broke through their customary restraints with the price of the scarcest factor, labour, naturally tending to rise fastest. The poor always have a high income elasticity of demand for food, and consequently the rise in wages helped to maintain food prices at a higher level than those for hand-crafted or literally 'manufactured' goods. This explains why a relative land surplus, coinciding with unprecedented high wages in a labour-intensive agricultural society, together with a drastic fall in total output led to reduced rents and profits for the landowners despite the marked tendency to forsake marginal land. Costs rose faster than profits; and this, quite apart from the appalling effects of the Black Death itself, reduced business and farming incentives and demoralized the nascent entrepreneurial spirit even in those sections of the economy – such as wool, cloth, wines, charcoal and metals – which were already sensitive to the normal market forces of demand and supply in medieval times. Although of course no nationwide figures of wages actually being paid are available, and whereas regional differences are known to have been considerable, a general picture of the rise in wages may be seen from the following examples given by Professor Hatcher (1977, 49): thus the daily wage rate for a labourer was about 1½*d*. in 1301, was still only 1¾*d*. in 1331, then rose much faster to about 3¼*d*. in 1361. A carpenter earned around 2¾*d*. a day in 1301, nearly 4*d*. in 1351 and about 4¼*d*. in 1361. Although by modern inflationary standards such rises may appear piffling, they seemed devastating to contemporary employers, and a violation of the accepted morality of the 'just' price.

The change from cheap to dear labour was strongly resisted by the landlords and by Edward III, who quickly issued a restrictive Ordinance in 1349, followed by a fuller and more formal Statute of Labourers from Parliament when it met, for the first time after the Black Death, in 1351. It had been called, according to Edward's own account, 'because the peace was not well kept, because servants and labourers would not work as they should, and because treasure was carried out of the Kingdom and the realm impoverished and made destitute of money' (Feavearyear 1963, 19). We shall therefore first examine Parliament's resultant policy on law and order, employment and wages, and then look at the measures adopted to cope with the damaging export of coin and bullion. The king saw clearly that these were but two sides of the same problem – of what we would call internal cost-push inflation and external exchange rates. The Statute of Labourers stipulated the maximum rates of pay, at pre-plague levels, which were to apply to all the main occupations; it also stated that all able-bodied men under sixty should be forced to work; and it severely restricted not only the mobility of labour between jobs, but actual freedom of movement between villages. These provisions were to apply to all workers and not just villeins. Despite the fact that such severe restrictions could not be uniformly enforced, the repeated attempts to do so unified the economic, political, religious and social grievances and led, eventually, to the Great Rebellion of 1381.

The law might hinder, but it could not prevent, the profound changes in the value of money from benefiting the labouring classes. Because wage rates rose much faster than prices, and because output per head also actually rose despite the decline in total national output, the *real* wages of the working classes tended to rise, with few reverses, for a century and a half throughout most of the fourteenth and fifteenth centuries. Hence the paradox of patches of real progress amid the general secular depression of these centuries; a paradox that helps us to see the compatibility of the apparently totally contradictory views such as 'Postan's tale of recession, arrested economic development and declining national income' and 'Bridbury's proclamation of an astonishing record of resurgent vitality and enterprise' (Hatcher 1977,

36). This patchy economic progress was accompanied by rising expectations among the working classes and a growing resentment against the established authorities of Church and state. What finally turned this smouldering resentment into open and widespread rebellion was the imposition of new taxes to meet the increasingly irksome costs of the Hundred Years War, a series of bloody conflicts that between 1338 and 1453 helped to destroy the old feudal system on both sides of the Channel.

If we use the generally familiar 'Fisher identity' of MV=PT to help to interpret the changes in the value of money in the century or so following the Black Death we can readily see that the enormous reduction in total transactions (T) combined with an initially unchanged quantity of money (M) would be bound to lead to a substantial increase in prices (P) which for the reasons already given, led especially to increased wages (I. Fisher 1911). However, the substantial decline in the velocity of circulation of money (V) acted to moderate the rise in prices. An even stronger and longer-lasting influence in preventing the huge surplus of money from having its full price-raising effect on the reduced quantities of goods being produced by the repeatedly decimated population was the enormous drain of money from England to the Continent chiefly because of the high cost of wars but also because of other monetary and trade factors. Among the most important of these other drains – or 'leakages' as we now term these reductions in consumer spending power – were the heavy taxes imposed by governments which diverted incomes from spending on internal consumption mainly to expenditures abroad to support the army. A similar leakage occurred through the importation of luxury goods, which partly explains the antipathy shown by John Wycliffe and his 'Lollards' against the debilitating and sinful influence of rich foreigners, who acted prominently as import agents in London, and who, as in the biblical parable of the tares, sowed their moral weeds or 'tares' on good English soil (Latin 'lolia' = tares). An external leakage exerting a direct influence on the money supply was the continued selection, or 'culling', of English silver and the new gold coins for export. Despite some replacement by debased imitations from abroad, the quality of these was such that they were not so readily accepted in payment, and therefore failed to do much to offset the persistent foreign drain.

The unofficial drain of gold and silver bullion and coinage stirred the wrath of the administration and caused it in 1351 to strengthen the previous prohibitions on export (such as that issued in 1299 and known as the Statute of Stepney), but to no great practical effect. The unofficial drain was supplemented by the government's decision to set

up an English mint to produce English coin in Calais, which remained
in existence from 1347 to 1440. This extension of circulation made it all
the easier for overseas imitators to pass their inferior 'esterlin'
currencies. The fact that foreign debasement proceeded at a faster pace
than that of the English currency tended to produce repeated strains on
the balance of trade, for the financial pressures of the strong pound
were bound to make it that much harder to export and easier to import
goods which again contributed to the export leakage of coin and
bullion. To try to eliminate, or at least to reduce, the temptation offered
to illegal exporters of coin, the weight of the penny, which had
remained almost unchanged for 200 years, was slightly reduced by
Edward III in 1344 and reduced more substantially by him in 1351, the
total reduction of the silver content of the coinage over those seven
years being 19 per cent. Parliament was not happy, and by the Statute of
Purveyors of 1352 expressed the hope that the king would no more
tamper with the coinage than with the standards of weights and
measures.

Two further aspects which contributed to a reduction of surplus
money relative to the gross fall in the national product were, first, that
during times of war and plague hoarding increased, so removing coin
from circulation, a process which applied also to much of the foreign
coin brought back by the victorious army. Secondly, coins wore out and
the mint was inactive for long periods, so that the previous replacement
rate was reduced. Thus the recoinage associated with the new policy of
devaluation stimulated an average annual rate of production of
£100,000 of gold coin and £50,000 of silver coin in the five years from
1351 to 1355 inclusive, whereas the average annual rates fell to only £9,500
of gold coins and £900 of silver coins in the whole of the thirty-nine
years from 1373 to 1411 inclusive. Thus instead of the same amount of
money chasing half as many goods and practically half as many
workers, the reduction of the excess money supply by these various
means considerably moderated the inflationary impact of the plagues.

So long as the war with France yielded its harvest of victories and
ransoms the burdens did not seem insupportable. The increased
revenues required for war were obtained at first by a combination of old
taxes and customs duties raised to new heights, supplemented by a
relatively small amount of borrowing. In the Middle Ages wool was by
far the principal export and the main source of royal revenue. The
export of 'England's golden fleece', the 'goddess of merchants', was
controlled by the Society of Staplers, the oldest company of merchants
in British overseas trade. They made Calais for two centuries their
'staple' port from the time of its capture by Edward in 1347 until its loss

by broken-hearted Mary I in 1558. Calais therefore was doubly important to the English monarch – as his mint and as his most abundant source of trade-based revenue. The customary duty on wool was raised from 6s. 8d. to an average of 40s. a sack in 1338, with foreign merchants having to pay a surcharge above that paid by English merchants. In the course of the next five years England's golden fleece lived up to its name by supplying more than £1 million to the royal Exchequer. Edward also profited directly by purchasing the greater part of the wool crop himself at low prices and selling it through Calais at much higher prices. Thus monetary, fiscal and trade-protection policies were neatly integrated. On balance the Calais mint was not therefore an abberation but a logical, convenient and long-lasting result of convergent military, monetary and taxation pressures. The high tax on raw wool exports, of around 33 per cent in value, combined with a low tax on cloth of only about 2 per cent in value, helped to stimulate cloth manufacture in England, but led to a substantial decline in raw wool exports and so, as an unfortunate by-product, resulted in a considerable fall in royal revenues from this source. This in turn contributed to the growing urgency to find other sources of taxation in the period 1377 to 1381.

The net military balance of ransom, loot, bounty and plunder tended to favour the English, particularly during the early stages of the war, as shown by the victories of Sluys in 1340, Crécy in 1346 and Poitiers in 1356, which latter yielded the highest prize of all when King John II of France was captured. A vast ransom of three million gold crowns (£500,000) was demanded, and though in the end only something a little less than a half of this was in fact paid, this still represented a massive amount, some four times larger, we may note, than the total of all the poll taxes which stirred up such turmoil a generation later. Part of the proceeds was used to rebuild the royal apartments of Windsor Castle, a permanent record of conspicuous expenditure typically engendered by such windfall riches. The 3d. a day paid to infantrymen, and the 6d. paid to archers with mounts, were poor incentives compared with the troops' customary one-third share of ranson money or booty (the other two-thirds shared equally between their captain and their king). When the tide of the long war turned against England, the net costs also grew far heavier, and were resented all the more since it was just at this time that the king's advisers decided that new forms of direct taxes had to be levied. New taxes are always detested, especially poll taxes, whether it be the 1380s or the 1980s.

Poll taxes and the Peasants' Revolt

There is no doubt that the three poll taxes of 1377, 1379 and 1381 acted as the trigger for the Peasants' Revolt of 1381, even though it was the long build-up of social and economic grievances 'between the landowner and the peasant, which had started with the Black Death and the Statute of Labourers' which formed the most important group of causes (Oman 1981, 5). The penalties of the Statute were repeatedly re-enacted and increased in severity while the yield of indirect taxes fell with the decline in national output.

The burden of taxes was soon to be grossly inequitable because, whereas the percentage fall in population varied from district to district, no reassessment of the customary burdens of tenths and fifteenths based on the new population was carried out. As time went on these distortions grew progressively worse, although the problem did not become pressing until the decade following 1371, when the frequency, amount and regressiveness of taxation were sharply increased. These new burdens, occasioned by the disastrous course of the war, were all the more resented because they stood in contrast to a preceding period of some twelve years (1359–71) during which no direct taxes were levied, 'this being one of the longest respites from taxation enjoyed in the fourteenth century' (Fryde 1981, xii).

The levying of flat-rate taxes on all 'adults' was felt by the king's tax commissioners to be fairer than trying to raise the same amount on the basis of out-of-date local assessments from shires and towns. Furthermore, many of the formerly poor labourers had now become relatively much better off and could afford to be taxed directly. They had, in the words of Piers Plowman, 'waxed fat and kicking', and it was widely felt that they should in all equity contribute their share. Contemporaries were quite aware of the regressive nature of poll taxes, but when all the arguments are taken into account there seemed in principle to be a perfectly good case for having recourse to such taxes. These poll taxes were therefore levied in addition to the ordinary tenths and fifteenths and certain other taxes on movables which were also being demanded concurrently. It was however the novelty of the poll taxes, and especially the greatly increased burden of the poll tax of 1381, which finally led to open rebellion. The first poll tax in 1377 was 4d. for all 'adults', from fourteen years old. The collectors recorded 1,355,201 such taxpayers, the total revenue being assessed at £22,586. 13s. 4d. Additionally, a miscellaneous body of 30,995 persons were recorded in the tax returns giving a total (underestimated) taxable 'adult' population of 1,386,196. This gives us the figure mentioned above as the base from which estimates of the total population of England in 1377 have been derived, such estimates being very considerably increased, by as much as a million or more, as a result of modern research (e.g. see Postan 1966).

The second poll tax of 1379, while also being based on a notional 4*d.*, was assessed at a slightly lower total of £19,304, because it was in fact carefully graduated according to social status and was therefore probably the most equitable of all the direct taxes of the fourteenth century. In harsh contrast, the third poll tax, that of 1381, was far more severe. It was assessed at £44,843, or double that of each of the previous taxes. Every lay person above the age of fifteen had to pay three groats or 1*s.*, triple the basic rate of the previous polls. Clerical persons were separately assessed. This heavy tax was felt even by the local assessors to be so unreasonable that they connived at an unprecedented degree of evasion by the poorest, upon whom the burden was clearly insupportable. In the two previous polls the heaviest tax paid by the poorest was 4*d.* In 1381 they were expected to pay the whole shilling with very few exceptions. The degree of evasion is shown by the fact that the recorded taxable population, though free of plague, fell by a fifth as a national average, with some regions registering an apparent fall of more than a half. When the commissioners of the tax attempted to punish the tax dodgers, open rebellion broke out in town and countryside involving over half the kingdom. Despite the promises of constitutional amendments, given by the young King Richard II (1377–99) to the rebellious hordes in London, the revolt was eventually suppressed, leaving at least a warning and a series of unanswered questions that still vex the experts to this day.

The revolt had been brought about by a whole complex of causes – social, political, religious and economic as well as fiscal. But the attempt to restrict, depress and overtax townsmen and agricultural workers who had for more than a generation been experiencing a *rise* in their real standard of living was a vital catalyst in this whole confused complex of causes. A key factor was the king's need to raise more taxes from a falling population which was individually growing somewhat richer but which in the aggregate was becoming markedly poorer. Wars, plagues and poll taxes proved to be a most inflammatory mixture. (The Thatcherite administration, 600 years later, had to relearn the dangers of trying to poll tax the populace.) Fleas and taxes, not just silver and gold, had become major determinants of the real value of money.

Money and credit at the end of the Middle Ages

During the Middle Ages as whole, however coinage dominated European monetary development. In England, a country which had uniquely reverted to barter in the fifth century, a new indigenous coinage based first on gold and then more firmly on the silver penny gradually emerged during the seventh century, and thereafter that little coin dominated England's monetary development for over 500 years until it became marginally supplemented by gold in the fourteenth century. Subsequently an uneasy bimetallic marriage was to last until the beginning of the nineteenth century. Medieval money was above all monarchical money, and monetary policy was among the most closely guarded personal prerogatives of the king, though the Great Council and Parliament were not without influence. The connection with fiscal policy, therefore, was direct and clear, and it was at first mainly in connection with the king's need to tax and borrow that credit instruments of a quasi-monetary character also developed. The bill of exchange was a foreign innovation which spread to England in connection with the trade in wool and wine and the collection and distribution of papal dues. Although the wooden tally had developed universally as a receipt, nowhere else did it reach the heights it achieved in England as a quasi-monetary instrument. Despite the considerable development of credit, its monetary significance still remained secondary to coins in England until after the end of the Middle Ages, a feature which in terms of its scale helps to distinguish modern from medieval times.

There were three types of coinage recycling prevalent in Europe during medieval times, and although evidence of all three is to be seen in England, only two of these types were resorted to extensively on the English side of the Channel. The three types, in rough chronological order, may be termed, first, revisionist or replacement; second, restoration or repair; and third, debasement or devaluation with or without adulteration.

Because of the high convenience of royally authenticated coinage as a means of payment, and with hardly any other of the general means of payment available in the Middle Ages being anything like as convenient, coins commonly carried a substantial premium over the value of their metallic content, more than high enough to cover the costs of minting. Kings could turn this premium into personal profit; hence the apparently puzzling feature of the wholesale regular recall of coinage which was described earlier, first at six-yearly, then at three-yearly intervals, and eventually about every two years or so. In order to make a thorough job of this short recycling process it was essential that all existing coins should be brought in so as to maximize the profit and, in order to prevent competition from earlier issues, the new issues had to be made clearly distinguishable by the authorities yet readily acceptable by the general public. These regular, complete changes in the whole currency long before wear and tear set in, have been dubbed 'revisionist' by numismatists, though 'replacement' might give a better indication of the system.

The regular wholesale recall and reissue of coinage was of course a wasteful and costly process which could moreover only be carried out without too much trade-crippling delay when every borough had its mint and when the total amount of money in circulation was small enough to be manageable. The process of centralizing minting in the eleventh and twelfth centuries in London, as opposed to operating the seventy-five or so mints of the 'revisionist' period, coincided with the rise in population, the growth of trade and an expansion of the money supply which together made the continuation of the old 'revisionist' cycle far less viable. Better methods of raising revenue rendered revisionism redundant. The 'revisionist' cycle therefore gave way to the 'restoration' cycle of a much less regular type since it depended on the supplies and prices of bullion available to the king on the one hand and the normal processes of wear and tear on the other hand. It 'topped up' the existing money supply rather than completely replacing it, and so it was more in the nature of a piecemeal repair job than a thorough renovation. Whereas under 'revisionist' policies complete recoinage took place only three or four times a decade, under 'restoration' policies such complete recoinages took place only three or four times in a century. The normal restoration rate was also strongly influenced by the loss of native coin, counterfeiting, clipping, sweating, hoarding and culling, and by the influx of inferior 'easterlins' to compete with native British issues. Although the king and his advisers soon became aware of any deterioration in the quality of the coinage, and although most of the kings of England and all of their counsellors (in contrast to the situation abroad) were concerned to maintain the quality of the circulating coin, the large-scale minting required from time to time to maintain the quality of coins in circulation had by then become a costly business with no guarantee of substantial profit. There was therefore a general tendency to postpone and to limit new issues.

The recurring shortage of coins relative to growing demand – a matter of recorded concern to the Parliaments of 1331, 1339 and 1341 – was such that the counterfeiter readily stepped in to fill the vacuum, thereby in effect, if not intentionally, performing a public service.

However, although the counterfeiter performed his dubious public service (at the risk of losing hand or head) by increasing the quantity of money, to the extent to which he succeeded, he reduced the quality of the coinage and hastened the date of the inevitable official restorative issue, as did the importer of foreign substitutes. When to these difficulties is added the variations in the relative value of gold and silver it was a considerable achievement on the part of English monarchs that they maintained the quality of sterling to such a high degree throughout the Middle Ages. The fact that England was the first country in northern Europe to have a single national currency no doubt helped to maintain the high reputation of sterling, whereas the numerous minting authorities on the Continent indulged in a form of continuous competitive devaluation, a profound difference of policy which widened the gap between sterling and the silver currencies overseas.

The third type of recycling, namely debasement, was therefore virtually absent for centuries in England and Wales (but common in Scotland), and when it did occur was very mild compared with that abroad. Debasement could occur either through making coins of the same nominal value lighter, e.g. the number of pennies minted from a given weight of silver, which was a simple 'devaluation'; or more drastically and deceitfully by mixing cheaper metal with the precious metal, i.e. 'adulteration'; or, of course, a combination of these two methods. Not until the middle of the sixteenth century did debasement, as operated especially by Henry VIII, become of major importance for royal revenue. As we have seen, the only substantial previous reduction, and this was in terms of lighter weight rather than adulteration, was that of Edward III, forced on him by the more rapid debasement of continental currencies next door to his Calais mint. Further debasements by weight, for the silver penny and the gold noble and their subsidiary coins, were carried through by Henry IV in 1412 of 17 per cent and by Edward IV in 1464/5 of 20 per cent. On average all the devaluations in England over the whole of the previous two centuries amounted to only one-fifth of 1 per cent per annum, which was hardly more than the ordinary loss of weight through normal circulation. The effects on the value of sterling were therefore relatively small. In short, debasement was not really a problem in England before the sixteenth century.

An indication of the wide extent of the differences as between English and continental debasement is given in the following comparison. Whereas the weight and content of the silver penny had been maintained practically unchanged for four centuries before 1250, the equivalent coins in France had fallen to around one-fifth of their original value, as had those of Milan. Venetian silver coinage depreciated to one-twentieth of its original value during that period. Between 1250 and 1500 even the pound sterling fell in weight by a half, and while the rate of depreciation of the silver currencies of France, Milan and Venice moderated, they still fell by 70 per cent, that is at a rate still appreciably greater than sterling. It was in the quality of their *gold* florins and ducats that the Italian mints took justifiable pride.

Generations of historians have praised the moral qualities of English kings in yielding less to the temptations of debasement than did foreigners. Some of the reasons for this difference have already been given but we should however add the warning that superior-quality money does not necessarily indicate a superior economic performance. Sound money is no guarantee of a sound economy, either today or in the Middle Ages. In matters of finance as in matters of trade, it was the foreigner with his poorer-quality silver coinage and his superior supplements and substitutes, such as gold and especially the paper bill of exchange compared to our wooden tally, who led the way. Consequently one should at least raise the question of whether medieval England was crucified on a cross of undebased silver. Admittedly, at this distance of time it is unlikely that anyone will be able to come up with a convincing answer. Nevertheless, unless such questions are raised, there is a danger of almost unconsciously equating praise for the moral qualities of English monarchs and their parliaments in upholding sterling with the unjustified assumption that the result was good for the economy in general – that what was good for the sovereign was good for the kingdom. The persistence of the external drain, the incentive given to counterfeiting, the peculiarly English insistence on using the primitive and clumsy tally are all indications that the quantity of money tended over the long run to lag behind demand.

Whilst this is not an argument for saying that bad money is good, a posthumous apotheosis of Gresham, it should however inhibit the equally false, damaging and insidious convention that intrinsically good money is necessarily good for the economy. There is a tendency among historians with a natural bias towards numismatology, such as Sir John Craig and, to a lesser extent, Professor Grierson, to stress the qualitative superiority of sterling without equally stressing its possible drawbacks. Feavearyear and Cipolla occupy a more neutral position and draw welcome attention to problems of quantity, or relative scarcity, inherent in maintaining the quality of sterling. Professor Cipolla puts the points lucidly thus: 'It is apparent that during the Middle Ages the countries which experienced the greatest economic development were also those which experienced the greatest debasement' (Cipolla 1981, 201).

The two views of money, one emphasizing the quality, and the other the quantity, of money are duplicated in similarly contrasting views about the quality and extent of the use of credit in medieval trade. Bishop Cunningham, writing at the end of the nineteenth century, was an early proponent of a 'primitivist' view of English credit, minimizing its importance: 'Transactions were carried on in bullion; men bought with coin and sold for coin . . . dealing for credit was little developed, and dealing in credit was unknown' (Cunningham 1938, I, 362, 463). In contrast Lipson, Postan and, above all, Spufford have propounded more 'modernistic' beliefs (Lipson 1943, I, 528 ff.; Postan 1954; Spufford 1988).

To some extent monetary constraints were alleviated by the growth of credit, not only in the special form of the tally but also in a variety of other ways of which we have a wealth of records. According to Professor Postan 'there cannot be many topics in the history of the Middle Ages on which the evidence is as copious as on credit' (1954, I, 63). The records of the larger and more important of such credits were formally 'recognized' by judicial tribunals and, after the passing of the Statute of Burnell of 1283, were centrally registered on special rolls. Although the abundance of these and of many similar but less official records of debts clearly demonstrates that credit commonly entered into commercial practice, unfortunately it leaves open the question as to the relative importance of credit as opposed to cash transactions. Wholesale trade in wool, cloth, wine, tin and so on was heavily dependent on credit, with the great Italian merchant banking houses, those of Bardi, Peruzzi and Ricardi being among the most prominent. All stages in the woollen clothing industry, although organized technically on the domestic system, were typically based on the wholesale extension of credit. Sales of land and of rents, which modern research shows to have been much more common than was formerly believed, were commonly conducted through extending credit. As we have already seen with regard to the tally and the bill of exchange, a significant proportion of such activities was 'fictitious' rather than 'real', a means of hiding the illegal payments of interest, but the great majority were genuine transactions pointing to the growing and pervasive use of credit in medieval trade – not only in London and other ports but also inland.

Such evidence enabled Postan to demolish a view strongly held by earlier economic historians that dealing *for* credit was little developed, and to cast doubt also on the belief that dealing *in* credit was unknown.

The evidence already given of the discounting of tallies and of bills of exchange shows clearly that dealing in credit had also in fact long been fairly common in medieval England. Whereas the quality of sterling was, if anything, relatively too high because its quantity was limited, both the quality and quantity of its credit instruments were crude and limited compared with the use of credit in the main financial centres of Europe. The prohibition of usury undoubtedly distorted the money markets of medieval Europe and tended to favour both a more extensive use of coinage and a greater recourse to foreign exchange in the form of coins and bullion and through 'fictitious' bills of exchange than would otherwise have been the case. Sterling was therefore much more widely used than simply within the domestic economy, being a preferred silver currency over much of northern Europe, though playing very much a secondary role in international trade when compared with the gold florins of Florence or Ghent, or the ducats of Venice (Spufford 1988, 321, 381).

Despite its sterling qualities, England remained a backward, primitive country in European terms, just as did Europe compared with China, throughout the Middle Ages, a feature made more and more obvious by the wider contacts and by the marked growth in trade towards the end of the period. Thus in the middle of the fifteenth century England was still, according to Professor D. C. Coleman,

> on the near fringes of the European world, economically and culturally as well as geographically . . . Aliens still controlled about 40% of English overseas trade . . . London was overshadowed in wealth and size by the great cities of continental Europe, and nothing in England even began to match such a manifestation of wealth and power as the Medici family controlling the biggest financial organisation in Europe. (1977, 48)

Although the continuity of economic life makes almost any precise date dividing medieval from modern times artificial and arbitrary, there would appear to be no sufficiently strong reason, from the point of view of financial development, to depart from the traditional date of 1485 or thereabouts. The end of the Wars of the Roses in 1485 plainly demonstrated the end of baronial power since all their fine castles, when put to the test (with the exception of Harlech) had been easily subdued by modern weapons. Already the longbow had, in the course of the previous century and a half, brought the knight in armour down from his high horse and so symbolized the end of feudalism. But it is not so much the fading of the old as the brilliance of the new which puts the appropriate dividing date conveniently near to the time when Henry Tudor plucked Richard III's crown from the thorn-bush in Bosworth Field. It would seem to be essential, therefore, to take the end of the Middle Ages as occurring just before the discovery of the New World by Columbus in 1492. The fall of Constantinople in 1453 provides a similar, roughly contemporary marker.

The modern monetary age thus began with the geographic discoveries, with the full fruition of the Renaissance, with Columbus and El Dorado, with Leonardo da Vinci, Luther and Caxton; in short with improvements in communications, minting and printing. A vast increase in money, minted and printed, occurred in parallel with an unprecedented expansion in physical and mental resources. The inventions of new machines for minting and printing were in fact closely linked in a manner highly significant for the future of finance. At first the increase in coinage was to exceed, and then just to keep pace with the increase in paper money; but eventually and inexorably paper was to displace silver and gold, and thereby was to release money from its metallic chains and anchors. The apparently complete victory of the abstract over the concrete, the triumph of fiction over truth, provides the main theme and interest of the story of the five centuries from Columbus to Keynes.

5

The Expansion of Trade and Finance,
1485–1640

What was new in the new era?

The most spectacularly obvious difference between the old era and the new was the discovery by Europeans of the New World of the West Indies and, at least in outline, North and South America, most of Africa, South-East Asia, and, after a long pause, Australia and New Zealand. The great oceans of the world had been opened up through the daring of the European seaman, supported by royal sponsorship and joint-stock finance. In less than a decade following Columbus's first voyage of 1492, the size of the world known to Europeans was more than doubled. Within a generation it was more than trebled. In no other age of history has geographical knowledge become so suddenly and breathtakingly extended. Thereafter new geographical discoveries suffered universal diminishing returns, and exploitation of the partially known replaced investigation of the vast unknown.

Of much more importance initially than the discovery of new lands was the finding of new routes to the already well-known trading centres of the ancient East. Among the many strong motivations, this was probably the main reason behind the early voyages of discovery. Authoritative records of the motives of the early Portuguese explorers make it 'clear that none of them ever trouble themselves to sail to a place where there is not sure and certain hope of profit' (Needham 1971, IV, 529). Columbus was known to be much impressed by Marco Polo's published accounts of the wealth of China and wished to achieve on a much greater scale by sea what had previously been interruptedly accomplished to a very limited extent by the traditional overland caravans. Consequently up to Columbus's death in 1506 he had remained singularly convinced that the (West) 'Indies' which he had discovered were just useful stepping-stones to the wealth of Japan, China and India. His voyages were therefore seen by his sponsors as well as by himself as simply complementary to the whole series of expeditions from Portugal and Spain, culminating in Vasco da Gama's successful arrival in India in 1498 via the aptly named Cape of Good Hope, previously the Cape of Storms. Apart from the belated, almost obsolete, crusading motives and the new spiralling, political and nationalistic rivalries, the main and constant inspiration which spurred the voyages of discovery was the profit to be derived from trade.

Not least among the desires of the richer sections of European society were the luxuries of the East – fine cottons, silks, carpets, porcelain, spices – including cinnamon, mace, cloves, ginger and pepper, indigo, slaves, pearls, precious stones, and above all the precious metals. Greed for gold was always a most dominant motive and it was the influx of precious metals which had the most direct and obvious effects on monetary developments in Europe, first in Spain and Portugal, but subsequently spreading in turn through Italy, France, the Low Countries and the rest of Europe, including Britain, during the sixteenth and seventeenth centuries. Thus, when it came to the objects traded – apart from the fish off the Grand Banks of Newfoundland and the crops indigenous to North America such as tobacco, potatoes, tomatoes, etc – it was not their exotic novelty but rather their quantity which gave a special significance to the age of discoveries. Again this was to be most easily seen with regard to first gold, and then silver, where the quantities previously available either locally in Europe or imported by the mainly overland routes from Africa and the Near and Far East, had become woefully inadequate in the face of rising demand, but were now to be vastly supplemented by capture from the Aztecs and Incas and by new mining methods applied to the rich mines of the New World.

The novelty of the Renaissance has been very much called into question by historians of the mid-twentieth century. It was no doubt a brilliant exaggeration to call the Renaissance 'the discovery of the world and of man'. Nevertheless, a new dimension in the trade of ideas accompanied, reflected and partially accounted for the new geographical discoveries. It may well be true that traditionalists laid excessive emphasis on the rise of the Ottoman empire and the capture of Constantinople in 1453 as causes of the dispersion of Greek scholars to the West and consequently of the rebirth of classical scholarship. But whatever the exact chronology, the resultant 'contraction of Europe' in the Near East was a vital factor in the expansion of Europe in the Far

East and in the new West, while the disruption of the ancient trade routes at the very time when demand for eastern luxuries was rising increased the relative scarcity of such goods and therefore the potential profitability of discovering sea routes to the East.

Production for a larger market, production involving new modes of transport over much wider distances and requiring much more time between its initial stages and acceptance by the final customer – all these factors had deep monetary and financial implications, including significant improvements of the embryo capital, money and foreign exchange markets. For each stage in the chain of production, and for each link in the chain, more finance was needed and in a form which would minimize the greater risks involved. Greater reliance on expanding amounts of gold and silver for wholesale trade was not enough. Supporting developments were also needed, including wider use of quasi-monetary instruments such as bills of exchange and extended reckoning for credit purposes in additional moneys of account. The pooling of resources was another essential method of reducing the novel risks associated with overseas trade to dangerous and far-away destinations, with the result that new experimental forms of equity capital were developed from which the basic structure of modern capitalism, the joint-stock company, eventually evolved.

Printing: a new alternative to minting

The three inventions which together provided the springboard for the new era, namely the mariner's compass, gunpowder and printing, all had Chinese antecedents, though printing may have been independently invented in Europe, especially in the form of movable metal types locked in a printing press. Modern runaway inflation is often literally seen as being due to resorting to the printing press, with, for example, all the German banknote presses of 1923 pressed into 24-hour service to provide the flood of notes in which the Weimar Republic was eventually drowned. It is one of the gentler ironies of history that German banking, minting and printing had very much closer causal contemporary connections than are generally supposed. Indeed the development of money as we know it would have been impossible without the printing press, while from the earliest days of printing, governments have fallen to the easy temptations of the press. China led the way in this as in so many others. Although China had produced block-printed books before AD 800, the modern press was invented by Johann Gutenberg in Mainz in about 1440, where he produced the world's first movable-type printed book in 1456. To finance his experiments he had borrowed 1,600 guilders from Johann Fust, a local banker, between 1450 and 1452. Inventors are not usually much good at running their affairs profitably. Gutenberg was no exception, while Fust, in contrast, was particularly hard-headed and hard-hearted. So aggressively impatient did Fust become, not only to see a positive return on his promising investment but also to seize the lion's share of any profits, that in 1455 he sued Gutenberg for repayment of capital and interest amounting to 2,026 guilders. When judgement was given in Fust's favour he foreclosed on his loan and installed his future son-in-law, Peter Schoeffer, to run the business instead of Gutenberg. Thus it came about that the world's first printed book to contain the date and place of publication, 14 August 1457 at Mainz, and the first to use more than one colour, the Great Psalter of 1457, was published by Fust the banker and his junior partner, Schoeffer. Thereafter the business never looked back, for if ever there was an invention whose time had come, this was it. By the year 1500 there were presses of the Gutenberg type in more than sixty German towns and in every major country of Europe except Russia. During the course of the fifteenth century more than 1,700 of the new printing presses were in operation and, including over 100 books of English literature printed by William Caxton in Westminster, between fifteen and twenty *million* copies of books had been printed.

An explanation of the rapidity of the spread of the new printing presses is to be found not only in the obviously huge pent-up demand, hungry for books of all kinds, but also in the fact, less obvious, but equally important economically, that the supply of the new presses was easily made available because traditional olive oil and wine presses had long been familiar in the very regions – southern Germany, northern Italy and much of France – closely surrounding the birthplace of the new invention. The outer framework and much of the basic structure of the printing press could thus readily be adapted from existing designs for oil and wine presses. Thus the huge potential demand was quickly and effectively answered with an elastic supply. For the same reasons competition among rival suppliers caused Europe to have a network of this vastly improved new 'internal' means of communication to complement the external geographical discoveries.

In due course the printing press designs became modified so as to lead to a significant improvement in the minting of coinage, a process in which, as mentioned briefly already, Leonardo da Vinci (1452–1519), that most brilliant all-rounder of the Renaissance, was himself actively involved. He was known to be a friend of Luca Pacioli, a mathematician and accountant, with whom he shared an interest in the new printing machines. Leonardo's mechanical drawings, held by many to demonstrate his original genius at its best, include detailed working designs for mechanical minting in the form of a press to produce both faster and more uniform coins. Faster production methods were urgently needed to cope with coining a high proportion of the increased output of the precious metals, already becoming available from new mines close at hand in the Tyrol and, later, by the flood of imports as a result of the geographical discoveries of the treasures of the New World. Leonardo's achievements in supporting improvements both in printing and in minting are, belatedly, given full recognition by A. P. Usher in his *History of Mechanical Inventions* (1962, 212–39). Sir John Craig (1953, 117) in contrast dismisses Leonardo in a line and a half.

Usher reproduces the working sketches and the detailed notes of Leonardo's printing press, and goes on to show how 'the utilisation of machinery to attain precision is further and perhaps more notably illustrated by Leonardo's projects for the improvement of the process of coinage'. He made provision for a water-driven mill driving seven hammers from a single shaft, a widely adopted innovation, so that the new money came to be called milled money.

> Although the introduction of the modern technique of coinage was long attributed to the goldsmiths and coiners of Augsburg and Nuremberg, it is now held that the beginnings of the new processes are to be found in Italy. We know that Leonardo was occupied at the Papal mint, though there is no record of any coins being struck under his supervision . . . His work was that of the forerunner – the work of conception. (Usher 1962)

In Europe, however, the knowledge that printing money could be a direct substitute for coining it took nearly two centuries to discover, and it was a further century before the abuse of the printing press was to lead to an inflationary flood of banknotes. It is appropriately to China, where paper, printing and the banknote were first invented, that we must turn for the world's first demonstration of banknote inflation. As a result the Chinese people lost all faith in paper money and became more than ever convinced of the virtues of silver, a conviction which lasted right up to the early part of the twentieth century. Because Europe in the fifteenth and sixteenth centuries had no real experience of banknotes, such an inflationary medium was not then possible. Instead its rulers debased the only acceptable and trusted form of money, namely coinage. Only when people have built up faith and confidence in a monetary medium is it possible for the authorities to take advantage of that faith. In China, paper money had enjoyed a long and trusted history before that trust was – or could be – destroyed. In

Europe a shortage of bullion led first to a new wave of metallic debasement, which in turn eventually led the monetary authorities back to the issuing of full-bodied, intrinsically sound coinage. It is, however, a further irony of monetary history that, not long after China finally abandoned its paper currency, European banks began increasingly to issue paper money notes about which they had first learned from the writings of travellers like Marco Polo, now suddenly widely becoming available in printed versions. Thus printing enabled Europeans to enjoy a renaissance not only of ancient classical civilizations but also of certain aspects of modern Chinese civilization, though without heeding the Chinese example of the dangers of paper-based hyper-inflation.

The rise and fall of the world's first paper money

Whereas in our account of the origins of proper coinage we had to cast doubt on Chinese claims to precedence, there is no gainsaying the facts of Chinese leadership in the systematic issue of banknotes and paper money. A short-lived issue of Chinese leather-money, consisting of pieces of white deerskin of about one foot square, with coloured borders, each representing a high value of 40,000 cash, dates from as early as 118 BC. There ensues a very considerable gap of 900 years before we hear of the next significant reference, this time to paper banknotes of a more modern type, in the reign of Hien Tsung (806–21). It appears that a severe shortage of copper for coinage caused the emperor to invent this new form of money as a temporary substitute for the more traditional kind. Another experimental state issue appeared around 910 and more regularly from about 960 onwards. By about 1020 the total issue of notes had become so excessive, amounting in total to a nominal equivalent of 2,830,000 ounces of silver, that vast amounts of cash were exported, partly as a form of 'Danegeld' to buy off potential invaders from the north, and partly to maintain China's very considerable customary imports, leading to a cash famine within China. The authorities attempted to replace the drain of cash by even greater increases in note issues, thus giving further sharp twists to the inflationary spiral. 'A perfumed mixture of silk and paper was even resorted to, to give the money wider appeal, but to no avail; inflation and depreciation followed to an extent rivalling conditions in Germany and Russia after the First World War' (Goodrich 1957, 152).

From time to time private note-issuing houses flourished, increasing the inflationary pressures and helping to devalue the official issues. By 1032 there were some sixteen such private houses, but the bankruptcy of some of these led the authorities to proscribe them all and replace the private notes with an increase in the official issue, with note-issuing branches in each province. As the old issues became almost worthless, so they were replaced with new issues until the total outstanding issues of these too became excessive. Thus, for instance, though a reformed new paper note was issued by Emperor Kao Tsung in 1160, by 1166 the total official issues had swollen to the enormous nominal value of 43,600,000 ounces of silver. 'There were local notes besides, so that the empire was flooded with paper, rapidly depreciating in value' (Yule 1967, 149). A series of inflations thus became interspersed with reformed and drastically reduced issues of paper, with the reforms effective only so long as the note issues were strictly limited.

With the rise of the Mongol empire, China became part of a vast dominion extending from Korea to the Danube. 'To standardize the currency throughout Asia, the Mongols adopted the paper money of China', and so repeated its financial history on an even grander scale (Goodrich 1957, 174). The Mongols' first note issues, of moderate size only, date from 1236; but by the time of the first issues of Kublai Khan in 1260 the note circulation had again become substantial. It was Kublai's note issues which were eventually brought to the attention of the western world by Marco Polo, who lived in China from 1275 to 1292. His tales of paper money were at first met with disbelief. However, in view of its subsequent importance, a brief reference to his account is relevant here. In Chapter XVIII of his famous *Travels*, entitled 'Of the Kind of Paper Money issued by the Grand Khan and Made to Pass Current throughout his Dominions', Marco Polo gives the following description.

In this city of Kanbalu is the mint of the grand khan, who may truly be said to possess the secret of the alchemists, as he has the art of producing paper money . . . When ready for use, he has it cut into pieces of money of different sizes . . . The coinage of this paper money is authenticated with as much form and ceremony as if it were actually of pure gold or silver . . . and the act of counterfeiting it is punished as a capital offence. When thus coined in large quantities, this paper currency is circulated in every part of the grand Khan's dominions; nor dares any person, at the peril of his life, refuse to accept it in payment. All his subjects receive it without hesitation, because, wherever their business may call them, they can dispose of it again in the purchase of merchandise they may have occasion for; such as pearls, jewels, gold or silver. With it, in short, every article may be procured. When any persons happen to be possessed of paper money which from long use has become damaged, they carry it to the mint, where, upon the payment of only three per cent, they may receive fresh notes in exchange. Should any be desirous of procuring gold or silver for the purposes of manufacture, such as drinking cups, girdles or other articles wrought of these metals, they in like manner apply at the mint, and for their paper obtain the bullion they require. All his majesty's armies are paid with this currency, which is to them of the same value as if it were gold or silver. Upon these grounds, it may certainly be affirmed that the grand khan has a more extensive command of treasure than any other sovereign in the universe. (Dent 1908, 202–5)

Even the Mongols failed, however, to spread the note-accepting habit to the citizens of the satellite states around the perimeter of their power, although short-lived imitative systems were developed in parts of India and Japan between 1319 and 1331. By far the most celebrated experiment, which brought knowledge of the Chinese system much closer to the West, was that in the kingdom of Persia in 1294. The depletion of the Persian king's treasury, as a result of the decimation of Kazakh's herds of sheep and cattle following an unusually severe winter, caused him to attempt to replenish his revenues by issuing 'chao' or paper money as in China. 'On 13th August 1294 a proclamation imposed the death penalty on all who refused to accept the new currency. Considerable quantities of Ch'ao were then prepared and put into circulation on 12th September' (J. A. Boyle 1968, V, 375). However the experiment, which lasted barely two months and was confined to the city of Tabriz, turned out to be a complete disaster, with the bazaars deserted and trade at a standstill. According to Professor Boyle, perhaps the most noteworthy aspect of this short-lived experiment is that it was the first recorded instance of block printing outside China. It is likely that the West first 'learned about printing from the commonly used paper money that was printed not only in Peking but also in Tabriz' (Goodrich 1957, 179). The first clear description of printing available to western scholars appears in a 'History of the World' written by Rashid al Din, a physician and prime minister of Persia around this period. His work, which became well known in European libraries also 'contains much information on China, especially on the use of paper-money' (Needham 1970, 17).

Rashid al Din's accounts were contemporary with, and so reinforced, those of Marco Polo. Together they helped to shorten the learning curve by which the West belatedly availed itself of Chinese experience. Thus the world's first hyper-inflation, based on paper banknotes, took place nearly 1,000 years ago, while the first Chinese books on coinage and numismatics and on the dangers of paper money, preceded those in the West by some 400–500 years. In 1149 Hung Tsun published the *Chhuan Chih* or a *Treatise on Coinage*, 'the first independent work on numismatics in any language . . . For European numismatics we have to await the late sixteenth century' (Needham 1971, II, 394). According to Sir Henry Yule's 'Collection of Medieval Notices on China', 'the remarks of Ma Twan-lin, a medieval Chinese historian are curiously like a bit of modern controversy,' which he demonstrates by quoting Twan-lin: 'Paper should never be *money* (but) only employed as a representative sign of value existing in metals or produce . . . At first this was the mode in which paper currency was actually used among merchants. The government, borrowing the invention from private individuals, wished to make a real money of paper, and thus the original contrivance was perverted' (Yule 1967, 150). In this way China experienced well over 500 years of paper currencies, from early in the ninth until the middle of the fifteenth century. By 1448 the Ming note, nominally worth 1,000 cash, was in real market terms worth only three, while after 1455 there appears to be no more mention of the existence of paper money circulating in China (Yang 1952). This was still some years before the concept was to enjoy a successful renaissance in the West, and nearly three centuries before printed banknotes became at all common. The West was eagerly ready for printing, where the small number of different type characters required for alphabets of only around two dozen letters provided an enormous advantage in ease of mechanization compared with the many hundreds required for Chinese characters. But the West was not yet ready for printed banknotes. Instead the printing machine was modified, as we have seen, for minting coins. Thus the minting press and the printing press shared a common parentage, occurring about the same time, developed in their earlier stages by the same inventors, sponsored by the same merchants and princes, and together playing a significant part in helping to bring about a common revolution in finance, trade and communications.

Bullion's dearth and plenty

It is the important conclusion of Dr Challis, in his expert study of Tudor coinage, and confirmed by the complementary work of Professor Gould, that 'In respect of the coinage, as in so many other fields, England was integral with Europe', so that she shared in the general shortage of bullion in the first half of the sixteenth century, even to the extent of adopting the sinful continental habit of debasement, and similarly experienced the mixed blessings of the influx of bullion from the New World during the second half of the century (Challis 1978, 300). Since Britain's economic and financial development was thus so closely connected with those wider economic and political forces influencing Europe and beyond, we shall first look at those aspects influencing the flows of bullion into western Europe before examining their impact on the financial history of the Tudors and early Stuarts.

The preoccupation of Europeans with the precious metals was long criticized by nineteenth- and early twentieth-century writers as a glaring example of the obvious follies of mercantilist doctrine. In truth, however, there was a very considerable degree of justification for the emphasis upon gold and silver in the sixteenth and seventeenth centuries, and for according bullion a very high priority as an incentive in the search for new avenues of trade. Quite apart from the importance of bullion as 'the sinews of war' (a feature to be examined more fully later), there were a number of excellent reasons for seeking gold and silver, the old, tried and tested commodities, in preference to many of the more exotic commodities that they were discovering, but which had a far more limited, experimental and riskier market than did the precious metals. Second among these advantages was their high value-to-weight ratios, all the more important given the vast distances now being regularly travelled for the first time in history. Although some of the new commodities, especially the spices required to make the salted meat of Europe palatable, also had, from time to time, exceptionally high value-to-weight ratios, these occasions were sporadic, hardly ever general or universal. In particular, spices could not long command high scarcity prices, except initially in Europe; and even here the natural scarcities, intensified by artificial 'corners', were in due course interspersed by long unprofitable periods of 'glut'. In other words there was a *limited* market in spices compared with an almost unlimited market for the precious metals. A few bags of pepper unloaded in Amsterdam or London could quickly depress its price far more than many tons of silver could depress the price of silver.

The exotic products of the East typically enjoyed a limited, inelastic demand in Europe, coupled with a long-term elasticity of supply in and from the new lands. Three examples of the resultant volatility of prices (highlighting the steadier high values of the precious metals) must suffice. As early as 1496 the importation of the new Madeira sugar caused a serious slump of sugar prices in Spain. It was one of the innumerable 'corners' in pepper, organized by the Dutch in 1599, which was the immediate cause of the founding of the London East India Company. So low did the price of nutmeg slump in Amsterdam in 1760 that in an effort to raise prices, a huge quantity of mace and nutmegs were burned (Masefield 1967, IV, 287–8). On a few exceptional occasions pepper was indeed preferred to the precious metals, being not only more than worth its weight in gold but used also on occasions as a unit of account. However these were precisely those occasions when normal gold and silver money was so scarce that resort had to be made to barter, to wages being paid in kind 'and to ersatz currencies like pepper on the busiest markets' of northern Italy (Day 1978, 4). Such crisis conditions quickly disappeared as soon as adequate supplies of the precious metals became available later. Thus in contrast to the extreme volatility of the market for spices, gold and silver were almost universally acceptable at high, though not inflexible, value-to-weight ratios, even when they became very much more plentiful as a result of the discoveries of new mines and new methods of mining.

The precious metals, especially gold, acted not only as a major incentive to the princes and merchants who sponsored or organized the voyages of discovery, but also and much more directly to the ships' crews, from their captains down to their humblest seamen. Thus Pierre Vilar, in his *History of Gold and Money* states that Columbus's diary of his first voyage makes mention of gold at least sixty-five times, while a prize of 10,000 *maravedis* promised by King Ferdinand and Queen Isabella to the expedition's first seaman to sight land in the New World – who turned out to be Rodrigo de Triana – was selfishly claimed by Columbus himself (Vilar 1976, 63). More normally, however, so interdependent for their very lives were all members of the crews of the small ships of that time, that, despite the iron discipline of the captains, some not inconsiderable share of the spoils could be expected by each member. It should not be forgotten, as Professor Kenneth Andrews graphically reminds us, that piracy was elevated to a preferred branch of policy by Britain, France and Holland as a means of obtaining a share of the riches of the New World claimed exclusively by Spain and Portugal. There were thirteen known English expeditions, supplemented by an unknown number of other piratical missions, to the Caribbean in the eight years 1570–7. From many of these all those crew members lucky enough to survive returned with small fortunes, such as Drake's expedition of 1573 (K. R. Andrews 1984, 119–31). Thus, quite apart from smuggling, the actual flows of specie exceeded probably to a substantial if unknown degree the total of the statistics compiled from more official sources, which naturally could not take adequate cognizance of piracy, plunder and illicit trading.

The precious metals were also avidly and steadily demanded in the East which, in demonstrating for the next three centuries that it was 'the sink of the precious metals', kept their values higher in the West than they would otherwise have been. One of the main reasons for this was, of course, the fact that many of the products which the Europeans produced were not keenly demanded in China or India, whereas their exotic products, on the contrary, enjoyed a keen and growing demand in the West. The lure of the precious metals therefore remained untarnished in the eyes of European merchants, all the more so since they provided an almost unfailing means of securing the luxuries of the East in exchange. England's famed wool and woollen cloth exports, keenly demanded all over Europe, were naturally scorned in the warmer countries of the East. The gap in the balance of payments could most conveniently be filled by the precious metals, especially silver, which generally enjoyed a higher ratio to gold than it did in the West. In this way total world trade was lifted to a far higher pitch than would otherwise have been possible, precisely because of this almost universal but varying preference for gold and silver. Consequently, fluctuations in the flow of specie relative to changing demands had a most pervasive and long-lasting effect on general economic development, as well as on money and prices both in the East and in Europe.

The 'Great Bullion Famine' of the fourteenth and fifteenth centuries was all the more keenly felt because of the still rather elementary state of European banking even in the most advanced centres of northern Italy and southern Germany. Over most of Europe trade depended fundamentally on adequate supplies of ingots and coinage, so much so that economic progress was held back by a persistent tendency for supplies to lag behind demand. 'Europe's indispensable but inadequate stock of bullion and coin, besides being subject to irretrievable loss in the process of coinage and recoinage and through "fair wear and tear", fire, shipwreck and forgotten hoards, was constantly being eroded by the large-scale export of gold and silver in all forms to the Levant' (Day 1978, 5). As already indicated, the return of barter, the introduction of fiat moneys of account and also the general decline in prices were all expressive results of the long-term bullion famine.

Portuguese probing along the African coast from the 1450s onward provided a new route for sub-Saharan gold channelled principally via Ghana and Mali. The increased supplies of gold then gradually raised the relative value of silver in Europe and increased the viability of European silver mines. This process, once begun, was intensified by the new supplies of gold reaching Europe from the West Indies during what has been called the Caribbean 'gold cycle' of 1494–1525. Briefly this consisted of first depriving the native Indians of their gold possessions; they did not use gold for money but mainly just for ornament. Then the natives were forced to work long hours in arduous conditions to pan for alluvial gold. Within a generation or less, disease and overwork practically wiped out the original Indian population of the initial gold-producing regions, and the first gold cycle was completed (Vilar 1976, 66–7). 'Out of all this emerged the profits of merchant financiers such as the Fuggers and Welsers of Augsburg' (Spooner 1968, 24).

Thus silver mining, minting and banking grew together in a notable example of profitable vertical integration. By the middle of the sixteenth century, however, a veritable flood of silver from Potosi brought about a sharp decline in the mine-owners' monopolistic mining profits, although by then they were successfully diversifying still further into a wide range of financial and industrial activities. Most of the German mines were closed down, leading to a wide dispersion of many of their skilled workers to such up-and-coming places as Almaden in Spain, Keswick in Britain and Potosi in 'Peru'. These were among the first of what were to be the much more powerful and widespread effects of the lure of the gold and silver of the New World on production, employment, migration and prices during the mid-sixteenth to the mid-seventeenth centuries.

Potosi and the silver flood

In the first half of the sixteenth century up to about 1560 the relative increase in gold exceeded that of silver; in the second half that situation was dramatically reversed, again with far-reaching effects on world trade and money. Until 1560 gold imports to Spain represented more than half the value (but less than one-twentieth the weight) of silver. Before concentrating our attention on the vast increase in silver from Mexico, Venezuela and 'Peru' (then a vast area which included Potosi, now in Bolivia) it is useful to recall the main features in the exploitation and exportation of gold from the New World. After the Caribbean sources had been exhausted, the next substantial amounts of gold came into Spanish-held territories on the mainland, with the period from about 1500 to 1530 being dubbed by Vilar as almost exclusively the age of gold, with silver production in those areas then being negligible. When from 1530 to 1560 silver production began to rise again its value was eclipsed by the sudden and huge increase in gold supplies following Pizarro's conquest of the Incas during his famous expeditions of 1531–41. Hamilton has calculated that, according to detailed records of gold production kept by the 'House of Commerce' in Seville, something between 1,000 and 1,500 kg of gold came into Spain from the New World each year on average between the years 1500 and 1540 (E. J. Hamilton 1934, 42). This was soon to be swamped by an upsurge of silver output from Mexico and Peru amounting to something around 300 tons per annum in the best years.

The Potosi deposits were discovered in 1545 in a 'silver mountain' of six miles around its base on a remote and desolate plateau, 12,000 feet above sea level. From being virtually uninhabited, for it was a most forbidding location, the population, entirely of immigrants, rose rapidly to 45,000 by 1555, and to a peak of 160,000 in 1610. The full exploitation of its resources depended on two factors: first the organization of a system of forced labour, and secondly the application of the newly discovered mercury process to enable cheaper, faster and fuller extraction of silver from its ores. The mines were so remote that, even more than in most mining areas, prices of everyday products were prohibitively expensive. Thus, despite the nominally high wages paid, insufficient free labour was attracted to enable full exploitation. Consequently the voluntary labour was supplemented by a conscript labour force, the 'mita' system, whereby all Indian villages within a certain radius of the mines were allocated a quota of their population to be sent to the mines. The mercury amalgam process of silver extraction was introduced first to the Mexican silver mines of Guanajuato and Zacatecas, with the mercury imported all the way from Almaden in Spain. However, in 1563 very productive mercury deposits were discovered at Huancavelica, situated between Potosi and the port of Lima, capital of Peru. Although it still took some two months for the trains of llamas to reach Potosi, this was still a far easier and more reliable journey than the long route from Almaden. Huancavelica supplied between a half and two-thirds of all the mercury used in the Americas, in the 100 years following its discovery, the other one-third or so still coming from Almaden. Without this mercury, the life of the American silver mines would have become very limited, not only because of the high costs of importing mercury from Spain but also because it would not have been worthwhile making use of the vast quantities of low-percentage silver ores once the richer seams, naturally chosen first wherever possible, had become exhausted.

The outpouring of silver to Europe produced a flood of pamphlets, articles and books in attempts to analyse its results, particularly with regard to responsibility for the long-term inflation in Europe in the sixteenth and first half of the seventeenth centuries. Most accounts concern themselves rather too exclusively with the influence of the precious metals on European economies, and tend to underestimate or ignore their effects on the economic fate of the Far East, except to the extent that the precious metals were re-exported from Europe. However, quite apart from the indirect drain to the Far East to compensate for Europe's chronic balance of payment deficits, the New World also exported its silver directly to the East in specially authorized ships for many decades. This direct export at its peak exceeded the indirect leakages which have captured the academic headlines.

Dr Atwell of the London School of Oriental Studies has amply demonstrated that the import of New World silver into China 'played an important part in the pace of China's economic development . . . but ultimately proved to be a mixed blessing and did much to undermine the economic and political stability of the Ming Empire (1368–1644) during the last few decades of that dynasty's existence' (Atwell 1982, 68). There were several routes by which Peruvian and Mexican silver reached the Far East, of which the most important were the direct sailings from Acapulco to Manila and thence to China. In the peak year of 1597 some 345,000 kg of silver were shipped by this route. In addition, silver in considerable amounts arrived in China via Buenos Aires, Lisbon, Seville, Amsterdam, London and from Goa and other colonial possessions in India, some legally, other shipments illegally. Dr Atwell indicates that silver from Chinese domestic mines during much of the fifteenth and sixteenth centuries had declined so much that the annual total was exceeded by the silver carried in just one Spanish galleon from Acapulco to Manila. With a population of 100,000,000 the world's most advanced economy had become dangerously dependent for its basic monetary supplies on New World silver. For as long as this source remained plentiful, Chinese commercial activity prospered, but eventually 'the sharp decline in bullion imports (from about 1640) had disastrous consequences for the late Ming economy. Without sufficient supplies of silver, many people in China were unable to pay their taxes, or rents, repay loans, or in some cases even to buy food' (Atwell 1982, 89).

Compared with its effects on China, at first stimulating and then debilitating, western Europe, with the exception of Spain (which changed its view of the New World specie from being God's bounteous blessing to becoming the curse of the devil) escaped lightly. On balance it probably gained considerably, despite the excessive emphasis conventionally placed on the role of the new specie in the price 'revolution' of 1540 to 1640, to be examined shortly. However, before looking at the causes and consequences of this overblown inflation in which England, like the rest of Europe, was closely involved, we shall see how the Tudors and early Stuarts coped with their own closely related fiscal and monetary problems at home.

Henry VII: fiscal strength and sound money, 1485–1509

Henry VII's first task was to reunite the country's previously warring factions so that internal peace and prosperity could again flourish after an absence of almost a century. Throughout his reign he showed himself to be a dedicated master of administration, keeping above all an especially firm grip on the purse strings. He extracted every penny of his legal dues, employing Morton with his infamous 'fork' and the notoriously keen Dudley and Empson for this purpose. His control of spending helped to swing the money pendulum towards higher quality. He modified the usual royal administrative and judicial machinery under the frightening authority of the Star Chamber, thus combining personal control with carefully delegated powers. In the days when the fortunes of royalty and those of government administration were still far from being clearly distinguishable but were properly considered to overlap to a considerable degree, the wealth of the monarch, and especially whether it happened to be rising or falling, was highly relevant to fiscal, financial and, indeed, to constitutional history in general. Parliament voted Henry his customary dues for life: Henry insisted with unusual efficiency that these came his way. To Henry sound money was essential to sound government, and 'no previous English King had ever realised so fully that money was power' (Pugh 1972, 116).

It was not that the mint in normal circumstances contributed anything more than a marginal amount to the king's finances. As Dr Challis has pointed out, Henry's average annual net return from operating his mints came to only between £100 and £200, a trifle when ordinary revenue was around £113,000 (1978, 248). Nevertheless Henry's same characteristics of ruthless penny-pinching efficiency were soon applied to his dealings with his mints, which were ripe for a shake-up. Henry's achievements in raising the general quality of the coinage to a very high standard are all the more remarkable, given the state of the coinage he had taken over from the defeated Richard III. Though not officially debased, the currency had suffered more than its usual share of wear and tear, clipping and counterfeiting, sweating and selective culling during the long period of the Wars of the Roses (1455–85). Good domestic currency was extremely rare, and much use had to be made, illegally, of imported European and Irish coinage, almost all also grossly underweight. Even the official scales sold by the mint for checking permissible coinage weights were found to be incorrect. Slackness and malpractices at the various mints were far too common. An example was made of one such unfortunate mint coiner who was hanged at Tyburn in 1505.

Before dealing with the important matters of the ways in which Henry improved the currency we may dwell for a moment on an early if unimportant lapse on his part, namely the issue of 'dandyprats', in order to indicate how even as sterling a character as Henry could, at a time when he was particularly hard-pressed, temporarily yield to the temptation of using the mints for a quick if small profit. Dwarf, substandard coins, deprecatingly dubbed 'dandyprats', nominally worth a penny, but soon circulating at only a halfpenny, were issued by Henry to help finance the siege of Boulogne in 1492. This short-lived misdemeanour was soon, however, corrected. Perhaps the two greatest numismatic events for which Henry is justly remembered are the first issues of coins exactly corresponding to the two age-old units of account, the pound and the shilling. Henceforth these abstract accounting units were to have their concrete counterparts in actual media of exchange, eventually considerably simplifying retail trading, while also supplying a heavy gold coin for larger, wholesale transactions. The quality of both these new coins was of the highest, the designs being made by Alexander of Bruchsal, who was brought over from Germany, and quickly came to merit to the full his description as 'the father of English coin portraiture'. Sir John Craig has made the bold claim that 'modern coinage begins with the shilling of Henry VII', while Sir Charles Oman similarly heaps superlative praise on the sovereign as 'the best piece ever produced from the English mint' (see Craig 1953, 100).

The shilling, also called the 'testoon', carried by far the best profile portrait of the monarch produced up till then on any English coin. Similar improvements were made in other silver coins, e.g. the groat, half-groat and penny, and in the gold ryal (10s.) and angel (6s. 8d.). Numismatically, therefore, there is no doubt that the quality of English coinage had been raised by Henry to an enviable excellence which stood in brilliant contrast both with what had passed for currency previously and still more when compared a generation later with the monstrous debasements carried out by his son. Chronologically the sovereign came first, being issued significantly in 1489, not only in order to imitate the heavy gold units then being issued on the Continent, but also to impress Europe with the power, prestige and success of the new Tudor dynasty (Challis 1978, 49). The shilling or testoon was not issued until 1504, but despite its excellence as a coin, was issued in such small amounts as to have little immediate economic significance. This contrast between the numismatic and economic importance of the coinage – where quantity and not just quality is the main concern of the latter – is also seen, though to a lesser degree, with regard to the sovereign. A marked encouragement to bring bullion to the mint so as to remedy the shortage of good coin was made when in 1489 the seigniorage and coinage charges were substantially reduced, from 7s. 6d. to 2s. 6d. per lb for gold and from 1s. 6d. to 1s. for silver. Although there were other factors influencing the result, there would appear to be little doubt that this reduction in mint charges was at least partially responsible for the average annual output of the mints doubling in the four years after 1494 compared with the similar period before 1489, with the silver output up from £5,334 to £9,116 (+71 per cent) and gold up from £8,207 to £18,425 (+125 per cent).

It took about seven years for the reduction of the mint price and the drive to supply new coins to satisfy the demand and so to enable the series of royal proclamations against the circulation of severely worn or clipped domestic coin and against foreign coin to become reasonably effective. By the end of the first decade of the sixteenth century it had become obvious that the general quality of England's coinage had been transformed. Royal proclamations were of course not infallible. It had taken several years to move the considerable influx of substandard Irish pennies and the even greater amounts of 'Roman' groats and half-groats issued by the Holy Roman Emperor, despite the continued administrative attempts to remove the former, and to prohibit the latter by the specific 'Proclamation Against Roman Coins' of 1498.

Though, compared with many of his other achievements, Henry VII's currency reforms may appear of secondary importance, this view would decry the quiet, undramatic but persistent benefits that good money brought to a country where commercial activities were not only obviously of central importance, but were at the beginning of a period of sustained growth. Henry had supplied a basic ingredient for growth, for when he died 'there was not a single coin in issue (which is of course not the same as in circulation) which he had not either introduced or modified, a point which tends to confirm the old-fashioned view that in England the Middle Ages ended when he came to the throne' (Porteous 1969, 151).

Henry VII's reformed currencies were maintained with few significant changes well into the reign of his son. For sixteen years, apart from changing the VII into an VIII, the father's fine portrait was retained on all issues of the large silver coins, constituting a most incongruous and misleading example of 'like father, like son'. However, in contrast to Henry VII's prudent economy and his ability to contain his expenditures well within his receipts, Henry VIII in his later years felt himself quite unable to cope without raiding the monasteries and picking the pockets of the people. These interconnected events, together with the religious reformation of which they were part, dominated the economic and financial history of the mid-fifteenth century. The contrast between the monetary successes of Henry VII and the adulterations of Henry VIII have been neatly summarized by Sir Charles Oman as a move from 'the finest, the best executed and the most handsome coinage in Europe' to 'the most disreputable looking money that had been seen since the days of Stephen – the gold heavily alloyed, the so-called silver ill-struck and turning black or brown as the base metal came to the surface' (1931, 244). We turn now to account for these glaringly contrasting financial experiences.

The dissolution of the monasteries

With the disadvantages of hindsight – which not infrequently enables historians to jump quickly to the wrong conclusions – it would at first seem credible to suppose that the profits, whether from the dissolution of the monasteries or from debasement if properly extracted, would have sufficed for the financial objectives which Henry VIII had in mind. However, that monarch would have been unimpressed when offered the kind of choice between alternatives beloved of economists, and in reply to the question 'which' would by inclination invariably answer 'both'. In fact there was no straight choice between one or the other: there was no master-plan either for all-out confiscation of the wealth of the Church nor a once-and-for-all general debasement of the coinage. Both were tackled a bit at a time, each supplementing the piecemeal proceeds available from the other, until ultimately both sources were pressed for all they could yield.

Although apparent precedents for both dissolution and debasement had occurred on a number of previous occasions in Britain, those of Henry VIII stand out as unique by virtue of their scale and rapidity, compared with which the previous examples were minor, gradual affairs. Furthermore, whereas the two policies had previously been unconnected, they were now to become contemporaneous and complementary events, the one, debasement being reversible, the other, dissolution, turning out to be irreversible. Though overlapping in time and largely in objective, they are, for ease of exposition, better dealt with separately.

The motives which prompted Henry VIII to take over possession of the monasteries were – including of course the religious – social, educational, financial and political. There can be no doubt, however, that by far the most important single cause was the king's desperate need for money to finance the defence of the realm. Henry VIII is justly renowned as 'the father of the Navy'. It was a costly business to equip the new ships and to build up the coastal fortifications in preparation for the inevitable conflicts such as the wars with Scotland in 1542 and France in 1543. It was defence and other similar costs which were specifically claimed in the various preambles to the Acts and Orders of the Suppression of the monasteries, shrines and priories as justification for the king's actions, as well as the unsurprising denunciations of the immorality and laxity of the monks. A recent authority on the history of the dissolution, Professor Woodward, has left us in no doubt as to the main reason for this series of confiscatory events. 'Finance is indeed the key to the proper understanding of the dissolution . . . the primacy of the financial consideration in governmental thinking . . . is to be seen in the title of the department established to supervise the dissolution, the 'Court of the Augmentation of the Revenues of the King's Crown' (1966, 4). Woodward has estimated that the total number of religious houses in 1530 in England and Wales was about 825, made up of 502 monasteries, 136 nunneries and 187 friaries. Their wealth came largely from being very extensive landlords, and it was mainly from their agricultural estates that they derived a gross annual income of up to £200,000. Official estimates in 1535 gave their net annual income as £136,000, but Woodward considers this to be a considerable underestimate, and puts the true net figure as 'nearer to £175,000, or nearly three-quarters as much again as the average annual income of the Crown' (1966, 122). This potential of nearly trebling the average ordinary revenues of the Crown was, however, never fully achieved for a number of reasons, the chief one being that the king's desperation for money meant that he was forced hurriedly to sell off much of the capital and so sacrifice what could have been an enormous annual increment to his income.

Henry's first attempt to increase the amount of revenue was not aimed at the monasteries alone but was a general imposition on the Church as a whole. Thus was the First Fruits and Tenths Act of 1534. This Act was almost immediately followed in the same year by the Act for the Suppression of the Lesser Monasteries, namely those with an annual income of less than £200. This comprised some two-thirds of the total of 502 monasteries, though only about one-third of those eligible for suppression were in fact dissolved under that Act. As soon as the bulk of the immediately realizable resources of this first suppression were used up, and with the pressures of expenditures still riding high, Henry authorized an extension of his policy of dissolution by suppressing the friaries in 1538 and the larger monasteries, mostly in 1539, though a few had already been 'voluntarily' persuaded to surrender their rights to the Crown in 1538. By 1540 the dissolution of all religious orders had been completed. The relatively few ecclesiastical guilds which remained were disendowed as the final part of the same policy by Edward VI in 1547.

The pressing need for money meant that the king began selling off parts of his monastic property almost as soon as it came into his hands, sacrificing future income for present gain. The most liquid of assets, namely all the gold and silver candlesticks, crosses, plate, together with jewels and so on, were speedily transferred to London, much of it to be coined or sold for cash, except for the best ornamental pieces, which were retained for the royal palaces. Excluding these latter pieces, the gold and silver sent to London were valued at £75,000. Although not all the monasteries were physically destroyed many of them were stripped of everything of value, including especially their bells and the lead from their roofs and gutters, the bells being melted and recast as cannon, while much of the lead was exported. Records of the values of proceeds sent to London are fairly complete, and these are usually the figures quoted in later texts; but where local sales took place no reliable consolidated figures of the total value of such sales appear to exist, but these are believed to have added quite substantially to the Crown's liquid resources. The most important fixed capital assets were of course the vast landed estates, sales of which began immediately and were carried on at a fairly steady pace, and at a steady price, in real terms, equivalent to twenty years' yield, directly for over a decade, and indirectly through a chain of agents, London merchants, and at least a number of specifically confirmed speculators for many decades subsequently. Most of the land went to purchasers who were already substantial landowners, although opportunities also existed for the newly rising gentry to acquire smaller and medium-sized estates.

Although most of the liquid spoils from dissolution had been sold within a decade, the Crown still retained considerable estates itself and decided, probably on Thomas Cromwell's advice, to dispose of much of the land by lease for limited periods, so that these lots reverted to the Crown at the end of their lease. The royal estates were also considerably increased by confiscations and escheats. Consequently, sixty years after the dissolution the Crown still owned substantial amounts of what were previously monastic lands, so that although the Court of Augmentations came to an end in 1554, the Augmentations office of the Exchequer continued to administer its 'monastic' lands. As Tawney has shown in his controversial but stimulating essay on 'The Rise of the Gentry', 'between 1558 and 1635 Crown lands to the value of £2,240,000 had been thrown on the market', including £817,000 sold by Elizabeth, £775,000 by James and £650,000 during the first decade of Charles I's reign. Additionally Charles made sales approaching a further £2,000,000 during the Civil War (1642–9). Tawney also confirms the views of previous experts on Tudor finance, views in turn reflected by more recent research, that 'few rulers have acted more remorselessly than the early Tudors on the maxim that the foundations of political authority are economic' and consequently 'had made the augmentation of the royal demesne one of the key-stones of their policy' (Tawney, 1954, 194–5).

Recent historians of the dissolution (such as Professors Woodward and Youings) have tended to play down the claims of the traditionalists that the dissolution was 'one of the most important events in the Tudor period or, indeed, in the whole of England's history', and have stressed other factors which, together with the dissolution, also played their part, e.g. the rise of the gentry, the increased secularization and commercialism of the Tudor Age, the confirmation of the Protestant Reformation, the increase in enclosures and in the market for land, and so on (Woodward 1966, 163). While such research thus moderates the extreme views of the traditionalists, it tends to confirm the economic, financial and fiscal importance of the dissolution, which is brought out with clarity and much statistical verification, especially by Professor Woodward. Taxation, dissolution and debasement were the three channels through which the Crown drew the revenues necessary to carry through its extraordinary duties of defending the realm at a time when the ordinary revenues were no longer sufficient to cover even the costs of normal, peacetime administration.

It was typical of Henry VIII, the rogue elephant of the Tudors, that he saw no reason to curtail his private expenditures, so that while such worthy public defence expenditures as repairs to Dover harbour, and to the fortifications of Calais, the south coast, etc., figure largely in the preambles to his acts of taxation, he still diverted large sums towards the construction of his palaces, 'over £1,000 in the financial year 1541–42 alone' (Alsop 1982, 22). In a desperate search for additional finance, innovations in taxation necessarily accompanied the drastic experiments in dissolution and debasement. No longer could the king 'live of his own'. Thus in the course of research on 'Innovations in Tudor Taxation', Professor J. D. Alsop reaffirms 'the presence of significant novelty within Tudor subsidy acts' (i.e. taxes), and 'confirms that taxation is most appropriately studied in relation to, and as a central aspect of, the evolving nature of Tudor finance' (1984, 91). However despite all the money squeezed by Henry VIII from taxing his subjects and from confiscating the property of the religious orders, he was still, in the early and mid-1540s, desperately in need of additional resources. Therefore, while his land sales were still proceeding, he turned to see what ruthless exploitation of the coinage could bring into the royal coffers.

The Great Debasement

The 'Great Debasement' of English history actually began, as it was to end, in Ireland, with an issue of 'Irish harps' in 1536, containing roughly 90 per cent of the silver in the similar coins then being issued by the English mints. This first, moderate, debasement was apparently accepted without demur, and so encouraged a further debasement in Ireland in 1540 and then in England in 1542, from which later time the general Tudor debasement is usually dated. Among the first to receive the debased Irish coins were members of the English army in Ireland. They had little choice but to accept, as did the Irish with whom they spent their pay (Challis 1978, 81–111).

However, the very much larger issues required in England demanded a more complex and subtle approach, at first based on attempting to secure the voluntary co-operation of the public. Before briefly charting the rake's progress of Tudor debasement we should remind ourselves that debasement has the three following possible elements: first the crying up, or calling-up, of the coinage, which means simply giving new coins, which in all essentials are the same as the previous issue, an officially decreed higher nominal value; secondly there is the not logically dissimilar method of making coins smaller or lighter, though of the same officially designated values as previously and out of precisely the same purity of metallic content; thirdly there is the process of making the metallic content of the coins out of cheaper metals than were previously used and officially attempting to enforce their acceptance as if they were issued in the previously unadulterated form. The Tudors were guilty of all three kinds of debasement and in practice it often became difficult to disentangle the degree of importance or, as we might nowadays say, the weight, to be attached to any one combination of these three elements of a debased currency.

Not all three forms of debasement were considered to be equally deplorable. In fact the first form, namely the enhancement of the values of either gold or silver, were fairly common and acceptable devices which had to be resorted to from time to time in order to try to keep the values of existing coinage in line with current bullion prices. If bullion prices were to rise substantially above their mint equivalents more coins would be leaked from domestic currency to foreign markets or would find their way into the melting-pots of the goldsmiths. The process would, of course, go into reverse whenever the price offered by the English mint exceeded bullion prices or the prices offered by foreign mints. Where an element of rightly deprecated debasement crept in was in those cases where the official enhancement of values noticeably exceeded that justified by differences between the mint and bullion prices. Following a considerable drain of gold to the Continent in 1526, involving considerable losses of sovereigns valued domestically at £1, the sovereign was cried up to 22s., with similar enhancements for the gold angel. Such enhancement was insufficient and the drain continued so that, later in the same year, two related methods were tried: the sovereign was enhanced to 22s. 6d. and the new sovereigns and other gold coins were issued not at the previous standard of 23.75 carats but for the first time at a lower standard of 22 carats.

However, all these changes were not unlike those previously accepted as tolerable, moderate changes fully justified by the circumstances of the time and not to be considered as belonging to the phase of Henry's real debasement. It was not therefore until the silver coinage began to be more substantially adulterated in the 1540s that the debasement movement really got under way. The Irish experiments had proved that the mints could become a much more profitable source of finance for the hard-pressed monarch.

Debasement was therefore a matter of degree and of conscience. Moderation might be successful in the sense of being generally accepted by the public since, with so many of the coins in general circulation being imperfect and underweight, even the new coins, as normally marginal additions to the currency, would seem preferable to the average coin in circulation. However, success in the sense of being accepted by the general public (if not by the professional money-changers) implied relatively modest profits for the Crown. If greater profits were sought then, by some means or other, attempts had to be made to hide from the public the degree of debasement actually being achieved, at least long enough for the king to receive his initial gains. Debasement thus became literally a *hidden* form of taxation from its inception.

Deception alone would not have been enough since professional coin exchangers, bullion dealers and merchants quickly became aware of such deception. The main engine of debasement was the official announcement of a higher mint price so as to induce voluntary offerings by such professionals of existing coin and bullion to the mint in order to receive *more* new coins, admittedly of a lighter, adulterated or enhanced valuation, from the mint. In other words the mint price had to be substantially increased in order to increase substantially the voluntary flow of silver and gold coins, bullion and plate to the mint. With regard to plate, the vast amounts coming from the monasteries, chantries and shrines were fed straight into the mint, and since these were involuntary supplies they did not of course require the inducement of a higher mint price. As Professor Gould has shown, in his authoritative, interesting and detailed study of the subject, it is certain that 'during the Great Debasement there was a substantial monetization of plate and ornament from the suppressed religious houses (Gould 1970, 33). Hence it was no accident that the 'ecclesiastical' mints of Canterbury and York were busily reactivated as being ideally placed to deal with the new flood of monasterial plate.

In May 1542 a moderate increase in mint price was announced followed by a series of more substantial increases, beginning in May 1544. Thereafter mint activity rose apace, for it was very much in the individual interests of those who could do so to take advantage of the higher mint prices. Thus, as Professor Gould shows in a most instructive example, if anyone in possession of sixty-four testoons (shillings) minted in 1544, and then worth £3. 4s., brought them to the mint for recoining in 1550, he would receive the equivalent of £4. 0s. 0d. worth of new coins, i.e. an increase of 25 per cent for each pound weight of silver (1970, 18). Indeed so successful was the king in attracting supplies to the mint after 1544 that in the following year or shortly thereafter, six new mints were opened or reopened to help the original Tower mint to cope with the flood from both voluntary and 'monasterial' sources. Three of these new mints were in London (another one in the Tower plus one at Durham House in the Strand and at Southwark), while the three others included, as well as those already referred to at Canterbury and York, a newly built mint at Bristol. The Tower's Irish coinage, where the first debasement experiments began in 1536, was also supplemented from time to time by issues from the Dublin mint. During the later stages of debasement the flow of gold and silver from the general public was greatly reduced, and so the greater proportion of bullion came from the government itself. One such means was through arranging loans from the German firm of Fuggers to purchase supplies of silver directly from its mines.

The process of physical debasement from the original pure sterling silver standard reached 75 per cent silver by March 1542, 50 per cent by March 1545, 33⅓ per cent by March 1546, and reached its nadir of 25 per cent under the young King Edward VI in 1551. The mainly copper-alloy coins were, in order to improve their acceptability, 'blanched' from 1546 onwards, by applying a thin surface coating of purer silver, a subterfuge which quickly wore thin to show the red copper underneath – hence Henry VIII's well-earned nickname 'old copper-nose'. In contrast to the gross adulteration of silver, the gold coinage remained close to purity throughout the debasement period, its least pure level being the twenty-two carats (or eleven-twelfths fine) which it had registered in 1526, and again (after restoration to over twenty-three carats) in 1542. It was rather through 'enhancement', or crying up its official price, that the policy of debasement was pursued in the case of gold, and even then to a much more moderate degree than with the silver coinage. Thus whereas the mint price of 1 lb weight of fine silver rose from £2.40 to £6.00 between 1542 and 1551, i.e. 150 per cent, the mint price of 1 lb weight of fine gold was raised only from £28.80 to £36.05 during that same period, an enhancement of only 25 per cent. The degree of change in the silver to gold ratio – from around 12:1 in 1542, to about 6:1 for a short time in the early part of 1551 – was clearly untenable, and a ratio nearer the customary 12:1 ratio was restored later in 1551, by almost halving the mint price of silver overnight.

These variations in the relative mint prices of gold and silver were not readily removed by what we might term 'arbitrage', at least not so far as the use of coinage within England was concerned, for the coins were almost invariably accepted at their face values. Although this was truly a bimetallic period, nevertheless silver was mainly the medium of retail and domestic trade, whereas gold became, during the debasement period especially, mainly the medium of wholesale and foreign trade. This is borne out by the statistics of the exchange rates between London and Antwerp. Instead of sterling falling to the weighted average of the silver and gold debasement, the £ sterling fell considerably less than that average on the Antwerp market, and was much more in line with the far more moderate debasement of gold. Indeed, in many foreign contracts the receipt of debased silver coin was unacceptable, while even the attempts of the King's Council to force foreigners to accept its declared enhanced price for gold was, much to their chagrin, ignored. They would not accept the Council's assurance that the pound in their pockets was not devalued.

The degree to which the fall in the value of the pound on the foreign exchanges acted as a stimulus to English exports and a constraint on imports has been very much a matter of lively dispute among economic historians in the past couple of generations. There are those, like George Unwin, who argued forcibly that the evils of progressive debasement followed by the uncertainties of reform, dislocated and drastically upset trade relations, thus reducing exports as well as imports (Unwin 1927, 149). Others, like F. J. Fisher, however, argued equally strongly that, like modern devaluations, after a time-lag (the J-curve effect as we would say) the cheaper pound led to a huge surge in exports and a decrease in imports (1940, 95–117). More recent detailed studies by Professor Gould, Dr Challis and others have demonstrated conclusively that Professor Fisher's claims were exaggerated, in that the figures he gave relating to cloth exports from London took insufficient account first of the continuing exports of wool, and secondly of the fact that London had for many years been increasing its share of total national exports at the expense of provincial ports. Basing national exports on London's experience was therefore bound to exaggerate the national increase in exports. Nevertheless, despite some debatable degree of exaggeration, there appears to be a consensus as to the main point, namely that the Great Debasement had a direct and considerable effect on terms of trade, raising the price of imports and reducing the price of exports. Since, however, the degree of gold debasement was so very much less than the silver debasement, and since money markets were less perfect in the sixteenth century than today, one should not attribute too much influence on commodity trade flows to debasement in the mid-sixteenth century, when there were other powerful structural factors also at work.

The extent of the profit gained by the Crown during the main period of the debasement, 1544–51 inclusive, had been considerably underestimated by economic and monetary historians until the painstaking researches of Dr Challis and Professor Gould. The main reason for this was that previous calculations were based almost exclusively on the output of the Tower mints to the neglect of the substantial contributions of the other six mints. If during the eight-year period in question one compares the revised figures of net profits from debasement, £1,270,684, with the other two main sources of finance available to the Crown, namely the net yield of all taxation, £976,000, and the net proceeds from the disposal of monastic properties, £1,056,786, then debasement is seen to yield more than either taxation or dissolution (Challis 1978, 254–5).

Debasement had run its main course by mid-1551 and had been squeezed dry, while the Crown still retained much of the monastic estates and taxable capacity remained practically intact. The Crown extracted its profits from debasement by arbitrarily and indeed fraudulently increasing its 'seigniorage', that is the difference between the total cost of producing the new coins and their face value, from a reasonable to a plainly unreasonable extent, and thus increasing the average annual rate of profit from minting from the negligible £100 or £200 received by Henry VII to the vast annual average of nearly £160,000 enjoyed by Henry VIII and Edward VI. Corresponding exactly to royal gain was the cost to the public – the cost of inflicting on the country the worst currency it had ever suffered (with the doubtful exception of that of Stephen and Matilda). It was the general public – who possessed and used mainly silver and rarely if ever aspired to gold – who bore the brunt of the diffused and hidden taxation brought about by debasement, rather than the richer sections. After all, only 7 per cent of the Crown's profit came from minting gold, compared with 93 per cent coming from silver. It was possibly the inconvenience rather than simply the increase in prices associated with debasement that was the major burden borne by the mass of the population – a matter which will be discussed later, as part of our examination of the long-term general inflation of European prices, in which debasement almost certainly played a relatively minor, though not unimportant, role.

Numismatically Henry VIII was plainly a disaster. Yet it would be wrong to judge that gifted, dynamic and hard-pressed monarch too severely simply by reference to the notoriety which he has earned through his related policies of dissolution and debasement. Had it not been for these two admittedly drastic and exceptional forms of taxation, then either there would have been no strong navy of seventy-one ships, or the normal burdens of taxation and borrowing would have been raised to unacceptable levels and thus possibly have brought forward the constitutional struggle that disrupted the Stuart monarchy and brought the return of civil war a century later. It was of course not the least of the advantages of debasement, so far as the king and his advisers were concerned, that coinage was a recognized royal monopoly and so its profits were independent of parliamentary approval. Although the main drive to debase the currency had exhausted its possibilities in England by mid-1551, the process was continued until 1560 in Ireland, where Henry's debasement policy was, as we have seen, first tried out. By 1560 Elizabeth decided on a vigorous policy for the reform of the debased currency.

Recoinage and after: Gresham's Law in action, 1560–1640

When the nine-year-old King Edward succeeded his father in 1547 his advisers were forced to maintain the fiscal policies inherited from Henry VIII. An early attempt to raise the quality of gold and silver coinage in mid-1547 was doomed to failure as it became obvious that such attempts were premature; the new king could not do without the fiscal support of continued debasement. Between 1547 and 1549 various attempts were made to combine increased purity with decreased weight, but the result was merely to increase the general confusion. The confusion and the degree of debasement reached its climax in 1551 when the 'three ounce' silver (i.e. only 25 per cent, full silver being 12 ounce) was issued in April 1551. In October of the same year the policy was changed; the main period of debasement had come to its inevitable end. Mint activity was drastically reduced, the mints outside London (except Dublin) were closed down, the values of the most debased silver issues were *down* to half their nominal values, the debased shillings being revalued at sixpence etc., and the future new issues of most of the coinage were brought up to or near the customary levels, at least for England and Wales, though not for Ireland. The existing circulation, however, still consisted mostly of the base coins issued in the previous years. Henry's policy of confiscating the wealth of the religious houses was also maintained not only by the suppression of the chantries in 1548–9 but also with seizure of the gold and silver plate from the parish churches in 1553 (leaving only the bare necessities for Holy Communion), a haul which brought in some £20,000 to the depleted royal coffers. In sum, despite ostentatious efforts at reform, the main fiscal policies of debasement and dissolution were still being carried out, insofar as any further yields were possible from these sources, in the six years of the unfortunate reign of Edward VI.

During the equally brief reign of Mary, the mints were modestly active, continuing the policy of producing good-quality coinage for England and base money still for Ireland. Much of the new supplies came from Spanish coinage purchased by Thomas Gresham, the royal agent in Antwerp, who was thus attempting to supplant, or at least supplement, bad money with good. Some of the most numismatically interesting issues were the sixpence and shilling coins bearing the busts of Mary and her husband Philip of Spain face to face, another small but significant example of the growing influence of Spain on English monetary history. Feavearyear probably underestimates Mary's contribution to the solution of Tudor monetary troubles not simply by his repetition of Ruding's assertion that 'the mints were inactive during most of the reign' (1963, 74), but more importantly by ignoring the investigations among her advisers on how best to reform the currency. Despite her strong encouragement to seek a solution, no action was taken. Nevertheless these preliminary discussions no doubt contributed significantly, in Dr Challis's view, to the speed with which Elizabeth was able to take action to end the curse of a thoroughly discredited currency.

Thus it was not until Elizabeth I had established herself that the problem of how to reform the deplorably bad coinage in circulation began to be tackled with any degree of vigour. The dual problem which had to be solved, if the country were again to enjoy a sound currency, was not simply to replace the base coins with good, but how to do so without saddling the Crown with insupportable costs. In the event this difficult task was accomplished with complete success – indeed with a surprising degree of profit coming to the Crown at the end of the operation. Again, as in the process of debasement, it was the general public who paid the price for enjoying once more the traditionally high standards of sterling silver and full-bodied gold – standards generally higher than those obtaining over the rest of Europe.

The task of replacing bad money with good was a most formidable one. Although Gresham's Law, that bad money drives out good, was well known long before Gresham's time, it was justly gaining prominence at this period because of its extremely urgent topicality and the enormous size of the debased circulation compared with the minuscule amount of new full-bodied coins. Consequently if the new unadulterated coinage were produced at the normal rate to add its marginal contribution to the existing debased currencies, the new would immediately have disappeared either legally, by simply being withheld from circulation, or illegally by being melted down or exported despite all the legal penalties against such action. Faced with problems of such a size and complexity, the reform of the coinage would have to satisfy the following conditions: first the recoinage would have to be done quickly, otherwise the old would swamp the new; secondly the scale of the operation would have to be so large as to enable as complete a replacement of the coinage as possible rather than simply gradually supplementing the old circulation; thirdly with the same sense of urgency and on the same large scale, the public had to be induced to hand in its old debased coinage in return for the new; fourthly the whole expensive programme had to be carried through without any final net cost to the Crown; fifthly to provide an initial supply of bullion to start the process going and to act as a reserve to meet the inevitable gaps between the flow of new coins into circulation and the counterflow of old coins back into the mint, it would be necessary to secure a large amount of gold and silver bullion from abroad. There were a number of other conditions subsumed in the above such as the ability to maintain secrecy at certain stages in the programme, the reinforcement of the fear of the consequences of breaking the law on the export or melting down of coinage, and the need to set up an agency network throughout the country to enable the exchange of currency to proceed as smoothly as possible.

Following a series of detailed investigations in which the queen herself was directly involved, an agreed plan was adopted and a series of royal proclamations were issued between 27 September and 9 October 1560 – the current equivalent of a modern 'white paper' – announcing the government's intention to proceed with the recall, revaluation and recoinage of all the base moneys, and warning the public that the legal punishments against exporting or melting coins would be carried out with the greatest severity. These proclamations also gave details of the 'crying down' or devaluation of the existing coinages (to an extent sufficiently less than their precious metal content so as more than to cover the costs of the whole operation). The less debased coins were devalued by 25 per cent, while the most grossly debased types were devalued by more than 50 per cent. A final date, 9 April 1561, was given after which the debased coins would no longer be legal tender, and further to speed the change a bonus of 3d. per £1 was given on certain types exchanged before the end of stipulated dates between January and August 1561. To assist the public in sorting out the tangle of the various issues goldsmiths throughout the country were appointed as agents for such exchanges.

The related difficulties of speed and scale were dealt with by greatly expanding the Tower mint by building the largest extension of any of the mints built during the whole Tudor period, by increasing the number and quality of assayers, craftsmen and metalworkers, a number of them being attracted from foreign mints, and by introducing for the first time the latest continental presses for producing 'milled' coin which, after early failures, eventually markedly improved the quality of the coins. This, combined with their increased purity, greatly aided their ready acceptability by the public. The total of base coinage in circulation has been variously estimated at between the low figure of £940,000 (given by Sir Albert Feavearyear) and the rather higher and more precisely accurate figure of £1,065,083 (given by Dr Challis). Recoinage of anything near such a vast amount could be accomplished only by taking in the debased currencies, separating the debased constituent from the varying degrees of precious metals they contained so as to form the basis of the new issues.

The main contract for separating the copper from the precious metals was already being negotiated by Sir Thomas Gresham in mid-1560, and as a result was given in November to a German company under Daniel Ulstate, which company ultimately separated about 83 per cent of the base metals, with the London company of Peter Osborne and the mint itself sharing the other 17 per cent. It was Gresham also who negotiated a loan of 200,000 crowns in Antwerp in January 1560 for the purpose of securing the reservoir of bullion required to supplement the main supplies coming from the influx of domestic debased coinage. Since the actual recoinage began only in December 1560 and yet was finished by 24 October 1561, the whole process, despite a frighteningly slow start, was actually achieved in a very commendably short space of time, thus minimizing the difficulties, bottlenecks and shortages inevitably associated with such a fundamental change in the basic – indeed almost the only – monetary medium. The currency had been transformed, its high prestige had been restored and the whole costly operation had been so finely managed despite the many difficulties that it yielded a handsome but not excessive profit to the queen of about £50,000. A grateful queen granted Sir Edward Peckham and three other mint officials the right to choose their personal coat of arms. The present Deputy Master of the Royal Mint, Dr Jeremy Gerhard, has kindly informed the writer concerning an interesting coincidence, in that Peckham's choice included the 'cross and crosslets' design, a feature which came to light again recently when Queen Elizabeth II granted the Royal Mint, now at Llantrisant (The Church of the Three Saints), its own smaller three-crosses mint mark, which appears on the edge of all current £1 coin issues.

Compared with the trauma of the Great Debasement and the curative surgery of Elizabeth's recoinage, the rest of Tudor and early Stuart monetary history turned out to be rather humdrum, with just one exception – the silent secular inflation from about 1520 to 1640, which baffled contemporary and much subsequent opinion. In debasement and recoinage the Crown had been betting with a double-headed penny, extracting profits both through crude adulteration and cunning recovery, but each time at the expense of the general public. The public never forgot the lesson and subsequently, until the coming of modern paper money, never allowed the monarchy to profit substantially again through debasement or reform, thus relieving the basic currency of the kingdom from its occasionally heavy fiscal burdens. By the 1580s Elizabeth's normal average annual income from the mint was down to around £700, or not more than about 3 per cent of her ordinary revenue. Her prudence and economy in expenditure, characteristics she inherited from her grandfather Henry VII, together with her share of the influx of treasure from the New World and her propensity to live off the backs of the barons whom she made a habit of visiting, complete with her courts and royal household, just enabled her to manage to balance her income and expenditure, despite the rise in prices which doubled during her reign and quadrupled during the Tudor period as a whole.

Among the relatively minor monetary problems which deserve mention were those associated with getting the right proportions of coin denominations in relation to the demand. The march of inflation made larger coins more and more necessary, and the Tudors correctly anticipated the demand with their issues of the golden sovereign and the silver crowns and shillings. It was the production of these that was given the greatest, but not exclusive, emphasis in the initial stages of the recoinage. Indeed so many shillings were issued in 1560 and 1561 that there was found to be no need to mint any more shillings for a further twenty-one years. It was at the other end of the range that the greatest difficulties occurred and from time to time there was such a shortage of pennies, halfpennies and farthings that local issues of copper tokens appeared in a number of towns including Norwich, Oxford, Worcester, and especially Bristol, a town granted official permission in 1577 to issue £30 worth per annum of copper coin. The main reason why the official mints tended to produce insufficient small coins lay in the fact that the rate of payment for producing small coins was unremunerative compared with that for the larger coins.

A fairly ingenious, though at first sight apparently peculiar, solution was the issue from 1572 to 1582 of a three-halfpenny and of a three-farthing coin. The latter could, for example, be given in change for a penny for any purchase of a farthing's worth of goods and thus to some extent it obviated the need to use or coin the impossibly small and unprofitable silver farthing. Silver farthings, like the silver groats, were no longer issued – with a very few, trivial exceptions. In 1583 the three-halfpenny and three-farthing issues were discontinued, with the more normal 2d., 1d. and halfpenny coins being issued as usual, until the silver halfpenny also ceased being issued in the 1650s. The silver penny continued to be issued right up until 1820 inclusive, thus ending an astonishing national numismatic record of around 1,100 years. In 1601 the price of bullion having again got out of line with the mint prices, the weights of the gold and silver coinage were reduced slightly, gold by rather more than silver, so that the gold/silver ratio was reduced from 11:1 to 10.8:1, just at the time when the plethora of silver was working, in the rest of the world, to increase the gold/silver ratio. Copper, having become synonymous with debasement, was not acceptable as subsidiary coinage until the memory of that era had faded, though some copper pennies for circulation in Ireland were produced at the London mint in 1601, another experiment later hesitatingly copied in Britain. Despite some particular shortages, Tudor tradesmen had a bewildering variety of coinage denominations to supply their needs, varying from the heavy 'fine-gold' sovereign (of 979 parts per thousand) valued at 30s., through the 'crown gold' sovereign (of 916 parts per thousand) valued at 20s., the half-pound, crown, half-crown, ryal, angel half-angel, quarter-angel – also in gold. Silver issues included the shilling, sixpence, groat, three-pence, the half-groat or two-pence, three-halfpence, penny, three-farthings, halfpenny and farthing. Obviously with such a variety to play the exchanges, traders were not too discomforted by the occasional lack of particular denominations, except for the smallest coins where the official issues remained insufficient to meet demand.

Turning to look at the circulation as a whole, at the peak of the debasement in mid-1551, the total coinage in existence, which was then by far the main component of the money supply, stood at £2.66 million. Whatever may have been the shortages immediately occurring, part of the increased world supplies of silver found their way to Britain so that, apart from difficulties between the balance of various coin denominations, the total circulation began to grow shortly after the debasement and continued throughout the rest of the sixteenth century. By 1600 the circulation was thus, at around £3.5 million, one-third higher even than the swollen total existing at the peak of the debasement in July 1551, so that, in macro-economic terms, the aggregate money supply seemed to be quite adequately provided with its basic ingredient when the last of the Tudors was succeeded by the first of the Stuarts.

When James VI of Scotland came to rule as James I of England (1603–25) the union of the crowns led naturally to a partial union of the coinage, celebrated first with the issue of the gold 'Unite', of exactly the same weight and purity as the 20s. sovereign, from 1604 to 1619. This was replaced with a slightly lighter 'Laurel', also valued at £1, in 1620. Not so easily assimilated, however, were the much more important issues of silver coins, since these were far more debased in Scotland which had long imitated the worst continental practices. For example, the Scots' silver mark had to be valued in England at the infuriatingly inconvenient valuation of 13.5d., whereas the English mark was still nominally worth 6s. 8d. At last the awkward, niggling problem of securing an adequate supply of low-value, subsidiary coinage for Britain as well as simply for Ireland had to be tackled.

To the annoyance of the Crown, the gap was being filled with token coins, most commonly made of lead. These were issued by a rabble of unofficial minters, which had grown by 1612 to the huge total of 3,000, and who paid the king nothing. Because the Royal Mint found the whole business of copper coinage unprofitable and undignified, and since it diverted skilled manpower away from the somewhat more profitable business of coining gold and silver, the king decided to resort to outside official agents, a device subsequently used on a number of occasions when the royal mints were under pressure. The first such outside agent, Lord Harington, began issuing copper farthings under licence in 1613. His contract had stipulated that half the profits were to go to the king, who had hoped thereby to gain around £35,000. When, six months later, Harington died, the total profits had amounted to only £300. The licence was next transferred to the Duke of Lennox and thereafter to a succession of hopeful buyers. Similar licences were later issued by Charles I to the Duchess of Richmond and to Lord Maltravers until all such private licences were revoked by the Commonwealth Parliament in 1644. Following this self-righteous act the shortage of low-value coins intensified, again leading to a mushrooming of municipal and other private traders' mints all over the country which issued tokens of copper farthings, halfpennies and pennies on and off for almost the next thirty years. Finally, in 1672 the Royal Mint itself took over direct responsibility for the issue of copper coinage. An interesting example of financial devolution and vertical integration was shown in 1637 when a branch of the Tower mint was established at Aberystwyth Castle, its coins being appropriately stamped with a three-feathers mint mark. Its main purpose was to handle the locally mined supplies of silver, during a decade when the London mint was intensively occupied coining vast amounts of silver brought, directly and officially, from Spain.

Throughout the sixteenth century and the first third of the seventeenth a considerable proportion of the net bullion supplies coming to the royal mints had come directly, by way of trade, plunder or piracy, from the New World, despite all the efforts of the Spanish authorities to limit such leakages. A new situation developed in the early part of the reign of Charles I (1625–40) whereby vast amounts of bullion came directly from Spain to the Tower mint with the full blessing of the Spanish authorities. It is useful to examine these fluctuations in the flow of specie in relation to changes in the mint prices of gold and silver during the first thirty years or so of the seventeenth century. The gold/silver ratio which, as we have seen, had overvalued silver in 1601, was responsible for a huge influx of £1.5 million of silver to the London mint in the decade to 1611. This inflow was abruptly halted in that year, however, when the ratio was altered again, this time by too much of a margin the other way, favouring gold and penalizing silver. The result was another even longer-lasting distortion in mint input and output. From 1611 to 1630 mint activity was mainly confined to gold, and the minting of silver coinage practically ceased to be of any importance. Consequently, by 1630 the general state of the silver in circulation had once more grossly deteriorated to an unacceptable level – not this time by conscious debasement, but simply through a combination of natural wear and tear and official neglect. Fortunately, by this time also the vast increase in world supplies of silver had so reduced its price as to make the unrealistically low mint price fixed in 1611 again attractive enough for merchants to bring in new supplies of silver, and profitable enough for the Crown to resume minting. Against this favourable background a new decade of feverishly sustained activity at the Royal Mint was ushered in particularly as a result of improved diplomatic relations between England and Spain. This new situation was signalled by the Cottington Treaty of 1630, so called after the English ambassador who negotiated not only the cessation of hostilities but also the detailed financial agreements which were to have a profound influence on subsequent monetary developments in Britain.

One of the largest and most persistent of the many drains on Spain's vast accumulation of gold and silver was the need to pay for her armed forces abroad and to subsidize her allies in various parts of Europe, as well as to support the Spanish administration in those parts of the Low Countries which were still under her control. In addition to the growing risks from piracy, the recurrent wars with England and Holland ruled out the possibility of sending supplies through the English Channel. The Spanish government had therefore come to a long-standing arrangement with the bankers of Genoa who assumed responsibility for transferring the specie to Flanders and other parts of northern Europe as required. The restoration of peace with England in 1630 not only removed the direct threat of the English navy but had the double blessing of enlisting that navy as a much-needed source of protection for the Spanish convoys to the Low Countries from the constant harassment of the Dutch navy (which hesitated to offend England) and from that of the Turkish, Barbary and other pirates who roamed the western Atlantic and the English Channel as well as the Mediterranean.

The Cottington Treaty thus opened a cheaper, better and more direct route to the Low Countries. Armies and administrators naturally enough needed ready money rather than bullion, and this urgent requirement was also neatly supplied by a special provision of the treaty. Henceforth all the money required to be sent from Spain to Flanders was first to be sent to London in English ships (for added security). Furthermore, at least one-third of the bullion was to be coined at the Tower mint while the remainder was available either to be subsequently sent on to Flanders or for use in buying supplies by means of bills of exchange drawn upon Antwerp. The Spanish treaty confirmed Charles's resolve to strengthen the navy by bringing the total of seaworthy ships up to eighty, and for this purpose he resorted to the hated 'ship money' taxes, which in 1634 came to £104,252 and in 1635 to £218,500 (Dietz 1964, 275). Although discussion of the wider financial and constitutional effects of ship money is deferred until the following chapter, it is relevant here to mention these heavy costs as possibly excusing Charles's determination to extract every penny of profit from coining the Spanish silver while at the same time overlooking the glaringly obvious need to replace the existing circulation. Nevertheless, on the positive side, the agreement with Spain meant that the Royal Mint was now assured of a vast and profitable supply of silver. A huge total of something between eight and ten million pounds' worth of silver was coined by the Royal Mint between 1630 and 1640 which 'was nearly twice the amount coined during the whole of Elizabeth's reign including the recoinage' (Feavearyear 1963, 91).

What was good for the king and his mint was also good for the coin-cullers, though not, as it happened, for the currency. If the success of the Elizabethan recoinage depended upon reversing Gresham's Law by first devaluing and then quickly taking in the great bulk of the debased currency, the failure of Charles's policy followed from simply adding the good, new coinage to the deplorably bad existing circulation. Rarely has Gresham's Law operated to greater effect, for no sooner were the new coins issued than they disappeared via the thriving goldsmiths (and the many agents whom they employed at a payment of 2–3 per cent of the net proceeds). The new coins were either melted down or exported with little delay. Notorious among such lawbreaking goldsmiths was Thomas Violet, who received a royal pardon in 1634 for his misdemeanours in return for informing on his fellow criminals, a dozen of whom were brought to justice. Despite all the efforts to prevent melting or export, most of the Spanish silver had disappeared from the country by the middle of the seventeenth century.

The so-called price revolution of 1540–1640

It is now time to turn to see how these tidal flows of finance affected the history of prices in general during the age of the Tudors and early Stuarts. Whereas the financial effects of dissolution and even of debasement had generally been relatively neglected by economic historians until the 1970s, in contrast the history of prices in the sixteenth century has exerted a magnetic effect on contemporary writers and historians ever since. While the fascination which the subject has held for investigators has considerably increased our knowledge of the prices of various commodities and the wages of various groups of workers in different regions, the key matter as to what were the causes of the inflation remains very much a subject of lively dispute. One would expect modern monetarists automatically to explain inflation as being clearly the result of a single simple cause – the expansion of the money supply relative to any increase in the output of final goods and services. Conversely modern Keynesians would be expected to look for a variety of non-monetary, as well as monetary, causes. The surprising truth of the matter, however, is that practically all writers up to the 1970s including especially Keynes himself, have adopted the simple classical approach of giving by far the greatest emphasis to monetary factors, whereas since about 1970, during the heyday of modern monetarism the supremacy of monetary factors as the main inflationary factor has been increasingly called into question.

Before trying to weigh up the relative roles of money supply and demand as compared with other changes it is as well to remind ourselves that to modern readers the inflation of the sixteenth and seventeenth centuries was a piffling affair and seemingly hardly worth all the ink that has been spilt upon it. Yet during those centuries there was a general belief that, temporary disturbances apart, there should be a *just* level for wages and prices, determined by equity and tradition, rather than by mere market equilibrium. Furthermore the new inflation followed a long period when most prices had been either stable or gently falling, so that when the new long series of unusually sharp price rises did not fall back to their traditional level, then contemporary opinion was troubled by events that were both strange and profoundly unsettling. Thus, although we today might gladly welcome as almost non-inflationary a rate of price increases which generations of economic historians have strangely persisted in calling 'revolutionary', yet on balance with deference to the views and reactions of people living at the time and, despite the obvious exaggeration, the use of the conventional term 'the price revolution' may still be accepted. What, then, were its causes and consequences?

Perhaps the first point which needs to be stressed in these monetaristic days is that no one simple, single cause can possibly be sufficient in itself to explain the selective, sustained, widespread and regionally differentiated rise in prices throughout Europe which lasted for more than a century. In other words the influx of precious metals from the New World, though without doubt a vitally important ingredient, cannot be taken as being so obviously and overwhelmingly responsible for the nature and extent of the rise in price levels that all the other influences can be ignored. However, so powerful was Professor Hamilton's explanation of European inflation being almost exclusively the result of the influx of American treasure that no less an economist than Keynes himself adopted his simplistic, monetarist stance (E. J. Hamilton 1934 and Keynes 1930, II, 152–63). His powerful advocacy diverted the main body of the subsequent generation of economic historians away from giving sufficient attention to other causative factors, and this despite the much more balanced view, carefully integrating monetary and non-monetary causes given by Bishop Cunningham at least as early as 1912, but subsequently brushed aside by the Hamilton-Keynes tide. In accepting Professor Hamilton's ideas, Keynes laid especial emphasis on his theory of 'profit inflation' as being the chief cause not only of economic growth but also even of political power. The fact that the rise in money wages lagged behind prices for decades gave entrepreneurs plenty of capital to invest wherever the incentives seemed greatest. 'Indeed the booty brought back by Drake in the *Golden Hind*' (variously estimated at between £300,000 and £1,500,000) 'may fairly be considered the fountain and origin of British Foreign Investment', claimed Keynes, who emphasized 'the extraordinary correspondence between the periods of Profit Inflation and of Profit Deflation respectively with those of national rise and decline . . . In the year of the Armada (1588), Philip's Profit Inflation was just concluded, Elizabeth's had just begun' (1930, II, 152–63). Keynes took his contemporary Cambridge historians to task for making no mention of these powerful economic factors which had made possible the greatness of the Elizabethan age. No self-proclaimed monetarist, not even Milton Friedman himself, could make greater claims as to the power of money, even though the stimulatory effects of the increased money supplies described by Keynes were critically dependent on very lagged and weak responses in the labour market. With the Keynes of the *Treatise* (1930), money is power: with the Keynes of the *General Theory* (1936) money is powerless – a remarkable change to which we will return in a later chapter.

Professor J. U. Nef of Chicago, a contemporary of Keynes, while admitting that 'the inflow of treasure from America helped to keep down the costs of labour and the land needed for mining and manufacturing', nevertheless warns us against the tempting assumption that the long period of rising prices was of compelling importance for the rise of industrialism' (1954, I, 133). Whereas Keynes referred mainly to the stimulatory effects of the influx of precious metals on England's overseas trade, Professor Nef looks rather at internal industrial developments, and makes the telling point that wages could not have been depressed so far or so long as Wiebe, Hamilton and Keynes had supposed, otherwise the home demand for the products of the new industries of coal, glass, soap, paper, salt, etc. would have been depressed rather than expanded. He also showed that the timing of these industrial developments does not fit very closely to the periods when overseas silver came in abundance to England in the second half of the sixteenth century, but rather had already been stimulated by the earlier periods of monetary debasement. It is no mere coincidence that the rate of inflation rose to its peak in the two decades following the beginning of the great debasement in 1542 and that the resulting gap between prices and wages widened. The resultant increase in labour unrest led in time to a national codification of local labour customs in the form of Elizabeth's Statute of Artificers of 1561. Its attempts to fix wages, to force 'vagabonds and vagrants' into the agricultural labour force and its lengthening of the standard period of apprenticeship to seven years may in retrospect be seen as obvious attempts to return to a traditional stability in industrial relations which had been deeply disturbed by accelerating inflation.

Some recent writers on the other hand, while drawing overdue attention to non-monetary causes, are again in danger of going to the other extreme in dismissing, ignoring or gravely underestimating the vital role played by the influx of gold and silver. Thus Professor Joyce Youings, in her stimulating and highly readable history of *Sixteenth Century England*, devotes a whole chapter to the twin 'Inflation of Population and Prices', in which she carefully and painstakingly underlines the inflationary force of the growth of population. However, apart from a few scattered references to debasement, she ignores what must surely be at least as important a cause, namely the increased money supply. Similarly, while one must agree with her analysis of the main consequences of the inflation, one can hardly agree to the almost complete neglect of the money supply. 'The growth of population,' according to Youings, 'itself the main cause of the increase in prices, ensured that those who suffered most were those most dependent on the earnings of wages' (1984, 304).

Why did the increase in population turn out to be so inflationary that some writers, like Professosr Postan, Youings, Brenner and Maynard tend, in one form or another, to give it pride of place? Plagues apart, the increase in population was fairly steady from its low point of little more than two million in 1450 to about four million by 1600. If the increase in population had led to a commensurate increase in output, its effect on prices would have been neutral; if it had been accompanied by a general increase in productivity, the results would have been positive and would therefore have moderated the inflationary pressures coming from other directions. In fact there were a number of powerful reasons why the increased output – especially in the key matter of foodstuffs –

increased less than proportionately with population. First the distribution of the population changed, with a pronounced drift to the towns, especially London. The greater occupational specialization which accompanied this drift reduced the degree to which people grew their own foodstuffs and made them more dependent on markets and retail outlets. Professor F. J. Fisher, in a path-breaking article on 'The Development of the London Food Market, 1540–1640', shows how

> By the early seventeenth century there was a general feeling that the city's appetite was developing more quickly than the country's ability to satisfy it . . . The high profiles of landlords were obtained in part by pinching the bellies of the local poor. The theory that the city was too large became generally accepted, partly because of this difficulty of obtaining food, and it became usual to fight unduly high prices by limiting the city population. (1954, I, 151)

Secondly, profits from producing wool, especially for export, led to a long period of diversion from arable to pastoral farming. Traditional arable farming was labour-intensive, sheep farming was not. The unemployment which resulted (for agriculture was as in all 'less developed countries' predominant) has been graphically portrayed in Sir Thomas More's vivid description in his *Utopia*: 'Your sheep, that were wont to be so meek and tame, and so small eaters, now, as I hear say, be become so great devourers, and so wild, that they eat up and swallow down the very men themselves' (1516, Book I). Thirdly, then, unemployment, caused not only by the enclosure movement, but by all the other many trials of those ages such as plagues, external wars and civil wars, was a powerful factor which reduced the actual supplies of goods, and especially of foodstuffs, below the potential suggested by the substantial increase in hands. Evidence of unemployment abounds (in the form of complaints regarding vagrants and vagabonds) from the days of the dissolution of the monasteries, which made the problem more obvious, up to 1601 when the Elizabethan Poor Law was enacted to try to set a national pattern for parishes to copy in dealing with the problem. Undoubtedly therefore population pressure played a significant part in helping along the rise in prices, especially of foodstuffs, during the so-called 'Price Revolution'.

The rise in population thus took the unfortunate form that it led to a greater increase in final demand than it did in output because of the lagged and insufficient increase in the productivity of agricultural labour. This feature helps to show how the increase in prices started to take place *before* any significant increase in monetary supplies from the New World. It also supports Professor Geoffrey Maynard's view that the prices of agricultural products rose faster than those of manufacturing goods because of the lower elasticity of supply of agricultural goods (Maynard 1962). It was these same pressures of providing for the requirements of an increased population which enabled landlords to continue to give further periodic twists to the inflationary spiral throughout the period 1540–1640 by their insistence on raising the rents they demanded from their tenants on every possible occasion (Kerridge 1953, 16–34). Yet, when all allowance is made for the direct and indirect effects of the substantial increase in population, the cost-push of rising rents would have been resisted more easily if product prices had not also been pulled up by an inflated monetary demand. The excellent advice of Dr Outhwaite, given in his brilliant summary of this highly controversial subject should be borne in mind: 'We must avoid making population pressure do all the work which was formerly undertaken by Spanish treasure' (1982, 44). On balance we might say that the size and persistence of the rise in population provided an inclined plane upon which the other inflationary causes, both monetary and non-monetary, exerted all the more effectively their own particular price-raising influences.

The rise in rents became a matter of repeated, vociferous protest because it affected an important sector of society. It provides us with a good example of how people were mainly concerned about increases in the price of a single commodity or at most in the prices of a narrow range of goods or services. Despite the many valuable studies which have been made of particular prices, such as those for grain, or oxen, or for the wages of agricultural or building labourers, they inevitably suffer from so many limitations that great care must be used in making temporal or spatial generalizations based upon them. Wide differences in regional and international 'baskets of goods', in exchange rates, in the extent to which people could produce goods for themselves, or were allowed benefits or perquisites in kind – these and other similar qualifications would seriously reduce the value of attempts to construct any wide-ranging index of prices, particularly when the appropriate weights to be given to its composite items are bound to be largely a matter of guesswork and during a period when fundamental changes were taking place in trade and expenditure patterns. Thus, although the very concept of a 'general index of Tudor prices' would have made no sense to contemporaries and probably remains impracticable for modern researchers, nevertheless there was ample evidence of a growing interest among leading members of society in the sixteenth and seventeenth centuries concerning the causes and effects of changes in the general level of prices. The strange phenomenon of prolonged if moderate inflation, by devaluing everybody's money, had kindled a new awareness of the related economic problems of the rate of interest, of the quantity theory of money and of the balance of payments.

Although it would be premature to describe the numerous, intense views which were being promulgated and published on these matters as being worthy of being called economic theories, nevertheless the protagonists were busily producing guidelines which they hoped would be adopted as official policy. In a sense these guidelines were exercises in applied political economy. In the course of the following century or so all this theorizing in bullionism and the balance of payments, on the relationship between the quantity of money, the level of prices and the rate of interest, on insurance and on taxation, developed via the rather narrow quantitatively biased study of 'Political Arithmetic' into the more general discipline of 'Political Economy'. But first the old medieval attitudes of mind and methods of computation had to be swept aside before the newer more commercial and capitalistic views could prevail.

Usury: a just price for money

Powerfully mixing his metaphors, Professor Tawney in his stimulating analysis of *Religion and the Rise of Capitalism*, showed how 'the revolution in prices, gradual for the first third of the century, but after 1540 a mill-race, injected a virus of hitherto unsuspected potency into commerce, industry and agriculture, at once a stimulus to feverish enterprise and an acid dissolving all customary relationships' (1926, 142). One of the most important spurs to commercial activities of all sorts was the gradual removal of the age-old prohibition against the payment of interest, a matter which had been debated throughout Europe for very many decades with little or no result, but which finally began to show such substantial changes in attitudes in the mid-sixteenth century that the law itself had belatedly to take note of them. Aristotle's simple but powerful belief that 'money was barren' and therefore that interest was unjust, was repeated in various forms both in the Old and in the New Testament (though the parable of the talents provided for some a debatable escape clause). In any case, from ancient times right through to early modern Britain, usury was frowned upon both by the Church and by the state, which quarrelled regarding the boundaries between their respective areas of control, all the more vigorously because of the money involved.

On the basis of 'an eye for an eye' the most common and appropriate punishment for greedy creditors was the extraction of as large a fine as possible – a great temptation to which both Church and state frequently yielded. Generally speaking however, provided certain niceties were observed, the law, whether canon or state law, turned a blind eye to the giving and taking of interest, except at times of exceptional religious or political zeal, or when the debtors were influential enough to attract the attention of the political or religious authorities to particularly harsh instances of extortion. While the Schoolmen argued, kings and popes, monasteries and republics, merchants and moneylenders, Jews and Gentiles, Italians, Spaniards, Germans, French, Dutch and English – all regularly borrowed, often paying high rates for the privilege, despite what the laws might say. It was partly because it had become so easy to find ways around the prohibitions that, during the later Middle Ages, these laws had actually been strengthened, so heightening the intensity of the debate as to what should or should not be permitted.

The word 'usury' throughout the Middle Ages had been synonymous with almost any sort of economic exploitation and not simply the charging of money for a loan. The actions of those who charged excessive prices for goods simply because they had become scarcer naturally or by 'engrossing', any form of monopoly or foreclosure, all were blackened by being called 'usury'. In a society where small craftsmen and peasants were far commoner than wage-earners and where free competition was the exception rather than the rule, the common people were easy prey to economic exploitation. It was their vulnerability to usury that, according to Wycliffe's sermon 'On the Seven Deadly Sins' made men 'curse and hate it more than any other sin'. In other words the question of the removal of usury was not simply a matter of pleasing the rising commercial interests of the gentry, the lawyers and the merchants: it was also a matter of protecting the everyday livelihood of the ordinary village craftsmen and small farmers, whose vulnerability was just as keenly felt in the sixteenth century as when Wycliffe preached, in the fourteenth. This fear of exposing the poor completely to the unscrupulous trader goes a long way towards explaining why such a seemingly completely anachronistic system as the maintenance of the ban on usury took such an incredibly long time to remove – and then only bit by bit. In fact it took no less than 300 years to remove completely the legal ban on usury in Britain. Even then total *laissez-faire* in money existed for only the short period of the last forty-five years of the nineteenth century. In the perspective of history – even modern history – total freedom for money is very much the exception and some more or less strict form of control has almost always been the general rule.

The increasing quantity of money and credit and the even stronger growth in lending money for commercial rather than simply for charitable purposes made the medieval attitudes to usury less and less tenable in the course of the sixteenth century when opinion and practice in England began to catch up with those on the Continent. By far the most modern in their approach to financial operations were the Lombards, or 'Long-beards', who operated not only in northern Italy but had their agents in all the other important economic centres of Europe, especially in the 'fair' towns of southern France and the Netherlands. The prosperity of these areas and the ease with which they overcame economic and social disasters which devasted other regions acted as an example to the rest of Europe. Since Milan, Genoa, Venice, Florence and Sienna were virtually independent city-states, a large proportion of their business which elsewhere would be considered regional or local could legitimately be taken as being 'international'. This was significant because by far the most common and widespread method of avoiding the ban on interest was to disguise credit transactions as dealings in foreign exchange. Thus, under the very nose of the Vatican, the Lombards developed a surprisingly modern money market successfully avoiding excommunications or fines which were the Church's usual punishments for usury. Indeed, the Italian banking houses regularly carried out such foreign exchange transactions on behalf of the papacy itself. Their system, based largely but not exclusively on the use of 'international' bills of exchange, became the basis of the modern forms of banking which were spreading over much of Europe including Antwerp, Amsterdam and London.

Precept followed practice so that various schools of thought emerged as academics and theologians began to find ways of modifying the traditional blanket prohibition of all kinds of usury. The first logical step in the process of changing accepted views was to allow claims to payment wherever *delays* occurred in the repayment of the principal of a loan. Such a payment by definition could arise only if the originally agreed maturity of the loan had expired. Such forms of payment became commonly acceptable and designated as interest ('id quod interest') and so escaped being stigmatized as usury. A second and more important step forward was to claim that periodic payments made during the course of a long-term loan were also legitimate. This first became regular practice when the Italian city-states began raising loans (some of them 'forced' instead of taxes) from their citizens. The arguments as to the legitimacy of such payments divided the Augustinian theologians, who were against them, from the Franciscans who were in favour of them. Already in 1403 the celebrated lawyer and theologian Lorenzo di Antonio Ridolfi successfully won his case on behalf not only of his creditors but also of the state debtor, the Republic of Florence, who did not want this source of funds from its rich citizens to be denied them. 'In such public lending then, interest was not due merely because of delay' (Gordon 1975, 197).

The exemptions thus granted to governments and their creditors were gradually extended to include commercial contracts between merchants where each was obviously so well able to look after himself that no possible stigma of extortion was implied. Prominent among the major creditors of governments were of course just such merchants, who could, in the prosperous regions around them, always find profitable avenues for their surplus funds, usually at better rates or with less onerous conditions than when they were forced, cajoled or induced to lend to the state. They felt very keenly the sacrifice involved when they lost the opportunities of making profitable use of their own funds whenever they lent them to the state. Furthermore since states were tending to become bigger and bigger borrowers, this problem of lost, more profitable alternative lending tended to grow ever larger. Such creditors began to demand, as an openly acknowledged right, rather than simply as a disguised privilege, an equivalent return from their debtors in the form of interest. Such payments were deemed 'lucrum cessans', that is payments for the cessation or loss of profits. As Professor Gordon and others have pointed out, this is the same thing as the modern concept of opportunity cost (Gordon 1975, 195). In this way, payments for delay, for compensation for loss of profit and for a range of other similar losses became semi-legalized and accepted even by orthodox Catholic theologians and lawyers, and consequently excused as 'interest' from the punishments still meted out for those antisocial practices which could still be construed as usurious. However, the definition of usury was shrinking as that of acceptable interest was growing: the financial exception was gradually becoming the rule.

The Reformation may have hastened the spread of these changes though, as we have seen, it can hardly be said to have caused them. Luther, Calvin and Zwingli, though loud in their denunciations of traditional forms of usury, nevertheless by questioning the very foundations of the beliefs of the established Church, raised questions among the public which they themselves failed to answer with clarity, at a time when others were keen to resolve their doubts. Ironically, Henry VIII first powerfully opposed the Reformation by publishing in 1521 his 'Defence of the Seven Sacraments', for which Pope Clement VII conferred on him the title 'Fidei Defensor' or 'Defender of the Faith', which has subsequently appeared on British coinage for 450 years, either as 'Fid.Def.', or simply as 'F.D.'. While it was more important matters of state, such as royal marriages and the sovereignty of the Crown over the Church, confirmed by the Act of Supremacy of 1534, that caused the rift with Rome, nevertheless its relevance to usury follows from the fact that once this break had been accomplished, there was no longer any overriding ecclesiastical impediment to the long overdue clarification of the legalization of the payment of interest. Thus, it so happened that the first Act to legalize the payment of interest in Britain was passed in 1545, when Henry was in the middle of his programme of debasing the coinage. Money and credit were equally capable of being manipulated by the monarch without undue parliamentary or ecclesiastical opposition.

The statute of 1545 is therefore of paramount importance in the history of usury and consequently in the history of money and banking also. Despite strongly upholding the traditional condemnation of usury in its preamble, it is the first official instance of the open acceptance of practices which though they had already become indispensable to England's economic life, had always been carried out under a cloud of debilitating suspicion. As well as paying lip-service to the old traditional views the preamble to the Act gave warnings against methods used for evading usury, in particular the commonly used device of fictitiously selling goods at a given price and buying them back at a higher price. This device need not, and quite often did not, involve the actual transfer of goods, but was simply a paper agreement or even a verbal understanding. By openly allowing payment for credit, *so long as the rate charged did not exceed 10 per cent per annum*, most genuine commercial interest transactions were now allowable. Naturally traditionalists were up in arms and managed to get the Act repealed in 1552. The new Act attempted to restore the old position, and repeated the condemnation of usury as 'a vice most odious and detestable, as in dyvers places of the Hollie Scripture it is evident to be seen'. This Act had no chance of long-term acceptance, though it did remain on the Statute Book for two decades, a tribute to the continuing strength of the opposition. Eventually in 1571 the regressive Act was in its turn repealed and replaced by the permissive Act of 1545, with the same maximum rate of 10 per cent, though this latter Act specifically excepted the Orphans' Fund of London from being lent out at interest, this detail again illustrating that the important protective, social aspects of usury had not been overlooked.

An ingenious solution to the problem of how to devise a scheme which would continue to give protection to the poor and yet allow greater freedom for commercial lending was proposed by Francis Bacon

(1561–1626), who lived through these changes. In his essay 'Of Usury' he advocated a two-tier rate of interest. First there should be a low maximum rate for lending the small amounts of money normally required by the poor. For this social purpose the rate, Bacon suggested, should be no higher than 5 per cent. However, because 'it is certain that the greatest part of trade is driven by young merchants upon borrowing at interest', there should be a second, higher, maximum rate of interest so as to allow full rein to such entrepreneurial drive. The maximum commercial rate, claimed Bacon, should be set at 9 per cent. However, there was to be no free-for-all. Only registered moneylenders properly licensed would be permitted to operate at these higher rates, and then only in London and a number of other main cities. Although his vision of socially and regionally differentiated interest rates was not implemented, nevertheless his idea that attempts should be made to bring down the maximum level found considerable support in the early decades of the seventeenth century, notably from Sir Thomas Culpepper who published his 'Tract Against the High Rate of Interest' in 1621. He 'devoted his life to the task of getting Parliament to lower the maximum rate' (Cunningham 1938, II, 384). As the result of such pressures a new, lower maximum rate of 8 per cent was established in the legislation of 1624, which in deference to traditional opinion (but by that time surely seen as lip-service), was entitled 'An Act Against Usury'.

Thereafter the way ahead was clear and an essential series of steps had been taken to remove the worst aspects of the ban on interest, without which the indigenous developments in banking which were to come to fruition in the second half of the seventeenth century would have been thwarted. Professor Lipson summarized the situation thus: 'The use of borrowed capital on a considerable scale was made possible by the abandonment of the medieval attitude towards the "damnable sin of usury." The legal toleration of interest marked a revolutionary change in public opinion and gave a clear indication of the divorce of ethics from economics under the pressure of an expanding economic system' (1956, II, xx–xxi). Whereas discussions about the appropriate rate of interest had always closely involved moral factors (and in a sense still do), the other burning contemporary topic, more easily divorced from ethics, but certainly not from politics, was the relationship between the supply of money and the level of prices.

Bullionism and the quantity theory of money

Because variations in the flow of precious metals played such an important role in international trade and the foreign exchanges, it should occasion no surprise that the foremost theoretical developments of the period came to be known in England by the term 'bullionism'. What money is to 'monetarism', so bullion was to bullionism, its theoretical great-grandparent. The bullionist approach to economic thought first came to full flower in the age of the Tudors and early Stuarts. Subsequently it has shown itself very prominently in later centuries, particularly in the Bullion Report of 1810 and the equally famous discussions of the Currency School which led up to the 1844 Bank Charter Act, which itself provided the basic constitution for British currency until 1914, and briefly again for the six years from 1925 to 1931. The narrower view of money as being based on the precious metals (whether gold or silver or both), stems directly from the bullionist doctrines of the sixteenth and seventeenth centuries, and although occasional references to such beliefs can be traced to earlier times, it was not until this later period, when a veritable spate of publications appeared on the subject, that anything worthy of being deemed economic doctrine emerged, and even then was subject to the conflicting views that commonly accompany most economic theories when these are closely related to current policies.

Basically, bullionism was the belief that trade, financial and fiscal policies should be so co-ordinated as to attract into the country the largest possible supply of bullion, and conversely to minimize those factors which, if not checked, would lead to a drain of bullion away from the country. This was not because of any naïve, miserly or particularly misguided adulation of the precious metals themselves, but because in the circumstances of the time, an adequate supply of such metals was believed to be absolutely essential for a number of powerful reasons. Among these were the need for a plentiful supply of sound coinage, rather than the debased coinage resorted to when bullion was scarce; the need to prevent a fall (or a low valuation) of sterling in the foreign exchanges; the need to give profitable employment for British capital and British workmen, rather than to stimulate foreign production and employment; the need to provide a ready reserve of precious metals so as to make it unnecessary for the monarch to have to rely on an illiquid, impoverished country or a recalcitrant Parliament for the special taxes required for defence purposes, and so on. Symptoms, causes, effects and irrelevancies were inevitably mixed up in many presentations of the bullionist case, though perhaps the extent of the confusion and irrelevancy may have been exaggerated by Adam Smith and still more by a number of other, later observers. The fundamental belief was simply that a plentiful supply of bullion was believed to be a prerequisite not only for economic growth but also, to a country perilously threatened by powerful enemies, for economic and political independence. Furthermore, given the fact that, despite all the efforts of monarchs and merchants to find any worthwhile amount of gold or silver within Britain, the only source of such vitally essential products was overseas, either by the dubious occasional means of war and piracy or by the apparently more certain and continuous means of trade. British bullionists therefore concentrated their attention on foreign trade and the foreign exchanges. Malynes, Milles, Mun and the whole army of bullionist pamphleteers would have heartily applauded von Clausewitz's conclusion regarding the essential similarity of objectives in war and peace; only the means differed. Unable to rely on a repetition of Drake's successful piracy, the bullionists had to content themselves with favourable balances of trade.

Differences between contemporary and subsequent definitions of 'bullionism' and 'mercantilism' loom large in the works of some historians but are minimized by others. The differences can be seen as both semantic and as a matter of substance. Contemporary English writers favoured the term 'bullionism' whereas continental writers preferred to refer to the 'commercial' or 'mercantilist system', a nomenclature adopted by Adam Smith. The matter of substance stems from the fact that bullionism tended to be given a narrow meaning as being especially concerned with international flows of specie resulting from *particular* trades, whereas mercantilism took a wider, more macro-economic standpoint, looking at the flow of specie resulting from the aggregate balance of trade and payments. Logically there were three stages in the supposed transition from bullionism to mercantilism: first, the balance of individual bargains or particular trades; secondly the bilateral balance between the home country and another; and thirdly the aggregate balance. Professor Viner notes, with some asperity as well as surprise, that the actual chronological development of the theory of international trade conspicuously failed to follow this logical arrangement. 'In some of the modern literature on mercantilism,' he complained, 'there is to be found an exposition of the evolution of the balance-of-trade doctrine in terms of three chronological stages . . . This is all the product of vivid imagination' (Viner 1937, 11). Professor Viner need not have been either surprised or angered, for yet again this is a most useful illustration of how in the imperfectly linked development of economic theory and practice, particularly where money is concerned, the logical and the chronological do not always march in step, even when nevertheless, they may be heading in roughly the same direction.

In pleasing contrast, Professor Eli Heckscher adopted a much more relaxed approach, barely mentioning bullionism as a separate topic, but including it simply as part of the general development of mercantilist theory. In his authoritative study, *Mercantilism*, he most conveniently and sensibly adopts the line that 'Everybody must be free to give the term mercantilism the meaning and more particularly the scope that best harmonise with the special task he assigns himself' (Heckscher 1955, I, 2). He then goes on to define mercantilism as a phase in the history of economic policy occurring between the Middle Ages and the age of *laissez-faire* in which the state was both the subject and the object of economic policy. 'Ideas on the balance of trade and the significance of money undoubtedly occupy a central position in mercantilism' (I, 26). Mercantilism was not only a practical policy by which the state attempted to increase its power and the wealth of its citizens but also 'there can be no doubt at all that mercantilist discussion was of importance to the final rise of economic science in the eighteenth century' (I, 28). If there is a dividing line, necessarily arbitrary and smudged, between early continental mercantilist doctrine (equivalent to English bullionism) and the later fully-fledged theory, this is to be found when the arguments of those based on the overall balance of trade prevailed over those concerned simply with particular balances. In England this transition began around 1620 and was almost completed by 1663 when the age-old prohibition of the export of bullion and of foreign coin was removed. But of course not all writers, as Viner overemphasizes, kept to this neat logical divide, for some quite advanced mercantilist views appeared before 1620, while many apparently crude and narrow-minded bullionist views appeared long after 1663. These latter views should not, however, necessarily be taken as evidence of bullionist back-sliding. Just as in our modern age, ever since the 1960s the general requirement of nationalized industries to 'break even' has had to be supported by stricter, narrower, particularized targets, and in the 1980s the general attempt to reduce the public sector borrowing requirement has had to be reinforced by insisting on particular cash limits for each government department, in exactly the same way the mercantilist target of a favourable balance of trade had to be supported then by strict limits on those particular items of trade where laxity had led to substantial leakages of bullion.

The first written evidence in England of a mercantilist viewpoint regarding the *net* flow of specie through foreign exchanges appeared as early as 1381, three centuries ahead of its time, when Richard Aylesbury argued that a legal ban on the export of bullion was unnecessary provided that total commodity exports at least balanced imports.

Similarly he argued that a legal ban would fail if exports exceeded imports. This not quite isolated but premature insight was, however, subsequently overlooked and forgotten in the rise of the main body of bullionist opinion in England, such as that of Hales, Malynes, Misselden and the Muns, father and son. Of critical importance as a link between the problems of debasement, the enclosures, inflation and the foreign exchanges was *A Discourse on the Common Weal of this Realm of England*, written in 1549, after the start of the Great Debasement and before the recoinage, the latter of which it strongly recommended. Thanks to the patient researches of Miss Elizabeth Lamond we now know the author to be John Hales MP, a Commissioner on Enclosures for the Midlands region. Woven into the *Discourse* are all the basic concepts which later bullionists were to develop.

Perhaps the bullionist viewpoint in its simplest, strictest and most dogmatic form was that put forward by Gerhard de Malynes, son of an English mint-master who, having emigrated to Antwerp, returned to England to assist in the Elizabethan recoinage. Malynes wished for stricter controls on the foreign exchanges, advocated the return of the office of the Royal Exchequer to oversee such exchanges, since 'exchange is the Rudder of the Ship of Traffic'. Trade should be monopolistically controlled, excessive imports discouraged and the exchange rate kept as high as possible. 'Throughout his active life, Malynes was constantly concerned with monetary questions and in 1609 was appointed a commissioner of mint affairs' (E. A. J. Johnson 1965, 43). The 'Harington' private monopoly of minting farthings which, as we have seen, was bought by the Duke of Lennox, was eventually purchased by Malynes – who made a loss on the deal. His ideas, as shown particularly in his main publication, *The Canker of England's Commonwealth* (1601), were similarly unsuccessful, in being rather too dogmatic even for other bullionists like Misselden and Mun to accept without violent verbal rejoinders.

The most celebrated of the arguments between Malynes, Misselden and Mun and their disciples concerned two important related matters, first the particular practical problem of whether to cancel or to allow the continued existence of the East India Company, and secondly the general validity of the balance of trade theory. Malynes was bitterly opposed to the company, Misselden first opposed but later supported the company, while Mun, after a very brief initial period of questioning, became even more firmly a convinced East India man. Edward Misselden, a member and later deputy governor of the Merchant Adventurers, was appointed to the royal commission of 1621 to investigate the trade depression, and in the same year published his initial views in his pamphlet *Free trade or the Means to make Trade Flourish*. In this he agreed with those who opposed the loss of bullion by traders like the East India Company, in contrast with the long history of the success of Merchant Adventurers in bringing gold and silver in to Britain. Within the short space of two years, during which he began part-employment with the East India Company, he published *The Circle of Commerce or the Balance of Trade* in 1623, completely reversing his previous view, and justifying his position by reference to the new theory, as the title suggests, of the balance of trade.

This was, according to Professor Viner's researches, the first time that the term 'balance of trade' had appeared in print, 'borrowed from the current terminology of book-keeping from the Italians about 1600' (1937, 9). As modern economists would describe it, the new micro-economic concept of balancing the books of an individual company was now transferred to the macro-economics of the state, a most timely and influential development which enabled the bullionists to judge the 'profit' or 'gain' from trade as a whole by means of its net acquisition of bullion. The first such computation for England had already been made jointly in 1615 by Sir Lionell Cranfield and a Mr Wolstenholme and was referred to by Sir Francis Bacon in an essay of 1616 (though not published until 1661). Thomas Mun, grandson of the Provost of Moneyers at the Royal Mint, became a member of the East India Company in 1615, and in 1621 published his first crude defence of the company, *A Discourse of Trade from England into the East Indies*. However, parliamentary criticism of the company, based on earlier bullionist theories, continued to threaten the East India trade, so much so that the company appealed to Parliament in 1628 in a famous and influential 'Petition and Remonstrance of the Governor and Company of Merchants of London trading to the East Indies'. This was largely written by Edmund Mun and formed the basis of the brilliant book published posthumously in 1664 by his son, Sir John Mun. If a true valuation were taken of the re-export trade and of numerous other benefits, the East India trade, he argued 'brings in more treasure than all the other trades put together' (E. A. J. Johnson 1965, 75).

Despite Mun's defence, attacks on the particular, adverse balances with India continued throughout the seventeenth century, and with France for much of the eighteenth. Nevertheless the mercantilist point of view, based on the overall balance of trade, was clearly winning the battle, both in theory and in practice, by about 1640. Where, however, neither the older bullionist nor the new mercantilist arguments could ever convincingly win the day was with regard to the ability of England (or any other country) to achieve through trade policy a *permanent* net inflow of specie. The question of what, in those circumstances, would happen to domestic prices relative to those abroad, and therefore to trade flows and the rates of exchange, brings us on to an examination of contemporary developments in the quantity theory of money.

The quantity theory in its fundamentals is the oldest, most simple and obvious of all monetary theories. Whether a particular society considers its money to be a special kind of commodity or not, money in actual fact, like all other commodities, obeys the universal economic law in that its unit value varies inversely with the total quantity. If we add, as we all must, 'other things being equal', as, for example, that reductions in quality may permit commensurate increases in quantity, we are of course simply relating the universal law to the particular circumstances of the time and place in question. During periods of monetary stability the general public does not bother about monetary theory and the theorists lie dormant. It is generally only during periods of substantial financial changes that interest is aroused as to the true nature and causes of such events. The usual result is to produce some up-to-date variation of the quantity theory appropriate to the particular circumstances obtaining at the time. The quantity theory has been the most popular of the general theories of money because it is almost infinitely adaptable. With the exception of Keynesian-type challenges, it has been almost all things to all men. Its ability to find renewed popular acceptance depends, however, on the age-old stock phrases being recoined form time to time. Friedmanism is just a modern example of a long line going back beyond Aristotle; for as we saw in chapter 3, it was the world's first substantial currency debasement, in Athens in 405 BC, that gave rise to the first recorded reference, by Aristophanes, to 'Gresham's Law'. It should therefore occasion no surprise that the first substantial treatment of the quantity theory to appear in western Europe was directly concerned with the need to re-establish monetary stability following a period of particularly severe monetary debasement.

The European roots of the quantity theory of money lead back to Nicole Oresme (1320–82). Since Oresme was undoubtedly the greatest economic thinker of the Middle Ages, concerned especially with monetary theory and policy, and because he had a very considerable influence on later writers, his contribution deserves at least some brief comment. Oresme was born near Caen around 1320, and in 1370 he was made chaplain and adviser to King Charles V (1364–80) and promoted to bishop of Lisieux in 1377. At the request of Charles, aptly known as 'the Wise', Oresme translated Aristotle's *Economics, Ethics* and *Politics*. Aristotle's influence and that of a large number of subsequent writers on economic matters, including Oresme's teacher at the University of Paris, Jean Buridan, are clearly to be seen in Oresme's own writings. In glaring contrast to the contemporary stability of the pound sterling, French currency had become the money box of its monarchs, manipulated at their pleasure. Between 1295 and 1305, the value of French currency was reduced by no less than 80 per cent, and in the next decade brought back up to its original value, only to fall back again during the reign of Charles IV (1322–8). He was known as the Fair – a reference to his appearance, not character: among his monetary misdemeanours was his confiscation of the property which the Lombard bankers held in France. Oresme's writings need therefore to be assessed against this background of volatile and arbitrary changes in the value of money which had been so violent that they threatened to destroy the monetary system. The first edition of Orseme's book, entitled *De Origine Natura Jure, et Mutationibus Monetarum* and consisting of twenty-three chapters, appeared in 1355, followed by an enlarged edition of twenty-six chapters in 1358. The first printed version appeared in 1477. Oresme's work represents a watershed in the development of economics, for his treatise 'was the first independent monograph on the subject . . . a comprehensive and well-built synthesis which must be regarded as one of the main landmarks in early economics literature' (Sarton 1948, II, 1, 494).

Oresme deplored debasement and insisted on maintaining the quality and therefore the stability of the monetary medium. Although he owed his office directly to the king he was no mere placid placeman. He insisted that the king was not the owner but rather the custodian of the currency with a duty on behalf of the public to maintain its value. Although Oresme was perfectly aware of the use of credit and in particular of bills of exchange, he saw money as being based absolutely on the intrinsic value of the metal and went into considerable detail on how best to arrange mint prices, exchange rates and the ratios of gold to silver and to other alloys in order to show what was necessary in practice to achieve the desired degree of stability. As a mathematician and physicist, his practical approach commanded respect, for he was an all-rounder, good with his hands, his head and his heart. His emphasis on the priority of maintaining the value of money and on his view as to what we would call the narrowness of the money base, show him to be the first bullionist and indeed in a sense the first monetarist.

The next important statement of the quantity theory came from an unexpected source, from someone whose genius in astronomy has perhaps blinded us to appreciation of his more mundane contributions to the ordinary business of life. Nicholas Copernicus (1473–1543) first became interested in the theory of money because, like Oresme, he was forced to suffer from successive debasements which were then occurring in a number of Polish provinces as throughout Europe, a problem made all the worse with their many local currencies and even more numerous systems of weights and measures. As a result of his studies he produced his *Treatise on Debasement* in 1526 (though this was not published in printed form until the Warsaw edition of 1816). In his treatise, though strongly condemning debasement, he nevertheless argued that it was the total amount of currency, as indicated by the total number of coins in circulation rather than the total weight of metal they contained that really determined the level of prices and the buying power of the currency. He grasped the essential fact that, for the great majority of everyday, internal transactions, coins had already become simply tokens of value. It was their number, not their intrinsic metallic content, their quantity rather than their quality, that fundamentally determined their true value. It was the duty of the princes therefore to limit total circulation, and the avoidance of debasement was seen as the best practical method of avoiding an excess issue of coinage and therefore of avoiding the gross instability of prices and of exchanges. Although, given the much more detailed treatment produced by Oresme, Copernicus can no longer be said to have made the first statement of the quantity theory (as some claim), nevertheless the emphasis which he placed on variations in quantity and not simply on quality at least justify his position as one of the important pioneers in the development of monetary theory *before* the influx of American silver rose to such a level as to make such ideas more easily and commonly appreciated.

Next in time, and again spurred on to his conclusions by the unusual spectacle of English debasement on the continental scale, came the *Discourse* of Hales, already described. In this connection, however, the common view, given by E. A. J. Johnson, among others, stands in need of correction. Johnson wrongly states, 'As every student of economic history knows, Hales gave the wrong explanation for the rise of prices' and 'Hales erred in assigning the cause of the rise in prices to debasement' (1965, 37). As Dr Challis in particular has shown, debasement in England was in fact the most important single cause of the high rate of inflation occurring during the decade when Hales wrote. Hales was right, and should not be blamed for failing to take into account the influx of American silver which did not enter England in any substantial amount until much later. Jean Bodin's *Reply to Malestroit* (1568) is rightly regarded as a milestone in the development of the quantity theory of money, although it again needs to be pointed out that while Bodin was the most influential contemporary writer to underline the role of New World specie as the main cause of inflation he was no crude bullionist. While he was clear that 'it is the abundance of gold and silver that causes, in part, the dearness of things', he also showed that other 'real' or non-monetary causes were at work such as 'the increase in trading activity, the rise in population and agricultural expansion' (Vilar 1976, 60–91).Bodin also related very carefully some of the main regional and temporal differences in inflation to the pattern of geographical dispersal of Spanish specie – first in Peru itself, then in Andalusia, then to the rest of Spain, then to Italy, France, Germany, the Low Countries etc. as waves going from the monetary centre to the periphery.

By the beginning of the seventeenth century therefore it was becoming clear to practically all writers on money (and they were many), whether they might be considered bullionists or mercantilists, that a persistent influx of precious metals would bring with it serious inflationary consequences. The decline of Spain was already becoming obvious. Nevertheless, the main body of bullionist/mercantilist opinion in England, while not being unaware of the difficulties, seemed to be of the general opinion that the Spanish disease could in fact be avoided. England was at the periphery and therefore just 'catching up' on her share of wealth from the rest of the world and especially from her European competitors. It was also emphasized that so long as England expanded her economy, developed her exports, encouraged the expansion of her merchant marine, and so on, the influx of precious metals would be put to good use rather than wasted in inflationary excesses. This vital necessity of expanding production by the proper investment of favourable balances was clearly emphasized by Malynes in his *Canker of England's Commonwealth*: 'The more ready money, either in specie or by exchange, that our merchants should make, the more employment would they make upon our home commodity, advancing the price thereof, which price would augment the quantity by setting more people on work.' As Heckscher (from whom Malynes's quotation is taken) points out, 'This was perhaps the first time that the claim that rising prices increase employment was ever clearly expressed' (1955, II, 227–8).

By giving the quantity theory of money this dynamic, Keynesian twist, the mercantilists were able to postpone the day of reckoning until 1776, when Adam Smith destroyed them in theory and the revolting American colonies in practice. But before that fateful date, bullionism merging into mercantilism enjoyed some two centuries or more of predominance as an economic theory based very largely upon a realization of the power of money as a liquid, macro-economic resource. It would be very wrong, however, to allow the brilliance of either Adam Smith or Thomas Jefferson to blind us to the positive achievements of mercantilism. It was during that period that the economic centre of gravity moved from the Mediterranean to north-west Europe in general and Britain in particular. It was during the latter part of that same period that British banking finally emerged to fame and fortune. But in 1640 that could not have been readily foreseen.

Banking still foreign to Britain?

Perhaps the single most important sign that England was determined to develop her own financial institutions rather than rely on foreign banks was the building of the Royal Exchange in 1566. This was the inspiration of Sir Thomas Gresham, and it received the royal seal of approval when it was officially opened by Elizabeth I in the following year. Yet it is significant that not only the very concept of the 'Bourse', which was its first name, was imported, but that the building itself was designed by a Flemish architect, that the skilled craftsmanship was supplied by Flemish carpenters and masons, and that even the bulk of the building materials such as the stone and glasswork were similarly imported. The most highly skilled workmen and the most highly skilled operators on the foreign exchange market (with the outstanding exception of Gresham himself) were all foreigners, especially Italians, Germans and increasingly the Dutch. Gresham had learned his skill mainly in Antwerp where he lived, on and off, for twenty-three years between 1551 and 1574, operating both on his own account and as royal agent. There he learned the art of large-scale lending and borrowing as well as foreign exchange so thoroughly that he frequently out-performed his foreign tutors. A famous instance of his skill was demonstrated in 1587 when Gresham arranged with a number of other operators to 'corner' so many bills drawn on Genoan banks that the build-up of the resources necessary to equip Philips II's Great Armada was delayed. Whether this was the main reason why his fleet failed to sail against England until the 'summer' of 1588 is doubtful, but it was at least a substantial contributory reason for the delay and illustrates how sophisticated the financial aspects of economic warfare had become by the 1580s. Another example of Gresham's many-sided financial genius was his proposal to set aside a fund of £10,000 to be used to counter adverse fluctuations in the exchange rates, a sixteenth-century equivalent of the Exchange Equalization Account of the 1930s.

Although this scheme failed, mainly because Elizabeth thought it too extravagant, it again indicates the affinity for finance that enabled him to amass the largest fortune of any contemporary commoner in England.

It is significant too that such examples of advanced financial development were concerned particularly with foreign exchange, where England was the eager pupil still lagging behind her European masters. As we have seen, a much wider range of banking expertise had long been developing on the Continent, where the gradual decline of the periodical meetings of medieval fairs had led to the more permanent provision of everyday banking facilities, including not only the issue of bills of exchange and foreign exchange facilities but also regular deposit banking and loan facilities for ordinary business as well as for rich merchants, princes, municipalities and state governments. The Bank of Barcelona had been founded as early as 1401; the Bank of St George, Genoa, in 1407, followed in 1585 by the public Bank of Genoa, which later occupied a strategic role in European finance; the Banco di Rialto in Venice followed shortly after in 1587. These are just a few examples of a mushroom growth of continental (especially Italian at first and later Dutch) banks, all the more important because they had numerous branches or agents in most of the main financial centres of Europe, including London. The financial and political power of the Bank of Genoa is illustrated by Andreades's description that it carried on 'a business very similar to that of modern banks' acting as 'a state within a state . . . The East India Company never held in England a position a quarter as great' (Andreades 1966, 79). A significant pointer to the northern movement of Europe's financial centre of gravity was the dominance of Antwerp during most of the sixteenth century. The Tudors borrowed considerable sums from time to time from the Low Countries, including as we have seen, the loan of £75,000 to assist Elizabeth's recoinage. As Antwerp declined, so the leading financial role was taken up by the public Bank of Amsterdam, known also as the 'Wissel' or 'Exchange Bank', founded in 1609; but part of Antwerp's loss was also eagerly taken up by London.

One of the most important and pervasive foreign influences which increasingly modified English business methods at this time was the introduction of 'Italian' double-entry bookkeeping. We have already seen how the idea of a balance between income and expenditure was transferred to the national accounts to support mercantilist views regarding the balance of payments. As in Italy, among the first to use the new methods in England were those merchants whose activities commonly included foreign exchange. Gradually, however, the new custom spread throughout most business, except that the Exchequer itself was slow in adopting double-entry. Foreigners resident in London were by their example our first tutors and 'the ledger of the Borromeo Company of London, covering the years 1436–9 is an example of an advanced technique that was adopted by English merchants only a century later' (Ramsay 1956, 185). Among the earliest examples of double-entry by an indigenous merchant, are the accounts of Thomas Howell covering the six years 1522–7. As well as the Italians, the Spaniards, French, Germans and Dutch had long been familiar with the new accounting methods before they became widely adopted in England, a development which had to await publication of translations of the standard Italian works on the subject.

Although the origins of double-entry bookkeeping appear to be uncertain, the system had been in operation for well over a century before the first Italian book on the subject was printed and published in Venice in 1494. This was the famous *Summa de Arithmetica, Geometrica, Proportioni et Proportionalita*, written by Friar Luca Pacioli, a mathematician and close friend of Leonardo da Vinci. His book consisted of five sections: 'On Arithmetic and Algebra'; 'Their Use in Trade Reckoning'; 'Bookkeeping'; 'Money and Exchange'; and 'Pure and Applied Geometry'. His work created an immediately favourable impression, and in 1496 Pacioli was appointed professor of mathematics at Milan. The popularity of the bookkeeping section of his *Summa* led to its being published separately as *The Perfect School of Merchants* in 1504. The new form of bookkeeping gave a further stimulus to the wider use of Arabic numerals. The first, but not particularly influential, translation of Pacioli's ideas to appear in English, was published by Hugh Oldcastle in 1543. Far more influential, however, was James Peele's *The Manner and Form How to Keep a Perfect Reckoning*, published in London in 1553.

Exactly how important the new accounting methods were to such broad matters as the pace of, and indeed, the very nature of, economic growth in Europe, remains a matter of dispute. Some see double-entry simply as a useful technical device of barely more than marginal importance to economic development as a whole, while others, notably Werner Sombart, have seen the new accounting methods as being of fundamental importance to the development of modern capitalism. Thus Sombart claimed that 'Capitalism without double-entry book-keeping is simply inconceivable . . . With this way of thinking the concept of capital is first created' (Sombart 1924, II, 110). A modern expert views the contribution of accountancy much less dramatically as not having 'the far-reaching consequences attributed to it by Sombart', but rather possessing merely 'modest practical utility' (Yamey 1982, chapter 2, p.21). In itself such an innovation in accountancy may well not amount to very much. However, taken in conjunction with all the other contemporary pressures on businessmen, double-entry may well have been a catalyst in the development of more capitalistic attitudes. The truth probably lies somewhat nearer the German exaggeration of Werner Sombart than the typical English understatement of Professor Yamey.

The Royal Exchange was far from being the only example of the important role played by the importation of skilled labour. Foreign labour and capital combined to raise the rate of economic growth above that of Britain's European neighbours, with the result that the gap between their standards of productive efficiency in agriculture and industry and therefore of average standards of living, was narrowed in favour of Britain. Professor Nef has shown, in his essay on 'The Progress of Technology and the Growth of Large-Scale Industry in Great Britain, 1540–1640' that foreign labour and capital helped both to transform existing industry and to introduce a range of new industries into Britain in this period, so reducing Britain's import-dependence and expanding her exports. By the end of this period, Britain was beginning to overtake her neighbours in certain areas.

> While the progress of large-scale industry in mining and metallurgy from 1540 to 1640 was stimulated by the application of technical processes introduced with the help of foreign artisans, it is probable that before the middle of the seventeenth century these processes were being more extensively used than in foreign nations. (Nef 1954, 98)

Similarly in agriculture the draining of the Fens was financed jointly by Dutch and English capital (including £100,000 supplied by the Duke of Bedford), under the experienced leadership of the Dutch engineer Cornelius Vermuyden with a core of skilled Dutch workmen. The scale of business, whether commercial, agricultural or industrial, was becoming greatly enlarged beyond the financial resources of individuals. The era of joint-stock enterprise was emerging, and with it the need for new, stronger financial intermediaries. The rise of these new financial institutions was integrally associated therefore with the increase in the scale of agricultural and industrial enterprise.

It is significant that the first of such joint-stock companies, the Russia Company of 1553, arose out of a search for the North-East Passage, and that German metalworkers were prominent in the development of the first of two inland joint-stock companies, the Mines Royal and the Mineral and Battery, both formed by Royal Charter in

1568. Among the founding stock of the Levant Company of 1581 was a large sum of £40,000 contributed by Elizabeth I as part of her proceeds from Drake's profitable circumnavigation. Foreign capital in one way or another found its way into most of these joint-stock companies, including the most famous of all such ventures, the East India Company, founded in 1600. The Royal Exchange was for many years more of a club for merchants engaged in overseas trade than simply a foreign exchange market. One of the main reasons for the net inflow of foreign investment into Britain was the fact that interest rates offered in Britain were considerably higher than those in Holland, and London remained a powerful magnet for overseas investors throughout this period. Nevertheless, though London was especially attractive for capital, it was no longer necessary for foreigners to be given special privileges in conducting foreign trade, and as a sign of this, the Steelyard, the London headquarters of the Hanseatic League, was closed down in 1597. Although Dutch influence, supplemented by that of the French Huguenots, continued to play a strong role in financial circles in London throughout the seventeenth century, that of the Italians and Germans declined, particularly from the onset of the Thirty Years War in 1618. By 1640 the foreigners who had helped to build and operate the Royal Exchange were no longer the dominant partners. Thus although 'banking' in the strict sense of the term was still largely foreign to Britain at the beginning of the seventeenth century, it had become much less so by around 1640. The financial apprentice was about to set up his own unmistakable brand of banking business.

6

The Birth and Early Growth of British Banking, 1640–1789

Bank money supply first begins to exceed coinage

Many of the most important aspects of modern banking emerged in Britain in the century or so after 1640, during which the forces of constitutional, agricultural and commercial revolution intermingled to prepare the way for the world's first industrial revolution. From being simply an industrial and financial apprentice of continental Europe, particularly Holland, Britain had by the end of the period clearly established a position of international leadership. The expansion of private debt and credit channelled mainly through London by new groups of financial intermediaries using new forms of notes, bills and cheques; the crucial change in government debt from a royal, personal obligation to the higher status of a national debt; the growth of overseas trade more commonly financed by bills drawn on London, and the modification of this system in order to finance the growth of domestic trade and production financed by internal bills; the growth of taxation made more viable through more efficient 'farming'; the increased importance of marine insurance, life assurance and, after the Great Fire of London, of fire insurance; the growing popularity of state lotteries and annuities; the growth in the business of the stock exchange and foreign exchanges – all the above were just some of the more significant among a whole host of changes which together stimulated the development of specialized financial institutions. Among these the goldsmith bankers were eventually to triumph over their early rivals such as the scriveners, brokers and merchants. By the end of the seventeenth century the popular clamour for a public bank to compare with those of Italy, Sweden and especially Holland, and to compete with the private goldsmith bankers so as to bring cheaper money to Britain, culminated in the establishment of the Bank of England in 1694 and the Bank of Scotland a year later.

These exciting entrepreneurial initiatives had by the end of the seventeenth century led to the position where the supply of bank credit in Britain was an essential and growing supplement to the stock of coins, so that by the time Adam Smith's *Wealth of Nations* was published in 1776, bank money clearly exceeded metallic money, a milestone in world monetary history. The important macro-economic results that would stem from supplementing coins with bank paper were remarkably well foreseen by a number of mid-seventeenth-century writers, most clearly of all by Sir William Petty (1623–87), a veritable polymath, professor of anatomy at Oxford, musician, inventor, founder member of the Royal Society and a most percipient political economist. In his *Quantulumcunque concerning Money* (1682) he stated prophetically, 'We must erect a Bank, which well computed, doth almost double the Effect of our coined Money', adding with some pardonable exaggeration that 'We have in England Materials for a Bank which shall furnish Stock enough to drive the Trade of the whole Commercial World.'

Nevertheless, important as the new banks were for the merchants, lawyers, goldsmiths and for the government, (their most important customer), coins and tokens remained the only currency handled by the vast majority of the population. Velocity of circulation varied usually as it still does inversely with the value of the transaction, with the small silver and copper coins changing hands in the ordinary daily business of life far more frequently than either gold or the ownership of the 'Running Cash Accounts' of the goldsmith bankers. In drawing attention therefore to the undoubted economic significance of the new sources of generally safe saving and convenient, cheap lending provided by the banks, we need to remind ourselves of the absolutely indispensable role played by full-bodied silver and gold coins in the economic life of the community, a situation that was to remain true, by and large, right up to 1914. The new forms of bank money brought a liberating, timely and essential extension to overcome the debilitating constraints of the metallic money supply, and in addition the bankers offered a range of new financial services beyond the ken of the Royal Mint. All the same, the healthy development of the banks themselves was crucially dependent upon the foundation of a sound and sufficient supply of the traditional and officially most important form of money; gold, silver and copper coins. Let us therefore turn now to consider the main features in the development of the coinage system in Britain in the century or so after 1640 with special but not exclusive reference to its interaction with the birth and growth of British banking.

From the seizure of the mint to its mechanization, 1640–1672

'Numismatically the reign of Charles I (1625–1642) is one of the most interesting of all the English monarchs' (Seaby and Purvey 1982, 164). We noted, in chapter 5, that the 1630 treaty with Spain had guaranteed Charles abundant supplies of bullion, mostly silver, so enabling him during his interrupted reign of twenty-four years to produce around £9 million of coins, almost double that issued during Elizabeth's long reign of forty-five years. The Tower mint in London became so busy that branch mints were opened, first at Aberystwyth in 1637, and then, when Charles was forced out of London by the Civil War, he opened a large number of mints, those at Oxford, Shrewsbury and Bristol being particularly active. In addition, use was made of mints at Colchester, Chester, Cork, Edinburgh, Dublin, Exeter, Salisbury, Truro, Weymouth, Worcester and York. Coinage, of a sort, was also turned out for the hard-pressed royal cause in the besieged towns of Carlisle, Newark, Pontefract and Scarborough. Apart from the rather strange pieces produced by the latter four towns it is important and, given Charles's character, surprising to note that the quality of this vast new issue was meticulously maintained.

Charles, habitually short of money, treasured the profits from minting, and by a royal proclamation in 1627 tried to add to them by reviving the Crown's ancient monopoly of exchanging and exporting coin. The king was forced to fume in vain against the growing power of the goldsmiths who had 'left off their proper trade and turned [into] exchangers of plate and foreign coins for our English coins, though they had no right'. Charles was strongly tempted on at least two occasions to go for the quick, rich profits to be reaped from debasement. His first attempt, made in 1626 just a year after he came to the throne, failed largely through the opposition of the Privy Council led by Sir Robert Cotton. His second vain attempt, in 1640, involved a plan to coin some £300,000 nominal value shillings but containing only a quarter of silver, enabling him to pocket the gross profit of £225,000 less the expenses of the deal. Yet again the opposition of the Council, stirred by a speech by Sir Thomas Roe – remarkably similar to that of Cotton – proved too strong, and the purity of the sterling standard was maintained. In the same year Charles forced the East India Company, to which he was already in debt, to sell to him on two years' credit its entire stock of pepper, a favourite commodity for speculation at that time. Charles agreed a purchase price of 2s. 1d. per lb and sold the lot immediately for 1s. 8d. per lb for ready money. Thus, although he considerably increased his medium-term debt, the deal gave him the cash he so desperately needed, but again at the further cost of alienating the City merchants.

Thwarted by the Council, by Parliament and by the City of London, which latter pointedly refused the king's request for a loan of £200,000, Charles turned to another rash expedient which was to lead to immediate and long-term results rather different from those he had anticipated. As from 27 June 1640 he decided to put a stop to the flow of coin from the mint, taking for himself most of the outflow which normally went to the merchants and goldsmiths to whom the king was permanently in debt. On the total amount of between £100,000 and £130,000 thus locked up in the Tower mint and which in normal circumstances would have been claimed, as and when coined, by his creditors, the king proposed to allow 8 per cent. The merchants and goldsmiths immediately raised such an outcry that Charles partially relented, allowing two-thirds of the total bullion to be coined and let out in the usual way, but he still insisted on holding back one-third for six months, paying his creditors 8 per cent. Thus although this partial stoppage of the vast flow of issues to which the merchants, goldsmiths and other creditors of the king had rightly become accustomed might not be quite accurately described with the confiscatory overtones of the common description of 'seizing the goldsmiths' deposits', and although the enforced creditors were eventually paid in full, royal credit had suffered a cruel blow in a most financially sensitive area. Consequently that growing body of influential persons desirous of setting up some form of national or public bank were now more determined than ever to prevent such an institution from coming directly under the power of the monarch to use as an extension of his mint, and thus granting him further independence from the growing power of Parliament over the royal purse – just another example of how monetary, fiscal and constitutional matters were inextricably intertwined in the history of the mid-seventeenth century.

Despite a couple of lapses in intention, Charles had in fact fully upheld the quality of newly issued money. Indeed during his reign the mint began to give some attention to the new inventions which were being more fully applied elsewhere. Although English mints had on the whole maintained the weights and purity of their gold and silver coinage at a higher level than on the Continent, they lagged behind in the technical developments taking place in the mechanization of minting, particularly in France and Flanders. The transformation of coin-making from the slow laborious hand hammering methods that had been in basic principle unchanged from the days of ancient Greece into a more mechanized form, able to produce a faster, cheaper and more uniform output, much more difficult to counterfeit, was not the result of a sudden, single invention, but emerged from a long process of trial and error, made all the longer and more difficult by the furious opposition of the established moneyers. It took many years of patient effort to produce horse-powered machines to roll the metal, to cut out the circular blanks, to stamp the engravings firmer and more quickly than was possible by hand and, perhaps more important than all else at that time, to be able to introduce various forms of graining around the circumference of the coins and to make inscriptions around the edges, both of these latter devices enabling the facile coin clipper finally to be outwitted. The fully mechanized or 'milled' coin with its famous milled edge first reached complete acceptance by 1645 in France when the hammer was finally banished from the Paris mint, a situation not achieved in England until after the Restoration.

'It was only with the employment of Eloy Mestrell at the [Tower] mint during the early years of Elizabeth's reign that mechanization really got under way', involving experiments with horse-powered machines for stamping, and in making counter-rotating hand screw machines for edging devices (Challis 1978, 16). His experiments were not well received. He was dismissed in 1572 and hanged ignominiously in 1578 for counterfeiting, the very crime his machines were intended to circumvent. Later immigrant French and Flemish engineers were to have better luck. Nicholas Briot, chief engraver at the Paris mint, having become frustrated by the strong opposition of the traditionalists, was lured to Britain in 1625 where he produced the first significant issues of milled silver between 1631 and 1640 both at London and at Edinburgh, though hammered money still prevailed. With the seizure of the London mint by the Parliamentarians in August 1642 Briot's influence declined. During the Commonwealth, 1642–60, practically all the coins struck were of the old-fashioned hammered variety, fittingly of very plain design and carrying their inscriptions in English rather than the Latin still used by the Royalists, which smacked too much of the papacy for the liking of the Puritans. The Parliamentarians were however very keen to proceed with the various experiments of the time, and with that in mind invited Pierre Blondeau, engineer at the Paris mint, over to London in 1649. Eventually the mint let him produce a small amount of milled silver, part of a vast treasure captured from a Spanish ship. His meagre £2,000 worth total of milled coins may be contrasted with the £100,000 worth of hammered coins produced from that same treasure in the same year, 1656, and while Briot's coins were not issued, all the hammered coins were issued as usual. Disillusioned, Briot left for France, but was recalled by Charles II a few years later. Meanwhile the Commonwealth government cancelled the private contracts issued by the Stuart kings for the production of farthings and halfpence, and since the very small silver halfpence were issued only sparingly and for the last time by the Commonwealth, the customary dearth of small coins grew to crisis proportions. These shortages were partially filled unofficially by a vast issue by merchants, manufacturers and municipalities, between 1648 and 1672, of copper tokens, mostly of farthings and halfpence.

With the Restoration of Charles II in May 1660 the age of lukewarm experimentation soon came to an end and vigorous preparations were made to mechanize minting as fully and as quickly as possible. For the first two years of his reign it was necessary to continue with the traditional hammered process and, as a transitional measure until such time as sufficient of the new regal coins appeared, the 'illegal' coins issued by the Commonwealth were still accepted. Charles's determination to press on with the new methods was made plain by an Order in Council of May 1661 by which 'all coin was to be struck as soon as possible by machinery, with grained or lettered edges, to stop clipping, cutting and counterfeiting' (Craig 1953, 157). Blondeau was immediately recalled from France and given a 21-year contract to specialize in producing improved forms of milled and engrained edges. For the major manufacturing processes of blanking, stamping and so on, a Flemish family of three brothers, John, Joseph and Phillip Roettier, were appointed to the Tower mint early in 1662. The new team was quickly put to work and produced in 1663 the new £1 coin that symbolized the true birth of modern mechanized minting in Britain – the golden guinea, so called because the gold came from west Africa, its origin also being indicated by carrying the elephant sign of the Africa Company (later the elephant and castle). The guinea was aptly edged with the motto 'Decus et Tutamen' – an Ornament and Safeguard – believed to have been copied from the clasp securing the purse of Blondeau's patron, Richelieu. In the same year, 1663, an Act for the Encouragement of Trade was passed which permitted the free export of foreign coin or bullion provided only that a declaration was made at the customs that it was actually of foreign origin, a declaration which many traders found as easy to make as it was profitable. The expectation was that free export would equally encourage a plentiful import of bullion, so necessary for minting and warring, as well as being essential for trade.

In 1666 an Act for the Encouragement of Coinage was passed by which the age-old seigniorage and other charges traditionally levied on customers of the mint to pay for coining were abolished. Henceforth the cost was to be met by import duties on wine, beer, cider, spirits and vinegar. A much more modern administrative system thus reinforced the beneficial effects of the technical improvements in the currency. As well as applying the new methods of minting to the silver and gold coinage, an important new step was taken in 1672 when the first proper state issue of a copper coinage appeared from the Tower mint, fully mechanized and bearing the famous Britannia insignia which has appeared on British coins in various guises for over 300 years. Britannia, seated on a bank of money, formed the official seal granted to the Bank of England in 1694 and still adorns the current fifty pence piece and the current notes of the Bank. The historian of the mint, Sir John Craig, seems perhaps too readily to have come to the conclusion that 'there is no foundation for the statement that the figure, in which the face is microscopic, was modelled from a lady of the Court' (1953, 174). However, the evidence given by Ruding in 1819 in his Supplement to his voluminous *Annals of the Coinage* still seems to be convincing: 'These coins were engraved by Roettier and the figure of Britannia is said to bear a strong resemblance to the Duchess of Richmond, in our coins and in a Medal, as one might easily and at first sight know it to be her.' He gives the evidence of contemporaries like Evelyn and Walpole, the latter believing that 'Roettier, being in love with the fair Mrs Stuart, Duchess of Richmond, represented her likeness under the form of Britannia on the Reverse of a large Medal' (Ruding 1840, Supplement, 59). Be that as it may, what is still more certain is that the new milled Britannia coinage was so attractive that instead of being circulated as was urgently required, it was initially most avidly hoarded, while the existing, badly worn, unattractive hammered coins and tokens continued to be used instead. As a not unimportant rider to Gresham's Law, bad-looking money chases out the good-looking money. Of course the new mechanized coins, as well as being attractive to look at, were appreciably heavier than the old coinage, so that although the clipper was made redundant, the culler and melter were still thriving. Many of the new coins, especially the silver coins, disappeared almost as soon as they were issued. Charles II had successfully revolutionized the techniques of minting and had introduced a freer administration of the currency, yet chiefly because most of the newly milled money had quickly vanished, another great reform of the coinage became obviously necessary within a few years of his death in 1685.

From the great recoinage to the death of Newton, 1696–1727

The main problem lay with the terrible state of the silver coinage, for it was still the old hammered silver that formed the bulk of the currency. The gold coins were circulated less frequently than silver (though their circulation was increasing) and they were handled more carefully than was the case with the battered and less valuable silver. Furthermore the gold coins were eagerly sought by the goldsmith bankers for use as reserves for their deposits. As for minting base metals like copper, this was considered by the mint at that time and even as late as 1751 to be simply a very reluctantly accepted social duty. Thus in that year Joseph Harris, assay master of the mint, considered that 'Copper coins with us are properly not money, but a kind of tokens' though admittedly 'very useful in small home traffic' (Craig 1953, 250). Consequently the recoinage, when it belatedly took place from 1696, was like that of all previous English examples, a recoinage of silver, still the major component of the currency. As more and more silver drained away to Holland and to the Far East the urgent need for reform grew cumulatively greater. Though, as we have seen, the Stuart kings were unable to debase the currency in England, James II tried it on in Ireland, to which country he fled via France, after abdicating in December 1688. A considerable amount of brass and 'mixed white metal' coinage was produced by the Dublin mint before James was defeated at the Battle of the Boyne on 1 July 1690. In the face of the heavy military expenditures facing the new monarchy of William and Mary, as war with France had broken out again in 1689, some argued that reform of the coinage should be deferred until the end of the war when the enormous strains on the state's finances would be alleviated. Others, including the key personage of the Chancellor of the Exchequer, Charles Montagu, argued on the contrary, that the successful prosecution of the war itself depended crucially on immediately reforming the currency, otherwise soldiers could not be paid in acceptable coin, nor could the army and navy secure the supplies they needed. The army marched on its money.

The sharply increasing price of the guinea was an incontrovertible index of the crisis in the coinage. Though originally issued at 20s. it had risen quickly to 21s. or just above until in March 1694 it rose to 22s. It reached a peak of 30s. by June 1695. Against such evidence the procrastinators gave way, and the decision to reform was given by the king in Parliament in November 1695. Now the arguments, which had been simmering for years, about what type of reform should be carried out, remained to be hastily settled. There were two main questions, the first one being whether to re-establish the old standard of metallic purity, or to reduce it. Given the lessons of monetary history regarding the previous slippery-slope results of debasement, those in favour of maintaining the purity won the day. Secondly there was a more even division of opinion as to whether the weights of the new coins should also be maintained at the old mint level, obviously at great cost, or whether they should be brought down somewhere near to the average weight of the worn and clipped coinage which formed the actual currency of the day, at a correspondingly lower cost to the Exchequer – but, it was feared, with loss of face and still more important, loss of public credit. The various views brought into the arena some of the foremost members of the Age of Enlightenment, including the philosopher John Locke and the world's greatest scientist, Isaac Newton, both of whom had been asked for their views by the Chancellor of the Exchequer, Charles Montagu. Locke argued strongly, in his *Short Observations* and *Further Considerations Concerning Raising the Value of Money*, both published in 1695, in favour of full restoration of the weights. The opposite school was led by William Lowndes, Secretary of the Treasury, and hence possibly a little predisposed to save the Treasury the very heavy costs of a full restoration. Lowndes had made a very thorough study of the history of the currency and made a number of telling points, widely supported by the goldsmiths and bankers, for writing down the value of the currency and stabilizing it at the lower level to which it had then fallen. Newton was in touch with both Locke and Lowndes, for both sides, the restorers and the devaluers, recognized the importance of getting a person of such outstanding stature on their side – as have later historians, especially since Newton's written views were supposed, by Feavearyear among others, to have been lost. Thus Feavearyear, incorrectly as it happened, believed Newton to be 'in substantial agreement' with Locke, while Craig though considering that Newton's view on the contrary 'was close to Lowndes's of which he had doubtless been informed', nevertheless fails to give Newton the credit for stating unequivocally his support for devaluation and his clear statement of the deflationary force of restoring the full value of the currency (Feavearyear 1963, 134; Craig 1953, 186).

Luckily Newton's 'lost' writings on the recoinage problem, along with those of Sir Christopher Wren, Sir John Houblon and others were rediscovered in 1940 in the aptly endowed Goldsmiths' Library of the University of London. In essence and shorn of their particular details, the arguments between Locke and Lowndes have been repeated frequently since then, Locke being the sound-money man conservatively opposed to the dangers of what a later generation of Americans would call monkeying about with money, whereas Lowndes thought that money could in certain circumstances and within reasonable limits be managed, and so believed the standard weight for the pound had not been immutably fixed for all time.

In substance, though not in every detail, Locke's views won the day, supported as they were by the Chancellor of the Exchequer, by the Court, and by most of the landed interest and conservative opinion. In January 1696 an 'Act for Remedying the ill State of the Coin' was passed, and for the first time since 1299 the weight standards were fully restored, and for the first time ever, the full costs were to be borne by the Exchequer. Locke's concept of the sanctity of the standard as a historically given weight of precious metal became enshrined in the minds of the authorities and was largely responsible for the ease with which the kingdom moved gradually during the eighteenth century towards the gold standard, which it did not officially embrace until 1816. The great 'Silver Recoinage' of 1696 thus turned out to have unexpected long-term effects in paving the way for the gold standard. The cost of the reform greatly exceeded the forecasts, coming to £2.7 million when total revenues were about £5 million. In addition hidden real costs of some £1 million were inflicted on those, mostly among the poor, who failed to send in their clipped coins by the due date. As well as the Tower mint, branch mints at Bristol, Chester, Exeter, Norwich and York were pressed into service to deal with the huge task of recoinage. A total of £6,800,000 new milled silver coins was produced during the three years of the recoinage period. The cost of the recoinage was to be met – rather perversely in the Age of Enlightenment – by a tax on windows. Because the proceeds of the tax naturally took a year or two to assess and collect, the immediate costs were met in a variety of novel ways highly relevant to the development of banking, to be examined shortly. Suffice it to say that by the time our greatest scientist was promoted from Warden to Master of the Mint on Christmas Day 1699, the enormous task of the full restoration of the coinage had been completed. Compared with what had gone before, the mastership of Sir Isaac Newton proved relatively uneventful, and he was luckily able to devote practically as much time as he liked to his researches in mathematics and natural science until his death on 20 March 1727.

During the latter years of his period as Master an attempt was made to reopen the Dublin mint so as to increase the amount and improve the standard of the copper currency of Ireland, but since there was no agreement regarding who should meet the costs nothing came of the plan. The lack of small money in Ireland had grown to such a pitch that 'manufacturers were obliged to pay their men in tokens in cards signed upon the back, to be afterwards exchanged for money' (Ruding 1840, II, 68). A more ambitious attempt to supply good-quality money followed in mid-1722 when Parliament granted William Wood a licence to manufacture halfpence and farthings for Ireland. Minting promptly began in Bristol in August 1722, but the intense opposition in Ireland led to the minting being stopped, even before its most famous opponent, Dean Swift, uttered his protests in two sermons later published in his *Drapier's Letters* (1724), which made it practically certain that the minting would never recommence. In his *Letters* the Dean 'could see no reason why we of all nations are thus restrained' from having their own currency produced in their own mint. Sir John Craig however makes the telling point that whereas in 1689 there were only thirteen Irish pence to the English shilling (of twelve pence), 'compared with autonomous Scotland, whose currency sank from parity to one-twelfth of English values in the two centuries before 1600, the English did not do badly' (Craig 1953, 369). Thus the Irish poor were left for many years further to suffer from their own tokens and quaintly endorsed promissory cards, a sort of anachronistic, involuntary, reverse credit card.

During the twenty-seven years of Newton's mastership, the emphasis at the mint changed dramatically from silver to gold. Indeed, during the whole of the eighteenth century only some £1,254,000 of silver was coined, whereas for just the forty-five years between 1695 and 1740 some £17,000,000 of gold was minted. At the same time much of the new silver minted during the recoinage had disappeared from circulation. When the principle so firmly established by the great reform, namely that the pound sterling was a given weight of metal, became linked with the revealed coinage preferences of the public, and particularly those of the bankers, merchants and rich individuals who could now afford more luxuries, then the gold standard had practically arrived, silently a century or more before its legal enactment. Now just as the narrow focus of the mint was changing from silver to gold, so the wider views of the community at large were changing from a preoccupation with coins into a growing appreciation of the role of various forms of paper substitutes for money such as bills, receipts, notes, drafts, orders and cheques and of the banking institutions that, in handling or issuing them, gave them greater acceptability or liquidity.

The rise of the goldsmith-banker, 1633–1672

Bits and pieces of the banker's many functions – including the safe keeping of gold, silver and deposits of money; lending out such monetary deposits as well as their own moneys; transferring money from town to town and person to person; exchanging foreign coin and bullion and discounting bills of exchange and tallies – had been carried out part-time as a by-product of other trading activities in various parts of Britain for a century or more before recognized indigenous 'bankers' emerged in London by about the 1640s. London, as by far the largest town in the country and with more than its fair share of the country's wealthiest people, was a rapidly expanding domestic market. It was also normally the centre of government, of domestic trade and, above all, of overseas trade. The development of financial intermediaries enabled rich persons to find profitable outlets for their surplus funds in London which attracted money in increasing amounts not only from the Continent but also internally. Provincial writers were loud in their condemnation of London's power in drawing to itself the liquid wealth of the country. The growing size and wealth of the city stimulated the growth of a vast market in coal and food, making available capital for further investment in agricultural improvements in a virtuous spiral which, after the Restoration, led to a sizeable export in grain and a corresponding balance of payments surplus financed by an influx of foreign capital. The greater degree of specialization in financial activities that evolved into fully fledged banking was thus largely the result of the insistent demands of businessmen engaged in three main areas centred in London: the new domestic markets in food and coal, the rapidly expanding markets concerned with exotic commodities, foreign exchange and shipping; and, in many ways the most important of all, the market in government debt. England, and this meant mainly London, was already challenging Holland as the world's entrepot. Its financial challenge in developing its own banking expertise was a natural consequence. Previously, as we have seen, the only true bankers in the sense of being full-time professionals were immigrants, mainly Italian, German and especially Dutch. It was true, as Richards (1929) says, that 'alien immigration helped to focus English public opinion on the problems of currency and of banking'. Although the initial impetus came from the Continent, the embryo capital and money markets in London were growing so fast that once indigenous banking began to take root it made rapid and sustained progress in this its foundation stage from around 1633 onwards, skilfully modifying the foreign models to its own particular requirements until the first major check to its development was clumsily administered by Charles II in 1672.

At the beginning of the seventeenth century there already existed a variety of different types of potential indigenous bankers, including the wool brogger, the corn bodger, the textile merchant, the tax farmer, the pawnbroker, the goldsmith and the scrivener. In so far as simple deposit banking is concerned it was the latter who first emerged into prominence. 'The shop of the Scrivener was the first English Bank of Deposit', for it was he who was the first financial intermediary in England to make a regular practice of keeping money deposits for the express purpose of lending to customers (Richards 1929). The scrivener was a clerical expert equipped with legal training or acquired legal knowledge, often an official public notary, who was customarily employed in drawing up contracts, wills, bills, bonds and mortgages, and so a respected, confidential adviser normally entrusted with large amounts of money – which he soon learned to put to good account, picking up many banking skills in the process. As far as lending is concerned, it was the tax farmer who grew to be particularly prominent in the Stuart period from 1604 onwards. Tax farming was a system by which a group of rich individuals paid the king in advance a licence fee for the privilege of collecting for him the various customs duties and taxes due locally, transferring to the king on a monthly or quarterly basis the sums so assessed, minus a generous allowance for their own expenses. The flow of taxes was thus speeded up, regularized and of course passed through the hands of rich and influential middlemen. In effect the farmers made loans to the king in anticipation of the revenue. Their loans were supplemented by collecting a stream of local deposits as well as customs which they profitably on-lent to the king. Thus they 'acted as a kind of collective banking syndicate, able to lend on a scale that no one individual (prudently) could' (C. Wilson 1965, 98). The transformation of the age-old occupation of pawnbroking into a more regularized form of lending was actively advocated in England. The model of the Italian 'montes pietatis', some of which grew into large-scale public banks, was not followed, though the pawnbroker was then and continued to be an indispensable lender for the poorer sort of trader. His functions remained too narrow in scope and size to be properly considered as banking. It was not the ubiquitous pawnbroker or tax farmer who grew to be a proper banker; rather it was the metropolitan goldsmith, further emphasizing and reflecting the rising importance of London as a European financial centre.

The first stage in the transformation of goldsmiths into bankers took place when a number of them became actively engaged as dealers in foreign and domestic coins, for reasons already discussed. Gradually a clear distinction emerged between the 'working goldsmiths', and the 'exchanging goldsmiths' from which latter group the true bankers typically emerged. The use of the goldsmiths' safes as a secure place for people's jewels, bullion and coins was obviously increased following the 'seizure of the mint' in 1640 and the outbreak of the Civil War in 1642. The goldsmiths' interest in exchanging coinage thus became linked with the keeping of demand deposits and the recording for the customer of his 'running cash' or current account. The insecurity of life and property, given the ravages of war, plague and fire during this period not only meant that customers sought the security of the goldsmiths as never before, but since the ordinary demand for goldsmiths to make objects of gold and silver for the customers had at that time practically ceased, the goldsmiths actively welcomed their new or enlarged banking-type business. Their outlets for lending to private customers and to government grew to be so essential and profitable that in order to attract more deposits they began to offer to pay interest on time deposits. Although current accounts were firmly established under the Commonwealth, 'there is no evidence of time deposits prior to 1660' (Richards 1929). Within the next few years there was a considerable expansion in this type of deposit, a position summarized in this oft-quoted comment by Defoe in his *Essay on Projects* (1690): 'Our bankers are indeed nothing but goldsmiths' shops where, if you lay money on demand, they allow you nothing; if at time, three per cent.'

It was the paperwork associated with these activities which formed the essence of the new banking initiatives developed by the goldsmiths at this time, in particular the cheque and the inland bill (which grew in imitation of the original internationally traded bill of exchange), and the banknote, which was an adaptation of the original goldsmith's receipt. What started out simply as paper records of credit transactions and transfer payments gradually became transformed into a significant extension of the metallic money supply. To the goldsmiths it was a natural step to add to their business of exchanging foreign coins that of purchasing, at a discount, bills of exchange. All the merchants of any size had long been familiar with the money market in bills, traditionally dominated by the foreign exchange markets in Antwerp and Amsterdam with literally thousands of members. The London goldsmiths now began to take over some of this business, for they were in a position to know the credit rating of the issuers and endorsers of the bills. They quickly extended their expertise in handling overseas trade bills to dealing in inland bills and, of crucial importance to the government, to the tallies and other assignable credit instruments being issued in a flood by the Stuarts and the Commonwealth. By their dealings in bills, the general liquidity of the money market was significantly enhanced, an increase in the quality again acting as a supplement to the traditional quantity of money.

The earliest extant cheque (now in the Institute of Bankers' Library in Lombard Street) dated 1659, is an order by a Nicholas Vanacker addressed to the London goldsmiths Morris and Clayton to pay a Mr Delboe 'or order' the sum of £400. The author of the *History of Negotiable Instruments in English Law* makes it clear that such cheques were modelled on the bill of exchange and that it was the goldsmiths, not the scriveners, who first developed cheques, although they were called by a variety of other names, such as notes or bills. 'It was not until well into the eighteenth century that the word "cheque", or "check", as it was then spelt (and still is of course in America), came to be applied to this type of instrument on the analogy of the real treasury or "exchequer"' (Holden 1955).

The earliest extant goldsmith's receipt appeared some twenty-six years before the cheque and was issued by Laurence Hoare in 1633. A goldsmith's receipt or note was evidence of ability to pay; of money in the bank. At first such receipts were issued to named customers who had made deposits of cash, and in time became negotiable just like endorsed bills of exchange. Then 'some ingenious goldsmith conceived the epoch-making notion of giving notes not only to those who had deposited metal, but also to those who came to borrow it, and so founded modern banking' (H. Withers 1909: 20). This position was reached by the 1660s. We owe our evidence for the earliest recorded case of a banknote being used for payment to that fount of social and economic knowledge, the famous diary of Samuel Pepys, Secretary to the Navy. In his entry for 29 February 1668 he casually mentions sending to his father a note for £600 – issued by the goldsmith Colvill. When the notes were issued not to a named person but to bearer, the modern bank promissory note had arrived, at least in practice if not in legal propriety. Difficulties occurred from time to time over enforcement of payment for endorsed bills and notes. Lord Justice Holt confirmed the negotiability of inland bills in 1697 but there still remained doubt about the negotiability of notes. It required a special act of codification and clarification, the Promissory Notes Act of 1704, to confirm the legality of the common practices and customs that had been developed by the goldsmith bankers since the 1640s, and thus belatedly to remove what had been an irritant to the bankers' progress. A far greater obstacle had however been royally thrown across their path early in 1672.

Tally-money and the Stop of the Exchequer

'To the Exchequer,' writes Pepys on 16 May 1666, 'where the lazy devils have not yet done my tallies.' We have seen, in chapter 4, how these notched sticks came to play a greater role in English government finance than anywhere else. Tallies were reaching the zenith of their importance in Pepys's time. The reason for the delay in producing tallies for Pepys's Navy Department and for all the other government departments was the inordinate increase in the number and size of tallies because of the vast increase in the number of creditors and the larger totals of individual loans respectively. When the Oxford Parliament of 1665 granted Charles II an 'Aid' or tax of £1.5 million, the issue of tallies, made as usual in anticipation of the revenue from this Aid, was accompanied by Exchequer Orders to Pay, allocating the revenues to the holder of tallies in strict rotation. Just like the normal tallies, the new orders were also assignable, i.e. the claim to revenue could be officially passed on to someone else on maturity. Furthermore just as the tallies had become negotiable by written endorsement, so, and much more conveniently, were the new paper orders, and they similarly carried interest. These two features of assignability and interest made the tallies and orders highly attractive to the goldsmith bankers who, buying them up at a profitable discount, became by far the major holders of outstanding government debt. J. Keith Horsefield in his 'Stop of the Exchequer Revisited' (1982, 511–28) shows that 'between 1667 and 1671 the practice grew up of issuing orders not against the proceeds of specific taxes, but against the revenue in general' with the important result that 'Since the orders were no longer tied to revenue already voted, there was no automatic limit to the number issued.' Charles had found the key to a new treasure house, an elastic increase to the revenue, and readily yielded to the temptation now available. The improved liquidity of the tallies and orders as a result of the market made in them by the goldsmiths virtually turned them into interest-bearing money. Their increased use economized on scarce coinage and allowed the small investor with just £20 or so to play his part in the greatly enlarged market in short-term government debt.

However, in order to induce the investing public in an increasingly saturated market to lend still greater amounts on the general security of an unbuoyant tax base, the king (who was believed to have authority to breach the usury laws) was forced to offer rates of 8 or 10 per cent, and even offered agents 2 per cent as an inducement to find large borrowers. Before the crisis broke, even the goldsmiths themselves, despite the 6 per cent legal maximum, were offering depositors of near-demand deposits 5 or 6 per cent regularly, in order to carry out discounting at very much higher rates. Pepys himself was getting 7 per cent from Viner for money at just two days' notice in 1666. With the expansion of the issues of Exchequer Orders the goldsmiths had reached a position in late 1671 of being so fully loaned up that they refused the king's request for moneys urgently required for the navy. In reply he issued a Proclamation on 2 January 1672 prohibiting payment, with certain exceptions, from the Exchequer. Such was the infamous 'Stop of the Exchequer', which contemporary opinion (and the earlier economic historians) viewed as having a disastrous effect on the goldsmith bankers. This opinion has, by and large, been recently reinforced by the careful researches of J. K. Horsefield, thus correcting the erroneous views of Richards (in his *Early History of English Banking*, 1929) which held fashionable sway for fifty years, namely that the goldsmith bankers had not been too badly affected. There is no doubt that it was the bankers who were left holding the vast bulk of assets made suddenly illiquid by the Stop in this grim game of musical chairs.

The first result of the Stop was the shock to royal credit. Had it not been for the Stop, Britain might have had a permanent issue of state notes. In fact for a time Exchequer paper orders had replaced tallies. But the Stop revived memories of the seizure of the mint in 1640, and Pepys echoed public concern in thinking that it demonstrated 'the unsafe condition of a bank under the monarchy'. Despite an immediate run on the goldsmiths, which forced them temporarily to suspend payment, they weathered the initial storm, and the fatal effects on their credit took some time to take their toll. This was largely a tribute to their original strength rather than to the exceptional payments allowed out of the Exchequer, for in contrast to the position in 1640, the goldsmiths as a group were never to be repaid in full, and the tardy, partial repayments that were eventually made merely prolonged the death agonies of the leading goldsmith bankers. The odium which rightly attached to the exchequer orders was undeservedly but understandably spread to include the notes issued by the bankers themselves. 'Goldsmiths' notes became unacceptable as a general means of payment 'partly because the Treasury itself altered its habits and stated them as 'not now money', so that 'it was not until 1680 that they again agreed to accept goldsmiths' notes' (Horsefield 1982, 523).

The Stop, which had originally been intended to last just one year, was extended for two more years and then indefinitely. Of the total debt, including accrued interest, which together totalled £1,314,940 in 1677, by far the greatest amount, £1,282,143, or some 97.5 per cent, was owed to the bankers. Horsefield's researches further show that Sir Robert Viner was owed £416,724; Blackwell £259,994; Whitehall £284,866; and Lindsay, Portman and Snow each between about £60,000 and £80,000. Eight other bankers were owed a total of just under £100,000 altogether. Reluctantly Charles agreed to pay 6 per cent interest – the legal maximum – but this itself failed to recoup their losses, for as we have seen, the goldsmiths had themselves been offering depositors that rate and more to purchase the debt in the first place. After the Glorious Revolution of 1688 William and Mary were hesitant in meeting the claims of the goldsmiths, who were blamed for having extracted an illegally high rate from the king and so deserved to have their fingers burned. In 1705 the interest on the bankers' debt was reduced to 3 per cent, and to 2½ per cent in 1714, when the capital sum was written down to about half its original nominal value. The remaining debt was then absorbed into the general national debt and no longer separately identified. Thus at long last the bankers or their inheritors were repaid only about half of their original debt and received an average true rate of interest of just about 1½ per cent.

No wonder the Stop had such a ruinous effect on most of the original bankers. All six of the largest holders of debt eventually failed. In 1684 the largest, Viner, failed, and then, in order of size, Blackwell was declared bankrupt in 1682; Whitehall was imprisoned for debt in 1685; Lindsay absconded in 1679; Portman became bankrupt in 1678 and Snow was in prison for debt in 1690. Five of the eight next largest debtors also failed. In addition, according to Horsefield's careful reckoning, some 2,500 depositors, including owners of funds supporting a number of widows and orphans, were adversely affected. A few famous names, such as Child's and Hoare's survived, while a new generation of unscathed goldsmiths arose to fill the gaps. Perhaps the greatest casualty of the Stop was the setback to all the many plans afoot in the 1660s and early 1670s to establish a large public bank on the continental model. Horsefield points out that whereas at least twenty new companies were formed between 1672 and 1694, not one of them was a bank. Thus, he concludes, 'the most significant effect of the Stop was to postpone for as much as ten to fifteen years the beginning of joint-stock banking in England' (1982, 528).

Foundation and early years of the Bank of England

Of the hundred or more schemes for a public bank put forward in Britain in the seventy years after 1640 (and most thoroughly analysed by J. Keith Horsefield in *British Monetary Experiments, 1650–1710),* only two successfully overcame the many pitfalls that caused all the others to flounder and fail. The various sporadic proposals tentatively suggested in the earlier years, and put into abeyance by the Stop of the Exchequer, reached an intensity of purposeful effort in the first half of the 1690s, for reasons about to be examined. Before doing so it will be of use to taste the flavour of some half-dozen of the earlier concepts, since the ideas contained therein greatly influenced the nature of the more mature discussions which reached their fruition in the 1690s.

The chronological leader is probably that of Henry Robinson who in 1641 published a 62-page pamphlet, *England's Safety in Trades Encrease*, based on the example of the long-established Italian banks. However when 'in the second half of the seventeenth century Amsterdam displaced Genoa as the world market for precious metals', Holland increasingly became the popular model for imitation in monetary experiments (Kirshner 1974, 227). To William Potter writing in 1650 the 'Key to Wealth' was to be found in a plentiful issue of banknotes to form the basis of tradesmen's credit. Samuel Hartlib, in his *Discoverie for the Division . . . of Land* (1653), set forth the Bank of Amsterdam, with which British merchants were becoming increasingly familiar, as his model for a Bank of England, but insisted that insofar as Potter's ideas for note issue were concerned, 'There be no way to raise this Credit in Banks but by mortgage of Lands', thus foreshadowing the land bank craze of the 1690s. Hartlib also outlined a scheme for country-wide money transmission using a primitive precursor of the cheque system (Horsefield 1960, 94–5). In 1658 Samuel Lambe, a London merchant, proposed a Bank in London governed by trusted leaders from the chartered companies, such as the East India, Muscovy and Levant companies, again in imitation of the Amsterdam Bank. Probably first written in 1663, but not published until 1690, was Sir William Killigrew's idea for a state issue of notes in anticipation of taxes, which may well have formed the source for the paper Exchequer Orders issued between 1667 and 1672, described earlier. Also in the mid-1660s a number of writers, such as Hugh Chamberlen, in his *Description of the Office of Credit* (1665), advocated 'Lombards' or 'Lumbards' where credit would be allied to pawnbroking, with varying emphasis on the dual purposes of providing working capital for traders and funds for charity. All the main aspects of the above proposals came to a head in the exciting and euphoric experiments in the dramatic three-year period from 1694 to 1696 which saw the founding of the Bank of England and the Bank of Scotland, the issue of Exchequer bills, attempts to establish the Land Bank and the Orphans' Bank, the Million Act, various new lotteries, poll taxes, excise taxes and window taxes, and of course, the start of the great recoinage already described.

The plethora of pamphlets in favour of a public, joint-stock bank gave rise to a number of optimistic projects of which the Bank of England turned out to be by far the most important. Dislike of the usurious practices of the goldsmith bankers was a prominent motive stirring on the projectors of potential new institutions. The maximum legal rate of interest, reduced from 10 per cent to 8 per cent in 1624 was brought down further to 6 per cent by the Commonwealth government in 1651 and legally reconfirmed at that level by the Restoration government in 1660. In 1690 a proposal to bring the rate down to 4 per cent was lost in Parliament by just three votes. There was a certain amount of wishful thinking about such maxima, but they did mirror the market trend. The laws were commonly flouted and, except for occasional vindictive cases, a blind eye was turned on marginal infringements. The usury laws were also more strictly interpreted for loans than for discounts. Even so rates of discount of 20 or 30 per cent, which were charged by a few goldsmiths at times of crisis when shortages of cash were at their height, or when the tallies or paper bills being discounted were of doubtful value or where it was uncertain that they would actually be paid on the due date, seemed inexcusable to the business community at large who turned the deserved particular condemnation of the relatively few into a general accusation against the monopolistic power supposedly exerted by all the goldsmith bankers almost all the time. A new public bank would thus achieve the dual related aims of reducing the rates of interest through breaking the goldsmiths' monopoly. Furthermore these beneficial micro-economic effects would work throughout the whole business world to bring about macro-economic gains in the shape of greater national wealth. Little wonder that commercial interests in the City in the 1690s were optimistic and impatient with regard to setting up their own joint-stock bank, confident of widespread support. If the one essential but hitherto missing ingredient, namely the support of the government could be secured, the battle for the Bank of England would be won.

Thus the Bank of England was born out of a marriage of convenience between the business community of the City, ambitiously confident that it could run such a bank profitably, and the government of the day, desperately short of the very large amount of cash urgently needed to carry on the long war against Louis XIV, the most powerful ruler in Europe. These needs were growing at a far faster pace than the lending resources of the goldsmiths, combined with the new forms of taxation, largely copied from the Dutch, could supply, despite the strong support of Parliament (see D. W. Jones, 1988). The tremendous increase in the financial demands being made by the government in the final thirty years of the seventeenth century are shown in the following revenue and borrowing statistics (taken from Chandaman 1975, 504). In the period 1670 to 1685 the total net fiscal revenue came to £24.8 million; it more than doubled to £55.7 million in the following corresponding period from 1685 to 1700. The figures for net borrowing show a spectacular seventeenfold increase from a total of just £0.8 million in the first period to £13.8 million in the second period. These figures indicate not only the growing cost of lengthy wars but also the government's need to rely much more on borrowing than previously. Even more significant for the history of banking and of the national debt was the need to be able to tap new sources of *long-term* borrowing, rather than simply relying on the short-term, hand-to-mouth expedients which the Tudors and Stuarts had been forced to adopt. It was thus from the urgent discussions of how to raise a 'perpetual loan' at a rate of interest economical to the government and yet readily acceptable to the lenders – because of the other benefits attached to the deal – that the Bank of England came into being. If Parliament (and no longer just the monarch) had the responsibility of repaying a substantial loan, even if long-term, then some future generation would be faced with heavy and possibly unsupportable burdens of taxation when taxable capacity was already thought to be at or near its limit. However, if the lenders could be induced to make a permanent loan then the additional taxation required to be raised at any time would be just a fraction of the total loan, being simply the annual interest or service charge. It was that canny and much misjudged Scot, William Paterson, who first conceived a viable plan for this sprat to catch a massive mackerel.

Paterson was born in Tynwald near Dumfries in 1658 – incidentally barely ten miles from the later birthplace of the Revd Dr Henry Duncan, father of the savings bank movement. Historians tend towards hysteria in their assessments of Paterson's life and work, for his gift for arousing controversy lives on after him. To some, e.g. Andreades, 'Paterson was a genius' but 'bold even to rashness', possibly still the best summation of this complex character. His contemporary, Daniel Defoe, spoke most highly of him, as did his compatriot, Sir Walter Scott, a view shared by the author of a brief, but well-researched recent biography (Evans 1985). However, the official historian of the Bank of England, Sir John Clapham, loftily dismisses Paterson as a 'pedlar turned merchant'; repeats Macaulay's cheap gibe that 'his friends called him a missionary, his enemies, a buccaneer'; states unequivocally that 'I think him an overrated person' not really worthy to have his portrait, if a fitting one were available, in the Bank's official history; and, more seriously, even questions whether he was 'strictly' the originator of the 'final' scheme for the Bank, or was 'merely the mouthpiece' of a City pressure group. But this final scheme was only one of at least three such schemes in which Paterson played the leading role and which were laid before various parliamentary committees and Charles Montagu,

Chancellor of the Exchequer, between 1691 and 1694, as is shown conclusively by J. Keith Horsefield in his detailed researches in *British Monetary Experiments 1650–1710* (published ten years before Clapham's official account, but nowhere mentioned by him). That Paterson's project was finally enthusiastically adopted, despite his awkwardness, speaks volumes for its merit, which was clearly recognized by Montagu, who rallied the Court and Parliament to the cause, and by Michael Godfrey, the three Houblon brothers, Sir Gilbert Heathcote and others who organized backing from the wealthy City interests. These all became founder members of the board of directors of the Bank of England, but Paterson was dismissed after seven short months, mainly because he had become involved with the supporters of the scheme by means of which the London 'Orphans' Fund' became transformed in 1695 into a bank, and therefore was seen by the Bank of England as a competitor and Paterson's position as disloyal. Paterson's claim to the gratitude of Londoners extends beyond the financial field, for it was largely owing to his energetic support that the Hampstead and Highgate Aqueduct Company was formed in 1691 to supply its citizens with fresh, clean water. Paterson failed however in his visionary ambition to set up in London a 'Library of Commerce', which among other benefits might have provided historians with a surer foundation for some of their generalizations about the City and its financial institutions, including the true merit of Paterson himself.

The Bank of England came into being by the Ways and Means Act of June 1694 and was confirmed by a Royal Charter of Incorporation (27 July 1694). The Act makes it clear that its real purpose was to raise money for the War of the League of Augsburg by taxation and by the novel device of a permanent loan, the bank being very much a secondary matter, though essential to guarantee the success of the main purpose. The Act was also known variously as the 'Tonnage' or 'Tunnage' Act, because the taxes were to be raised from both ships and wines, for the carrying capacity of ships was then commonly measured either by the 'weight of water displaced' method, or, which came to very much the same thing, the number of large casks or 'tuns' of wine (of 252 gallons, equalling when allowance is made for evaporation, 2,240 pounds or one ton weight approximately), which the ship could carry. This explains the preamble of 'An Act for granting to their Majesties several Rates and Duties upon Tunnages of Ships and Vessels, and upon Beer, Ale, and other Liquors; for securing certain Recompenses and Advantages . . . to such persons as shall voluntarily advance the Sum of Fifteen hundred thousand Pounds towards carrying on the war against France'. The £1,500,000 was to come from two unequal sources;

£300,000 from annuities, and the major sum of £1,200,000 from the total original capital subscriptions to the 'Governor and Company of the Bank of England'. In return the Bank was to be paid 8 per cent interest plus an annual management fee of £4,000. Thus for just £100,000 a year, and some vague privileges to a bank, and with no capital repayment burden to worry about, the government received £1,200,000 almost immediately. The whole amount, 25 per cent paid up, was subscribed within twelve days, and the total sum was in the hands of the government by the end of 1694. This was an astonishing success given the abject failure of a number of rival banking-type institutions, but not so surprising given the speculative boom in other kinds of companies being formed around the same time. From the government's point of view it was an object lesson of the advantages of borrowing as compared with taxation to meet sudden emergencies. Paterson was right in saying that, to the government, the bank was only 'a lame expedient for £1,200,000' – but the government had other priorities.

During its passage through Parliament two significant amendments were made: to placate the Tories the Bank's power to carry out commercial trading was strictly limited, while to please the Whigs a more important limitation was placed on its power to lend to the Crown. The by-laws of the Bank did allow for the sale of any merchandise received through pawnbroking, then considered by some to be an acceptable ingredient of a proper range of banking services; but apart from an initial flurry, such operations soon dwindled to insignificance. It was quite a different matter with regard to the Bank's lending to the government, and it did not take long for the Bank and the government together to find ways around the restriction which the Whigs first intended to fix at a ceiling of the original £1,200,000 capital. Even the Whigs relaxed their attitude when it became obvious that Parliament had discovered new ways of limiting the powers of the king. The capital of the Bank was widely spread by limiting the maximum ownership of the original shares to £10,000. King William and Queen Mary each subscribed the maximum. The pattern of ownership, with medium and large holdings together taking up 92.3 per cent in value terms, is shown in table 6.1.

Although the Bank had thus got off to an excellent start it was soon to experience difficulties so immense that its continued existence seemed very doubtful. The natural antipathy of the goldsmith bankers was to be expected, and concerted withdrawals of cash did occasionally occur. Such opposition was in the main short-lived and was less damaging than earlier writers, like Clarendon and Andreades had

Table 6.1 Bank of England stock holdings, July 1694.

Size	Holdings		Total value	Total
	No.	%		% value
£300 & under	561	37	£92,550	7.7
£300–£1,999	778	52	£530,350	44.2
£2,000 & over	170	11	£577,100	48.1
	1,509	100	£1,200,000	100

supposed. A few important goldsmith bankers, especially Charles Duncombe remained stubbornly hostile, but the value and convenience of having an account with the Bank soon began to be widely appreciated, so that in general the goldsmiths followed the example of Richard Hoare and of Freame and Gould (forerunners of Barclays) who both opened accounts in the Bank in March 1695. In course of time the goldsmiths gave up their own note issues and used Bank of England notes instead, to their mutual advantage. What the Bank feared most was the threat posed by the establishment of rival public banks, though in retrospect such fears are seen to have been largely unjustified. We have noted the Bank's furious reaction to Paterson's support for the plan by which the City of London Orphans' Fund transformed itself into the Orphans' Bank in 1695. By 1700 it had petered out of existence. The Million Bank was also founded in 1695 and combined its main activities of dealing with lotteries and annuities with more general forms of banking. However it also soon relinquished its banking, but it continued to carry on acting as an investment fund for government securities for a century.

Daniel Defoe's idea that 'land is the best bottom for banks' was widely and uncritically held. It was naturally very popular with Tories and landowners who hoped that by setting up some form of land-based i.e. mortgage-based bank, they would compete destructively with the Bank of England, felt to be too wedded to the Whigs, and at the same time turn part of their valuable but fixed assets into something more conveniently liquid and spendable. A series of such projects emerged, backed by impressive personages such as Dr Hugh Chamberlen, John Briscoe, John Asgill, Dr Nicholas Barbon (prominent in insurance) and Thomas Neale (who had preceded Sir Isaac Newton as Master of the Mint). The two most prominent among these schemes merged their forces and so managed to bring a bill before Parliament for a National Land Bank which received royal assent on 27 April 1696. Its supporters hoped to outdo the Bank of England by raising a total subscription of

£2,564,000. The result was utter fiasco. When the subscription list was closed the total came to £7,100 of which the cash, at the initial call of 25 per cent, was, apparently, £1,775. But the subscription included the king's promised £5,000, so that when allowance is made for this the total subscriptions promised by the public came to only £2,100 and the total cash reluctantly handed over by them came to the derisory amount of £525. The boom for land-banks had burst, and the concept was only to be revived in a much modified form a century later when the first building societies emerged.

Two matters of far greater concern to the Bank, both of which drained it of cash, were, first what was known as the problem of the 'Remises', and secondly 'the Ingrafting of the Tallies'. The former involved the speedy and reliable remittance of hard cash to pay the troops in Flanders. This task was undertaken with deadly enthusiasm by the Bank's deputy governor, Michael Godfrey, who during the siege of Namur in July 1695 and despite royal warnings against exposing himself to unnecessary danger, insisted on standing alongside the king – until he was struck by a French cannonball, and thus, to use Clapham's phrase, the Bank lost its best head. But Godfrey had succeeded in establishing a system whereby the army received its funds promptly – yet another example of how the Bank helped the government in its efforts to defeat Louis XIV. The abject failure of the Land Bank left the government with no support for its tallies, which fell to a discount of 40 per cent; indeed some tallies of distant maturity had become virtually undiscountable.

This lack of public confidence in the new credit institutions coincided with the great shortage of cash because of the recoinage and reacted upon the price of the stock of the Bank of England which fell from 108 in January 1696 to only 60 by October. Nevertheless in this crisis the government was forced once more to turn to the Bank, which agreed to take up most of the problem tallies, upon which the Treasury agreed to pay 8 per cent. By an Act quickly rushed through Parliament on 3 February 1697 the Bank's authorized capital was increased by £1,001,171, subscribers being allowed to pay up to 80 per cent in tallies and the rest in banknotes. Thus instead of a diffused and difficult multitude of public debtors holding tallies requiring total repayment of both interest and capital within a definite period of time, the government was now simply faced with a single, more manageable creditor and had exchanged a series of short-term debts into part of the permanent or 'funded' debt on which interest only was payable. By such means a sizeable proportion of the government's outstanding tallies were 'ingrafted' into the Bank's capital stock. In return a grateful government, as well as allowing the Bank to increase its capital – and therefore also its permissible note issue (by £1,001,171) – granted the Bank four other privileges. First, the death penalty was prescribed for forging its notes, i.e. the same penalty as for counterfeiting the king's money. Secondly, the Bank's property was exempt from taxation. Thirdly the Bank's charter was extended until 1711. Fourthly, and in retrospect the most important, no other company 'in the nature of a bank' could legally be established during its existence. The Bank had weathered another storm, and the price of its stock rose almost to parity, reaching 98 when the Peace of Ryswick was signed in September 1697.

The Bank's supposed monopoly did not however remain unchallenged for long for, between 1704 and 1708, a number of companies ostensibly not 'in the nature of banks' began issuing notes, in particular the Mines Adventurers Company and the Sword Blades Company. Responding to the Bank's complaints, an Act passed towards the tail end of 1708 sought to clarify the position by specifically forbidding associations of more than six persons from carrying on a banking business, of which note issue was then considered to be an indispensable part. The Act authorized the Bank to double its capital and granted it a long-term renewal of its charter to 1733. Thus in 1709 under its new Governor, Sir Gilbert Heathcote, and with its total capital and note-issuing powers standing at £6,577,370, the Bank seemed supremely confident and secure. Any such complacency was however quickly banished when its physical security was threatened by the London riots of 1710, while its financially favoured position was put at risk by the same Tory-inspired activities of the South Sea Company. The Bank, said to be 'Full of Gold and Whiggery', was about to face its greatest threat.

The national debt and the South Sea Bubble

The process by which the personal royal debt became transformed into a parliamentary-controlled public or national debt was neither simple nor sudden, but formed part of a complex series of hesitant steps over a period of thirty years from the 1660s to the 1690s. We have already traced certain essential aspects of this development immediately after the Restoration of Charles II in 1660 in the practice of occasionally borrowing, though for relatively short periods, in anticipation of taxes or 'funds' granted by Parliament, a device which became both more regular and for much longer terms after the Glorious Revolution of 1688, when the words 'the funds' came to mean the securities (tallies and, increasingly, paper documents) issued by the government to back such loans. It was not possible to raise really long-term loans on reasonable terms until parliamentary control over the monarchy had been secured and royal credit replaced by parliamentary guarantees. Long-term or permanent debt required as an essential counterpart the guarantee of permanent institutions rather than merely mortal monarchs. Stuart extravagance had simply made this lesson all the plainer. Thus although the foundation of the Bank of England in July 1694 is rightly taken as the origin of its *permanent* component, it is the 'Tontine Act', which passed through Parliament during December 1692 and January 1693, which strictly speaking should be taken to mark the origin of the *national* debt.

The term 'tontine' is derived from its initiator, Lorenzo Tonti (1630–95), adviser to his fellow Italian, Mazarin, at the French court where he put his financial ideas to good effect. The tontine, which had many variants, was a method of raising money from subscribers with the rewards weighted heavily in favour of the longest survivors. By the Tontine Act as modified during 1692–3 the government attempted, and eventually succeeded, in raising £1 million. Its first alternative was to promise subscribers 10 per cent until 1700 with an increasing share thereafter for the dwindling number of survivors. The longest survived until 1738 with an annual pension in his later years of around £1,000 on his original investment of £100. Generally speaking, however, this first alternative was unsuccessful, and managed to bring in only £108,000. However the government's second alternative, a simple 14 per cent for life, proved far more attractive and raised £773,493. The remaining £118,507 required to make the first £1 million of the national debt was raised later in 1693 by the issue of tax-free annuities, a rather costly precedent. A further Annuity Act in 1694 enabled subscribers to nominate their beneficiaries (within limits, they could usually nominate the youngest of the participants) and hence was particularly though not exclusively taken up by families. It raised some £300,000.

The annuity principle meant that the government could raise a really long-term loan without ever having to repay the principal – one of the key concepts behind the scheme for the Bank of England – and also meant that it was faced, depending on the choice of scheme, with a progressively declining interest payment, thus relieving the burden on posterity. In the same hectic year of 1694 the government brought in the so-called Million or Lottery Act, intending to raise that amount by issuing 100,000 shares of £10 at 10 per cent with the added attraction of the possibility of sharing in the total of £40,000 put up each year for prizes. Shares in these lottery tickets were subdivided by zealous agents into smaller sums, despite which the scheme failed to reach the total anticipated. The successful launch of the Bank of England more than made up for this disappointment. The lottery tickets and shares for both the Million Funds of 1693 and 1694 were accepted as subscriptions to the capital of the Million Bank, which, as we have already seen, soon dropped its initial ambitions to compete in banking activities with the Bank of England and settled down instead into being an investment fund for government securities, acting as agents for the general public, particularly the small investor. However it was not the small, private investor, but rather the large joint-stock companies that took up the major portion of the national debt, and in so doing became powerful rivals of the Bank of England in courting the favours of the government, to the great discomforture of the Bank. Prominent among such competitors were the two East India Companies (reunited in 1702), and above all the South Sea Company, the rise and fall of which was to play a crucial role in the history of finance and of company law, and hence had long-lasting effects on industrial development as well as on banking, not only in Britain but also in the USA.

The parliamentary Act incorporating the 'Governor and Company of Merchants of Great Britain trading to the South Seas and other parts of America, and for encouraging the Fishery' was passed in 1711. Apart from stimulating whale fishing, its main purpose was to break into the Spanish monopoly of trade with Central and South America. Following Marlborough's successes in the War of Spanish Succession the 'Asiento Treaty' was signed on 26 March 1713 by which the South Sea Company gained the right to send 4,800 Negro slaves annually to the Spanish colonies and to send out to Portobello annually one general cargo ship of up to 500 tons – quotas not regularly achieved. On balance its trading activities turned out to be only moderately successful, and its special privileges were subsequently abolished by the Treaty of Madrid (1750) in return for a useful sum of £100,000 in compensation, while its slave trading was abolished by the general Anti-Slave Trading Act of 1807. The limited success of the company's first voyage in 1717 did nothing to dampen the enthusiasm of its promoters, a confident posture increased when George I accepted the company's invitation to become its Governor in 1718. It was not however through humdrum matters of trade, but rather through its role as leader of the speculative boom during 1719 and 1720, particularly in bidding for the national debt, that the company has made its mark in international financial and commercial history. The post-war boom was reflected also in France, where John Law's banking experiments similarly had their exotic counterpart in the Mississippi Company. The failure of Law's ambitious schemes did not check the advance of the boom in company formation and stock prices in Britain, where some 200 new companies were formed between mid-1719 and mid-1720. Such buoyant conditions seemed to provide the government in Britain with an ideal opportunity to reduce the burden of the national debt.

King George's speech in opening Parliament in November 1719 therefore voiced the government's view to see an early and significant reduction in the debt. The resulting committee of Parliament endorsed a proposal made by Sir John Blunt on behalf of the South Sea Company that this company would take over all the state's outstanding debts at 5 per cent until 1727 and 4 per cent thereafter, and that in addition the company would pay the government £3.5 million for the privilege. Parliament decided however to see what other companies might offer. The Bank of England, fearful of losing its special position in the City, rashly promised £5.5 million for a roughly similar scheme. It was saved from its folly when the South Sea Company in reply raised the value of its bid to £7,567,000 in return for converting all the outstanding debt, amounting to £31 million, not already held by the Bank of England and the East India Company. In modern terminology, the South Sea Company was offering to 'privatize' the national debt; in contemporary terms and methods it was 'ingrafting' the national debt into South Sea Company shares. Investors could buy South Sea Company shares, then rapidly appreciating and expected to pay very high dividends, with their government stock, which was also appreciating though at a much slower rate. The higher the price of South Sea shares, the greater the amount of government debt which could be acquired by such transfers. It was an apparently painless procedure, like betting with a double-headed penny, so long as business confidence was maintained.

Credit was easily available from the new financial institutions. The South Sea Company's speculative activities were strongly supported by the Sword Blade Bank with which it shared common directors. South Sea Company shares and those of other mushrooming companies rose to record heights on a wave of easy and cheap credit. Holders of unglamorous government securities rushed to exchange them into South Sea Company shares. The speculative mania was such that its shares, which had traded at 128, moderately above par, in January 1720, rose to 330 in March, 550 in May and reached their peak of 1,050 in August. Most of the 200 or so companies that had sprung up in the previous twelve months were not fully paid up, since their shares had been issued for quite small initial subscriptions, a feature which greatly multiplied the effect of the credit base on the total volume of equity. Junk companies were formed for the most unlikely or most vague purposes – perpetual motion, coral fishing, to make butter from beech trees, to extract silver from lead, gold from sea water, and, most quoted of all, 'for carrying on an undertaking of great advantage which shall in due time be revealed'. During July and August as more and more calls for cash for the remaining subscriptions were being made, so the business atmosphere began to change.

Ironically the prick that actually burst the bubble was administered by the South Sea Company itself, which while impatiently awaiting parliamentary legislation, issued a writ questioning the legality of eighty-six new companies. Rarely, has the proverb about digging holes for others been better illustrated, for by focusing public attention on the weaknesses and illegal status of so many of these new companies, it exposed the vulnerability of credit-inflated companies in general, chief of which was the South Sea Company itself. The company was particularly concerned that the cash being called into these new companies was weakening the potential flow into its own coffers and so might endanger its grandiose scheme for taking over the whole of the national debt before its task could be completed. To check this drain to other companies, an Act, subsequently popularly dubbed the Bubble Act, was introduced, following the South Sea Company's urgent pressure, in May 1720 and became effective on midsummer day. The main section of that Act set up two new insurance companies, the Royal Exchange and the London Assurance. The bubble clauses were tacked on. They declared that no joint-stock company could be established without a charter authorized for a specified, definite purpose, and laid down severe penalties for operating illegally, ranging from heavy fines through forfeiture of all goods and chattels to imprisonment for life. Strictly speaking, only the Crown could legally authorize a company and only Parliament grant it exclusive privileges; but it had become the general custom from the time of the Glorious Revolution of 1688 to allow unauthorized companies to exist. These were now in for a rude shock.

Financial consequences of the Bubble Act

Contemporary opinion and later popular history have claimed that the 'Bubble' had deep and widespread effects on the economic and financial development of Britain. Despite some attempts by specialists to play down its effects, the popular view is by and large the correct one and is strongly supported by expert research. The strength of its immediate effects is not in dispute. Almost before the ink of the Bubble Act was dry, the rush for liquidity began, affecting initially the shares of the first two 'illegal' companies taken to court (from its list of eighty-six) by the South Sea Company. By the end of August 1720 the rush had turned into a general panic, leading before the end of September to wholesale bankruptcy and the ruin of many hundreds of speculators. Already by 2 September South Sea stock was down to 700, falling to 200 before the end of the month, and reached its low point of the year at 124 on 24 December – still significantly above par and roughly at the level of the previous January before the boom had properly got under way. Bank of England stock, though much less volatile, had slumped from its 1720 high point of 265 to 135, its lowest point of the year. The notorious Sword Blade Bank failed on 24 September. This 'bank' had been highly favoured by the South Sea Company despite bitter attacks by the Bank of England which accused it of infringing the monopoly of joint-stock banking conceded to the Bank of England in 1708 and confirmed in 1709. The Bank was now rid of its most awkward competitor as far as its commercial banking operations were concerned. The South Sea Company remained in existence until 1853 passively handling its much-reduced, but still sizeable, portion of the national debt. But it had failed ignominiously in its bid to take over the whole, or the major portion, of the debt. Never again was the supremacy of the Bank of England's position challenged as the major manager of the national debt, whether funded or unfunded. Were it not for the 'Bubble' British governments might well have had their own 'pet' banks, as later did the USA, with government deposits and loans shuffled from one bank to another with every change of government. The benefit to the nation resulting from the removal of this destabilizing competition has never been fully appreciated.

On the other hand the strengthening of the Bank of England's monopoly deprived England and Wales of strong joint-stock banks during the early part of the industrial revolution and delayed their rise for over a century. Perversely, however, the Bubble Act, which remained on the Statute Book until 1825, made industry more dependent upon banks for working capital than they would have been if company formation had been easier. The Bubble Act made it difficult and costly to set up a company formally, while the articles of incorporation, to be legally acceptable, tended to stress the limitations on corporate action just at the time when the utmost flexibility was required.

Deprived of equity capital, the rising industrial partnerships turned to the partnership banks which supplied them with renewable loans as a not inconvenient substitute for permanent capital. As Rondo Cameron has made plain, in his study of *Banking in the Early Stages of Industrialisation* (1967), 'the mere existence of the Act hindered the flow of capital into industry' and so 'served to increase the importance of short-term finance for working capital provided by banking and other sources of credit'. Similarly Professor A. H. John, in his work on *The Industrial Development of South Wales* (1950) asks us 'to reverse the accepted view of a rigid division between the growing industrialism and the early banking system and to substitute one in which the latter played a not unimportant part in the industrial development of the period'. Professor Pressnell's authoritative study of *Country Banking in the Industrial Revolution* (1956) shows how the banking restrictions brought in during the period 1708 to 1720 'long outlasted any reasonableness and by the time they were abolished in the legislation of 1825, 1826 and 1833 they had done much harm by depriving the country of a banking system commensurate with a period of rapid economic growth'. He goes on to show how many industrialists entered banking, 'some to provide means of payment for workers and raw materials' and others to provide

> protracted short-term borrowing which added up to long-term borrowing. Where deposits were received from the public, their employment in the banker's own business resulted in a useful compromise between the limitations of the contemporary law of partnership and the advantages in the mobilisation of capital of the modern joint-stock company.

Thus the Bubble deeply influenced the form and methods of operation of the banking system of England and Wales (but not so much in Scotland) and also influenced the operation of the capital market and the legal structure of companies in general for a hundred years or more, not only in Britain but also overseas. It is clear that both company and banking law in the USA were closely affected by the events in England. 'Ever since I read the history of the South Sea Bubble,' said President Jackson to Nicholas Biddle, head of the Bank of the United States, 'I have been afraid of banks.' So the President vetoed the extension of that bank's charter in 1832 as being unconstitutional. In France, where the corresponding Mississippi crisis had peaked earlier, John Law's banking experiments perished in the flames of inflation, similarly delaying but for even longer the establishment of a modern system of banking in France.

Following Parliament's committee of inquiry into the Bubble crisis, which reported in February 1721, the South Sea Company was completely reorganized. Its directors were heavily fined, imprisoned and had their estates confiscated, as did a number of others involved in the general corruption. Among the large number of influential persons convicted of bribery was the Chancellor of the Exchequer, John Aislabie, who was expelled from Parliament, imprisoned in the Tower of London and had his property confiscated to help to compensate the victims of the crash. His replacement, Robert Walpole, who had prophesied and profited from the Bubble, was brought back into office, as Chancellor of the Exchequer and first minister, 'to save the country in the crisis'. As the world knows, as well as solving the financial crisis Walpole played a key role in three basic constitutional reforms, namely the strengthening of the Treasury as the predominant department, the development of the cabinet form of government and the emergence of a prime minister as 'primus inter pares'. Here once more, partly as a result of the Bubble, we see fundamental financial and constitutional changes going along hand in hand. Walpole took a most active part, along with the Governor and directors of the Bank of England, in the reconstruction of the South Sea company and in the consequent redistribution of the major part of the company's holdings of the national debt. The Bank took over nearly £4 million of debt from the company and in return was allowed to increase its own capital by a similar amount. A grateful government also renewed the Bank's charter for twenty-one years from 1721. As in the original South Sea scheme, the general level of interest on outstanding government debt was reduced in 1727 from 5 to 4 per cent, for Walpole had always been very keen on reducing, and indeed if possible, eliminating the burden of the national debt. (For a scholarly account of Walpole's role in the 'Rise of the British Treasury' see D. M. Clark 1960.)

It is perhaps fitting that the idea for eliminating the national debt should have come from none other than William Paterson who of course had been largely responsible for the form in which it was first set up. His 'Sinking Fund' concept was taken up in 1716 by Stanhope, Chancellor of the Exchequer, and strongly supported by Walpole. They arranged that all surpluses from taxation were set aside in a special fund which, wisely invested, grew to a size substantial enough to reduce the debt, and eventually, as the experiment was repeated, might even have eliminated the total debt. Walpole persevered, and despite having to 'raid' the sinking fund in 1734–5, managed to reduce the total debt by £4 million by 1739. However, the outbreak of war in that year and the even more costly and more frequent wars which followed rendered the sinking fund concept inoperative, until it was temporarily revived when the Younger Pitt set up the Commission for the Reduction of the National Debt in 1786. In the mean time a few other reforms in debt management are worth noting. Pelham successfully took advantage of the low market rates of interest which prevailed in mid-century to bring about a large 'conversion' of the national debt from 4 per cent to 3½ per cent in 1749 and followed this up by reducing the rates to 3 per cent for a large portion of the debt, the 'reduced threes', as they became known, in 1750. In 1751 he brought together a whole untidy series of annuities into a single new general stock, the famous 3 per cent Consolidated Stock, or 'Consols'. Thus by the second half of the eighteenth century most of the main aspects of a modern system of debt management had already been established, efficiently administered by the Bank of England as unquestionably the government's main agent, acting as the key link between the growing markets for money and the most secure form of capital available anywhere in the world.

The operations of other financial institutions such as the stock exchange, insurance companies and friendly societies were also considerably affected by the aftermath of the 1720 crisis. Investors, cured for a time of their urge to speculate in equities, turned back to dealing mainly in government securities, which continued to dominate the capital market throughout the century. They also turned favourably towards the expanding insurance companies, although these latter confined their operations in the main to the London area. It was the stock jobbers who felt the full venom of public abuse after the crisis, and eventually their wings were clipped by Barnard's Act of 1734 which was expressly intended 'to prevent the infamous practice of stock-jobbing'. That Act however soon became very much a dead letter and so was belatedly repealed in 1867, although in the same year Leeman's Act was passed to make sure that the legal prohibition against option dealing in *bank* shares, which had never been a dead letter, was firmly maintained. Friendly Societies – the poor man's combined savings bank and insurance company – grew steadily more important throughout the century, even though they were in the eyes of the Bubble Act of doubtful legality, as were the early building societies, at least until the Friendly Societies Act was passed in 1793 in an effort to clarify the situation and give some limited protection to members. Another method commonly used to circumvent the Bubble Act was to arrange for groups of persons, sometimes even numbering hundreds, to be represented by what we would now call a 'front' of prestigious and highly respected persons who acted as 'trustees' for the business or organization – a method later to become very popular with the savings banks. By such means business carried out by partnerships, associations, trustees, societies, unions and other such groupings in course of time 'had become almost as liquid as it was with the incorporated companies' (Dubois 1938, 38). Nevertheless the vigilance of the Bank of England saw to it that banks at any rate were strictly limited to a maximum number of six partners – except in Scotland where financial institutions developed upon interestingly different lines.

Financial developments in Scotland, 1695–1789

A series of innovatory financial developments in Scotland in the century or so following the establishment of the Bank of Scotland in 1695 were to have far-reaching effects not only on the economy of that country but also had a significant influence on monetary theory and policy and on practical banking habits in England and Wales and abroad. Consequently Scottish monetary history, interesting enough in itself, is of far greater importance than might at first glance be supposed. Scotland was the only region of Britain, outside the London area, where indigenous banking had made substantial progress by the middle of the eighteenth century. If we begin by looking at the state of the currency, this was in a much worse condition in general even when compared with the pre-1696 coinage in England and Wales, so that when banking grew so as to supplement the metallic currency, the benefits were more immediately obvious. Furthermore Scotland, much poorer than England, could not afford the luxury of relying on a gold currency to the extent that was becoming common south of the border. As in England, the first traders to carry on banking business in places like Berwick and Edinburgh were the Italian 'Lombards', but apart from teaching some familiarity with the discounting of bills of exchange, little else was learned.

Not only were the bankers foreign, so was most of the better-quality coinage, what little there was of it. As C. H. Robertson shows in her study of 'Pre-banking financial arrangements in Scotland' (1988),

> The available currency was to a considerable degree made up of coins of the countries with which it traded and of the native coins of which there were comparatively few in circulation . . . Gold and silver were extremely scarce and most payments were made in the clipped, worn, crudely made discs which passed under the name of coin of the realm.

The attempt by James following the union of the Crowns in 1603 to unify the coinage failed dismally, despite the minting of the gold 'unite'. The scarcity of gold in Scotland also prevented the Edinburgh goldsmiths from developing into banking business in imitation of the London goldsmiths (though John Law's father, an Edinburgh goldsmith, did manage to pursue some very elementary credit business roughly akin to banking). Clearly Scotland would have much to gain from supplementing its lamentable metallic currency by adopting paper credit and payment systems such as those which had grown up in London during the seventeenth century and which had culminated in the establishment of the Bank of England as advocated by William

Paterson. This example immediately fired the imagination of a number of influential London Scots, who, led by Thomas Deans and by the Englishman John Holland, got together to set up a public Bank for Scotland superficially similar to the Bank of England.

A rival to the planned Bank of Scotland appeared on the scene immediately, led by none other than William Paterson, who far from being the 'founder of the Bank of Scotland' as a number of writers wrongly persist in claiming, strongly opposed the bank, fearing that investors' money would be diverted from the much more grandiose plans for his Darien project, a sort of Scottish East India Company. The Act which established the 'Company of Scotland trading to Africa and the Indies' was passed successfully by the Scottish Parliament on 26 June 1695. Although its main purpose was to set up a colonial entrepot at Darien on the isthmus of Panama, strategically seen as 'the key to the universe', Paterson was also keen to see it carrying on a banking business. In the event, the Darien venture turned out to be an unmitigated disaster involving the colonists in much disease and many deaths and the investors in heavy losses. Nevertheless it was to exert considerable influence on the constitutional and financial history of Scotland. Despite the fierce opposition of Paterson and his friends, the Act authorizing the Bank of Scotland was passed by the Scottish Parliament on 17 July 1695. A new era in Scottish economic history had dawned.

Thomas Deans and his fellow promoters in Edinburgh and London asked John Holland, a private banker and merchant in London, to draw up the proposal for the bank's charter as quickly as possible. Thus, apart from the Bank of England being the obvious and most recent model, the urgent need for haste to tap a limited market for capital was one of the main reasons for the similarity between the charters of the two banks. The capital seemed nominally the same, at £1,200,000 Scots, which of course was merely £100,000 sterling. Only £10,000 sterling was called for the initial subscription and the shareholders enjoyed limited liability up to the total subscription. Like the Bank of England, the Bank of Scotland and the Darien Company sought to attract foreign subscribers, the latter two companies going to the extent of allowing such subscribers to be granted Scottish nationality. Nevertheless, to prevent take-over, a minimum of two-thirds of the shares in both companies had to be held by persons resident in Scotland. Again like the Bank of England, the Bank of Scotland was forbidden to indulge in trade (though the Darien Company was allowed to carry on banking business as well as trading). The Bank of Scotland was, just like the Bank of England, not allowed to lend to the monarch without the consent of Parliament, but, different from the case of the Bank of England, this also applied to its initial capital subscription. Yet, quite apart from its much smaller size, there were a number of important differences between the two banks which grew to influence in important aspects the monetary practices of the two countries just when, constitutionally, they were becoming more united.

Whereas the Bank of England had to struggle through its formative years until 1709 when its monopoly of joint-stock banking was made explicit (but was thereafter extended on or before expiry well into the nineteenth century), the Bank of Scotland was expressly given a monopoly for twenty-one years, but this was *not* extended afterwards. Furthermore, whereas bank partnerships were limited in England to a maximum of six, there was no such maximum limit to co-partnery under the distinctly different Scottish legal system. The much greater freedom for joint-stock and larger-partnership banks was to be a vital feature in the role played by banks in the economic development of England and Scotland, with Scotland becoming eventually the model to be copied. The Bank of Scotland was not involved, as was the Bank of England right from its commencement, in acting as the major holder and manager of the national debt. As Professor Checkland, the eminent historian of Scottish banking explains, the Bank of Scotland has many claims to uniqueness, being 'the first instance in Europe, and perhaps the world, of a joint-stock bank formed by private persons for the express purpose of making a trade of banking, solely dependent on private capital . . . wholly unconnected with the state' (1975, 23). Although the Bank of Scotland's monopoly as the 'only distinct Company or Bank' was almost immediately challenged by the Darien Company, the bank received a further special privilege in that its profits were not to be subject to tax for its first twenty-one years. Under its first Governor, John Holland, it began to issue notes – significantly denominated in pounds sterling – for £100, £50 and £10, thus increasing uniformity of accounting between the two countries, although when it began issuing smaller notes in 1716 valued at £1 sterling these still carried the inscription 'Twelve pounds Scots'.

Hardly had the bank begun issuing notes than the Darien Company tried to bring about its downfall by suddenly presenting for payment in specie a very large quantity of notes which it had previously amassed with this purpose in mind. By promptly calling on its subscribers for a temporary loan and by economizing by closing its recently, and prematurely, opened branches at Aberdeen, Dundee, Glasgow and Montrose, the bank weathered this first serious challenge to its existence during 1696 and the early part of 1697. During 1704 the effects of the drain of specie from Britain to pay for Marlborough's army was intensified in Scotland because of the huge losses suffered by the Darien Company. In December 1704 the bank suffered another run and had to suspend payment, paying interest on its suspended notes until repayment became possible in May 1705 following a second temporary call for capital from its subscribers. In this crisis the bank availed itself of the 'Optional Clause' by which banknotes could be paid *either* on demand *or* up to six months later provided interest was paid as compensation.

By March 1700, after the battered remnants of its three disastrous expeditions to Panama finally withdrew, the Darien Company virtually ceased to exist. The Scottish subscribers had lost the whole of their investment of £153,000 sterling, while in addition the company owed around £80,000 to hard-pressed creditors, almost all of whom were Scots. The potential English subscribers were fortunately saved the £300,000 they had originally promised, because legal proceedings brought by supporters of the East India Company showed that the latter's existing monopoly would have been infringed. This dismal end to the Darien scheme not only removed the main rival to the Bank of Scotland but also put paid to any lingering ambition Scotland may have had of independently establishing its own colonial trading posts, or even being allowed, in that mercantilist age, to partake substantially in exotic international trade, except with the acquiescence of its larger southern partner. Consequently the Darien fiasco became one of the important factors leading towards the Act of Union of 1707, which laid down that trade was to be 'free and equal throughout Great Britain and its dominions'.

The financial clauses of the Act laid down that Scotland, in return for losing its own customs and excise and other taxes and for assuming a share of responsibility for the English national debt, was to receive in compensation an 'Equivalent' of £398,085. 10s. sterling, plus a further sum, the 'Arising Equivalent', being the expected increased yields to Scotland from 1707 to 1714 of the new uniform fiscal system combined with the increased volume of trade stimulated by the fact of Union. Perversely, however, the yields in the initial years turned down – an early example of the frustrating effect of the notorious 'J-curve' on the direction and extent of eventually beneficial adjustments in international trade.

The largest claim on the Equivalent Funds was that by the shareholders and creditors of the Darien Company, which amounted to £232,884. Almost as much, some £200,000 was required to pay off holders of public debt. Thirty thousand pounds was allocated to pay for the administrative costs of carrying through the Union, while industrial development funds were set up to assist the fishing, textile and other industries over the seven years from 1707 to 1714. The Act of Union further decreed that 'from and after the Union the coin shall be of the same standard and value throughout the United Kingdom', and to this end some £50,000 was allocated to cover the costs of recoinage. The gap in the currency during the three years of recoinage was largely met by the issue of notes by the Bank of Scotland, which acted as government agent in the process. After the recoinage was completed the Edinburgh mint was finally closed down on 4 August 1710. The Bank of Scotland and its notes had most opportunely arrived on the scene in good time to supplement the coinage, the total value of which was then given as £411,117 sterling.

Only the most influential or otherwise fortunate of creditors with claims on the Equivalent were paid in cash in Scotland. Some were paid or credited in Bank of England notes, Exchequer bills and similar short-term paper, whereas the majority had to accept long-term debentures and so had to suffer a capital loss if they chose to discount these, as a number of desperate Scottish holders felt forced to do, with English holders via the London money market. Thus by 1719 as much as £170,000 or 68 per cent of the total of £248,550 Equivalent debentures were held in London (Checkland 1975). There was thus double pressure for repayment, or for some other means of recompense, to the increasingly impatient holders of these debentures. Strangely, in this roundabout manner, Scotland came to acquire its second public bank, arising phoenix-like out of the long-dead ashes of the Darien scheme. During the 1715 Rebellion the Bank of Scotland was felt to have been far too openly favourable to the Stuart cause, a fact pressed home by those who wished to establish a rival bank, chief among whom were the Equivalent debenture holders, who had meanwhile formed themselves into the Equivalent Company purposely to improve their chances of gaining such privileges. As a belated result, on 31 May 1727, the Equivalent Company was incorporated by royal charter as the 'Royal Bank of Scotland' with an authorized capital of £111,347 sterling. As with the case of the Bank of England, the holders of public debt had managed to persuade the government to allow them to form a joint-stock bank, an aptly Royal rival to 'the Old Bank'.

The Royal Bank of Scotland's most important claim to a place in banking history stems from its innovatory 'cash-credit' system from which in due course the simple, effective and flexible 'overdraft' was to emerge. If an applicant for a loan, e.g. a newcomer, unknown to the bank, could produce two or more guarantors of good standing, a 'cash-credit' could then be opened in the applicant's favour to draw cash (generally notes) as required, interest being payable only on the amount so withdrawn. Because of the strong competition between the Scottish banks, this most useful of lending practices soon spread throughout Scotland, and duly modified, in course of time was copied by the English banks. Thus the extension of note issue and the development of business activity grew hand in hand; though naturally the pace diverged from time to time.

A third public bank – though not at first so called – came into being when the British Linen Company was granted a royal charter on 5 July 1746 with an authorized capital of £100,000 and empowered to 'do everything that may conduce to the promoting of the linen manufacture'. This came to include financing the putting-out system by paying for produce with its own notes, discounting bills of exchange and carrying on a number of other banking practices. In 1763 it gave up linen manufacture to concentrate on banking: 'the only British bank to be formed on the basis of an industrial charter' (Checkland 1975, 96).

As well as these three publicly chartered banks, a considerable number of banking institutions of varied kinds were setting themselves up in all the main towns of Scotland, so that by 1772 some thirty-one banks were in operation covering with their branches and agencies most of the country. Special mention should be made of the emergence of the Ship and the Arms banks formed in hitherto neglected Glasgow in 1749 and 1750 respectively, deriving their popular names from the designs on their notes. Both had developed out of 'agents' of the two old Edinburgh banks, the Ship being promoted by agents of the Bank of Scotland, while the Arms Bank was promoted by former agents of the Royal Bank. The 'agency' system was another distinctive feature of Scottish banking, whereby a small sub-branch could discreetly and most economically be set up in part of the premises of some other prospering business e.g. a draper's shop, or a solicitor's office, and if it proved itself a success, could be hived off into a full branch. This was a most cheap and well-tried way of setting up branches, and by its means Scotland became the first in the world to establish an almost nationwide branch banking system.

Two other distinctive features of Scottish banking deserve examination, namely the importance of small notes in the currency and secondly the early legal confirmation in Scotland of the principle of 'free banking', by which was meant a steadfast refusal to allow the two chartered banks a monopoly of banking, especially with regard to the essential function of note issue. During the 1750s and 1760s a veritable small-note mania had broken out in Scotland with notes as small as 5s.

and even 1s. being common and being commonly issued by non-banking firms of little standing. In order to protect themselves, the Bank of Scotland and the Royal Bank of Scotland campaigned with considerable support to be granted a monopoly of note issue so as to secure the integrity of the note issue in general. In opposition stood the smaller banks and an important section of public opinion in favour of the practice of free trade. The result is to be seen in the Banking Act of 1765 'to prevent the inconveniences arising from the present method of issuing notes and bills by the banks, banking companies and bankers in that part of Great Britain called Scotland'. First it forbade the issue of notes of less than 20s. sterling. Secondly it forbade the use of the optional clause, so that notes had to be payable on demand, and it strengthened the legal position of note holders claiming immediate payment. But equally important was its determination to allow freedom, within the above limits of note size and immediate payment, for *all* 'banks, banking companies and bankers' to issue notes (then and for a century or more to come, seen to be the essential mark of being a bank). In contrast stood the situation in England where the Bank of England's monopoly was reconfirmed and the maximum six-partner rule was strictly adhered to. Furthermore the minimum note permitted in England and Wales was for £5, and in practice few for less than £10 were commonly issued. Thus banknotes grew to supplement the currency of the general public to a much smaller extent in England when compared to contemporary Scotland.

Any complacency that the Scottish Bank Act of 1765 had removed the dangers of excess note issue was however rudely shattered by the bank crisis of 1772, a financial disaster 'comparable to the collapse of the Darien Company' (Rait 1930, 164). In 1769 the Ayr Bank was founded by Douglas, Heron and Co. with the extensive backing of a number of very rich landowners such as the Duke of Queensberry and the Duke of Buccleuch, patron of Adam Smith. The Ayr Bank was of unlimited liability, relying on the fortunes of its backers, so that it became in practice the private embodiment of the 'land bank' principle, with its notes directly supported by landed wealth. The Ayr Bank was also a sort of public protest against the over-cautious attitude of the Edinburgh-based banks and their tardiness in forming branches. It quickly built up some half a dozen branches, carried on a large amount of business with Anglo-Scots in London and pushed out its circulation of notes by means of aggressive banking to around £200,000, a total much exceeding the combined circulation of the Bank of Scotland and the Royal. The failure of one of its main London customers, a newly established private banking firm of Neale, James, Fordyce and Downe in June 1772, quickly brought down the Ayr Bank and with it some thirteen private bankers in Edinburgh. Once again the land bank principle exploded itself through excessive speculation and too rapid a rate of lending via note issue. However, in contrast to Rait's extremely gloomy view given above, Professor Checkland shows that the failures of 1772 did no long-lasting harm to the development of Scottish banking. It did however confirm the old banks in the rightness of their more stolid traditional conservative approach to the principles and practices of sound banking. Whether this was at the cost of also slowing down the growth of the economy remains an open question.

The same Parliament that had set up the Darien Company and the Bank of Scotland also passed in 1696 an 'Act for the Settling of Schools' in every parish. The resultant high level of literacy, unusual for any country at that time, supplied bankers in Scotland and abroad with a steady and reliable stream of cheap, juvenile clerks, who played a not unimportant role in the spread of Scottish banking practices. A more notorious 'export' was John Law, who, having failed to get the Scottish Parliament in 1705 to adopt his aggressive land bank concept, emigrated to France in 1714 and successfully persuaded the Duke of Orleans to set up such a bank which helped to drive the speculative excesses of the 'Mississippi Mania' in 1719. More worthy exports may be seen in the two prestigious London banks of Coutts and of Drummonds, and of the House of Hope in Holland, all well established by the middle of the eighteenth century, by which time Scotland had developed one of the most advanced banking systems in the world.

The money supply and the constitution

The recoinages of 1696 in England and of 1707 in Scotland enable fairly accurate estimates to be made of the total of the traditional, metallic circulation of the currencies of the two countries. In addition, various estimates of less certain value have been made by writers like Davenant and Adam Smith of the total of supplementary forms of paper money. Taken together they provide a rough guide to the total money supply, and more importantly to the relative significance of precious metal coinage as compared with paper money. The estimates, by ignoring copper money and metal tokens, probably understate to a minor degree the continuing importance of metallic currency, but when every allowance is made, the main fact stands out: already by the beginning of the eighteenth century paper forms of money exceeded metallic money in total in England and Wales, and by the middle of the century, paper money considerably exceeded specie money in Scotland also. Table 6.2

is based on Davenant's 1698 estimate of the total money supply in England and Wales. (See Horsefield 1960, 256).

Table 6.2 Davenant's estimate of the money supply in 1698.

	£ million	as % of e.
a. Silver coins	5.6	21.1
b. Gold coins	6.0	22.5
c. Total coins in circulation	11.6	43.6
d. Tallies, banknotes, bills etc.	15.0	56.4
e. Total of coins plus liquid paper	26.6	100.0
f. Land securities i.e. mortgages	20.0	75.2

Although the land market had become very active in Davenant's time, it would be stretching matters too far to include mortgages in even the widest definition of the money supply. Indeed, elsewhere in his writing Davenant gives the proportion of assignable paper to coinage as 5:4, that is similar to that given in the table above, *excluding* mortgages. In any event it is clear that Davenant already saw coins as being less in total than the most liquid forms of paper money.

The situation in Scotland, though initially more primitive, was soon to point even more decisively in the direction of the superiority of paper. As we have seen, some £411,117. 10s. of silver was brought to the mint in 1707 to be recoined. Adam Smith believed that the value of the gold in circulation was rather more than that of silver so that, making some allowance for hoarded silver but again excluding copper and tokens, the total metallic circulation in 1707 was 'around £1 million'. By 1776 Smith reckoned that bank money had grown to be so important that of the current total circulation of £2 million 'that part which consists of gold and silver most probably does not amount to half a million'. He claimed that 'silver very seldom appears except in the change of a twenty-shilling bank note and gold still seldomer'. Smith was also in no doubt that the banks could claim a large part of the credit for the enormous expansion in the growth of trade and industry in Scotland between 1707 and 1776. By that time banknote penetration and bank density (the number of bank ofices per 10,000 of the population) were much higher in Scotland than in England, although the convertibility of notes throughout the kingdom rested ultimately on the gold reserves of the Bank of England. The immediate security of the notes rested upon prudential management reinforced occasionally by the harsh discipline of bankruptcy for the gross overissuer, like the Bank of Ayr.

The fact that more than half of the total money supply was now being created, not by the mint under the dictate of the monarch, but rather by the London money market and the provincial bankers gave rise to the most profound constitutional consequences. First, in order to carry out his much more burdensome civil and military duties, the monarch, after a painful but vain struggle, had been forced to call parliaments annually. Secondly because of the state's need to supplement taxes regularly and substantially with various forms of short-, medium- and long-term borrowing, the state had been forced to take into account the views and interests of the moneyed classes and the nature of the institutions which its borrowing had very largely brought into being. The national debt not only created the Bank of England but also virtually created the London money and capital markets in recognizably modern form long before an equity market in industrial shares became of importance.

Provided that the government's general policy was acceptable in the City, the government's sources of finance, though no longer directly under its control, had been enormously increased. Trevelyan's traditional view that 'the financial system that arose after the Revolution was the key to the power of England in the eighteenth and nineteenth centuries' (1938, 1797) is strongly supported by modern research. Thus P. G. M. Dickson in his detailed study of the development of public credit from 1688 to 1756 shows how these fiscal changes in stimulating the growth of the London money and capital markets financed external imperialism as well as internal economic growth. The changes 'were rapid enough and important enough to deserve the name of "the Financial Revolution"' (Dickson 1967, 12). The financial and constitutional revolutions were thus closely and causally intertwined.

Not only had the money supply been elastically increased in total amount, but in addition the drastic reduction in interest rates, which allowed the government to borrow at around 4 per cent in the mid-eighteenth century compared with real rates of 12 per cent or more in the previous century, greatly increased the liquidity of the whole range of Exchequer bills, bills of exchange and other near-money substitutes. Cheap, plentiful and yet generally sound money provided a double blessing – for the economy as a whole as well as for the Treasury.

Another aspect of the financial revolution has in general been overlooked. It was not simply that the monarch had to *borrow* that limited his power. When paper money began to exceed metallic money the power of the royal purse became thereafter permanently, irreversibly and progressively diluted. The Royal Mint had always been a main source as well as a symbol of royal power. Money creation had always been the undoubted and exclusive prerogative of the king. As recently as 1630 Charles I had shown how to gain independence of Parliament, at least for a time, by bringing Spanish bullion to his mint. But those days were gone for ever as soon as money could be created independently of the monarch, and even of the monarch as advised by his ministers. The symbol was still gold, but the substance was paper; and much of the real financial and political power had been silently transferred from the Tower to the City and beyond.

No longer either was the nation's money created in the single centre of London, for although London's money market was to remain the predominant source of paper money, the growth of banks throughout the country diffused money creation regionally. Furthermore whereas the supply of minted money was arbitrarily and centrally decided and at a predetermined, definite amount, bank money in contrast arose spontaneously and flexibly, but to a total amount not known in advance, in accordance with the vague but insistent demands of local trade and business. Again whereas, except for export drains and the occasional recoinage, metallic currency was downwardly inflexible, paper money was easily adjustable in both directions.

For the first time in history money was being substantially created, not ostentatiously and visibly by the sovereign power, but mundanely by market forces so vividly and aptly described by Adam Smith as the 'invisible hand'. From the days of the Greek and Roman empires, as we saw in chapter 3, coinage had been a major instrument of state policy and of far-reaching propaganda. With the coming of bankers' notes no longer was the head of state the sole or main source of money. The aura of monarchy was removed from money, which was now not the creation of the ruler but of the humblest of his subjects. Ordinary people, 'pedlars turned merchants', drovers of cattle, innkeepers, iron masters, linen makers, shopkeepers, indeed almost any Tom, Dick or Harry could now share the royal prerogative. This was an unconscious, unplanned and still underestimated transfer of constitutional sovereignty; a partial financial democratization that preceded and facilitated the advent of political democracy.

In conclusion, it is clear that the century or so after 1640 is of quite fundamental importance in the development of a modern financial system. Before the period, modern banking was unknown in Britain; after it, Britain led the world in financial, agricultural and industrial development. It had taken many centuries to establish the rules of metallic money creation. The rules by which the optimum amount of paper money should be decided required a long period of experimentation and legislation to supplement the internal disciplines of bank management and the harsher lessons of bankruptcy. It required also the growth of a central banking system of control linked to the heavy anchor of a gold standard. This was to be the path of monetary development in the next period from 1789 to 1914.

7

The Ascendancy of Sterling, 1789–1914

Gold versus paper . . . finding a successful compromise

Although it is quite true that economic history, unlike political history, has no abrupt turning-points, yet monetary, financial and fiscal history share with political history certain decisive dates which mark changes in policy, and share also with economic history the gradual evolution of the factors which help to bring about those more abrupt changes in policy. Thus, as all the world's schoolchildren know, the French Revolution began on 14 July 1789; but many esoteric and controversial volumes have been written concerning when the industrial revolution started. All however agree that the world's first industrial revolution took place in Britain and was in full swing during the French revolutionary period with mutually interacting effects, not least with regard to substantial changes in gold, silver and copper currency, banknotes and the national debt. Consequently the year 1789 may be taken, necessarily somewhat arbitrarily, as our approximate starting point for the monetary history of the nineteenth century. There is much less room for doubt concerning the century's naturally convenient terminating date. The outbreak of the First World War on 4 August 1914 marks the virtual end of a uniquely great monetary era during which Britain had evolved a universally admired gold standard system of national and international payments, when sterling's prestige reached its zenith and when the City of London's position in the world's money and capital markets was unrivalled. The following chapter traces the salient features of this historic development.

We have seen that the world's first coins were made of gold around 700 BC and that a number of Greek city-states established their own forms of 'gold standard' which concept was extended empire-wide by Alexander and later by Roman and Byzantine emperors. The Italian cities, led by Florence in 1252, revived the popularity of gold coinage in medieval Europe, imitated in England very briefly, as a knee-jerk reaction as early as 1257, but more regularly from the mid-fourteenth century. Even so, despite such a long experience, the situation at the beginning of the nineteenth century was that no modern state had developed what could fairly be called a gold standard system. Officially Britain was still on the sterling silver standard that had been in existence for many centuries. Similarly, though certain forms of paper credit had been in existence in the ancient world, though bills of exchange had been in fairly common use in Europe for over 400 years, and though banknotes had been popular in London since the mid-seventeenth century, yet, at the beginning of the nineteenth century no proper system existed for controlling the flood of notes issuing from a motley collection of many hundreds of banks which were springing up over most parts of Britain. Needless to say, no country had by then devised an effective working link between a high-quality gold coinage on the one hand and a controlled yet sufficiently elastic supply of paper money on the other hand. The British monetary authorities, after starting the century with no sign that they knew the answer to this problem, then had to turn their energies to financing a long and burdensome war as a result of which the pound became depreciated and inconvertible for the first quarter of the century, and finally took a series of well-studied and deliberate steps between 1816 and 1844 to solve the problem. First, gold was at last officially made the standard of value and then the ground rules were laid down by which a non-inflationary and yet sufficiently elastic supply of paper money could be practically guaranteed. Consequently, by the middle of the century most of the problems which had led to a recurrence of internal drains of gold from the Bank of England's reserves and from the reserves of the unit banks had at last been overcome.

The second half of the century was to demonstrate how the Bank of England, with astonishingly low reserves, could also successfully deal with potentially very heavy external drains and with import surges of gold, while fully maintaining the convertibility of the pound. During the course of the century the total supply of gold increased substantially, but in irregular spurts; yet it could not keep pace with the steady increase in population and the increase in the average standard of living. The more manageably elastic part of the money supply was provided by the banking system, and was made available, thanks to the links maintained with gold, in a manner that kept the general level of prices remarkably steady, in a most flattering contrast with the 'managed moneys' of the twentieth century. The authorities, consciously seeking for an 'automatic' monetary system, had managed to establish, in an open economy sharing the risks and benefits of free trade, a most successful compromise between the disciplines of gold and the incentives of banking. The British empire may well have been built up in a fit of absent-mindedness, but the gold standard which helped to sustain it was by contrast the result of consciously learning from the experience of practical bankers, those who failed as well as those who prospered, and from the willingness of the authorities to accept the wisdom and reject the folly of countless parliamentary debates, committees, books, journals, pamphlets and papers with which the period abounded.

Of course a certain amount of luck was involved in the shape of a spate of gold discoveries in far distant parts of the world, but the British monetary system was so devised that it was able to take full advantage of these new sources of supply. The continents were being more closely connected by steamships, telegraph and cable – and by the final golden fling of the Clippers. Meanwhile the interiors of these continents were being opened up by the railways, 'England's gift horse to the world', most of such development being heavily financed by British capital and the bill on London. A successful monetary system supported a successful economy – or so it was confidently thought. We shall have to consider in some detail later whether, and if so to what extent, the train of causation was the other way round. We turn now from this first glimpse at the successful compromise which linked paper to gold and which formed the background to the picture of monetary development in the century as a whole, to a more detailed analysis of the new banking system which created most of the increased money supply, and then turn to examine the state of the metallic currency and the importance of the belated recognition that gold had finally replaced silver as the official standard of value.

Country banking and the industrial revolution to 1826

Professor Pressnell's authoritative and comprehensive research on this subject (1956) has confirmed Edmund Burke's contemporary view that by the middle of the eighteenth century, which is approximately the traditional starting date of the industrial revolution, barely a dozen banking houses existed in England and Wales outside the London area. Sir John Clapham also gives good reason for thinking that probably not more than half a dozen were regularly constituted banks worthy of the name (1970). The earliest was that established in 1658 by Thomas Smith, a draper in Nottingham. James Wood of Bristol began issuing notes in 1716 which were accepted eagerly by businessmen in that area, the success of which some years later led to a similar bank being set up in Gloucester. The Gurney family of Norwich had entered banking by about 1750, by which time there is evidence of a second bank in Bristol and another in Stafford. After 1750 the pace noticeably quickened, so that by 1775, depending on how strictly one uses the term 'bank', there were between 100 and 150. One cannot be precise because unit banking, by its nature, and even more especially in its infancy, is a risky business; the numbers fluctuated, on a rising trend, from slump to boom. Furthermore banks were not required to have licences to issue notes before 1808, and not every bank issued notes, though the majority of country banks did so. Growth became really strong from the 1780s, rising from 119 in 1784 to 280 by 1793, while the number of licensed banks in the peak year of 1810 was 783, which together with a reasonable allowance for unlicensed banks gives a total of over 800. This increased momentum of bank formation lends support to Rostow's view that between 1783 and 1802 Britain experienced the world's first 'take-off into self-sustaining growth' (1971), while the wide geographic and industrial spread of such banks would favour the 'broad push' rather than the narrow 'leading sector' view of the basic economic causes of the industrial revolution (Hartwell 1971).

The fascinating variety of the origins of country banking may be gleaned from the following list of some of the main industries or occupations in which their founding partners were engaged when they first became bankers: army agents, agents for packet-boats, and attorneys; barristers, brewers, butchers and button-makers; chandlers, church treasurers, coal factors, colliery owners, copper miners, corn merchants and cotton manufacturers; drovers and drapers; engineers and excisemen; farmers of all sorts; gun makers, grocers and goldsmiths (the latter not as prominent as in London); haberdashers, hatters, hop-growers, hosiery makers and hemp merchants; innkeepers, iron ore dealers, iron smelters and owners of iron foundries; jewellers and manufacturers of japan-ware; lace makers, leather merchants, linen merchants and of course land owners; mercers, millers and naturally money lenders; pewter makers; revenue collectors; scriveners, ship-owners, shoemakers, snuff-box makers, stockbreeders, solicitors and sword makers; tanners, tea merchants, tin miners, timber merchants and tobacco dealers; varnishers; weavers, wine merchants and wool merchants, etc.

Perhaps the strangest of such origins is that of Fryer's Bank in Wolverhampton, formed when an oak chest full of French gold coins left behind by the followers of Bonnie Prince Charlie in 1745, was eventually opened by Richard Fryer in 1807 to provide the initial capital used for investing in what by then had become one of the most fashionable of ventures, banking (Sayers 1957). However diverse the origins might have been, Pressnell shows that it was industrialists and transmitters of funds who were the most common sources of bank partnerships, together with lawyers, who, like the London scriveners, had long been accustomed to handling other people's money.

Thus almost all the early country banks grew up as a by-product of some other main activity. This mixed apprenticeship not only further explains the minor point concerning the inexact nature of early banking statistics but also has a number of much more important economic aspects. For one thing it made for easy trial and error, giving the potential banker an opportunity to test the water before plunging in. Typical of such early tentative ventures is that of Birmingham's second bank, founded by Robert Coales around 1770, described in that year's *Business Directory* as 'Sword-Cutler and Merchant' without even mentioning his banking. By 1789 he was known as 'Banker and Sword-Cutler', and by 1797 simply as 'Banker'. This process was typical of country banking in general, for gradually the non-banking business which subsidized the fledgling banking activities was separated, sold off or just dropped, the country banks emerging as specialized financial institutions all the more able to appreciate the needs of other business customers through having themselves been closely involved in such affairs. A further generally overlooked advantage of mixed parentage sprang from the fact that being a banker, even in the small way typical of the early starters, gave the partners a strategic overview of the local business scene, clearly indicating opportunities that might otherwise have been missed. For the early bank partners commonly had their fingers in half a dozen business pies, not always confined to their own localities. Having a banker as partner not only assured the other concerns of priority in banking services but also enabled bank partners to share in partnerships elsewhere, especially since the demands on the time and financial resources of the entrepreneur made by running the early small-unit, local banks were not too severe. The part-time banker is therefore frequently seen setting up businesses, including other banks, elsewhere, a feature which helps to explain why, after the initial lag of a hundred years behind London, country banking, once it caught on, spread so rapidly and so widely. A lot of banking eggs were being hatched in a large number of small nests, the geographic and industrial spread acting as a macro-economic insurance policy for a basically risky industry.

One of the main reasons for setting up a bank was the simple one of securing on a regular and reliable basis the wherewithal to pay for goods and services, given the unreliability of supply and the very poor quality of most of the official metallic money supply and the limited geographic coverage, lack of knowledge of or faith in the notes of the Bank of England, especially during the periods when its notes were issued only in large denominations. From among the many industrialists who came into banking through finding it necessary to produce their own coins or notes or both, we may take as an example the Wilkinsons, iron masters and colliery owners, originally of Bilston, then known as 'the largest village in England' with a population of 6,000. They issued token coins mostly of iron and copper and notes of various denominations through a number of banks in which they were partners in the Midlands and North Wales, most of which eventually became absorbed into today's Midland Bank. Of the 114 banks which had by the 1930s been so absorbed into the Midland, some forty-one were originally small country banks. It was the iron trade that also supplied the greater part of the family wealth that enabled Sampson Lloyd to join with John Taylor, a manufacturer of buttons and japanned ware, to set up what was probably Birmingham's first proper bank in 1765. Of the 142 banks listed by Professor Sayers as having been merged into Lloyds by 1957 no less than 126 had been country banks. It was thus that the industrial heartland of England gave birth to what by the 1920s were to be the world's two biggest banks, the Midland and Lloyds respectively. Barclays, the largest of today's Big Four, originated in the rural corn-growing area of East Anglia where John and his brother Henry Gurney set up a banking house in Norwich in the 1750s. This famous Quaker family, through its relations, friends and co-religionists, spread its influence widely to as far as Keswick and Ireland, as well as establishing in London what was to become the largest bill-broking firm of the mid-nineteenth century.

The role of remittance activities in banking development may be illustrated by the drovers' banks of mid-Wales, such as the Black Ox Bank set up by David Jones of Llandovery in 1799 with its notes aptly depicting the Welsh Black breed of cattle. The drovers' regular and growing trade with London's Smithfield market became a convenient and relatively secure way of transmitting bills of exchange readily discountable in London. Similar pastoral origins are seen in the Bank of the Black Sheep which supplemented the short-lived Banc y Llong or the Ship Bank, again so called from the designs on its notes, which had been formed in Aberystwyth around 1762 when, significantly, a new customs office opened in the town (Crick and Wadsworth 1936).

Pressnell, while questioning the importance of the 'bovine paternity of banking', yet gives a number of examples of so-called 'cattle banks' in small market towns, such as Peacock's which was operating in Sleaford in Lincolnshire by 1801, and cites at least one Smithfield merchant, Joseph Pilkington, who in 1828 was known as a 'money taker and banker'. He also suggests that the excessively large number of banks in the East Riding of Yorkshire arose because of the needs of drovers buying Scottish cattle. Of equal if not greater importance in helping to give rise to country banking were the remittance activities of revenue collectors, such as that of the Exchange Bank of Bristol set up by Samuel Worral in 1764 and Joseph Berwick's bank formed in Worcester in 1781. The French wars, in necessitating much greater revenues and public money transmission, especially to pay troops stationed in various parts of the country, also indirectly substantially stimulated the further growth of country banking and its links with London.

Links with London were of vital importance on both the micro- and macro-economic levels, that is for the security and profitability of the individual bank and for the progress of the economy as a whole. Most country banks were individual, single offices; there were very few branches before 1800. Nevertheless they were not isolated units, but through contacts built up in a variety of ways with London banks they had recourse to or contributed to, as occasion demanded, the monetary reserves centralized in the City. This enabled country banks to operate with lower capital and reserves than would otherwise have been the case, or, what amounts to the same thing but viewed more positively, enabled them to issue a larger total of loans through expanding their note issues or discounting more bills than they could have done without such linkage. Thus the country banks, while not yet able to develop the fully integrated system which had to await the branch banking developments of the second half of the nineteenth century, managed to overcome many, though not all, of the more obvious disadvantages of a basically unit banking system. Of the 119 country banks in 1784 only seven (or 6 per cent) had any branches at all, a situation practically unchanged so far as the trend in branching is concerned by 1798, when only fourteen (or 5 per cent) of the 312 banks then operating had branches. Of the 483 banks listed by Pressnell for 1830 some 362 banks (or 75 per cent) still had just a single office each. Of the other 121 banks which operated branches, some sixty-six had just one branch. The total number of offices in the branch banks, at 359, came to almost exactly half the total of 721 bank offices then in existence. Quite exceptionally, the firm of Gurneys, operating mostly in East Anglia, already had a network of twenty-one branches, prematurely pointing the way to the natural development of the second half of the nineteenth century (Pressnell 1956, 127). Integration, such as it was in the heyday of country banking, therefore, came about not through branching but through establishing representative agencies and sometimes shared partnerships with London banking firms which in turn had direct access to the Bank of England for its notes and bullion. In this way the excess savings of the City and of the rural areas via the City were made available to the country banks in the industrial areas where demand for funds generally exceeded local supplies.

Although the existence of such links had long been recognized by economic historians, the importance of this linkage has not usually been sufficiently appreciated because of a general failure to realize the value of working capital – as opposed to the traditional emphasis on fixed capital – in business investment in the early and mainstream days of the industrial revolution. When Britain became the world's first workshop, it was the small workshop, the small mine, the small bank and so on, all needing very modest amounts of fixed but large amounts of working capital, which in the main brought about this economic transformation. This is not to decry the importance of large factories, mines, canals, ships and major inventions such as the steam engine, which required large amounts of equity capital, but rather to give more needed emphasis to the countless small improvements all around the country, surrounding the more spectacular developments, which together enabled the growth of national output regularly to exceed the rise in population.

Early banks were very properly called 'houses' and the manager's office, usually the only room, containing a clerk and a safe, was known (and still is) as the 'parlour', reminders of how little in the way of fixed capital was needed to set up the country bank of those days. Even the parlour was sometimes borrowed from one of the partners so that the initial capital could be used for till money, printing notes, the clerk's wages and so on. As Mr R. A. Hodgson in his path-breaking study of 'The economics of English country banking' (1976) states, 'A few hundred pounds would in all probability cover the outlay necessary to fit out the establishment . . . the rest of the capital sum was available to finance its initial activities and to open an account with a London banker'. Because of the limitations following the passing of the Bubble Act and the vigilance of the Bank of England in policing its monopoly, the maximum number of partners in banks in England and Wales was six. The dangers of unlimited liability were in addition so strong that in fact only twenty-six of the 552 banks in 1822 had six partners; the average was only three. Thus A. H. John, in his book on *The Industrial*

Development of South Wales (1950) quotes William Crawshay, the Merthyr iron-master as follows: 'I don't say that banking capital partnerships may not be good, but without I was the sole controlling manager I would not be a partner even in that of England if my whole property was liable' as it would have been. The weakness of English as compared with Scottish banks has already been mentioned. In 1810 the average capital of the Scottish joint-stock banks was £50,000 compared with the £10,000 estimated for English country banks.

Despite the irksome restrictions of the law on partnerships and the strict policing of its monopoly privileges by the Bank of England, the small country banks effectively supplied Britain's agriculture and industry, in that order of magnitude, with the working capital they required during the agricultural and industrial revolutions from about 1760 to around 1826. As Rondo Cameron shows in his study of *Banking in the Early Stages of Industrialisation* (1967), only recently have economic historians been able to judge the quantitative importance of the various forms of capital investment. Most firms grew by reinvesting their own profits, and only 'rarely did the representative firm invest as much as 50 per cent of its total assets in fixed capital. Of greater importance collectively were the liquid funds or access to credit needed for the purchase of raw materials, the payment of wages . . . and the extension of credit to buyers.' This the country banks were almost ideally placed to supply. We have already noted that there was a very close connection between banking and industrial investment with the customary renewal of short-term loans so as to supply much of the medium- and long-term needs of the entrepreneur. Furthermore, by supplying businessmen with so much of their working capital, the firms' own profits were the more fittingly available for ploughing back into fixed capital. The close connections between banking and industry – so markedly different from later developments in Britain – sometimes through shared partnerships and more generally through a common commitment to the growth of the local economy from which they all drew their major profits, was in the main a symbiotic relationship. Although on occasions the failure of the bank would bring down other businesses, in which case banking was seen as a parasite, on balance there can be no doubt that the mushroom growth of country banking played a vital role rather than merely a passive one in stimulating the world's first industrial revolution. Without the banks the revolution would have been strangled in its infancy.

Currency, the bullionists and the inconvertible pound, 1783–1826

The state of the currency by the end of the eighteenth century was, once again, deplorable. Sir John Craig shows that 'The mint had been deprived of copper coinage; silver coinage was dead; and gold minting was only undertaken on a small scale' (1953, 255). Gold coins had however been minted at a record level in the last quarter of the century, some £46,000,000 of gold having been minted between 1774 and 1795, while only £68,609 worth of silver was minted between 1760 and 1816. It was in silver and copper coins, the bread and butter of everyday life, that the shortage was of a crippling severity. Faced with a woefully inadequate and unreliable supply of official coinage, businessmen in the provinces in particular were forced increasingly to improvise. There were five main methods used to try to fill the currency gap: tokens of metal; truck, or payment in goods; paper notes issued by company shops and quasi-banks; the use of foreign coins, especially silver; and eventually and by far the most effectively, as we have seen, by proper banks, which issued bills as well as notes, and could usually draw on the official currency, such as it was, from their London agents. Even though the gold circulation was never allowed to deteriorate to the extent of silver and copper, its poor state was demonstrated when Matthew Boulton was able in 1772 to buy more than a £1,000 worth of gold coin of the realm with a £1,000 banknote. Patchy geographical distribution added to the difficulties arising from the overall inadequacy and the very poor intrinsic standard of the coins in circulation.

Mr F. Stuart Jones, in his research into 'Government, currency and country banks in England 1770–1797' (1976), records the fairly typical struggles of Samuel Oldknow, a Lancashire cotton manufacturer, to get enough money to pay his workforce. Relatives would send him cash hidden in bundles of cloth; he went into the retail trade for the sole purpose of garnering enough cash to pay the wage bill, and when that scheme failed he was forced to ration cash payments to his workers for eighteen months from 1792 to 1794 paying them mainly in 'Shop notes' of one guinea down to 1s. 6d. redeemable in certain company shops. Because of its later abuses the whole of the truck system has been given a bad name. Admittedly, at its worst it meant the arbitrary payment of cotton workers in yards of cloth, miners in tons of coal, and so on, together with gross exploitation through charging high prices in the 'Tommy', 'Truck' or 'Company' shops where the truck, tokens or notes were redeemed, often at large discounts on their nominal values, the workers losing at both ends of the scale. But there were legitimate and honest reasons for many of the early company shops set up in industrial areas remote from established towns and villages, and for the issue of tokens and notes by many desperate and helpful employers. 'So many manufacturers were forced to adopt such measures that the first decade of the nineteenth century witnessed the heyday of the private token coin. When this stage was reached the government had almost completely lost control over the metallic currency of the Kingdom' (F. S. Jones 1976).

Token coins were not in actual practice, and with some exceptions, illegal, provided that they were not copies of the designs on the official coinage, in which latter case they were counterfeits carrying the direst penalties, including death, to the manufacturer and to the user of counterfeits. Economically all three kinds of coin performed most of the functions of currency almost equally well, the bird in hand being worth two in the bush; but the social consequences which frequently included death for tendering forged notes as well as for counterfeiting, could hardly have been greater. But genuine tokens, if one might use such a phrase, were fair game. The first great era of token production during the Industrial Revolution began with the issue in 1787 by the Anglesey Copper Company, using the high-quality ore from its local Parys mine, of a very attractive 'Druid Penny' which could be exchanged for official coin at full value, if so desired, at any of its shops or offices. Soon practically every town in the country was producing its own tokens, often buying the blanks, dies and designs from Birmingham and elsewhere. By the turn of the century the total supply and velocity of circulation of tokens, foreign coins and other substitutes very probably exceeded those of the official coin of the realm. A worried government was partially relieved to hear from the Royal Mint that the tokens were 'not illegal'; indeed some of the chief engravers of the mint were making a good profit from selling new designs (not official ones of course) to the free market in coinage.

Much of the token coinage was so obviously superior in appearance to the official coinage that the government itself decided that the free market could probably supply copper currency better than could the Royal Mint. Consequently Matthew Boulton was given a contract in 1797, initially for just 50 tons of two-penny and one-penny pieces, accompanied by an Act of Parliament and a Royal Proclamation to place the legality of his new coins beyond doubt. To assist the immediate circulation of the new money Boulton managed to obtain early orders from bankers in Scotland as well as from the larger number of smaller bankers in England and Wales, while the government agreed to use the coin straight away to pay the armed forces and their suppliers in Deptford, Greenwich, Woolwich, Chatham, Skegness, Portsmouth and Southampton (Cule 1935). Boulton's partnership with James Watt had led to the application of steam to many new forms of production at the Soho works in Birmingham, including coinage not only for tokens for English towns but also for the East India Company, for customers in Newfoundland and the USA and, despite the war, for the large French banking house of Monnerons. Two other contracts followed from the British government for whom Boulton's Soho works minted 4,200 tons of copper between 1797 and 1806. His 'Cartwheel' two-penny pieces, weighing a full two ounces, as well as his smaller copper coins, were extremely popular as soon as issued and 'the public demand for the new pence continued to be almost insatiable' (Cule 1935). After supplying mints embodying his new steam-powered machinery in Russia, Spain, Denmark, Mexico and India, Boulton was employed to erect the Royal Mint's new manufactory on Tower Hill just before his death in 1809, the new mint being completed in 1810.

Meanwhile the desperate shortage of silver coinage continued. Old French twelve- and twenty-four-sou pieces circulated in Britain as sixpenny and shilling pieces. Given the inactivity of the mint, the Bank of England itself stepped into the breach and issued silver coins, altered in design to varying degrees, from its reserves of foreign coins. Half a million pounds' worth of Spanish dollars issued by Charles IV were overstamped in 1797 with a small engraving of George III and made current at 4s. 9d. – hence the ridicule 'Two Kings' heads and not worth a crown', and more crudely 'The head of a fool stamped on the neck of an ass'. The issue failed because the overstamping was readily applied unofficially to the plentiful supplies of light or base Spanish dollars. Consequently Matthew Boulton was employed in 1804 to erase completely the existing design on full weight Spanish coins and re-stamp them as 'Bank of England Five Shilling Dollars', the price being raised to 5s. 6d. in 1811. In the latter year the Bank also took the very significant step of issuing token, i.e. light-weight as opposed to full-bodied, silver coins for 3s. and for 1s. 6d. By thus appearing to usurp the royal prerogative the Bank was considered to have given the green light to manufacturers around the country, who in the second great era of token production in 1811 and 1812 issued a flood of silver coins.

However, the silver currency was plainly still in a mess and most contemporary observers realized that silver's days as the official standard of value were over, in fact if not quite yet in legal form. Because of the poor condition of the silver coinage its legal tender status had already been limited to £25 by an Act of 1774, silver payments in excess of that amount being legally acceptable by weight at 5s. 2d. per ounce. The issue of silver tokens by the Bank of England was a further open, if belated, admission of the subsidiary role to which silver had been reduced. Boulton's copper was limited legal tender up to 2s; there was no limit on gold, while notes, even of the Bank of England, were not yet deemed worthy of consideration of legal tender status. But towards the end of the war the situation was changing and much thought was to be devoted to this question and to the best way of establishing a sound metallic currency. The official position with regard to banknotes swung from *laissez-faire* to restriction and back again. A series of Acts, usually forced on Parliament after financial crises, first tried to limit the use of notes through forbidding small denominations, then was forced to allow them, and later tried again with partial success to restrict them. In between the restrictive Acts the supply of unofficial paper swelled to meet the growing demand in a fundamentally new way which meant that no longer had provincial businessmen to go cap in hand to the monarch, or to Parliament (or even to London as they had to in previous and in later years) in order to increase the money supply. Instead the money was being created locally, on the spot, when, where and to the degree demanded. This most useful but unstable volume of credit was being created 'by the needs of trade', or in modern terminology, endogenously by the effective demands of business and not exogenously by the central monetary authority – by the market rather than by the Royal Mint.

As Peter Mathias shows, in his study of *English Trade Tokens: The Industrial Revolution Illustrated* (1962), 'Local money gives dramatic evidence of the state of economic life and insights into the aspirations of the men who led it' (p. 62). When Wilkinson, the 'iron king', stamped his own head regally on his own coinage, with his tilt-hammer and forge pictured on the reverse, this symbolism, which appeared exaggerated to his contemporaries and to most later historians, was in fact much more fully justified than was apparent. It gave a true picture of how the money supply in general, partly in metal but mostly in paper, had become an endogenous product, being created provincially as an essential ingredient of the world's first industrial revolution. Taken together, the country banks and the token makers were providing almost the whole range of currency needed and certainly the bulk of its most elastic and responsive component. Further support of this viewpoint is given by Stuart Jones: 'Bank deposits may have increased the volume of currency available to entrepreneurs by considerably more than ten-fold' and thus 'the banks, by means of their deposits alone, were stimulating industrial expansion' and so indicating 'the importance of re-assessing the role of banks in promoting industrialisation' (1976, 264).

The second spurt of token production in 1811 and 1812 alarmed the government, for whereas it had been willing to turn a blind eye to copper tokens, the unofficial production of silver money seemed a much more direct challenge to traditional monetary authority. Most silver token producers took great care to make clear the ancillary nature of their product. Thus the 1811 Merthyr silver token bore the cautionary inscription 'To Facilitate Trade Change Being Scarce', while at the other side of Britain the Ipswich 1s. token of 1811 was issued 'To Convenience the Army and Public'. A Bristol businessman, a Mr E. Bryan, however, was less circumspect and confidently issued a 6d. token with the strange device: 'Genuine Silver Dollar'. The currency of most tokens was restricted to their own localities, and they were subject to an increasing discount with distance. To overcome this a 1s. token issued in London in 1811, inscribed 'To Facilitate Trade', also carried a design of four hands joined and the names of the four towns of 'London, York, Swansea, Leeds' where they were accepted (R. Dalton 1922). Forgery, even of tokens, was rife, many being 'mules' which combined the obverse of one coin with the reverse of another (though not all mules were forgeries). The technical requirements for producing tokens were of course the same as those needed for forgery; it was an easy, profitable but highly dangerous temptation. Thus William Booth, to give just one example, a farmer of Perry Bar, produced not only his 'Wheatsheaf' tokens but also forged Bank of England 3s. tokens. On 15 August 1812, at the third gruesome attempt, he was finally hanged for counterfeiting and forgery.

An abortive parliamentary bill attempted to suppress the making and passing of tokens in 1812, but they continued to be traded in considerable volume until an 'Act to Prevent the Issuing and Circulating of Pieces of Copper and other Metal usually called Tokens' was eventually passed in July 1817; but even then certain exceptions were allowed, for instance the tokens issued by Poor Law unions, until 1821, by which time the official supply of coinage had increased enough to make tokens redundant. Before seeing how this official control over coinage was re-established, it is necessary to examine government policy regarding the financing of the wars of the time and their inflationary consequences, together with contemporary opinions in the great debate between the 'bullionists' and the 'anti-bullionists' which provide one of the most famous examples of the perennial swing of the pendulum between the narrow and the wide interpretations of the meaning of money.

The sudden outbreak of war with France in February 1793 was quickly followed by the failure of a number of country banks and a decline in their note circulation with consequential difficulties for the many businesses that had come to rely on them. But the degree of failure and possibly the amount of decline in circulation has been greatly exaggerated. Instead of the hundred bank failures commonly given, and repeated by Sir John Clapham, Pressnell's researches show only sixteen bank failures for the whole of 1793 – grim, but not devastating. Between 1750 and 1830 the total number of country banks which failed was 343. Clearly the country banking system was unstable; yet the exaggerated picture usually painted lent undeserved force to the general underestimation of the positive part played by the banks in Britain's industrial growth (Pressnell 1956, 443). Be that as it may, the 1793 crisis led to such a severe drain from the Bank of England that the government set up a 'Committee on the State of Commercial Credit' as a result of which the Treasury was permitted to issue up to £5,000,000 Exchequer bills, of which some £2,202,000 in denominations of £100, £50 and £20 were actually issued.

In addition the Bank, as we have seen, first began to issue notes as low as £5. In thus helping to alleviate the shortage of currency and in effect acting as lender of last resort (although that concept was for future discovery) the Bank and Treasury together helped the country to weather what has been described as 'the worst financial and commercial crisis it had yet known' (Clapham 1970, II, 259).

No sooner had the Bank of England rebuilt its reserves of gold coin and bullion from their low point of £4 million in 1793 to some £7 million in 1794 than severe new drains, both internal and external, began to occur. Lending to the government itself was one of the biggest drains. Early in 1793 the directors of the Bank of England were becoming increasingly concerned that in agreeing to such lending they were in danger of infringing a clause in their original charter which forbade them to lend to the government without the express approval of Parliament. The directors therefore proposed that the government should bring in a bill granting them legal indemnity in making any loans to the government up to £50,000. William Pitt, the Prime Minister, readily agreed to the Indemnity Bill – but got it modified cleverly without any limit! Obviously in the earlier part of any war the brunt of any expenditure has to be met from borrowing before the slower yield from taxation can catch up.

In addition to increased expenditure on Britain's own armed forces Pitt sent large subsidies to her allies, a total of more than £15 million between 1793 and 1801, including a loan of £1,200,000 sent to Austria in July 1796. The external drain was considerably intensified when the grossly inflationary issues of *assignats* (paper notes originally based on the value of Church and other lands confiscated by the French revolutionary government) were replaced in July 1796 by a gold-based currency. This had the effect of drawing bullion back from Britain. Although an attempted French invasion of Ireland in the winter of 1796 was thwarted, an invasion of Britain was imminently expected. On 22 February 1797 French troops landed at Carreg Wastad near Fishguard: it could hardly be called a raid, let alone an invasion, for the French troops, mistaking a distant gathering of women in Welsh costume as uniformed troops, ignominiously surrendered. However when rumours of the landing reached London, a run on the banks quickly ensued, bringing down the reserves of the Bank of England on 25 February to their lowest point in the war, at £1,272,000. An emergency meeting of the Privy Council was called on Sunday morning, 26 February, which resolved that 'the Bank of England should forbear issuing any cash', a situation confirmed by the 'Bank Restriction Act' of 3 May 1797. The restriction, then expected to be of very short duration, was in fact to last until 1 May 1821. A new era of inconvertible paper had arrived.

By the Bank Indemnity Act Pitt had eased his path to securing the bulk of the short-term funds he required. According to Andreades, 'No government had ever had such a formidable weapon placed in its hands' (1909, 191). Before long Pitt had found an even more powerful weapon for securing longer-term finance, namely the income tax. This came into operation in April 1799 at 2s. in the pound (10 per cent) on incomes over £200, with lower rates down to £60, below which no income tax was levied. On average in its first three years, to the great satisfaction of the government, the new income tax raised £6 million annually. The range of indirect taxes was widened as far as possible. In the immortal words of Sidney Smith, in the *Edinburgh Review* of January 1820, there were:

Taxes upon every article that enters the mouth, or covers the back, or is placed under the foot – taxes upon everything which is pleasant to see, hear, feel, smell or taste – taxes upon warmth, light, locomotion – taxes on everything on earth, and the waters under the earth – on everything that comes from abroad or is grown at home – taxes on the raw material – taxes on every fresh value that is added to it by the industry of man – taxes on the sauce which pampers a man's appetite, and the drug that restores him to health – on the ermine which decorates the judge, and the rope which hangs the criminal – on the poor man's salt and the rich man's spice – on the brass nails of the coffin, and the ribands of the bride – at bed or board, couchant or levant, we must pay. The school-boy whips his taxed top; the beardless youth manages his taxed horse with a taxed bridle, on a taxed road; and the dying Englishman pouring his medicine, which has paid seven per cent, into a spoon that has paid fifteen per cent, flings himself back upon his chinz bed, which has paid twenty-two per cent, makes his will on an eight pound stamp, and expires in the arms of an apothecary, who has paid a licence of £100 for the privilege of putting him to death. His whole property is then immediately taxed from two to ten per cent. Besides the probate, large fees are demanded for burying him in the chancel. His virtues are handed down to posterity on taxed marble, and he will then be gathered to his fathers to be taxed no more.

It is abundantly clear that the weight of the fiscal burden, both through taxation and through long-term borrowing, by removing so much purchasing power from the people made the task of monetary policy that much easier. As well as heavy taxation the government raised so much money by long-term borrowing that the national debt, which had been £273 million in 1783, rose to £816 million in 1816 of funded debt, plus a large amount of £86 million of floating or short-term debt. Between the same years the annual interest or service charge on the national debt had risen from £9.5 million to £31 million. If the taxation had been lighter or if the national debt had been lower, then the government would have had to rely, however unconsciously, on the hidden taxation of a much more inflationary monetary policy than actually occurred. To modern observers imbued with strong inflationary expectations of what governments may feel forced to do in wartime, the price rises of the early nineteenth century seem laudably modest. To contemporaries, stalwart believers in the virtues of a stable value of money, the general rising trend of prices seemed deeply disturbing and puzzling. Matters were brought to a head by the publication on 8 June 1810 of the 'Report from the Select Committee of the House of Commons on the High Price of Bullion', one of the most famous monetary documents of the last two centuries.

The science of index numbers of prices was in its infancy at the beginning of the nineteenth century and never really entered into the arena of public discussion until much later. Consequently other indicators were needed in order to gauge whether and to what extent general price changes were taking place. The two basic indicators of the changes in the value of the paper pound, related to and confirming each other, were on the one hand the state of the foreign exchanges with other major trading countries and on the other hand, the 'premium on gold', by which was meant the extent to which the price of gold had risen above its pre-inconvertibility mint parity. The mint par value of the pound sterling was 123.25 grains of 22 carat gold, i.e. eleven-twelfths fine, or at the rate of £3. 17s.10½d. per ounce. This was the price paid by the mint, and naturally involved the customer in a certain amount of cost and inconvenience and in waiting his turn, and so was not worthwhile for smaller transactions. The much more convenient and immediate exchanges at the Bank of England, covering the whole range of personal, retail or wholesale customers was priced at the official rate of £3. 17s. 6d., the 4½d. difference being simply a token contribution towards the much higher real costs saved by using the Bank as intermediary. Those persons who wished to return as soon as possible to this traditional convertibility were therefore known as 'bullionists', while the supporters of the government and of the Bank of England in its policy of deferring such convertibility until after the end of the war and meanwhile emphasizing the practical advantages of the suppression of cash, i.e. gold, payments, were known as 'anti-bullionists'.

The remit of the Bullion Committee was thus 'to enquire into the Cause of the High Price of Gold Bullion, and to take into consideration the State of the Circulating Medium, and of the Exchanges between Great Britain and Foreign Parts'. In bald summary the committee's well-supported and lucidly expressed findings were that the premium on gold and the depreciation of the value of the pound on the foreign exchanges were to a substantial degree caused by the creation of an excessive amount of credit, principally by the Bank of England through issuing too many notes but also through being too liberal in discounting bills of exchange. Therefore the only cure was to return to full convertibility of Bank of England notes after two years, and of the notes of the country banks and of the chartered banks of Ireland and Scotland shortly thereafter, whether or not the war would be over by then.

The chairman of the committee was Francis Horner, son of an Edinburgh merchant, and educated at Edinburgh High School and Edinburgh University, but with two years spent in England 'to rid himself of the disadvantages of a provincial dialect' (Rees 1921). Apart from being co-founder of the *Edinburgh Review* this report was his only but amply sufficient claim to fame. The committee's vice-chairman was William Huskisson, who was to become a liberalizing President of the Board of Trade, and who suffered the final dubious distinction of being killed by a train at the ceremonial opening of the Liverpool to Manchester Railway in 1830. These two, together with the banker-economist Henry Thornton, actually wrote the report, which was promptly laid before Parliament on 10 June 1810, but was not formally debated until May 1811. The views it contained were widely debated outside Parliament, with most of the economists, including Malthus and Ricardo, strongly supporting the bullionist side, but with most of the practising bankers and businessmen supporting the anti-bullionist position of the Bank of England and of the government. But there were cross-currents of opinion and some notable changes of position over the years, in a debate which reflected the controversies of over a century earlier, preceding the great currency reform of 1696, and which foreshadowed the Currency versus Banking School arguments of the mid-nineteenth century and the monetarist as opposed to the neo-Keynesian beliefs of today. Those interested in controversial cross-currents should read Viner (1937) or Clapham (1970), while those wishing a straightforward, neutral account with a full copy of the report should see Edwin Cannan's *The Paper Pound* (1919).

With the clarity of our hindsight, the views expressed to the committee by the Governor and former Governor of the Bank of England were incredibly perverse. They put forward the view that (a) there was no need to consider the state of the foreign exchanges or the premium on gold when they decided their policies on note issuing or discounting, providing that they dealt only with bills of exchange raised in the course of sound commercial business; (b) subject to the same proviso, it was impossible to overissue or to overdiscount; c) raising or reducing the rate of discount would have no effect on the volume of business, because no businessman would incur the costs of borrowing unless it was essential for carrying on his trade. Thus Mr Whitmore, the Governor, states quite categorically: 'I never think it necessary to advert to the price of Gold, or the state of the Exchange, on the days on which we make our advances' (Cannan 1919, 34). When asked if the temptation to overissue or overdiscount would be increased by reducing the rate from 5 per cent – the maximum permitted by the usury laws – to 4 or even 3 per cent, the Governor replied that the result would be 'precisely the same'; while the Deputy Governor dutifully supported him in replying 'I concur in that answer' (Cannan 1919, 48). That the reliance on sound commercial bills – the famous 'real bills doctrine' – was an insufficient safeguard against an excess issue of notes or of advances was easily demonstrated by the committee: 'While the rate of commercial profit is very considerably higher than five per cent there is in fact no limit to the demands which Merchants may be tempted to make upon the Bank for accommodation and facilities by discount' (Cannan 1919, 51).

The committee went on to show how the note issue had in fact increased from £13,334,752 in 1798 to £19,011,890 in 1809, an increase of 45 per cent, but with an increase of 170 per cent in notes under £5, which rose from £1,807,502 in 1798 to £4,868,275 in 1809. The committee also stressed the importance of the velocity of circulation and financial innovation – views of surprising modernity insufficiently stressed by most historians. Thus the report shows that 'The effective currency of the Country depends on the quickness of circulation, and the number of exchanges performed in a given time, as well as upon its numerical amount', while 'Your Committee are of opinion that the improvements which have taken place of late years in this Country, with regard to the use and economy of money among Bankers, and in the modes of adjusting commercial payments, must have had a much greater effect than has hitherto been ascribed to them, in rendering the same sum adequate to a much greater amount of trade and payments than formerly.' Not all the economic verities were, however, possessed by the bullionists. They underestimated the autonomous nature of much of the country banks' money-creating powers and, using the quite plausible excuse of the unreliability of the figures on the total of note issues by these banks and the lack of figures on their discounts, came rather too readily to the conclusion that 'the amount of the Country Bank circulation is limited by the amount of that of the Bank of England' (Cannan 1919, 54) and so absolved the country bankers from their share of the blame for excess issue by heaping it all on to the Bank of England.

Even Sir John Clapham is forced to admit that 'the Bank witnesses showed up badly as economists' (he could hardly do otherwise); but he makes the supremely telling point that 'many of their critics showed up no better as politicians' (1970, II 28). For there was a war on, and any serious attempt by the Bank to return during the war to full convertibility would have led to such strong deflationary pressures that the economic strength of the country would have been gravely imperilled at the most critical of times. As the Chancellor of the Exchequer, Spencer Percival, wrote at the time, the Bullion Report's recommendations were equivalent to 'a declaration that we must submit to any terms of peace rather than continue the war'. It was this vital matter, rather than any fine points of economics, that carried the day when the time came to vote on the debate in Parliament. Horner had drawn up the main conclusions of his report in the form of Sixteen Resolutions which he laid before parliament, every one of which was rejected. The government's views, and that of the anti-bullionists, were put forward by Nicholas Vansittart, who, going one better than Horner, put forward seventeen Counter-Resolutions, which were all carried, despite the weak economic basis of many of them.

Vansittart's third resolution, based on a mixture of wishful thinking and the inertia of the general public in their monetary customs, asserted that 'the promissory notes of the Bank of England have hitherto been, and are at this time, held in public estimation to be equivalent to the legal coin of the realm'. This brazen denial of any depreciation at all in the paper pound was immediately challenged by Lord King, who in a letter to his tenants demanded payment in gold or in an additional sum of notes equal to the market price of that gold. As a result Stanhope's Act of 1811 was hurriedly passed which had the effect of safeguarding payments in bank notes at the nominally contracted prices. The Act refused to take the clear-cut and logical decision of making Bank of England notes legal tender, but at least it was a step, awkward and stumbling, in that direction.

When the end of the long, burdensome war came at last in 1815 it seemed at first as if the Bank would be able to return to convertibility within six months just as the government had already intended; but a renewed drain on the Bank's reserves forced a further postponement. The government did however set about establishing gold as beyond doubt the official standard of the currency. A report of the Privy Council on the coinage recommended in May 1816 that gold should be the only standard, at the traditional parity of 123.25 grains per pound sterling, and that a new coin, the 'sovereign' of 20s. should be issued. By the Coinage Act of 1816 these recommendations were put into effect utilizing the new mint which had been ready for such large-scale demands, awaiting the return of peace, since 1810. Britain thus legally and most belatedly recognized the gold standard towards which the country had very largely moved early in the previous century. It required the resumption of convertibility to confirm the legality of the new gold standard in practice. The long-awaited Act for the Resumption of Cash Payments was passed in 1819, allowing free trade in bullion and coin, and stipulating that full convertibility would have to be restored by 1 May 1823. As it happened the Bank's reserves improved so strongly that cash payments were resumed in full from 1 May 1821 – without having had to resort to the intermediate stage of the 'ingot exchange system' advocated by Ricardo – after twenty-four years and two months of a paper pound. A related Act of 1819 had once again removed the Bank's indemnity in lending to the government for more than three months without the permission of Parliament, which had been granted in 1793. The coinage system, still held to be the obvious and unquestioned foundation of the country's monetary system, was thus soundly reconstructed. It was now time to turn public attention to what in fact had already become the far more important component of money, not only in London and Scotland, but throughout the kingdom, i.e. the banking system.

The Bank of England and the joint-stock banks, 1826–1850

The three legislative landmarks in the history of the development of banking in the nineteenth century are those of 1826, 1833 and 1844. In each case the Bank of England's monopoly position in banking, particularly with regard to note issue, was the central feature, although other aspects of banks' credit-creating powers, such as those concerning the discounting of bills of exchange, also attracted considerable attention. It is interesting to see how the opinions of practical bankers, politicians and economists, in an era of prolific publicity, were all changing to embrace either a wider definition of money, or the acceptance of the view that a wider range of financial instruments needed to be controlled in order to control the quantity of money. Gradually the bullionist versus anti-bullionist arguments changed into those of the Currency versus the Banking School, described below, again illustrating the eternal swing of the pendulum between the narrower and the wider vision of a money supply that everyone now agreed was larger and wider than was previously in existence. For even those who had previously held the narrowest, most blinkered view, now openly accepted notes as money and not simply as a money-substitute, while even the Bank of England had before the end of the 1820s explicitly admitted that its total issue of notes was dependent upon variations in the rate of interest which it charged for discounting bills; and – a further significant change – this was so even in circumstances where all such bills were generated in the course of genuine and sound commercial transactions. The anti-bullionists now conceded the bullionist case that note issues could thus be increased or decreased at the discretion of the Bank; and this carried the corollary that the achievement of convertibility, even when combined with a conservative and cautious policy of discounting, was not enough to supply the right amount of money to satisfy the demands of trade. Convertibility merely carried the micro-economic advantage of guaranteeing to a person the ability of changing paper money into gold at a fixed price. Everyone now had to concede that convertibility could not also carry any macro-economic guarantee of supplying the country with the optimum quantity of money. Some additional controls over paper money as well as over metallic money, over the relationship between the notes of the Bank of England and those of other banks, over discount rate policy and over the metallic backing of notes, were all seen to be required, although the light did not dawn in a single blaze of knowledge. As usual it was the recurrence of financial crises that crystallized the debates into legislative form. The closely related developments of theory and practice may thus conveniently be traced in three stages, to 1826, 1833 and 1844 respectively.

The Banking Acts of 1826

The revival of prosperity in the early 1820s, after an initial depression, gradually gathered momentum into a speculative boom that culminated in an economic crisis and a banking panic at the end of 1825. When the Resumption of Cash Payments Act was passed in 1819 it was the stated intention to end the circulation of banknotes under £5 two years after the actual resumption. But the depressed state of agriculture, still by far the country's largest employer, coupled with the vested interests of the country bankers, led the government to adopt a reflationary, expansionist policy through a combination of monetary, fiscal and administrative means. Already in 1821 the Bank of England extended its normal maximum period of acceptance of bills for discount from sixty-five to ninety-five days, thus increasing the liquidity of bills in general. In 1822, reversing the previous policy, the government passed an Act to prolong the life of small notes by ten years, from 1823 to 1833, a lease of new life which was not to be fully consummated. Coincident with this increase in liquid funds, market rates of interest began to fall, a move confirmed in June 1822 when the Bank of England reduced its rate of discount from 5 per cent to 4 per cent. The Bank's lending policy, even on very long-term loans, was similarly expansive, for beginning with a loan of £300,000 at 4 per cent to the Duke of Rutland in 1823, the bank granted over fifty mortgages totalling more than £150 million, secured by landed estates, during the next two years (Clapham 1970, 82–4).

The Chancellor of the Exchequer, F. J. Robinson, aptly dubbed 'Prosperity Robinson', together with Huskisson, now President of the Board of Trade, developed fiscal policies to reinforce the reflationary monetary policy. In his budgets of 1823, 1824 and 1825 Robinson substantially reduced the rates and narrowed the range of taxes. The government took advantage of the lower rates of interest to reduce the burden of the national debt. Vansittart converted £150 million of 5 per cent stock to 4 per cent in 1822, while Robinson followed this up by converting £70 million of 4 per cent stock to 3½ per cent in 1824. The successful revolt of the Mexican and South American colonists against Spain opened the doors wide for the export of British goods – the economic counterpart of Canning's famous 'calling the New World to redress the balance of the Old'. The greater liberality of the government towards company formation was shown by the repeal of the Bubble Act in 1825. Between 1824 and 1826 some 624 new companies were provisionally registered with a nominal capital worth nearly £400 million, but since a large number of these never really got going the actual totals were considerably less. All the same there was something of a company mania reminiscent of 1720. As well as domestic new investment on a large scale there were considerable exports of capital, some to rebuild European business and governments, some in riskier deals in Mexico and South America. The fashion for wealthy Britons to make the Grand Tour of Europe led to a sizeable deficit on the 'tourist account'. Huskisson's freer trade policy though, undoubtedly to the long-term general good of British producers and consumers, had the initial result of contributing to a surge in imports (as well as permanently destroying the Spitalfields silk weaving industry). The net result of these various drains was to reduce the reserves of the Bank of England from the exceptionally high figure of £14.2 million in 1823 to the dangerously low point of only £1,260,890 by early December 1825. Belatedly the Bank reacted by raising its discount rate back up to its legal maximum of 5 per cent on 13 December.

Already in September 1825 several banks in Devon and Cornwall had failed, including the fairly large firm of Elfords of Plymouth. Much more serious was the failure, despite help from the Bank of England, of the London firm of Pole, Thornton and Co. since, with forty-three country correspondent banks, the effects of its failure were quickly felt throughout the country. During December 1825 some thirteen country banks failed, and during the crisis as a whole a *net* figure of sixty banks failed (a figure rather smaller than the seventy or more commonly given, but some of these latter 'failures' were branches, while a few were temporary failures of banks which eventually managed to reopen). Nevertheless the failure of sixty banks demanded urgent action and some fundamental reform of the banking system.

The immediate panic was alleviated by the Bank of England's liberal acceptance of collateral and by issuing £1 notes printed in 1818 which had lain half-forgotten since then in a large storage box. The mint was also pressed into overtime to produce as many sovereigns as possible to help to overcome the liquidity shortage that always accompanies a financial crisis. Despite the blame attached to the Bank of England and government policy in general for having overstimulated the economy, there was almost unanimous agreement that the single most important cause was the elastic supply of small notes by the small and weak country banks, weak especially when compared with the joint-stock and co-partnership banks of Scotland, where only one bank had failed since 1816. The Prime Minister, Lord Liverpool, in introducing the remedial legislation, made his famous criticism: 'Any small tradesman, a cheesemonger, a butcher or a shoemaker may open a country bank, but a set of persons with a fortune sufficient to carry on the concern with security are not permitted to do so.' Stronger banks issuing larger-denomination notes, those were the key reforms that experience had shown to be urgently required. By an Act of 22 March 1826 no more notes of less than £5 were to be issued and all outstanding small notes had to be redeemed by 5 April 1829. By a second Act, passed on 26 May 1826, the Bank of England's century-old monopoly was partly broken, by allowing joint-stock banks with note-issuing powers to be set up outside a radius of sixty-five miles of the centre of London. In return the Bank of England was explicitly authorized to set up branches, or 'agencies' anywhere in England and Wales. Daniel Defoe's Bank of 'London' was about to become in truth the Bank of England.

Branches of the Bank of England were quickly opened in 1826, at Gloucester (19 July), Manchester (21 September) and Swansea (23 October). Five more were opened in 1827, at Birmingham, Liverpool, Bristol, Leeds and Exeter. The Newcastle branch opened in 1828, followed by those of Hull and Norwich in 1829, Plymouth and Portsmouth in 1834 and Leicester in 1844. Apart from the London branches – the 'Western' in 1853 and the 'Law Courts' in 1881 – the only other branch was that of Southampton, opened in 1940, the same year that a Glasgow 'Office' was opened for exchange control purposes, not being strictly speaking a 'branch' or 'agency'. The branches received a mixed reception, being warmly welcomed in some towns, such as Gloucester and Swansea (and invited in vain to others, such as Carlisle) and actively opposed in towns like Exeter; the local newspaper, the *Exeter Flying Post*, lamenting 'of all men who are sinned against by this uncalled-for interference on the part of the Bank of England, none are less deserving it than the Bankers of our own City' (*BEQB*, December 1963, 280). The new branches for the most part saw themselves as aggressively active competitors with the local banks, whether old country banks or new joint-stock banks. In particular they discounted local bills at most competitive rates, – discounting nearly £5.5 million for 1,000 clients in 1830, so exceeding the totals for Threadneedle Street – and entered into special agreements with local banks in order to boost the issue of Bank of England notes, partly for their own profit but also for the economic and social reasons behind the legislation of 1826. The Bank had always had a particular dislike for small and other easily forged notes. Between 1797 and 1829 some 618 persons were capitally convicted for forging notes and many of these were hanged. The harshness of the death penalty not only led juries to ever greater reluctance to condemn culprits but dragged the prosecuting

Bank into public distaste. There is therefore a great deal of truth in a Bank historian's comment that 'for reasons both financial and humane, the Directors ceased issuing small notes as soon as they could' (Giuseppi 1966). Nathan Rothschild, and Overend and Gurney were prominent in persuading Peel to bring in an Act of 1832 which reduced the maximum penalty for forgery from death to transportation for life. (Francis 1862, 230–1).

The prohibition of small notes was intended to apply also to Scotland despite the much greater role played there by small notes and the much greater strength of the Scottish banks. The proposal aroused the wrath of the Scots and the powerful ridicule of Sir Walter Scott, who wrote a series of letters which appeared in the *Edinburgh Weekly Journal* in February and March 1826 under the pseudonym Malachi Malagrowther. After demonstrating the superiority of the Scottish banking system and the disastrous consequences that would follow abolition of their customary small notes, he asks: 'Shall all be lost to render the system of currency betwixt England and Scotland uniform? In my opinion Dutchmen might as well cut the dikes and let the sea in upon the land.' The letters forced the government to allow Scotland its small notes; no wonder that Scott's portrait still adorns some current issues. The letters, though triggered off by mundane matters of finance, went on to question the politics of the Union. As P. H. Scott wrote recently in a new edition of Malachi Malagrowther's *Letters* (1981), 'they dealt in a way which is still topical with the whole question of the relationship between Scotland and England'. Scottish notes had circulated in the bordering counties of England for many years, and despite the 1826 Act and a further motion by the Chancellor of the Exchequer in 1828 'to restrain the circulation of Scottish notes in England' they continued to be popular in those districts up to 1845 (Phillips 1894).

The Bank Charter Act 1833
In December 1827 the Bank of England minuted its acceptance of the bullionist view that its volume of discounting could indeed influence the value of the pound on the foreign exchange markets. By this admission of its previous fundamental error the way was opened for discussing the removal of the 5 per cent maximum rate under the usury laws. But the volume of the Bank's discounts and the related volume of Bank of England notes could not be logically discussed in isolation either from the matter of how to control the issues of other banks or the legal tender nature of Bank of England notes, in the absence of which the other banks would always insist, whenever they faced the slightest

strain, on drawing gold rather than notes from the Bank. As soon as the 1826 Act had become law a series of joint-stock banks were set up, growing to around fifty by 1832, of which thirty-two were new and the rest enlargements of previous partnership banks. Thomas Joplin, a Newcastle timber merchant, well versed in the superiority of Scottish banking, was actively involved in promoting a number of these, for fittingly enough, he had been one of the most powerful driving forces in bringing about the modification of the Bank of England's monopoly. He was also busily planning an ambitious 'National Provincial Bank of England' with branches in the main towns, though this did not come to fruition until 1833. In the mean time he took his quarrel with the Bank of England a stage further. According to his meticulous reading of the original Acts, joint-stock banks, *provided that they did not issue notes*, could quite legally be set up even within sixty-five miles of London, an opinion hotly disputed by the Bank. The difference arose from the fact that when the Bank was first granted its monopoly, note issue was considered inseparably essential to banking. That this was no longer the case seemed a large loophole for Joplin and his supporters, but a mere, unjustified quibble to the Bank of England.

As it happened, the Bank of England's charter was due for renewal in 1833, and so the time seemed right to seek further clarification of the matters in dispute. Early in 1832 the government set up a committee of inquiry which considered all aspects relevant to the renewal, including the usury laws, the Bank's monopoly, the legal position of non-note-issuing banks and the granting of legal tender status to Bank of England notes. The Bank could not be complacent about the concessions it might be forced to make to secure the renewal of its charter, for at a time of great public unrest the Bank had become associated in the minds of some of its most vociferous critics with that section of ultra-conservative opinion that resisted parliamentary reform. Hence radicals were ready to follow leaders like Francis Place who invented the slogan 'To Stop the Duke [of Wellington] Go for Gold', an incitement which led to an ineffectual but frightening run on the Bank in May 1832, and the dispatch of pikes and sabres to its branches, some of which still form an eye-catching display at the Bristol branch. After much heated debate, in and out of Parliament, the Bank Charter Act was finally passed on 23 August 1833.

The Act renewed the Bank's charter for twenty-one years from 1 August 1834, but with a break clause after ten years. Bank of England notes were to become legal tender (against the wishes of Peel and a sizeable minority) in England and Wales, a privilege not extended to Scotland or Ireland. This would help to stop internal drains. Bills of exchange up to three months were removed from the ambit of the usury laws. In this quiet way, what was to become the famed 'Bank Rate' instrument of policy for the next 150 years was born, though the first breaking of the 5 per cent ceiling did not take place until 1839. In order for the government to be able to monitor Bank policy more closely a weekly return of the Bank's accounts, including its note issue and reserve of bullion had to be sent confidentially to the Treasury, while a monthly summary was to be published in the *London Gazette*. Accompanying legislation required all other banks to publish quarterly returns of their note issues so that any tendency to excess issue could more easily be exposed to public view. After this seven-year spate of investigation and legislation one might be forgiven for expecting a period of agreement or at least compromise and financial calm. On the contrary, the debate hotted up to reach a new pitch of intensity as the views of the two opposing monetary camps became more stridently and more dogmatically asserted.

Currency School versus Banking School

Believers in the 'Currency Principle' were so called because, naturally enough, they believed that gold and bank notes, especially Bank of England notes, were the only proper money or currency; all other forms of bank credit were simply second-rate substitutes, of use only because they allowed people to economize in using real money. Their logical starting point was the London foreign exchange market in which gold provided the link and value indicator between internal and external currencies. Britain's currency, i.e. gold plus notes, should be made to behave as if it were entirely of gold. Experience had shown that convertibility was not enough to guarantee this. Any loss of gold to other countries should require the banks to reduce their note issues by the same absolute amount so that UK prices would fall, and foreign prices rise, together acting to restore equilibrium on the foreign exchanges and in the relative price levels. It was little wonder that convertibility alone did not suffice when hundreds of banks were, in a totally uncoordinated fashion, allowed to issue their own notes. The response was not, in those circumstances, quick enough to prevent excessive fluctuations in finance and in trade. Ideally, as Ricardo advocated, a single state note-issuing authority would be the best way of making note issues increase or decrease in line with the 'influx' or 'efflux' of gold. Since this ideal could not be brought about overnight, the next best alternative would be to encourage the Bank of England in its policy of taking over the issues of the other banks. (We have seen how the Bank came to special arrangements with many country banks for the latter to give up their own issues in favour of Bank of England notes, receiving privileged access to bill discounting at the cheap rate of 3 per cent.) In modern terminology the Currency School (by the 1840s both camps were calling themselves 'schools') was a classic example of money being conceived in the narrowest possible way consistent with the circumstances of the time and, typical of all such narrow views, they obviously believed that money should be created and controlled by the central monetary authorities – exogenously as we would say – in the financial and administrative capital of the country, the City of London and the Parliament at Westminster.

The main supporters of the Currency School were Samuel Jones Loyd, a banker who later became Lord Overstone; Robert Torrens, ex-colonel of Marines and a keen amateur economist; G. W. Norman and W. Ward, both directors of the Bank of England, a fact that helped to strengthen the natural predilection for central banks to be in favour of the narrower view of money. Exceptionally, as we saw at the time of the Bullion Report of 1810, the Bank then felt constrained to support the anti-bullionist position of the government, a view happily recanted in 1827, and in practice years earlier. As early as 1832 J. Horsley Palmer, Governor of the Bank, together with G. W. Norman, had formed the view that it was essential for the Bank to hold about one-third of its assets in the form of bullion, the rest being in government securities. Thus all liabilities payable on demand, i.e. notes and deposits, were backed by a reserve of one-third in bullion. This so-called Palmer Rule was not, as Clapham shows, strictly followed: 'Palmer and Norman were describing the fair weather practice of a single decade, not promulgating a dogma' (1970, II, 125). As it turned out, to the discredit of the Palmer Rule, the volatility of bank deposits was greater than that of notes, so that when customers drew down their deposits to get gold from the Bank, its note issues were not correspondingly reduced. And as Loyd made clear in his evidence to the Committee on Banks of Issue, 1840, 'Whenever the aggregate paper circulation of the country fails to conform to the fluctuations of the bullion then mismanagement is justly said to occur' (Feavearyear 1963, 262). The Currency School was desperately seeking a better method than the Palmer Rule for linking the supply of notes more closely to variations in the flows of bullion.

The Banking School was led by the Revd J. Fullarton; Thomas Tooke, author of the compendious *History of Prices*; J. W. Gilbart, founder of the London and Westminster Bank; and James Wilson, founder-editor of *The Economist*. It was a strongly talented group with a wide and varied experience of business and finance. The Banking School started from the opposite pole to that of the Currency School, for the former insisted that the banks supplied money in a wide variety of forms to suit the demands of their customers, and notes were just one form among many other functionally similar forms of money. It was the flow of trade in all parts of the country which generated the issue of banknotes, or the volume of cheques or of bills of exchange and so on. Although followers of the Banking School were not always consistent or in full agreement on matters of method, they were unanimously and steadfastly of the opinion that in practice money was much more than simply gold and notes. 'Bank notes' said Fullarton are simply 'the small change of credit.' It followed therefore that 'it was absurd to attempt to regulate prices by attending to notes only, for they were merely a part, and were rapidly becoming a minor part, of the total paper circulation' (Feavearyear 1963, 266). The Banking School was, however, too blind to see that the freedom which the banks possessed in granting credit could be used to excess, excusing themselves by Fullarton's 'law of reflux' according to which every note issued in response to a demand for a loan would automatically be returned to the bank when the loan was repaid, so that 'The banker has only to take care that they are lent at sufficient security, and the reflux and the issue will, in the long run, always balance each other' (Fullarton 1845, 64). Urgent events were to prevent the complacent acceptance of long-run tendencies. Clearly the Banking School represented the classical case of a wide interpretation of the meaning of money and of the important and as yet still geographically dispersed role of the banks as (passive) providers of money. In modern terminology money was mainly bank money, endogenously created throughout the country by market forces, and not just exogenously and arbitrarily by the mint and the Bank of England in London.

Each school realized that their opinions were of much more than purely academic concern. The country had suffered from two crises in three years, in 1836 and 1839. The government had set up a Committee on Joint Stock Banks which met from 1836 to 1838 and was then supplemented by a Committee on Banks of Issue in 1840. Clearly the government was about to legislate once again on matters of money and banking, as concern rose over how to deal with the interrelationship between bank failures, business bankruptcies and the severe drain of gold from the reserves. In November 1836 one of the apparently strongest of the new joint-stock banks, the Northern and Central Bank of England, failed. Based in Manchester, it had rapidly built up a network of thirty-nine branches in the north-west which had been enjoying a boom induced by trade with a buoyant market in USA.

The bimetallist controversies in the USA (see chapter 9), the failure of the Agricultural and Commercial Bank of Ireland in November 1837 and of the Bank of Belgium together with a run on the French banking house of Lafitte and other failures on the Continent around the same time, led to recurrent drains of gold from the reserves of the Bank of England. Although it managed to scrape through the 1836 crisis without too much difficulty and had built up its reserves back to a creditworthy level of £9.5 million in January 1839, in the following months the drain became so severe that it was forced to take the historic step of raising bank rate for the first time to 5½ per cent on 20 June, and then more boldly to 6 per cent on 1 August. It had also to face the humiliation of borrowing £2 million from Paris and £0.9 million from Hamburg. Even so its reserves fell to the dangerously low level of £2.3 million in October. Fears of an inconvertible pound had been narrowly averted by these stop-gap expedients. Obviously a new way of ordering the nation's finances was urgently required.

The Bank Charter Act of 1844: rules plus discretion

With the possible exception of the 1694 Act which set up the Bank of England, no other piece of financial legislation has caused so much ink to be spilled as the Bank Charter Act of 1844, both at the time and subsequently. It combined most of the rules demanded by the Currency School and by the Bank of England with just a little of the discretionary powers demanded by the Banking School for the commercial banks but grabbed by the Bank of England, which in the national interest, as it saw it, managed to get the best of both schools. Perhaps the most flattering and telling summary of the importance of the Act in helping to secure real, non-inflationary growth over most of the following seventy years is given, ironically enough, by the Radcliffe Committee of 1959, whose report marks the nadir of belief in the importance of money, and not unnaturally heralded the most rampant period of inflation in British history:

> The Act remained on the statute book because the ceiling it fixed (on note issues) had come to be regarded as an assurance against any collapse of the value of the pound. For this reason the 1844 legislation, despite all its shortcomings, was one of the pillars of the English monetary system, and has left its mark on later statutes, even until quite recent times. (Radcliffe Report 1959, para. 522)

In the 'Act to Regulate the Issue of Bank Notes, and for giving to the Governor and Company of the Bank of England certain Privileges for a limited Period' – to give the 1844 Act its full title – some eighteen of its twenty-eight clauses deal directly with the problem of note issue either of the Bank of England or of the other banks, while a number of other clauses do so indirectly. Clause 1 states that 'the issue of notes of the

Bank of England . . . shall be separated, and thenceforth kept wholly distinct from the general Banking Business'. As Peel later explained, 'The Issue Department might be in Whitehall and the Banking Department in Threadneedle Street', thus clearly expressing the generally held concept of rigid rules for the currency and apparently unfettered discretion in carrying on its ordinary banking; a discretion soon to be limited by the need to develop its central banking functions. The Issue Department was to receive from the Banking Department some £14 million of government securities to back its fiduciary issue of notes, any issue above that to be fully backed by gold and silver, the latter not to exceed one quarter of the gold. (Since 1861 the Bank has kept none of its reserve in silver.) Notes were to be given on demand at £3. 17s. 9d. per ounce; this price, rather than the previous official rate of £3. 17s. 6d. had arisen thanks to the bargaining power of Nathan Rothschild who in 1836 insisted on dealing directly with the mint at £3. 17s. 10½d. until the Bank raised the price for him, and so for everyone else, by 3d. The Bank had now to send a weekly return to the Treasury, the famous 'Return' then being published. According to one historian, writing on the hundredth anniversary of the Act, this weekly return was its most important provision – a pardonable exaggeration. (It was a great time for economic enlightenment. James Wilson, of the Banking School, had just issued the first *Economist* on 2 September 1843, while the *Bankers' Magazine* followed in 1844.) The Bank of England was empowered to increase its fiduciary issue by up to two-thirds of any lapsed issue, while other clauses of the Act aimed to make sure that the issues of the other banks would be ended as quickly as possible (although this was to take more than seventy years, not the dozen or so expected by Peel and his Currency School supporters). The final clause contained various definitions, including 'the term Banker' which 'shall apply to all Corporations, Societies, Partnerships and Persons carrying on the Business of Banking, whether by the Issue of Bank Notes or otherwise'. As it turned out it was certainly 'otherwise' than by the issue of banknotes that banking subsequently developed, and in so doing prevented the British economy from becoming severely constrained in its later growth.

These constraints on other banks' notes were as follows. No new note-issuing bank was to be set up anywhere in the UK. With regard to the existing issuers in England and Wales any merger, except where the combined partners remained less than seven, was to cease issuing; a penalty also applying to any bank opening an office within sixty-five miles of London. Any temporary cessation of issue, and of course any bankruptcy, entailed cancellation of issue. The maximum issue allowed to any bank was its average issue in the twelve weeks before 26 April 1844. Until 1856 the Bank of England could pay a commission to induce other banks to cease issuing their notes voluntarily. The Act thus made it clear that 'real money' should properly still be the prerogative of the centralized state. Scottish banks however retained their existing issues, as did those in Ireland, according to the Bank Acts of 1845 which sought to apply some of the provisions of the English Act to those countries. Important differences remained. They could (like the Bank of England) increase their issues if backed by bullion. Amalgamation carried no penalties, nor did setting up an office in London; and they retained their £1 notes, as in 1826: positive Celtic discrimination, though with eventually diminishing returns.

Amalgamation, limited liability and the end of unit banking

Although mergers between the private banks of the eighteenth century took place from time to time it was not until after the legislation of 1826 that amalgamation became of any significance. One of the earliest examples of a London private bank merger was that of Humphrey Stokes of the Black Horse, founded in 1662, which joined with John Bland in 1728, and again with Barnett and Hoare in 1772. One of the first country mergers (also like the former to become eventually part of Lloyds) was a Caernarvon bank which was taken over by a Chester bank in 1796, the owner of the former bank staying on as manager of what was now a branch. Although such examples were not rare, the pace of merger remained very slow until after the crisis of 1825. In the next nineteen years, until the legislation of 1844 put the brakes on, there were 122 amalgamations. In contrast, in the eighteen years from 1844 to 1861 inclusive there were only fifty-four amalgamations in England and Wales (Sykes 1926, 18). This change in the pace of merger was to a large extent because of the restrictions on note issue laid down in the 1844 Act, for although the London banks and those in most of Lancashire had given up their note issue, by far the greater part of the country banks were still heavily dependent on their own notes. The new Act denied these banks their traditional method of growth and inhibited and distorted amalgamation by making mergers between most medium and large banks costly, while still allowing small banks with just two or three partners to merge without having to face such a heavy penalty in lost note issue. Similarly at a time when trade and communications between London and the provinces were being speeded up and growing in scale as never before, the natural process of amalgamation between banks in the capital and the regions was heavily penalized.

The situation with regard to the volume of note issue in 1844 was that some nineteen banks in Scotland were authorized to issue notes to the total value of £3,087,000, while the 280 note-issuing banks in England and Wales (208 private and 72 joint-stock) had a total authorized issue of £8,632,000. In addition to its fiduciary issue of £14,000,000 the Bank of England had a fluctuating gold-backed issue which in 1844 averaged £5.1 million, giving a total issue for the country as a whole of around £31 million. The sacrifice of a note issue of £8.6 million for the English banks was not easy, since the banks involved had to change their style of banking. Furthermore note issue was not only profitable but it also was a cheap and effective way of advertising and carried with it a certain amount of esteem and prestige. Nevertheless the new trend towards deposit banking combined with the use of cheques rather than notes was already clearly visible before the legislation of 1844 gave the banking system as a whole a hefty push in that direction. Thus whereas 93 (or 82 per cent) of the 114 banks formed between 1826 and 1836 were note-issuing, only 7 (or 19 per cent) of the 37 banks founded between 1837 and 1844 issued notes (Pressnell 1956, 159).

A further barrier to banking progress was erected in 1844 in the shape of an 'Act for the Better Regulation of Joint-Stock Banking', although its constraints were to apply only to new banks. No new bank could be set up without obtaining a twenty-year charter granted by the Crown. The minimum nominal capital was to be £100,000 and no bank could begin operating until at least 50 per cent of its capital had been paid up. The minimum denomination of shares was to be £100, statements of assets and liabilities had to be published monthly and annual accounts had to be independently audited. These conditions were at that time felt to be so stringent that only three banks were set up in the following decade and only ten by 1857, by which time the government decided to repeal such obviously excessively onerous legislation. Other factors in addition to inappropriate legislation deterred new bank formation during this period when capital was drawn to railways and other financial institutions at home and abroad in such a speculative frenzy that the new Bank Charter Act had to be suspended twice, in 1847 and 1857. Just as the bad harvests of 1845 and 1846 led to the repeal of the Corn Laws, which had previously restricted imports, in 1846 – a victory for the Anti-Corn Law League – so the pressing need for greater liquidity at the height of the railway mania of 1847 seemed to justify the claims of the 'Anti-Gold Law League' that the 1844 Bank Charter Act was far too restrictive. The Treasury's letter suspending any penalty on the Bank of England from exceeding its fiduciary limit, coupled with a high bank rate, was sufficient to restore calm (as we shall see later in tracing the development of the discount houses). In 1857 the Bank was however forced to print £2 million additional notes, of which some £928,000 were actually issued. By 1857 it had become clear to all that, however useful the Bank Charter Act might be, there was no purpose at all in retaining the 1844 Joint Stock Banks Act in operation. Its repeal was bound up with more comprehensive reforms in company law. Most of the irksome provisions of the 1844 Joint Stocks Act were therefore repealed in 1857 and the rest in 1862, by which time two further questions relevant to banking structure, including amalgamation, were becoming matters for public discussion and legislation. These two burning issues concerned the granting of limited liability to shareholders and the 'reserved liability' inherent in a company's authorized but uncalled capital.

The growth of the economy depended largely on the effective mobilization of savings and their distribution via an efficient capital market in a way in which any risk to shareholders was limited to the share of capital subscribed by them. Generally speaking, the new privileges granted to shareholders as the market for capital grew were made available to non-bank company shareholders before being granted to bank shareholders, who were considered a special case: and even when the new legal freedoms were extended to banks, many bankers at first preferred not to take advantage of them. Companies lost their automatically illegal status when the Bubble Act was repealed in 1825, but shareholders in general were still liable for the debts of their company without limit unless the company had a Royal Charter or was specifically authorized by Act of Parliament. It was this latter aspect, as much as its technical promise which caused railways to be the major attraction for Victorian investors, and 'it was the railway that won the acceptance of general limited liability' (Shannon 1954, 376). However, despite doubts about limited liability, 'after railways, banks were among the most important objects of joint-stock company formation in nineteenth-century Britain' (Anderson and Cottrell 1975, 598).

The year 1844 was also a milestone in company law, for in that year an 'Act for the Registration, Incorporation and Regulation of Joint-Stock Companies' was passed. It did not apply to Scotland or to banks, which had already been fully dealt with. It set up a Registrar with whom prospective companies had to register, and it laid down conditions regarding shares and prospectuses. By this Act companies could now be legally recognized and regulated, but still shareholders faced unlimited liability, partly because public opinion was divided on this question. Even a report by the Royal Commission on Mercantile Law (1854) had a majority against general unlimited liability, and although perversely the resultant Limited Liability Act of 1855 followed, it was such a half-hearted and ambiguous affair that it was repealed almost immediately and replaced by a much more effective Joint Stock Companies Act 1856. At last 'General limited liability had come, and with it the modern era of investment' (Shannon 1954, 379). Banks however had to wait a couple of years, until the 1858 Limited Liability Act, to avail themselves of this privilege, a concession made even easier to obtain when the great consolidating Companies Act of 1862 was passed. As W. T. C. King (1936) says, 'A steady trickle of banking formations, which had its source in the Limited Liability statute of 1858 became by 1862 a rushing torrent', twenty-four new banks being formed between 1860 and 1875. A company mania was in full swing, culminating in the banking crisis of 1866, when the 1844 Bank Act was suspended for the third and last time in the nineteenth century. The company mania was triggered off by the coming of limited liability; but the fact that Overend and Gurney, the main culprit in the crisis, had suddenly made itself a limited company just before the crash, reopened the sharp divisions in opinion as to whether or not banking companies should take advantage of the new legislation. In any case note issues were not covered by limited liability, a further cause of the declining trend in country bank notes.

Those bankers who opposed limited liability for banks argued that the proprietors of banks should be confined to persons of substance whose fortune and probity formed the bank's true guarantee in the eyes of the public and especially its customers. For the same reason they were opposed to the issue of shares of small denomination which would allow men and women of little wealth to become shareholders. Furthermore limited liability would tend to make bankers more recklessly supportive of risky business ventures, while competition from bankers with limited liability, by attracting business away from sounder banks, would act to the long-term detriment of the community at large. These conservative opinions were found chiefly among the long-established and most prestigious banks. Those who favoured limited liability, coming chiefly from among the new joint-stock bankers, saw the need for banks to grow rapidly in line with the growth in other businesses by attracting capital from a widely dispersed base of shareholders from all over the country. The vast new army of small investors in high-saving Victorian Britain (many of them spinsters and widows), needed the protection which only limited liability could give to their savings. The arguments continued indecisively for twenty years from 1858 to 1878, for the custom of many banks to retain a large percentage of their nominal subscribed capital in uncalled form acted to some extent, though far less than unlimited liability, as a deterrent against encouraging investment too easily by persons of little means. The events of 1878 brought matters suddenly to a head, by dramatically demonstrating the dangers to shareholders in the absence of limited liability, irrespective of the form in which the bank's capital was structured.

In October 1878 the City of Glasgow Bank failed, involving its 1,200 shareholders with calls of five times their paid-up capital. Since its formation in 1839 the Glasgow Bank had grown to be one of the largest in Scotland – and so one of the largest in Britain – with 133 branches, deposits of over £8 million and a note circulation of £800,000. Overexpansion and deliberate fraud had gone hand in hand, but could no longer be hidden from public gaze. Although hundreds of innocent shareholders, mostly in Scotland, were either ruined or severely pressed, the banking system in Scotland and Britain as a whole weathered the storm. It became painfully obvious however to all doubters that the time had come to bring about a form of banking legislation which would incorporate limited liability in a manner fully acceptable to the great majority of bankers. This was largely the work of George Rae. Rae was born in Aberdeen in 1817 and joined the North of Scotland Bank at Peterhead as branch accountant in 1836. In 1839 he was appointed inspector of branches at the North and South Wales Bank head office in Liverpool, and went on to become the bank's chairman and managing director in 1873. When the 'Wales' Bank was finally absorbed by Midland in 1908 it was the largest bank they had taken over up until that time.

Rae was clearly a banker with the highest credentials, and apart from his successful work in bringing in limited liability in a legislative form which banks would readily adopt, he is best known for his authorship of *The Country Banker: His Clients, Cares and Work, from an Experience of Forty Years*, published in 1885. Rae's advice helped to steer the new Companies Bill quickly through Parliament, despite opposition for political reasons unconnected with banking from Irish MPs. The Companies Act 1879, also known from its chief provision as the Reserved Liability Act, allowed banks, whether previously of limited or unlimited liability to register under the new Act with their capital divided so as to provide a 'reserved liability' callable only if the company were to be wound up. In the next few years there was a widespread rush by banks to register under the new Act and to avail themselves of limited liability. Banks which had previously hesitated in taking over others with unlimited liability were able to re-register so as to preclude such dangers, in this way stimulating further amalgamations. This rush towards limited liability was accompanied by a stronger movement towards the regular publication of balance sheets, for as George Rae put it, 'a strong balance sheet attracts business'.

In the period between the Companies Act of 1862 and the Baring Crisis of 1890 there were 138 amalgamations, with the joint-stock banks being by far the largest amalgamators, absorbing sixty-six mostly small private banks and forty, usually larger, joint-stock banks. Private banks absorbed thirty-one other private banks and one joint-stock bank. In this way the structure of banking was rapidly changing from unit to branching, and from note-issuing to cheque-using and deposit-taking. Apart from the National Provincial, no bank had set out from the beginning to cover the country with a network of branches. They had started as single-office local banks, and in a few cases, before the amalgamation fever took control, they had grown organically into regional banks. Organic growth was slow compared with taking over one or more branches of another bank, which had already made its contacts with local businesses and which had trained staff already in position (though having to transfer its loyalties). If amalgamation in practice almost always meant a reduction or a complete loss of note issue, on the other hand it usually meant the possibility of a more rapid attraction of deposits. As the competitive process of amalgamation continued, so the field was left to ever larger banks with a disappearing note issue. There were still in 1880 some 157 note-issuing banks in England and Wales with a total issue of £6,092,123. By 1900 there were 106 banks, but only fifty-five were by then still note-issuing, with a total of £2,618,465. By the end of 1914 there were only eleven note-issuing banks left, with a total issue of just £401,719. Apart from those of the Bank of England, which insisted on its right to increase its issues by two-thirds of the lost issues of the other banks, country bank note issues ceased in 1921 when Lloyds absorbed Fox, Fowler and Co. of Wellington, Somerset, with its fifty-five branches. Unit banking had virtually come to an end – except for the non-note-issuing Gunner and Co. of Bishop's Waltham, absorbed by Barclays in 1953.

We have seen how the 1844 Bank Charter Act was especially hard on attempts by country banks to enter London, or London banks which sought to take over note-issuing country banks. A key date in this connection is 1866, when the National Provincial Bank gave up its lucrative and substantial note issue of around £400,000 (without receiving any hoped-for compensation from the Bank of England) in order to establish a London branch: its existing London office had been purely used for administration and had carried out no banking business. In course of time all the other large country banks did likewise. 'When Lloyds Bank, hitherto confined to the Midlands, absorbed two well known houses in 1884, when the Birmingham and Midland Bank took over the Central Bank of London in 1891, and when Barclays united fifteen private firms into one large company in 1896, it was plain that the day of the small local bank, whether private or joint-stock, was very near its end' (Crick and Wadsworth 1936, 37). Lloyds was at first reluctant to move its head office from Birmingham to London, but eventually the pull of London was so strong that all head office business was transferred to London in 1910, a pattern followed by the other banks.

Because of their larger size and growing international business the Scottish banks had recognized the importance of having a branch in London long before most of the English banks. Thus as early as 1864 the National Bank of Scotland opened its London office, and around the same time efforts were made jointly by the Bank of Scotland, the Union Bank and British Linen Bank to set up a commonly owned joint-stock bank in London. When it became clear by 1866 that these complex negotiations would fail, the separate banks sought their own solutions, the Bank of Scotland opening its own London branch in 1873. In 1874 the Clydesdale Bank began to open a number of branches in Cumberland. The English bankers greatly resented the Scottish 'invasion' and thought that the Scottish banks should be forced to give up their note issues when coming to London. However the nine Scottish banks involved presented a 'Memorial' in March 1875 to the Chancellor of the Exchequer, Sir Stafford Northcote, as follows: 'We do most strongly protest against our freedom to carry on the business of banking in England, distinguished from issue (especially in the Metropolis of the nation, where all our operations centre and are ultimately settled), being made dependent upon the surrender of our rights of issue in Scotland' (Rait 1930, 305). The Scots turned out to be clear winners in the Anglo-Scottish banking war of 1874–81 (Gaskin 1960, 445–55). This was a tribute not only to the strength of their legal case but also an acknowledgement of the superior average size and standing of Scottish banking.

One of the main reasons why the country banks wished to secure a footing in London was to be able to get their accounts, increasingly in the form of cheques, settled through the London Clearing House. The private bankers of London first set up their clearing house in 1770, but they did not admit any joint-stock banks until 1854, nor any country banks until 1858. The privilege was far from being automatic, and a good presence in London was held to be a strong recommendation. The reduction of stamp duties on cheques to a uniform duty of a penny, irrespective of distance, in 1853 was a further expanding and centralizing stimulus. The Bank of England was admitted in 1864, greatly simplifying the clearing process. The importance of such developments is shown by the rise in the value of clearing (mostly cheques) from £954 million in 1839 to £12,698 million in 1910, an increase of more than twelve times. By 1914, of the total of sixteen members of the London Clearing House Association no less than thirteen were joint-stock banks.

By this time Britain had become, compared with other countries, a highly banked nation. Whereas in 1851 there was only one bank office in England for every 20,000 persons, by 1914 there was one office per 5,000 (and one for about 3,000 in Scotland). These were, however, average figures, and although banks had become indispensable not only for the wealthy but also for all business and professional persons of any size, the vast bulk of the population had still never been inside any of the commercial banks so far described. The working classes had been developing their own financial institutions parallel with, but to a large extent not directly connected with, the main banking system.

The rise of working-class financial institutions

Friendly societies, unions, co-operatives and collecting societies

It was money for a rainy day that provided the main stimulus for setting up working-class financial institutions in the nineteenth century, and it was the various kinds of savings banks that achieved solid success rather than the wild and sporadic attempts at other forms of banks for workers. Money transmission for small sums did not become an item on the working-class agenda until the latter half of the century, apart from the short-lived experiment by Owenite trade unions in the 1830s in issuing 'Labour notes'. Of the many thousands of burial clubs, benefit clubs, box clubs (with triple locks and three keys kept by separate individuals for greater security), friendly societies, building societies, trade union collectors, ancient 'orders', church and chapel associations, and industrial insurance societies which sprang up in bewildering profusion in the latter part of the eighteenth and early part of the nineteenth centuries, it was the friendly society which first became both prominent and acceptable enough in the eyes of the authorities to gain some form of legal recognition. Support for legislative encouragement of saving among the poor was widespread and included influential public figures such as T. R. Malthus, Jeremy Bentham, Samuel Whitbread, William Wilberforce, Patrick Colquhoun, and, above all, Captain George Rose, RN, MP, whose forceful initiative led to the Friendly Societies Act of 1793 and to other legislation even more directly responsible for protecting the growing savings of the working classes.

The protection which the Friendly Societies Act offered was eagerly sought after by a number of working-class organizations which, chameleon-like, assumed the outward appearance of the friendly society at a time when official opinion was not only still influenced by the Bubble Act's dread of unbridled organizations, but in addition was obsessed by a consuming fear that the subversive fever of the French Revolution might spread throughout Britain under cover of all sorts of apparently innocent organizations. Yet at the same time even governments wedded to *laissez-faire* wished to strengthen the saving habits of the poor if only to relieve the rapidly rising burden of the poor law. Furthermore a large number of the new collecting agencies were either weak or fraudulent or both. If the rules which governed the best of them could be used as a general guide for those who sought the protection of the new Act, under the supervision at first of local justices of the peace, then not only would these numerous new organizations be made visible to the authorities but they would also escape from the general prohibition under the Bubble Act (and the strengthened specific legislation against potential revolutionaries embodied in the Anti-Combination Acts of 1799 and 1800). Thus the Friendly Societies Act 1793 became an umbrella giving shelter to all sorts of working-class organizations, especially the building societies. It was not surprising to find that when a Registrar of Friendly Societies was set up later he became responsible for supervising the building societies also.

There was a great deal of overlapping in the functions, membership and leadership of these various organizations with, for example, building and benefit societies becoming combined and with the co-operative movement setting up its own insurance, building society and banking affiliates. Before the trustee savings banks were properly set up a series of 'Sunday Banks' were formed by church ministers in Bishop Auckland, Wendover, Hertford and elsewhere. An intense rivalry developed between church and chapel on the one hand and the public houses on the other as centres for collecting local savings. For the working classes, savings as well as socialism owed more to Methodism than to Marxism. Before turning to examine the growth of the two major savings institutions to emerge from these rather amorphous early developments, the building societies and the savings banks, we shall first look briefly at the dismal failure of British trade unions to set up their own banks, at the moderate, if belated, success of co-operative banking, and at the substantial growth of the industrial life assurance societies.

In 1833 and 1834 Robert Owen and his followers set up a National Equitable Labour Exchange with its headquarters in Charlotte Street, London, and with branches in most of the major towns. Antedating in this very practical manner by some thirty years Marx's labour theory of value, the National Labour Exchange under its Governor, Robert Owen, issued Labour Notes to the value of one, two or five hours, redeemable at designated 'Exchange Stores' scattered throughout the country. This multi-branch, quasi-bank crashed however when the Grand National Trades Union, of which it was the financial counterpart, failed towards the end of 1834. This dismal failure helps to explain why trade union banks failed to re-establish themselves in Britain, in contrast to their great successes in other countries such as Germany.

Co-operative banking also exhibited a half-hearted and belated growth in Britain when compared with continental co-operatives. Legal opinion in Britain was divided on whether banking was a proper activity for co-operative societies, the negative view being made explicit in an Act of 1862, although this same Act, by allowing societies to own shares in each other's associations paved the way for the integration of the separate co-operatives into the Co-operative Wholesale Society, which with its stronger clout managed to get the clauses prohibiting banking repealed in 1872. The first Co-operative Congress held in 1869 had pressed strongly for a co-operative bank, so that as soon as the legal bar was removed the CWS Bank was formally established in 1872. The various local co-operatives were encouraged to deposit their surplus funds in their new bank. By the end of the first quarter of 1872 the bank's assets amounted to the not very significant total of £8,000; but renewed propaganda on its behalf saw its assets rise to as much as £2 million by 1900. Its banking functions were very limited in range, consisting mainly in accepting the deposits of its member societies, and later of an increasing number of trade unions (and later still of local authorities), which it invested in government securities and gilt-edged stock, while it also undertook the financing of bulk purchases on their behalf, e.g. of Danish dairy produce, and dealt with the foreign exchange aspects of such trading. The CWS Bank used the services of the Westminster Bank for clearing purposes, while the local societies in which the CWS Bank's branches were first based still had to have accounts with branches of one of the clearing banks for the many banking functions which their own bank failed to provide. However, despite its limitations, the CWS Bank had already by the 1890s become 'both a settling house for the cooperative movement on its trading side and an investment institution for groups or individuals attached to the movement' (Fay 1928, 418). By 1914 its assets had grown to £7 million, but it had not yet shown its ability to compete for business and customers by providing a wider range of banking services for the general public.

A number of the collecting clubs and friendly societies, particularly after the local groups were drawn into regional and national 'Federations' and 'Orders', such as the Oddfellows, the Druids, the Foresters, the Hearts of Oak and the Rechabites, in the middle decades of the nineteenth century, were able to grant higher interest as a result of the much larger aggregate sums now being invested. Typically they expanded from simply gathering the basic minimum sums needed to avoid the stigma of a pauper's funeral to being able to provide substantial life assurance and sickness benefits based on increasingly sound actuarial principles. Whereas the old-established insurance companies such as the Sun, Royal and London Assurance companies appealed to the relatively wealthy, who made their premium payments monthly or quarterly by cheque, the new collecting societies, such as the National Friendly Collecting Society, the Wesleyan and General, the Salvation Army Assurance Society Ltd and the Royal Liver Friendly Society, and the so-called 'industrial' life assurance associations such as the Pearl, the Pioneer, the Prudential and the Refuge Assurance Companies – all these depended very largely on the door-to-door canvasser and collector, who timed his regular weekly visits just after the breadwinner arrived home and was of course paid in cash. Although in legal form the societies, in being owned by their members, differed from the companies, which were owned by their shareholders, in practice and in the competitive process of time they converged in the type and value of the services which they offered. Their economic effects were also similar in that they both provided affordable sickness benefits and life assurance, and gathered together the small rivulets of local working-class savings from scattered towns and villages into large, easily investible reservoirs in the City of London.

They provided an essential ingredient in the successful growth of working-class savings and so helped to increase the wealth, welfare, security and stability of Victorian society. By the time Lloyd George introduced his legislation for compulsory health and unemployment insurance in 1911 the voluntary collecting societies had provided him with an admirable model, and so the existing twenty-four industrial insurance offices were offered as officially 'approved societies' for the workers' choice. By that same year of 1911 when the welfare state was born, the total assets of the twenty-four life offices had grown to £118,842,000, and the total accumulated payments to policy-holders had by then amounted to £181,418,000. By looking after the pence, which without the kindly, self-interested intervention of 'the man from the Pru' would have been frittered away, the pounds had looked after themselves. According to no less an authority on the Victorian age than Professor Asa Briggs, 'there are few books in history which have reflected the spirit of their age more faithfully and successfully than Smiles's "Self-Help", published in 1859. Samuel Smiles himself, in his chapter on 'Money: Its Use and Abuse' summed up saving as being 'an exhibition of self-help in one of its best forms' (Briggs 1958, 27). Two other groups of savings institutions, tailored mainly to meet the needs of the working classes, remain to be examined, namely the building societies and the savings banks.

The building societies
Among a number of initiatives which seemed at first likely to give rise to quasi-building societies but which in the event turned out to be false starts was the Land Buyers' Society of Norfolk which was in operation from about 1740. As its name suggests, its relatively well-to-do members clubbed together to purchase a fairly large plot of land, which was then subdivided into their own individual plots for erecting houses surrounded by their own gardens. Their activities fell away into obscurity after a few years, possibly because the larger landowners objected to the whittling away of large estates and 'the making of a parity between Gentlemen and Yeomen and them which before were labouring men' (Davies 1981, 14). What is now generally accepted as being the first genuine example of a British building society was that formed by Richard Ketley, landlord of the Golden Cross Inn, Snow Hill, Birmingham. In 1775 Ketley formed a group of his customers and friends into a society for saving regularly to finance the purchase of their own houses. Most, though not all, of the early societies closely combined saving with building, the membership therefore being generally confined to purchasers of houses within their own scheme. The oldest existing stone-and-mortar evidence of the soundness of these early self-help societies is still to be seen in the sturdy shape of Club Row, Longridge, near Preston, which was built between 1793 and 1804. In the fifty years between 1775 and 1825 at least sixty-nine such societies have been definitely authenticated, but if the term 'building

society' is less strictly defined, the number may well be as high as the figure of 'over 250' given by one of the earliest historians of the movement, Seymour Price (1958). The movement spread gradually from the Midlands to the West Riding and Merseyside, reaching Scotland in 1808 in the shape of the Glasgow and West of Scotland Savings, Investment and Building Society, its name indicating the greater flexibility now being given by a few even of the newer societies in not tying saving inseparably to building. The first London society did not appear until 1809 when the Greenwich Union Society was formed. The Greenwich soon became involved in a legal case of considerable general interest to the movement. In 1812, in the case of Pratt v. Hutchinson, the bogey of the Bubble Act was raised threatening the future existence of the movement. Hutchinson, a guarantor for a delinquent member of the Greenwich, sought to avoid making overdue payments on the grounds that 'the Society was a mischievous and dangerous undertaking and should be declared a public nuisance' under clause 18 of the Bubble Act, and that 'raising a sum by small subscriptions for building houses' was specifically condemned by the framers of that Act. Although the court found in favour of the society it was not until 1836, significantly after the repeal of the Bubble Act in 1825, that some sort of legal recognition was given to building societies as such and not simply from their assumed similarity to friendly societies. Building societies had at last arrived on the Statute Book as legal entities in their own right.

Until 1845 all the building societies considered themselves as temporary associations, terminating when all their members had secured the houses financed by their joint funds, but in that year the first of the permanent societies was formed. Sometimes second, third or fourth terminating societies, occasionally coexisting would bear the same name (hence making it rather difficult for researchers to be certain of the precise number in being in the earlier days of the movement, as indicated above). It was a quite natural step from temporary to permanent status, though in the first instance it was coupled with the rivalry between public house and chapel which split the Woolwich supporters of the original terminating society (which met regularly at the Castle Inn under the chairmanship of its landlord, Mr Thunder), from the teetotal followers of Dr Carlile, pastor of Salem Chapel, Woolwich, who chose a schoolroom as their meeting place. England's first permanent building society, after protracted negotiations, was duly registered in 1847 as the Woolwich Equitable Benefit, Building and Investment Association. The movement as a whole was rather slow to see the benefits of permanency, especially in the North, which 'remained steadfast to the original aim – a house for every member'. Thus the majority of the 2,000 societies which registered in the ten years after 1846 were terminating types, although the powerful advocacy of Arthur Scratchley, examiner of the newly founded Institute of Actuaries (1848) turned the movement increasingly towards the permanent principle. Even so it was not until March 1980 that the last British example of the terminating society, the First Salisbury, finally expired, by which time it had become merely an interesting historical relic, for of the 287 permanent societies in existence in 1985 some 200 were established as permanent societies in the period from 1846 to 1879. The bedrock of existing societies was formed within a remarkably brief but highly productive period of fifteen years after 1845, thus fully justifying their founders' faith in first calling them 'permanent'.

In order to operate permanently, the societies separated the investor in a flexible manner from the borrower to the greater benefit of both, and so assisted in the faster rate of growth and sounder security of most of the new societies formed around the early part of the second half of the nineteenth century, which included all of today's so-called Big Five. The Woolwich, which as we saw, became permanent officially in 1847, had its germination in 1843; the Leeds was formed in 1848; the Abbey National (or at least its 'national' part) in 1849; the Halifax in 1853; and, a little late, the Cooperative Permanent, now known as the Nationwide, in 1884. In 1890 there were 2,795 separate building societies, more than treble the peak number, at around 800, which the banks had reached in 1810; and there were still some 2,286 societies in 1900, in contrast to the 106 banks in England and Wales. Almost all the building societies were small, local and with few branches. Yet their ubiquity testified to their indispensability in providing mortgages and acting as a vehicle for the savings of the working class – mostly with considerable security.

Amalgamation would not disturb the unit structure of the building societies until well into the second half of the twentieth century, but the societies felt the need for some common organization to safeguard their interests, particularly in view of the incomplete and insecure legal status grudgingly granted in 1836. Local associations were set up in Liverpool and in Birmingham in the early 1860s, following which a national Building Societies Protection Association came into being on 1 January 1869, the occasion being marked by the first issue of the *Building Societies Gazette*. Among the strongest of the external pressures that gave rise to such protective devices was the Royal Commission on Friendly Societies which was, following a number of scandals and after some delay, set up in 1870, and again exposed to public view the failings of the friendly and building societies. The *Gazette* and the Association became deeply involved in the Commission's investigations and managed to bring about very favourable modifications in the proposed legislation to control the societies. Consequently the Building Societies Act 1874 turned out to be so favourable to the societies that it became known as their Magna Carta, remaining in essence unchanged for over a hundred years. All building societies, whether they were the old 'unincorporated' type set up under the 1836 Act, or the new 'incorporated' type under the new Act, were now unambiguously placed under the control of the Chief Registrar of Friendly Societies. The liabilities of individual borrowers were limited to the amount due on the mortgage (the previous bad habit of some societies in levying ridiculously heavy penalty payments being abolished). Although terminating societies were still allowed, the Act favoured the permanent principle, marking a further stage in the decline of temporary societies. The Act laid down that amalgamation or 'transfers of engagements' required the consent of three-quarters of the members involved holding at least two-thirds of the value of the shares. The fact that the building society movement had been able so skilfully to turn the strictures of the Royal Commission into a benevolent 'Charter' is eloquent testimony to the enormous surge of progress achieved in the first few decades of the life of the permanent societies, some of which were beginning to establish branches; but in the main the barriers against amalgamation delayed for almost three-quarters of a century the development of a nationwide system of societies, when compared with the growth of joint-stock banking.

Despite certain restrictions laid down by the 1874 Act (to curtail activities felt to be dangerous), such as limiting the average borrowing to not more than two-thirds of the value of the mortgaged property, and preventing societies from owning land or buildings except for their own use (to prevent speculation), some of the more aggressive societies found ways round these obstacles. Thus the failure of the Sheffield and South Yorkshire Society in 1886 can be traced back to its rash policy of industrial investment, including loans of £65,000 to the Dunraven Colliery in south Wales. It had strayed dangerously too far from investing locally in housing. Failure however did not always mean loss for members, whether as lenders or borrowers, for there were many cases like that of the Wandsworth Equitable, which, forced into failure in 1889, had its engagements prudently transferred to the neighbouring Woolwich. But the movement was about to be shaken to its foundations in the early 1890s by the failure of what was then by far its largest and most flamboyant member, the Liberator Building Society.

The Liberator was first registered in 1868 and soon achieved, under the leadership of Jabez Spencer Balfour, an unprecedented rate of growth, securing £1 million of assets within its first ten years. The important single factor contributing to its rapid growth was the strong support of its membership in chapels and temperance associations, stimulated by a vast network of hundreds of agents among ministers, elders and laymen who found the cause appealing and the commissions paid equally acceptable. The enormous and well-founded success of its first decade led on to unjustified excesses by which the nature of the society was changed into something approaching a speculative investment holding company. It had direct connections with seven other companies including the London and General Bank, the House and Land Investment Trust and J. W. Hobbs and Co. – a speculative builder to which company alone the Liberator made advances of over £2 million, much of this being 'secured' merely by second or third mortgages. Thus the society became involved in the partial ownership of banks, hotels, chapels, collieries, chemical companies, land reclamation sites and harbour constructions, including involvement in the repeated rebuilding of a vulnerable sea wall (with a valuation in the books equal to its total repeated rebuilding costs!).

The failure of Balfour's London and General Bank in September 1892 brought down the whole house of cards, with total losses of over £8 million to the depositors and shareholders of the Liberator and its associated companies. Six of the directors were altogether sentenced to a total of thirty-seven years' imprisonment, ranging from four months to fourteen years. The fall of the Liberator brought down a number of other societies, including the London Provident Society. The inevitable parliamentary inquiry of 1893 led on to the Building Societies Act of 1894 which attempted to achieve a number of objectives mainly by means of greater publicity. First, it demanded fuller information from every registered society and required annual accounts to be properly audited and certified before being sent on to the Chief Registrar. It gave the Registrar much greater powers, including the right to suspend or cancel any society's certificate after due investigation. Thirdly, advances on second or subsequent mortgages were forbidden; and fourthly, the various systems for balloting in mortgages were ended so far as new societies were concerned. In view of the considerable if temporary importance achieved by various balloting and similar unconventional societies during the years 1850–90, the subject requires at least a brief discussion.

The originator of a host of imitative societies based on balloting members for priority in being allocated a house was Dr Thomas E.

Bowkett, who first put his ideas into practice in Poplar, London, in the mid-1840s. The main feature of these societies was their accessibility to a poorer section of the community, for no interest was credited or charged and the voluntary administrative work was unpaid. The houses were sound, but small and cheap, and repayments were minimal. Weekly subscriptions as low as 9½d. (or 4p) were charged until a house was allocated – by ballot – after which, a higher charge, just like a rent, of 8 shillings (40p) was payable until the total debt of the bare capital value of the house without interest (based on £200) was repaid. Bowkett's idea was taken up so enthusiastically by Richard Benjamin Starr, – who flamboyantly promoted the concept for personal profit – that over 1,000 Starr–Bowkett societies had been set up by 1892. The Chief Registrar had always been hostile to the gambling element of these societies, a feature enhanced when persons lucky enough to gain an early allocation for a house sold out at a premium, while in many cases cash prizes rather than actual mortgages were issued to winners of the ballots. Consequently both the Registrar and the Building Societies Association, keen to preserve the reputation of their members, were pleased to see the prohibitive clauses inserted into the 1894 Act. The effect of this prohibition was further to reduce the number of terminating societies. The principle of the best balloting societies was simple, but the practice became complicated, particularly in an increasingly mobile society when the luckiest members had already been satisfied, and the initial faith, hope and charitable enthusiasm had given way to a prolonged anticlimax of resigned and reluctant re-payment.

Another experimental type of society tried to combine the rising popularity of deposit banking with normal building society operations. By far the most prominent of these was the Birkbeck Building Society registered in 1851. Right from the beginning its founder, Francis Ravenscroft, decided that 'at least three-quarters of its deposits should be invested in Consols or other convertible securities'. Its banking business, including the issuing of cheque-books, had grown to such an extent that by 1891 it was reckoned by *The Economist* to be the sixth largest *bank* in Britain. Little wonder therefore that the Bank of England decided to come to its rescue when it suffered a run following the Liberator crash in 1892. Nevertheless its days were numbered, for with excessive investments in gilts it was always vulnerable to abnormally high withdrawals at any time when the capital value of such investments happened to be low. This was just the state of affairs when the failure of the Charing Cross Bank in September 1910 led to another run on the Birkbeck in October. Despite its long struggle to hold out it was eventually forced to suspend payment in June 1911. 'Throughout the years of its prosperity it was known as the Birkbeck Bank . . . on its collapse it immediately became known as the Birkbeck Building Society' (J. S. Price 1958, 363). This again undermined public confidence which had hardly recovered from the Liberator crash.

Societies in general underwent a considerable decline in membership, and a complete recovery was not attained until after the First World War. The history of the Birkbeck may go far to explain the stubborn reluctance which persisted for ninety years thereafter in Britain regarding the degree to which building societies should be allowed to compete with banks by providing some banking services – a burning issue again in the 1980s and 1990s. The year 1895 saw the official agreement – the Composite Agreement – between the Inland Revenue and the Building Societies Association which allowed the societies to pay a composite tax based on a sample of the incomes of their investors; and since many of these were too poor to be assessed for income tax it followed that the composite rate was lower than the basic rate – thus giving the societies, in the view of bankers, an unfair advantage, which again persisted for over ninety years. In contrast to the centralizing cash flows of the banking system, the main body of the building societies gathered their savings locally and invested them locally, even if these investments were mainly in the relatively unproductive form of housing, a bias officially encouraged by the composite agreement which laid the seeds of greater distortion in the higher tax regime of the twentieth century, providing a partial explanation for Britain's long-term relative industrial decline, and an unintended blemish on the success story of the building society movement. Investing in industry has for a century or more in Britain been penalized compared with investing in housing.

The savings banks: TSB and POSB

Oliver Horne, the unrivalled historian of savings banks, fully justifies the conventional claim that the Revd Dr Henry Duncan, 'the amiablest and kindliest of men', should rightfully be reckoned as the 'father of the savings bank movement' in Britain and in many countries abroad, a claim more recently confirmed by the Page Report of the Committee to Review National Savings (Cmnd 5273, June 1973). Earlier examples of savings banks exist before 1810 in Britain and abroad: the Sunday Banks have already been noted, while a more worthy claim for precedence may at first sight seem to exist in the Tottenham Benefit Bank opened by Mrs Priscilla Wakefield on 1 January 1804, to receive the savings of all and sundry, rather than being in the main confined to church and chapel members, as was the case with the Sunday banks. In Scotland the West Calder Friendly Bank, founded by the Revd John Muckersy in 1807, successfully preceded Duncan's example by three years. The earliest continental example, the Hamburg Institution was founded in 1778, but was more in the nature of an annuity institution than a savings bank. The savings banks set up in Berne in 1787 and in Zurich in 1805 – the latter having the longest continuous history among European savings banks – had little influence beyond their own localities, whereas Duncan's experiment quickly became imitated worldwide. Thus while there is no doubt that a number of examples can be found on the Continent and in Britain of institutions which handled small savings before 1810, 'the British savings banks seem to have been the first to be systematically established on a national basis' (Horne 1947, 88). The founder of the French savings banks, Benjamin Delessert, had studied in Edinburgh and never disputed the fact that he had copied the British idea; while in Holland the Workum (1817) and Rotterdam (1818) Savings Banks were the direct result of following the Edinburgh model described in a Dutch translation of an article in the *Edinburgh Review* of 1815, which gave instructions on just how to set up such banks. Since the new banks were the children of the social conditions brought about by the world's first industrial revolution, it was natural that British preachers and philanthropists should have been prominent in providing parental leadership in creating a nationwide system of such banks.

Henry Duncan was born near Kirkcudbright and educated at Dumfries Academy and, with interruptions, at three of the old Scottish universities. After leaving St Andrews at the early age of fourteen he worked in Heywood's Bank in Liverpool for three years, but being determined to enter the ministry he returned to study at Edinburgh for three years and at Glasgow for a further two. In 1799 he became minister of the kirk for the small and poor parish of Ruthwell near Dumfries at a stipend of less than £100 a year. In 1809 he founded and edited the *Dumfries and Galloway Courier* in which he expounded his concept for a kind of savings bank where the poor would receive strong encouragement for sustained saving combined with obvious security and with the discipline required to discourage too easy withdrawal of deposits. He determined to practise what he preached, putting his theories to the test by opening the Ruthwell Savings Bank in May 1810, convinced that if it could be made to succeed in such a small and poor parish, it would thrive anywhere. Deposits from £1 to £10 were accepted, but interest was paid only on whole pounds, at a rate of 4 per cent, rising to 5 per cent after three years. As with Friendly Societies, trust-inspiring community leaders such as the Lord Lieutenant, Sheriff, and local MPs were enrolled as honorary members. After the first year total deposits had risen to £151, and by the end of 1814 they had reached £1,164. The good minister was delighted, and his many friends and his very few enemies were convinced, for by this time its success had been widely noted and plans for copying it were being drawn up in Scotland and elsewhere. In December 1813 the Edinburgh Society for the Suppression of Beggars established in that city a savings bank with rather simpler rules than Dr Duncan's strict constitution, so that subsequent imitators had a choice of two good models, which could be modified to suit local circumstances and preferences. By the end of 1815 almost all towns of any size in Scotland had their own savings bank. In England and Wales the need was just as great but there were barely half a dozen such banks in 1815. There was however such a ferment for establishing such banks that in 1816 seventy-four were set up in England, four in Wales and four in Ireland. It was clearly time to see that their legal position was assured, and not simply assumed as an extension of the Friendly Societies Act of 1793. It was most fitting that George Rose, initiator of that Act was also mainly responsible, in his dying years, for this new legislation on which the savings bank movement in Britain was founded.

George Rose – another Scot – was born in Brechin in 1714. He joined the Royal Navy as a boy and, having been twice wounded in action, was invalided out of the service when just eighteen. He then entered the civil service as a humble clerk and rose steadily to become a Member of Parliament, Vice President of the Board of Trade and Treasurer of the Navy. His philanthropic energy was boundless, even towards the end of his life when he became determined to see that the savings bank movement should be built on a sound legislative basis. Despite the vociferous opposition of radicals like William Cobbett, Rose's Savings Bank Act received the Royal Assent on 12 July 1817. The three fundamental provisions of the Act were, first, that each bank had to be under the (undefined) supervision of an honorary board of trustees; secondly, all the accumulated savings surplus to the everyday working requirements of the bank had to be invested with the National Debt Commissioners, for which purpose a 'Fund for the Banks for Saving' was opened in the Bank of England; and thirdly, the rate of interest allowed on this fund was fixed by the government. These three principles were to become matters of continuing controversy throughout the century and beyond. Following the Act the growth of savings banks 'was one of the most rapid and spontaneous movements in our social history' (Horne 1947, 81). At the beginning of 1816 there were only six savings banks in England and Wales. By the end of 1818 there were 465 separate savings banks in the British Isles; 182 in Scotland, 256 in England, 15 in Wales and 12 in Ireland. Some banks had as many as eighty honorary 'trustees' or 'directors' or 'managers' busily encouraging thrift, and by 1847 the Trustee Savings Banks had amassed just over £30 million of small savings, with only one really significant pause in their steady growth – during 1826 following the panic of December 1825; but even in this instance there was only a net fall of £120,000 out of a total value of £15 million in deposits, and this fall was quickly restored in the following year.

Nevertheless, despite these impressive statistics of success, all was not well, as is attested by a series of frauds, investigations and remedial Acts of Parliament, seven such Acts being passed between 1818 and 1844. Of the many frauds, that of Cuffe Street, Dublin, which came to light in 1828, was important in highlighting the problem of the proper degree of responsibility assumed by trustees. Mr Tidd Pratt, who in 1828 was appointed as the Certifying Barrister for Savings Banks, and looked into the Cuffe Street affair, gave his opinion that trustees were unlimited in their liabilities unless their certified rules had expressly stipulated such a limitation. Almost all the banks formed up to then had carried no such written limitation in their rules. There was therefore an imminent danger that the savings bank movement would be destroyed by the wholesale withdrawal of trustee support. However this danger was averted by the Savings Bank Act of 1828, when the liability of trustees was limited to 'their own acts and deeds where guilty of wilful neglect or default'. The same Act also reduced the rate of interest paid by the Debt Commissioners from 3*d.* to 2½*d.* per day per cent, a reduction from the originally generous 4.56 per cent per annum to 3.8 per cent. There was a great deal of controversy, led by Cobbett and fed frequently by *The Times*, against such generosity by the state made, it was alleged to the rich more than to the poor, for the rich could open a number of accounts (despite apparent safeguards against this) and save up to the maximum limits, whereas many savings banks did not start paying any interest until a minimum amount, say 12*s.* 6*d.*, had been deposited, obviously by those who were quite poor.

In the 1820s the return on Consols was about 3.75 per cent, so the Commissioners of the Debt were running a deficit on their 'Fund for the Banks for Saving'. Supporters of the Savings Banks argued strongly that the poor needed the encouragement of a small subsidy especially since this would relieve the poor rates. Furthermore whereas the large and wealthy Scottish commercial banks paid their depositors, including their savings bank customers, interest on their accounts, English banks did not do so, at least to any extent; therefore it seemed right that the state had to step in. Figures given by Mr Horne of the distribution of savings among various classes of depositors show that in fact the great majority were servants, labourers, small farmers and small tradesmen. Thus some 615 of the total 670 depositors in the York Savings Bank in 1817 were as described, the largest number, 332, being servants. Nevertheless whenever there was a scandal, new attempts were made by opponents to reduce the rate of interest paid and the maximum amount of individual deposit; as again in 1844 when the Savings Bank Act of that year reduced the rate payable to trustees to 3.25 per cent and stipulated that the maximum rate that any trustee savings bank could pay to an individual depositor should not exceed £3. 0s. 10d. per cent. Even so the Savings Bank deficiency remained 'a bogy constantly resurrected by the critics of savings banks for fifty years or more' (Horne 1947, 162). Further strong ammunition for such critics was supplied by the case of the failure of the Rochdale Savings Bank in November 1849, when it came to light that its actuary, Mr George Haworth, had managed to defraud the bank of the huge amount of £71,715 over the years, almost three-quarters of the total savings of the poor townspeople of Rochdale. This fraud was the largest of some twenty-two cases of fraud that came to light between 1844 and 1857. Opinion was hardening against the trustee savings banks in favour of some other forms of savings, such as co-operation – in which Rochdale led the way – and also resurrected older ideas of a post office bank.

In 1859 a Huddersfield banker, Mr C. W. Sikes, despairing of ever getting his pet Postal Savings Bank idea officially accepted, determined to cut through the red tape by writing directly to the Chancellor of the Exchequer, Mr Gladstone, craftily explaining the moral significance as well as the mechanics of his scheme. Gladstone was highly receptive of the main part of Sikes's plan, for he shared his disillusion with the trustee savings banks. In 1861 a large number of the 638 TSBs then in existence were small, insecure and incompetently managed. Some 300 of them managed to open for business on only one single day each week, while their geographic coverage was very patchy, especially in the south of Britain. In contrast, Sikes planned a secure, nationwide network for, as he stated in his letter to Gladstone, 'Wherever a Money Order Office is planted let the Savings Bank be under its roof . . . and you virtually bring the Bank within less than an hour's walk of the fireside of every working man in the Kingdom' (Davies 1973, 55).

The huge sums which could thus be placed at the disposal of the government at the cheap rate of only 2½ per cent appealed strongly to two sides of Gladstone's character – his love of economy and his dislike of the big banking interests in the City. 'It was only by the establishment of the Post Office Savings Banks and their progressive development that the finance minister has been provided with an instrument sufficiently powerful to make him independent of the Bank and City power when he has occasion for sums in seven figures' (Morley 1911, III, 43). Little wonder that Gladstone opposed Sikes's original plan to set up an independent commission for investing the proceeds of the POSBs. The unquestioned security offered by the government had to be paid for by giving the Treasury complete control over investment – and at a rate ½ per cent below that then offered to the TSBs. It took another TSB failure, that of the Cardiff Savings Bank in April 1886, to set in train a series of steps by which the rates of interest, maximum holdings and other such technical matters were harmonized between the two sets of savings banks. The TSB movement was shaken to its foundations by the failure of the Cardiff Bank, which brought down the Bristol Savings Bank, led to fatal runs on a number of other such banks as far afield as Yorkshire and Kent and caused three London savings banks to fail also. Huge amounts were transferred to the POSBs. When cheap money in 1888 enabled Goschen to convert £40 million of the national debt from 3 to 2½ per cent, advantage was taken to press the rate for TSB depositors similarly downwards to the 2½ per cent level, thus ending a period of twenty-seven years in which the TSBs had enjoyed a ½ per cent premium when compared with the POSBs. Nevertheless the much greater convenience, longer opening hours, better administration and above all the superior security of the POSBs guaranteed the greater success of the latter during the period from its formation in 1861. Whereas the total deposits in TSBs which had totalled £41.7 million in 1861 fell to £36.7 million by 1866 and rose only slowly to an undulating plateau of around £41 million to £46 million for the next twenty years, already by 1870 the POSB had deposits of £15 million, rising to nearly £51 million to equal those of the TSBs in 1886 when the Cardiff TSB failed. In the next four years 101 TSBs closed, mostly voluntarily, with depositors transferring nearly £5 million to the POSB – except in Scotland, where the TSBs such as that of Glasgow, the country's largest, remained strong. Eventually 'Rollit's Act' of 1904 re-established the TSBs in the country as a whole on a sounder basis; but by then the superiority of the postal banks as the favourite recipient of working-class liquid savings was unchallengeable.

Although the penny banks, with the exception of the Yorkshire example, never amounted to very much, they deserve at least a brief mention, partly because they introduced the very poorest and youngest of customers into the savings and other banks. Perhaps the earliest

British example is that established by Mr J. M. Scott of Greenock in 1847 as a nursery for the 'parent' Greenock Savings Bank. In England it was the father of the POSB, Mr Sikes, who as early as the 1850s established a number of penny banks in Mechanic Institutes in and around Huddersfield. His ideas inspired Colonel Edward Ackroyd to open the most successful of all such banks, the Yorkshire Penny Bank, on 1 May 1859. By 1865 it had accumulated savings of £100,000, reaching £1 million by 1884 from 140,000 accounts. By 1900 its total deposits had reached £12.5 million.

A most useful supplement to the narrow range of services provided by the savings banks was the introduction by the Post Office of the Postal Order in 1881, as an alternative to the issue of 'Post Office Notes', which would have been rivals of the commercial banknotes. The suggestion that the Post Office should issue banknotes (put forward by the Committee on Postal Notes in 1876) was rejected, and the much weaker version of a postal order system was eventually introduced some five years later. It was an immediate success, for nearly 4½ million orders to a value of over £2 million were issued in 1881. For the following ten years postal orders were used as currency in some areas. By 1907 the annual number of postal orders issued had passed the 100 million mark and represented a value of £43 million.

Generally speaking, no credit was made available by any of the savings banks for their customers, who could obtain access only to moneys they had themselves previously deposited. A number of Clothing and Rent Societies, Slate Clubs, Christmas and Holiday Clubs managed to provide a very limited and tightly controlled amount of credit to their members. The working classes as a whole had to await the coming of consumer hire purchase to gain specific and limited amounts of credit. Bank credit remained the privilege of the relatively richer customers of the commercial banks. Nevertheless, starting from a negligible amount at the beginning of the century, working-class savings had shown a remarkable growth to approach some £500 million by 1914, of which the greater part consisted of deposits in the POSB, at around £182 million; TSB deposits totalling £71 million (of which £54 million was in ordinary deposits and £17 million in investment and other accounts); Friendly Society Deposits came to over £67 million, with the rest in the penny banks and in the various clubs and insurance societies. Most of these savings, like those of the amalgamated banking system as a whole, were being drained from all over the country to centralized governmental or private sector headquarters in London, to be redistributed to the provinces or abroad as the bankers and administrators in the City thought fit. It was the discount houses and the merchant banks that played leading roles in this financial redistribution process. Working-class savings supplied a steadily rising rivulet into the lake of City liquidity.

The discount houses, the money market and the bill on London

The discount houses were so called from what has been their distinctive but never their sole activity for the greater part of their pertinacious existence, namely the purchasing of bills of exchange at a discount or lower value from their nominal or terminal price and either holding them to maturity or selling them to other dealers in bills. Because bills perform three functions – they transmit funds, they provide credit and they supply holders with a most convenient and highly liquid reserve – the discount houses, as wholesale dealers in bills, came to occupy literally and figuratively a central and strategic role in the London money market, and hence in domestic and international finance. During the latter quarter of the eighteenth and the first quarter of the nineteenth centuries bills of exchange (as we have already noted) were also used as currency in London and even more so in parts of Lancashire and Yorkshire, until banknotes and cheques took their place. As the volume of bills handled multiplied during the nineteenth century so the 'bill on London' assumed a role whereby bilateral trade between countries far distant from London, such as the woollen trade between Sydney and Tokyo, became dependent upon the smooth functioning of the discount market. Short-term money rates were immediately affected by the demand and supply of bills, as were the liquid reserves held by the amalgamated banking system, during the last quarter of the nineteenth century. The government itself was so impressed with the advantages of bill finance that it developed its own Treasury bill for meeting its own short-term needs, flatteringly in direct imitation of the London money market's bill of exchange. Because of the key position held by the discount houses the Bank of England had found it essential to grant them special, and for most of the time, exclusive privileges in rediscounting their bills. These impressive operations were performed by one to two dozen houses employing a skilled and adaptable, but surprisingly small number of employees, of about 300 to 400, situated mostly in and around Lombard Street. Mr W. T. C. King, in his *History of the London Discount Market*, is not guilty of exaggeration in pointing out that 'from the days of Bagehot to those of the Macmillan Committee successive authorities have recognized that it is to her possession of a specialized discount market that London largely owes her supremacy as an international financial centre' (1936, xi).

The development of the discount houses in the nineteenth century may be conveniently divided into two periods, the first up to the failure of the City's largest house, Overend and Gurney, in 1866. During this period it was the *domestic* bill that predominated. In the second period, from 1866 to 1914, the decline of the domestic bill was more than compensated by the vast increase in the importance of the international bill on London. After the domestic bill first obtained legal status in 1697, its growth was gradual until the 1780s, when it grew to be used so rapidly that by 1800 bills had become the normal method of payment between traders and, in the absence of overdrafts which had not by then been discovered in England, and in the relative rareness of loans, bills were thus also the normal method of obtaining short-term credit from the hundreds of banks that were by then covering the country. Country banks with surplus funds invested them with their correspondent banks in London who used such funds for investing in bills not just in London, but also for purchasing the bills raised in the deficit districts in the industrial areas of the country. The growth of the economy was thus reflected in and facilitated by the growth of the London bill brokers, some of whom began to withdraw from general banking business in order to concentrate on bill broking, the first such 'true' bill dealer being Richardson and Gurney, formed in 1802 and joined by Overend as partner in 1805. Until about 1817 the London brokers and the country bankers all charged the same rate of discount – 5 per cent – the maximum then allowed by law, but from then until the end of 1825 there was a glut of money, particularly in London, stimulated by the excessive issue of small notes. London brokers during that period began to compete by reducing their rates of discount, causing industrialists in the country to use the London brokers rather more than their local banks for discounting.

Until the 1826 crisis the London *bankers* had relied on being able to gain immediate access to cash whenever required by rediscounting their bills with the Bank of England, but as a result of the crisis the Bank ended this facility, limiting the privilege only to the specialized bill brokers, further stimulating their growth. The rise of joint-stock banks after 1826 and the stricter limitation of note issuing meant that bill dealing was again encouraged. In economic function bills and notes were virtually interchangeable, so that whereas amalgamating or opening a London branch might entail loss of note issue, there was no such bar to issuing more bills. The Bank of England itself aggressively competed in bill discounting until it recognized that it was partially to blame for the 1847 crisis after which it toned down the fervour of its competition, beginning to learn that the 1844 Act had not completely liberated its Banking Department from the growing responsibilities of a central bank. It could not be both poacher and gamekeeper. It was during this period, 'roughly from about 1830 until the 'sixties or 'seventies, that the bill market as an agent for the *domestic* distribution of credit reached its highest point, in terms both of the scale of operations and of importance in the body economic' (W. T. C. King 1936, 41). In their zeal to assist domestic (and external) trade, and in contravention of the lingering belief in the 'real bills doctrine', discount houses like Overend and Gurney began issuing large amounts of 'accommodation' or 'finance' bills, even for financing fixed capital such as railway building. Economic difficulties following the outbreak of the Crimean War in 1854 rose to crisis point when the news of the Indian mutiny of May 1857 reached London, again causing the discount houses to rediscount exceptionally large amounts with the Bank of England, so draining it of reserves that the 1844 Act had again to be suspended, and a legally exceptional issue of £928,000 of notes was put into circulation.

There followed ten years of strained relations between the discount houses and the Bank of England, which latter showed its teeth in the 'Rule of 1858' by which the Bank reversed its decision of 1825. No longer were the discount houses to be allowed in the normal course of business to have rediscount facilities at the Bank – a retrograde step which prevented the Bank from keeping an oversight on the quality of the bill business of the houses at a period when such a brake on the activities of houses like Overends would have been most salutary. Suspicion and spite were mutual. In 1860 in a single day Overend and Gurney withdrew £1,650,000 from the Bank, all in £1,000 notes, thus forcing the Bank to raise bank rate to 5 per cent. (The Bank remembered this action and stood aloof in 1866, leaving Overend to fall – a victim of its own excesses.) The general movement during this period towards limited liability led to the formation of a number of joint-stock discount companies, the first of which was the National Discount Co. Ltd, formed in February 1856, followed by the London Discount Co. later in the same year, and by the General Discount Co. in the next year. Both the latter were to fail after a short and troubled existence, the London Discount Co. being involved in June 1860 in the 'leather crisis', in which no fewer than thirty leather firms collapsed with liabilities of around £3 million. Overend and Gurney were also involved, but managed to weather the storm. Half a dozen other discount company formations followed before Overends themselves became a limited company in July 1865, a decision described by the *Bankers' Magazine* of the time as the 'greatest triumph of limited liability'. The triumph was short-lived. After heavy withdrawals in the first months of 1866, the crisis came with a legal decision questioning the status of the company's securities in the Mid-Wales Railway, and hence the value of its heavy involvement in other railways also. By the next day, 10 May 1866, Overend and Gurney, the world's biggest and best-known discount house, had suspended payment, with debts of over £5 million.

The repercussions were immediate and spectacular, but surprisingly not widespread beyond the City. Bank rate was pushed up to the unprecedented rate of 10 per cent, but at that rate the Bank discounted freely. Among the banks, the English Joint Stock Bank of London and the Agra and Masterman Bank were the two most important of seven that eventually failed. Fortunately for the rest of the economy the crisis remained mostly financial, and despite the ruinously high rate of interest commercial failures were relatively few. The Chancellor's letter again allowed the Bank of England to exceed the fiduciary note issue's normal limits, but this time, as in 1847, no excess notes were actually issued. In the course of time calm was restored and bank rate was brought down in July 1867 to the remarkably low level of 2 per cent, a level only previously touched on just two occasions (April 1852 and July 1862). Although most of the discount houses incurred heavy losses, the National Discount and Alexanders the two largest after Overends, escaped relatively unscathed. Overends' fall seemed to open the door for a number of new entries to the discount market with partnerships like Gillett's, Sanderson's and Shaxson's being among the most prominent of eleven new private houses formed between 1866 and 1870. In terms of size the Union Discount Co. which had absorbed the General Credit Co. in 1885 was the first of the 'Big Three' to reach deposits of £10 million – in 1894, a position not achieved by the National until 1904 nor by Alexanders until 1913. By the latter year the total deposits of the Big Three, now consisting mainly of call money placed by the head offices of the amalgamated banks in the City, came to £46.6 million, double the total reached in 1891. By 1913 there were also some twenty private discount houses together with a dozen or so money brokers who fed the houses with business, which by then included only a negligible amount of domestic bills.

Although the decline in the inland bill may, according to King, have begun as early as the 1857 crisis it did not become very significant until after the 1866 crash, the decline accelerating markedly in the 1880s and 1890s. The three main, connected reasons for its decline were, in chronological order: first, the revolution in transport and communications; secondly, the resulting reduction in the need for merchants to hold their customary vast stocks of goods, a costly necessity previously; and thirdly, the amalgamation movement in banking. Already by 1880 Gillett's dealing was mostly in overseas bills and by 1905 their country business had declined to a 'negligible percentage' (Sayers 1968, 45). Professor Nishimura, in his study of 'The Decline of Inland Bills' has emphasized the fact that 'Inventory investment . . . must have been a great burden on the money market' until after the 1870s when 'telegraphs and steamers' not forgetting internal railways 'did away with both the enormous amount of inventory of goods and the middlemen merchants. Branch banking absorbed money into the banking system. Thus the demand for money for inventory finance dwindled and the supply of money increased, enabling banks to lend in the form of overdrafts, which in turn caused [inland] bills to decline' (1971, 78). The amalgamation movement of the 1890s provided the final, culminating pressure to a decline that was already well on the way. The discount houses, always adaptable, took this decline in their stride, by new dealings in Treasury bills, and even more importantly, by vastly increasing their international bill dealing.

In 1877 the Chancellor of the Exchequer, Sir Stafford Northcote, annoyed with the unpopularity of the Exchequer bill as a means of raising short-term finance, asked the advice of Walter Bagehot, editor of *The Economist* and author of the classic *Lombard Street*. Bagehot suggested a short-term security 'resembling as nearly as possible a commercial bill of exchange'. His idea was incorporated in the Treasury Bills Act, 1877. Originally the bills could be used only for finances authorized under the Consolidated Fund, but from 1902 the purposes for which they were permitted were widened, so that the volumes outstanding were considerably increased, reaching a pre-war peak of £36,700,000 in 1910: a preparation for their massive use in the First World War and subsequently. This offered more London-based grist for the discount houses' mills, and even for foreign financiers who were substantial purchasers of Treasury as well as of commercial bills. By 1890 the Bank of England had re-established the traditional privilege by which the discount houses enjoyed almost automatic rediscounting with the Bank. Once the crisis of that year (shortly to be examined) had been overcome, 'the organisation by which all free British capital was sucked into the London money market was functioning almost perfectly . . . a smooth channel had been cut down which the aggregated northern surpluses flowed south. The channels from East Anglia, the South West and rural England generally, had been cut long before' (Scammell 1968, 166, quoting Sir John Clapham).

The call money which the banks loaned to the discount houses was now being almost entirely used in the finance of Treasury bills and, above all, international bills. London had become a truly international market much more powerful than the foreign centres with which it was in hourly contact. By the first decade of the twentieth century 'the most active and powerful factors in it are of foreign origin' with 'foreign interests to serve, which may frequently clash with British interests'. This was the view of W. R. Lawson, writing in the *Bankers' Magazine* of 1906 (King 1936, 282). The London merchant bankers had almost always been even more myopically international in their vision than the discount houses for whom they 'accepted' a large proportion of their bills. Only the building societies escaped the powerful centripetal pull of the City; and even they of course did nothing to finance local industry. The seeds of future industrial decline, relatively speaking, were being widely sown during the period of sterling's unchallenged supremacy.

The merchant banks, the capital market and overseas investment

Merchant banks, like elephants, are difficult to define but instantly recognizable. Most merchant banks began as merchants and expanded into banking, but movement the other way was not uncommon. 'Scratch an early private banker and you will find a merchant' (Carosso 1987, 3). Because of their mixed origins and functions the term 'merchant bank' has 'no precise meaning, and is sometimes applied to merchants who are not bankers, to bankers who are not merchants, and even to Houses which are neither merchants nor bankers'. This is the considered view of Baring Brothers, who, if anyone, should know what a merchant banker is (Baring Brothers 1970, 9). Most merchant bankers in Britain came originally from overseas; from Germany especially, such as the Barings, the Brandts, the Hambros (formerly Levys), the Kleinworts, the Rothschilds, the Schröders and the Warburgs; but also from Holland, like the Hopes (originally from Scotland) and the Raphaels; and from the USA, such as Brown Shipley, the Seligmans, and the Morgans (from Wales, via Bristol and New England, back to London). Not surprisingly therefore in experience, outlook and interests they remained predominantly international, as if created to be the ideal catalysts of international trade and development. With a number of important exceptions, such as the Barings and the Morgans, most were Jewish, for the international nature of their business naturally attracted Jewish bankers. Twenty-four of the thirty-one merchant bankers who died as millionaires between 1809 and 1939 were Jewish.

As merchants, whatever their origin, they were used to buying and selling in substantial amounts on their own account, a skill they readily sold to other wholesalers and manufacturers. Their knowledge of the credit standing of foreign traders, acquired through long, painstaking, personal or family involvement, was put directly to use in arranging loans and purchases; and indirectly by the important development of their 'acceptance' of bills of exchange, their endorsements greatly enhancing the saleability of bills, enabling issuers to quote much finer i.e. lower rates. The merchant banks thus played an indispensable role in building up the unrivalled reputation of the bill on London.

In the same way, the mere knowledge that the merchant banks were associated in raising capital, whether for foreign railways, mines, harbours, bridges, canals or waterworks, and so on, was normally sufficient to guarantee that the general public in Europe (and later in the USA) would eagerly take up such loans at a greater speed and at higher prices than would otherwise have been the case. The influential borrowers could thus afford to be generous in their rewards – monetary, social or political – to the merchant bankers, thus contributing to other reasons (examined below) for pushing City money in a biased fashion towards overseas rather than home investment. Perhaps the most powerful influence of the merchant bankers is to be seen in arranging loans for governments and for propping up kings, princes and potentates in the anachronistic ways of life to which they could not afford, either politically or financially, to have become accustomed. Because the achievement and maintenance of the highest esteem, trust and prestige are essential ingredients of true merchant bankers, their economic and political influence became inextricably intermixed, their political influence facilitating their economic deals, while their economic weight enabled them to intervene strategically on a number of occasions in international politics. Thus Count Corti, in one of the earlier examples of what has become a deluge of dynastic histories, stated that 'the object of this work is to appraise the influence of this family [the Rothschilds] on the politics of the period, not only in Europe, but throughout the world' (Corti 1928, 11). Brief glimpses of the salient features of the two leading houses, the Barings and the Rothschilds, must suffice to give an inkling of the fascinating, controversial and economically strategic history of the merchant banks in general.

The Baring family, originally woollen merchants in north Germany, first became associated with England through importing wool, mainly from the West Country. John Baring, son of a Lutheran minister in Bremen, was sent to Exeter in 1717 where he married into a rich local family and rapidly expanded his business. His sons moved to London, where they set up their merchant banking business, 'John & Francis Baring & Co.' in 1762. By the beginning of the war in 1793, Barings had already become one of the strongest houses. When Hope and Company, fearful of their future, fled to London to escape from the French invasion of Holland in 1795, they were befriended by Barings. In return their mutual links with the USA were considerably strengthened. By 1803 almost half the $32 million of US stock owned by foreigners was held in Britain, with Barings being very heavily involved. In the same year Napoleon, being hard-pressed for cash, offered to sell the whole of Louisiana to the USA for $15 million. Even this bargain price was beyond the immediate purchasing power of the American government. However Barings and Hopes together were willing and able to advance the money to Napoleon, and so the famous Louisiana Purchase was successfully completed (despite the hostilities). Subsequently when the Bank of the United States wished to set up an agent in London, naturally enough it chose Barings. After the war ended in 1815 Barings were active in sponsoring a huge loan of 315 million francs for the French government. Hence arose the often repeated catch-phrase, attributed to the Duc de Richelieu, that there were 'six Great Powers in Europe: England, France, Prussia, Austria, Russia, and Baring Brothers' – a phrase used in the title of the latest official history of that house; though even that author's meticulous research has failed to prove that Richelieu ever did really utter that inspired remark (Ziegler 1988, 85).

Throughout most of the nineteenth century Barings still kept a wary eye on opportunities for direct commodity trading, dealing in a wide variety of products such as coffee, copper, indigo, rice, tobacco and corn. They sometimes managed to make a 'corner', such as that in tallow in 1831, and even challenged Rothschild for a share in Spanish mercury in the 1830s and 1840s. Ziegler shows that the fact that Barings were not Jews significantly affected, particularly in their formative years, the people with whom they preferred to deal, and the countries in which, from time to time, they specialized: though by the 1870s the need for co-operation and the opportunities of a wider range of business increasingly overcame ethnic loyalties. The larger merchant banks did engage in some degree in long-lasting but never rigid geographical specialization, such as the Hambros in Scandinavia, the Rothschilds in Spain, and the Barings in Canada, but in the larger markets of Russia and North and South America keen competition was the rule. All the same, the minor degree of tacit separation of markets reduced the number of occasions for head-on rivalry, and helps to explain how in their hours of need, the main competitors were able to co-operate closely and offer each other much-needed support – most notably for Barings in 1890. Before examining that crisis, a brief summary of Rothschilds' progress is appropriate.

The Rothschilds originated in medieval Frankfurt on Main, their house, in the days before houses had numbers, being aptly marked by a red shield. They had enjoyed many decades of banking and merchanting experience before Nathan Mayer Rothschild was sent to Manchester in 1798 to deal in the thriving cotton industry. Nathan's activities grew apace during the French wars (just like Barings), when he was able to demonstrate his skill in transferring financial 'subsidies' to the allies, and moneys to the armies abroad, quickly and in the correct mix of currencies, using his family's network of couriers for this purpose, and for gathering sensitive information generally more quickly and reliably than other operators, whether banking competitors or official sources. The London branch of Rothschilds raised over £100 million during the war for the allied governments. It was Rothworth, one of Rothschild's agents (and not the fabled pigeon) that first brought the news of Wellington's victory at Waterloo on 18 June 1815, to Nathan Rothschild by the early morning of 20 June, some twenty-four hours before the government's official envoy arrived in London. Rapid information was obviously a valuable asset both for commodity trading and for banking – and there was only jealous admiration rather than a legal ban on 'insider' dealing in those days. On the other hand merchant bankers often refrained from taking short-term advantage, for the sake of building up a long-term, continuous relationship with customers, the integrity, discretion and loyalty of merchant bankers being thus built into a largely unwritten but most valuable, influential and impressive 'code of conduct'.

In contrast to the wide range of commodities in which the Barings traded, the Rothschilds normally confined themselves to the goods traditionally traded in Europe by court Jews, namely diamonds, gold and silver, and the mercury which was used, among other things, for refining silver – hence the Rothschilds' early partial monopoly of the mercury from Spanish mines. For most of the nineteenth century Rothschilds were more important than Barings in bullion dealing, foreign exchange and also in government loans in Europe; but Barings always played the leading role in the 'bread and butter' bill-accepting business and in loans to America. The senior Rothschild normally became head of the Jewish community in Britain, while the interconnections between finance and politics were further confirmed by Lionel Rothschild's becoming the first Jewish MP, in 1858, and his son Nathan the first Jewish peer, in 1885 – though in this rivalry they did not quite match up with the Barings. By 1890 by far the most prominent role in bill acceptance business in London was still handled by Barings, with a total value in that year, despite the storm which almost engulfed them in the autumn, coming to £15 million. Second came Brown Shipley with £10.6 million; Kleinworts came third with £4.9 million; Hambros fourth with £1.9 million; while N. M. Rothschild could only manage fifth place with £1.4 million (Chapman 1984, 121). But Barings were about to be toppled from their perch.

The 'Baring Crisis' of 1890 is correctly so called, for without any doubt it was the excesses of that house which led to the near-disaster of that year; yet, if Barings had been left alone, like Overends in 1866, to try to undo the consequences of their own folly, it would have become everybody's crisis. As it happened, the unprecedented degree of timely co-operation in the City, led by Lord Lidderdale, Governor of the Bank of England, was so effective that it has been said that the significance of the 1890 crisis lies in the fact that there was no crisis. By saving Barings the City saved itself. In the previous decade Barings under Lord Revelstoke had become grossly over-committed in South America in general and in Argentina in particular. In 1880 the total value of British investment in Argentina was £25 million. By 1890 nearly half of Britain's external investment was to that country, by which date its total value had risen to £150 million, and a 'strikingly large' proportion of it was financed by Barings (Ziegler 1988, 236). The particular investment that led most directly to Baring's difficulties was the failure of the 'Water Supply and Drainage Company' to complete its contract for Buenos Aires in time or up to the designated standard. These financial and commercial matters were further complicated when a revolution broke out there in August 1890. By 24 November Barings were within twenty-four hours of bankruptcy. By the next day Lidderdale brought to fruition three days of frantic effort in securing promises of support from all the major City banks. Not only did all the main merchant houses, including Rothschilds (after a show of reluctance) give their support, but, in addition to the £1 million promised by the Bank of England itself, the London and Westminster, the London and County, and the National Provincial Banks each offered £750,000. The final total of the guaranteed sum came to £17 million. Thus armed and pulling together, the City weathered the storm. Bank rate, which was raised to 6 per cent in November was back down to 5 per cent in December and fell to 3 per cent by the end of January 1891. The economy was back to normal, though many lessons in central, deposit and merchant banking were taught by the blistering experience of those three months.*

*See p. 664 below for the Barings crisis of 1995.

Barings were so badly shaken that, despite their previous disdain for limited liability, they followed the fashionable trend they had previously attacked by becoming a limited company. All the same, family members have to this day (May 1994) continued to play the major role in the company's affairs. Although Barings' fall had been caused by their issuing activities, it was inevitable that their acceptance business, based as it was on the indivisible attributes of esteem and indubitable credit, also suffered gravely. By 1900 they had made a laudable degree of recovery, handling in that year £3.9 million worth of acceptance business, though this was just about a quarter of that of 1890. They had been demoted to third place, behind Kleinworts with £8.2 million and Schröders with £5.9 million. These latter were typical of the newer generation of German houses which were now playing a more aggressive and more energetic role in the London money and capital markets than were the old-established families. They all shared however in the great expansion of world trade and in the issuing of foreign loans, which in the period 1890 to 1914 – though the total size has been revised downwards by recent research – rose to heights which were unprecedented and remain impressively substantial by any measure. Whereas the role of London-based merchant banks in facilitating British exports and world trade in general has received universal acclaim, their role in exporting capital has remained a subject of much controversy throughout the twentieth century, although the arguments sometimes resemble attacks on sprinters for not engaging in marathons, or blaming thoroughbreds for not making good cart-horses.

It was not for what they did but for what they failed to do that the City's merchant bankers have been blamed; for sins of omission not of commission. They have become the scapegoats for the alleged weaknesses of the London capital market, in which they played such a key role, for diverting domestic savings from home investment, particularly in manufacturing industry, to overseas destinations. Any harm to domestic investment would depend on a large number of factors, including the actual size of such investment, whether savings not invested abroad would have been invested at home, whether the risks and returns were properly evaluated, whether the timing of external investment coincided with or compensated for rises and falls in home investment, whether the UK's total savings was a fixed amount which determined the total amount of investment either at home or abroad (what was later called 'the Treasury view') or whether it was total investment which really determined what the total of savings would be (that is the 'Keynesian view' available to writers after 1936). A whole library of books, theses and papers has been written on this compellingly attractive subject, chiefly because the period marks the zenith of Britain's political and economic 'salt water' imperialism, in contrast to the 'manifest destiny' of continental expansion in North America, Russia and China. In recurrent surges throughout the nineteenth century British capital was lured abroad, via the services of the merchant banks, induced by generally higher rates of interest. The Royal Commission on the London Stock Exchange (1877–8) explained that the 'craving for high rates of interest' had been a 'leading cause' for the export of enormous sums of money since the 1850s (Platt 1984, 178).

The thorough and painstaking research of Professor Platt has shown that the basic statistics of British overseas investment before the First World War, which have been almost universally accepted and endlessly repeated for seventy years, were seriously at fault. Professor Paish's original figures of the value of British overseas investment in 1913 came to £4,000 million, of which £3,700 million was in portfolio investment and £300 million in direct investment. Professor Platt's revised figures come to a total of only £3,130 million, of which £2,630 million was in portfolio and £500 million in direct investment (1986). This gives a total reduction from Paish's standard figures of £870 million or 21.7 per cent – a considerable but not a shattering reduction, except perhaps for those brave cliometricians who have built too heavy a load of complex calculations on what was, before Platt, taken too readily to be a firm foundation. Further revisions, not necessarily in one direction, will doubtless be published, though the most recent are not of course bound to be the most correct (see Feinstein 1990).

It was not merely the size of foreign investment that benefited the recipient countries, but also the fact that such investment was made in sectors of the economy critical to the growth of such countries. Furthermore the export of capital was accompanied by an export of expertise in the form of an army of civil and mechanical engineers, surveyors, professional, technical and skilled labour of all sorts that together made the financial contribution very much more worthwhile. Without such skills the financial seeds would have remained unwatered and unweeded (as many twentieth-century examples show). 'The United States was a prime beneficiary' of the work of London's merchant banks; 'European capital, especially from Britain, accelerated the pace of nineteenth century America's economic progress; and English banking practices, most notably those of London's merchant banks, influenced the organization of the country's financial system', for bankers and banking skills closely accompanied the export of finance (Carosso 1987, 12). In Australia, as Sir John Habakkuk has shown, whereas smaller investments could be supplied from indigenous savings, 'loans for large scale construction had to be obtained from London' as was most long-term capital for Britain's colonies in general (1940, II, 787). There was therefore much to justify the bias of the London capital market towards overseas investment – and despite the doubts of the revisionists, such a bias remains convincing. As Sir Alexander Cairncross has rightly emphasized, the London merchant bankers 'did not possess the apparatus of investigation necessary for home industrial flotations, but were admirably placed for the handling of loans to foreign governments and corporations . . . They were under no temptation to dabble in home industrial issues (except the very largest)' (1953, 90).

Even in the latter half of the nineteenth century, one half or more of investment in Britain's manufacturing industry came from ploughed back profits. Of the rest, most came from investments made by friends and relatives of the business, and some, where necessary, was financed by the provincial stock exchanges. Most business was still small in scale, too small to call for the services of the London capital market. Private companies in 1913 still comprised nearly 80 per cent of the existing total, and formed five-sixths of all new companies registered in 1911–13. But most of the British merchant banks for most of the time avoided becoming embroiled in British industry even when opportunity arose. Their attitude is exemplified in Lord Revelstoke's statement in 1911: 'I confess that personally I have a horror of all industrial companies and that I should not think of placing my hard-earned gains into such a venture', the venture being a coal product at a time when coal was king (Ziegler 1988, 286). Barings, like the other merchant banks, did all the same participate in the large issues in what Ziegler calls the 'infra-structure of British industry', such as London United Tramways and Mersey Docks and Harbour Board; in their minds, hearts and interests they concentrated on overseas business. They were financial extroverts.

In certain periods when foreign issues were at a low ebb the total of home issues, counting provincial as well as London issues, considerably exceeded that of foreign issues, e.g. during the period 1896 to 1903. But an enormous surge of foreign investment again dominated the next decade, rising to its highest peak in the years from 1911 to 1914. There remained however a vital difference in that a considerable portion of home 'investment' merely represented changes in the organization and ownership of existing British businesses, from partnerships or private company status into public limited company status, whereas overseas issues mainly represented new, real, asset formation, further strengthening its relative economic importance. (A lively debate on this issue is to be seen in A. R. Hall versus A. K. Cairncross in *Economica*, February 1957 and May 1958 respectively.) Thus although the merchant bankers did from time to time handle a number of large home issues, they did not much relish the business. At the close of the long nineteenth century, as in the beginning, they remained predominantly international in outlook. As Ziegler dramatically states, 'International trade was their bread and butter; international loans their jam; the financing of British industry was fare for the servants' hall, or worse still, fit only for the dogs' (1988, 290).

This unenthusiastic attitude towards industrial investment, particularly in the smaller, domestic, manufacturing industries – Revelstoke's horror in attenuated form – permeated the City of London, partly because of the general political and economic power of the merchant bankers in Westminster and in City boardrooms, but particularly because of their naturally heavy representation as directors of other banks, including the Bank of England. As early as 1873 Walter Bagehot pointed to bias in that merchant bankers like the Rothschilds were invited to become directors of the Bank of England, even though 'they have, or may have, at certain periods an interest opposite to the policy of the Bank' (1873, 226–7). Cunliffe (of that merchant banking house), and Montagu Norman (of Brown Shipley) later became Governors at key periods of the debate as to whether the international interests of the City conflicted with the needs of the industrial regions. It was in the couple of decades before the First World War that the seeds of this division were being sown. It was the combination in timing of bank amalgamation and the centralization of savings and decision-making in London, coinciding with the surge of overseas investment, that diverted savings in a biased manner from investment in manufacturing at home to all sorts of investment abroad. The fact that the industrial revolution took place later abroad at a time when the Americans and the continental Europeans maintained their local and regional banking structures meant that there were not such strong centripetal forces elsewhere breaking the link between local savings and local investment decision-making. Compared with the hundred or so banks in the UK, with the Big Five already about to emerge, the USA then had 35,000 separate banks, with the major European countries similarly having large numbers of local banks dependent on the prosperity of their own localities and with no one having a distant head office to turn down their lending decisions, however risky for the banks and however stimulating for local development. This overseas picture was reminiscent of the earlier close connections between Britain's unit banks and local industries. But Britain's centralized, amalgamated banks could now, it was erroneously thought, leave investment in British industry to the stock market, and concentrate their own lending on short-term commercial loans repayable on demand.

The deposit banks, with their imposing new headquarters, for most of them, in the City, away from the smoke and din of the industrial areas, no longer thought it their business to lend for plant and machinery; while the merchant banks, being predominantly wholesale bankers, could similarly wash their hands of the problem. Industrial investment in Britain was not their problem; they had their hands and purses full elsewhere. Professor Sidney Pollard authoritatively confirms the view that 'the London capital market was simply not interested in Britain', and although 'on some criteria the Victorians did right to channel such a large part of their savings abroad, it is difficult to avoid the conclusion that they must have contributed thereby, to an unknown extent, to the deterioration of the British economic growth rate' (Pollard 1989, 93, 114). Bankers and brokers steered Britain's savers to 'safe' investments abroad rather than towards more risky, pioneering investment in the newer industries at home.

The City's bias abroad was officially reinforced by the Colonial Loans Act of 1899 and the granting of trustee status to colonial stocks in the following year, both acts reflecting Joseph Chamberlain's policy of imperial preference. Dr Kennedy's researches also show that

> because of the withdrawal during the mid-Victorian years of the British banking system from the close relationship with domestic industry that had developed over the previous century, by the late nineteenth century equity markets were more important than they had ever been before. That they were not adequate for the tasks that confronted them may be clearly seen by the Victorian economy's stunted growth and marked inability either to create or to exploit new technologies. (W. P. Kennedy 1982, 114)

Although, along with Beales, one may question whether 'the Great Depression' in the two decades after 1873 was really as great as has usually been assumed, and even concede that it was 'a period of progress in circumstances of great difficulty', one must also admit the obviously painful relative decline of Britain, as other countries such as the USA and Germany developed more rapidly not only in a catching up process but also with a pronounced bias towards new industries (Beales 1954, I, 415). Furthermore, although the entrepreneurial sins of omission blamed on our Victorian forefathers may commonly have been exaggerated, they should not be dismissed as negligible. Donald McCloskey's stirringly controversial article 'Did Victorian Britain fail?'

seems rather too laudatory in giving 'a picture of an economy not stagnating but growing as rapidly as permitted by the growth of its resources and the effective exploitation of the available technology'. The strictures of Cairncross, Pollard, Kennedy and many others can no longer be cavalierly dismissed as 'ill-founded' (McCloskey 1970, 459, 446).

The argument often put forward that in any case the banking system adequately met domestic industrial demand is weak in that it assumes a non-creative passivity on the part of the banks, as if they could only ever simply respond to customers' explicit demands, and could not themselves take the initiative in such a way that their supply of credit could stimulate a latent into an actual demand, so giving a twist to a virtuous spiral. The passive 'armchair' theory of banking, though falsely applied internally, certainly did not fit the essentially aggressively entrepreneurial way of life of the merchant bankers who from their infancy went out from Germany and elsewhere to places like Exeter, Liverpool, Manchester and London to create business, before using the latter city as their base for opening up the world. Thus the Barings, undeterred by their Argentinian fiasco, were already by the late 1890s taking the leading role in introducing Japanese business ventures to the London capital market. Where there's a will there's a way: but our leading bankers were complacently and profitably unaware of any connection between the over centralization of savings and the structure and operations of the banking system on the one hand, and the lack of dynamism in British manufacturing industry on the other hand. That the banks were not alone to blame goes without saying; but, whether they recognized it or not – and they did not – they were inescapably part of the problem. The infamous Macmillan Gap was being conceived at the height of sterling's supremacy, though it did not become delinquently of age until the 1930s.

The final triumph of the full gold standard, 1850–1914

After thousands of years of continual usage commodity money reached its culminating excellence in the form of the gold standard as it operated in and from the United Kingdom in the period from about 1850 to 1914. This formed a short golden interlude in monetary history and an outstanding example of the contemporaneous 'sailing-ship' effect'. For just as the best sailing ships ever, such as the *Thermopylae* (1868) and the *Cutty Sark* (1869), were built well after the steamships which were to replace them had already become commonplace, so the supreme development of commodity money based on the age-old concept of intrinsic value took place long after bank bills, notes, cheques and other forms of abstract 'fiat' money that were to supersede gold had similarly become well established as essential elements of everyday life. But whereas it was obvious to contemporaries that the decline of the sailing ship, despite its final flourish, was inevitable, contemporary opinion regarded the future of the gold standard as permanently guaranteed by the very degree of near-perfection so obviously achieved by such an ideal form of currency. The British gold standard had, by the middle of the nineteenth century, become the British Imperial Standard and, in the last quarter of the century, the International Gold Standard, as all the major trading nations of the world hastened to imitate the currency system of what was still the supreme financial centre of the world. As an American economist admits, 'the period of the ascendancy of the gold standard throughout the world corresponded with the apogee of the British Empire. Britain was the most powerful nation on earth, and the money market centre of the world was the London money market' (Cochran 1967, 25). The gold standard seemed to have finally embodied the hard-learned monetary experience of mankind throughout its long history and was internationally acclaimed irrespective of the different forms of government or the contrasting natures of the banking systems of the countries which were belatedly rushing to imitate Britain's successful example. Even after the devastating changes brought about by the First World War, most influential opinion on both sides of the Atlantic sought to put the clock back to Britain's finest financial hour, without appreciating the essentially transient nature of the full gold standard system.

As we have already seen, the 'pound sterling' for well over a 1,000 years signified silver, not gold. Gradually in the eighteenth century because of two self-reinforcing causes, namely, first, the poor quality and shortage of silver coins, and secondly the rise of money substitutes in the form of metal tokens and bank paper, gold became increasingly to be the preferred standard metal in practice. Unlike the situation in many countries abroad, silver in Britain never regained its former standing, so that by the nineteenth century she was spared the conflicts between gold and silver supporters and the confusing chimera of bimetallism that plagued countries in Europe and America for much of the century. In 1816 gold became at last legally recognized as the official standard of value for the pound, though it was not until the restoration of convertibility in 1821 that the domestic gold standard was in full operation. We have also traced how the Bank of England came to be the monopolistic issuer of bank notes with a fixed fiduciary issue of £14 million and also came to hold the main gold reserves of the centralizing banking system. From the middle of the century the previous concern about internal drains of gold from the Bank was replaced by a more single-minded concern with external drains, while, by means of trial and error, the Bank experimented with various devices for safeguarding its gold reserves, the most effective of which turned out eventually to be the combined use of bank rate with open market operations in such a way as to make the market follow the Bank's chosen rate (Sayers 1936). Even before the Bank of England had mastered these techniques, the major trading countries had become so favourably impressed that they too gave up their flirtations with silver and bimetallism and adopted full gold standards with internal circulation of full-bodied gold coinage and more or less freely allowed imports and exports of gold, as the rules of the international gold standard system demanded. Following the new German Empire's decision in 1871 to base its mark on gold, Holland, Austro-Hungary, Russia and the Scandinavian countries soon did likewise, while in 1878 France abandoned its bimetallic experiments in favour of gold. Thus by the end of the 1870s, without being consciously planned, the international gold standard system had fallen fittingly into place, (though internally the USA still flirted with bimetallism).

Taking any two countries, A and B, say America and Britain, operating a full gold standard, the relative gold values of their internal coinage would give the 'mint par' of exchange. Thus with the US dollar valued at 25.8 grains of gold nine-tenths fine, and the sovereign at 123.3 grains at eleven-twelfths fine, the mint par of exchange was £1 = $4.866. The actual rates in the foreign exchange markets fluctuated very closely to this parity, the outside limits, known as the 'specie points', being determined by the costs of making payments in gold rather than pounds or dollars, the three main costs in determining the width of the specie points being the costs of freight, insurance and the loss of interest for the time in transit. The enormous improvements in transport and communication occurring at this time caused the specie points, and therefore the range of fluctuations between currencies, to become even narrower, making London, as the dominant market, more 'perfect' to the economist as to the foreign exchange dealer.

The market not only worked micro-economically to smooth out surges in the demand and supply of currencies but also helped, macro-economically, in equilibrating the levels of economic activity among members adhering to the international gold standard. The three chief elements in this important equilibrating mechanism were, first, the price effects; secondly, the income effects; and thirdly, the interest-rate effects. In practice all three worked together though with differing contributions in time and place. In theory the analysis of the various elements has kept the midnight oil burning from Hume and Adam Smith to the present day. (An excellent recent summary appears in Eichengreen 1985.) Let us suppose that prices in country B rose relatively to those in A, then following the fall in B's currency to its export specie point, gold would flow from B to A, directly reducing the money base in B and raising it in A, and therefore changing their relative money supplies by a multiple of the money base, depending upon the size and fixity of the bank multiplier, thus in time restoring equilibrium and eliminating the need for further gold flows. These ultimate price effects were associated with and speeded up by the effects of relative changes in incomes and interest rates in the different countries. Thus the country with the relatively high prices – B – would lose exports and gain imports, depressing the incomes of workers and the profits of employers in B, first in the export industries and then more generally. The lower levels of income in B required a smaller money base, easing the release of gold to A and so reinforcing the price effects. The initial pressures in B that had caused prices to rise would also cause rates of interest to rise, while the increased gold base in A would lead to a fall in interest rates in A, so assisting in the restoration of equilibrium.

All these were relatively short-term effects and depended on the lack of rigidity – or to put it more positively, on the existence of a high degree of responsiveness or 'elasticity' – in wages and other factor prices in the economies of the countries concerned. It also assumed the willingness of the authorities, whether long-term believers in *laissez-faire* or zealous new converts, not to impede these so-called 'automatic' effects. The central banks did of course use their 'discretion' either to thwart the rules or to assist them (bringing to a higher level of public awareness the debate, mostly critical of discretion, first developed in the Bullion Report of 1810). By early and judicious anticipatory action the central banks could influence the movement of interest rates in the direction which would eventually have resulted from the working of the 'automatic' forces, and so reduce the size of the fluctuations in gold flows and in the size of 'barren' reserves, and so too moderate the disturbing changes in incomes and employment. Certainly the Bank of England became much more active in its use of bank rate, and although other factors were involved, its role in safeguarding the gold reserves was of increasing importance. Between 1845 and 1859 bank rate changed on average just four times a year; between 1860 and 1874 it averaged twelve times a year, with the record twenty-four times in 1873.

From 1875 to 1914 it averaged seven times a year, varying from none in 1895 to a dozen in 1893. It was during this time that bank rate gained a veneration bordering on the worship of the gold standard it helped to maintain.

Since all the world needed sterling for its trade it might at first seem that the Bank of England would require to keep much vaster gold reserves than the other central banks. Bagehot and Goschen among others constantly warned of the need for bigger gold reserves in the City to back up its worldwide responsibilities, though they differed as to the proper distribution of such reserves between the clearing banks and the Bank of England. As a matter of fact, although the Bank's reserves were enlarged in the second as compared with the first half of the century, yet they remained on average very much smaller than those of other central banks, and 'never between 1850 and 1890 exceeded four per cent of the liabilities of Britain's domestic bank deposits' (Viner 1937, 264). From the 1880s to 1914 the Bank of England's reserves fluctuated between an average of about £20 million and £40 million. In contrast the Bank of France customarily averaged around £120 million of gold reserves, the Imperial Bank of Russia held around £100 million and even the Austro-Hungarian Bank held around £50 million. Such reserves were largely 'barren' in that they yielded the banks concerned no return in interest and, as reserves, were not at the same time available for financing trade. Holders of sterling enjoyed the convenience and liquidity of the world's favourite currency, and London was by far the world's largest gold market. Because sterling was more liquid, more heavily demanded and supplied and, together with gold, more perfectly marketed than elsewhere, the Bank of England could and did manage to operate with a much smaller, more active and less barren reserve than was the case in other countries. 'It is small wonder that contemporaries were torn between criticism of the Bank and admiration for the efficiency of a system that enabled such vast transactions, both domestic and external, to be handled with so small a reserve' (Feavearyear 1963, 314).

Luckily, the world's stock of monetary gold increased substantially during this period, from £519 million in 1867 to £774 million in 1893, an annual rate of increase of 1.5 per cent; and to £1909 million by 1918, at an average annual rate of 3.7 per cent; helping to give confidence to a financial world that still worshipped gold, while in fact relying on bank deposits at least twenty times as large. Minimum reserves were thus a glowing testimony to the skills of the City and of the Bank. Yet there was a price to pay. As Viner has shown,

the practice of extreme economy in the maintenance of bank reserves did have as an accidental by-product the beneficial effect that it guaranteed to the metallic standard world that so far as England was concerned there would be no hoarding of gold and that all gold reaching that country would quickly exercise an influence in the appropriate direction for international equilibrium . . . But it tended to intensify the growing tendency for instability of business conditions within England itself. (1937, 269)

London was becoming, during the second half of the nineteenth century, the headquarters not only of most of the large banks in England and Wales but also of a growing number of overseas banks, the main business of which lay in the former colonies and dominions, including groups of banks variously known as the Imperial Banks and the Eastern Exchange Banks. One of the earliest of these was the Chartered Bank of India, Australia and China, registered in 1854 after some years of struggle against the East India Company which was still jealously trying to guard its monopoly. James Wilson, originally from Hawick, and as we have seen, leader of the 'Banking School' and founder of *The Economist*, was chiefly responsible for its foundation and for its early progress. (The story of its first hundred years is skilfully portrayed by Sir Compton Mackenzie in *Realms of Silver*, 1954.) The Standard Bank of South Africa, originally formed by John Paterson and five other British businessmen in Port Elizabeth in 1857, became one of the first banks to be registered in London under the 1862 Limited Liability Act. Grindlay's, the British Bank of the Middle East, the Chartered Mercantile Bank of India, London and China, the Oriental Bank Corporation, the Hong Kong and Shanghai Bank, the Bank of London and South America, and Barclays, Colonial, Dominion and Overseas were all banks with similar ambitions, spreading out from London to assist the development of trade in 'colonial' goods in the second half of the nineteenth and first half of the twentieth century. A late nineteenth-century example of such a bank, engaged in trade with Nigeria (including its initial provision of a modern currency), was the British Bank of West Africa (BBWA). It was founded jointly by Alfred Lewis Jones of Carmarthen and George Neville of London, first as an offshoot of the business of the Elder-Dempster shipping line, and began carrying on a banking business from their Lagos office in the early 1890s. Having demonstrated their abilities, they were duly registered in London as a limited company in 1894.

The interlocking directorates of the boards of these banks with those of the London merchant and clearing banks and with the Bank of England, a pattern which existed right from the early formation of the overseas banks and which persisted well into the twentieth century, further reinforced the external bias of the City of London. Thus Lord

Milner, who had been Governor of South Africa from 1899 to 1902, and director of the London Joint Stock Bank (later the Midland), was chairman of BBWA from 1910 to 1916. The 1st Viscount Goschen, member of the merchant banking family Goschens and Cunliffe, became a director of the Bank of England at twenty-seven, wrote the classic 'Theory of the Foreign Exchanges' (1861) and went on to become Chancellor of the Exchequer in 1886. A close relative, Sir Henry Goschen, was a director of the Chartered Bank and Chairman of National Provincial Bank. Lord Harlech was not only a director of BBWA and of Midland Bank but carried on for a number of years as chairman of both, and at a time when the Midland was the world's largest bank. Lord Inchcape was concurrently a director of BBWA and of National Provincial, while Sir Cyril Hawker, after forty-two years with the Bank of England became chairman of Standard Bank (which took over BBWA) and later of the combined Standard-Chartered Group. Such examples could be multiplied almost indefinitely. Suffice it to say that at the very time that the formerly diffused country banking system was being transformed into a centralized system based largely in London, the City was increasing its export not only of capital but also of its banking expertise throughout the whole range, from junior clerks to managers and directors, quite a few of the latter having had the highest experience of colonial government. The effect of this influential concentration of administrative and financial experience was greatly to strengthen the external bias of the City of London.

The supply of trained persons to take up the key positions in overseas banks came from a surplus of young bankers from all over Britain, particularly from Scotland. The Scottish Institute of Bankers, the world's first, was set up in 1875, four years before that of England and Wales. The British banks were soon training, or at least employing, far more young people than could readily find promotion at home, hence the drain of young bankers to complement and fructify the export of capital. Professors Lythe and Butt give it as their view that 'Scotland almost certainly invested more abroad and not enough at home . . . foreign competition was assisted and at the same time new industrial development at home was sacrificed' (1975, 238–9). The growing centripetal powers of the City might leave Britain's industrial hinterland rather neglected, but those same powers greatly strengthened the financial links with all the major trading centres overseas, in many of which British or British-type banks employing a core of British staff were becoming increasingly active by the turn of the century. It was this close, personal integration of the overseas banking institutions based on common experience, training and methods of operation that underlay the efficient working of the commodity markets, the bill on London and the money and foreign exchange markets; while in similar fashion the closely connected merchant banking communities facilitated the smooth working of the London capital and gold markets. The freedom and flexibility of those markets enabled the Bank of England to carry out its duties of running the gold standard system within a range of real economic costs that seemed politically tolerable and appeared to yield a clear balance of advantage, at least up to 1914. (It was this same personal network overseas which helped to guarantee the more limited, less spectacular but still very significant success of the sterling area system after 1931 by which time the gold standard was justifiably vilified as a barbarous relic.)

The international crisis of 1907, which had its most dramatic effects in the USA, where it brought about widespread bank failures, served to confirm public belief on both sides of the Atlantic in the superiority of the British financial system, and the efficiency of its central banking operations in particular. Bank rate was raised to 7 per cent on 7 November 1907, the highest since 1873, and attractive enough to draw into the Bank £7 million of gold from Germany, £3½ million from France, £2½ million from India and £6 million from gold-mining countries, enabling the Bank very quickly to rebuild its reserve to more than the figure of £21 million which existed before the crisis began. By May 1908 bank rate had been brought down to 2½ per cent. Thus bank rate again proved itself 'A technique associated with a most satisfactory maintenance and improvement in industrial equilibrium' (Clapham 1970, II, 389). This result helped the American official investigators of the crisis to recommend a similar central banking system, suitably adapted to their continental conditions, for the USA. Yet these victories were already being won at a heavy price, for despite the quick restoration of the reserves and of financial equilibrium, cheap money failed to bring down unemployment, which averaged 8 per cent over the two years 1908 and 1909, with the rate in shipbuilding rising to 13 per cent in 1909 and with most of the building trades suffering 11 per cent unemployed. Nevertheless, because of its glittering advantages in other directions, the harsh discipline demanded by the rules of the gold standard game remained politically acceptable until after 1914. As C. R. Fay has explained: 'When the world lived on Lancashire cotton, Cardiff coal, and the London money market, the policy of free trade [and he might well have added, its financial counterpart, the gold standard] was justified by the facts. But this situation passed away with the War' (1948, 323). Hobsbawm fully agrees: 'The stability of the British currency rested on the international hegemony of the British economy, and when it ceased, no amount of bank rate manipulation did much good' (1968, 200).

Two further (generally overlooked) costs are associated with the acceptance by the Bank of England of responsibility for safeguarding the country's gold reserves, for this involved giving up its profitable competition with the clearing banks and downgrading the operations of the Bank of England's branches. The first meant the reduction of a most powerful competitor, and hence a strengthening of the growing monopoly powers of the big, amalgamating banks, while the downgrading of the Bank's branches meant a reduction of its daily involvement in, and consequent close awareness of, business conditions in the industrial regions around places like Leeds, Birmingham, Liverpool, Manchester, Newcastle and so on. 'There were sustained differences of opinion,' states Sir John Clapham, 'about the policy of the branches' (1970, II, 402). Ernest Edye, Inspector and Head of Branches from 1897 to 1914, argued with annoying and vigorous persistence in favour of expanding branch lending in direct competition with other banks. But the lesson, already well learned by the Bank of England by 1890 (and subsequently painfully relearned by a number of other central banks), was that you must not compete with the commercial banks if you wish to control or even influence their policies or hold part of their reserves. Although Ernest Edye kept up his campaign against the Bank's 'soft-pedalling' of branch banking, the requirements of the gold standard at that time inevitably meant a reduction in the importance of the branches. Here again the centripetal force of London reduced the Bank's direct involvement in assisting businesses in the regions in competition with the clearers, whose monopoly powers were to that extent thereby increased. Again the City wins, the regions lose: perhaps not a lot in each instance, and therefore easy to overlook at the time; but the cumulative results of these many different elements of centripetal bias were significant and long-lasting, forming a delayed-action economic bomb destined to wreak considerable damage on the industrial regions in the inter-war period.

Cheap coal, cheap iron and steel, and cheap capital from Europe in general and from Britain in particular, helped in creating the infrastructure, such as the ports, waterworks and railways, in the undeveloped world. To what extent this should be praised as 'development' or castigated as 'exploitation' remains largely a subjectively political rather than an objectively economic question. Similarly an assessment of the balance of benefits over costs which accrued to Britain from operating the gold standard system – in which many other countries were free riders – depends on a mixture of economic and political considerations. Certainly sterling and the City of London gained enormously, while the losses in the form of unemployment and belated industrial reconstruction occurred mainly after 1914, when these evils could be blamed on the war and when in any case the gold standard had ceased to operate, ar at least to operate fully. The import of expensive munitions and cheap food during the war, largely paid for by Victorian investment, and cheap food for the unemployed in the inter-war period, were of immense political importance. But by then the period of the ascendancy of sterling had passed, and the gold standard, which internally had enjoyed a long run but internationally had been short-lived, was permanently dead, as the failure of the stubbornly misguided attempts to revive it, described in the next chapter, abundantly prove.

At the beginning of the nineteenth century Henry Thornton, in his *Enquiry into the Nature and Effects of the Paper Credit of Great Britain* (1802), laid down what Schumpeter has called the 'Magna Carta of Central Banking', namely:

> to limit the total amount of paper issued, and to resort, whenever the temptation to borrow is strong, to some effectual principle of restriction; in no case, however, materially to diminish the sum in circulation, but to let it vibrate only within certain limits; to afford a slow and cautious extension as the general trade of the kingdom enlarges itself; to allow of some special, though temporary increase in the event of any extraordinary alarm or difficulty; and to lean to the side of diminution in the case of gold going abroad, and of the general exchanges continuing long unfavourable; this seems to be the true policy of the Bank of England. To suffer either the solicitations of merchants or the wishes of government to determine the measure of bank issues is unquestionably to adopt a very false principle of conduct. (Quoted in Humphrey 1989, 9–10)

The 'vibrations', or the swings of the monetary pendulum, from broad quantity to narrow quality and back again were repeated many times in the course of the long nineteenth century as the bullionists, the Currency School and similar restrictionists attempted to keep the money supply within narrow limits and emphasized the golden core, while the anti-bullionists, the Banking School and other expansionists tried repeatedly to widen the type and quantity of what could legitimately be accepted as money, and emphasized the importance of the peripheral, paper money substitutes. By and large the Bank of England, aided by the legal restrictions on the note issue, kept the dynamic balance remarkably well, through timely intervention using bank rate, open market operations and other devices, although on occasions getting the timing wrong, unsurprisingly. Even in the latter circumstances, the Bank could flexibly retrieve the situation, for its discretion was inspired by a traditional pragmatism rather than by any rigid dogma. Thornton's 'Magna Carta' turned out therefore to be a true guide and prophecy; but even he could not have foreseen the extent to which the full gold standard would achieve not only a high degree of stability within Britain, but would also allow sterling to become during the nineteenth century the most extensively used currency up to that time in world history. But in 1914, in contrast to the Pax Britannica and the stability of the sterling-centred full gold standard, a more violent century was about to explode into existence, with many more competing central banks giving in too readily to the short-term demands of their governments, entailing far wider swings of the monetary pendulum.

8

British Monetary Development in the Twentieth Century

Introduction: a century of extremes

Every success and every failure experienced in all previous monetary history have been repeated, with additions and on a vaster scale, in the twentieth century. In money as in economic, social and political life in general, this has been a century of extremes. Only in the case of money, however, have the violent oscillations repeated themselves quite so faithfully in their familiar reversible pattern in the advanced countries of the world. Primitive commodity moneys were still in use over large tracts of the 'undeveloped' world as recently as the 1960s, as described in chapter 2; while throughout the developed world the most successful and traditional of all commodity moneys – gold – reached its highest peak of operational perfection at the beginning of the twentieth century. It remained a dazzling ideal to which governments sought to return until the outbreak of the Second World War and was again being flirted with as a potential international price stabilizer, in theory if not in actual practice, in the last decades of the century. Despite such outstanding examples of the appeal of stable money, inflation of unprecedented proportions repeatedly interrupted attempts to adopt sensible monetary policies.

Monetary management, with mismanagement the beguiling obverse of the same coin, became a tool universally available to all governments as the century unfolded; a management no longer physically constrained by the supply of gold. In these circumstances it might at first be assumed that at least one of the recurrent failures of earlier history, namely an actual shortage of money, would not be repeated. Not so: in the 1930s a dire monetary scarcity, brought about directly by governmental mismanagement, intensified and was a strong contributory cause of the world's most severe economic depression. Nevertheless the bias in twentieth-century financial policy has undoubtedly been in the opposite direction, that is towards excessive money creation, so much so that some form of gold or general commodity anchor is again being internationally investigated as the twentieth century draws to a close.

Against this violent background the swings of the monetary pendulum between quality and quantity and the changing monetary theories behind actual policies have also been alternating to an extreme degree. Apart from a precious few examples of long-term stability, notably in small, traditionally neutral countries like Switzerland and Sweden, extreme fluctuations have held global sway. Even Britain, with its long tradition of political moderation, has experienced swings to an unprecedented degree, from price stability to deflation with mass unemployment and to inflation, first with over-full employment and then mass unemployment again; and with the associated theories which acted as the explanation or excuse for policy lurching suddenly from stolid classicism through confident Keynesianism and defiant Friedmanism back to an uncertain but more realistic pragmatism.

Given Britain's influence on both monetary practice and theory, stemming in turn from its vital role in the operation of the international gold standard, the export of its commercial and central banking expertise, the prestige and following of Keynes, the bold embodiment of Friedmanism in the Thatcher experiment, the City's irresistible attraction for foreign banks and the stubborn eminence of London's foreign exchange market, the financial development of Britain in the twentieth century, notwithstanding the decline of its empire and the erosion of its lion's share of world trade, still remains of central importance in world monetary history

Financing the First World War, 1914–1918

Despite relatively minor conflicts such as the Crimean War (1854–6) and the Boer War (1899–1902), the national debt had been modestly reduced in nominal terms, and very significantly reduced as a percentage of national income, in the century after 1815, falling from £830 million in 1815 to £650 million in 1913. Such reductions had been brought about by the generous use of frequent budget surpluses, the result of good housekeeping by Victorian Chancellors, some of whom also took advantage of recurring spells of cheap money-market rates to convert large chunks of the debt into lower rates. Thus Goschen in 1888 converted the 3 per cent stock to 2¾ per cent, a rate which was to fall to 2½ per cent in 1903. Edwardian Chancellors were bolder and bigger spenders, though Asquith in his three budgets between 1906 and 1908 managed to redeem much of the debt incurred during the South African war. Lloyd George's budgets of 1909–11, 'which may not unfairly be described as the most revolutionary series of proposals ever laid before a British Parliament' (Muir 1947, II, 757) introduced far greater progression into the fiscal system, tapping far more copiously the wealth of the rich. Although the purpose of Lloyd George's fiscal policy was for financing social welfare benefits, the fiscal framework had thereby been fundamentally transformed on the eve of the First World War into a much more buoyant source of revenue, ripe for the insatiable demands of the military machine. What had been introduced, at the cost of a seething constitutional crisis, for welfare thus became a timely godsend for warfare.

The tax base which had fortuitously been put in place to support the First World War was much more progressive, buoyant and effective than that which had been available to finance the French wars of 1793–1815. Nevertheless borrowing had to be resorted to still more drastically, so that the national debt rose tenfold during the four years of the First World War, compared with just a trebling during the twenty years of war from 1793 to 1815. It was not until March 1920, some sixteen months after the war ended, that the national debt rose to its peak of £7,830 million. Some £1,230 million or 15.7 per cent was owed to people abroad. Only a very small amount, £315 million or just 4.0 per cent was permanently funded or very long term, while around £5,000 million or 63.9 per cent had varying maturity dates, mostly of medium term, a feature which was to cause considerable re-funding problems in the inter-war period. As much as 16 per cent or £1,250 million consisted of the highly liquid 'floating debt', mostly made up of three-month Treasury Bills. In short, the borrowing and taxable capacity of the country had been put under immense strain, yet both at the time and subsequently considerable controversy has raged concerning whether the correct balance had been struck between borrowing and taxing, and as to whether the best available methods for fund-raising had been put into practice.

Keynes, writing twelve years after the end of the war, was too pessimistic in fearing that 'perhaps the financial history of the war will never be written in any adequate way' because 'too many of the essential statistics' were unavailable; but, given his close involvement as Treasury adviser and his analytical genius, he was quite right when, modestly including himself in the condemnation, he admitted that 'looking back he was struck by the inadequacy of the theoretical views we held at the time as to what was going on and the crudity of our applications of the Quantity Theory of Money' (1930, II, 170–1). Theoretical refinement was a luxury that had to await the peace. Keynes's pessimism – a characteristic not unknown among the profession – was not confined to worrying about statistical deficiencies. In September 1915 he circulated what Lloyd George has called an 'alarmist and jargonish paper' to the Cabinet in which he gave his considered opinion that 'it is certain that our present scale of expenditure is only possible as a violent spurt to be followed by a strong reaction: the limitations of our resources are in sight'. He went on to warn of British bankruptcy by the spring of 1916 (Lloyd George 1938, I, 409). Fortunately although McKenna, the new Chancellor, was frightened stiff by the gloomy forecast of his chief adviser, Lloyd George, in his typically modest way, 'knew more about the credit resources of this country' than either the current Chancellor or his 'pessimistic, mercurial and acrobatic economist'. Keynes was 'much too impulsive a counsellor for a great emergency': he was 'an entertaining economist whose bright but shallow dissertations on finance and political economy, when not taken seriously, always provide a source of innocent merriment to his readers' (Lloyd George 1938, I, 410). Keynes himself returned similarly effusive compliments about Lloyd George: 'a Welsh witch . . . rooted in nothing, void and without content; a prism which collects light and distorts it; this syren, this goat-footed bard, this half-human visitor to our age from the hag-ridden magic and enchanted woods of Celtic antiquity' (1933b, 35–6).

Keynes was not alone in considering the rate of expenditure reached in the early part of the war to be unsustainable. As early as the autumn of 1914 *The Economist* assured its readers of 'the economic and financial impossibility of carrying on hostilities on the present scale' (Mackenzie 1954, 240). Before turning to see how such an 'impossible' rate of expenditure was substantially exceeded and how the rising balance between taxation and borrowing was managed, we must first consider briefly how the immediate crisis facing the country's financial institutions in August 1914 was successfully overcome.

The first financial reaction to the assassinations of Archduke Ferdinand and his wife in Sarajevo on 28 June 1914 was a series of banking panics in Europe, intensified as the Balkan conflict widened. So far as Britain was concerned, the initial effect was to increase the flow of hot money into the traditional safe haven of London. However, by the end of July the growing probability that Britain would become directly involved frightened the City so much that the vastly increased desire for firms and persons to make their assets more liquid than normal, particularly by selling vast quantities of securities, brought about the closure of the Stock Exchange, temporarily, on 31 July. Bank rate was raised from 3 to 4 per cent on 30 July, to 8 per cent on 31 July, and to the panic rate of 10 per cent on 1 August, when, accompanying the announcement, the Chancellor's letter to the Governor of the Bank of England permitted an excess issue of fiduciary notes if this were to prove necessary. Fortunately for the deliberations of the monetary authorities, Monday 3 August was a normally scheduled Bank Holiday. To gain time to decide on their plans three additional days, up to and including Thursday, were also declared to be Bank Holidays. To stem any pre-emptive drain of gold the Chancellor announced that specie payments were *not* to be suspended. A series of steps were taken to avoid the possible domino effect of bankruptcies. On 3 August Parliament passed a 'moratorium' in the form of a Postponement of Payments Act followed by a Royal Proclamation deferring the maturity of bills of exchange for a month with government guarantees following later to enable the Bank of England to advance virtually all the funds required by the discount houses and the banks to deal smoothly with the increased volume of bills. A Currency and Bank Notes Act, rushed through both Houses of Parliament on 6 August, empowered the Treasury to issue notes of £1 and 10s. denominations, and granted temporary legal tender status not only to Scottish and Irish banknotes but also to Postal Orders, which latter became negotiable instruments despite still having the words 'not negotiable' plainly printed across them. A Courts (Emergency Powers) Act was passed on 31 August to relieve debtors in general who were not able to pay because of war circumstances, thus complementing the earlier special Acts of moratorium; and a Government (War Obligations) Act was passed on 27 November to indemnify government ministers for the emergency measures they felt forced to take.

This urgently arranged and costly battery of protective devices saved the City from any further signs of panic, and business quickly returned to normal, except of course for trading with the enemy, aspects of which could be cunningly concealed through third parties. It was the need for someone with long experience of discerning the true origins of trade bills, and so able to prevent London's first-rate services being used to finance enemy trade, that brought Montagu Norman in April 1915 from Brown Shipley full-time into the Bank of England (where he had been a director from 1902) as adviser to the Deputy Governor. Because of the four-day Bank Holiday the panic 10 per cent bank rate was in operation for only a single working day and was quickly brought down to 6 per cent on 7 August and to 5 per cent the next day. As to the foreign exchanges, sterling, by far the world's most coveted currency, actually rose for a time well above its mint par of $4.86 to as high as $6.50 before settling down fairly close to par, with the Bank of England avoiding the dangers of shipping gold overseas by using its gold deposits in Ottawa to pay North American creditors. The public in England and Wales took to the new small notes of the Treasury – called 'Bradbury's' after the signature of the Permanent Secretary – like ducklings to water, despite the very poor quality of the first issues. They met a long-felt need, and their ready acceptance allowed the banks, and through them the Bank of England, gradually to gather in the gold circulation to add to its war chest. This quiet, unofficial cessation in specie payments which accompanied and was made possible by the public's welcome of the new notes, did not bring forth the dire consequences that had been feared by many, including notably 'Mr J. M. Keynes' (who) 'at this time firmly predicted national ruin if specie payment was suspended' (Owen 1954, 265). The cessation of internal gold circulation, then conceived simply as an urgent temporary expedient, thereafter became permanent. Thus ended without fuss or fanfare nearly 700 years of intermittent gold coinage circulation, including a century of the full gold standard, ousted ignominiously by bits of scrappy paper. It took the stock exchange rather longer than the other financial institutions to resume normal working, which it eventually succeeded in doing from 4 January 1915.

Although the motto 'Business as usual' was a tribute to the resilient spirit of the country, the mood of normality was carried to excess and so worked against public acceptance of the true scale of effort, in finance as in other areas, demanded by the enormous challenges of this new type of war. It lulled the public and most of the government into complacently delaying the acceptance of physical controls like requisitioning and rationing, so placing too much of the burden of transferring resources from civilian to military uses on voluntary market forces and normal financial mechanisms. It helped to push the balance of government funding too heavily towards borrowing, and especially short-term borrowing, ably assisted by eager and efficient financial institutions, rather than relying more heavily on taxation. The government's revenue from taxation increased from around £200 million in 1913–14 to nearly £900 million in 1918–19, i.e. by about four and a half times. But expenditure soared during the same period by nearly thirteen times, from just under £200 million to around £2,580 million. On average only about a third of government expenditure during the war was raised by taxation, leaving two-thirds of an ever-rising total to be cajoled voluntarily by borrowing, generally at an unnecessarily increasing cost.

The first emergency provision of cash was a vote of credit granted by Parliament on 8 August 1914, followed on 26 August by an enabling 'War Loan Bill' giving the government the power to raise 'any sum required' for war purposes, a blank cheque of which Lloyd George and subsequent Chancellors took full advantage. A further vote of credit of £225 million was granted on 17 November, when Lloyd George introduced the first war budget. Income tax and supertax rates were doubled, the duties on tea were raised by 60 per cent, and on beer by a massive 300 per cent, while the first War Loan, redeemable 1925–8, was issued for a nominal £350 million at 3½ per cent, but by being issued at 95 brought in £332.5 million at a true rate of approximately3⅔ per cent. In his second war budget in May 1915, Lloyd George being too pleased with the influx of revenue, left tax rates unchanged, thus missing the chance of raising revenue closer to the spiralling expenditures, and thereby set quite a problem for his successor as Chancellor, Reginald McKenna. McKenna raised the rates on indirect taxes and both the rates and progression of income and supertax. Notably he introduced an Excess Profits Duty at 50 per cent (later raised to 80 per cent) and placed import duties of 33 per cent on cars, motor-cycles, clocks, watches and film. The Excess Profits Duty was not only welcomed as catching unscrupulous profiteers but turned out to be a most lucrative tax, yielding around a quarter of total revenue during the latter half of the war. By so tapping the inequitable 'profit inflation' of wartime 'the British Treasury, by trial and error, had got as near to the ideally right procedure [of taxation] as could be expected' (Keynes 1930, II, 174). McKenna's import duties, imposed as a temporary infringement of free trade in order to raise desperately needed revenue, were later to be strengthened to protect domestic industry. However praiseworthy his tax policy might be judged, his borrowing policy was less inspired. The second War Loan, which he issued in July 1915 at 95, carried a nominal rate of 4½ per cent, a full 1 per cent higher than that of Lloyd George, and set a bad precedent. The third War Loan, February 1917, and the post-war Victory Loan of June 1919 both issued at 95, carried a 5 per cent coupon (a 4 per cent tax-free option was largely ignored). Furthermore all three latter loans carried what might be called 'reverse conversion' privileges whereby owners of previous, cheaper stock could convert into the new longer-dated but higher-rated stock, in effect raising rates retrospectively, and so intensifying the service and transfer burden in the post-war deflation.

What had started under Lloyd George as a moderately cheap war at around 3⅔ per cent turned into a dear war financed at rather more than 5 per cent. Not only was the total quantity of borrowing excessive, a weakness understandable given the cumbersome unpopularity of taxes, but so was the price, for which there was no acceptable excuse. The loans were oversubscribed and reached in very short time their target sums. Thus the third War Loan issued by Bonar Law in February 1917 (when the Governor of the Bank of England insisted on keeping to the high 5 per cent rate) received applications for £1,000,000,000 from some 5,289,000 subscribers within six weeks. The first billion-pound loan in world history was thus raised with surprising ease and speed, prompting the government to follow this up by a system of continuous borrowing 'on tap' by the issue of National War Bonds, four series of which were issued between October 1917 and May 1919. Instead of the government using its monopsonistic power as the only purchaser of really large loans in wartime to get such loans at a cheap rate, it perversely paid higher rates than was necessary, a feature which increased the service burden both during and after the war, when it also imposed the hidden cost of higher unemployment and lower private sector investment than would otherwise have been the case. Lloyd George's criticism is fully justified: 'The adoption of the principle that the British Government had to pay the commercial rate . . . had a costly sequel. McKenna's action had no doubt the fullest authorisation from the leading circles of banking and finance, but these circles are by no means to be reckoned as infallible advisers' (1938, I, 74).

These strictures applied even more strongly to short-term borrowing where the Bank of England's desire to keep the pound strong on the foreign exchanges was an added factor helping to raise market rates of interest, e.g. the rate on the issue of Exchequer Bonds, 1916 was at 6 per cent, bank rate in July 1916 was also raised to 6 per cent where it remained until the following January; and 5 per cent was paid on the 'special deposits' which the banks kept with the Bank of England. A conflict inevitably arose between the government's need, however weakly expressed, for cheap finance and the Bank of England's worship of the market and its belief that it was still operating the gold standard, a conflict made all the more bitter by the overbearing attitude of the Governor, Sir Walter Cunliffe, by common consent an autocratic bully and 'one of the nastiest men ever to be Governor' *Banking World*, August 1989, 55). Cunliffe not only pressed the imperative need for high rates on the Chancellor, Bonar Law, but interfered with mailed instructions from the Chancellor to the Treasury in Ottawa regarding sales of gold. The Cunliffe quarrel was 'the worst blot ever known on the relations between Governors and Chancellors' (Sayers 1976, I, 99).

Only an immediate threat by Lloyd George to nationalize the Bank caused Cunliffe to cave in; he promised to 'consult the Chancellor on general conditions affecting credit' but 'did not propose then or at any time to obtain the Chancellor's special sanction in regard to such changes as might be contemplated in Bank Rate' (Clay 1957, 104). The question of monetary sovereignty as between Treasury and Bank was thus postponed for thirty years, until the Bank was nationalized in 1946. It could at least be said in Cunliffe's favour that with the assistance of the Bank's agent in New York, J. P. Morgan & Co., the pound was kept within 2 per cent of its mint parity for most of the war, so enabling Britain to get full value for the loans it raised abroad totalling £1,365 million, chiefly from the USA, which partly helped to compensate for the larger total of £1,741 million that Britain lent to its allies. On balance Britain paid for much more than its own war effort; yet despite the war's debilitating burden there was a universal euphoric desire to return as soon as possible to the gold standard that was believed to have been the symbol, and if not the cause, at least an indispensable condition of Britain's recently held position of financial and trading supremacy.

The abortive struggle for a new gold standard, 1918–1931

In strictly legal terms the gold standard was still in operation during the war, though mines and U-boats by making insurance costs prohibitively expensive effectively prevented the free import and export of gold. Consequently it was not until after the war had ended that the law caught up with the fact that Britain had gone off gold in August 1914. Under the Regulations for the Defence of the Realm, 1 April 1919, the export of gold was legally prohibited, but these regulations were modified by the Gold and Silver (Export Control) Act of 1920 in such a way as to facilitate the re-establishment of London as the chief market for gold. This would be the means whereby, supported by an attractively high bank rate, a sufficient gold reserve could be drawn into the Bank of England so as to go back to the gold standard in all its essential forms. Unequivocal guidance towards this promised land was provided by the Cunliffe Reports. When Lord Cunliffe retired after his five-year stint as Governor (1913–18) he was appointed to chair a 'Committee on Currency and Foreign Exchanges after the War', which promptly issued its Interim Report (Cd 9182) in August 1918, followed by the Final Report (Cmd 464) in December 1919. Cunliffe was a man of few words, so, unlike most inquiries into money, the reports are brief, brisk and to the point, and came to clear, confident conclusions calculated to please the City – and to crucify the economy on an outdated cross of gold.

The interim report, some half-dozen pages priced 6*d*. (or 2.5p), considered that the 1844 Act 'has on the whole been fully justified by experience' and therefore 'an effective gold standard should be restored without delay'. Even in its single and apparently bold innovation, in believing that 'the internal circulation of gold was neither necessary nor desirable' it was conservatively harking back to a suggestion first made by Ricardo in 1811. In proposing that convertibility should be restored in terms of ingots of bullion, Ricardo had argued that a gold standard could be re-established with an economy of gold usage, a minimum drain on the world's supply of gold, and full reliance on cheap paper for internal circulation (Viner 1937, 177). Cunliffe saw as an essential precondition to convertibility the reduction of government borrowing, especially of the floating debt, even if this meant a politically unpalatable 'caution with far-reaching programmes of housing and other development schemes' – a swipe at Lloyd George's vote-catching policy of 'homes fit for heroes'. The 1844 principle of a fixed fiduciary note issue should be restored with the Treasury note issues to be amalgamated with, and under the control of, those of the Bank of England. As we have seen, Cunliffe when Governor (for a period longer than any of his 107 predecessors) had struggled unscrupulously to maintain as high a degree of independence for the Bank from government as was possible, and this cessation of government note issue was seen as being much more than simply a symbol. So the final report asserted, 'We have found nothing in the experiences of the war to falsify the lessons of previous experience that the adoption of a currency not convertible into gold is likely in practice to lead to overissue.' It considered it to be essential to reduce the outstanding issue of Treasury notes by suggesting that the actual maximum issue each year should be reduced until there was no strain on the Bank's gold reserve of around £150 million, the level which Cunliffe had obtained by hook or by crook during the war. The supremacy of bank rate was reaffirmed in the report's statement that 'the recognized machinery which operated to check a foreign drain and the speculative expansion of credit in this country must be kept in working order and should not be evaded by any attempt to continue differential rates for home and foreign currency'.

It took far longer than expected to set up the new 'Gold Bullion Standard' and even longer to merge the Treasury notes with those of the Bank. Once the wartime restrictions were relaxed, the pound quickly fell from the rate of $4.76 to which it had been pegged – and which looked delusively close to the pre-war rate to which it was then almost universally assumed Britain should return – down to the record low (up till then) of $3.21 in February 1920. Prices had risen much faster in the post-war boom of 1919–20 than in the four years of war, and to stem the speculation and lift the external value of the pound, bank rate was raised to 7 per cent in April 1920, the highest level (except for the one-day increase to 10 per cent in August 1914) since 1873, and kept at this penal level for the unprecedently long period of twelve months. The boom was quickly deflated: prices fell, unemployment soared; but the targeted dollar exchange rate recovered gradually to make the coveted gold standard attainable, whatever the harsh internal effects. *The Economist*'s index of prices, with 1913 = 100, had barely doubled during the war and had only reached 212 by March 1919, but shot up to 310 in March 1920, only to fall abruptly to 158 by March 1922. Registered unemployment was just 4 per cent in October 1920 but rose sharply to 15.4 per cent by March 1921 and to 18 per cent before the end of that year. The pound rose substantially to fluctuate between $4.70 and $4.33 during 1923. In June 1924, in the knowledge that the Gold and Silver (Export Control) Act was due to expire by the end of 1925, the government set up a Treasury committee to prepare finally for the implementation of the Cunliffe proposals. In its report it reaffirmed the City view that 'as a practical present-day policy for this country there is, in our opinion, no alternative comparable with a return to the former gold parity of the sovereign' (Report of the Committee of the Treasury on the Currency and Bank of England Note Issues, 1925, para. 8). On 13 May the Gold Standard Act 1925 became law, obliging the Bank to sell gold in minimum amounts of gold bars of 400 troy ounces at £3. 17s. 10½d. per fine ounce.

Cunliffe's proposals were completed ten years late, by the passing of the Currency and Bank Notes Act 1928. One of the purposes of the old Bank Charter Act of 1844 had been to replace private banknotes with those of the Bank of England – though it was a long process which took nearly seventy years before the last note-issuing joint-stock bank, Fox, Fowler & Co., gave up issuing when absorbed by Lloyds in 1921, so enabling the Bank of England to increase its fiduciary issue to its eventual maximum under the 1844 Act, i.e. to £19¾ million. It took just a few weeks for the huge Treasury note issue, under the terms of the new Act, to be absorbed through an increase in the Bank's fiduciary issue to £260 million. The considerable profit from the Bank's note issuing was henceforth to go to the Treasury, and more importantly a more elastic limit was placed on the Bank's power to vary the fiduciary limit. The Act, as a safety valve for emergencies, allowed the Bank to exceed the prescribed maximum, with Treasury consent, for a period up to six months, after which Parliamentary authority would be required. Thus in fact and almost unconsciously, a door was opened which would allow the supply of notes to be varied arbitrarily, according to the judgement of the Bank or Treasury, instead of being dependent directly on variations in the gold reserve – an open door which within three years was to be fully used.

In outward form the basic 1844 structure had been laboriously rebuilt to face the much stronger storms of the 1920s. It soon became plain to see that it could not stand the strain. A worried government wondered what more could be done. To help them find out they set up in 1929 under the chairmanship of Lord Macmillan, a Committee on Finance and Industry, a forum in which the trade unionist Ernest Bevin, Professor T. E. Gregory and above all, Mr J. M. Keynes, tried to drag the gaze of the City, and particularly that of the Governor of the Bank of England, Mr Montagu Norman, away from the international scene which always seemed to mesmerize the financiers, to the dismally mundane spectacle of the internal industrial scene and the long lines of the unemployed. The composition of the Macmillan Committee guaranteed that the linkage in its title and remit between 'finance' and 'industry' turned out to be a polarization between the combined classical views of the City of London and the Treasury on the one hand, and those of the industrial regions of the North and West allied with emerging Keynesian economics on the other.

Before turning to trace the rise of this internal conflict, which has continued in various vigorous forms throughout the present century, it is first necessary to see how the external financial policy of the British government throughout the inter-war period was influenced to an unusually strong degree by the Bank of England under its 110th Governor, Montagu Collet Norman. Norman was elected Governor on 15 April 1920 and was deemed so indispensable that he continued in that office for an unassailable record of twenty-four years. Arguments still rage as to the merits of his rule, but friend and foe agree that after such an experience it is certain that no Governor will ever again be granted anything like such a long reign, or therefore be able to acquire the personal power that such a long period of office inevitably grants its incumbent.

No one was more involved in the financial reconstruction of Europe after the war than Norman. Surprisingly his most influential ally in this part of his external policy was Keynes. Keynes was the official representative of the Treasury at the Paris Peace Conference, but resigned on 7 June 1919 as a protest against the attempt to extract what he considered to be dangerously high reparation payments from

Germany. Within barely six months he published *The Economic Consequences of the Peace* (1920) where, in his brilliantly fluent style, he advocated aid for German and Austrian reconstruction, rather than inflicting revenge (much to the disgust of the French) and a mutual cancellation of the allied war debts (to the consternation of the United States). He pointed out that 'the US is a lender only. The UK has lent about twice as much as she has borrowed [while] France has borrowed about three times what she has lent' (p.254). 'The existence of the great war debts is a menace to financial stability everywhere,' he wrote, adding prophetically that 'there is no European country in which repudiation may not soon become an important political issue' (p.261). Although he supported French claims to Ruhr coal, in general he felt that it would be impossible for central Europe, 'starving and disintegrating before our eyes' (p.211) to rebuild its economy without outside assistance. 'I am therefore', he said 'a supporter of an international loan' to assist immediately with such a task. The idea of a loan to Austria, initially easier to sell politically, and then to Germany, was taken up enthusiastically by Norman. In the face of American pressure, however, Norman was not willing to press for Keynes's other aim of securing the mutual cancellation of allied debts. Norman insisted, as he thought any good banker should, on paying British debts to America in full – and moreover at the pre-war parity, for anything less would be cheating – no matter who else defaulted, and no matter how heavy the burden on Britain. How else could the City of London's superlative reputation be maintained?

Norman strongly influenced the two League of Nations conferences, at Brussels in 1920 and at Genoa in 1922, in their attempts to get the gold standard widely re-established in Europe, and boasted about how the Bank of England 'managed to get a more or less dear money report out of a more than less cheap money committee' (Sayers 1976, I, 154). The League of Nations, with Norman's influential backing helped to raise an international stabilization loan to Austria in 1923 and to Hungary in 1924. Meanwhile runaway inflation in Germany was approaching its climax (see chapter 10). A commission under the chairmanship of the American General Charles G. Dawes, advocated a modification which would ease Germany's reparation burden, the payment of which was to be supervised by a Reparations Commission. It also pressed the urgent need for an international loan of £40 million together with allied supervision of Germany's financial institutions to the extent necessary to guarantee the payment of the new schedule of reparations without placing too much strain on the process of stabilization then being successfully carried out by Hjalmar Schacht,

President of the Reichsbank and a firm, close friend of Montagu Norman. Renewed difficulties led in 1929 to a new allied commission under the chairmanship of Owen D. Young, a prominent American banker. As well as helping to raise a new international loan to Germany and reconstituting the flow of reparations, perhaps the most important outcome of the Young Commission was the establishment in 1930 of the Bank for International Settlements, initially to help, as its name states, in overcoming the problems involved in such huge financial transfers but later playing a key role as a forum for central bankers. The French were not greatly enamoured of what they saw as too soft a treatment of Germany and laid a large part of the blame, so far as financial matters went, on Keynes and Norman, with results that were to lead to increased difficulties for British attempts both to maintain the gold standard and to widen the British system into an international gold exchange standard.

Apart from their similar pro-German policies, Norman and Keynes were complete opposites. Norman despised intellectuals: he used to boast that he came bottom of his form at Eton (though he was wrong even about that). He detested being put on the mental rack by Keynes during the Macmillan Committee's inquiries, and though he could never hope to win a war of words with Keynes (who could?), Norman's contemptuous and arrogant attitude to his critics is summed up in the final sentence of his speech when guest of honour at the Lord Mayor's banquet in London in October 1933: 'The dogs bark but the caravan moves on' – confidently, but in the wrong direction, one might add (A. Boyle 1967, 289). Norman gave himself single-mindedly, selflessly and completely to the Bank full-time for twenty-nine years during which he drew not a penny in salary. He saw Britain's and the City's interest as one, and best served by putting the external aspects of monetary policy first. By so doing he had raised the international prestige of the Bank by 1930 to possibly its highest level. But by relegating internal economic growth and the problem of unemployment to second place, his cherished gold standard was doomed to face collapse, and with it much of the painfully built prestige of the Bank of England.

Keynes's attacks on the gold standard were no mere flashes of hindsight. Just before the return to gold he wrote 'The British Public will submit their necks once more to the Golden Yoke, as a prelude, perhaps, to throwing it off forever at a not distant date' (1925a, 287). His reasons for considering the parity of $4.86 to be at least 10 per cent too high were spelt out in his 32-page pamphlet *The Economic Consequences of Mr Churchill* (1925b), a veritable polemical bombshell. Churchill later admitted that episode to be the greatest mistake of his political career. Keynes's warning of the strikes that would follow attempts to reduce prices and wages sufficiently to compete overseas were quickly followed in the shape of the nine days' General Strike from 4 May to 13 May 1926, sparked off by the miners' strike which lasted for more than six months. Admittedly there were many other causes of conflict besides the parity of the pound, including chronic underinvestment, obstructive unions, the uneconomic size of most of the pits, the loss of markets because of French annexation of the Saar and their occupation in January 1923 of the Ruhr, the switch of the Royal Navy from coal to oil and so on – but the high value of the pound and the high rates of interest required to support the pound were much more than simply being the last straws. What we would today call supply-side remedial measures, however necessary, were ineffective given the strong deflationary thrust of government policy which inevitably followed from government insistence on following the City's instinctive attachment to the pre-war parity.

All these arguments were paraded at length in the Macmillan report, the only novelty of which was its emphasis on what has thereafter been called 'the Macmillan Gap', namely that insufficient provision was being made by the otherwise excellent financial institutions of the country to enable small- and medium-sized firms to get the long-term or permanent funds they required for growth. Although little was done to fill that alleged gap in the inter-war period, it reappeared in almost every similar monetary report in the subsequent half-century. At that time and later, traditional bankers denied or played down its existence, giving what has become the stock reply: 'Today, however, the main trouble is not a limitation of the amount of available bank credit, but the reluctance of acceptable borrowers to come forward' (Cmd 3897, 1931, p.131). The Macmillan Committee confirmed the idea that domestic currency management could no longer be 'automatic' but had to be placed under the authority of the Bank of England, which it went out of its way to praise for its ready acceptance of evolutionary changes: 'It would not be a true picture to portray new and lively elements of contemporary thought . . . held down by the weight of conservatism of the Bank of England.' That whitewash soon wore off.

Externally, said the report with undeniable evidence, the rules of the gold standard game were not being adhered to. Countries which like the USA had received large amounts of gold neutralized the normal effects on their price levels, while that traditionally large hoarder of gold, France, had set the value of its currency at too low a standard when compared with the pound, as had a number of other countries including Belgium, Japan, Germany and Italy, so making it much harder for British exports to compete, and also making it necessary for the Bank of England to try to maintain much larger gold reserves than had been necessary in the days when London alone was the predominant world financial centre. Nevertheless the Macmillan majority report stubbornly rejected devaluation, which would be 'a shock to our international credit'. Perhaps its most notoriously confident pronouncement concerned the role of bank rate: 'There is no doubt that Bank rate policy is an absolute necessity for the sound management of a monetary system, and that it is a most delicate and beautiful instrument for the purpose.' The report was published in June 1931; in a few months Britain went off gold and in June 1932 threw bank rate into the dustbin for twenty years.

This is yet another vivid illustration of the suddenness of the swing of the pendulum from one extreme position of excessive reverence of a key feature of monetary theory and practice to the opposite extreme of complete dismissal. There are few things more impressive than the haughty analytical certainty with which fundamental theories of money are for a time almost universally held, only to be discarded in favour of a diametrically opposite but equally firmly and widely held new orthodoxy which in turn lasts until the whole process reverses itself suddenly a generation or so later. It is this process of polarized change which is the long-term constant in the history of money, the points of change naturally occurring during short periods of such obvious crisis in monetary affairs that thoroughgoing investigations by the monetary authorities take place accompanied by an intensification of theoretical discussion by economists and others such as financial journalists, and even by the usually reticent body of bankers. Born of the crisis, new monetary practices come quickly into being, accompanied at a rather more leisurely pace by the appropriate theories which rule until the next crisis or series of crises cause a reverse swing in the whole process. Going off gold, discarding the folklore of bank rate, changing from dear money to cheap money, from free trade to protection, and from perfect competition towards monopoly marked the beginning of the revolutionary and more general change from classical to Keynesian economics in the 1930s. Together these constitute one of the clearest examples of a number of such dramatically polarized changes during the headlong course of the twentieth century partly caused by and largely reflected in public attitudes towards monetary theories and practices.

'In recent years,' wrote Keynes, with untypical understatement, 'most people have become dissatisfied with the way in which the world manages its monetary affairs' (1930, II, 405). By 1936 Keynes was beginning to convince the world that 'the characteristics . . . assumed by the classical theory happen not to be those of the economic society in which we actually live, with the result that its teaching is misleading and disastrous if we attempt to apply it' (1936, 3). When the gold standard was dethroned – by accident not design – the traditional importance which monetary policy occupied in classical theory was also demoted, not to be restored for forty years, during most of which Keynesian concepts (not necessarily quite the same as Keynes's concepts) were to hold sway.

The trigger which led to the end of Britain's attempt to maintain the gold standard was the failure of the Austrian Creditanstalt Bank in June 1931, which led on to the failure of a number of German banks and started a new wave of 'hot money' around the world's financial centres. The heightened volatility of such large deposits meant that gold reserves which in pre-1914 days would have seemed ample were now plainly inadequate, while money intent on finding security was much less sensitive to high bank rates than formerly. The City's deposits were much more vulnerable to political fears, including antipathy to Britain's Labour government, which since its election in 1929 had seemed to the bankers to be too weak to take the tough measures deemed essential to cure its poor balance of trade and its unbalanced budget. The Macmillan report, at an unfortunately critical moment, had exposed the dangerous extent to which Britain's reserves were dependent on short-term and therefore potentially volatile deposits. Fears on this account were increased by the government's hesitation in following the recommendations of the May report, published on 31 July 1931, for drastic cuts in expenditure on unemployment and public sector pay. Despite the Bank of England's success in borrowing £25 million from New York, and the same from Paris on 1 August, the external drain continued, partly because on that same day the Bank, with Treasury consent, had increased the fiduciary note issue by £15 million. Although this increase was intended only for the three weeks of the peak holiday season, it sparked fears of an inflationary trend that would push British prices still higher than those of the country's competitors.

The intensification of the crisis led to the fall of the Labour government and its replacement under the same Prime Minister, Ramsay MacDonald, by a 'National' government on 24 August. The new government managed to overcome the 'bankers' ramp' sufficiently to raise a new loan on 31 August of £80 million shared equally again between New York and Paris. An emergency budget on 8 September included among its economy measures drastic cuts in public sector pay.

A week later as a protest the lower ranks of three Royal Navy ships at Invergordon refused to muster, a reaction blazoned across the world as a 'mutiny'. The inevitable acceleration in the loss of the already low reserves of gold remaining led on 20 September to the official announcement of the decision 'to suspend for the time being the operation of the gold standard'. Ironically Norman was not involved in the decision to go off gold, for at the time he was sailing back from Canada. He even misinterpreted his Deputy Governor's cable – 'Old Lady goes off on Monday' – to be about his mother's holiday plans (A. Boyle 1967, 268). The necessary bill was passed on 21 September. With not a little understatement it was entitled 'The Gold Standard (*Amendment*) Act 1931', but this 'temporary amendment' turned out luckily to be a permanent abandonment. The gold shackles had been broken for ever. After an inevitable lag the new freedom to adopt a cheap money policy helped to give rise to a steady recovery of economic activity. The forces which led to this momentous decision are fully analysed by (among others) Professor Moggridge in *The Return to Gold 1925* (1969) and its results followed through in his study of *British Monetary Policy 1924–31* (1972). The policies of the period remain highly controversial, rekindled by the ERM crises of the 1990s.

Cheap money in recovery, war and reconstruction, 1931–1951

The banks were able to cope successfully with the dramatic change from dear to cheap money despite the onset of the world depression because of their structure and mode of operation. Unlike the still localized, regional banks in the USA and Europe, British banks had become strong national monopolies and confined their lending almost entirely to short-term, liquid loans. Thus British banks did not fail, despite widespread industrial failure. So far as the general public were concerned during the inter-war period the 'Big Five' referred not so much to the great powers that emerged victorious from the great war but rather Barclays, Lloyds, Midland, National Provincial and Westminster banks, which had completed their amalgamation conquests during the war and emerged to control some two-thirds of the total bank deposits of the country, which in 1918 came to £1,500 million. The 115 banks of 1900 had fallen to half that number by 1918 and to thirty-six by 1930 when the Big Five controlled over 70 per cent of total deposits. By 1939 that proportion had risen to well over three-quarters of the then total deposits of £2,200 million. The market share of total deposits in the hands of the Big Five was at least maintained, if not indeed increased, during the twenty years of cheap money, for in

December 1951 the Big Five still accounted for nearly 80 per cent of total UK bank deposits. Their monopolistic power had been increased despite considerable opposition.

This opposition first showed itself in any prominence as early as March 1918 when the government set up a Treasury Committee under Lord Colwyn. Its Report on Bank Amalgamations (Cd 9052, 1 May 1918) recommended that, 'because of the exceptional extent to which the interests of the whole community depend on the banks', legislation should be introduced to limit amalgamation and to restrict interlocking directorships. Next year a bill to that effect was introduced much to the disgust of the bankers who 'felt that the mere fact of special legislation, apparently based on the assumption that the Banks are a danger to the nation, is a slur upon them which they are in no way conscious of having deserved' (Sayers 1976, I, 236). The bill was withdrawn and a compromise reached in the 'Treasury Agreement' of December 1919 by which the banks were to refer any proposed amalgamation to the Treasury. It was assumed that no amalgamation would be allowed between big banks, but that smaller bank mergers would in general still be permitted. In fact some twenty-five mergers took place between 1919 and the end of 1951, mostly of quite small banks, and it was not until the 1960s that the basic assumption of the Treasury Agreement against permitting the large banks to merge with each other was again called into question. By then new forms of competition were emerging to challenge the monopolistic structure of British banking and to change its banking practices from those that had shown themselves most clearly during the twenty years of cheap money to be basically risk-averse and industry-shy.

There were however some notable exceptions to British bankers' aloof attitude towards medium- and long-term lending, all the more significant and surprising because of the lead taken in this innovatory process by none other than Montagu Norman. As early as 1925 he encouraged the establishment of the United Dominions Trust to provide hire purchase facilities for industry. In 1928 Norman persuaded all the big banks (except the Midland) to join with the Bank of England in providing capital to set up the Agricultural Mortgage Corporation, so that long-term mortgages, eventually of up to thirty years, could be made to help tenants purchase their farms. The Bank helped to set up the Securities Management Trust in 1929, the Bankers' Industrial Development Company in 1930 and, in 1934, as an immediate response to the suggestions of the Macmillan Committee, Credit for Industry, to supply the capital needs of small firms. Norman helped vigorously in the 'rationalization' of the engineering, shipbuilding, cotton and steel industries. Because of its importance in the defence industry, Armstrong-Whitworth, long-time customers of the Bank, were helped to merge with Vickers in the early 1930s. The Bank arranged a loan of £150,000 for Fairfields Shipbuilding Company in 1933, followed by further assistance to Cunard which, after absorbing the troubled White Star Line, went on to build the *Queen Mary* and the *Queen Elizabeth*. In the rationalization of the steel industry the Bank helped to modernize Stewarts and Lloyds at Corby, GKN & Baldwin at Cardiff, and most notably enabled Richard Thomas at Ebbw Vale to complete by 1938 Britain's first continuous strip sheet steel mill.

Professor Clay showed that Norman was motivated by a desire to forestall more direct government intervention in industry – rationalization was a preferred alternative to nationalization. He also makes a valiant but unconvincing case that the Bank was simply extending its traditional role of acting as lender of last resort from the banking sphere to industry (1957, 359). A more correct interpretation is probably that given by Professor Sayers who described 'the intrusion of the Bank into the problems of industrial organisation' as 'one of the oddest episodes in its history: entirely out of character with all previous development of the Bank' (1976, I, 314). There can be little doubt that Norman's most unusual but warmly welcomed initiatives played a vital role in re-equipping the engineering, steel and shipbuilding industries to face the unprecedented military challenges soon to burst upon them in September 1939, and thus to make some significant if exceptional recompense for British mainstream bankers' reluctant attitude towards lending for industrial development. Before dealing with the benefits of cheap money in wartime it is necessary first to see how cheap money helped to lift the burden of the national debt and stimulated the housing drive over considerable, if patchy, areas of Britain; both features which contributed to the general economic recovery of the country in the 1930s.

If economists view the inter-war national debt as a 'burden' it is not because it is created by one generation and carried by posterity, but rather from the fact that it is carried inequitably and unevenly by a posterity divided into a relatively few, usually rich, dividend receivers on the one hand and the majority of relatively poorer taxpayers on the other hand. Such burdens and benefits are not evenly cancelled out and are subject to quite arbitrary alteration because of changes in the general level of prices, with the majority of relatively poor taxpayers being particularly penalized by deflations – such as that which occurred in the 1920s. This caused the government to set up a Committee on National Debt and Taxation, in March 1924, under Lord Colwyn. The committee's rather dismal report appeared three years later (Cmd 2800, 1927), and while the thirteen members of the committee were in broad agreement as to the heavy burden of the debt, they were in dispute as to whether such a burden was likely to fall (if prices rose), or to rise still further (if prices continued to fall). The majority, despite the contrary evidence of Keynes, believed that it would all come right in the end, especially because in some strange way they believed the gold standard would help to raise prices. 'If the course of history were any guide, prices were certain to rise, and as far as can be judged . . . the future level of prices will be higher' (para. 741).

The four signatories of the minority report were less optimistic, and after showing how the annual service costs of the national debt had risen from 10 per cent of total revenue in 1913 to 39 per cent in 1925 and 38 per cent in 1926 (and thus confirmed the popular estimate that the payment of interest on the debt cost a million pounds for every working day), concluded that 'Expenditure upon new enterprises such as assistance to housing schemes, and on the development of existing services, such as education, is inevitably restricted' (Cmd 2800 356–8). This was an early, painful, example of public sector investment being crowded out.

Events were to prove that it was the fall, not the maintenance, of the gold standard that enabled the burden of the debt to be alleviated. As soon as the major part of the £130 million of the foreign debt borrowed in a vain attempt to support the gold standard had been repaid, the Bank of England was able to bring short-term rates down, confirmed as we have seen by fixing bank rate at 2 per cent in June 1932. Long-term rates, much more important than short-term rates insofar as investment in physical resources was concerned, could not be brought down so long as investors could, without any risk, earn high returns from government stock. The 'Great Conversion' of over £2,000 million loan stock from 5 per cent to 3½ per cent, successfully arranged by the Bank of England in July 1932, was therefore of critical importance in laying the foundations for the house-building boom of the 1930s which itself was the leading sector in the general economic recovery. Cheap money thus arose by accident rather than by design, but having been born, the policy was, with just one hiccup, vigorously sustained for a generation, with results that were more than coincidentally beneficial (see Nevin, 1953 and Moggridge 1972).

The reduction of the rate paid on consols, combined with the dampening effect of the world slump on investing abroad, diverted British savings into physical investment within Britain to build new houses and factories for the newer industries. The building societies took full advantage of the new situation provided by cheap and ample money. The annual total of new houses built in Britain jumped from 220,000 for the four years 1929–32 inclusive to around 350,000 for each of the five years 1933–8. The fall in the birth rate coupled with a fall in construction costs increased the *effective* demand for houses just when the supply of funds was being substantially increased. Competition among the numerous building societies – they numbered 1,026 in 1930 – caused them to lend a higher proportion of the cost of a house and to increase the repayment period. As a result the length of the average mortgage rose from twelve years in 1933 to sixteen years in 1938. Three-quarters of these new houses were privately owned (except in Scotland where over two-thirds of its inter-war housing was built by local authorities). The bulk of this construction, together with the multiplier effects (contemporaneously being expounded by Kahn and Keynes), took place in the Midlands, London and the South-East where most of the new, light industries were being established. On the other hand an emerging regional policy was already trying to divert some of this expansion to the 'Special Areas' of the North and West even before the Barlow Report of the Royal Commission on the Geographical Distribution of the Industrial Population (Cmd 6153, 1940) and the Luftwaffe's bombs speeded up the process in the 1940s. For the first time in centuries official policy was attempting, however weakly, to oppose the centripetal market pull of the City of London. It is also significant that the many hundreds of building societies widely spread over the regions had, quite unlike the monopolistic banks, resisted the pull of London, so that the societies' savings were for the most part invested locally rather than centrally (Davies 1981).

While cheap money stimulated the building societies it almost led to the complete bankruptcy of London's discount houses. The severe slump in international trade and new methods of cabled bank transfers drastically cut the volume of commercial bills, while the government's determination ever since the publication of the Cunliffe Report, reinforced by a similar recommendation in the Colwyn Report (para. 102), to reduce the volume of the floating debt to as low as possible caused a similarly sharp reduction in the supply of Treasury bills. The reduced supply of bills during this inter-war 'bill famine' was eagerly fought for, not only by the various discount houses but also increasingly by the big powerful banks for, given the depressed state of industry, they had ample liquid funds available. After bank rate was reduced to 2 per cent they squeezed the houses even more strongly. The competition grew so cutthroat that the Treasury bill rate during much of 1934 was brought down to ⅓ per cent – indeed to take the extreme case the rate was forced down to ⅛ per cent – and this at a time when the banks were reluctant to lend the call money on which the houses depended for buying the bills at any rates below 1 per cent.

To prevent the threatened wholesale bankruptcy of the discount houses, which were considered by the authorities to be vital for the health of the monetary system, a series of cartel agreements was arranged by the banks, the houses, the Treasury and the Bank of England (the latter two sometimes actively conniving and at other times benevolently looking the other way). The salient features of the resulting 'syndicated tender system', finally agreed in 1935, were, first, that the banks would henceforth not compete for newly-issued Treasury bills nor purchase any less than one week old, thus allowing rates to rise. Secondly, the houses would no longer compete against each other for new bills but would jointly tender for the Treasury's weekly issue at a prearranged price and distribute the total among themselves according to a prearranged quota. This was again a move calculated to raise the rate above bankruptcy level. In practice these two conditions came in time to lead to a third feature, namely that the houses would agree to bid for the whole of the bills on offer (to 'cover the tender'). In the 1930s this latter condition was of no consequence in view of the small amounts of such issues, but it became of more importance later. A fourth feature was the agreement of the banks to support the houses in their new policy of dealing in short-term government bonds by lending to the houses on the security of such bonds at a rate of 1 per cent. In this way the discount market came increasingly to be a bond market, a fact which was to be of great benefit to official war and post-war finance. This system was in full working order in 1935 (not 1938 as stated by the Radcliffe Report), and thus well tried and tested before the demands of war had to be met.

In the 1930s three roughly distinct financial trading regions or 'blocs' emerged: the sterling area, the dollar area and the franc area. When sterling went off gold, almost all those countries which carried on the lion's share of their trade with Britain followed Britain off gold – otherwise they would have priced their goods out of the large market which Britain provided. These countries included all the Commonwealth (except Canada), Ireland, the Scandinavian countries, Egypt, Iraq, Portugal and Siam (Thailand), and a number of South American countries like Argentina. The dollar area comprised most of the two American continents, while the franc bloc comprised France and most of Europe south of the Scandinavian countries. Generally speaking, by going off gold or otherwise resorting to devaluation a country cheapens its exports and makes its imports dearer, thereby increasing employment in its own country but reducing employment abroad. Retaliation would lead to successive rounds of this 'beggar-my-neighbour' policy, resulting, in the classic example of the 1930s, in an intensification of the slump. This led to calls, especially by the League of Nations, for more sensible policies, in particular a greater emphasis on finding new ways of currency stabilization in place of the eroded gold standard.

Quite apart from the need to avoid the nonsense of competitive devaluation, some relative stability of rates of exchange was necessary to restore business confidence in order for international trade to recover from the depths to which it had sunk in the early 1930s. As early as April 1932, after the pound had fallen to $3.45, an Exchange Equalization Account was set up by the Treasury and was further strengthened in September 1936 when, in conjunction with the devaluation of the franc and its departure from gold, the UK, USA and French governments established their Tripartite Agreement. They promised to co-operate in achieving the greatest possible equilibrium in the system of international exchanges by mutually supporting each other's currencies. They did at any rate manage to limit the degree of fluctuation between the currencies of the three blocs, which comprised by far the greater part of international payments, and so helped to lift world trade from the abysmal depths to which it had fallen in 1933. The Exchange Equalization Account was further strengthened in 1939 on the eve of war when the vast bulk of Britain's gold reserves were transferred to it in order to enable it to maintain the 1939 rate of $4.03 throughout the war. The slump of 1929–33 had been the worst in economic history, yet despite its devastating effects on the 'special areas', Britain came through it rather better than did most countries. The causes and extent of Britain's recovery still remain matters of considerable controversy, ranging from the optimistic assessment given by H. W. Richardson in his stimulating portrait of *Economic Recovery in Britain 1932–39* (1967) to the brilliantly-written but depressing picture painted by Corelli Barnett in his book *The Audit of War: The Illusion of Britain as a Great Nation* (1986). Whatever might be said of other industries or of our armed forces, it was undoubtedly true that Britain's financial institutions were well prepared for the exigencies of total war.

Despite its peacetime benefits, for one brief moment on the eve of the war it looked as if cheap money might be abandoned. Bank rate was raised from 2 to 4 per cent on 24 August 1939. However, unlike the situation of August 1914, the City showed not the slightest sign of panic when war was declared on 3 September 1939. Consequently bank rate was quickly reduced to 3 per cent on 28 September and back again to its customary 2 per cent on 26 October, where it was to remain throughout the war and beyond. Thanks in part to the selective adoption of Keynesian policies, Britain was to run a 'three per cent war' – or less, as we shall see – in contrast to the 5 per cent or more of the First World War.

By the beginning of the Second World War Keynes's ideas had already so permeated Whitehall and Westminster that high interest rates were rejected as unnecessary, costly and perverse. Keynes was a member of an expert committee, chaired by Lord Stamp, which on 20 July 1939 submitted to the authorities a report on Defence Expenditure and Financial Problems. It is clear that it was Keynes who stiffened the committee's determination to adhere to really cheap money, which could readily be achieved if backed up by financial controls on capital issues and on foreign exchange, and by physical controls like the rationing of food, clothes and other essentials. However in the crucial matter of a cheap-money war, the men of action, those with the primary responsibility, particularly the Governor of the Bank of England, the Prime Minister and the Chancellor of the Exchequer, were already convinced by the experience of the First World War that dear money should be avoided if at all possible. The experience of successfully managing cheap money since 1932 convinced them that it was perfectly feasible. The City and the establishment had now also in practice become, reluctantly and despite themselves, converted to Keynesianism (Sayers 1956, 143–6). With just a few unimportant exceptions, 3 per cent became in fact the *maximum* rate at which the government borrowed within the United Kingdom.

The government was able to perform this remarkable feat by adopting a variety of devices additional to those physical and financial controls just mentioned. First, the British Bankers' Association agreed to the government's request that as from July 1940 they should refuse to offer the public a higher rate than 1 per cent for deposits, thus removing at a stroke the government's most powerful competitor for short-term funds. Secondly, all government departments with excess funds used them as necessary to purchase appropriate forms of government debt, so helping to keep their prices up and of course their rates of interest down. Similarly Treasury bills were made available 'on tap' not only to UK government departments as previously, but also to overseas monetary authorities etc., thus both extending, and smoothing the market for short-term debt. Thirdly, the government was careful not to swamp the market with excessively large loans all at one go, but issued them in more reasonable sizes at fairly regularly spaced out intervals with similarly spaced maturities to appeal to different segments of the market, and then going on to place longer-term debt virtually 'on tap' to the general public. Fourthly, the government's marketing of all kinds of savings, from the very small individual sums garnered by the National Savings Movement to the huge amounts available from the large financial institutions, was ably assisted by its control of the propaganda machine. Fifthly, the government began a system of borrowing directly from the banks through Treasury Deposit Receipts (rather than having to rely on indirect borrowing via issues of Treasury bills bought first by the discount houses). The TDR, introduced in June 1940, was a non-negotiable receipt deposited in a bank against a six-month loan to the government at a fixed (and low) rate of 1⅛ per cent. To a large extent the TDR supplemented the Treasury bill and grew to a peak of £2,186 million in August 1945, representing 41.4 per cent of total bank assets. Sixthly, the discount houses were encouraged by the Bank of England to amalgamate and to strengthen their capital bases to enable them to act much more substantially than before as dealers in bonds. By such means the liquidity of government debt as a whole was considerably improved and hence made more saleable initially and more attractive to the holder in general. Thus the government, as by far the largest borrower, had by means of what the layman would call a policy of divide and rule, and what the economist would call acting as a discriminating monopolist, perfected a remarkably cheap and efficient system of financing the war.

The internal national debt rose from £7,245 million in March 1939 to £23,745 million in April 1945. The bulk of this increase of £16,500 million was raised as follows: £2,800 million of Savings Bonds with maturities of from twenty to thirty years at 3 per cent; £3,500 million of War, Defence and Exchequer Bonds (five to ten years) at rates from 2½ per cent to 1¾ per cent; £4,000 million of small savings (POSB, NSB, TSB etc) at 2½ per cent; £2,000 million of Treasury Deposit Receipts (six months) at 1⅛ per cent; and £3,500 million of Treasury bills (three months) at 1 per cent. The general pattern is clearly one where the more liquid the maturity, the lower the rate of interest. The key to the structure was the stabilization of the Treasury bill rate at 1 per cent. This was achieved through the Bank of England being willing to repurchase bills at that rate. This was its so-called 'open back door' policy. Thus actual short-term rates were usually very much lower than the formal, front door bank rate of 2 per cent might lead one to assume. The weighted average even of the funded debt is nearer to 2½ rather than 3 per cent, while if, as it should be, the floating debt is included, then the average rate for the total internal debt is *less than 2¼ per cent*.

To call it a 'three per cent war' is an exaggeration which undervalues the success of the new policy: a 'two per cent war' would be a truer description than the label historians have generally attached to it, for 3 per cent was the maximum rather than the average rate. The most grievously costly war in history, in real, human terms was thus financed by incredibly cheap money.

The financial lessons of all previous wars had been 'the more you borrow, the higher the rate'. The revolution in economic thought led by Keynes had helped the government to borrow far more money than ever before at rates of interest far lower than ever before in such circumstances. If the Keynesian miracle could work with war finance, then perhaps with the return of peace the doctrines of his *General Theory of Employment, Interest and Money* could combine with those of the Beveridge Plan to bring in the brave new world of full employment and the welfare state. Unfortunately, accompanying these benefits there was a third partner – inflation, an unwelcome cuckoo in the nest, barely noticed in the beginning, but which was to grow later to threaten full employment and limit the subsidies on which the welfare state depended. Before turning to examine the relationship between internal inflation and the ultra-cheap money of the immediate post-war years it is necessary first to look briefly at how Britain's external wartime deficit was financed, for this too had profound consequences on subsequent monetary policy.

Britain's external wartime expenditures were financed in three main ways. First by the sale of British investments abroad, which brought in goods to the value of £1,100 million. Secondly, purchases made in the sterling area were credited by the build up of 'sterling balances' in London which amounted to £3,000 million. Thirdly, American Lease-Lend, which began in March 1941 and was intensified when the USA was herself forced to enter the war after the Japanese attack on Pearl Harbor in December 1941. This vital source of food and war material was ended with brutal suddenness by President Truman on 20 August 1945, without prior consultation with Britain. Keynes's last major service to Britain was to negotiate in the following months the Anglo-American Loan of some $4.4 billion for fifty years at around 1.6 per cent. The rate was generous enough, but the conditions attached to the loan with regard especially to the convertibility of sterling and non-discrimination in trade were very soon shown to be as impossible to fulfil as Keynes had prophesied. These problems, plus the overhang of the huge sterling balances, much of which was kept in very liquid form, bedevilled financial and fiscal policy for at least a decade after the war, thwarting a war-weary nation's desire for a rapid reduction in taxation and contributing substantially to the massive total debt, much of which was actually or potentially highly liquid. Part of the cost of keeping rates of interest so low was this inevitable counterpart of far too much potential money chasing the post-war scarcity of goods in Britain and even more so in Europe, channelling world demand in an unsustainable rush to America. After barely a month of premature freedom, restrictions on sterling convertibility had to be reimposed when the various Orders in Council were consolidated into the Exchange Control Act 1947. The dollar drain brought convertibility to an abrupt end (Bell 1956, 55).

Meanwhile a seemingly grossly ungrateful electorate replaced Winston Churchill with Clement Attlee as Prime Minister. Attlee's government, keen to nationalize the 'commanding heights' of the economy, had strong memories of the deflationary bias of the Bank of England at the time of mass unemployment between the wars and of the 'bankers' ramp' that contributed to their losing the 1931 election. It is not without significance therefore that the Bank of England became the first post-war institution to be nationalized. In practical economic terms this was an unnecessary gesture, for the Bank had in the last resort almost always been under governmental control, as had been demonstrated most plainly when Lloyd George forced Cunliffe to cave in to Bonar Law in the First World War. Yet the Bank of England Act 1946 made this power much more explicit, particularly in its double-barrelled directives contained in clause 4: (a) 'The Treasury may ... give such directions to the Bank as, after consultation with the Governor, they think necessary in the public interest'; and (b) 'The Bank may request information from and make recommendations to bankers, and may, if so authorised by the Treasury, issue directions to any banker.' Although these directives have never been used – and have been overtaken and strengthened by later legislation – the threat they posed strengthened the power of the monetary authorities over the financial sectors of the economy, at least in the short run. However, as the Labour Chancellor of the Exchequer, Dr Hugh Dalton, was about to learn, the government's power to influence the City's longer-run expectations remained much more limited than he imagined, despite his apparently newly extended powers of control over the monetary system.

Having nationalized the 'citadel of capitalism', the Labour government was determined to demonstrate its power over the rate of interest also, by introducing its 'ultra-cheap money policy'. As well as cutting the cost of servicing the huge national debt, Dalton claimed his policy would benefit the local authorities, industry at large and the

British Commonwealth as a whole. So much depended on the success of this policy. He started to work first on short-term rates and soon achieved his aims. In October 1945 the Bank of England raised the price at which it would purchase Treasury bills (by its 'open back door') sufficiently to reduce the rate of discount from its wartime 1 per cent to a record fixed low of ½ per cent, so helping to bring down the whole range of associated short-term rates. Those dealers and investors seeking higher rates naturally bought Consols, the price of which – assisted also by governmental purchases – rose to par by October 1946. Dalton took advantage of this to issue nearly £500 million of Treasury 2½ per cent stock (1975) thus apparently signalling his success in bringing the long-term rate of interest down also. However this rate was unsustainable. Fears that the price of securities would fall from these unnatural peaks stimulated a wave of selling. For the first six months of 1947 departmental purchases absorbed these sales, but at the cost of a rapid increase in the public's bank balances. The national debt was being monetized at a rate where even the Labour government, previously expecting a post-war deflation, became frightened of its inflationary consequences. The final blow, in the shape of the convertibility crisis of August 1947 caused the government to give up its attempt to hold down the long-term rate – but it continued with its ultra-cheap short rates, based on a Treasury bill rate of ½ per cent, until it left office in 1951.

At that time there was no belief in either the need or the efficacy of a restrictive monetary policy in restraining inflation. The wartime faith in planning rose in fervour under the socialist government so as to push monetary policy into abject subservience. The dollar shortage, which had quickly ended the abortive experiment in convertibility in August 1947, was temporarily relieved during 1948 and early 1949 by America's generous help to Europe in the form of Marshall Aid (or the European Recovery Programme). Britain's gold and dollar reserves were insufficient to support sterling at the overvalued rate of $4.03 fixed during the war, and again confirmed in the post-war agreement with the International Monetary Fund. Intensified speculation against the pound in late summer 1949 forced the government to devalue sterling on 18 September from $4.03 to $2.80. This large downward step of a 30 per cent devaluation was considered necessary to put beyond doubt Britain's ability to defend the new rate. It sparked off the most extensive and rapid realignment of exchange rates – in the form of a devaluation by almost all the rest of the world against the dollar – ever carried out up till then. For Britain the success of such devaluation depended on the extent to which foreign consumers (especially in America) increased their purchases of goods and services from Britain and the rest of the sterling area, plus the extent to which the latter curtailed its dollar expenditures. In more technical terms, the success of devaluation depends to a considerable degree on the sum of the elasticities of demand for traded and tradeable goods and services after allowing for the short-term disadvantages of the change (in the form of the initial J-curve effect). It turned out that the devaluation was only a partial success. The initial difficulties were quickly overcome, the medium-term results were good, but the longer-term results were overridden by the effects of the Korean war on the volume and terms of trade between the USA and the sterling area. At any rate, the forced devaluation of 1949 had enabled Britain to make the fundamental readjustment in its exchange rate required to reflect the true state of its war-weakened economy and to set the new level at a rate where it could again build up its reserves and act once more as a long-term lender to the sterling area. Throughout the five post-war years no recourse had been made to the part that might be played by higher interest rates in managing the economy. Renewed inflationary pressures following the outbreak of the Korean war in June 1950, followed by the fall of the Labour government in October 1951, offered the Conservative government under Churchill an opportunity to reassess the role of monetary policy in a Keynesian world, particularly when the fourth of the post-Second World War series of roughly biennial crises duly turned up in late 1951.

The new Chancellor of the Exchequer, R. A. Butler, signalled his intention of reviving monetary policy by raising bank rate to 2½ per cent in November 1951 – and to 4 per cent in March 1952. Thus bank rate policy, virtually unused for twenty years was back into flexible operation. It was then changed seventeen times between November 1951 and December 1960. At last it appeared that the era of Keynesian cheap money had officially ended. This was true only to a very limited degree. To the consternation of the Conservatives, monetary policy, despite the restoration of classical techniques, did not seem to work any more; if anything it worked perversely. In truth, far from monetary policy regaining its classical importance and replacing Keynesianism, it was to remain subservient to Keynesian-based policy-making for another twenty-five years, right up to 1976. Little wonder that the trend of inflation rose decade after decade.

Inflation and the integration of an expanding monetary system,
1951–1973

A general perspective on unprecedented inflation, 1934–1990
It is a remarkable fact that the general level of prices in Britain rose
continuously every year from 1934 up to 1990. Moreover, until the deep
depression of 1990–3, there was little sign that this persistent inflation,

Index of prices
with 1935 = 100

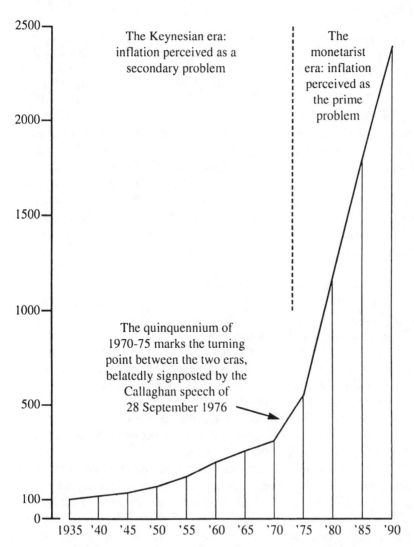

Figure 8.1. Fifty-five years of continuous inflation, 1935–1990.

Table 8.1 Index of retail prices 1935 to 1990*: a non-stop escalator.

Year	Index	Quinquennial inflation %	Year	Index	Quinquennial inflation %
1935	100	–	1965	279.4	11.7
1940	121.5	21.5	1970	344.7	12.3
1945	141.2	16.2	1975	587.3	70.4
1950	160.4	13.6	1980	1200.2	104.4
1955	207.1	12.9	1985	1760.5	46.7
1960	238.4	11.5	1990	2277.0	29.3

*Constructed from: (a) Cost of Living Index 1935–47; (b) Interim Index of Retail Prices 1947–56; (c) Index of Retail Prices 1956–90 – all rebased with 1935 = 100. Quinquennial inflation measures the rise in prices over the five years to the date given.

unprecedented in British history, was likely to end in sustainably stable prices. Even moderate rates of inflation if they persist for decades can lead to startling results in drastically reducing the value of money and, inversely, raising the index of prices soaringly above its starting baseline. Thus the figures given in table 8.1 and illustrated in figure 8.1 show that prices in 1990 were in general more than twenty times as high as in the mid-1930s. They also show that this 55-year period of continuous inflation divides itself into two sections; the first from 1935 to the early 1970s, during which period though the trend was upwards, inflation remained moderate compared with the surge in rates during the second period from the mid-1970s to 1990. For most of the first period, governments persisted in pursuing Keynesian-type policies – until the 25 per cent inflation of 1975 caused even a Labour government, at the insistence of the IMF but against the outspoken opposition of the trade unions, to attempt to adopt monetarist policies. However even after more than a decade of such policies the average annual rate of inflation exceeded the average of the Keynesian years from 1935 to 1970. The monetarist medicine not only failed to eradicate the Keynesian virus; in actual fact, with the admittedly glaring exception of the mid-1970s, monetarism was far less successful than Keynesianism in curbing inflation up to the early 1990s.

Measuring inflation in five-year intervals not only smooths out the irregularities of exceptional or unrepresentative years, such as the record low rates of around 1 per cent achieved (because of a 20 per cent fall in basic import prices) in 1958 and 1959, and the record high rates of 24 to 25 per cent achieved (following Latin American-type wage increases) in the mid-1970s, but also enables one to appreciate and compare more easily the underlying inflationary pressures of different periods. Figure 8.1 clearly demonstrates the sharp turning-point in the 1970–5 quinquennium between the Keynesian and monetarist eras, while table 8.1 shows that the average rates of inflation in the two halves of the 1980s, at over 45 per cent and around 30 per cent respectively, when hard-headed Thatcherite policies ruled, were two to three times higher than the average rates existing from 1945 to 1970, when 'soft' Keynesian policies predominated. Keynesianism was more deep-rooted in Britain and took longer to be eradicated than elsewhere. Thus the UK's long-term inflationary record stands in markedly poor contrast with most of the competing countries. Between 1957 and 1992 annual percentage inflation in the Group of Seven major economies was as follows: Germany 3.4; USA 4.7; Japan 4.9; Canada 5.0; France 3.4; USA 4.7; UK 7.2; Italy 8.5, (M. King 1993, 269). Table 9.3 enables a more detailed comparison to be made with annual inflation rates in USA from 1950 to 1990. These long-run statistics underline Britain's lax anti-inflation record. Having thus outlined the basic facts of the unprecedentedly long age of persistent inflation from 1935 to 1990, we shall now look at the two eras, Keynesian and monetarist, separately.

Keynesian 'ratchets' give a permanent lift to inflation
Up to 1951 Britain's inflation could be excused as the inevitable consequence of war and immediate post-war difficulties. Compared with most other belligerents, Britain's inflation was very mild. Many European currencies had collapsed completely, the world record for inflation still being that of Hungary, where by July 1946 its 1931 gold pengo was equivalent to 130 trillion paper pengos. Such runaway inflations simply repeated post-First World War experience, and were so extreme that they were usually followed by thoroughgoing currency reforms. Britain, despite its infinitely milder inflation, was beginning to experience a new kind of long-run persistent inflation, in which price levels seemed to have lost their previous tendency to fall during cyclical recessions. Thus, when energy prices rose substantially (coal in the 1950s, oil in the 1970s), the general level of prices was pushed up, but failed to reverse itself when energy prices stabilized or even fell substantially. Part of the blame for this must be laid at the door of a defunct economist.

Although Keynes died in 1946, Keynesianism became more abundantly alive than ever. Keynesianism facilitated the godsend of full employment and encouraged the governmental management of money throughout most of the world. In so doing, it helped to build into national economic systems, at first unconsciously, a series of powerful inflationary ratchets whereby economic and socio-political forces act asymmetrically to raise, but hardly ever to reduce, the general level of prices. Each general price rise becomes, even if initiated by some temporary cause, consolidated into a basis for further increases, with the natural fluctuations in prices occurring above an inclined plane, the pitch of which, in Britain's case, turned steeply upwards in the early 1970s.

The Keynesian ratchets are of two main types, 'real' and 'financial'. The 'real' ratchets are mainly of the cost-push variety and include the inflationary effects of rising import prices and especially rising wages, both being of particular relevance to Britain, given its strong demand for imports and strong supply of unions. Together these explain why successive devaluations (and depreciations) were of little avail. Thus Harold Wilson's famous pronouncement, after the pound was again devalued, in November 1967, this time by 14 per cent from $2.80 to $2.40, that 'the pound in your pocket is not devalued' was soon rendered totally invalid when the import and wage ratchets combined to cause inflation to accelerate. By far the most pernicious and persistent ratchet has been the wages-and-pensions ratchet, with the increasing resort to index-linking effectively writing inflation into the constitution. For most of the Keynesian period Jack Jones, Secretary of the Transport and General Workers' Union, and other union leaders, had more effective control of Britain's money supply than did Lord O'Brien and other Governors of the Bank of England. Discussion of these other causes of inflation in any detail would take us too far away from our subject of money, though because they are directly linked with the value of money, it is imperative to recognize not only that inflation has powerful non-monetary causes (contrary to the beliefs of most monetarists) but also that to cure inflation requires supply-side measures as an essential complement to monetary policy.

Keynesianism was selectively based on those most influential works of Keynes which were written during the world's worst slump, a period of mass unemployment and savage deflation, when very naturally he ignored the inflationary effects of wage rises and welcomed rather than deprecated moderate inflation. In a neglected passage of his *General Theory of Employment* Keynes notes (quite correctly up to then) that 'full or even approximately full employment is of rare and short-lived occurrence'. But he then goes on more sanguinely to suggest that 'fluctuations tend to wear themselves out before proceeding to extremes and eventually to reverse themselves. The same is true of prices'. Still more optimistically he believed that 'Workers will not seek a much greater money-wage when employment improves' (1936, 250–1). Yet

Keynes goes on to give a warning, ignored by almost all Keynesians at great cost, that his observations concerned 'the world as it is or has been, and not a necessary principle which cannot be changed' (p.254). Thanks largely to Keynes's influence, full employment became long-lasting; but the wage ratchet which he gravely underestimated became even more long-lasting. Not only did the wage ratchet help to overthrow Keynesian policies, it also undermined much of the credibility of the apparently opposite policy of monetarism.

Keynes's repeated and trenchant attacks on saving and his encouragement of spending – by governments if private spending fell below the full employment level – gave yet another strong inflationary bias to post-war policy; while, following the universally welcomed implementation of the Beveridge Plan, welfare payments became not only massive in size but adjustable virtually upwards only. Given this fertile background, new financial institutions flourished and a large number of new financial instruments and methods were devised by new, and usually copied later, by well-established, institutions. Together these developments increased both the nominal amount of money and, through assisting its increased velocity, added still more to the country's effective money supply. Once a new monetary habit is adopted, e.g. an addiction to hire purchase, or an existing monetary instrument is given extended use, e.g. cheques issued by savings banks and building societies, thus widening the market, a permanent lift is given to the potential money supply, thus acting as a 'financial ratchet', more easily raised than reduced, although fluctuations around the new higher level will of course continue. Furthermore, while increases in the efficiency of a monetary system are to be welcomed, yet in circumstances where inflation is under way strongly enough to give an artificial boost to the financial sector, such developments, if uncontrolled, may add significantly to the ready availability of money and credit (bank credit being money) and so further increase the inflationary potential. Before turning to examine some of the more important of these developments in financial institutions we shall look first at the increased velocity of money, which both reflected and contributed to the inflation of the Keynesian era, and consider how these matters impinged on the most influential monetary report of the post-war period.

Although bank rate policy had been restored in 1951, experience in the following years cast doubt on its efficacy. A perplexed government set up in May 1957 a high-powered committee under Lord Radcliffe 'to inquire into the working of the monetary and credit system, and to make recommendations'. Shortly after it began to sit, another crisis intervened in September 1957, necessitating what contemporary opinion deemed a 'spectacular rise' in bank rate from 5 to 7 per cent and thus underlining the urgent need for the Radcliffian recommendations. The report (Cmnd 827), published in August 1959, marks the zenith of the Keynesian concept of broad liquidity and the nadir of any belief in the quantity theory of money, whether this is interpreted as the old-fashioned classical version or the re-emerging modern variant of Friedmanite monetarism. No official report has ever in British history (nor I believe elsewhere) shown such scepticism regarding monetary policy in the sense of trying to control the economy by controlling the quantity of money. By delaying for a decade or more serious consideration of the ways in which the supply of money could be controlled, one of the essential means of curbing inflation was thrown away. Warnings such as those given by the Institute of Economic Affairs in its polemic *Not Unanimous: A Rival to Radcliffe on Money* (Seldon 1960) were arrogantly ignored by the new establishment.

For a time the influence of the Radcliffe Report in Britain was all-pervading, so that it became fashionable for currently published economic textbooks to ignore the quantity theory even to the point, in one very popular text, of not mentioning the term at all. The fact that Milton Friedman in the USA had already by the mid-1950s powerfully restated the theory in modern form was completely ignored by Radcliffe, and in the few brief pages where any mention is made of the supply of money (there is no mention of the quantity theory as such) the treatment is negative and dismissive, e.g.

> If, it is argued, the central bank has both the will and the means to control the supply of money . . . all will be well. Our view is different. It is the whole liquidity position that is relevant to spending decisions . . . The decision to spend thus depends upon liquidity in the broad sense, not upon immediate access to money . . . *Spending is not limited by the amount of money in circulation.* (emphasis added; paras. 388–91).

The two main reasons why the report turned against the use of monetary policy as commonly understood were first the fact that money-substitutes abound in a modern economy, and secondly that any given quantity of money (even if it could be defined) could easily be increased in effect by simply using it more intensively, that is by increasing its velocity of circulation. In a key passage the report states: 'We cannot find any reason for supposing, or any experience in monetary history indicating, that there is any limit to the velocity of circulation' (para. 391). If that really were the case then all the world's trade could be carried on with a halfpenny.

In a highly developed financial system the theoretical difficulties of identifying 'the supply of money' cannot be lightly swept aside. Even when they are disregarded, all the haziness of the connection between the supply of money and the level of total demand remains: the haziness that lies in the impossibility of limiting the velocity of circulation. (para. 523)

It was for such reasons that they reached their astounding conclusion that monetary policy was secondary: 'We envisage the use of monetary measures as not in ordinary times playing other than a subordinate part in guiding the development of the economy' (para. 511).

It is perfectly true, as the Radcliffe and other official reports such as the First Report of the Council on Prices, Productivity and Incomes (1958), pointed out, that the velocity of circulation had increased steadily and substantially during the 1950s. Table 8.2 shows this trend with the velocity in 1947 at 1.64 rising each year to reach 2.68 in 1957. Expenditure had doubled even though the money supply had risen by

Table 8.2 The supply of money and its velocity, 1947–1957.*

Year	I Note circulation	II Net deposits London clearing [banks]	III Money supply (I+II)	IV Total domestic expenditure	V Velocity of circulation (IV÷III)
	£m	£m		£m	
1947	1351	5454	6805	11181	1.64
1948	1229	5703	6932	11837	1.71
1949	1238	5761	6999	12457	1.75
1950	1244	5800	7044	12911	1.83
1951	1291	5918	7209	14975	2.08
1952	1370	5844	7214	15644	2.17
1953	1462	6012	7474	16803	2.25
1954	1551	6225	7776	17721	2.28
1955	1657	6171	7828	19154	2.45
1956	1765	5998	7763	20296	2.61
1957	1828	6059	7887	21139	2.68
Increase % 1947–57	31.2	23.1	26.1	104.8	–

*Constructed from Council on Prices, Productivity & Incomes (HMSO 1958), appendix VIII.

only about a quarter. The traditional measure of money supply, banknotes plus net deposits in the London clearing banks, had thus grown only at a very moderate pace in pre-Radcliffian years and so the inflationary effect of the money side of the problem was underestimated because the contributions of the fringe financial institutions were either completely ignored or substantially overlooked as potential creators of money. Only the banks, it was thought, could create money; and in any case, in the Radcliffian view as we have seen, money supply did not matter very much at all – a view that was very widely held. Thus the Fourth Report on Prices, Productivity and Incomes, in making the glaringly obvious point that 'One outcome of inflation is the rise of prices' went on to make the Freudian slip that 'stopping this rise is not the main end of Policy' (HMSO 1961, 2–3). Nowhere do they refer to the need to control the money supply, even to complement their other and correctly diagnosed objectives of raising productivity and controlling demand and money incomes by fiscal means.

An attempt to draw attention to the inflationary contribution of the secondary banking institutions was made by the writer in November 1970 as follows:

> Corresponding to cost inflation ratchets such as those caused by the current wage explosion . . . are those monetary ratchets emanating largely from the dynamic financial fringe. These supply an elasticity in the provision of finance especially for borrowers initially rejected by traditional sources. The result is to increase the availability and efficiency of money supply over the long term, despite the slow growth of deposits in the traditional banking system . . . A flexible and discretionary monetary policy as part and parcel of a variety of other instruments of control – the Radcliffe package deal, but with the significant difference that money plays a much larger role – is therefore essential if inflation is to be curbed.

The writer added that belatedly the Bank of England had seen the necessity of widening its definition of money from M1 to M2 and M3; narrow, medium and wide. Furthermore, he noted that 'the wider the definition, the faster had been the growth exhibited over recent years. Thus between 1964 and 1969 M1 increased by 14 per cent, M2 by 25 per cent, while the dynamic M3 rose by 37 per cent. A large part of the fringe has (belatedly) arrived within the official definitions of money' (Davies 1971). Although the process, as shown later, had further to go, the belief that only the 'undoubted' banks could create money and thus inflation, had at long last been publicly discredited by the monetary authorities themselves by the end of the 1960s. Despite such growth in finance, gaps in credit persisted.

Filling the financial gaps

Like the poor, a fringe of unsatisfied borrowers is always with us, so that complaints of 'gaps' in the supply of credit are never-ending. Banks protect themselves by rationing the supply of credit that they themselves create, not only by raising the price, that is the rates of interest (and fees) they charge, but also and more commonly by simply refusing to lend to what they deem to be uncreditworthy borrowers. Only when reasonably viable sectors of the borrowing public are normally refused accommodation by banks can the case for the existence of a gap be justified. We have already seen how the Macmillan Committee in 1931 exposed the gap in medium-term finance for the smaller firm. The Radcliffe Committee in 1959 examined four alleged gaps in the finance available for the following sectors: agriculture; exports; research and development; and money transfer. With regard to agriculture, the committee was 'not able to reach the conclusion that there is any obvious and serious gap in the provision of credit' (para. 931). However with regard to exports the committee did find 'a gap in the capital market for debts between eight and twelve years' maturity' (para. 894). This gap existed despite the useful work done by the Export Credits Guarantee Department which had been set up under the Board of Trade in 1919. The gap had arisen partly because the ECGD, together with the other members of the Berne Union (or the International Export Credits Association), wished to show that it was 'taking a firm stand against demands for excessively long credits' (para. 888). The committee also feared that 'this country is not likely to be the main beneficiary of an international credit race' (para. 894). Nevertheless this gap was largely filled shortly thereafter by the scheme for refinancing private export debt set up by the Bank of England. Following its philosophy of reducing governmental involvement in business, ECGD was 'privatized' by the Thatcher government in 1990, using the merchant bank Samuel Montagu as the vehicle for the transfer.

The gaps facing small business tend to change over the years, with new gaps emerging and old gaps changing their guise. Thus although the Radcliffe Committee praised the achievements of such institutions as the Industrial and Commercial Finance Corporation (later called Investors in Industry and later still '3i') and the Finance Corporation for Industry, the committee remained strongly of the opinion that various gaps still existed and suggested that banks should provide 'term loans' for a fixed period of from five to about eight years. This advice was gradually followed (probably as much the result of aggressive competition by American banks as of the Radcliffe Report). The

Radcliffe Committee expressed particular concern that 'There are special problems about the provision of finance for the commercial development by small businesses and private companies of new inventions and innovations of technique' (para. 948). These might however be overcome 'by setting up an Industrial Guarantee Corporation with government backing' (para. 949). This view was strongly reinforced by the conclusions of the Bolton Enquiry into Small Firms which published its report in November 1971 after it had commissioned the Economists' Advisory Group to make a detailed examination of the 'Financial Facilities for Small Firms'. The EAG found an 'information gap' (p.191) which has been subsequently largely filled by the establishment of a network of Small Firms Advisory Centres. Yet the Bolton Report's recommendations appeared to be weak in the face of its own evidence. It rejected adopting the admittedly most successful model of the American Small Business Administration, and even at one point went as far as saying that 'There is now no gap corresponding to the famous Macmillan Gap' (p.188). Even so it could not escape the conclusion that

> We have found that small firms have suffered and still suffer a number of genuine disabilities, by comparison with larger firms, in seeking finance from external sources . . . What is required above all is an economic and taxation system which will enable individuals to acquire or establish new businesses out of personal resources and to develop these on the base of retained profits. Without this no institutional financing arrangements can preserve the small firm sector. (p.192)

Six years later the Wilson Committee which was set up to 'review the functioning of financial institutions' was however still so dissatisfied with the flow of finance to industry that it decided to make this the most urgent part of its inquiry and published the results in 1977 three years ahead of its main report. 'Whether or not the terms of finance are biased against small firms, there is an "information gap" for them: they do not know enough about the facilities that are available, and they often lack the skills that are needed in putting forward propositions for finance' (Wilson Report 1977, para. 144). Although the information gap has been partly filled, the gap in actual finance has, despite all previous efforts, re-emerged on such a scale as to worry the Bank of England. In its *Quarterly Bulletin* for February 1990 the Bank gave its view that

> A number of developments suggest that the gap might have widened in recent years. Two possible gaps have been identified: seed-corn capital and second-stage growth capital . . . While the industry disagrees on the extent

to which, if at all, there is a gap in the availability of second-stage growth capital in amounts of £100,000 to £250,000, there is considerable agreement that seed-corn capital of less than £100,000 is hard to obtain. (February 1990, p.82).

Gaps, like history, repeat themselves.

Undoubtedly the most successful result in filling one of the four Radcliffian gaps has been in the case of transfer payments or 'giro'. The committee were convinced that 'the experience of other countries suggests that some simple mechanism for transferring payments . . . would be an amenity which might be welcomed and used by the public in this country . . . a giro system operated by the General Post Office' (paras. 963–4). This recommendation, despite the fierce opposition of the banks, was accepted by Harold Wilson's Labour government, with the announcement by Mr Wedgwood Benn, the Postmaster General, on 21 July 1965, that a postal giro would be set up. It began operating from its Bootle headquarters in mid-1968. 'National Giro was the first public sector bank to be established in Britain for over a century and it was the first bank in the world to be set up from its beginnings so as to give a fully computerised nationwide service' (Davies 1973). Although it failed to equal the achievements of its continental counterparts or to reach the heights anticipated by its more euphoric supporters, National Giro, later called Girobank, widened its originally restricted services and was operating profitably within its first decade. Perhaps its most successful results have been achieved in its 'business deposit service', handling the cash, cheque and credit-card takings, mainly of retailers (which amounted to £39 billion in 1989 and £55 billion in 1992) and using these to dispense pension, unemployment and other social security payments via some 20,000 Post Office branches. After twenty-one years in the public sector it too was 'privatized' by the Thatcher government when, after a public auction in which a number of British and foreign banks showed some interest, it was eventually purchased by the Alliance and Leicester Building Society in July 1990 at a cost of £72.8 million, proving a large mouthful to swallow. It is notable as the first clearing bank to be bought by a building society. In short the giro had been a worthwhile public experiment, but it had been introduced too late to carve out the large and profitable market share of the kind enjoyed by the continental giros. By the time it came on the scene the clearing banks and the building societies were busily extending their custom among the working classes that giro had hoped to capture largely for itself.

Stronger competition and weaker credit control

In May 1971 the Bank of England issued a consultative document entitled 'Competition and Credit Control' the chief proposals of which, after taking into account the views of interested parties, were put into effect from September of that same year. Competition and Credit Control had two main objectives, first to stimulate strong but fairer competition among the various growing financial institutions, and secondly to provide an improved method by which the Bank of England and the Treasury could control the total amount of credit now being supplied by a wider range of institutions than just the traditional clearing banks. As it turned out, the banks and other financial institutions immediately swallowed the carrot of competition but skilfully evaded the cudgels of control – so much so that the controls had to be substantially strengthened to try to curb the so-called 'Secondary Banking Crisis' barely two and a half years later.

Prominent among the non-bank financial institutions were the finance houses. The contemporary Crowther Report on Consumer Credit, which was published in March 1971, showed that although the earliest of such houses had appeared in the mid-nineteenth century in order to finance the hire of coal wagons, their mushroom growth in Britain did not occur until after the Second World War and involved financing the supply of consumer durables such as furniture and furnishings, radios, televisions, washing machines, refrigerators and (of rapidly dominating importance) motor cars. 'Figures as high as 1,900 have been quoted for the total number of houses, but there appears to be about 1,000 active houses, the bulk of actual business being in the hands of less than a hundred', of which forty-one were members of the Finance Houses Association, while the majority of the dozen largest were subsidiaries of the banks (Crowther 1971, 866–7).

The inflationary power of hire purchase was made evident by the combination of rising discretionary incomes with the widely advertised financial facilities offered by the finance houses, and later, by the banks themselves. As a country's real income rises so its discretionary income rises by a greater proportion. Keynes had considered it to be a 'fundamental rule' that it was savings that increased more than proportionally as incomes increased; but now, with the increased importance of hire purchase, with substantial annual increases in wages, and with the safety of the welfare state umbrella, it was possible for such increased spending power to be anticipated, resulting in a marginal propensity to spend rising temporarily to unity or even higher. The aggressiveness of the finance houses and the attractions of hire purchase for a wealthier working class proved a powerful engine of inflation. (An excellent early, though generally overlooked and neglected, analysis of the contribution of hire purchase to the persistence of inflation was given by Dr Paul Einzig in 'The dynamics of hire-purchase credit', 1956.) If customers could get the credit they demanded from non-bank financial intermediaries (and many of them were not then considered worthy of being traditional bank customers), then trying to control the aggregate supply of credit just by means of the Bank of England's traditional controls over the clearing banks was bound to fail. Increased competition meant that new and wider methods of control had become essential. This accounts for the fundamental change attempted by the Bank in 1971.

By its new policy of Competition and Credit Control the Bank changed from rationing bank credit through quantitative ceilings on bank advances and qualitative or selective guidance – which as well as being unfairly restrictive in being confined to the clearers also gravely distorted the flow of credit. Instead the Bank wished to rely on the more generally pervasive influence of the price mechanism, with variations in the rate of interest becoming the main weapon, although it retained its power, as recommended by the Radcliffe Report, to call for Special Deposits from the 'banks', now more widely defined. The two former ratios of control, the old 8 per cent 'cash ratio' and the rather newer 28 per cent 'liquidity ratio' were replaced by a stipulation that all the banking institutions had to keep a minimum of 12½ per cent of their deposits in the form of 'eligible reserve assets' (which included balances at the Bank of England, Treasury bills and money at call with the discount market). The clearing banks agreed to end their interest rate cartel (which they had established in the 1930s) and thus began to compete for loans and deposits by means of more competitive interest rates. The Bank of England abandoned its age-old bank rate and replaced it with a Minimum Lending Rate which was henceforth normally to be determined automatically by market forces, rather than set arbitrarily by the Bank (though it retained the right to do so). At about the same time the controls over hire purchase were removed. All was set for an unsustainable boom, a daredevil dash for growth, led by Anthony Barber, the Conservative Chancellor of the Exchequer from 1970 to 1974. (He later became Chairman of Standard Chartered Bank, which in November 1973, just a few weeks before the crash, purchased Julian S. Hodge & Co. Ltd, the example *par excellence* of the new post-war finance house.) The deal was termed 'one of the best-timed multi-million pound sales in history' (Reid 1982, 80).

The year 1970 marks a watershed in the relative position of the London clearing banks when compared both with the building societies and with the overseas banks in Britain, for it was in that year that personal savings in the building societies first exceeded those in the London clearers, and also it was the first year for the total of deposits in American banks in Britain to exceed that of the London clearing banks. The dominance of the clearers in the British monetary system, a dominance which had lasted for just over half a century, was over. At that time it was the American banks that formed by far the most important sector of the overseas banks stationed in London, but the whole of the overseas sector was growing rapidly at a pace much greater than the growth of the clearers, even after their shackles were removed in 1971. The whole of the British financial system was in the process of rapid change, facing the authorities with unprecedented challenges of how to control this more complex, and expanding flood of credit. In trying to see how they coped – or failed to cope if the control of inflation is the measuring rod – we shall look first at the changes in building societies and savings banks before going on to examine the growth of the American and other overseas banks, together with the rise of the Eurocurrency market.

The building societies were able to steal a march on the clearing banks and to capture a growing share of a substantially rising total of personal savings partly because they greatly enlarged their branch network and partly because they were in the lucky position of being generally ignored insofar as monetary policy was concerned; for according to the generally accepted theory, only the banks could create money and hence needed to have such powers controlled. The Keynesians, especially after Radcliffe, tended to ignore or play down the importance of money, while the monetarists focused their monocular vision solely on the narrower ranges of money – the non-bank financial intermediaries were beyond their pale. The building societies, unconstrained, were able to overtake the banks in their share of the lucrative, growing personal savings market. The total of personal savings rose substantially in the thirty years after 1950, during the whole of which time the personal savings ratio also rose – as is shown in table 8.3 – despite the erosion of the unit value of savings in the highly inflationary 1970s. It takes a long time to change personal habits, so that it was not until the 1980s that the ratio fell significantly. The building societies and the insurance and pension funds took an increased share of this market; the banks' share increased only sluggishly; while that of the national savings movement fell substantially. Until 1969 the banks' share exceeded that of the societies, but throughout the 1970s, with the single and very marginal exception of 1974, the share held by the societies exceeded that of the banks. At

Table 8.3 The rising trend in the personal savings ratio, 1950–1979.*

Year	%	Year	%	Year	%
1950	1.6	1960	7.4	1970	8.6
1951	1.7	1961	8.9	1971	8.5
1952	3.5	1962	7.6	1972	9.3
1953	3.9	1963	7.6	1973	10.7
1954	3.4	1964	8.1	1974	13.7
1955	3.9	1965	8.6	1975	13.5
1956	5.5	1966	8.7	1976	12.8
1957	5.1	1967	8.2	1977	12.3
1958	4.3	1968	7.7	1978	12.8
1959	5.3	1969	7.8	1979	14.4

Average for the 1950s = 3.82%
Average for the 1960s = 8.06%
Average for the 1970s = 11.66%
(From 1980–88 the ratio fell, then rose in 1989–90, averaging 9.30 per cent for the 1980s.)

*Percentage of personal disposable income at current prices.

Sources: 1950 to 1971, Page Report (Cmnd 5273) para. 28; 1972 onward, CSO Financial Statistics.

first the banks did not seem to be very worried by the growing competition of the societies, and in any case the banks were precluded from competing by the severity and duration of their inequitable constraints; but even after the restrictions were removed and a more equitable regime came in with Competition and Credit Control in 1971, the banks felt that there was plenty of room for both institutions in the still rapidly expanding savings market. The total amount of personal savings soared during the 1970s, trebling from £3,123 million in 1970 to £10,044 million in 1975, and almost doubling again to reach £19,264 million in 1979 (CSO, Financial Statistics, August 1980).

The building societies were able to tap this growing reservoir of savings through their basic strategy of greatly extending their network of conveniently sited and 'homely' branches. Branch numbers grew from 659 in 1952 to 2,016 by 1970 and to 5,147 by 1979. The number of share and deposit accounts in building societies rose from 2,910,000 in 1950 to 10,883,000 in 1970 and to 31,551,000 in 1980, while their total assets grew from £1,255,872,000 in 1950 to £10,818,772,000 in 1970 and to £53,792,870,000 in 1980 (Davies 1981, 52). The building societies thus thrived by being ignored, overlooked or underappreciated by the monetary authorities and by their potential competitors. The Radcliffe Report, in outlining the Registrar's duties of control over the building societies, stated simply that 'the purpose of supervision is the protection of the public from the consequences of imprudent or fraudulent management, and *it has no monetary significance*' (para. 296, emphasis added). Not until the mid-1970s did the Bank of England really begin to show much concern about the societies. By 1980 opinion as shown in the Wilson Report was surprisingly hostile to the societies' aggrandizement, yet even Wilson was forced to admit that 'Societies in the course of expanding their branch networks appear to attract more new business than might otherwise be expected and have lower than average administrative costs' (para. 375).

Because savings are a residual from large totals, one cannot be too adamant about the exactness of the percentage for a given year; but the averages for the decades smooth out such variability and show very closely the rise in the trend of the personal savings ratio from 3.82 per cent in the 1950s, through 8.06 per cent in the 1960s to the unusually high level, for Britain, in the 1970s of 11.66 per cent and 9.30 per cent in the 1980s. It was this mainly rising trend that helped the building societies to achieve such a successful growth rate throughout most of the post-war period. (An excellent assessment of the 'Fall and rise of saving' from 1980 to 1990 is given by Professor K. A. Chrystal 1992.) International comparisons for the period 1970–92 show average personal savings ratios of around 19 per cent for Japan, 16 per cent for France and 13 per cent for West Germany – but with only 10 per cent for the UK and 7 per cent for the USA (Bundesbank Monthly Report, October 1993).

The success story of the building societies was not repeated by the savings banks, which were thoroughly investigated by the Committee to Review National Savings set up under Sir Harry Page in June 1971 and which published its report in June 1973 (Cmnd 5273). Sir Harry tried to move the stolid national savings 'movement' on to a more modern plane, and in particular attempted to push the Trustee Savings Banks into becoming 'the third force' in British banking; but the inertia of their old-fashioned ways greatly delayed the implementation of what had become plainly well-overdue reforms. A few telling examples must suffice. The rate of interest paid on ordinary deposits by the post office and TSBs had remained unchanged at 2½ per cent from 1888 until 1971 when, one hundred years after the founding of the POSB it was raised to 3½ per cent, and to 4 per cent in 1973. The moneys raised went into government coffers: a policy of robbing the poor to pay the rich. The authorities ignored Page's despairing plea that the National Giro might 'in the longer term' be combined with the National Savings Bank (para. 400). The TSBs were painfully slow in carrying out Page's recommendations on mergers and on extending the banking services which they needed to provide. Eventually the seventy-three separate TSBs were combined into fifteen groups and then into two main groups, one for Scotland and one for England and Wales, together with a Central Bank in London. For most of the post-war period the virility of the building societies stood in stark contrast to the senility of the national savings movement and the slow progress of the TSBs. By the 1980s both the building societies and the savings banks were successfully trespassing on ground that had previously been the preserve of the clearing banks.*

Further competition was provided by the Scottish banks, which needed 'Lebensraum' and therefore intensified their activities south of the border. Thus for example in 1977 the Royal Bank of Scotland fully absorbed William and Glyn's network of branches in England and Wales, while the Bank of Scotland which had already taken over North West Securities in 1958 went on to absorb Sir Julian Hodge's second banking creation, the (Commercial) Bank of Wales, in 1986. In quite a contrast to the 'Anglo-Scottish War' of a century earlier this new southern incursion produced no hostility. On the contrary, the Bank of Scotland was voted, according to a 1989 survey by *The Economist* and Loughborough University 'the most admired bank' by its banking peer group. A related, significant but generally neglected, aspect in the growth of secondary banking was its regional dimension, seen perhaps most clearly in the rise of Cardiff as a financial centre, largely as a result of Sir Julian Hodge's entrepreneurial initiatives. The formation of new banks (not simply changes in designation) is rare in modern Britain compared for instance with hundreds annually in the USA. It is therefore noteworthy that a third new Welsh bank, the Julian Hodge Bank Ltd, was opened in Cardiff in 1988. Despite the recession of the early 1990s, which saw the Bank of England having to keep forty small banks 'under particularly close review', its successful progress was indicated by an independent research report on 'Top Performing Banks, 1993' which placed Julian Hodge Bank Ltd third out of the 239 authorized institutions surveyed (Searchline Publishing 1993). A further indication of financial development in Wales is shown by the rise in employment in 'banking, finance and insurance' from 37,000 in 1971 to 90,000 in 1991, compensating to a welcome degree for the decline in employment in its traditional heavy industries (*Welsh Economic Trends* No. 13 1992). (Moreover in Britain's qualitative social balance-sheet, jobs in banking are infinitely safer and much more congenial, cleaner,

---

*Economic logic finally prevailed when Lloyds Bank merged with TSB and Cheltenham & Gloucester Building Society in 1995–6 to form Britain's biggest bank. See also p. 429.

less arduous and more open to both sexes than coal mining and have a smaller import-content than steel making. This is not to decry the economic significance of manufacturing.) Still much more important with regard to direct competition with the core business of the clearing banks, discount houses and merchant banks, was that pressed home aggressively by banks from overseas, magnetically attracted to London, the major pole of global banking.

The American-led invasion and the Eurocurrency markets in London
Although about a dozen major foreign banks had established themselves in London in the thirty years before the First World War (including Comptoir National, Crédit Lyonnais, Société Générale; the Deutsche and the Dresdner; the Swiss Bank Corporation and the Yokohama Specie Bank) only some seven US banking-type institutions, of no special importance and carrying on a variety of financial and commercial operations, had managed to set themselves up in London. US legal restrictions had held up such developments until after the Edge Act Amendment of 1919; even thereafter no real growth took place until the 1960s saw a headlong rush of US banks into London. There were still only seven American banks in London when, lumped together with the other overseas banks, they were cursorily examined by the Radcliffe Committee in 1959. This committee was barely curious about overseas banks: 'We did not take oral or written evidence from foreign banks . . . only their relative unimportance in the domestic financial scene can excuse our summary treatment of them' (para. 197). The original Trojan horse, while equally cursorily examined, had at least excited more interest. Two years later, when the United States Commission on Money and Credit reported, they took even less notice of their own Trojan horse strategically positioned in central London (*Money and Credit: their Influence on Jobs, Prices and Growth* 1961). The Radcliffe Committee did however note that 'American banks have ventured further and more actively into (domestic) business than the other overseas banks', yet consoled themselves by going on to say that 'this domestic business is negligible in comparison with the activity of the clearing banks' (para. 201). Within ten brief years the situation was dramatically changed, though even then its significance was still complacently underestimated by the authorities and by most academic commentators.

In 1959 the total value of deposits in American banks in Britain, at £163.2 million, came to only 2.5 per cent of the £6,552.4 million held in the London clearers, and was equivalent to only 24.3 per cent of the £670.9 million held in the Scottish banks (Radcliffe 1959, Memoranda of Evidence, II, 215). Between 1959 and 1970 twenty-nine of the most powerful American banks rushed to join the seven already there, starting with First National Bank of Chicago in 1959, Chemical Bank in 1960 and Continental Illinois in 1962. Six others followed in the next three years, culminating in a rush of no less than twenty new arrivals in the three years from 1968 to 1970, all of these being 'billion-dollar banks'. Such growth continued afterwards, but it is clear that by 1970 a fundamental change had already taken place. As Dr Ian Thomas, one of the earliest economists to note the significance of these events, explains:

> It is unique in financial history for banks of another country to have established installations on such a large scale and for their activities to have grown to occupy a significant position in such a highly developed and sophisticated market as the U.K. For this to have occurred within such a short period of time is in itself notable. For it to have taken place with so little public discussion or academic treatment is even more remarkable. (Thomas 1976, ii)

By the end of 1970 deposits in American banks in Britain, at £11,566.5 million had increased seventy-one times since 1959 and for the first time exceeded the £10,606 million then in the London clearing banks. They were now ten times larger than the £1,118.6 million in the Scottish banks. Meanwhile the deposits in other overseas banks were also growing, but not at the spectacular rate achieved by the American banks, which were outright and aggressive leaders.

The challenge which such new developments posed for monetary management was underlined by Sir Leslie O'Brien, Governor of the Bank of England, in the First Jane Hodge Memorial Lecture given in Cardiff on 7 December 1970:

> It was not so many years ago that domestic banking in this country was conducted virtually entirely by the deposit banks; that is primarily the London clearing banks . . . Only some dozen years ago the other banks in London accounted for little more than 10% of the deposits held with the banking sector as a whole. Since then their deposits have increased twenty times to over £17,000 million . . . Their resident sterling deposits are now approaching £3,000m. This represents around 20% of such deposits with the whole banking sector. (BEQB, March 1971)

The oligopoly of the Big Four had ended. From being the world's biggest banks in the inter-war and immediate post-war period, they had now been well and truly overtaken even in their home capital. At the same time the financial system had, largely on foreign initiative, built up a new market for money alongside – or 'parallel' as it came to be called – the old traditional discount houses, so that the banking institutions were now able to borrow directly from each other in the 'inter-bank market' rather than having to use the discount houses as the intermediary. No longer could the City be ruled by the nods, winks and eyebrow-raising of the Governor, nor even by the simple cash and liquidity ratios that, as we have seen, with various modifications, previously provided the levers by which the Bank of England with the help of the discount houses controlled the supply of credit. But just at the time when new sources of finance from so-called 'secondary' British and foreign banks began to flood the City – a situation crying out for stronger controls – the monetary authorities welcomed such competition so enthusiastically that the old, admittedly outworn, controls were abandoned. Their more equitable but far looser replacements were totally unable to hold back the precipitate boom which led inevitably to the crash of 1974. Because that crisis barely halted the foreign invasion we shall first continue to trace the subsequent scale of the influx and then examine how the related parallel markets came into being before considering the salient features of the secondary banking crisis.

The sizes of the various kinds of British and overseas bank deposits as at July 1980 are given in table 8.4 and their most striking aspects are shown graphically in figure 8.2, from which may clearly be seen the predominant position held by the overseas banks. Insofar as total deposits are concerned their share had increased to 70 per cent, while their holdings of sterling deposits had risen from the 20 per cent noted by the Governor in 1970 to 25 per cent in 1980. Only 11 per cent of non-sterling deposits and only 30 per cent of total deposits were held in British banks; the Trojan herd had taken over the stables. The American banks were still the major operators in 1980 with 28 per cent of total deposits and 34 per cent of non-sterling deposits: but, significantly, the Japanese banks with 16 per cent of total deposits and 23 per cent of non-sterling deposits were beginning to show the shape of things to come. By December 1989 Japanese banks' holdings of sterling, at £33,315 million were practically double those of American banks, at £17,338 million, while Japanese holdings of other currencies in their London banks, at £246,342 million were 2½ times those of US banks, at £96,836 million. American banks had led the invasion, but other foreign banks, particularly the Japanese giants, had enthusiastically followed their example. The Japanese banks had gained 43 per cent of overseas banks' share of non-sterling deposits by December 1989 (*BEQB*, February 1990). As with deposit sizes, so with the number of officially

Table 8.4 Bank deposits, sterling and non-sterling, in all banks in UK,
July 1980 (£ million)

Bank type	Sterling	%	Other currencies	%	All currencies	%
London clearing	36649	58	10095	6.5	46744	22
Scottish	4477	7	1370	1.0	5847	3
N. Ireland	1325	2	18	–	1343	–
Accepting houses	4548	7	5853	3.5	10401	5
Total UK	46999	75	17336	11	64335	30
American	7821	12	51296	34	59117	28
Japanese	782	1	33759	23	34541	16
Other overseas	7302	12	48490	32	55792	26
Total overseas	15905	25	133545	89	149450	70
Total all banks	62904	100	150881	100	213785	100

Source: BEQB (September 1980).

categorized banking institutions, overseas banks had been in the majority in Britain for two decades by 1990. Thus as table 8.5 shows, of the 588 institutions included by the Bank of England within United Kingdom Banks as at 12 January 1990, 361 or 61 per cent were overseas banks compared with 227 indigenous banks (and some of the latter, such as Northern Bank, Clydesdale and Yorkshire Bank are now owned by an Australian bank, Guinness Mahon by a New Zealand bank, and Morgan Grenfell by a German bank). Public awareness of this phenomenon has been muted in the country at large because only in the City of London does the physical presence of overseas banks become visibly marked. The ubiquitous and costly branch network of the clearers and the branching mania of the building societies so essential for retail deposit gathering and money transfer in the past, have disguised for most of the public the externally induced transformation in the British financial scene.

Among the many reasons which had enticed the American banks into London in this period was, first and foremost, the freedom from the irksome constraints they suffered in their home country, such as

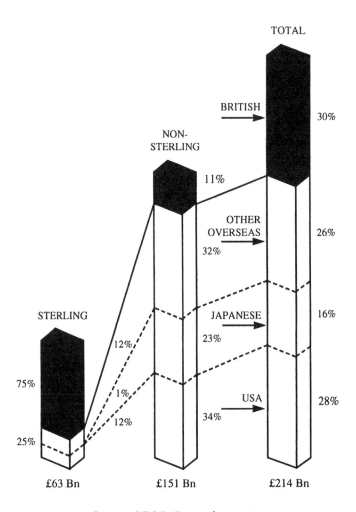

Source: BEQB (September 1980)

Figure 8.2 Sterling and non-sterling bank deposits in UK: British and overseas banks' market share in mid-July 1980.

restrictions on branching, the ceiling on interest rates (Regulation Q) and compulsory reserve deposits. Second came the need to follow their US corporate customers who were substantially expanding their business interests in Britain. Thirdly, there were the strains produced by the large US balance of payments deficits which led to restrictions on raising dollar loans in the USA – but not on dollar loans raised abroad. Fourthly, the US Interest Equalization Tax of 1963 similarly gave an incentive to hold dollars outside the USA, London being easily the most

Table 8.5 Numbers and types of British and overseas banks within the United Kingdom, January 1990

British banks	Number	Overseas banks	Number
Retail	21	American	44
Merchant	31	Japanese	29
Discount houses	8	Other overseas	288
Other British	167		
British total	227	Overseas total	361

Total number of officially designated banking institutions in UK as at 12 January 1990 = 588 (formerly officially known as 'the Monetary Sector').

Source: BEQB (February 1990).

convenient haven. Fifthly, the Voluntary Credit Restraint Program, intended to limit inflation within the USA, stimulated the raising of dollar credit abroad. Sixthly, added to these economic factors was the strongly held political fear that foreign-owned dollars within the USA might be expropriated or at least frozen, and so become unavailable for repatriation. That this fear had a concrete basis in fact was repeatedly demonstrated by US governments. The USSR had long kept for that reason a significant amount of dollars in their Moscow Narodny Bank branches in Paris and London; and it was the vigorous use of such balances that is generally held to be the model origin of the Eurodollar market. When as a result of the Suez War of 1956 the US government temporarily froze the dollar assets held in the USA by the belligerents, such political fears were revived with the result of diverting much of the rising flow of Arab oil money into Europe – fears later reinforced during the American quarrels with Iran. Seventhly, the widespread adoption during 1958 and 1959 of convertibility of currencies into dollars (especially) and into each other gave an enormous fillip to the marketing of loans in other nations' currencies: the foundation of what was to become the trillion-dollar Eurocurrency and Eurobond market had been established. The Bank of England – not usually given to hyperbole – rightly stressed the connection between convertibility, foreign deposit growth and the rise of the Eurocurrency market. In Governor O'Brien's speech, already noted above, he showed that 'This *phenomenal expansion* came after the widespread move to the convertibility of currencies at the end of 1958 and has been associated with the growth of the euro-dollar market' (*BEQB*, March 1971 emphasis added).

An eighth causative factor was the rise in the use of the 'certificate of deposit' by which a bank certified that the original holder had made a large deposit of cash for a fixed time. This gave the bank the certainty that the deposit would not be removed until its fixed maturity date (ranging from one month to two years) but yet enabled the depositor to sell his deposit, at the sacrifice of some part of the interest, if he wished to obtain cash before the maturity date. Certificates of Deposit first originated in New York in 1961, and dollar CDs were first issued in London by Citibank on 13 May 1966, with sterling CDs being issued by American and British banks two years later. Their liquidity was further enhanced when First National Bank of Chicago introduced a secondary market for such negotiable CDs. Already by 1971 the value of CDs outstanding on the London market exceeded £2,000 million. Complementing the growth in deposits was that of borrowing, and as our ninth contributory factor in the rise of the parallel market was the very substantial rise in borrowing by local authorities after 1955, when their traditional access to the Public Works Loan Board was restricted and they were pushed out on to the private sector, stimulating a specialized market in local authority deposits in which foreign as well as British banks participated. A tenth factor goes under the awkward description of 'disintermediation', whereby large borrowers, instead of borrowing from their bank, used their bank (or banks) as agents to arrange borrowing directly from the public, including other large companies with surplus cash, who found such loans more profitable than passively depositing their surplus funds with their bankers. A particular aspect of many variants of such devices is the market in commercial paper, although this market in London did not quickly take on the popularity it had acquired in New York. An eleventh factor was the increasing importance of specialist money brokers and similar agents who helped to bring the various newly developing forms of borrowing and lending into fruitful contact, so that the new and old money and capital markets became more fully integrated.

Just as bank rate had been the key rate in the traditional discount market, so the London Inter-Bank Offer Rate, or LIBOR, became the key rate in the parallel markets. In the development of these new markets, no single cause among those mentioned above would have sufficed; but together they produced a financial revolution in which the Eurodollar plays perhaps the most spectacular but certainly not the only major role. The City of London had gained its world status on the strength of sterling; it had retained that status as sterling declined by becoming the most convenient and efficient centre of operations in Eurodollar and other foreign currencies by international banks, especially, as well as by indigenous banks. Just when these new, highly competitive, markets were at full stretch in the early to mid-1970s the City was stunned by the secondary banking crisis.

The monetarist experiment, 1973–1990

The secondary banking crisis: causes and consequences

Since most modern money is bank money, bankers' attitudes, beliefs, fashions, moods, philosophies or theories (call them what you will) profoundly influence the creation and distribution of money. Thus in addition to the institutional metamorphosis explained above, the underlying cause of the excessive credit creation which led up to the 1973–5 banking crisis was a change in banking theory, from 'asset management' to 'liability management'; and the main consequence of the crisis was a sudden and profound change in bankers' attitudes, and in the public's attitude to bankers, that led to Britain adopting, for the first time in its history, a written financial constitution, something that had previously been completely alien to it. There have been four main banking theories which, consciously or unconsciously, have guided bankers' actions in the course of the twentieth century. First was the 'neutral' or 'cloakroom banking' theory; secondly the 'asset man-agement' theory; thirdly the 'liability management' theory; and finally the 'weighted capital adequacy theory' which now rules the roost. One does not have to assume universal acceptance of these theories, for all bankers do not think – or act – alike. However, the historical evidence of the herd instinct is so overwhelming (witness the fashionable surge to property lending and to Third World loans in the 1970s and to mortgage lending in the 1980s) that the acceptance of the proposition that most banks think alike supports some variant of the theoretical outline now being suggested.

The 'neutral banking theory' was put forward most influentially by Sir Walter Leaf (1852–1927) classical scholar, a founder member of the Institute of Bankers and chairman of Westminster Bank, in the early 1920s. The theory held that bankers could lend only what the public had decided, in the course of their everyday business activities, to deposit with their banks. It was the public, not the banks, – with the exception of the Bank of England – that caused any variation in total bank deposits. The banks could not 'create money out of thin air': they were neutral and simply changed deposits into cash and vice versa as demanded by their customers. It was of course very convenient at a time when the trade unions and socialists were crying out for nationalization or at least for some greater measure of control over the monopolistic 'Big Five', for the bankers to play down their power. The theory seemed to accord with plain common sense and with the cautionary practices of the thousands of bank managers throughout the country. The theory was however easily demolished: micro sense made macro nonsense.

Bank deposits already exceeded cash by around ten to one and bankers were clearly much more than cloakroom money-changers for the public. 'Practical bankers, like Dr Leaf,' said Keynes in his *Treatise on Money*, 'have drawn the conclusion that the banks can lend no more than their depositors have previously entrusted to them. But economists cannot accept this as being the commonsense which it pretends to be.' In a closed banking system a loan made by a banker soon reappears as a deposit in that or some other bank. Every loan creates (with certain exceptions that are subsidiary to the main argument) a deposit. As Keynes explained: 'Each Bank Chairman sitting in his parlour may regard himself as the passive instrument of outside forces over which he has no control; yet the "outside forces" may be nothing but himself and his fellow-chairmen and certainly not his depositors' (1930, I, 25, 27).

From the 1930s to around the mid-1960s the 'asset management' theory prevailed almost unchallenged, whereby the limit on the banks' power to create credit depended on keeping a certain ratio of liquid assets to total deposits, the ratio being arrived at by practical experience and confirmed by the authority of the Bank of England. By means of open market operations the Bank of England could influence the size of bankers' balances which the clearers needed to keep at the Bank as part of their cash reserves; and by means of bank rate it could also influence the rates which the discount houses paid the banks for call money and the price at which the banks could sell or buy their other main liquid assets, viz. Treasury and commercial bills. Conventional banking customs and central bank control were thus neatly dovetailed together. As we have seen, the banks in that period did not compete for deposits (except very indirectly); for part of their cosy cartelized agreement was to refrain from paying any interest on their current account deposits, and only low agreed rates on their deposit accounts (or 'time deposits'). Management of deposit liabilities was therefore passive, and all the emphasis was on how best to manage their assets so as to achieve an acceptable level of profit – cushioned by the cartel and partially hidden from public gaze by accounting privileges – in the long run. This long run ended with the rise of the secondary and foreign banks in the 1960s, when appropriately the old theory was displaced by the craze for 'liability management'.

The practice and theory of liability management was first developed in the USA with the expansion of the 'Federal Funds' market in the 1950s. It came to Britain with the American bank invasion during the 1960s and was therefore contemporaneous with the rise of the Eurodollar and the parallel markets. The time was just ripe for eager acceptance and further development of this transatlantic innovation.

Since the banks and quasi-banks could now borrow as much as they wanted whenever they wanted from the parallel markets, a number of micro- and macro-economic consequences followed. First, they could sidestep the discipline associated with borrowing from the central bank, whether directly, as in the USA, or indirectly, as in the UK via the discount houses. Secondly, they needed no longer to keep nearly so much as formerly in low-yielding liquid assets, for these could be purchased with borrowed funds just as and when required. Thirdly, they therefore could and did switch to holding a much higher proportion of higher-yielding 'earning assets' such as loans and advances. Fourthly, since a range of longer-term deposits could also be bought, banks could grant a higher proportion of longer-term loans (or, which apparently came almost to the same thing, they could more willingly 'roll over' short- and medium-term loans). These again were usually more profitable for the banks than being confined to short loans, and much more profitable than the traditional overdraft. Fifthly, banks needed no longer to wait to see whether they had sufficient funds before they agreed to make a loan (or at least they needed to be much less hesitant) because they felt confident, backed by their growing experience in 'matching' or 'marrying' loans to deposits, that they could always get the kind of funds they required, in the time periods and currencies as necessary. The City became a happy hunting ground for innovative schemes of liability management. All these developments worked together to hold out the promise, given skilled liability management, of achieving permanently more profitable and dynamic banking than that typified under the old asset-management regime. The road to crisis was paved with golden intentions. Only as a result of that crisis was the popularity of the liability management theory replaced by the more cautious 'weighted capital adequacy' approach. Before examining this latest theory we must therefore look first to see how the shock administered to the British banking system in this period led to a re-examination of basic principles.

An invaluable account of the crisis is given by Margaret Reid (1982). The earliest direct indication of impending disaster occurred in the spring of 1973 when the Banking Department of the Scottish Cooperative Wholesale Society, which had grossly overextended its operations in Certificates of Deposit, had to be rescued by the Scottish and London clearers, under the guidance of the Bank of England – a harbinger of things to come. By December 1973, with the public knowledge of the harsh difficulties facing London and County Securities Group and of Cedar Holdings in particular, it had become obvious that a major crisis, worse than any in Britain since 1890, was threatening the banking system as a whole with collapse. To meet the danger, a rescue committee under Sir Jasper Hollom of the Bank of England, with George Blunden as his deputy, and with senior representatives from all the major clearers, went into vigorous action as from 29 December 1973: the famous 'Lifeboat' was launched. As Sir George Blunden later explained, at a speech at Cardiff Business Club on 25 October 1976

> Though these secondary banks had not previously been under the surveillance of the Bank of England, it was to the Bank that London and County turned when faced with crisis. And it was obvious to the Bank that it had to marshal defences against what might otherwise become a tidal wave sweeping through, and probably overwhelming the financial system.

About thirty secondary banks were supported directly by the 'lifeboat', and at least another thirty such banks received other forms of assistance. 'Without these supporting operations virtually all of them would have collapsed . . . and undoubtedly many of the primary banks would have been swept away in the maelstrom. As it was, by protecting the secondary banks, the Bank of England and the clearing banks ensured that not one of the inner ring of primary banks had to be supported' (Blunden 1976). Even so, at the height of the panic the false rumour that National Westminster needed such support had to be denied both by its Chairman and by the Governor of the Bank.

The 'Lifeboat' operation was an outstanding triumph for the Bank. Not a single ordinary depositor lost a penny, while most of the suspect banks were successfully restructured or absorbed by stronger banks. But the fact remained that widespread disaster had been very narrowly avoided. This alerted everybody to the urgent need for comprehensive and drastic reforms in the ways in which banking was carried on and how it was (or was not) supervised. Bankers' attitudes recoiled from aggressive liability management in favour of safer banking. It was clear that every bank should make sure that its capital base was strong enough in relation not only to the total amount of business it took on its books, but also that its free capital base should be used as a yardstick to provide a strict limit to the special risks associated with particular types of activity e.g. foreign currency exposure in an era of floating rates, or lending to property development companies – two of the main causes of failure in the mid-1970s. General agreement was reached between the Bank and the City, after years of discussion culminating as we shall see in legislation, chiefly but not only in the Bank Acts of 1979 and 1987, on the operation of the new system which was being first developed step by step on a voluntary basis. Among important specific provisions were that no bank should make a single (or aggregated to connected companies) loan of 25 per cent or more of its free capital base without having first to obtain the permission of the Bank of England, while all loans of from 10 per cent up to 25 per cent of a bank's capital had to be specifically disclosed to the Bank on a regular and timely basis. In other words, all banks had to embrace the 'weighted capital adequacy' theory, with liabilities of greater risk requiring proportionately greater capital backing, as an unavoidable guide to their operations. Although the Bank's prestige throughout the banking world was greatly heightened by the way it successfully 'saved the City' in the mid-1970s, it was obvious that in its task of helping to build up and maintain a sound banking system, now that this system was far more extensive than ever before, it would require to have its traditional authority very considerably strengthened. What was required was something quite new in British banking history: a written financial constitution.

Supervising the financial system

A basic reform in the theory and practice of financial supervision in Britain following the secondary banking crisis concerned the definition of a 'bank'. For nearly one hundred years banking students had both laughed at and admired the circularity and the foggy imprecision of the accepted definition in the Bills of Exchange Act 1882 which said that 'bankers' were simply those people 'who carry on the business of banking'. However the law's laxity and its very vagueness kept the door wide open in Britain for new entrants and new experiments. It was through this door that hundreds of secondary 'banks', armed with new tools, surged aggressively in the run-up to the crisis. When the legal status of United Dominions Trust, the largest of the secondary banks, was challenged in 1966 by a Mr Kirkwood, a bankrupt owner of a garage business, the resulting important legal case led the judges, with a bare majority of two to one, to agree first that UDT could for all practical purposes rightly be considered to be a bank, and secondly to advise each aspiring bank, in order to remove any doubt, to seek a certificate from the Board of Trade that it was 'bona fide carrying on the business of banking'. This recommendation, rapidly entrenched as section 123 of the Companies Act of 1967, became a potent factor in the stimulation of secondary banking because it enabled such banks to borrow (and therefore lend more competitively) at more favourable rates than before. At a stroke, not only the legality but also the competitive powers of a vast new army of aggressive bankers were increased, thus putting an end to most of the remaining monopolistic privileges of the traditional and hitherto complacent clearing bankers. However although the Board/Department of Trade could grant a licence, it had neither the power nor the ability to supervise. In the crisis, as we have seen, the Bank of England was urgently left to take over such responsibilities. Putting such a wide burden on sounder legal foundations was one of the most pressing reasons for the Banking Act 1979, which came into full operation in a formal sense from 1 April 1980, but which had been gradually and informally approached in practice by the City during the previous five years – during which all the main participants co-operated in the knowledge that legislative powers were certain to follow. The objects of the Act were 'to regulate the acceptance of deposits, to confer functions on the Bank of England with respect to deposit-taking institutions' and 'to restrict the use of names and descriptions associated with banks and banking'.

The 1979 Act, with all-party support, used the popular cause of consumer protection to bring some degree of order and control over a previously amorphous banking system of some 600 institutions. It set up a two-tier arrangement that divided the banking sheep from the deposit-taking goats, giving to the Bank of England (not the Treasury or the Department of Trade and Industry) the power to decide, according to certain criteria, whether an institution could be regarded as a 'recognized bank', and so be allowed to use the terms 'bank' and 'banking' in its title, stationery and advertising, or whether it was just a 'licensed deposit-taker' (LDT), and so could not call itself or advertise as a 'bank'. The minimum criteria for being a recognized bank, stipulating both quantitative and qualitative ingredients, included having 'enjoyed for a considerable period of time a high reputation and standing in the financial community' and the provision of either 'a wide range of banking services' (in which case a minimum of £500,000 of net assets was required), or 'a highly specialised banking service' – a device to let the discount houses into the top tier to which they undoubtedly belonged – in which latter case the lower minimum of £250,000 of net assets was required. Net assets were defined as 'paid up capital and reserves'. The minimum criteria for being accepted as a licensed deposit-taker included also 'net assets of a minimum of £250,000' plus the qualitative stipulation that 'every person who is a director, controller or manager is a fit and proper person to hold that position'.

The second part of the Act was concerned with the setting up and regulation of a Deposit Protection Board and Fund, administered by the Bank of England, to which all banks and LDTs had to contribute 0.3 per cent of their total deposits, between a minimum contribution of £2,500 and a maximum of £300,000. This Protection Fund would guarantee repayment of all individual deposits – but significantly only up to 75 per cent of the total, again subject to a ceiling of £10,000. The 25 per cent residual and the ceiling acted as cautionary warnings to depositors and banks – emphasized by the widespread failure of 'Thrifts' in the USA. As it turned out, the numbers of recognized banks and of LDTs were evenly balanced, at 295 each in 1983, and with 290 banks and 315 LDTs in the peak year for numbers in 1985, when of the total of 605 institutions 250 were overseas institutions with UK branches, 65 were subsidiaries of overseas institutions and 24 were joint ventures of mixed parentage. Perhaps the most important feature of the Act was the power granted to the Bank of England for the first time in law, to call for statistical and other information as required by the Bank from every licensed institution, including 'its plans for future development' (clause 16). The legislation had teeth, for the Bank could (and did) revoke licences where it felt necessary. Experience with the working of the Act in the first five years seemed on the whole to be satisfactory, but there were a few groans. A minor irritant was the feeling by the big banks that they were contributing the most to a fund to protect depositors from smaller and more risk-prone banks which paid much less. (They were already seeming to forget one of the main lessons of the mid-1970s crisis, that the failure of even the smallest secondary banks brought general discredit and loss of confidence throughout the City – penalties worth paying to insure themselves against.) Of more substance was the complaint by indigenous LDTs that overseas LDTs as well as banks could use the terms 'bank' and 'banking' in circumstances denied to native institutions. This led to a number of 'David and Goliath' type struggles as, for example, between the (Commercial) Bank of Wales and the Bank of England, with the little protagonist maintaining its title.

Most serious of all was the failure of a recognized bank, not on or of the fringe but right in the centre of the City. In the late summer of 1984 Johnson Matthey Bankers Ltd, which had close connections with the Bank of England, failed and had to be directly rescued by the Bank of England, much to its embarrassment and much to the annoyance of the Chancellor of the Exchequer. This failure brought right home to the City the need for still stronger supervisory powers, particularly with regard to the ways in which the banks' accountants and auditors were involved in the supervisory process. Consequently the Chancellor of the Exchequer, Nigel Lawson, announced in December 1984 the setting up of yet another committee, under the chairmanship of the Governor, Robin Leigh-Pemberton, to consider amendments required to be made to the Banking Act. The resulting Bank Act 1987 abolished the two-tier division of recognized banks and LDTs, which were all henceforth known as 'authorized institutions'; it laid down a uniform net assets requirement of £1,000,000; it increased the ceiling for individual protected deposits from £10,000 to £20,000; it gave a legal basis for a Board of Banking Supervision; it gave the Bank discretion to decide whether authorized institutions need set up audit committees and have non-executive directors (to which the answer was 'yes' unless the bank was a very small one); it considerably strengthened the requirements for banks to maintain adequate records and strictly audited systems of control; and it allowed any authorized institution, provided it had a minimum capital of £5,000,000, to use the name and description 'bank'. Forty-six institutions immediately rushed to take advantage of this last provision, proof that a bank by any other name does not rank so highly. The growth in the number of staff employed in the Bank of England's Supervision Division, from 75 in 1983 to 200 in 1989 and to 270 in 1993, gives another pointer to the increasing importance of supervision; although, to keep it in perspective, the Bank's total staff during this period numbered around 5,400.

In the twenty years following 1971 the Bank shed all vestiges of its former traditional image as an aloof, taciturn and reticent Old Lady. The Bank's staff have poured out a stream of consultative papers, and by these and other means have carefully prepared its policies only after the most detailed discussions with interested financial institutions and individuals, in order to try to make sure that when its proposals are finally crystallized into law and practice, they are tried, tested and workable, and that they help to maintain an essential degree of co-operative goodwill between the central bank and the financial community at large, both indigenous and that from overseas. 'In particular it has been a major policy initiative of the Bank to enlist the assistance of the accountancy profession in the process of bank supervision' (Annual Report, Bank of England, 1987, 29). Under the terms of the Bank Act every authorized institution has via an approved accountant to submit an annual report on internal control systems and records, make regular prudential reports and submit to being the subject of *ad hoc* reports as and when felt necessary by the auditors. Apart from these reports the Bank keeps itself closely informed of the situation in each of its 600 reporting institutions by means of direct interviews and visits. Over 3,000 such interviews were carried out during 1988, an average of six per bank, as well as 126 review team visits, some lasting over a week, in order to provide more detailed knowledge of the management, control systems and procedures of the bank concerned. Supervision is thus comprehensive and continuous. In addition the Bank has been involved in the preparation, among many other matters, of the Consumer Credit Act of 1974, the Financial Services Act of 1986 and the Building Societies Act of the same year, the 'Report on Banking Services: Law and Practice' – the Jack Report of 1989 (Cm 622 February 1989) – and the government's White Paper 'Banking Services; Law and Practice' (Cm 1026 of March 1990), from which like-thinking parentage a voluntary Code of Banking Practice was to emerge. Internationally the Bank was involved in discussions with the Federal Reserve System of the USA and with the Bank for International Settlements on the 'convergence of capital' and with the other members of the European Community on the European Directives on Banking and Credit Services and the Delors Report on 'Economic and Monetary Union in the European Community' (1989), of which committee Governor Leigh-Pemberton was a member and signatory. Perhaps it is not surprising that a former economic adviser of the Bank, Professor Charles Goodhart, has complained of 'overkill'; and one begins to wonder how soon experience may show that the law of diminishing returns applies even to banking rules and regulations.

Although the basic causes of the British secondary banking crisis were very much internally generated, it was accompanied, and to some extent aggravated, by financial failures in the USA and in continental Europe. Failures of scores of small US banks from among its then 15,000 total are not unusual, (see table 9.4). Yet the failure of larger banks such as the National Bank of San Diego in 1973, of Franklin National in 1974 (and even more of the near-failure of the giant Continental Illinois in 1982) strengthened the general concern among the international financial community for stronger and wider-reaching forms of banking supervision. In 1974 Lloyds Bank branch in Locarno suffered severe losses, because of poor supervision, on its foreign exchange operations, as did Westdeutsche Landesbank and the Union Bank of Switzerland. However it was the sudden collapse of the West German Bankhaus I.D. Herstatt on 26 June 1974 which precipitated an international crisis and led to the temporary paralysis of the Eurodollar market. Widespread failure was avoided by the prompt co-operative action of the monetary authorities, again led by Governor Richardson, who quickly organized an international version of the 'lifeboat'. Such crises provided the spur to a long series of contemporary and partially linked discussions, nationally and internationally, on how best to avoid such difficulties while yet preserving full and equal competition, with the suitably chastened participants being far more amenable to realistic compromise than would otherwise have been the case.

In July 1988 the Governors of the ten major central banks meeting in

Basle agreed to implement a series of proposals based firmly in fact (though without mentioning the word 'theory') on the capital adequacy theory. Banks in all member countries were to converge to a *minimum* capital base of 8 per cent of assets. (In Britain the actual base was already in general considerably higher.) The 8 per cent capital base had to consist of at least 4 per cent paid-up capital or its equivalent for 'Tier 1' capital, plus 4 per cent reserves and general provisions for losses for 'Tier 2'. As well as an agreed definition of capital, the risk-weights to be attached to a bank's assets were also agreed, ranging from a nil risk for cash, bullion and certain loans to OECD governments, through a 10 per cent weight on loans to the discount market and on Treasury and other eligible bills, and a 50 per cent weight risk on residential mortgages, up to a 100 per cent weight risk on loans for most other purposes to private and corporate customers. (Bank of England: 'Implementation of the Basle Convergence Agreement', October 1988.) Any complacency regarding the adequacy of these measures was blown away when the Bank of England was forced to close the British branches of the Bank of Credit and Commerce International on 1 July 1991, so exposing the world's biggest banking fraud and eventually bringing about a much-needed strengthening of supervisory co-operation between home and host monetary authorities (see Sir Thomas Bingham's 'Inquiry Into the Supervision of BCCI' 22 October 1992). Global money and global vulnerability had thus produced a large measure of international agreement on both the framework and much of the method of bank supervision.

Accompanying the supervisory regime to hold the banks in check there arose a whole host of rules and regulations under the umbrella Financial Services Act of 1986, administered mainly by self-regulatory organizations but backed up by statutory sanctions, covering investment, insurance and the stock exchanges. Similarly the Building Society Act of 1986 attempted both to give the societies greater freedom to carry out a much wider range of financial transactions than ever before while also tightening capital and other controls under the watchful eye of a Building Societies Commission. Because bank loans, securities and building society loans compete over a growing part of their range it had become inevitable that the pendulum of freedom followed by control should eventually apply more or less at the same time across the whole of the financial spectrum. The first of the building societies to take advantage of the provisions in the new Act enabling them to change at the same time into a public limited company (from a mutual organization) and into becoming a fully authorized bank, was Abbey National, the second largest society in

1989. Halifax, the largest society, together with at least half a dozen other large societies, had second thoughts, and preferred first to take step-by-step advantage of the many new opportunities offered in the Act short of becoming fully fledged banks. At any rate legally speaking, the barrier between bank and building society had by the mid-1980s become paper thin and easily passable by the bigger societies.* Economically speaking, the dividing line had for many years been non-existent, as was most obviously seen during the long-drawn out attempts to define the money supply and especially the increasingly important concept of 'broad money'. These were essential steps in the never-ending struggle to control whatever was thought to be the actual money supply as a key factor in controlling the economy.

Prudential supervision, triggered off, as we have seen, by concern for the safety of customers' bank deposits, thus became inextricably interwoven with the fundamental macro-economic struggle of the last quarter of the twentieth century, namely how to control the economy by controlling (if possible) the money supply. Thus the main indicator of the government's economic success, or lack of it, was the rate of inflation. In the words of Nigel Lawson, Chancellor of the Exchequer from 1983 to 1989, inflation was to be both judge and jury of the government's efforts. Ironically, Lawson, who (with Sir Geoffrey Howe) was the chief architect of the Thatcher government's 'Medium-Term Financial Strategy', himself became the first major casualty of the government's painfully slow progress in containing inflation.

Thatcher and the medium-term financial strategy

The term 'monetarism' was coined by Professor Karl Brunner (1916–89) as a convenient label for the counter-revolution against the Keynesian economics that had dominated theory and policy in many countries, but especially Britain, for much of the three or four decades after 1936. This counter-revolution was triggered by Milton Friedman's famous *Restatement of the Quantity Theory* as early as 1956, and thanks to Brunner, made quicker progress in Switzerland and West Germany, countries of markedly low inflation, than in the USA or Britain, where Democratic and Labour Party politicians were much more loath to depart from what had now become orthodox and embedded Keynesian opinion. It is therefore of the greatest significance that the signal rejection of Keynesian policies was made by a British socialist Prime Minister, James Callaghan, in 1976 after inflation had been running at over 25 per cent and when recourse had ignominiously to be made to the IMF to support sterling. In a bold, unequivocal, speech (written after consulting with his eminent economist son-in-law,

*Thus by early 1996 mergers and flotations among the big societies, including the Halifax, had fundamentally changed the structure and nature of the building society industry – outstanding examples of a world-wide trend towards more integrated and competitive financial systems.

Peter Jay) made to the Labour Party Conference in Blackpool on 28 September 1976, at the height of a financial crisis, Lord Callaghan dramatically challenged the cosy conventional Keynesian viewpoint:

> We used to think that you could spend your way out of a recession and increase employment by cutting taxes and boosting Government spending. I tell you in all candour that that option no longer exists, and that insofar as it ever did exist, it only worked on each occasion since the war by injecting a bigger dose of inflation into the economy, followed by a higher level of unemployment as the next step. Higher inflation followed by higher unemployment. We have just escaped from the highest rate of inflation this country has known; we have not yet escaped from its consequences: higher unemployment. That is the history of the last twenty years. (Callaghan 1987, 426).

The Governor of the Bank of England confirmed ten years later that Britain's conversion to monetarism occurred under a socialist administration in 1976: 'The foundations of our present monetary policy were in fact laid down in 1976' (BEQB December 1986, 499). Furthermore, although statistics for narrow, medium and broad money had been published by the Bank from September 1970 it was not until 1976 that an explicit *target* for the growth of the money supply was first announced publicly. The apparatus of a new monetary policy was in place – but it required the iron will of Margaret Thatcher to bring in a full-bodied monetarist policy when she became Prime Minister in May 1979.

In its first budget of 1980 the new Conservative administration announced its Medium-Term Financial Strategy (MTFS), setting out the broad fiscal and monetary policy for the next four years, with a much greater and explicit emphasis on the medium term than had customarily been the case. There was to be a targeted progressive decline in monetary growth with the stated ultimate aim of stable prices. Fiscal policy was to support monetary policy, which latter was unequivocally to hold pride of place. Thatcherite policy thus suddenly caught up with that branch of monetarism that embraced what is known as the 'Rational Expectations Hypothesis' (REH), which correctly but overoptimistically lays great stress on the role of the public's expectations in the inflationary process. 'The new challenge to Keynesian policies . . . not only argued that Keynesian theory cannot handle inflation, but also that Keynesian policies are themselves the cause of inflation; only by discarding Keynesian policies will we be able to control inflation. This influential challenge is made in the name of "rational expectations"' (Colander 1979, 198). (Incidentally when Professor Colander wrote that, he was Visiting Scholar at Nuffield

College Oxford, long thought to be the last bastion of unrepentant Keynesianism.) Only if the government held to its declared course, come hell or high water, could its credibility be assured and hence the public's expectations of future inflation be moderated – a prerequisite for actually reducing inflation.

There was thus to be no room for Keynesian demand management through a flexible fiscal policy, even with rising unemployment, nor for monetary 'fine-tuning'. Instead an attempt was made to set the path along a more fixed anti-inflationary timetable with annual reductions in the Public Sector Borrowing Requirement (PSBR) (which had previously swollen to such an extent as to generate excess liquidity and crowd out private sector investment) coupled with pre-announced target ranges for what was considered from time to time to be the most relevant form of the money supply. Thus a target of 7 per cent to 11 per cent for 'Sterling M3', the currently favoured definition, was announced to cover the period from February 1980 to April 1981. The actual rate of growth turned out to be 18.5 per cent: such overshooting became common throughout the 1980s. Nevertheless, because of the ruthless force of other anti-inflationary measures, the rate of inflation fell until the late 1980s when, for a number of specific reasons, it picked up again. The anti-monetarists could claim that their repeatedly stated view (e.g. see Kaldor 1970) that there was no close correlation between the money supply and the rate of inflation was thereby proven; in contrast the monetarists could – until 1987 – claim, that despite the unfortunate slippage of the money supply brake, their general policy of bearing down on inflation was working. In any case there was a heavy cost to pay in the form of the minimum lending rate raised to 17 per cent in 1979, and of a trebling of unemployment from around one million to three million in the three years from 1980 to 1983, accompanied by a decimation of manufacturing industry which left the industrial base so small as to be unable to satisfy home or export demand in subsequent recoveries, so increasing Britain's high marginal propensity to import and her chronic balance of payments deficits.

After ten years, with Britain's increased rate of growth at long last on average exceeding that of its major competitors, and with unemployment rising again, after having been brought back down to around one million, coupled with inflation of over 10 per cent, the tentative judgement on the Thatcherite experiment must be a mixed one. It turned out to be highly successful in some respects, e.g. in the continued progress of the City of London and more widely in stimulating sounder management, stronger personal incentives, less militant unionism and a higher rate of productivity in industry, even though the average levels of productivity, employment-training skills and the size of the manufacturing base remain far too low. Strangely enough in what should have been the decisive sector for monetarism, the rate of inflation, the success of the mid-1980s, despite being purchased at so high a cost, appeared short-lived. As stated above (pp. 395–97) the average rate of inflation during the long period of Keynesianism from 1934 to 1976 (with the painful exception of the mid-1970s when Britain seemed in danger of becoming an ungovernable banana republic) was much lower than the inflationary average of the explicitly and abrasively monetarist decade of the 1980s. As the Governor admitted in the Bank of England's report for 1990: 'No central banker could regard as successful a year in which the value of money fell by as much as 8 per cent in terms of what it will purchase at home, and by 10 per cent in terms of overseas currencies.'

Because the money supply is a leading indicator (prices following with a variable lag but usually about eighteen months later) while unemployment is usually a lagging indicator (employers being reluctant to shed labour they have already trained and to incur redundancy costs) the year 1990 saw prices and unemployment rising together, threatening a return to the stagflation nightmare of the 1970s. A deflationary high interest rate was contributing visibly to raise unemployment and yet without any visible effect on inflation even after a year of base rate at 15 per cent. By 8 October 1990, when base rate was reduced to 14 per cent, both unemployment and inflation were still rising and were significantly higher than when Margaret Thatcher became Prime Minister in 1979. Obviously monetarism, the essence of Thatcherism, was not the simple infallible cure its more immoderate protagonists had confidently trumpeted. It cannot be too emphatically stated that a consistently firm and therefore credible monetary control is a necessary but not (particularly in Britain) a sufficient cure for inflation, which has mainly, but certainly not exclusively, monetary causes. Among the reasons for the failure indelibly indicated by the rise in inflation to double figures, after having fallen to 3 per cent, were first, the government's (initially understandable) reaction to the stock market crash of October 1987; secondly, the pernicious role of the distorted housing market; thirdly, the government's mistaken persistence in a lax tax policy; fourthly, the monetary authorities' confusing plethora of money targets and indicators; and fifthly, the government's ambiguity in deciding whether it should be the money supply, however measured, or the exchange rate which should be the main determinant of policy.

Just as the London Clearing Banks' monopoly was eroded by the revolutionary changes of the 1970s, so eventually was that of the

London Stock Exchange. In 1984, to forestall legislation expected to be at least as restrictive as that of the Securities Exchange Commission of the USA, agreement was reached between the stock exchange and the Department of Trade and Industry which involved abolishing fixed commissions and replacing the traditional single-capacity system of separate jobbers and brokers with a combined dual-capacity system which would be open to new competitors. These changes were made to coincide with a new system of automated operations. Because these and other improvements were all timed to begin together on 27 October 1986 (instead of being introduced bit by bit) the change was known as 'Big Bang'. The creation of this brave new competitive world was assisted by and in turn further stimulated the booming bull market. Average daily turnover of UK equities increased from £643 million in the first nine months of 1986 to £1,156 million in the corresponding period of 1987, an increase of 80 per cent – and if intra-market transactions are included turnover increased by almost 250 per cent (*BEQB* November 1987). The number of dealers (or 'equity market-makers' as they became known) rose to thirty-four in that same period compared with just thirteen jobbers before the Big Bang. The company merger mania and the growth of 'securitization' (i.e. the process by which corporate borrowers, instead of taking loans from their banks, issued saleable securities) further increased the volume of trading on the world's stock exchanges. This system reached its extreme form in the 'junk bonds' of Wall Street (i.e. the issuing of high-yield but therefore high-risk bonds classified as 'speculative' by credit agencies such as Moody and Standard-and-Poor). The speculative fever was further stimulated by the growth of 'indexed' and other forms of 'programmed trading' whereby computerized dealings in a whole range of securities were automatically triggered at prearranged price levels.

Suddenly just one year after the Big Bang came the Great Crash, when all this frenzied bullish activity went into reverse. It frightened monetary authorities the world over into adopting what turned out to be, for Britain especially, an excessively relaxed and expansionary monetary policy, thereby rekindling the previously ebbing inflationary fires. The downturn started on Wall Street on 6 October 1987, set off by fears that equity prices were too high to be sustained and by rumours that the existing international agreement to support exchange rates in general and the dollar in particular (the Louvre agreement) was in imminent danger of breaking down, this latter acute fear being built on the chronic anxiety caused by the huge size of the US 'double deficit', viz. its budget deficit and its balance of payments deficit. The fall on Wall Street reached record levels on Friday 16 October. It so happened that, adding woe to the general foreboding, a devastating hurricane that same evening of 16/17 October swept across southern England including in its full severity London and the stockbroker belt. Therefore New York's record fall was not reflected in London until 'Black Monday', 19 October, when what were certain to be record insurance claims added their weight to the crisis. Hurricanes apart, the newly automated world markets reacted with greater speed than ever before: and so also, to be fair, did the curative actions of the world's monetary leaders. Alan Greenspan, head of the Federal Reserve System, promised immediate help to the US financial system; the Governors of the central banks of 'G7', the major economies of the world (excluding USSR), jointly issued a similar statement regarding the need for adequate liquidity and support for exchange rates; and the Bank of England reduced base rates from 10 per cent by ½ per cent on 23 October and again on 4 November, with the downward trend continuing, falling to 7½ per cent by May 1988.

At the time, these moves were universally and enthusiastically welcomed by politicians, bankers, industrialists and academics, whether Keynesian or monetarist. Among the reasons for this unusual economic unanimity were first the fact that the falls on the stock exchanges were by far the worst since 1929, so generating a widespread fear that these falls would, unless quickly and decisively checked, lead on, as in 1929 to 1934, to a worldwide slump of devastating proportions. While no ink should be needed to see why Keynesians would react immediately to welcome almost any action which might prevent such a calamity, without worrying too much about the opposite danger of feeding the still existing inflation, the fact that monetarists also, despite their more sensitive fears regarding inflation, similarly welcomed such actions does require some explanation. The answer is to be found in no less an authority than Milton Friedman himself, who with co-author Anna Schwartz had in 1963 made a scathing attack which blamed the 'inept' Federal Reserve for having turned the stock exchange crisis of 1929 into the modern world's worst slump. They fully justified their criticism in a typically robust and plain-speaking form which no one with any claim to monetarist leanings could possibly afford to ignore. Because the Fed was so inept, 'the monetary system collapsed but it clearly need not have' (1963, 407). Furthermore

> the great contraction [in the money supply] shattered the long-held belief that monetary policies were important . . . and opinion shifted almost to the opposite extreme that 'money doesn't matter'. However, the failure of the FRS to prevent the collapse reflected not the impotence of monetary policy . . . but is in fact a tragic testimony to the importance of monetary forces (p.300).

Faced with the Great Crash of 1987 therefore all monetarists, from the most full-blooded fanatics to the most diffident (if any) were united in their determination to seize this opportunity to demonstrate to the world the truth of their leader's gospel. Money could save the world from slump. For far too long Thatcherite monetarism had seemed, at least with regard to the money supply, to have been a negative doctrine, preaching monetary restriction whatever the pain (and despite the *cri de coeur* of 364 economists, not all of them Keynesian, who in a letter to *The Times* following Sir Geoffrey Howe's savage budget of March 1981, rightly feared the decimation of British manufacturing industry). In contrast to the gloom of the 364, monetarists like Professor Minford had, with incredible optimism, predicted that any loss of output would be 'temporary' and of 'modest significance' and that unemployment would show merely a short-lived increase of around 300,000 – 'wrong by a factor of four' (Gilmour, 1983, 143). Now in 1987 the monetarists could demonstrate in a directly benevolent and positive manner that the most powerful weapon in any government's economic armoury was the monetary lever. Monetarists like Chancellor Lawson were determined not to repeat the mistakes of the 1930s and so turned a blind eye when the money supply rose well above its target limits, with the later inevitable result that the rate of inflation rose strongly again, to reach 11 per cent by autumn 1990 – by which time a new Chancellor, John Major, had been installed. What still remains to be explained is why Britain's inflation rose more strongly and then declined much later than was the case with its main competitors. Strong contributory factors flow from the built-in market distortions in the British economy, such as the cost-push of annual wage rises (already noted) and in particular the distortions in the housing finance market (see Muellbauer 1990).

Contrary to expectations and thanks only in part to the prompt curative actions of the world's monetary authorities, the Great Crash did not lead immediately to a general, severe slump: the world's major economies were much stronger than in the 1930s. In the UK one special result of the equity slump was to divert personal savings from unit trusts, stocks and shares and privatized projects like a badly timed BP issue, increasingly into the already buoyant housing market, so contributing to a housing boom of record dimensions. 'The housing market thus became the main engine of the current burst of inflation which reached 10.9 per cent in September 1990' (Riley 1990). In boom conditions houses, which are normally stolidly fixed assets, became to a considerable degree liquid, spendable assets, or assets on which liquid funds could readily be raised. The euphoric 'wealth-effect' of asset inflation stimulated both monetary demand and supply, since not only did spenders and borrowers so blessed feel confidently richer but lenders also felt more able and ready to lend on the security of the rising value of property and the greater personal wealth of the borrower. Although the principle of the 'wealth-effect' (which works both ways) has been known to economists for many generations, and was for example emphasized by the pre-1914 Cambridge School under the name of the 'Pigou effect', never has the principle been so widely and clearly demonstrated as in the latter half of the 1980s. Since around fifteen million, or two-thirds, of the UK's dwellings are now owner-occupied, with an aggregate value of around £1,000 billion, the total effect of a rising housing market on general expenditure, and therefore on inflation, became of considerable weight, particularly since the UK has a higher percentage of home ownership than most of its major competitors.

A flood of finance stimulated the housing boom (see Chrystal 1992). This still came mostly from the building societies, but with the banks now free to add much more than previously to the total sum. In the four years after 1984 the societies doubled their annual mortgage lending, with the largest increase ever made in the house-buying mania of 1988. Given this record expansion, the societies could then face with equanimity the growing competition of the banks. Loans made by the larger banks for house purchase trebled between 1984 and 1989, rising from £14.4 billion to £43.1 billion (Bank of England Report for 1989/90). Regardless of the original source or stated purpose of the loan, much of this huge flood found its way into general expenditure. This process of turning the inflated value of housing into consumer expenditure or into the repayment of short-term (and dearer) debt, a process known as 'equity withdrawal', soared to record heights reflecting the 'increasing sophistication of the personal borrower and the blurring of the distinction between mortgage and non-mortgage finance' and of course of the distinction between banks and building societies (Bank of England Report for 1989/90). The money supply tap was turned on full.

Not only were there too many institutions eagerly supplying too much credit, but also they were doing so at heavily subsidized rates of interest, since tax relief on mortgage interest was granted at the borrower's marginal, i.e. highest rate, up to the current limit of £30,000. Between the late 1970s and the mid-1980s the tax relief per mortgagor in real terms rose by 50 per cent. Yet in the March 1988 budget Nigel Lawson reaffirmed the government's commitment to the principle of mortgage interest relief, which was enjoyed by 8.4 million borrowers, including 500,000 single persons with joint or multiple mortgages.

The multiple mortgage, an inequitable and costly tax on legitimacy, was ended on 1 August 1988. In the mean time this otherwise welcome and overdue reform led to a stampede for joint and multiple mortgages before the deadline, creating a paradise for estate agents and a further sharp spur to inflation. Each downward step in interest rates (with base rates as we have seen down to 7½ per cent by May 1988) coupled with the budget's generous reductions in the rates of income tax, increased the euphoria and the scope for higher mortgages and equity withdrawal. Furthermore as well as thus stimulating powerful surges of demand-pull inflation, the cost of mortgage repayments formed a significant element in the cost-push pressures of wage bargaining, particularly as such payments rose progressively when in its belated and narrow-visioned response to inflation the government pushed base rates upwards to reach 15 per cent by 5 October 1989. A powerful polemic on this matter is given by the Oxford economist, Dr John Muellbauer, in his study of *The Great British Housing Disaster and Economic Policy* (1990). Just as mortgage finance, partly through 'equity withdrawal', spurred on the boom of 1988 to mid-1990 so thereafter as house prices fell below mortgage indebtedness, 'negative equity' helped to intensify and prolong the slump of the following three years.

The next two interrelated causes of Britain's differentially high and stubborn inflation, namely the confusing array of ever-changing monetary definitions, targets and indicators, and the vacillation with regard to the precise role of the exchange rate, lie at the heart of any evaluation of Britain's monetarist experiment. Although the quantity theory is the world's oldest explanation of the relationship between money and prices and was known to the ancient Greeks and has had a continuous existence in Europe since the sixteenth century, yet official statistics categorizing the money supply into narrow, medium or broad bands were not published in the UK until 1970, while official 'targets' date from as recently as 1976 – a further reason for choosing this latter year as the watershed between a Keynesian and a monetarist Britain. Since then there have been about as many changes in the definitions of money as there have been in the official definitions of unemployment, in both cases well over a score, reflecting adaptation to changing institutional and social practices coupled with political expediency. Already by 1982 the Bank of England had grown tired of pointing out that 'there is no single correct definition of money' and went on to analyse no less than 'twenty-four classes of assets, some of which are included in the aggregates and some not' (*BEQB* December 1982). Since then many more have emerged. The selection of aggregates reflected not only changing functions and institutions but also the varying exigencies of political pressures, informed or confused by changing economic theories. These monetary aggregates have included: M0, M1, NIB M1, M2, M3, M3C, Stg.M3, M4, M4C, M5, PSL1, PSL2, DCE, etc. The list is illustrative, not exhaustive, and the coverage has changed as, for example, hire purchase companies became banks or as a building society, such as Abbey National, the second largest, likewise became a bank; as the proportion of interest-bearing deposits rose significantly; and as the value of foreign as compared with sterling deposits changed in importance. These developments may be seen as modern elaborations of Keynes's original, simple but inspired dual classification in which the total money supply is 'the amount of cash held to satisfy the transactions and precautionary motives, M1, and the amount held to satisfy the speculative motive, M2 . . . Thus M = M1 plus M2' (Keynes 1936, 199). In the mid-1990s the argument which still rages, after twenty years of inconclusive experimentation, relates fundamentally to whether narrow or broad money, or some weighted combination of them, makes the best target.

In practice, money breaks down all artificial barriers; which explains how 'savings' from housing rushed into spending, and why the intermediate monetary categories get pulled and pushed from both sides, becoming unstable and unreliable over time, just as happened to the former officially favoured target 'Sterling M3'. Targets may be secret or publicly announced; they may be points or ranges. Insofar as monetary policy requires firm public expectations, a target must be publicly announced, and preferably hit; while the flexibility obviously allowed by a range gives the authorities a much greater chance of claiming success than when faced with the over-precise imperative of a stark point. Only aggregates which have demonstrably acted as good measures of, or good pointers to, inflationary pressures should be chosen as targets. Unfortunately 'Goodhart's Law' has often intervened to undermine the reliability of indicators promoted into targets. Professor Goodhart, when economic adviser at the Bank of England, very wisely (though at first jocularly) commented that 'any observed statistical regularity will tend to collapse once pressure is placed upon it for control purposes'. This scepticism was thus not confined to anti-monetarist outsiders. By the mid-1980s it had infected the highest ranks inside the monetary authorities. Thus Governor Leigh-Pemberton himself publicly wondered whether 'the unpredictability of the relationship between money and nominal incomes could reach a point – as in some other countries – at which we would do better to dispense with monetary targetry altogether . . . and whether that point has arrived in relation to broad money' (*BEQB*, December 1986). Broad money ceased therefore to be a target at the beginning of the next financial year. The fractious baby had been thrown out with the bath water; and this was at the very time when the Lawson boom, fuelled by record equity withdrawal, was being frantically signalled by the newly discarded and discredited broad money target. There remained as a target only M0, or narrow money (although to confuse the uninitiated this is always termed officially in the Bank's statistics 'the wide money base').

Little wonder that public credibility, a vital feature in inflationary expectations, had evaporated. Sir Ian Gilmour, one of Mrs Thatcher's many ex-ministers, captured the public's sceptical mood perfectly when he wrote: 'Monetarism may be termed the uncontrollable in pursuit of the indefinable' (1983, 142). Though difficult to interpret, the plethora of monetary statistics stood in contrast to a fall in the quantity and quality of general economic statistics – a costly parsimony. The Governor of the Bank was thus fully justified in protesting that 'policy mistakes and forecasting errors' were in part the result of the 'misleading information provided by official statistics' (*BEQB*, May 1990). This statistical fog not only caused both the Governor and the Chancellor to underestimate the strength of the combined consumer and investment boom, consequently overstimulated by their reductions in interest and income tax rates, but also helped to excuse their delay in taking the necessary remedial actions.

There had thus been three stages in monetary targetry since its introduction in 1976: first the emphasis was on broad money, mostly Sterling M3; secondly in the mid-1980s equal weight was also given to narrow money, mostly M0; and finally from 1987 M0 remained the only target until 8 October 1992 when for the first time the rate of inflation itself (within a range of 1–4 per cent) became the officially declared target. Without becoming trapped in the maze of definitions, it is essential to note briefly how, belatedly, building society and other similar savings deposits, which have been responsible for releasing so much of the inflationary potential of recent decades, came to be incorporated into the monetary aggregates. The relevant figures first appeared – as an 'experiment' – in the Bank's *Bulletin* of September 1979, as 'Private Sector Liquidity'; and after a continued existence in slightly differing guises, still form an important and essential ingredient in M4, the main broad money aggregate for policy purposes. Like Russian dolls, the broader aggregates enclose the lesser, but with surprisingly differing shapes. Faith in M0 at first resided in the simplistic theory that changes in its shape would bring about corresponding changes in the broader categories, or (to change the metaphor) that the whole broad inverted pyramid of money and credit not only rested on, but was also controlled by, the money base, whether M0 or by some similar or even narrower measure, the size of which could be directly determined by the Bank of England. In countries without bank-like building societies and where the reserves kept by the commercial banks in their central banks are substantial, such devices work reasonably well; but unfortunately for 'little M0' and its worshippers that situation no longer applies to the UK.

In June 1990 the narrow aggregate M0, which consists of notes and coin in circulation (comprising over 99 per cent of the total) and bankers' operational balances at the Bank of England (which comprise less than 1 per cent) came in all to only £18 billion, equivalent to £320 per head of population or under two weeks' national income, a proportion which has been tending to fall over recent years. In contrast the stock of M4, which comprises the private sector's holdings of cash plus sterling deposits at banks and building societies, came to £455 billion or almost £8,000 per head, and equal to about ten months' national income, a proportion which has tended to rise with national wealth over recent years (*BEQB* August 1990). It appears increasingly unlikely that, in British circumstances, M0 even when hit, will *control* the massive M4, but it may well *reflect* changes in inflationary pressures. The big advantage of M0 is that it is used practically entirely for transactions to be made now or in the very near future, so that it is the best quick indicator of expenditures and of changes in the rate of expenditure. It is a very good coincident or concurrent economic indicator, but not nearly as good a predictor of future spending as many monetarists had claimed. It tells us where we are and where we have just been, but not where we are going: and it tells us nothing about cheques or plastic money. M4, which is a changing mixture of moneys kept for actual and anticipated expenditure as well as for saving, does at least indicate potential inflationary pressures up to one or two years ahead, although not in anything like a mechanistic manner.

After fifteen years of targetry, neither the Bank nor the Treasury, which though wounded, are surely best placed to make a judgement, seemed at all confident with regard to which aggregates (if any) to target. Unfortunately, to paraphrase Yeats, the best lack all conviction, while the rest are full of passionate intensity backed up by models of economic certainty. Official scepticism towards targetry has allowed some monetarists to argue (against all other evidence) not so much that monetarism has failed but that it has not been properly carried out. In a letter to *The Times* (28 September 1990) a self-appointed Shadow Monetary Policy Group of ten influential monetarists, including Tim

Congdon, Patrick Minford, Gordon Pepper and Sir Alan Walters wrote that

> it is right and timely to emphasise the strong need for a coherent and credible domestic monetary policy . . . Given the complexities of the modern deregulated financial environment it would be appropriate to monitor and probably target a spectrum of monetary aggregates including both the narrow (M0) transactions measure currently targeted and broader measures of money and credit.

In the light of the dire limitations of the UK's internal monetary indicators and targets, Nigel Lawson very understandably decided to make use of the exchange rate, long deferred to as an additional indicator, in the form of 'shadowing the D-mark', to act as a brake on UK inflation. No money can serve two masters, the internal money supply and the external exchange rate; nor can the economy be expected to give credence to the two diametrically opposed views seen to be struggling for mastery in the Cabinet of the late 1980s, namely that of the official Chancellor and that of Mrs Thatcher's private economic adviser, Sir Alan Walters, who advocated freely floating exchange rates and single-minded concentration on internal control of the money supply. The City and then the country became aware of these incompatibilities, and as the crisis intensified the Bank of England forced base rates up step by step to reach 15 per cent on 5 October 1989. By 26 October Nigel Lawson felt constrained to resign, followed almost immediately by the resignation of Sir Alan Walters from his part-time appointment (probably the only instance in history of an economic adviser resigning because his advice was preferred by the head of state). Yet just a year later, on 5 October 1990, the Prime Minister herself announced from outside 10 Downing Street that with effect from 8 October Britain was to enter the Exchange Rate Mechanism of the European Monetary System (and that the Bank was bringing its Minimum Lending Rate down from 15 to 14 per cent). This was much more than a tactical monetary manoeuvre. However unintended, it seemed to herald the end of the sovereignty of the pound sterling, and led within two months to the overthrow of Mrs Thatcher. Monetary policy dominated politics. As it turned out Britain remained in the ERM for less than two years – only until Black (or White) Wednesday, 16 September 1992.

EMU: The end of the pound sterling?

Radical currency reform, while rare in England's long history, has been endemic on the Continent: a contrast which may help to explain

Britain's uniquely strong reluctance to accept the currency changes involved in European Economic and Monetary Union (EMU), and which the other members more readily welcome. Most European countries, large or small, have repeatedly had to carry out changes which have drastically altered their internal currencies. Admittedly Britain's actual coinage, ever since Anglo-Saxon days, has undergone cycles of debasement and reform. Admittedly too, 'the pound in our pocket', despite Prime Minister Harold Wilson's denial in 1967, has been grossly devalued. However, the pound as a unit of account has never had to be replaced by a 'new pound' or any other designation in 1,300 years, in contrast to the French franc or the various German currencies such as the Reichsmark, Rentenmark, Ostmark and Deutsche Mark, to mention merely some of the more modern changes. In contrast to such major changes, the two minor changes even remotely comparable in twentieth-century Britain were, first the cessation of the internal circulation of the gold sovereign and half sovereign in 1914, and secondly decimalization in 1971. The former had been proposed by Ricardo a hundred years earlier and took place without a hitch; as did the latter, after attempts at reform spread leisurely over 150 years. A proposal by Lord Wrottesley in 1824 in favour of currency decimalization was rejected by Parliament, as were similar proposals following a number of other reports, including those of the Select Committee of 1853 and the Royal Commissions of 1857 and 1918. At long last, following the Halsbury Report of 1963 currency decimalization arrived with effect from 15 February 1971, and turned out to be, despite the irrational fears of opponents, so successful as to be termed a 'non-event'. For Britain the changes proposed by EMU are uniquely different in kind from those faced in her previous history: for most of the other countries such changes simply represent their own history repeating itself on a larger scale.

A second basic difference between sterling and continental European currencies springs from the fact that the pound had been paramount in international trade for two hundred years but remained (except for Scandinavia and Portugal) relatively unimportant in intra-European trade. Conversely even the major European currencies were unimportant in international trade outside their own colonies. Thus when sterling went off the gold standard in 1931 the Scandinavian countries and Portugal chose to join the Commonwealth countries as part of the sterling area, since Britain was their major trading partner. But this situation was interrupted with the outbreak of war in 1939, which temporarily severed and permanently weakened the connection with the European members of the sterling area. France had managed to cling to the gold standard until 1936 and thereafter continued until the war to be the centre of a franc bloc which included most of the non-German European countries south of Scandinavia. Until the First World War the pound had no rival overseas, nor, except for the US dollar, until after the Second World War. On the Continent however it had always faced strong competition, especially from the French franc. Throughout the long era of sterling supremacy it was the other countries that had in the main to adapt their currency arrangements to fit in with sterling. From 1945 to 1972 Britain, like other countries, had to fit its currencies to the exigencies of the dollar. From the time that Britain belatedly entered the EEC on 1 January 1973 she too had to undergo the difficult transition involved in adapting sterling to the currency arrangements of her EEC partners, a change in attitude greater than that required from these other participants.

Continental Europeans have long been accustomed to currency unions: for Britain before 1990 they have been either unnecessary or peripheral. Thus in 1861, under French initiative, a Latin Monetary Union was formed comprising France, Italy, Belgium, Switzerland and Greece. The primary gold and silver coins of each country were made legal tender and circulated throughout the Union, though subsidiary, token coins were legal tender only within their own country. The Union lasted until the 1920s, by which time the strains of the wars and the widening differences between the value of gold and silver caused its gradual demise. A rather similar pattern was seen in the Scandinavian Monetary Union formed in the 1870s, until, under similar pressures it was effectively dissolved by Sweden in 1924. By far the most successful of all such currency unions, but embracing much more than just the currency, was the Zollverein of 1834, whereby the separate currencies, weights and measures of the previously independent thirty-nine German states were gradually combined, leading to the unification of Germany in 1871, with the chief Prussian bank becoming the Reichsbank. We have already noted how the formation of the Bank for International Settlements at Basle in 1930 emerged from the inter-war arrangements regarding German reparations, and we shall see how in a similar way the disbursement of Marshall Aid to Europe after the Second World War paved the way for new forms of European monetary co-operation.

During and immediately after that war almost every country on the European continent experienced the destruction and reform of their currencies. Germany reformed her currency in 1948 (on which her subsequent success was based) after having suffered two hyper-inflations in a generation. The former German-occupied countries, from France to Norway, got rid of their wartime inflation by means of overnight currency reforms whereby their grossly inflated wartime currencies were reduced by up to a hundredfold or more, thus not only providing the basis for a sound new currency but also penalizing collaborators, profiteers, tax-evaders and similar unworthy holders of swollen money balances. At the same time, it provided the grandest and most perfect example of the effectiveness of the quantity theory of money administered at a stroke and, most unusually, in a price-reducing manner. Thus in glaring contrast to the British, most continental families or their parents have personally experienced drastic currency reform, followed by unprecedented growth in their living standards. For them EMU was just another logical step, not the leap in the dark it seemed to a considerable section of British opinion, especially among the older and more influential generation. In the light of this geographical contrast the main steps taken since 1945 in Europe towards greater currency convergence and exchange rate stability will now briefly be outlined in order to place in perspective the Delors 'Report on Economic and Monetary Union' of April 1989, which, when and if fully implemented, would in effect, and possibly also in name, mark the end of a dozen currencies, including the pound sterling, and their replacement by a single currency serving the whole Community.*

The Bretton Woods agreement of 1944 envisaged an idealized post-war world of convertible currencies, fixed exchange rates and free trade. It had become painfully obvious by 1947 that the transition towards such a system would require substantial assistance to Europe from the USA. The immediate dollar shortage from which the war-torn countries of Europe suffered was in large part met by the European Recovery Programme proposed by General George Marshall in a speech at Harvard on 5 June 1947. To help ensure the effective distribution of Marshall Aid, an Organization for European Economic Co-operation was formed (becoming enlarged in 1961 to the permanent Organization for Economic Co-operation and Development), which also helped during the period 1948–50 to broaden the existing restrictive bilateral payments system into wider multilateral clearings. By 1950 sufficient progress had been made to set up the European Payments Union, which enabled its fifteen member countries mutually to offset deficits and surpluses, up to the limits of their quotas. These quotas were set according to each country's share of world trade in 1949. Significantly Britain's quota at $1,060 million was over one-quarter of the total, with France's at $520 million and Germany's at only $320 million. The Bank for International Settlements fittingly acted as the agent for EPU with the accounts reckoned in a new abstract common denominator, the

*See p. 662 below.

European Accounting Unit (EAU) initially equal to one US dollar or 0.888671 grams of fine gold. In that same year of 1950 the European Coal and Steel Community was established, which grew by means of the Treaty of Rome (25 March 1957) into the EEC of the original Six: Benelux, France, Germany and Italy. Britain remained insular. By December 1958 Britain and most other European countries made their currencies convertible to such a degree that EPU became superfluous and was terminated. An enlarged role was found for its replacement under a new European Monetary Agreement with a larger fund to assist currency stabilization. The Treaty of Rome had also set up the European Investment Bank to counter overcentralization and to foster regionally balanced growth through granting long-term loans for infrastructural projects and also 'global finance', through intermediaries like Britain's ICFC, to smaller enterprises. Whereas the origins and constitutions of BIS and EIB differed, they were complementary institutions with close and continuous co-operation facilitated by sharing at least one director and by both using the EAU as their official accounting currency. This latter point was much more than being the technical detail it might first appear; and it was to become later of strategic importance with regard to British participation in EMU. It prepared the way for the Ecu.

The extreme and apparently persistent dollar shortage of the 1940s and 1950s gave way in the next two decades to an increasingly stubborn dollar glut. Foreigners' liquid claims on US dollars increased tenfold from around $7 billion in 1953 to around $70 billion in 1971. Over the same period US gold reserves fell from over $22 billion to less than $11 billion. The inescapable decision facing the US authorities was taken on 15 August 1971 when the convertibility of the dollar at the fixed price of $35 per ounce of gold was ended. The foundation of the Bretton Woods system of fixed exchange rates collapsed. After some five months of severe dollar turbulence a meeting of the 'Group of Ten' major economies was held in December 1971 at the Smithsonian Institute in Washington, as a result of which dollar currency parities were realigned and the participants agreed to keep fluctuations within 2¼ per cent either side of their new parities (compared with the 1 per cent swing allowed under the Bretton Woods regime). This realistically allowed much greater rate flexibility while yet providing a framework of settled parities with the world's major trading currency. In a brave but abortive search for still greater stability, the UK joined the EEC's 'narrower margins scheme' (the so-called 'snake') on 1 May 1972; but after only six weeks and despite the member central banks' strong support for the weak pound, the government decided on 23 June to float the pound.

Thus for the first time since 1939 sterling floated freely against all currencies – and was to remain floating for eighteen years until October 1990.

The British monetary pendulum had thus swung suddenly from firm faith in the virtues of fixed exchange rates, to an equally fervent belief in the extreme monetarist doctrine espoused by Milton Friedman and his followers in favour of floating rates and of 'letting the market decide' (Friedman 1953). Protagonists of floating exchange rates could point to the long experience of Canada, to the release from 'stop-go' restrictions, to steadier, more sustained growth now that there was no need to keep idle reserves to defend a fixed rate, etc. In the quiet, uncomplicated model world of both classical and monetarist economists the Purchasing Power Parity theory might well work in the long run (during which British manufacturing industry nearly died). Although the PPP theory – that the underlying exchange rate in free markets is a reflection of countries' relative prices of traded and tradeable goods and services – has some merit, that does not justify claiming that an equilibrium rate, and far less that an equilibrating or stabilizing rate, will arise from the untrammelled working of market forces. The foreign exchange market has rarely been a perfect market which would allow a supposed 'equilibrium' rate to emerge such as would necessarily be superior to the arbitrarily judged rates fixed by the monetary authorities.

The effects of relative price levels as determinants of exchange rates in free markets are swamped by capital transfers, arbitration and financial speculation. Even leaving aside such transfers, in modern conditions dealings in key commodities alone are sufficient to cause de-stabilization. The experience of that most volatile commodity, oil, in recent decades had shown that 'unfettered markets have had a record of making monumental mistakes endangering the livelihood of millions. The spot markets, selling and reselling cargoes, turn over a hundred times as many "paper barrels" as the real stuff and over-emphasize transient factors' (OPEC *Bulletin* August 1990, 3). Even in normal periods foreign exchanges not based on actual goods predominate. A study made for the European Parliament noted that 'the volume of financial transactions exceeded turnover in world trade in real terms by a factor of 25' (*The European Financial Common Market*, June 1989, 17). This imbalance is especially so in the UK, given that London is still the world's largest foreign exchange market but has long ceased being the world's largest importer or exporter of goods. A co-ordinated survey of foreign exchanges by the Bank of England, the Bank of Tokyo and the Federal Reserve Bank of New York in March 1986 showed their average total daily turnover at nearly $200 billion, with London's at $90 billion, New York's at $50 billion and Tokyo's at $48 billion (BIS 57th Annual Report, 1987, 163). Little wonder then that free foreign exchange markets, far from being naturally equilibrating, in actual fact often tend to be volatile and destabilizing, while even the authorities' corrective measures themselves not infrequently lead to 'overshooting'.

Such overshooting occurred repeatedly during the eighteen years of Britain's monetarist experiment with floating rates. Despite enforced interventions (castigated by the more extreme monetarists as 'dirty floating') to control the most violent movements, the value of the pound swung from around $2.45 in 1975 to $1.60 a year later, back to over $2.40 in 1980, only to fall to a record low point of just above $1.0 in 1983. In no way could swings of such amplitude be said to be caused by changes in relative price levels. While speculators might profit from such wild swings, the uncertainties facing producers and traders in real goods and services was obvious. Although all the world's currencies suffered from the gyrations of the dollar (mainly), yet the EEC's system of combining a joint float against the dollar with narrower margins for their own currencies gave greater security than isolated floating, and even for a time attracted countries outside the EEC such as Sweden and Norway to join this 'snake inside the tunnel'. Britain's stance with one foot in Chicago and one in Brussels was becoming too painful to endure. It was thus becoming increasingly conceded by the late 1980s that Britain needed the sort of anchor that the rest of the EEC had forged since 1979.

On 13 March 1979 the EEC began operating its European Monetary System (EMS) to create a zone of monetary stability in Europe and to strengthen the economies of its less prosperous members. The Bank of England was heavily engaged in preparing the structure and operational details of the new scheme, thus smoothing the way for the UK's hesitant, step-by-step approach to full membership. The main features of the EMS include an Exchange Rate Mechanism (ERM) which was a replacement and improvement on the original 'snake', allowing similar fluctuations of 2¼ per cent either side of an agreed central rate but with a 6 per cent swing initially allowed for weaker entrants such as Italy, Spain and eventually Britain. Secondly, the European Monetary Co-operation Fund, originally formed in 1973, was strengthened by the deposit of 20 per cent of each member's gold and dollar reserves. Thirdly, a new European Currency Unit, the Ecu, was formed, based on the weighted average of ten European currencies, including the pound and the drachma though neither Britain nor Greece were initially full participants of the ERM.

The UK became from the start a contributor to the Monetary Co-operation Fund and a most enthusiastic promoter of wider use of the Ecu; but decided not to join ERM. This refusal sprang not only from the influence of monetarism, with its inbuilt preference for floating rates, but also from the government's more practical consideration that the pound's position as a petro-currency would expose it to greater and more divergent pressures than those facing the other EEC currencies. In keeping with the UK's more market-related philosophy, it decided on 23 October 1979, just six months after the start of EMS, boldly to remove all foreign exchange controls. The removal after some forty years of these protective devices gave a lead to the rest of the EEC in this field and further strengthened the role of the City in the world's financial markets. When, for the reasons given above, the UK finally turned its back on the dubious joys of isolated floating and with typical belatedness joined the ERM on 8 October 1990, the EEC had moved on to consider the still greater challenges of the Delors Report: challenges not easily dodged by procrastination.

By December 1985 all members of the EEC had agreed to a 'Single European Act' to create by the end of 1992 a unified economic area in which goods, services, people and capital would be able to move freely. As part of the implementation process, the European Council invited M. Jacques Delors, President of the European Commission, to chair a committee with the task of studying and proposing concrete steps leading to economic and monetary union. Among its other sixteen members were the heads of member central banks 'in their personal capacities', including Robin Leigh-Pemberton, and Karl Otto Pöhl; and Alexandre Lamfalussy, General Manager of BIS. The subsequent Report on Economic and Monetary Union in the European Community (April 1989) proposed a three-stage programme with 1 July 1990 as its starting date. Although no dates were proposed for the subsequent stages, 'the decision to enter upon the first stage', said the report with expectation bordering on arrogance, 'should be a decision to embark on the entire process' (para. 39). What proponents saw as an integrated and logical progression, opponents saw equally clearly as a slippery slope towards an irrevocable loss of economic and political sovereignty. Furthermore, unlike previous and premature attempts at EMU, such as the Werner Report of 1970, which failed not only because of the oil shocks of that decade but also primarily because the French and German economies had not converged sufficiently, the Delors Report came at a time when the economies of the inner core comprising France, the reuniting Germany, Benelux and possibly also Italy had already converged to a degree sufficient to provide a seemingly firm foundation for its bold proposals. The unconverged UK remained unconvinced.

The main proposals for Stage One were that (a) 'a single financial area' should be established 'in which all monetary and financial instruments circulate freely and banking, securities and insurance services are offered uniformly throughout the area'; (b) 'all Community currencies are in the exchange rate mechanism'; and (c) 'all impediments to the private use of the Ecu should be removed' (para. 52). During Stage Two the Community would (a) 'set precise rules relating to the size of annual budget deficits and their financing'; (b) see that a 'European System of Central Banks (ESCB) – would be set up'; and (c) require that 'the margins within ERM be narrowed' progressively to zero (paras. 56, 57). Thus 'Stage Three would commence with the move to irrevocably locked exchange rates' (para. 58); 'The transition to a single monetary policy would be made with the ESCB assuming responsibility for the formulation and implementation of monetary policy'; while 'the change-over to the single currency would take place during this stage' (para. 60). Rarely has the publication of such a brief report (of just forty pages) had such a wide, deep and controversial impact: irrespective of the timing and extent of its possible eventual implementation, the Delors Report gave public notice that neither the Bank of England nor the pound sterling would ever be the same again. The days of the sovereignty of the pound were numbered.

The increased sovereignty of the consumer in a greatly enlarged single market of 350 million people could no longer be coterminous with national boundaries of 56 million under the authority of a sovereign parliamentary executive and of the Bank of England as much as had previously been the case.

> Once every banking institution in the Community is free to accept deposits from, and to grant loans to, any customer in the Community and in any of the national currencies, the large degree of territorial coincidence between a national central bank's area of jurisdiction, the area in which its currency is used and the area in which its banking system operates will be lost. (Delors Report, para. 24)

For such reasons Delors very logically proposed that 'the domestic and international monetary policy-making of the Community should be organised in a federal form in . . . a European System of Central Banks, consisting of a central institution and the twelve national central banks' (para. 32). (Because ESCB has many eye-catching, but mostly superficial, similarities with the US Federal Reserve System it has often been dubbed 'Eurofed'.) 'The ESCB would be committed to the objective of price stability', consequently 'the ESCB Council should be independent of instructions from national governments and Community authorities' (para. 32). Given the dismal failure of Britain's monetarist policies to eradicate inflation even after twenty years of making that objective its explicit target, the need for such independence cannot reasonably be gainsaid. British experience merely brings forcibly up to date the unmistakably clear lessons of history that governments without specific constitutional safeguards cannot be trusted to control their money-making powers sufficiently to achieve stable money. Furthermore monetary policy alone, unless this is taken to include key aspects of fiscal policy, cannot bring price stability. Hence there must be *effective co-ordination between budgetary and monetary policy* with 'upper limits on budget deficits, exclusion of access to direct central bank credit and limits on borrowing in non-Community currencies' (para. 33). This provides another example where consumer sovereignty requires the limitation of political sovereignty.

Now whereas the Delors formula might well suffice for the majority of EEC countries to succeed in their fight against inflation, in Britain's case something more is vitally necessary, as was clearly recognized by Nigel Lawson right from the early days of MTFS. 'To achieve stable prices', he wrote, 'implies fighting and changing the culture and psychology of two generations. That cannot be achieved overnight. But let there be no doubt that that is our goal' (1984, 11). It was most unfortunate for Mr Lawson and for the UK that British attitudes are so infuriatingly slow to change. But when the time is overripe they *can* change dramatically.

It was largely in order to gain time for Britain to adjust to the demands of EMU that the Major/Butler plan for a 'hard Ecu' was devised. This envisaged that, instead of the EC's twelve currencies being suddenly replaced with the (ordinary) Ecu at a specific time in Stage Three, the 'hard Ecu' would be a parallel or common currency growing in use naturally according to the demands of the financial markets, competing with and possibly eventually supplanting the other currencies. In essence the idea is neither new nor peculiarly British. Thus within a year of the start of the Ecu, Daniel Strasser, the European Commission's Director-General for Budgets, wrote that 'There is every reason to suppose that step by step the point will be reached when conditions will be ripe for a European currency to take its place alongside the national currencies. This development will certainly be speeded up by the introduction of the Ecu' (Strasser 1980, 30). The case for the UK's 'hard Ecu' was put very strongly by the Governor of the Bank of England to European parliamentarians at Strasbourg on 11 July 1990, where he pointed out that the 'hard Ecu' would be 'quite different from the current Basket Ecu' which simply mirrors the average values of the twelve currencies, whereas the hard variety would not only be as strong as the strongest of these but also 'could never be devalued' (*BEQB*, August 1990).

Opposition to the hard Ecu as an unnecessary thirteenth currency (or possibly fourteenth, since it differs from the basket version) has come from influential quarters; and Mrs Thatcher herself has damned it with faint praise. At a conference at the London School of Economics in November 1990 Karl Otto Pöhl, president of the Bundesbank, roundly condemned the hard Ecu proposals as 'the worst possible recipe for monetary policy'. At the same time a report from the Select Committee of the House of Lords on EMU and Political Union firmly rejected the hard Ecu in favour of the single currency, as being the only sensible route to EMU. The committee, chaired by Lord Aldington, was composed mainly of Conservative and Independent peers and, significantly, included two former Governors of the Bank of England, Lord Cromer and Lord O'Brien. Fears that Britain might be relegated to a 'lower tier' within the European Community was shared by the City and industry. Reference has already been made to London's leading position in foreign exchange shown by a survey in 1986. A new survey carried out in April 1989 confirmed London's lead, with daily foreign exchange turnover of $187 billion compared with $129 billion for New York and $115 billion for Tokyo. A third survey, taken in April 1992, showed that London had impressively extended its lead, with its daily turnover of foreign currencies rising to $300 billion compared with $192 billion in the USA and $128 billion in Japan, (*BEQB* November 1992). London's lead in foreign equity dealing is even more impressive. 'In 1988 London's turnover in foreign equities at $71 billion was nearly one and a half times that of New York and ten times that of Tokyo' (*BEQB* November 1990). These advantages might well be put at risk if the UK were in the lower tier, while the benefits to industry of lower transactions costs enjoyed by any possible top tier business would likewise be lost.

Because Thatcherism depended so singularly on monetary policy, any transfer of decision-making power in the financial area, such as is bound to occur with EMU, was certain to be keenly felt. As the EEC progresses by whatever route towards EMU, 'the shift from national monetary policies to a single monetary policy is inescapable' (Delors Report, para. 24). Furthermore because 'transport costs and economies of scale would tend to favour a shift in economic activity away from less developed regions especially if they were at the periphery to the highly developed areas at its centre', structural adjustments would have to be made to 'help poorer regions to catch up with the wealthier ones' (Delors Report, para. 29). The interventionist nature of stronger structural and regional policies had either been rejected, or accepted with great reluctance, by Mrs Thatcher, despite being seen as a welcome necessity by her European partners – and by many of her former ministers. e.g. Michael Heseltine, Sir Ian Gilmour and Peter Walker.

The inter-governmental conferences and the treaty amendments required to implement the next stages of EMU should offer all members enough opportunities to adjust their parities so that they could be finally fixed in such a way (e.g. at arithmetically convenient rates) so as to meet both the demands of a single currency for wholesale and larger retail trading throughout the Community while still retaining national currency names for internal, mostly small-scale retail trade (which will always amount to the overwhelming number of transactions). However if a substantial majority of the twelve eventually carry out their stated intention of going directly to a single currency, there is little to be said in favour of Britain's attempt to jump the gap in two hops. As previously indicated, many of the apparently most difficult problems – decimalization, currency reform, and the most recent and telling example of the merging of the two German marks – turned out to be much easier than had been anticipated. With regard to the last, academics, lawyers, economists, bankers and civil servants in endless committees could have enjoyed decades of discussion backed up by shoals of published and most erudite papers in order to come to ineffective and controversial decisions as to whether one D-mark was worth 7.36 or 3.27 or 2.73 East-marks, for 'hardly any reliable benchmarks were available for the "correct" conversion rates' (Monthly Report of the Deutsche Bundesbank, July 1990, 14). In the event Chancellor Helmut Kohl determined swiftly, simply and boldly on round figure one-for-one and one-for-two rates for different categories, to be worked out in detail by his 'independent' Bundesbank and the East German monetary authorities with immediate effect from 1 July 1990. But only a strong economy with a strong currency could make such a decision work. The sovereignty of the people depends on their productivity. In Euro-jargon effective 'subsidiarity', or rule by the lower levels of government, depends on the economic clout of the nation or region in question.

In concluding this analysis of British monetary development in the twentieth century, the key to understanding its complexity has been shown to be the inherent tendency of money, both in practice and in theory, to swing like a pendulum between periods when there is an institutional and theoretical compulsion to press for increased quantity and decreasing quality, and then suddenly to veer back to periods when all the emphasis returns to efforts at restoring quality through controlling the quantity. As a new century approaches, the intervening stage before universal money displays similar pendulate tendencies, since global finance will be operating with tri-polar currencies; the dollar, the yen and, last but not least, the adolescent Ecu: an uneasy troika.

The timetable for the prematurely agreed Delors Report and, possibly some of its essential principles also, seemed in danger of being thrown overboard during the speculative storms which lasted intermittently from mid-1992 to August 1993. Even Sweden, normally a most stable sound-money economy, raised its official short-term interest rate in September 1992 to 500 per cent. The date of 16 September 1992, when international speculators forced Britain to leave the Exchange Rate Mechanism, was at first called 'Black' Wednesday, by the narrow sound-money men, but then dubbed 'White' or 'Bright' Wednesday by those with a broader view of economic realities, because it paved the way for an overdue and substantial fall in British interest rates sufficient to revive the economy form the dismal slump of 1990–2. Less than a year later the hungry and expectant speculators turned their attention to a number of other currencies, especially the franc, forcing a hurried general reorganization of the ERM. As from 1 August 1993 the official currency bands were hugely extended, from 2¼ per cent to as much as 15 per cent on either side of the central parity. With permissible swings of up to 30 per cent between the strongest and weakest currencies (another case of overshooting) the drive towards a single currency had for the time being gone rapidly into reverse. Even more than the break-up of the Bretton Woods system of fixed exchange rates in 1971, the disruption of the ERM in 1992–3 demonstrated in a most disconcerting manner to the world's monetary authorities and to the over-confident planners in Brussels that few nations, armed as they are with the relatively puny reserves of their central banks, even when they manage, painfully, to act in concert, can stand out against the vast resources at the disposal of the international speculators who seize their profitable chances whenever rates of exchange are perceived to be unrealistic. Their actions provide a most instructive example of the increasing global sovereignty of the consumer, which greatly limits the degree of sovereignty previously enjoyed by national monetary authorities. It is becoming ever harder to 'buck the market'. Granted that the central banks can normally be the largest single operators, yet even the UK's official reserves which stood at $43 billion in September

1993, form little more than a drop in the ocean of the trillion-dollar-a-day foreign exchange market.

The dawn of a single European currency, planned with complacent confidence in the 1980s, seemed by mid-1993 to have been pushed much further away, at least into the early decades of the next millenium. This was certainly then the view of the British government, with the 'fault lines' of the ERM pointedly exposed by the rare appearance of a signed article by the Prime Minister, John Major, in *The Economist* (25 September 1993). Such pessimism was roundly rejected by most of the other EC leaders, especially Chancellor Kohl and President Mitterrand. No doubt the number of countries willing and able to attach themselves to the inner core and its single currency will wane and, mostly, wax, in the usual pendulate fashion, as their economies diverge or converge. The EC had already officially become a 'single market' with no barriers to capital, labour, goods or services, from 1 January 1993, while the Maastricht treaty had also come into force from 1 November of the same year, reconfirming the timetable for a single currency by the end of 1999 at the latest. Despite possible slippage, the momentum towards European Monetary Union appeared to be too great to be halted indefinitely. To re-echo Montagu Norman, the dogs bark but the caravan moves on – this time roughly in the right general direction.

Germany's long record of financial rectitude was rewarded by the decision to set up the headquarters of the European Monetary Institute – and so eventually of the European Central Bank – in Frankfurt. The head fittingly chosen for this new supra-bank was Baron Alexandre Lamfalussy, the Belgian General Manager of the Bank for International Settlements, which had long acted as a quasi-central bank for thirty or so central bankers and had, ironically, originally been set up, as described earlier, in 1930 in order to reorganize German reparations. It is painfully apparent that the change from national moneys to larger regional money blocs is fraught with problems as yet only partially resolved. The even more remote goal of a single, universal money still beckons, a vision for bloodless world citizens and a nightmare for nationalists. In the mean time the foreign exchange markets, in which London is still likely to play the major role, will be operating with three main currencies; the dollar, the yen and an untidily changing group of European currencies which will increasingly include the new Euro as the symbol of wider and deeper financial, economic and probably also political, integration.

9

American Monetary Development
since 1700

Introduction: the economic basis of the dollar

The American dollar, by far the world's most important currency for most of the twentieth century, is the natural product of what has long been and still remains easily the world's strongest economy. Nevertheless the strength of the dollar relative to gold, and (much more importantly) relative to other currencies, has fluctuated widely so causing greater problems and creating greater opportunities for traders and speculators than has been the case with any other currency, including gold. The role held undisputedly by sterling for a hundred years before 1914, based on the world's first industrial revolution, has been overtaken by the US dollar since about 1931, reluctantly at first, but all the more inevitably because the choice of the dollar as the world's major trading currency was made by the practical everyday decisions of the rest of the world. The dollar climbed to its international eminence on the back of its factories and farms. The strength of the dollar was not derived from the strength of the American financial system; rather the reverse, for time and time again throughout its history the dollar, weakened by endemic failures, has been restored to strength through the robust power of American agriculture, forestry, mining, manufacturing industry and managerial expertise. The fact that major international institutions like the World Bank and IMF set up their headquarters in Washington simply endorsed and reinforced a choice that had already been made by the world's markets and underlined universal acceptance of the belief that the value of the dollar was too important a matter to be left to the decisions of American politicians alone.

The role of the dollar made economic isolation obviously impossible for the USA and, only a little less obviously, political isolation also. Such integration has meant that increasingly during the second half of the twentieth century global finance speaks with an unmistakably American accent, for far more trade, internal and external, is carried on in dollars than in any other currency. The almighty dollar was not something consciously forced on the rest of the world by American politicians skilfully aware of their growing power; it was a role voluntarily chosen by the rest of the world with only occasional and ineffectual cries of protest from (mainly French) politicians and of course from academics on both sides of the Atlantic. The process by which the dollar rose to such prominence from its humble and inauspicious origins two centuries ago will now be examined with particular reference to the ways in which the American constitutional and legal framework has influenced the structure and operations of its financial system.

Colonial money: the swing from dearth to excess, 1700–1775

Colonial America offered a clean slate where the immigrants repeated their age-old European monetary habit of swinging from an initial dire monetary shortage to reach eventual inflationary excess. In the early years, for at least two or three generations, particularly but not exclusively in the frontier zones, the colonists were drastically short of money – not just in the simplest sense that everyone feels that he or she could do with more money – but in the realistic, economic sense that the colonists' actual, and still more their potential, productive capacities were curtailed by an obvious lack of currency. Actual money supply chronically fell short of demand; and in such circumstances those lucky enough to possess money held on to it more cautiously than they would otherwise have done, so decreasing monetary velocity and thus intensifying the shortage. In money matters, as in so many other fields, the colonists had to compromise and experiment, compensating for the dire shortage of official coins by resorting to a wide variety of money-substitutes, many of which they would have disdained to use in their countries of origin. A large proportion of immigrants, such as indentured labourers, servants and slaves were so poor that they brought few if any possessions and little or no money with them. No silver or gold mines were found in these early colonies to supply indigenous sources of money. Furthermore the trade balance with Britain was generally heavily adverse, thus exerting a strong and sustained pressure to drain bullion and specie away from what little reserves the colonists had managed to build up. This drain from the weak to the strong accorded well with contemporary European mercantilist thought, but it ran counter to the needs of an undeveloped country heavily in debt to Britain and finding it increasingly difficult to service its debt in sterling – an economic and monetary conflict of interest which underlay the political forces leading to revolution.

The main sources which provided the colonists with their essential money supplies fall into five groups. Essential for frontier trading with the indigenous population, but also thereafter widely adopted by the immigrants themselves, were the traditional existing native currencies such as furs and wampum. Such adoption greatly increased their monetary significance. Second, and in some ways similarly, since they were mostly natural commodities, came the so-called 'Country Pay' or 'Country Money' such as tobacco, rice, indigo, wheat, maize etc. – 'cash crops' in more than one sense. Third, and playing an important role in distant as well as local trade, came unofficial coinages, mostly foreign, and especially Spanish and Portuguese coins. Fourth came the scarce but official British coinage, the golden guinea, the silver crown, shilling etc. and the copper pennies, halfpence and farthings. Fifth, and of greatly increased importance in the colonies' later years, was their own paper currency of various kinds, eagerly accepted as a welcome deliverance from the irksome restrictions of commodity money and coinage. Rates of exchange between the various types of money varied considerably over time and space. An indication of the shortage of official coins and of the resultant wide variety of substitutes is given by the fact that during 1775 in North Carolina alone as many as seventeen different forms of money were declared to be legal tender. However it should be remembered that all these numerous forms of means of payment had a common accounting basis in the pounds, shillings and pence of the imperial system. To some extent this reduced the internal exchange rate problem. Obviously opportunities for profitable arbitrage-type operations remained in plenty, the obstacles themselves thus creating an incentive to overcome them. But what was profitable for the individual imposed a needless social cost on the community. Before briefly examining each of the main groups of money, it is easy to see that the colonial monetary 'system' lacked any systematic cohesion. The colonists improvised in different ways in different localities. Any attempt at a coherent overall solution had to await the deliberations of the post-revolutionary governments in the last decade of the eighteenth century.

The most popular of the indigenous types of money by far was wampum (already described in some detail in our chapter on primitive money). We noted its ready acceptance by the immigrants as legal tender and the large-scale production in factories for turning the raw shells into wampum money-belts. We noted further that wampum was used not only for small payments but also for large credits, such as the loan in wampum worth over 5,000 guilders arranged by Stuyvesant in 1664 for paying the wages of the workers constructing the New York citadel. Wampum became for many years a widespread, durable, attractive, versatile and absolutely essential supplement to the more conventional but scarcer forms of currency. What long-established wampum was to indigenous moneys, tobacco quickly became as the leading type of the new forms of 'country pay money' developed by the immigrants as they began making more general monetary use of the crops best grown in their particular localities. Tobacco, introduced from the West Indies, first began to be used as currency in Virginia as early as 1619, barely a dozen years after the colonists' first permanent settlement was founded in Jamestown in 1607. As Professor Galbraith shows in his most readable account of *Money: Whence It Came and Where it Went*, tobacco was used as money in and around Virginia for nearly 200 years, so lasting about twice as long as the US gold standard (1975, 48). In order to overcome the workings of Gresham's Law, by which good tobacco was driven out of circulation by bad, a system of authorized certificates began to be used, attesting to the quality and quantity of tobacco deposited in public warehouses. These quasi-certificates of deposit, or 'tobacco notes' as they became known, circulated much more conveniently than the actual leaf and were authorized as legal tender in Virginia in 1727 and regularly accepted as such throughout most of the eighteenth century. Colonial experience with other forms of 'country money' such as wheat, maize, rice, beans, fish, indigo, and derivatives such as whisky and brandy, duplicated, though less successfully, that with tobacco.

The use of foreign coins as currency had been so common in Europe and elsewhere for hundreds of years that its reappearance in America was in the main regarded as simply an unsurprising, unfortunate, inconvenient but unavoidable if rather old-fashioned necessity. It enabled the official British currency to be economized in general use and to be given priority as and when required for official payments. There were, however, a number of factors of special significance with regard to America's resort to foreign coins and other unofficial forms of money. First was the unusual extent and duration of such enforced dependence on uncertain and costly foreign supplies. The uneven geographical distribution of the slippery supplies of foreign coins led to intense rivalry among the colonies, which in their scramble for greater shares resorted to a historically early series of competitive devaluations, foreshadowing in their beggar-my-neighbour results the international devaluations of the twentieth century. A further feature was the bitter frustration caused when many of the attempts by the colonists to print or mint their own money were strictly forbidden by the British government. The underlying constitutional conflict was aggravated when Britain subjected the colonies in the mid-eighteenth century to stricter controls over their trading with the West Indies, Mexico and South America, with which they had a favourable balance of trade, and from which therefore they gained the bulk of their foreign coins. Familiarity with foreign coins, coupled with the difficulties encountered in securing enough sterling, led Carolina and later the country as a whole to adopt the dollar and not the pound as the basis of its currency.

The first and only colonial mint of any consequence was that set up by a successful merchant, John Hull, in Massachusetts, in 1652, coining silver threepences, sixpences, and, most famous of all, the 'pine-tree shillings', all of which contained about three-quarters of the silver content of their newly minted English equivalents (seventy-three grains compared with the ninety-three in the English shilling), but intrinsically equal to most of the old, worn and scarce official silver actually in circulation. The popular pine-tree currency circulated widely until the mint was forced to close down in 1684. Hull made his fortune in thus partially and temporarily filling the currency gap, but this success apart, the colonies continued to rely on the confusing variety of all sorts of foreign coins, but with a marked and growing preference for the Spanish peso minted in Mexico City and Lima and the Portuguese eight-real piece. Both these large silver coins were practically identical in weight and fineness, being based on imitation of the famous 'thalers' which had been produced from the silver mines in Joachimsthal in Bohemia for centuries – hence the designations 'pieces of eight' and 'dollars'. The English parity of these coins was 4s. 6d., a rate confirmed by Isaac Newton, Master of the Mint, in 1717; but as indicated above, competition between the colonies pushed the market rate much higher. Thus already in 1700 a piece of eight in the Bahamas exchanged for 5s., in New York for 6s. 6d. and in Pennsylvania for 7s. In 1708 an Act of Parliament laid down that 6s. was to be the maximum rate which any of the colonies should use in exchange for the dollar, but in practice this was of no avail. Similar attempts by the Board of Trade around the same period to introduce uniform rates throughout the American colonies were also doomed to fail. These efforts came about not so much as conscious attempts to prevent competitive devaluation but rather in order to try to get value for money in official purchases, especially for the army's pay and provisions. Inflation was, for example, blamed for the lack of equipment and the 'fatal delay' which led to the defeat of General Braddock at Fort Duquesne in 1755. General Wolfe similarly complained of lack of funds in his Quebec campaign in 1759: a victory this time, proving that an army does not always march on its stomach. Such complaints did, however, stiffen the government's determination to increase taxation and revenue in America, so spurring the revolution. As Dr D. M. Clark has shown in her study of *The Rise of the British Treasury: Colonial Administration in the Eighteenth Century* (1960), a shortage of currency 'combined with the necessity of paying the new duties in sterling aggravated the money problem in the colonies', concluding that 'in the years between 1766 and 1776 the Treasury bore the major responsibility for measures inciting to revolution' (1960, 123, 197).

Much the most important economic result of the currency shortage was that it caused Americans to turn with the greatest enthusiasm to printing paper money, especially State-issued notes, generally sooner and to a greater extent relative to population size than any contemporary country, despite many attempts by the British authorities to curtail such issues. As Galbraith inimitably puts it: 'If the history of commercial banking belongs to the Italians and of central banking to the British, that of paper money issued by a government belongs indubitably to the Americans' (1975, 45). Although the frequently made claim of American priority in note issuing in the Christian world cannot be substantiated, what was novel was the source of the notes, being issued either directly by the government or under its express authorization by its agents (see for example Bogart 1930, 172). The first such State issue of notes was made in 1690 by the Massachusetts Bay Colony. These notes, or 'bills of credit' as they were first termed, amounting to £40,000, were issued to pay soldiers returning from an expedition to Quebec. The notes promised eventual redemption in gold or silver and could immediately be used to pay taxes and were accepted as legal tender. Just as the war against France in Europe gave rise to the Bank of England, so just four years earlier the same military necessity against the same enemy on the other side of the Atlantic gave rise to America's first governmental issue of notes. Such issues avoided the higher costs and uncertainties of borrowing and the still greater evil, especially for American citizens, of taxation. However, it is important to notice that money creation was given as an explicit reason for issuing these notes, for the Act authorizing the first Massachusetts issue saw the bills of credit as a way of overcoming 'the present poverty and calamities of this country and through scarcity of money the want of adequate measures of commerce'. Further issues of such notes were made by Massachusetts, and its example was avidly copied in other colonies, not simply as a military expedient but to save or at least postpone the raising of taxes for expenditures in general and in each case to supplement inadequate supplies of currency. The notes' promise of future redemption was soon seen as less valuable than cash in hand, so despite the fact that some of the issues carried the carrot of dividend or interest payment, most paper issues began to be exchangeable only at a discount – or, what amounted to the same thing, higher prices were charged than if payment was made in specie. In Massachusetts by 1712 there were still around £89,000 worth of bills in circulation, exchangeable at a discount of 30 per cent. By 1726 a Spanish dollar was worth twenty paper shillings, and by 1750 was worth fifty paper shillings. Differential inflation was the other side of the coin to competitive devaluation, and complaints of unfair competition multiplied, both within the colonies and to London.

The temptation to overissue was far too strong, except for Virginia, which was a late entrant into this business, and especially Pennsylvania, which was most circumspect. Maryland, Delaware, New Jersey and New York were only moderately inflationary, while South Carolina and especially Rhode Island gave way with such carefree abandon in note issuing that by 1750 a Spanish dollar passed in Rhode Island for 150 paper shillings and by 1770 its paper money had become practically worthless. As well as State issues, a number of public 'banks', beginning again with Massachusetts in 1681, were founded and began issuing bills and notes to swell the rising tide of paper money. In such early cases the term 'bank' simply meant the collection or batch of bills of credit issued for a temporary period. If successful, reissues would lead to a permanent institution or bank in the more modern sense of the term. Many of these were 'Land Banks' issuing loans in the form of paper money secured by mortgages over the property of their borrowers. One of the best examples was the Pennsylvania Land Bank, which authorized three series of note issues between 1723 and 1729, the first issue totalling £45,000 followed by a further two issues each of £30,000. From this authorized total, individual loans ranging from £12 to £100 were granted on the security of the borrower's land for a term of eight years at 5 per cent. This bank received the enthusiastic support of the young Benjamin Franklin who published (on his own press) his disarmingly 'Modest Enquiry into the Nature and Necessity of a Paper Currency' (1729). His advocacy did not go unrewarded, for he was then granted the contract not only for the third issue of the Pennsylvania Bank but also became the public printer for Delaware, Maryland and New Jersey. Many years later, when he was in London in 1766, he tried to convince Parliament of the case for a general issue of colonial paper money. Unfortunately his sensible advocacy was in vain for by that time Parliament had already been forced to take the opposite course of action, chiefly because runaway inflation had followed the excessive issues in a number of colonies, including Massachusetts and especially Rhode Island.

There were three stages by which the mother Parliament felt itself progressively constrained by the sound-money men in the colonies as well as in its own perceived interest to intervene in order first to restrict and finally to ban completely the issue of colonial paper money. The first action arose as a result of the quarrel between the supporters of a new 'Land Bank or Manufactory Scheme' in Boston in 1740 and its opponents. The proposers, who included 'notorious Debtors', faced the powerful opposition of the governor of Massachusetts and a number of prominent Boston merchants who took their case to London. Parliament ruled in 1741 that the bank was illegal in that it transgressed the provisions of the Bubble Act of 1720. To clarify this piece of retrospective legislation Parliament formally extended the Bubble Act to cover the colonies so that only companies legally authorized could carry out the specific functions for which such authorization was originally granted. The second, harsher restriction followed in 1752 when, following a petition from creditors in Rhode Island who had understandably become alarmed by its sky-rocketing prices, Parliament forbade all New England colonies from issuing new bills of credit and insisted that outstanding issues should be promptly redeemed at maturity. The third and final such prohibition came in 1764 when a complete ban on issues of legal tender paper – except when needed for strictly military purposes – was extended to include all the colonies, so punishing the saints with the sinners, causing widespread hardship and bitter resentment.

It would, however, be quite wrong to see the paper money controversy as simply a question of the prodigal colonial son thwarted by an overstrict, imperious parent. The colonists were themselves deeply divided, and although the 'frontier versus the north-east' did not emerge with full clarity until half a century later, yet its blurred outlines in embryo were discernible in colonial times. Many of the small farmers in a highly agrarian society, together with the retail shopkeepers and above all the ever ready speculators, joined forces in a shifting group in support of easy credit and liberal note issue. Rather than be without business they eagerly accepted the bills of credit that facilitated their activities and they greatly benefited from the inflation which lightened their debt repayments. The virtues of paper money in America's most inflationary colony were roundly defended by Richard Ward, governor of Rhode Island, in an official report of 9 January 1740. 'If this colony,' he wrote 'be in any respect happy and flourishing it is paper money and a right application of it that hath rendered us so. And that we are in a flourishing condition is evident from our trade, which is greater in proportion . . . than that of any Colony in His Majesty's American dominions' (quoted by Bray Hammond in his most stimulating and detailed assessment of *Banks and Politics in America* 1976, 20). Ranged against such 'irresponsible venturing' was a numerically smaller but very influential group comprising most of the creditors outside the issuing agencies, many of the larger farmers, the wholesalers and merchants who had important trading links with England requiring sterling payments for imports. Their views are typified by Lieutenant-Governor Hutchinson of Massachusetts who claimed that 'the great cause of the paper money evil was democratic government. The ignorant majority, when unrestrained by a superior class, always sought to tamper with sound money' (Fite and Reese 1973, 54). Naturally taking the same stance were most of the influential English creditors who had by 1776 invested some £800 million in the American colonies.

Not only contemporaries but also economic historians have swung between the extremes of self-righteous condemnation and complaisant indulgence in judging colonial monetary experiments. Adam Smith, a contemporary observer, was fully aware of the benefits of paper money in stimulating business enterprise in the colonies as in his native Scotland. 'The colonial governments find it in their interest to supply the people with such a quantity of paper money as is sufficient and generally more than sufficient for their domestic business . . . and in both countries it is not the poverty, but the enterprising and projecting spirit of the people . . . which has occasioned this redundancy of paper money' (1776, 423-4). Most classical economists since then up to about the 1940s or 1950s indiscriminately condemned the colonists' inflationary proclivities without giving attention to the benefits of economic growth or to the moderation of colonies like Pennsylvania. Subsequently, impregnated by Keynesianism, perhaps the sympathy for the inflationists has been overplayed. More recently the prevalence of monetarist theory with its obvious similarities with sound-money classicism pushed the pendulum to the opposite extreme. The rather limited success of monetarism in practice in the last decades of the twentieth century should restore a more pragmatic position of balance between the poles of inflationary easy credit and of growth-inhibiting sound money: back in fact towards Adam Smith.

The constitutional conflict between Britain and the colonies, between the distant, authoritative centre and the quarrelsome peripheries, regarding the power to create money and to control banking was handed down as an unresolved legacy to the post-revolutionary administration, and has continued down the long years to bedevil the relationship between the State and federal authorities. Admittedly there are a number of other reasons, apart from the obvious geographical ones, rekindling such conflicts. However the fact that ambiguity was built into the new constitution with regard to the precise but changing balance of power required to control such a dynamic, mercurial, mundane yet mighty matter as money was a problem directly carried over from the late colonial period.

The early colonists were desperately short of currency. Later they were blessed or cursed with too much self-made money. When Parliament tried to swing the pendulum right back from quantity to quality, it found its authority repudiated by revolution. The erstwhile colonists, forced by freedom to seek their own solution, did not find it an easy task.

The official dollar and the growth of banking up to the Civil War, 1775–1861

'Continental' debauchery

When the war broke out the monetary brakes were released completely and the revolution was financed overwhelmingly with an expansionary flood of paper money far greater than had ever been seen anywhere previously. Any thoughts of monetary reform, though vastly reinforced by such experience, had to wait until after the end of the war for their implementation. Meanwhile the opposite course of financial debauchery was deliberately chosen, and the American Congress financed its first war with hyper-inflation. Not that other methods were not resorted to; but compared with note issuing, all other ways were very much less effective. Direct requisitioning of goods and services was used on occasion, but this method suffered literally from rapidly diminishing, indeed vanishing, returns and alienated, by its arbitrary imposition, influential sections of the population. Taxation was hated by the Americans, for that had been a major cause of the revolt against Britain in the first place. The even higher taxes now being demanded could be raised only after much discussion and delay, such obstruction being made worse by the lack of appropriate administrative machinery for tax, excise and custom collection, and by the fact that the British army occupied much of the land while the Royal Navy blockaded the ports. Borrowing was disliked because repayment was generally made in heavily depreciated notes. In contrast the people had grown accustomed to the only slightly less obvious form of daylight robbery – note issuing. Furthermore now was the chance for a uniform national or 'Continental' note issue such as had long been advocated by Benjamin Franklin and others. Little wonder that the First Continental Congress jumped at the opportunity.

The overwhelming reliance on note issuing is shown by the fact that the central government between 1775 and 1780 itself authorized forty-two batches or 'banks' of notes totalling $241 million. In addition (though competing with as much as complementing the 'Continentals') the States issued their own notes totalling $210 million. Compared with this paper mountain of $451 million only about $100 million at most was raised by domestic borrowing, and much of this was paid in Continental and State notes, so giving a further twist to the inflationary spiral. Only about 11.5 million of such borrowing was paid in 'real money', i.e. in specie, mostly in Spanish dollars. Foreign loans totalling $7.8 million in real money equivalents became available in the later stages of the war, granted first and most eagerly by France which loaned $6.4 million or 80 per cent of the total. Spain lent just $174,000 while, very belatedly, $1.3 million was raised privately on the Amsterdam capital market.

The faster the Continental and State notes were issued, the faster they depreciated. Attempts were made repeatedly to hold back the resultant inflation by means of edicts fixing the prices of essential commodities, but to little or no effect. By 1781 the value of Continental notes in terms of specie fell to one-hundredth of their nominal value, falling later to 1000 to 1. Although the phrase 'not worth a Continental' has subsequently, with good reason, symbolized utter worthlessness, nevertheless in the perspective of economic history such notes should be counted as invaluable as being the only major practical means then available for successfully financing the revolution. Yet however necessary such temporary wartime expedients might have been, it meant that when the founding fathers met to draw up their constitution they could hardly have been faced with a more chaotic and intractable monetary situation. The inflationary flood of paper issued during the war and its greatly uneven distribution afterwards, coupled with a severe post-war slump in the market values of agricultural products, sharpened the divisive interests within and between the States. With the end of the war in 1783 'Continental' issues ceased and five of the States also refrained from issuing notes. The eight other States carried on regardless, including Rhode Island where the farmers were again the main supporters of a 'paper bank' of £100,000 authorized in 1786 to supply long-term loans of up to fourteen years at a bargain rate of 4 per cent against individual mortgages valued at twice the loan. Most of such loans were naturally taken up by the farmers who had supported the bank's foundation against considerable opposition.

As with previous issues the notes were considered by the bank – but not by the opposers – to be legal tender. Many shopkeepers and merchants refused to accept them at their face value, and when the matter was taken to court their refusal was upheld (Myers 1970, 40). Dr Myers's examples show that Bray Hammond's emphasis on the ultra-conservatism of farmers and on 'agrarian dislike of paper money' was excessive (B. Hammond 1967, 35). Similar struggles between debtors and creditors took place in other States, notoriously 'Shay's Rebellion' in Massachusetts, also in 1786. Captain Shay led a rebel force of debtors and other disaffected farmers and ex-soldiers to try and secure debt relief, issues of paper and other reforms. The rebels were finally captured by an official army financed by Boston merchants.

The constitution and the currency

Financial chaos had led to violence, and the alarm spread throughout the country, leading to demands that a national solution should be urgently sought. The Constitutional Convention which convened in May 1787, just two months after Shay's Rebellion was put down, tackled the problem as best it could, its conclusions finally being ratified in 1789. The essence of their deliberations is contained in three clauses of article 1 of the Constitution: (a) 'Congress' (not the States) 'shall have power to coin money, regulate the value thereof and of foreign coin'; (b) 'No State shall coin money, emit bills of credit, make anything but gold and silver tender in payment of debts'; and (c) Congress is to have 'the power to lay and collect taxes, duties and excises, and to pay the debts . . . of the United States'. These three clauses formed the foundation of the USA's fiscal and financial constitution. At the time their meaning seemed clear enough, but varying interpretations of these interrelated clauses by interested parties and unforeseeable changes in monetary practices led to results far different from those anticipated by the founders. The drafting and initial implementation of these crucial financial precepts were in the main the work of three gifted men: Robert Morris – a Pennsylvanian merchant and banker who had already been extolled as 'the financier of the Revolution' – Thomas Jefferson and Alexander Hamilton. We shall look first at coinage and then examine the interconnections between debt and banking.

Since coins were universally considered to be the only real money it was felt to be essential to study the subject thoroughly before formulating the basic currency of the new country. Official monetary studies and desultory experiments were spread over fourteen years, beginning with the appointment of Robert Morris to chair a committee on money and finance in 1778. In 1782 Morris, now promoted to Superintendent of Finance, published his long-awaited report. After looking at this, Jefferson presented an amended report to Congress and as a result the Confederation Congress passed the first, and quickly aborted, Mint Act of 1786. Its only practical result was the coining of just a few tons of desperately needed copper coins to replace, among other shortages, the 1-, 2- and 3-penny paper tickets that New York City Council had felt forced to issue. It was not until five years later, under the leadership of Alexander Hamilton, the first Secretary to the Treasury, that a new report, based on an amalgam of the previous reports, was presented to Congress and debated with painful slowness. Eventually, with the direct support of President Washington, the Coinage Act of 1792 reached the Statute Book.

That Act officially adopted the dollar as the American unit of account (so confirming Confederate legislation). As we have seen, among the chronic general scarcity of coins the Spanish dollar was relatively less scarce and very popular, while refusing to give the pound its status as the official accounting unit was furthermore a fitting symbol of independence. Secondly, the Act laid down that the currency was to be subdivided into cents according to the decimal system – as advocated, (though in different ways) both by Morris and by Jefferson. This was put into effect in America 179 years before a similarly simple practice was adopted by Britain. Thirdly, the dollar was officially to be bimetallist, being defined as equivalent to 371.25 grains of silver or 24.75 grains of gold. The mint ratio was thus 15:1 – a rate that in practice was found slightly to overvalue silver. It was Jefferson's advice that edged the decision towards bimetallism, for reliance on a single metal would, he said, 'abridge the quantity of circulating medium' and lead to the continuation of 'the evils of a scanty circulation' (Kirkland 1946, 239). Fourthly, both gold and silver coins were to be unlimited legal tender, while the minting of copper coins and half-cents as tender for limited amounts was also authorized. All foreign coins were to lose their status as legal tender three years after the American coins came into circulation. Fifthly, a national mint was to be set up with no seigniorage charges for minting. The mint was built in Philadelphia and rather significantly was thus the first purpose-built structure authorized by the United States. It began minting gold, silver and copper coins in 1794. In legal form the USA had established a system that seemed to its proposers to guarantee a sound and adequate basic money supply.

In practice things were vastly different. Because of the slight overvaluation of silver in the 15:1 mint ratio, it was, after a short while, mostly silver that was brought to the mint for coining and relatively little gold. Consequently the shortage of gold coins persisted. An even greater problem arose with silver because the bright new American dollars disappeared from circulation almost as soon as they were minted, being keenly preferred to the older, duller Spanish variety even though the latter were heavier by 2 per cent. It was thus found to be profitable to melt down the Spanish dollars, take them to the mint for coining gratuitously, pocket the profit and repeat the process. At best this simply would have meant changing the composition of the existing inadequate money supply instead of increasing it. In fact, since many of the new dollars were exported to Latin America and elsewhere, the net position inside the USA was made much worse. The intended removal of legal tender from foreign coins had therefore urgently to be suspended. By a presidential proclamation of 22 July 1797 legal tender was extended indefinitely to 'the Spanish milled dollar and parts thereof' – and in actual practice to most other foreign coins also. By 1806 these and other unanticipated results of the Coinage Act had become so marked that President Jefferson was forced to suspend all minting of silver – a suspension that was to last for twenty-eight years.

The shortage of gold coins in America was intensified during the same period by an external drainage caused not simply by a generally adverse balance of payments with Britain, but also because the mint ratios in Europe were more favourable to gold. Thus in 1803 France established a ratio of 15.5:1, while from 1816 a still more favourable 16:1 existed in Britain. After almost interminable delay the USA in 1834 came into line with the British ratio of 16:1 and so was able to resume minting its silver coins. In the mean time the USA still had to make do with a confusing mixture of all sorts of coins, supplemented by various devices – for instance the paper warrants issued by Ohio State for 5, 10 and 20 dollars, which acted as a currency between 1809 and 1831. It was not until 1857 that the federal government felt it safe finally to repeal 'all former acts authorising the currency of foreign gold or silver coins, and declaring the same a legal tender in payment for debts'. By then metallic money, though still as necessary for retail trade as ever, had become merely the small change of commerce. In metallic, as in other forms of money, for most of its first century after independence America saw the pendulum swing between occasional strong attempts by the central government to improve the quality of money, and practical efforts by farmers, businessmen and some of the States to overcome these restrictions and so increase the quantity of money not just by trying to get more coins minted but mainly in multiplying its banks. The silver cloud had a golden lining in that it forced the pace of progress in banking and so stimulated the economy in general so as more than to make up for the glaring deficiencies of the formal currency.

The national debt and the bank wars

Thomas Paine in his pamphlet *Common Sense,* published in Pennsylvania in 1776, stated that 'No nation ought to be without a debt' for 'a national debt is a national bond.' Judged by this criterion the new States were very much a nation, for debts, bonds and banks were to climb high on each other's backs in the following decades. The first 'bank' formed after independence, with Thomas Paine's support, but mostly because of the lead given by Robert Morris, was the Bank of Pennsylvania, hastily established in June 1780. It was however little more than a temporary means of raising funds to pay for the desperate needs of a practically starving army. Although it had received its charter (despite doubts about its legality) from the Confederacy it performed very much like the former colonial 'banks', with none of the functions of contemporary European banks. Nevertheless as well as coming to the aid of the army at a critical juncture, its supporters learned from the experience and were foremost in forming shortly afterwards a more advanced and more permanent institution, the Bank of North America, which by a narrow margin of votes was granted a charter by Congress in 1781 and began operations in Pennsylvania on 1 January 1782. Notwithstanding continued doubts about Congress's power to grant bank charters, the new venture proved to be a great commercial success, providing a range of services to the government and to the public so that it may in truth be described as the first modern type of bank on the American continent. Not only did it issue notes but it took deposits from governments and merchants, transferred funds to a limited degree, dealt with bills of exchange and granted short-term loans to merchants (initially of not more than thirty days). Its undoubted success prompted others to follow its example. The Bank of New York (the oldest existing US bank) and the Bank of Massachusetts both opened for business in 1784, followed by the Bank of Maryland in 1790. Meanwhile Alexander Hamilton had become Secretary to the Treasury and set to work to create order out of the chaos of the national and state debts, to build up the credit standing of the new government at home and abroad and, a related task dear to his heart, to set up a major public bank much more like the Bank of England than the existing banks. In January 1790 he presented to Congress his proposals in a *Report on the Public Credit*, followed in December by his *Report on a National Bank*.

The size of the national debt, as is its nature, grew for some time after the war had ended, before an efficient peacetime fiscal regime could be set up, which was obviously a bigger task than usual in the case of a new nation. The problem was not simply the unpaid interest which had accrued, but in addition the magnitude of the major portion of the debt, the domestically owed part, was unclear and depended on assumptions about what allowances should be made for variations in the rates of wartime hyper-inflation and a number of other still unresolved factors as between the States and the Union. Hamilton dealt first with the comparatively straightforward matter of the foreign debt, which had risen, with added interest, by 1789 to over $10 million. His proposal for a complete repayment over a fifteen-year period was quickly agreed to by Congress and creditors, a move that soon restored US credit abroad to a high level, assisted partly by the progress of the French Revolution, which frightened funds away from Europe in general and France in particular. With regard to the domestic national debt this, however estimated, represented only the minor portion of the real, economic costs of the war, which had been in fact borne by the general public every time anyone had parted with goods or performed services in return for rapidly depreciating money or money-substitutes. Out of many millions of such transactions only an unknown proportion still held written evidence of claims, valued at fancy prices, on their State or on the Union. The domestic 'national' debt thus consisted of a chaotic 'mass of virtually worthless paper money, loan office certificates, IOUs signed by the Quartermaster, lottery prizes, certificates given to soldiers in lieu of pay, Treasury certificates and various evidences of debt' (Hession and Sardy 1969, 96). Since many of these claims had been passed on many times at varying rates of discount questions were naturally raised as to whether only current holders should be repaid, and at what rate.

Hamilton sensibly decided to allow only existing owners of the old debt to receive in exchange new specie certificates at the rather generous rate of 100 to one; a bold but successful move. The most difficult problem by far to resolve – foreshadowing the endemic fragility of the Union – was the vital matter of the amounts and rates at which the Union should assume the debts of the State governments. Indebtedness varied greatly with a number of the southern States such as Virginia, having either already repaid much of their debt or having little to repay in any case, whereas others, mostly in the north, having large unpaid debts and so having much to gain from the Union's generosity. Agreement was finally reached when Hamilton granted Virginia the privilege of being allowed to have Washington, the newly-designed US capital, built within its territory. Pride was salved and the national debt had thus become a national bond in both senses of the word. Hamilton had the foresight to see the advantages to America which could flow from a reservoir of sound securities, which would help to mobilize diffused or idle domestic savings and attract foreign investment, thus stimulating the economic progress of the nation. Integral to his plans was a National Bank.

In no other country in the history of the world has the subject of money and banking given rise to such long-sustained, deep-rooted, widespread, acrimonious, publicly debated and eagerly reported controversy as in America. Admittedly money everywhere touches so many people's interests every day that disputes ranging from petty differences in retail payments up to public policy discussions of the most major consequences, e.g. regarding high unemployment caused by high rates of interest or the sharing of monetary power between Treasuries and central banks, recur from time to time. Supporters of rival monetary theories then rise to claim much public attention. Thereafter the rivals normally subside into long periods of peace and relative obscurity from public gaze. Not so in America, where monetary quarrels have right from the start been deeply divisive and almost never-ending. The divisions have run from paupers to presidents, from State to State, from States to the Union, from North to South, from coast to frontier, from farmers to manufacturers, from bank to bank, from politicians to philosophers, and above all from lawyers to lawyers. In comparison, economists, even when furiously engaged in their not uncommon pursuit of supporting rival theories, have been far less acrimonious.

One might have expected the newly independent Americans to have welcomed with unanimous enthusiasm their freedom to set up their own banks despite the novelty of such institutions. However, the experience of the early years of the first true American bank indicated the alarming extent of opposition to such institutions. Unpaid soldiers were only with great difficulty prevented from looting the Bank of North America in June 1783: a government-chartered bank should, it was thought, see to it that its soldiers were paid. More serious was the opposition from Pennsylvanian farmers who got their representatives in the Assembly to debate the legality of the bank's existence. After two years of bitter wrangling its congressional charter was repealed by an Act passed on 13 September 1785. Although the bank managed to get a new charter from Delaware, this, in playing off provincial versus central authority, was merely the first pointer to much bigger things to come, as was quickly revealed when Hamilton unveiled his ambitious and far-sighted proposals for the first Bank of the United States. He had five objectives in mind. First, he wished the new bank to be, right from the start, much bigger than the three existing banks so that its power could be wielded quickly and effectively. Secondly, he expected the bank to stimulate the growth of the economy: in his own words 'to enlarge the mass of industrious and commercial enterprise'. As well as thus acting as a commercial bank, his third objective was vital, viz. to act as a government bank, thereby strengthening the Union. This would help in his fourth aim, to improve the credit standing of government securities, and so 'turn the national debt into a national blessing'. Fifthly, by having a soundly based note issue it would answer the demands for a much-needed but safe increase in the currency.

Hamilton's proposals were debated with fierce passion in the two months following the introduction of the bill in December 1791. Eventually the Senate passed the bill, with an unknown majority, and the House of Representatives also voted, by thirty-nine to twenty, in its favour. President Washington asked his Attorney General, Edmund Randolph, and his Secretary of State, Jefferson, for their advice. Their view was that the bill was clearly contrary to the Constitution. Their doubts weighed so heavily with the President that he was about to use his veto when Hamilton finally persuaded him of its merits. On 25 February 1791 the Bank of the United States received its twenty-year charter. To signalize its dual nature, its large authorized capital of $10,000,000 was split so that the national government was to contribute 20 per cent. Of the $8,000,000 to be contributed by the general public only a quarter needed to be paid for in gold or silver, with the remaining $6,000,000 payable in government securities. By a sleight of hand (which in Britain today would lead to either ennoblement or imprisonment, the dividing line being razor-thin) Hamilton and the board of the Bank managed to grant the government the means whereby the government's contribution also was paid in full in government securities or in its own notes which had been paid to the government for this purpose. The price of government securities rose substantially – an intended and welcome result of this wide increase in demand. The Bank was authorized to issue notes and to begin operations as soon as just $400,000 had been paid by the public. The issue was heavily oversubscribed within the first hour of the offer being opened. The Bank proved to be a great economic success – to the increasing chagrin of its opponents. Its business with the public and with the government soon grew too big to be confined to its head office in Philadelphia, so it opened branches in New York, Boston, Baltimore and Charleston in 1792, followed later by branches in four other towns. Its size and success, despite the accompanying cries of 'monopoly', did not in fact prevent the rise of new banks. From just four banks in 1790 the total number increased to eighteen by 1794, twenty-nine by 1800 and as many as ninety in 1811. Clearly there was a growing market for new banks to share. A bone of contention more justified than the complaint of monopoly was the loss by other banks of what they saw as their deserved share of lucrative and safe government deposits. According to Professor Myers, around 90 per cent of treasury deposits were by 1804 being placed in the Bank of the United States. When the Bank's charter came up for renewal in 1811 its enemies closed in.

The opposition's extreme but yet widely held view was simply that *all* banks were evil. Not only did they print paper money which in American experience was likely to become worthless, but they tempted yeomen and other reliable citizens to overextend themselves, becoming forced in the end to sell their lands and property at bankrupt prices to the banks or to their rich associates, many of whom were foreigners. The Bank of the United States, though initially owned predominantly by Americans (who alone could vote), came in time to have a substantial number of British shareholders. Barings for instance purchased 2,220 shares from the US government in a single lot in 1802. By 1811 shares to the value of $7 million were held abroad. Was this not clear evidence that British imperialism was being re-established by aristocratic merchant bankers? Eighty worthy citizens of Pittsburgh made a written protest dated 4 February 1811 that the Bank 'held in bondage thousands of our citizens who dared not to act according to their conscience for fear of offending the British stockholders and Federal directors' (B. Hammond 1967, 213). Apart from such extremes the most dangerous opposition, again led by Jefferson, came from those who argued that the Union was exceeding its constitutional powers, for banking was not mentioned in the Constitution, and silence meant prohibition rather than the consent that the Federalists were taking for granted. Supporters of the Bank claimed that the powers expressly withheld from the States and given to the Union 'to coin money' and 'to regulate its value' gave the Union the right to charter and control banking. The States jealously guarded their own right to charter banks and even to 'emit bills' so long as formal legal tender was not enforced. The Bank's undoubted success counted little against such dogmatic beliefs, so that when the renewal of the charter came to be voted on, the House voted against by just one vote, sixty-five to sixty-four, while the Senators' votes were tied, seventeen to seventeen. This time the vice-

president cast his veto against renewal. The Bank was killed; but the
case for a government bank and for a federal monetary power remained
so belligerently alive that within five years a second such bank was
born.

Almost as soon as the First Bank of the United States closed its doors
the American financial scene reverted to its familiar inflationary
pattern. The most obvious cause was the outbreak of the war of 1812
but a more deep-seated cause was the mushroom growth of new banks
which issued far too many notes backed by far too little specie, and now
with no government bank to exert a restraining hand. By far the largest
specie deposits had normally been kept in the First Bank of the US. Not
only was this dispersed but some of it had to be sent abroad to redeem
foreign-owned shares. To help finance its rapidly increasing expenditure
the government issued a series of interest-bearing Treasury notes
redeemable after one year but in the mean time accepted by government
departments for official payments. Altogether some $36 million such
bills were issued between 1812 and 1816. To this mass of near-money
was added the note issues of new, mostly small and weak banks, many
of which had very little specie to back such issues. The ninety banks of
1811 had grown to 260 by 1816, while their note issues had increased
from $28 million to $260 million. Even non-bank companies were
issuing notes. According to Jefferson – in his own words 'ever the
enemy of banks' – the actual circulation of paper money in 1814 was
$200 million, and rising, he feared, towards $400 million. Whatever may
have been the total it was plainly grossly excessive. Most paper money
for most of the four-year period was unredeemable into specie; and
although the British invasion could be blamed for the initial cessation
of cash payments, the undisciplined rise in note issuing would have led
inevitably to the same result even had there been no invasion. In such
circumstances sentiment at the end of the war swung back firmly in
favour of a more secure banking system including a Second Bank of the
United States.

The new bank received its twenty-year charter in April 1816 and
began operating from its Philadelphia head office in January 1817.
Apart from being much larger, the Second Bank was very similar in
form and function to those of the First Bank. Thus its $35 million
capital came one-fifth from the government, with specie contributions
from the public equal to at least one-quarter of their contributions,
though the Bank itself patiently assisted its new shareholders to fulfil
this latter condition. Its first heavy responsibility was to help restore the
health of the currency through a general resumption of the
convertibility of the paper notes into cash, a task it carried out within

two years, except that in a few, mostly remote, areas some banks' notes still remained inconvertible into the 1820s. The most effective method used by the Bank for restraining the excessive note issues of other banks, and which had been used to a smaller degree by the First Bank, was to present, on a regular basis if necessary, such notes to the issuing banks for payment in specie. This not only forced such banks to increase their holdings of specie but to refrain from excessive loans in future; and since note issuing was still the customary method of making loans, to make lending more difficult. Although the quality of the currency and of bank lending was thus raised, the potential for speculative profits by the more adventurous banks was also curtailed, while a number of small banks were forced into closure, leaving some communities 'bankless'.

Before turning to assess the forces which eventually swept away the Second Bank, a brief examination of its positive achievements will help to provide a balanced picture. It performed well in functioning as a government bank, receiving deposits and transferring funds on behalf of the Treasury and other government departments, paying pensions and dividends on government stock, all such services being free of charge. It centralized and economized on the use of specie. It soon established itself as the largest operator in the foreign exchange market where its growing expertise prevented excessive external drains of specie and so moderated what would otherwise have been harmful domestic monetary contractions. It found itself becoming relied upon by other banks as a convenient and dependable source of specie during emergencies, thus acting as what would later become known as a lender of last resort. In day-to-day trading the Bank greatly encouraged directly and indirectly the market in bankers' 'acceptances', i.e. bills of exchange were 'accepted' and thereby guaranteed by the Second Bank and by a few of the other more prestigious banks, on behalf of both external and domestic traders. The value of acceptances grew almost tenfold between 1820 and 1833. The Second Bank pursued vigorously its policy of branching, aiming to set up at least one branch in each state, with twenty-nine in operation by 1833. By such means the Bank was able to bring about what was probably its most important and obvious result so far as the general public was concerned, the provision of a desperately needed uniform national currency, for its notes were the only ones to circulate throughout the country at face value.

All other banknotes circulated at a discount, if not locally, then at a distance from the issuing bank. Not only did the Second Bank thus furnish a good currency directly, but as we have seen, by presenting other notes for cash at their parent bank, it improved the quality and reduced the discount on other paper money. Other notable improvements in banking were made independently of the national Bank. The Suffolk Bank of Boston developed from 1824 onwards in co-operation with six other local banks a system whereby inter-bank accounts were offset and cleared while each member bank's notes plus those of a growing number of designated country banks were accepted at par. In 1829 the New York legislature passed a Safety Fund Act which became a model for securing greater care in the subsequent chartering of state banks and contained provisions which foreshadowed later developments in deposit insurance. While giving all due credit to such improvements in banking law and custom it was mainly through the instrumentality of the Second Bank of the US that the foundation of what could reasonably be called a national system of money and banking was being established in the USA in the period 1816–34; but it was doomed to failure following the election of Andrew Jackson to the presidency in 1828. Resentment of the Second Bank's justified strictness towards other banks was aggravated, especially during its first seven years, by considerable laxness in controlling the activities of its own branches: little wonder, perhaps, for its first president, Captain William Jones, was a declared bankrupt. Gradually but cumulatively the hostility of jealous bankers, frustrated borrowers, desperate debtors and populist politicians built up into what has aptly been called 'the Bank War', a repetition with heightened intensity and on a larger scale of previous mixed monetary and constitutional conflicts.

'General Jackson,' said Bray Hammond, 'was an excellent leader in the revolt of enterprise against the regulation of credit by the Federal Bank' (1967, 349). Although Jackson never made the Goering-like remark 'Whenever I hear the word "banker" I reach for my revolver', he did admit saying at a meeting in November 1829 to Nicholas Biddle, the cultured third, and last, president of the Second Bank: 'Ever since I read the history of the South Sea Bubble I have been afraid of banks.' His fear was of the kind that leads to attack, for he was 'a pugnacious animal'. Within ten days of his meeting with Biddle, in his first message to Congress, he questioned the legality, the necessity and the policy of the Bank. However because of the progress that had been made by the Bank by 1829, and particularly because of two earlier favourable decisions by the Supreme Court, Biddle was arrogantly confident that his Bank would weather the storm. In earlier attacks a dozen States had tried by various devices to prevent the Bank from operating within their borders. In the two years 1818–19, Maryland, North Carolina, Ohio, Tennessee and Kentucky had imposed annual taxes on the Second Bank's branches ranging from $15,000 in Maryland to $60,000 in

Kentucky. The Bank refused to pay. In 1824 Illinois declared all branches illegal. Luckily for the Bank these devices were overruled by the Supreme Court in two celebrated cases which set important constitutional precedents much wider than just banking – McCulloch v. Maryland (1819), and Osborn v. the Bank of the United States (1824). So confident were Biddle and his supporters that in January 1832, four years before the expiry of the Bank's charter, a bill was introduced to renew the charter. This successfully passed the House by 167 votes to eighty-five, and the Senate by twenty-eight votes to twenty.

Jackson promptly vetoed the bill, repeating his objection that the Bank was unconstitutional, that foreign ownership was excessive and that the influence of the 'monied oligarchy' was oppressive. The issue became his rallying call against Henry Clay, the Bank's supporter, in the 1832 presidential election. Jackson's electoral victory was overwhelming, with 219 electoral votes to Clay's forty-nine. Jackson's support was widespread and even included influential New Yorkers jealous of the retention of financial power by Philadelphia, which contained the Bank's head office. His main fighting support came predictably from the 'frontier' regions of the South and West. Typifying this attitude in the West, Senator Thomas Hart Benton of Missouri declaimed against the Bank that 'All the flourishing cities of the West are mortgaged to this money power. They are in the jaws of the Monster' (Kirkland 1946, 144). In the South in 1831 Nicholas Biddle's hot-headed but short-sighted brother, manager of the Bank's branch in St Louis, felt forced to defend the Bank's honour by reaching for his pistol and fighting, at a range of 5 ft, a doubly fatal duel (Galbraith 1975, 80). During 1833 Jackson removed government deposits from the Second Bank and placed them in State banks – the 'pet banks' as they came to be known. To protect itself the Bank recalled specie and deposits from other banks and curtailed its own note issues and in this way forced other banks and curtailed their note issues also. This had a deflationary effect and further reduced its popularity. Jackson had killed the Bank, and with it had ruined any hope of a sensibly regulated banking system, for this would not in fact be re-established for another eighty years.

A banking free-for-all, 1833–1861

When the Bank of the US existed under Biddle the American banking scene was beginning to show signs of convergence towards a national pattern; untidy and incomplete, but at least discernible in outline. With the ending of the Bank, that emerging pattern broke up into chaotic, confused and diverging pieces with little if any cohesion and with no central institution to pull the discordant elements together. Almost any and every monetary belief, theory or fad, however sound or silly, positive or negative, was given an airing and put on trial somewhere or other in the States in this period. It was a free-for-all where some States tried to prevent the rise not simply of a national bank but of any banks of any kind and so to do away with paper money altogether. Some wished to encourage their particular State, despite the apparent prohibition in the Constitution, to issue notes and to conduct the whole range of banking as it was then understood. Others wished simply to see the State, under strict rules and regulations, allow private citizens to become bankers, while yet others wanted the State to allow anyone, with the fewest possible limitations, to set up as many banks as they wished. All these forces pulled and pushed against each other with varying strength in different States. But all the while there was a rising tide of money and credit supplied by a motley collection of banking institutions to meet the increasing demands of a nation where the population and, with occasional setbacks, the gross national product, was growing at record pace. Despite this inevitably confused picture, it becomes possible to give tentative answers to that chicken-and-egg question concerning the causes of economic development relative to money: namely, did an initial rise in the supply of credit stimulate the growth of production, or was the supply of credit simply called into being by the growth of the real economy?

In general it would probably be true to say that the spectacular growth of America in earlier as in some later periods took place despite rather than because of its monetary sector. And yet for much though not all of this period easy money and credit, though unreliable, undoubtedly acted especially in the ever-moving frontier regions as an active spur to growth. It is equally an important part of the truth to say that if the 'sound' or 'hard' money men of the more settled communities, such as those that typically supported the Second Bank, had had their way throughout the country, the average rate of growth nationally would probably have been considerably reduced. As it happened, the more settled areas, such as New England, veered towards sounder money, while as we have noted it was the frontier States (with some exceptions) that tended to welcome easier money. Given such conditions, American money was far from being 'neutral' in its effects; there was an uneven and unfair distribution of gains and losses. The burdens of bank failures, unpaid loans, highly discounted notes and bankruptcies fell unequally and arbitrarily on certain unlucky individuals, while other individuals, especially the entrepreneurs, and on balance the community as a whole gained. It was after all during this period, from around 1840 to 1860 that, according to Professor Rostow (1960), the United States experienced its critically important 'take-off' into self-sustaining growth.

For a brief period before the quarrel regarding rechartering, Jackson had relied on Biddle in the task, successfully accomplished, of repaying the national debt. Here the plain, blunt, self-made frontiersman and the brilliant, erudite aristocrat were in full agreement on this aspect of financial rectitude. Buoyant revenues plus the saving in having no national debt to service, together with other hard-money measures led to substantial government surpluses. Among these measures was Jackson's 'Specie Circular' of 11 July 1836 which laid down that future purchases of government land had to be paid in gold or silver, or their strict equivalent rather than as in previous lax administrations, in local notes or even in promises to pay. Although the sales of public land never again achieved the peak of $25 million recorded in 1836, and although ways of paying by credit were not entirely discontinued, yet for some time the circular had the desired effect of swelling the government coffers with specie. In buoyant years the government's surpluses had become so large as to pose a problem of how to dispose of them. This was managed in part by distribution to the States, an incentive to profligacy camouflaged as 'loans', and in part by deposits in the government's 'pet' banks. By the end of 1836 such deposits had been placed in as many as ninety-six banks, some of them far too small, too risky or too unreliable politically to be endowed with such responsibility. Attempts to relate the amount of government deposit to the size of the receiving bank's capital proved ineffective.

The logical step for hard-money men in their attempt to divorce the central government from the banking system altogether was to set up an independent Treasury, a measure first enacted tentatively in 1840 and then more definitely in 1846. By means of its central Treasury in Washington, together with a growing number of sub-treasuries spread across the country, the Treasury attempted to carry out its own banking requirements, working towards its ideal as far as possible, of relying mainly on specie for government payments and receipts. Interestingly it was at about the same time that the British government was seeking to separate its responsibilities for sound money from the tentacles of banking. As we saw in chapter 7, Prime Minister Peel's view of the 1844 Bank Charter Act was that in effect the issuing department was in Whitehall, leaving the Bank of England free to concentrate on its banking business in Threadneedle Street. In fact no such separation was possible. The extreme American solution of abolishing the central bank left the Treasury to attempt for eighty years to carry out the increasingly difficult task of being its own banker. In practice it found it impossible to work purely independently of the banking system. Meanwhile the States in their various ways tackled or failed to tackle the problems associated with the surging growth of the commercial banks.

The death notice of the Second Bank was a green light to the States to charter their own banks or to encourage their citizens to set up banks for themselves. A half-hearted attempt by Chief Justice Marshall to uphold the Constitutional denial of the power of the States 'to emit bills' was pushed aside and specifically reversed in 1837. A 'Free Banking' movement sprang up which claimed that citizens had a right to set up banks rather than being dependent on seeking a privilege granted by the State. Yielding to such pressures the State of Massachusetts in 1837 passed an Act allowing any resident the right to set up a bank with only the very minimum of safeguards.

A more sensible and moderate approach was shown in the Free Banking Act of New York in 1838 which laid down conditions regarding capital requirements and the necessity of keeping a reserve of specie of at least 12.5 per cent behind any note issue. Banks roughly modelled on these two examples varied from worthless 'wild-catters' that profited from making quick note issues and then quickly moving on, to the opposite example of prudently managed institutions. Bruising experiences with weak and fraudulent banks led nine States during this period to pass laws – which soon turned out to be quite ineffective – prohibiting banking of any kind. The virtuous and prudent banks included most of those in New England that had joined the Suffolk Clearing Scheme, already mentioned, and which by 1857 had grown to handle the issues of 500 banks circulating at par. In the South the Louisiana Bank Law of 1842 required its banks to keep a specie reserve of at least one-third of the combined total of notes and deposits, and also laid down useful stipulations regarding adequate liquid assets to back the remaining liabilities. Thus some large islands of sanity and security were to be found in the general sea of financial chaos.

The total number of banks more than doubled between 1830 and 1836, rising from 330 to 713. The crisis of 1837 at first merely reduced the rate of increase, the number reaching 901 in 1840. Then, after falling to 691 in 1843, the numbers rose again, slowly in the 1840s but rapidly in the 1850s to reach the pre-Civil War peak of 1,601 in 1861. These banks, operating under the differing laws of thirty States, varied enormously in quality, as did the notes by which they were most readily judged. They poured out a flood of notes most of which were accepted only at a discount from their face value. Not only every banker but every trader of any importance had to make constant reference in the course of his everyday business to one or other of a series of banknote guides. Thus *Hodges Genuine Bank Notes of America, 1859* listed 9,916 notes issued by 1,365 banks, and even then around 200 genuine banknotes had been omitted. In addition there were, according to the *Nicholas Bank Note Reporter*, counterfeit notes of 5,400 different kinds in circulation, and this despite the best efforts of the banks themselves, which had set up in 1853 their Association for the Prevention of Counterfeiting.

The condition of the coinage, starting from a deplorable level, improved markedly by the end of this period. As already noted, no silver dollars were minted between 1806 and 1836, while gold coins tended to disappear through internal hoarding or through export. Thus much reliance continued to be placed on foreign coins, e.g. the specie reserve of the Second Bank in 1831 consisted of $9 million in foreign coin and only $2 million in US coin. By the Coinage Act of 1834, slightly modified in 1837, the mint ratio of 15:1 established in 1792 was changed to 16:1. While this encouraged gold to be brought to the mint it hastened the disappearance of much of the remaining silver in circulation. Retail trade was badly affected, though relieved to some extent by certain banks issuing notes of fractions of dollars. By the Subsidiary Coinage Act of 1853 the silver content of half-dollars, quarters and dimes was reduced by about 7 per cent, making it no longer worthwhile selling such coins to the silver metal dealers. The same Act limited the legal tender of such silver to a maximum of $5; and in 1857 legal tender could safely and finally be removed from foreign coins. Thus although the new silver coins now remained in circulation, their importance had been diminished. After the discovery of gold in California in 1848 gold came into the mint in great quantities. Between 1850 and 1860 the mint issued $400 million in gold coins, around twice as much as had been coined in all its previous history since 1793. In practice the USA had moved towards a gold standard, though the move was fought tooth and nail by a growing silver lobby who struggled to maintain bimetallism for half a century until the law finally recognized the economic facts at the very end of the century.

The gold discoveries directly stimulated the economies of the frontier mining areas within an astonishingly short space of time; and indirectly, more steadily but equally certainly led to a diffused and general increase in confidence and economic growth by allaying the fears of even the most conservative of sound-money men in the established money centres, not only in the USA but also worldwide. In the ten years following J. W. Marshall's find at Sutter's Mill on 24

Table 9.1 Banking and the growth of the money supply, 1830–1860.

Year	1830	1840	1850	1860
Population (millions)	12.866	17.069	23.192	31.443
Number of banks	330	901	824	1562
Pop. /banks	39000	18944	28145	20130
Banknotes $m	61	107	131	207
Specie $m	33	83	154	253
Deposits $m	21	76	110	254
Money total $m	115	256	395	714
Supply per head $	9	15	13	23

Sources: *Historical Statistics of United States, Colonial Times to 1957*; Fite and Reese (1973); American Banker's Association, *The Story of American Banking* (New York 1963).

January 1848, California produced over $500 million of gold, an abundance for home and export. Also swollen by Australian discoveries in 1851, the world's stock of gold available for money increased from £144 million sterling in 1851 to £376 million in 1861, an increase of 161 per cent (Final Report of the UK Royal Commission on Gold and Silver, 1888, part I, 10). Given such a substantial increase in the USA and in the rest of the world, even the sound-money men became expansionist, so that the developing banking system was able to build up with greater security than in the previous decades its inverted pyramid of credit, increasing its banknotes and deposits by an experimental multiple on a growing and universally acceptable money base. America's ramshackle financial superstructure was thus, by a fortunate accident of geography, being supplied in abundance with a growing monetary base of the highest quality. The salient features of this growth of banking and of the money supply are indicated in table 9.1.

First one must give a loud and clear warning that, with the exception of the population figures, pre-Civil War statistics are notoriously subject to wide margins of doubt and error, and even when they appear to be reliable their significance is subject to differing interpretations. All the same, when taken as indications of orders of magnitude they may usefully provide evidence of significant trends during this critically important period in American economic history. The population figures are essential to bring what would otherwise seem astronomical rates of growth down to earth. Thus the almost fivefold increase in the number of banks between 1830 and 1860 turns out to be a more moderate though still significant doubling in per capita terms. To give an opposite example, the apparently minor 8.5 per cent fall in the number of banks in the financially dismal 1840s turns out, when allowance is made for population, to be more like a very substantial 50 per cent reduction per capita. The much criticized increases in note issues in the same decade, however well deserved from the point of quality, did not in money supply terms keep pace with the growth of population.

From the economist's standpoint counterfeit notes and coins, so long as they are accepted, carry the same power as their legal counterparts. Legally the counterfeiter is always a malefactor, but economically speaking he may often be a public benefactor. Given the pressure of population, one can see why, in the absence of better and above all adequate money, America's chaotic currency was eagerly pressed into creative use, and why the large but unknown total of counterfeit notes and coin were called into being. The figures for specie and deposits are much less precise than those for notes, but both indicate a strongly rising trend throughout the period. Bank deposits on which cheques could be drawn were emerging into use in the larger towns of the north-east by the 1830s and spread south and west gradually with urbanization. But there was no separation into time and demand deposits in aggregate, and it is probable that the 'moneyness' of deposits was a smaller proportion of total deposits in the early years before the banking habit had spread. Consequently the deposits reckoned as part of the money supply have been arbitrarily adjusted slightly for 1840 and more so for 1830. In case the 'money supply per head' figures in table 9.1 look incredibly low, it should be pointed out, first, that this average relates to all the population and not only to adults; secondly, this static sum makes no reference to the velocity of circulation; thirdly, the vast majority of people were engaged in agriculture, and thus were largely self-supporting. Farmers then had neither the desire nor the opportunity to participate in the kind of insistent, frenetic weekly or even daily shopping that fuels modern economies.

Although the money supply grew decade by decade there was a fall per capita in the 1840s followed by a spectacular rise in the 1850s. During most of the 1830s the supply of finance, though of shocking quality, increased faster than population and probably stimulated demand as a whole. The 1837 crisis was however followed by one of the worst depressions in American history, lasting until 1843 with only a very weak and slow recovery. During this period, when the increase in population is taken into account, the supply of money lagged behind and was a brake upon effective demand. Thus to answer chronologically the chicken-and-egg question of the relationship of money supply to development, the 1830s saw demand lifted upwards by a rising flood of finance, the cumulative and excessive growth of which inevitably led to the crisis of 1837. Thereafter and for most of the 1840s the money supply, contracting in relation to the real needs of an expanding population, acted as a brake on development. From 1848 for nine years an enormous increase in gold gave one of the clearest examples in history of the stimulative power of good-quality money. Business and especially banking confidence built an excessive super-structure of credit on this golden foundation, leading in the autumn of 1857 to 'what has been called the first really world-wide crisis in history . . . in which all the feverish and gold-dazzled activities of the mid-fifties ended' (Clapham 1970, II, 226).

Although there were significant differences between the crises of 1837 and 1857, both highlighted the interconnections between the American and European, especially British, economies and provide an important reminder that the economic development of the USA was not dependent solely on its own supplies of money, credit and capital. Some $300 million of new foreign capital flooded into America between 1850 and 1857; while, already by 1853, 58 per cent of States' securities, 46 per cent of US government securities and 26 per cent of railway bonds were owned by foreigners (Hession and Sardy 1969, 263–4). As well as thus supplementing American savings and investment in key areas British bankers also supplied large amounts of working capital and trade credit. The closest personal relationships were built up between British and American merchant banks and commodity traders, such as Barings, Rothschilds, Brown Shipley, Morgans, and the '3 Ws', Wilson's, Wiggin's and Wilde's. All these not only helped in the flotation of American loans but also financed the growing export-import trade, arranged for the 'acceptance' of large volumes of bills and negotiated 'open credits' of substantial amounts in British banks, including the Bank of England. Even the Bank of the United States, private and no longer national, but still the largest bank in the world, turned in the 1837 crisis to the Bank of England for assistance, though Biddle haughtily laid down conditions the Old Lady could not accept. When the US Bank crashed in 1841 it failed to repay any of its capital. In contrast to the long-lasting effects of the 1837 crisis, that of 1857 although perhaps more dramatic did less permanent damage. 'There was never a more severe crisis nor a more rapid recovery,' wrote the London *Economist* of 5 January 1858. Certainly the American economy was immeasurably stronger than it had been twenty-one years earlier when every bank was forced to suspend specie payment of notes.

Although 1,415 banks in the US suspended payment in the single month of October 1857 yet a number of banks in New Orleans, Indiana and Kentucky maintained their specie payments. One result of the crisis was to cause more banks to follow their shining but exceptional example of keeping higher gold reserves. But just as the American economy was showing strong recovery from that crisis, the looming struggle for supremacy between the States and the Union, which we have traced only on the financial side, brutally interrupted the country's resumed progress with the onset of its bloody Civil War.

From the Civil War to the founding of the 'Fed', 1861–1913

Contrasts in financing the Civil War

Intense political rivalry and fierce financial competition were inseparably interconnected throughout the half-century from 1861 to 1913, during which the USA finally grew into a world power, which was achieved without the benefit of central banking. We have noted how America's citizens decisively rejected the logical steps Biddle was taking towards a sounder, more disciplined and centralized banking system, and how instead they favoured *laissez-faire* run wild. After thirty years of such chaotic freedom, opinion was slowly swinging back the other way towards greater discipline and uniformity when the outbreak of war, as it usually does, forced the pace of change. The war required a rapid transfer of resources from diffused and decentralized civilian expenditure to concentrated and centrally controlled military expenditure, by means of some combination of taxing, borrowing and printing money. The mixture actually chosen differed so markedly between the Unionists and the Confederates as to offer the most instructive – and apparently clear – lessons of how governments can use and control money or abuse it and capitulate to inflation.

Among the various estimates of the financial costs of the war, that given by David Wells, the Special Commissioner of Revenue, in 1869 may be taken as a guide (Myers 1970, 170). Wells estimated the costs incurred directly by the Union government as $4,171 million, with directly incurred costs for the Confederates of $2,700 million. A large remaining sum of $2,323 million, not divided as between North and South, included such items as pensions, state and local government debts, and losses to shipping and industry, making a total of $9,194 million. Despite America's ingrained antipathy to direct taxation, the Union government levied from mid-1861 two types of such taxes. The first was levied on each of the States in proportion to population rather than ability to pay, and therefore was felt by the poorer States to be very unfair. It was paid tardily and reluctantly and was not very productive. Rather better yields were obtained by a general income tax, the rates on which ranged from a basic 3 per cent through 5 per cent to an eventual maximum of 10 per cent on the highest incomes. In all, such direct taxes yielded less than $200 million. Much more important were the indirect taxes, levied from the middle of 1862 onwards, with the rates of tax and the coverage widened from year to year so that they almost became what today would be called a general expenditure tax, yielding at their maximum rates a revenue of over one billion dollars. Tariff revenues on imports were increased by the Morrill Act of 1861, eventually raising the average rate from 20 per cent to 48 per cent, but because imports were depressed by the war, total revenue was not very responsive. In any case since the tariffs were intended partly as protection for domestic producers, what was lost in revenue was gained in encouraging home-based manufacturers.

The Northern government's initial attempts at long-term borrowing by the issue of $500 million twenty-year bonds at 5 per cent were not very successful until an Ohio banker, a Mr Jay Cooke, was put in charge of their sale and was given a commission as an incentive. He was a marketing genius, employed 2,500 agents, advertised widely in local newspapers and appealed in all sorts of ways directly to the pockets and patriotism of the public. By mid-1863 the issue was oversubscribed, and all taken up by the end of the year, mostly by the public, thus moderating its inflationary impact. During 1863 and 1864 another $900 million bonds of various kinds were issued, again initially at only 5 per cent. This low rate did not any longer, despite Cooke's best efforts, appeal to the public, and consequently variations in conversion conditions and redemption facilities were granted. More significantly, to ensure the sale of such large amounts of both long- and short-term debt instruments, the Union had to rely on the assistance of the banks. It was in this way, through the imperatives of war, that long-needed changes in the banking system were brought about. The absorption of government paper, including both notes and bonds, thus became an integral part of the fundamental reform of the banking system – a topic which is most conveniently studied after considering the contemporary but glaringly different fiscal and monetary experience of the Confederacy.

One similarity for both sides was the early suspension of specie convertibility for notes. Priority in the use of the nation's supply of gold and silver was given for government purposes, and the drain of specie from the banks led to the formal declaration of suspension by Congress at the end of December 1861. Since one of the main reasons for the war was opposition to the power of central government, the general American aversion to taxation was strongly reinforced in the South. The imposition of adequate taxes and their collection was very much a case of too little and too late. A tax on property and a progressive income tax with a top rate of 15 per cent, seemingly more severe than in the North, in fact yielded so little that payments of taxes in kind, direct physical requisitioning (or 'impressment') and financial requisitioning on the States had to be enforced. Though its borrowing policy was more impressive than its woefully inadequate taxation, yet it still fell far behind that of the North. The Southern States, relying too optimistically on Europe's dependence on 'King Cotton', did manage to use that commodity in attempts to raise loans of $15 million from Europe, but because of the blockade only around a quarter of the expected supplies came from such sources. The blockade similarly reduced the actual yield from the South's increased customs duties to negligible amounts. Nevertheless up to one-third of Confederate expenditure was covered by borrowing, including that raised by the States. As much as it could, the army lived off the land.

The one seemingly unlimited resource was the printing press, which was resorted to quickly and with great abandon. A flood of notes, some interest-bearing, others convertible into bonds and yet others promising redemption in specie 'two years after the ratification of a peace', answered the most pressing needs of the moment. The first issue of $100 million was made in August 1861, with later issues bringing the total up to around $400 million by the end of 1862 and $600 million by the beginning of 1864. A few futile attempts were made to convert certain notes to lower denominations but the total continued to rise until the end of hostilities, reaching by then an estimated $1,555 million. In addition to the Confederate notes, the States, and railway, insurance and other companies, were also issuing notes. Depending on how one defines the term, the money stock probably increased by about eleven times in four years. Estimates of the rise in prices indicate an increase by about twenty-eight times, from a base of 100 in January 1861 to 2,776 in January 1865. There was obviously a 'flight from money' with a marked increase in the velocity of circulation, while at the same time the quantity of goods available for purchase was drastically reduced. Thus far too much money was ever more rapidly chasing a diminishing quantity of goods – the perfect recipe for hyper-inflation.

In comparison the inflation of the North was very mild, with the estimated index of prices rising from 100 in January 1861 to 216 at the beginning of 1865. Not only is this mild inflation extremely creditable when put alongside the infamous record of the South, but it stands up well in comparison with the experiences of victorious countries in later wars and is infinitely better than the experience of occupied or defeated countries in most subsequent wars. Even if the South had resorted earlier to the imposition of higher taxes, and even if it had managed to borrow more (though it is difficult to see how this could have been done), heavy resort to the printing press was inevitable. The lessons to be gained from the more virtuous policies of the North could have been applied in the South only had it possessed something more like equivalent resources. In terms of population, the South with 9 million, of which 3.5 million were slaves, confronted the richer 22 million of the North, which possessed over 70 per cent of the country's railway mileage, nearly 75 per cent of its initial bank deposits and over 80 per cent of its manufacturing plant, much of which continued to prosper from the demands of war to a greater extent than did the new industries encouraged to spring up in the south. Northern agriculture also prospered. Wheat production was immensely stimulated by British as well as Northern demand, by the new railways and the Homestead Act of 1862, which all worked together to increase the prosperity of the West just when the productive capacity, including that of the railways, in the South was being severely reduced. The mix of fiscal and financial policies available for the Union was just not possible for the Confederacy to put into practice. Thus it could at best have escaped only to a marginal degree from the hyper-inflation it suffered, and which led finally to Confederate paper becoming worthless, so repeating the history of the 'Continentals'. Meanwhile the basic monetary reforms the whole country needed were being put into effect in the North.

Establishing the national financial framework
The secession by the anti-federalists opened the way for nationwide monetary solutions by the Union government. Most urgent was the immediate granting of purchasing power to the central government by means of the Legal Tender Act of February 1862 whereby the Treasury was given the right to issue $150 million 'United States Government Notes'. A second issue of $150 million was authorized in July 1862, and a third, also of $150 million, in March 1863. These issues of $450 million, popularly known as 'Greenbacks' from the vivid colour of the printing on their reverse, formed a fiat currency, specifically not convertible into specie but authorized as legal tender for all purposes except the payment of customs duties and interest on government securities. Furthermore it was generally understood that the greenbacks

were to be a temporary, wartime issue; they were however destined for a long and controversial life, dividing the nation sharply between the 'Greenbackers' and their opponents. A second type of nationwide paper money, intended right from the start to be permanent and to replace the chaotic State banknote issues, came into being as the result of the Currency Act of 1863, amended and expanded as the National Bank Act of 1864. Like former 'free banking' Acts passed by New York and other States, this Federal legislation allowed any group of five or more persons to set up a bank, with a minimum capital of $50,000 in small towns with up to 6,000 people, a minimum capital of $200,000 in large towns of 50,000 people or above, while for the medium-sized towns in between a capital of $100,000 was required. In order to secure the privilege of note issue (still thought indispensable for banking) each bank had to buy government bonds and deposit them with the Comptroller of the Currency, who had been newly established to authorize and supervise the national banks. The national banks thus provided a greatly enlarged market for government stock and supplied the country, instead of the immensely varied and insecure State banknotes, with a 'National Bank Note' currency of uniform size and design (except for the name of the particular national bank), with the important additional advantage of guaranteed acceptance at par by every other national bank: a pleasing contrast to the infuriating discounts commonly charged when State banknotes were used at any distance from their issuing bank.

To speed up the change to national notes a 2 per cent tax placed on State bank issues in 1862 was raised to 10 per cent in 1866, so taxing such notes out of existence. It did not lead to the expected disappearance of State banks, for these, after declining from their pre-war peak in 1861 of 1,601 to their lowest post-war number of 247 in 1868, rose stubbornly thereafter to ensure that the USA continued to enjoy or suffer the distinction of its 'dual banking' structure. Actually the term 'dual' is bland and misleading, for it implies that the United States operates only two kinds of banking jurisdiction instead of more than fifty confusing varieties actually or potentially existing. In the United States, the textbook home of *laissez-faire*, even the term 'free banking' is subject to fifty limiting interpretations, for it is freedom to operate under fifty potentially widely differing sets of restrictions. It was just in this period when the chaotic banknotes had at last been replaced by uniform notes that bank deposits transferable by cheque grew to become the main currency for business. Already by 1890 over 90 per cent in value terms of all transactions were carried out by cheque. The supply of the main and growing source of money thus became subject not to uniform rules, controls and supervision but to a large number of different authorities using varying and sometimes conflicting guidelines with widely contrasting degrees of strictness or laxity. Even the 'national', federally chartered banks could not in fact operate uniformly but were subject to different constraints in different States, notably for example in such a vitally important matter as whether they could open branches. Thus national banks in Illinois or Texas have not operated in the same way as their neighbouring national banks in Iowa or Louisiana, to say nothing of the much greater differences from the national banks in California or New York and the still greater contrasts with their State counterparts. In this way the so-called dual system divides even the apparently uniform national banking system into a number of starkly different varieties. This peculiar dual banking system is thus in part connected causally with another distinctively American feature, namely the persistence of a high degree of unit banking throughout the nineteenth and twentieth centuries. This and other related factors such as the high incidence of bank failures will be examined later; but first we trace the remarkable growth in the number of banks in the USA up to the peak year of 1921 – remarkable because, in glaring contrast, bank numbers in other advanced countries were falling steeply during the same period (see table 9.2).

Reference to table 9.2 shows that the total number of banks increased by over nineteen times between 1860 and 1921 to reach a peak of nearly 30,000. The vigour of State banks is shown by their staggering eighty-eight times increase from 1868, rising through equality of numbers with national banks in 1892 to their high point of 21,638, or 73 per cent of the total number of banks in 1921. Typically, however, State banks were significantly smaller on average, so that their proportion of total deposits has generally varied between one-third and a half. State banks more than trebled in number in just fifteen years between 1900 and 1915, rising from 5,000 to over 18,000, during a period of intense competition with their national rivals, which though not growing so fast yet managed to double their numbers from 3,731 to 7,589. In order to enable the national banks to compete more directly at the small-town level, the Currency Act of 1900 reduced the capital requirement for banks in towns with a population of less than 3,000 from the previous minimum of $50,000 to $25,000.

This competition in weakness is another instance of the debilitating effect of the dual system, dragging national standards downwards. Naturally the State banks enjoyed a number of perceived offsetting advantages to put before their shareowners and customers, otherwise they could never have grown so fast or have persisted so long as they

Table 9.2 State and national banks, 1860–1992.

Year	Total	State banks		National banks	
		Number	%	Number	%
1860	1562	1562	100	nil	-
1865	1643	349	21	1294	79
1868	1887	247	13	1640	87
1870	1937	325	17	1612	83
1875	2662	586	22	2076	78
1880	2726	650	24	2076	76
1885	3704	1015	27	2689	73
1890	5734	2250	39	3484	61
1892	7532	3733	50	3759	50
1895	8084	4369	54	3715	46
1900	8738	5007	57	3731	43
1905	14682	9018	61	5664	39
1910	21486	14348	67	7138	33
1915	25875	18227	71	7598	29
1921	29788	21638	73	8150	27
1929	25113	17583	70	7530	30
1935	15478	10053	65	5425	35
1955	13719	9027	66	4692	34
1975	14570	9838	68	4732	32
1980	14836	10411	70	4425	30
1989	12912	8636	67	4276	33
1990	12572	8458	67	4114	33
1991	12384	8368	68	4016	32
1992	12050	8175	68	3875	32

Sources: Board of Governors of the Federal Reserve System; *Annual Statistical Digests* and *Federal Reserve Bulletins*.

have. State banks have outnumbered national banks for a hundred years, and by about two to one throughout almost the whole of the twentieth century, remaining in its closing decade a most vigorous apparent anachronism. There are a number of strong reasons for their stubborn survival, not all of them good. Their generally much smaller initial capital requirements enabled them to capture a large market share among the small country towns and to grow with the growth of these towns: hence their particular appeal in the States of the Midwest. State banks have also for most of their existence been required to hold much smaller reserves. Ten States, even as late as 1910, stipulated no reserve requirements at all. Supervision of State banks was generally less onerous, and examinations less frequent, than was the case with national banks. State banks were able to carry out a wider range of bank-related services, many of which were specifically forbidden for national banks, including the important practice of being able to lend on the security of real estate. State-chartered banks were generally felt to be more flexible in responding to local demands. Fewer costly restraints, combined with these other advantages, gave them the ability to operate at a size so small as to be forbidden to or unprofitable for the national banks. The prohibition of branching and the legal bias against bank mergers preserved the small unit bank and prevented the generally larger national banks from being able to take over their smaller rivals or to compete with them as effectively as would have been the case in a free market. National banks were not generally allowed to purchase the stock of other banks whereas most State banks could do so. Similarly while national banks were not allowed (at least until 1906) to lend to any one borrower an amount exceeding 10 per cent of their capital, State banks were usually free from such constraints, which otherwise would have impinged most heavily on the smaller banks.

While banks and their money-creating powers thus grew in a fast but haphazard manner, the attention of the public was mainly turned to other aspects of money. The essence of the great 'money question' which dominated the waking thoughts and actions of the politicians between the Civil War and the end of the century was not so much a concern about the silent financial revolution brought about by abstract bank deposits but rather with the much more concrete, highly visible and emotionally explosive matters of gold and silver and the convertibility of notes into one or both of these metals.

Bimetallism's final fling
The United States and France played the leading roles in trying to establish international agreement on bimetallic monetary systems in the latter part of the nineteenth century, during which the world was awash with monetary remedies for economic instability. It was realized that external drains of either gold or silver could create strains so strong that any single country might find it impossible to maintain its bimetallic system, but that if the major countries could all agree on the same mint ratios then the supposed advantages conferred by bimetallism would more easily be maintained. Among these advantages were first, the securing of a less restrictive money supply than would be the case were only one metal (in practice the much rarer gold) chosen as standard and, also that by having paper money anchored firmly to a combined metallic base, inflation would be avoided. Bimetallism thus seemed the best bet for stability. France widened its influence in 1865 by

establishing the Latin Union with Belgium, Switzerland and Italy (with Greece joining in 1868). These countries agreed a common 15½:1 silver/gold ratio, and that the gold and silver coins of each country were to be accepted by all. In 1867 an International Monetary Conference was held in Paris, to which the USA sent representatives, where attempts were made to widen still further the area of common currencies based on the French gold and silver 10- and 5-franc pieces. By then the world was moving strongly towards a preference for a British-type gold standard, a model which the newly united Germany adopted in 1871, followed by Austria, Holland, Scandinavia and Russia. A further such conference was held in Paris in 1878, greatly reviving, through wishful thinking, the hopes of US bimetallists, but otherwise falling flat. The Bank of England had refused to send representatives to either conference: the Old Lady considered them to be both too political and too theoretical – a shrewd but correct interpretation. Vast increases in world supplies, first of silver, then of gold, unsettled even the Latin Union's bimetallic stance. In 1879 France had to discontinue its silver coinage, and only gold coins were universally accepted in practice in the Union, which thereafter could manage only a 'limping bimetallism', with silver as its broken leg. Theoretical variants of bimetallism rose – and fell without trace. Such was the 'Parallel Standard' where mint ratios were to be adjusted frequently whenever significant changes in market ratios of gold and silver demanded such changes (but this left the problem of the value of existing coins unsolved). The so-called 'Great Depression' of 1873–86 had caused the monetary authorities even in Great Britain to question the merits of the gold standard and ask the advice of its Gold and Silver Commission of 1886 as to how best to overcome the fall in prices. Two of the most famous economists of that period, Alfred Marshall and F. Y. Edgeworth, advocated 'Symmetallism', where the legal standard unit would consist of a fixed weight of both silver and gold, 'a linked bar on which a paper currency may be based' (Edgeworth 1895, 442, quoted in Friedman 1990, 95). On the analogy of a clock's compensating pendulum their combined values would vary less than that of either silver or gold – correct but impractical. It is against this international background, battling valiantly but vainly against the tide, that America's 'blundering enrapturement' with bimetallism as part of its great money question has to be judged (Nugent, 1968).

From 1865 to 1873 opinion in the USA moved strongly against silver and towards gold as the dollar standard, but suddenly from 1873 to 1896 bimetallism surged into a crusade. Supporters of the gold standard were mostly concentrated in the established cities of the north-east. They wished to reduce the inflationary dangers of excessive note issues by taking measures which would lead to full gold specie convertibility for greenbacks and national banknote issues. Silver's supporters were to be found mainly in the West and South where the silver miners easily gained the backing of the rural communities. During much of the second half of the nineteenth century prices in general tended to fall, while agricultural prices and farmers' incomes (because of the inelasticity of demand for their products) fell even farther. At the same time the newly formed States of these western and southern areas were each bringing their two representatives to Congress, so giving the silver lobby a political influence much greater than their population justified. At the end of the Civil War the greenback circulation of $450 million was worth only half as much in gold as in nominal value. Consequently the hard-money men wished to see a quick reduction in such note issues (which after all had been intended only as a temporary wartime expedient). By the Contraction Act of 1865 they persuaded the government to begin withdrawing the greenbacks at a rate of $10 million a month. Unfortunately these reductions coincided with, and reinforced, a general depression, so that the government was forced to halt further note withdrawals in 1868, and in the following years even began making some increases in greenback circulation. A Greenback Party was formed in 1875, and by 1878 had managed to attract a million voters and returned fourteen members to Congress determined to secure at least the maintenance and preferably an increase in the greenback note circulation. A compromise between the opposing factions resulted in the fixing of the greenback circulation in 1878 at the then current amount of $346,681,016. The trend towards scarcer and dearer money was thus halted.

Around the same time two further aspects of the money question were being resolved, namely the demonetization of silver and the resumption of convertibility into specie, the specie concerned being gold. By the Coinage Act of 1873, passed while the silver lobby was sleeping, the silver dollar ceased to be the standard of value: the USA was now virtually on the gold standard. The gold premium carried by notes was clearly falling during the early 1870s, so that the government felt it safe, by the Resumption Act of January 1875, to promise full redemption by 1 January 1879. One of the factors strengthening the value of the greenbacks and so making resumption easier was the case of Knox v. Lee of May 1871 by which the legal tender quality of the greenbacks, which had previously been drawn into question, was widened and confirmed. The restrictions on note issue, the fall in prices, the legal confirmation of greenback status and an increase in world gold supplies all helped to make resumption completely successful. But a further feature, insufficiently stressed before the monumental researches of Friedman and Schwartz, was the greatly increased output of goods and services achieved despite the depression in prices. America simply grew up to its money supply (Friedman and Schwartz 1963, 41–4).

By the time convertibility had been resumed a 'free silver' movement had suddenly awoken and bestirred itself into furious activity. This movement claimed the right to bring unlimited amounts of silver to the mint for coining, thus keeping up prices in general and of course silver prices in particular. The silver lobby's first success in undoing what had belatedly come to be called the 'crime of 73' was registered in the Bland–Allison Act of 1878 whereby the Treasury was obliged to buy between $2 million and $4 million of silver each month to be coined at the 16:1 ratio. Still better, the Treasury agreed to purchase a fixed amount of 4.5 million ounces each month according to the Sherman Silver Purchase Act of 1890. This situation could not last long for, as every student of economics soon learns, monopoly power does not bestow the ability to fix both price and quantity; and although the government had not promised to buy unlimited amounts, and although the American silver miners were not alone in the world, yet the government did purchase an enormous amount of over $500 million of silver between 1878 and 1893. The abundance of silver on the world markets meant that gold could be purchased in the USA at favourable rates, so that there soon ensued both an internal and an external drain on the US gold reserves. This grew so severe as to bring them by 1893 below the level of $100 million considered to be the minimum to guarantee the convertibility of an enlarged note circulation; for although the greenback circulation had been fixed, the Resumption Act had in 1875 removed the $300 million limit on national bank note circulation. The gold drain therefore forced President Cleveland, despite fierce opposition, to cancel the silver purchase laws as from 1 November 1893. Gradually, with the aid of the merchant banking house of Morgan (there being no central bank), the gold reserves were again restored so as to maintain convertibility. However, Cleveland paid the price by being rejected by the Democratic Party in favour of someone who, more than anyone else in history, has come to embody the bimetallist cause, William Jennings Bryan (1860–1925).

Bryan trained and practised as a lawyer; but he was also a gifted journalist and publicist, a brilliant and tireless orator and political organizer who stimulated, bullied, cajoled, inspired and unified all the disparate factions that shared some interest in the silver question into fighting single-mindedly for the bimetallist cause. Among such factions were the Populists or People's Party, formed in 1891 but already numbering a million members by 1896. They advocated mildly socialistic policies, e.g. government ownership of the communication industries, postal savings banks, etc.; but being strongly in favour of unlimited silver coinage they were natural allies of Bryan. The American Bimetallic League and the National Bimetallic Union similarly combined to fight for Bryan in his bid for the Presidency in 1896. During this campaign in one of the first 'whistle-stop tours' Bryan made a political convenience of the newly expanded railway system, travelled over 18,000 miles in thirty-seven States and made some 600 speeches, culminating in the Democratic National Convention in Chicago where he repeated his rallying cry against the stultifying restrictions of the gold standard: 'You shall not press down upon the brow of labour this crown of thorns, you shall not crucify mankind upon a cross of gold.'

Yet for all Bryan's brilliant oratory and energetic campaigning it was his more realistic opponent, the Republicans' William McKinley, who won the election, by 271 votes to Bryan's 176. All the same, so frightened had McKinley's supporters been made by the rhetoric of the bimetallists that they hedged their bets, favouring America's continuance on the gold standard only until such time as the major trading nations would agree to coin gold and silver at the same fixed ratio – an event which naturally never occurred. In retrospect it is easy to criticize Bryan. Yet during the first part of the 1890s, as we have seen, America was losing gold; and Bryan could hardly be blamed for not seeing the immense increase in world gold supplies that were already beginning and which were to grow into a flood in the next decade or so. The annual world output of gold rose from 5,749,306 ounces in 1890 to 12,315,135 ounces in 1900. The USA, which had been a net exporter of gold to the extent of $79 million in the year from mid-1895, became, thanks to running a favourable balance of trade, a net importer of $201 million of gold altogether in the next three years. This, together with its retained portion of domestic production, caused total US monetary gold stocks to rise from $502 million in 1896 to $859 million in 1899 (Friedman and Schwartz 1963, 141). World gold supplies continued to grow in the next decade and a half. This enormous increase came in part from new discoveries in Alaska, Africa and Australia, and in part from the invention of the cyanide process which made extraction from low-grade ores profitable. Together these gold supplies helped to stimulate the world economy and led to a doubling of America's monetary gold stock from 1890 to 1900 (and a trebling between the earlier date and 1914). This was the economic reality that moved the balance of opinion decisively away from bimetallism and led at last to the confident enactment of the Gold Standard Act of March 1900: gold monometallism had, belatedly, legally captured what was to be its most powerful convert.

From gold standard to central bank(s), 1900–1913
That Act, as well as unequivocally confirming in legal terms the already established economic fact that the dollar was defined in terms of gold alone, contained a number of other provisions which had a considerable effect in expanding the basic money supply – and hence is also known as the Currency Act. The first of these was the increase of the minimum gold reserve which the Treasury had to hold to maintain the convertibility of greenbacks, Treasury notes and the national banknotes from $100 million to $150 million, thus substantially raising public confidence in the government's ability and determination to maintain the gold standard, and the convertibility of notes, which latter for most people symbolized that standard. Secondly, as already noted, the minimum capital for the smallest national banks was halved to $25,000, so stimulating not only a rapid increase in their numbers but also leading to a much-needed increase in national banknote circulation. Thirdly, and still more important in this connection, was the raising of the limit on a bank's note issue from the previous 90 per cent to 100 per cent of the value of the required backing of government securities deposited with the Comptroller of the Currency, though the valuation was still reckoned on the lower of either the market price or the par value of such securities. Although, in terms of quantity, bank deposits were by far the most important part of the money supply, yet in times of crisis and more commonly in rural areas and in retail trade the greater liquidity of cash was preferred. It was hoped that the increased note issues encouraged by the Act of 1900 would answer the insistent demands for a more 'elastic' currency. When the greenback circulation had been fixed at a maximum of $357 million in 1878 it had been expected that the national banknote circulation, which, as we saw, had already had its previous ceiling of $300 million completely removed in 1875, would rise in line with the demands of a rapidly growing economy.

Unfortunately it was not the needs of the economy but rather the state of the government's own finances that governed note supply; a continuously increasing deficit would have been required to provide a sufficiently cheap supply of government securities to make it profitable for the banks to increase their note issues. In fact the opposite tendency towards fiscal surpluses prevailed. Thus, after a slight rise to $352 million in 1882, the circulation of national banknotes fell drastically by 54 per cent to only $162 million in 1891. In 1898 they had risen, but insufficiently, to $221 million. The influence of the Currency Act thereafter becomes apparent, for the circulation rose to $349 million in 1901, just exceeding that of the greenbacks, to reach $598 million in the crisis year of 1907 and then continued to rise to reach a pre-war peak of $745 million in 1913. These developments alleviated but did not solve the clamorous need for an 'elastic currency' for the simple and increasingly apparent reason that the key ingredient to be flexibly controlled in line with the needs of the economy was not the gold or the notes which had been dominating public discussion, but rather bank credit. Following the severe bank panics of 1873 and 1893 this lesson was finally underlined with unmistakable clarity by the crisis of 1907, which demonstrated that just being on the gold standard was no guarantee of either monetary stability or of the safety of the banking system.

The chief financial factors responsible for the recurring instabilities of the national banking era (apart from those severe fluctuations in the real economy for which the banking system could not directly be blamed) were, first, the pyramiding of deposits, and secondly, the absence of an effective lender of last resort, i.e. a central bank. Small country banks naturally found it convenient, indeed essential, to keep part of their total deposits with a larger 'correspondent' bank in (usually) the nearest large town; and banks in such towns similarly kept a larger amount with their correspondent bank(s) in the big cities, especially New York, Chicago and St Louis. These arrangements were codified into law by the National Banking Acts of 1863–4, with country banks having to keep reserves of 15 per cent of their deposits (plus, originally, notes), while the forty-seven reserve cities and three central reserve cities, whose bankers acted as bankers to the country banks, had to keep a higher reserve, of 25 per cent. Whenever banks throughout the country, for example at seed-time and harvest, found it necessary to draw more heavily than usual on their deposits from their correspondent banks in the reserve cities, these latter banks were forced to sell securities and call in their loans to brokers, thus leading to high money market rates and falling security prices, so as frequently to cause severe stringency, and in the extreme cases runs on banks and thus general financial panic.

It was at such times that the lack of an efficient lender of last resort – able and willing to supply sufficient liquidity promptly enough to quell the crisis in its early stages – was keenly felt. Instead, the domino effect turned local difficulties into widespread panics with bank failures being far too common. To some extent certain alleviating measures were taken from time to time by local bank clearing houses and also, though more rarely, by the wealthy Treasury, whenever it decided to reverse its 'independent' stance. (A most useful summary of both kinds of such measures is given by Ellis Tallman 1988.) In particular, members of bank clearing houses would issue and accept among themselves 'clearing house certificates' for settling inter-indebtedness, leaving the precious notes and gold more exclusively available for their more fearful and impatient retail and personal customers. Thus during the height of the 1893 crisis 95 per cent of all clearings in value in New York were settled with clearing house certificates. As for the Treasury's tentative central banking activities, these became most prominent when Mr Leslie M. Shaw was Secretary of the Treasury, from 1902 to 1906; in the latter year, with pardonable exaggeration but with little foresight, he claimed that 'No central or government bank in the world can so readily influence financial conditions throughout the world as can the Secretary' (Friedman and Schwartz 1963 150). However, as the events of the following year were to prove, such sporadic and patchy actions were far from being the proper way to run the banking system of what had now grown to be the world's largest economy.

Whereas previous crises had usually started in the weak country banking regions and had spread via the reserve deposit system to involve the sounder, bigger banks of New York, the 1907 crisis started within New York itself led in particular by the powerful and fashionable trust companies. The trust companies could carry out financial services denied to the commercial banks, were less keenly supervised and could operate with lower reserves. Unfortunately, partly for that reason, they were not members of the New York Clearing House which otherwise might have saved them by prompter action when the 1907 crisis broke. The trusts were important customers both of the large New York commercial banks that held most of the reserves of the nation's banks and of the merchant and investment banks like J. P. Morgan, Jay Cooke and Kuhn Loebe, the whole nexus forming together the heart of the country's famed and feared 'money trust'. It was the hidden danger of this money trust, purported to be the strongest part of the country's financial system, that was cruelly exposed by the 1907 crisis and the lengthy public investigations that followed.

As the country's banking system had grown, so had the extent of concentration of reserves in New York City, both in absolute and relative terms. Thus whereas in 1870 some 40 per cent of all national bank reserves were held there, by 1900 three-quarters of the very much larger total of reserve deposits of all the country's correspondent banks were held by the six largest New York City banks. Much of this money was, either directly or indirectly via brokers and investment trusts, invested in the stock market, prices on which could of course be very volatile. To deal with the growing scale of investment business the competing brokers combined to form the New York Stock Exchange in Wall Street in 1896. Only twenty industrial companies were quoted on this exchange in 1898 but by 1905 eighty-five were listed. A company merger mania in the early 1900s stimulated by professional promoters like Charles R. Flint, the 'father of the trusts', caused a boom in the investment trust movement that sucked in these rapidly growing bank deposits. Thus John Moody in *The Truth about the Trusts* shows a growth from ninety-eight trusts with a capital value of one billion dollars in 1898 to 234 trusts with a total capital of six billion dollars in 1904. This euphoria lasted until 1907.

The crisis began when five New York banks were forced to seek assistance from their clearing house on 14 October. This at first seemed to quell the trouble, but a week later the country's third largest trust, the Knickerbocker Trust, failed, followed shortly after by the second largest, the Trust Company of America and another large trust. Despite the issue of Clearing House Certificates, the deposit of $36 million by the Treasury in the New York banks and a frantic effort by J. P. Morgan to mount what we today would call a 'lifeboat' rescue, a general banking panic spread rapidly throughout the country. This mainly took the form of a restriction of cash payments, which lasted in many areas until January 1908. In the two years 1907–8 some 246 banks failed, much fewer than in the previous panic of 1893. The restrictions on convertibility rationed the existing gold reserves and thus had the effect of inhibiting the runs on banks from producing the larger number of failures that would otherwise have taken place. The Knickerbocker Trust itself reopened in March 1908. In fact the rise of new banks soon exceeded the number of failures, so (as seen in table 9.2) the total annual number of banks continued to grow. Nevertheless the long period of inconvertibility coupled with the painfully telling fact that the crisis had first arisen, not among the small, weak, country banks, but among the country's largest financial institutions right in the central reserve city of New York, led to a ready acceptance by all sections of business and political opinion of the urgent need for a fundamental reform of the banking system.

The first major step towards an 'elastic currency' was taken when

Congress passed the Aldrich–Vreeland Act in May 1908. It enabled, as an emergency measure, groups of a minimum of ten national banks to form National Currency Associations to issue temporary currency up to a maximum for the country as a whole of $500 million. Secondly, the Act set up a National Monetary Commission of nine Representatives and nine Senators including Nelson W. Aldrich as Chairman. This Commission authorized some forty-two separate reports, which were published in twenty-four volumes, most of which contained studies of foreign banking systems. In all, they constituted the most comprehensive investigation of money and banking seen up to then in history. It took five years for Congress to digest the information sufficiently to come to its decisions. In the mean time two other relevant aspects require a brief mention. First, in 1911 the US Postal Savings System was established, thus apparently answering the demands the Populist Party had made in the 1890s; but the opposition of the commercial bankers saw to it that the rates of interest the postal banks were allowed to give prevented them from ever becoming really serious competitors. Secondly, in February 1912 a committee under the chairmanship of Arsene Pujo of Louisiana was set up to investigate the extent of the powers of the alleged 'money trust'.

The Pujo Committee reported in 1913 that it had 'no hesitation in asserting that an established and well-defined identity of interest . . . held together by stock-holdings, inter-locking directorates and other forms of dominion over banks, trusts, railroads' etc. 'has resulted in a vast and growing concentration and control of money and credit in the hands of a comparatively few men'. The oft-repeated warnings of William Jennings Bryan, now the newly appointed Secretary of State, had been amply vindicated. The days of *laissez-faire*, particularly for New York money men, were over and some form of central banking control inescapable and imminent. In introducing the bill for banking reform Senator Carter Glass stated plainly that 'Financial textbook writers in Europe have characterised our banking as "barbarous" and eminent bankers in this country have not hesitated to confess that the criticism is merited.' The Act establishing the Federal Reserve System was eventually signed by President Woodrow Wilson on 23 December 1913, its declared objects being 'to provide for the establishment of Federal reserve banks, to furnish an elastic currency, to afford means of re-discounting commercial paper, to establish a more effective supervision of banking, and for other purposes': almost a blank cheque to be filled in as circumstances demanded. The President, in the course of the debate, added: ' We shall deal with our economic system as it is and as it may be modified, not as it might be if we had a clean sheet of paper to write upon; and step by step we shall make it what it should be.' That journey has no end, for like the liberty with which it is so closely related, the price of sound money is eternal vigilance.

The banks through boom and slump, 1914–1944

The 'Fed' finds its feet, 1914–1928

Before the buildings of the new Federal Reserve System were completed and staffed, the outbreak of the First World War in Europe in August 1914 caused such a large sale of US securities and a drain of gold that the US authorities were forced, for the first and only time, to make use of the emergency facilities of the Aldrich–Vreeland Act for National Currency Associations to issue temporary notes, some $380 million of which were put into circulation. This turned out to be a successful example of monetary elasticity, filling the gap before the new central banking system took over. The checks and balances that characterize the American constitution were strongly reflected in forming the kind of banking system appropriate to a large subcontinent with widely different economic interests. Memories and myths of the monsters of the past – the First and Second Banks of the United States – ruled out any single central bank. Instead twelve Federal Reserve Districts, each with its own Reserve Bank, were established, with the larger districts having a number of branches, currently twenty-five, plus twelve other separate offices. All national banks had to become members of the new system while it was hoped (overoptimistically) that the conditional permission given to State banks to join would be taken up rapidly enough to eradicate the acknowledged weaknesses of the dual banking system. The member banks 'owned' their local Reserve Bank by each member contributing the equivalent of 3 per cent of their own capital (with another 3 per cent on call) to form the capital of their Reserve Bank.

Each member bank had to deposit stipulated reserves with their Reserve Bank, with the latter having to keep a minimum reserve of 35 per cent in lawful money against its deposits, with a 40 per cent gold reserve behind its issues of Federal Reserve notes. Each Federal Reserve Bank has a board of nine members comprising a balance of control between small, medium and large local banks, local businessmen and the main board in Washington. In this way each Reserve Bank became a regional and local institution integrated into a nationwide system. Borrowing facilities, mainly at first by rediscounting, were made ubiquitously available for member banks all of which had to clear cheques at par. Thus for the first time this basic business boon was available nationwide – but mainly for member banks (with few exceptions). Central control of this regionalized system was based not in the economic capital, New York, but in Washington, the political capital, so as to counterbalance the 'money trust'. In Washington sat the seven members of the Federal Reserve Board (as it was originally termed) comprising the Comptroller of the Currency, the Secretary of the Treasury and five other members all appointed by the President but having their independence strengthened by being appointed for fourteen years and with membership later staggered by one member retiring every two years. Regional equity meant that no two Central Board members could come from the same Reserve District.

The massive compromise that determined the structure of the 'Fed' has proved its merit by remaining basically unchanged; while it has been flattered by imitation in the constitution of a number of central banks not only in the Third World but also notably in the case of post-Second World War Germany. Even in its operations, apart from the disasters of the 1930s, the 'Fed' has been widely praised by economists, with the exception of the strangely united Professors Milton Friedman and Kenneth Galbraith. We shall now judge its progress, together with that of the banks in general, first in its formative years up to 1928, secondly during the catastrophic years of collapse from 1929 to 1933, and then during the more positive period of reform and of wartime finance up to the international conference at Bretton Woods in 1944.

During the period from 1914 to 1928 a central banking system which had with great care and deliberation been formed as a regional structure where local economic demands were in large part to determine policy, became transformed operationally into a centralized system based in reality in New York, where policy was determined predominantly by the demands of Wall Street and of the international money market, moderated, if at all, by whatever influence the Washington Board of Governors could exert against the dominant personality of Benjamin Strong, Governor of the Reserve Bank of New York. Even the Treasury's greatly enhanced wartime powers, although exercised nominally from Washington, were in practice largely carried out through the agency of the New York Federal Reserve Bank. No other federal reserve district carried anything like the economic weight of that of New York, and the larger the number of Federal Reserve Districts, the more prominent was the influence of New York. Intense parochialism defeated its own object and played into the hands of the nation's economic capital. As Professor Chandler has emphasized in his brilliant biography of *Benjamin Strong: Central Banker* (1958): 'The division of the rest of the country into eleven reserve districts rather

than a smaller number' (such as the minimum of eight permitted under
the Act of 1913) 'served to decrease the size and probably also the
prestige of the other reserve banks relative to New York' (p.46).

The New York Federal Reserve District was by far the country's most
important economic region, with its largest ports, most concentrated
banking centre and with the largest domestic and international money
market in the USA. New York was also easily the largest capital market,
whether dealing in private or government securities. Thus the Federal
Reserve Bank of New York quickly began to act as agent for purchasing
securities for the other reserve banks, whose staff, from top to bottom,
lacked the experience of those in New York. Issues of government
securities increased enormously after the USA entered the war in April
1917, the total national debt rising from around $1 billion in 1916 to
$25 billion in 1920. This again acted both in an obvious and in a more
subtle manner to increase the relative power of the New York Federal
Reserve Bank. The obvious and direct manner arose from the simple
fact of the immense size of government security dealings, the great bulk
of which was handled via New York. Before turning to the more subtle
and indirect results, it is necessary to take a brief glance at how these
events were moulded by that master technician and financial strategist,
Benjamin Strong; for even more obviously than is the case with
commercial banking, central banking is about people – particularly in
this period.

A triumvirate of exceptionally powerful central bankers towered
above their financial markets in the 1920s so as to achieve far-reaching
economic and political, as well as financial, results. These three,
Montagu Norman, Benjamin Strong and Hjalmar Schacht worked
closely together, the two former continuing their close wartime co-
operation; and all three, together with Émile Moreau, president of the
Bank of France, helped to overcome in the financial field America's
post-war political lurch back into 'isolation'. Benjamin Strong first
came into public notice when he was made Secretary of Bankers Trust
in 1904. Bankers Trust had been formed in the previous year by a group
of New York bankers, led by H. P. Davison, who had become
increasingly concerned that the mushrooming growth of financial trusts
was depriving the commercial banks of many of their best customers.
Such trusts, being less constrained by minimum reserves and rules
restricting lending, could carry out a wider range of financial business –
with the exception of note issue –, grant higher rates on deposits and
lend at cheaper rates than could the conventional banks. On the well-
tried principle 'if you can't beat them, join them', Davison and his
colleagues therefore set up their own 'Bankers Trust' which, though

formed only in 1903, had grown sufficiently strong so as to play a prominent role in aiding other banks and influential businesses during and in the aftermath of the 1907 crisis. Thus Strong was well known, well connected and had gained a wealth of highly relevant experience when he was chosen as the first Governor of the Federal Reserve Bank of New York in October 1914 and was thus launched 'on his way to becoming the dominant personality and *de facto* leader of the entire Federal Reserve System' (Chandler 1958, 41).

Strong quickly drew the threads of power into his own hands by getting the agreement of the other eleven governors to form an unofficial yet powerful Governors' Conference which met from time to time under his chairmanship to lay down the system's operational guidelines during the formative years from 1914 to 1917. Inevitably it was Strong who was chosen to represent the American banking system in dealings with foreign central bankers, duties which grew to crucial importance during the war and post-war period. Here again the glamorous attraction of striding across the international arena diverted attention from the more humdrum regional financial scene. In Britain's case, as we have seen, Montagu Norman gave a higher priority to preserving the City of London than to curing the depression and unemployment of the North and West. In America the combined and related priority given to the interests of New York and international finance inhibited the powers of the other Reserve District Banks and allowed excessive domestic speculation to continue to grow until the terrible climax of 1929.

The most subtle method by which the regional reserve system became effectively centralized was however by a change in emphasis in monetary policy from reliance on *regionally* determined discount rates to the development under Strong's leadership of open market operations, aided as this was by the enormously increased size of the national debt. There had been general agreement by the framers of the Federal Reserve Act that the desired 'elastic currency' could best be supplied through 're-discounting commercial paper' at rates set by each district according to its perception of the business needs of its particular region. Such discount rates were 'subject to review and approval by the Federal Reserve Board', the exact significance of which was later to become a contentious issue. In addition each Reserve Board had discretionary power as to which bills were 'eligible' for re-discount, with short-term bills for financing 'real' goods being given preferential acceptance and rates, compared with bills financing longer-term or speculative deals. By 1917 at least thirteen different and confusing eligibility categories had been established; but all such complexities were swept away for the duration of the war, during which government paper rather than commercial bills became the fastest-growing and most 'elastic' asset held by the banking system. The primary objective of the Fed therefore changed from meeting the regionally differentiated needs of business to that of meeting the centralized demands of the Treasury. At the same time member banks that needed cash had a ready alternative to borrowing from their Reserve Bank, by selling securities themselves or using government paper rather than commercial paper to back any such borrowing. Thus the formal independence of action jealously assumed by each Federal Reserve Bank in setting its own rates and deciding eligibility became of declining importance when the prices of government securities were increasingly influenced by the operations of the Federal Reserve Bank of New York and when variations in the volume of sales and purchases were being determined by an emerging open market committee dominated by Benjamin Strong. The war thus clearly demonstrated the weakness of the false 'commercial loan' or 'real bills' theory as the key determinant of the money supply; but inevitably it also undermined the regional foundations of the system.

After the war 'control over discount rates' again became 'an important and far-reaching power', according to the Board's Annual Report for 1921; but here again the lead was taken by Benjamin Strong. To give an important example, when the Federal Reserve Bank of New York raised its rate in June 1921 to the then record level of 7 per cent to curb excessive borrowing, it was followed shortly afterwards by all the other Reserve Banks. About a year later the previous independence of District Reserve Banks in purchasing or selling securities was modified when, to prevent the policies of one Reserve Bank being cancelled out by another's actions, Strong in May 1922 set up a committee of five governors to co-ordinate open market operations. According to Professor Chandler, 'Never before 1922 had the Reserve Banks bought or sold government securities for the purpose of regulating credit conditions'. This tentative policy of restraint was flexibly and more forcefully used in the opposite direction a couple of years later: 'The easy money policy of 1924 was of historic importance, [being] the first large and aggressive easing action deliberately taken by the Federal Reserve for the purpose of combating a decline of price levels and business activity and of encouraging international capital flows' (Chandler 1958, 205, 241). This action helped Strong's friend, Montagu Norman, to import enough gold to restore Britain's gold standard in 1925. In such ways Strong, between 1922 and 1928, skilfully and successfully made combined use of the classical twin tools of central banking, discount rate and open market operations, so as to turn the potentially divisive Fed into a prestigious, unified and effective central bank. Yet just a year after his death came the Great Crash of October 1929.

Feet of clay, 1928–1933

Although the 1929 Wall Street crash has had an impact on financial history just second to that of the South Sea Bubble, it far exceeded its earlier rival in scale, bringing to ruin the fortunes of hundreds of thousands of speculators directly, and insofar as it led on to the great slump, indirectly helping to impoverish many millions of innocent workers in the USA and abroad who had never indulged themselves in speculation. Nevertheless the financial crash did not lead to mass defenestration in Wall Street nor even to an increase in the rate of more normal forms of suicide. That tenacious myth has been fully exposed as completely false in the statistics given in Galbraith's elegant and brilliantly entertaining study of *The Great Crash 1929*. In our brief glance at the world's greatest crash, as measured by its economic rather than by its historical weight, attention will be focused mainly on the extent to which American monetary policy may be held responsible first for initiating the boom, secondly for not restraining it when it had obviously got out of hand, and thirdly for turning the financial crisis into a general economic slump of world record proportions.

In contrast to the paeans of praise lavished on the Fed during the years of Strong's leadership, its subsequent sins of permission, omission and commission in the following six years have been widely and cruelly exposed to public scorn by economists on both sides of the Atlantic and of both monetarist and Keynesian persuasion, though with subtle differences of emphasis. The particular fashionable object which fascinates the public into joining the speculative spiral lies mainly in the imagination of the speculator: tulips, exotic products from the south seas, land in Florida, common stock command over consumer durables, home ownership – all these and many other less substantial items have furnished the excuse for exercising the cumulative and contagious gambling instinct inherent in speculation. Without that mad, mass instinct, money remains modestly used, with the velocity of turnover of tulips, houses, etc. similarly remaining unremarkable. In such circumstances monetary policies appear to be either neutral or under control. However when mass hysteria strikes, monetary policy by itself alone appears powerless to control the surging speculation: thus historical explanations of a purely monetarist nature fail to be completely adequate. If the mood of the masses becomes infected with the speculation virus, then sufficient finance, in some form or other, will readily be found to feed a boom on to its inevitable crash. This is not to say that economic, monetary and fiscal policies working together are powerless to moderate the upsurge – far from it – but it does show that monetary causes alone are insufficient to account for such extreme cyclical phenomena, and it also follows that the power of monetary policy alone is insufficient to give rise to, or to undo, the savage effects of speculative financial cycles. These aspects are brought out with crystal clarity not only in the actual development of the causes and consequences of the 1929 crash but also in the significant differences which remain (despite a wide measure of overlapping agreement in certain other respects) between Professor Milton Friedman's deeper, more technical but almost exclusive emphasis on the money supply, and Professor Galbraith's wider economic and psychological view which places much greater emphasis on the gambling instinct shown in the 'get-rich-quick' mentality of the speculators. Modern readers may greatly benefit from combining the results of both streams of research.

That the speculative instinct was eagerly on the look-out for a plausible excuse in the 1920s first became evident in the Florida land boom which intensified from 1925 onwards, until halted by the devastating hurricanes of September 1926 followed by similar storms in 1928. By that time the focus of speculation had moved from subtropical property to common stocks traded on the New York Stock Exchange, aided by the leverage provided by the fashionable craze for investment trusts and the additional credit from the device of buying stock 'on margin'. Thus just as the demand for stock multiplied, so did the effective supply of credit. The New York Federal Reserve Bank cut its rediscount rate from 4 per cent to 3½ per cent in the spring of 1927 partly in order to help Britain maintain its gold standard, a goal more easily achieved if US rates were lower than those in Britain – and causing President Hoover to describe Benjamin Strong as 'a mental annex of Europe'. The Fed also expanded credit by purchasing securities. Nevertheless Galbraith colourfully dismisses conventional claims that by such actions the Fed encouraged the speculation shown in the early stages of the boom as 'formidable nonsense' (1955, 15). Similarly Professor Schumpeter mistakenly 'saw no connection between Reserve policy in 1927 and the stock market boom of 1928–29'. Yet 'it is hard to see why the Reserve System (can be) absolved from fault for making these additional funds available' (Friedman and Schwartz 1963, 291). The balance of argument in blaming the Fed for stimulating the boom in its early stages seems to the writer to be tilted strongly in favour of Friedman's condemnation rather than towards the exoneration shown by Galbraith and Schumpeter.

The increased supply of credit went further to stimulate speculation because brokers needed to put down only a percentage – the 'margin' – of the purchase price of the stock, which stock in turn acted as security for the brokers' borrowings from their banks. Thus banks could borrow from the Fed at around 5 per cent and re-lend it to the call market to finance brokers and other speculators at 12 per cent, making this 'possibly the most profitable arbitrage operation of all time' (Galbraith 1955, 27). In such circumstances discount rate policy – at least at rates then felt to be acceptable – was largely ineffective as a brake on speculation. At the same time the generally booming trends of the 1920s gave rise to budget surpluses, thus reducing the Fed's holdings of government securities. At the end of 1928 when it was becoming obvious that the boom should be restrained the Fed held only $228 million of government stock: clearly insufficient ammunition to reduce bank credit by open market sales to anything like the required degree. Furthermore at that crucial time the death of Benjamin Strong, in October 1928, left the Fed divided, drifting and leaderless. The Board of Governors in Washington no longer deferred to New York, while all twelve District governors assumed the role of the Washington board to be a purely passive one, at most pursuing reactive co-ordination and supervision. The seriousness of the situation did however cause even the board to issue a statement in February 1929 asking the public for restraint in security speculation; but at the same time it dithered and delayed in taking any firm action. A month later when the Federal Reserve Bank of New York proposed to raise the rediscount rate to 6 per cent the move was opposed by the Washington board and by President Hoover, delaying such necessary, if insufficient, action until August 1929. The Fed must thus also share considerable responsibility for the continuation of the speculative mania.

By 3 September 1929 the great bull market had ended, and after a short-lived plateau, the market crashed, typified by Black Thursday, 24 October, when nearly 13 million shares were sold at plunging prices. Having fed the fever, the monetary authorities now proceeded to starve the sick economy, persisting in a contraction of credit which is probably the most severe in American history. The Fed which had been set up to provide an elastic currency strangled its patient. Here Galbraith, Friedman and practically all others who have conducted research into the matter unreservedly blame the Fed for its actions. We have already noted in the previous chapter Friedman's castigation of the Fed's inept policy, while according to Galbraith, 'the Federal Reserve Board in those times was a body of startling incompetence'; and President Hoover, who was in the best contemporary position to know, described them as 'mediocrities' (Galbraith 1955, 33).

Businesses of all kinds went bankrupt, in part (but only in part) because so many banks failed, and because even those banks that did not fail still drastically cut their lending to customers in a downward spiral so that between 1929 and 1933 total bank deposits fell by 42 per cent and net national product by 53 per cent (Friedman and Schwartz 1963, 352). Some 2,000 banks failed in 1931, rising to around 4,000 in the peak year for failures in 1933. Altogether 13,366 incorporated commercial banks failed between 1920 and the end of 1933, including 8,812 in the four years from 1930 to 1933 inclusive. Even in the boom years of the 1920s bank failures had averaged around 600 annually. The banking system, always chronically weak, had, in the 3¼ years following the Great Crash, once again drastically failed the nation and obviously needed urgent and fundamental reform.

Banking reformed and resilient, 1933–1944

Franklin D. Roosevelt's first action on becoming President on Saturday 4 March 1933 was to declare a national Bank Holiday from Monday 6 March. Every bank in the country, including even the Federal Reserve Banks, were thus closed and allowed to reopen only after a special investigating team, hurriedly rushed into action, had declared each bank to be solvent. A number of States had already declared partial Bank Holidays, but this was the first time in American history for such a complete stoppage to occur in the country's main monetary artery, and the natural domino effect of the increasing rate of bank failures was brought at a stroke to its logical conclusion by presidential decree as a necessary prelude to enforced reform of the whole financial system. The world's largest economy was thus virtually bankless for at least ten days. More than $30 billion of bank deposits, in a country more dependent on such deposits than any other, were thus temporarily immobilized, causing a desperate money shortage which the almost simultaneous increase of around $1 billion in notes did little to alleviate. The end of the Bank Holiday was signalized when the Federal Reserve Banks reopened on 13 March, while by the end of the month around half the pre-crisis number of banks had been allowed to start up again. Many areas including many large towns in the industrial regions remained without any banks for several months.

Meanwhile a vigorous legislative programme was being prepared which, together with the harsh lessons of the crisis and the weeding out of most of the weaker half of the banking system, considerably strengthened the remaining structure. Insofar as the effectiveness of such reforms can be gauged by the statistics of bank failures, these show that from an average failure rate of over 2,200 banks annually in the first four years of the 1930s they fell to an annual average of forty-five during the rest of the 1930s. In the years from 1943 to 1960 the number of annual failures never exceeded nine, and in 1945 only one bank failed. It seemed that significant bank failures, of the kind that had inevitably plagued the unit banking system of the USA for 150 years, had been ruled out by the reforms of the 1930s. Such a welcome conclusion, eagerly seized on by contemporary politicians and bankers and even by certain prominent American economists up to the 1970s, was later seen to be a display of premature optimism. Nevertheless the enormous improvement in the bank failure rate does summarize the salutary effect of the legal improvements which the financial crisis forced the country to accept.

The implementation of Roosevelt's policy of reviving industry and agriculture and of reducing the country's appalling total of 13 million unemployed required a restoration of business confidence derived from building a sound basis for the country's banking system. The New Deal required a new banking system. The first relief agency, which had already been set up by President Hoover in January 1932, was the Reconstruction Finance Corporation. Its initial $15 million capital was given by the Treasury and subsequently increased under Roosevelt. Its stated purpose was 'to provide emergency financing for financial institutions and to aid in financing agriculture, commerce and industry'. With such a wide remit and under its energetic chairman, Jesse Jones, the RFC provided supplementary capital to over 7,000 reopened banks, subscribed $10 million of the $11 million capital of the first US Export-Import Bank in 1934 and made loans for infrastructural improvements to almost every State in the 1930s. From 1941 to 1944 it supplied vitally needed investment for military purposes. After the Second World War the private sector financial institutions complained increasingly of unfair competition, and in an era of full employment the RFC was seen as redundant and so was eventually abolished in 1957, by which time it had made investments of over $15 billion. Certainly it played a major role in pump-priming the recovery of the 1930s. To supplement housing finance eleven Federal Home Loan Banks were set up in 1932, supplemented by the Home Owners Loan Corporation of 1933, while, with the ubiquitous assistance of the RFC, such finance was still further increased when the Federal National Mortgage Association ('Fanny Mae') was formed in 1938.

On the agricultural side a number of existing but diverse financial institutions were given greater resources and their efforts more effectively co-ordinated through the Farm Credit Administration set up under the Agricultural Adjustment Act of 1933. That innocuous-sounding Act led, via the Thomas Amendment, to surprisingly far-reaching results in that, first, it authorized the Treasury to expand the note circulation by $3 million; secondly, it authorized the President to devalue the gold content of the dollar; and thirdly, as an echo of the old bimetallist days, it promoted and subsidized official purchases of silver. Although substantial in themselves and also very significant as indicating a Keynesian willingness by the US government to involve itself more directly than ever before in the country's business affairs, these developments were supplementary to the core legislation dealing directly with the banks and the stock exchanges, the two main institutional scapegoats that had acted to provide irresistible encouragement and naked excuses for man's cupidity, elation and depression; cursing 'the system' is modern man's variant of Adam's blaming 'the woman'. The financial panic and slump produced a corresponding legislative panic with over fifty financial bills being introduced advocating all sorts of monetary cure-alls, such as Sylvio Gesell's 'stamped money' (to encourage people to spend their way out of depression) and Major C. F. Douglas's reflationary 'Social Credit' schemes. But the winning formula, in banking as in the New Deal itself, was based on a vague but pervasive acceptance of the essence of Keynesian economics.

A driving force behind some of the more commonsense and effective pieces of legislation was Marriner Eccles, newly appointed Governor of the Federal Reserve Board. He was believed to be strongly influenced by his staff economist, Lauchlin Currie – hence Eccles's proposals were dubbed 'curried Keynes' (Hession and Sardy 1969, 731). The various bills overlapped and borrowed ideas from each other. As we have seen in the case of the Agricultural Adjustment Act, substantial reforms in banking were contained in bills on other subjects as, with greater logic and relevance, was done by the legislation on the stock exchange, namely the Securities Act of 1933 and the Securities Exchange Act of 1934. Together these two Acts increased the penalties for rigging the market, insisted on better licensing of members of the exchanges, demanded that fuller information be given to the public on new issues, and above all set up a new Securities and Exchange Commission with power to examine and approve most new issues. It was armed with strong investigative powers: the SEC was equipped with a fine set of teeth which it has subsequently used to good effect. The 1934 Act also gave the Federal Reserve System responsibility for regulating the amount of credit based on securities. This was the origin of the brake on speculative credit through variations of 'margin' requirements:

Regulation T, limiting credit to brokers; and Regulation U limiting lending by banks for other security purchasers.

The more purely banking legislation comprised the Glass–Steagal Act of 1932, the Banking Act of 1933 and the Banking Act of 1935. The purpose of the Glass–Steagal Act was to enable an easier increase in the money supply, or at any rate to prevent its further harmful reduction following recent substantial exports of gold from the USA. First, it allowed government bonds to supplement gold to some extent as backing for note issues. Secondly it made it much easier for member banks to borrow from their Reserve Banks by widening the range of acceptable collateral. The Banking Act of 1933, in a classical version of belated stable door locking, sought to prevent member banks from extending credit 'for the speculative carrying of or trading in securities, real estate or commodities or any other purposes inconsistent with the maintenance of sound credit conditions'. Investment banking and ordinary commercial banking had to be completely separated, and commercial banks had to sell off their investment affiliates. Because it was believed (with some justification despite Professor Friedman's denial) that the payment of interest on demand deposits led to banks being tempted to take on too risky business to compensate for the high interest costs, the banks were henceforth prohibited from paying interest at all on demand deposits and were limited on the rates of interest which they could pay on time deposits by maxima laid down by the Federal Reserve Board: an authority exercised as Regulation Q. Important changes were made in the administration of the Fed, which because they were taken further in the 1935 Act will be described shortly. In retrospect, by far the most important feature of the 1933 Banking Act was the establishment of the Federal Deposit Insurance Corporation: 'in all American monetary history no legislative action brought such a change' (Galbraith 1955, 197). Through the payment of a small premium by practically all the banks, a substantial sum was available to guarantee the repayment of customers' deposits, technically up to a certain maximum but in practice without limit. Not only Reserve member banks but almost all other banks joined, so that soon after FDIC came into operation in January 1934, 97 per cent of total bank deposits were guaranteed. A condition of membership of FDIC was the submission to inspection by corporation staff, thus significantly improving the coverage and quality of such inspection especially in areas where bank inspection had previously been notoriously weak.

The Banking Act of 1935 confirmed and placed on a more permanent basis most of the reforms relating to banking in the previous legislation. The changes it proposed in the administration of the Federal Reserve

System shifted power further away from New York and the Federal Reserve Districts towards Washington. The former 'governors' of the twelve Districts were demoted simply to 'presidents'. The Federal Reserve Board was renamed the Board of Governors of the Federal Reserve System, and the members of its Open Market Committee were given greater independence by having their period of appointment lengthened to fourteen years. The board was given authority to vary the reserves that member banks were required to hold at their Reserve Banks, with the amounts increasing from country districts, through reserve cities to central reserve cities. Finally the system was encouraged to give the public more information on its decisions and the reasons for reaching such decisions. American monetary policy has thus subsequently been conducted in a white blaze of publicity in a courageous attempt to bring money and the bankers who create it under more democratic control. This transfer of power to Washington coincided with and reflected massive disillusion with monetary policy and thus led to an increasing acceptance of the superiority of fiscal and planning mechanisms. This slide to Keynes is further illustrated both by the adoption of cheap money techniques and by the devaluation of the dollar. Internally and externally, Keynesian ideas of managed money were adopted. To try and prevent such 'monkeying about with money' and to eradicate all forms of the new Keynesian heresies, some forty established economists led by Professor E. W. Kemmerer of Princeton united to form the Economists' National Commission on Monetary Policy. Despite such powerful opposition, Keynesianism triumphed, becoming initially more enthusiastically welcomed in the United States than in Britain. This early influence on policy in the USA was largely the result of the ability of Lauchlin Currie to recruit a number of gifted young Keynesian economists, such as J. K. Galbraith, to work in key government departments and in the Fed in the 1930s and 1940s.

The breakdown of America's internal monetary system in 1933 necessitated a correspondingly urgent readjustment in the external value of the dollar. As soon as the national Bank Holiday was declared controls had to be introduced on the sale and purchase of gold. Eventually in January 1934 the Gold Standard Act of 1900 was replaced by the Gold Reserve Act. This raised the official price of gold from its old level of $20.67 to $35 per fine ounce – a substantial devaluation of 69.33 per cent. In this new gold standard the internal circulation of gold was ended and all private and bank-held gold was transferred to the Treasury. The value of official gold stocks rose by $2.8 billion, of which $2 billion was used to set up a Dollar Stabilization Fund to maintain the new fixed gold price. (Part of the remainder was most aptly used later to help pay the US contribution to the original capital of the IMF and World Bank.) The silver lobby used this occasion to press with success for the Silver Purchase Act of June 1934 whereby the government was forced to purchase silver in sufficient quantities to comprise a quarter of the total metallic money stock. Such vast purchases at first raised the world price of silver to such an extent as to force China off its silver standard and to cause many other countries to demonetize their silver currencies. Thus, perversely, the long-term result of the silver lobby's action was a drastic fall in the demand for silver (outside America) and therefore in its free market price, and a further disruption to international trade. However, such was the lingering power of the silver lobby that the Silver Purchase Act was not repealed until 1963.

Eventually the slow pace of economic recovery rose substantially when Europe again became embroiled in war in September 1939, and rose still more after America's entry in December 1941. Thereafter monetary policy was still further subordinated to government imperatives, with the Fed strongly supporting the seven War Loans and the Victory Loan raised between 1941 and 1946. The national debt, which was only $16 billion in 1930, rose to a peak of $269 billion in 1946. Interest rates were kept low by the readiness of the Fed to purchase government paper. The rate for Treasury bills of ninety-day maturity was fixed at ⅜ of 1 per cent; medium-term paper rates earned between ⅞ and 1 per cent while even bonds of between five and twenty-seven years earned only up to 2½ per cent. Government debt had become interest-bearing money, forming a huge reservoir of liquidity which made normal techniques of monetary control useless. New direct controls on credit were used instead, one of the most effective of which was Regulation W, which laid down minimum deposits and maximum maturities for consumer durable goods, thus quickly freeing resources for defence purposes. By such means the war was successfully financed at cheap rates, while the physical controls and rationing, though nothing like as severe as in Britain, suppressed most of the inflation until after the war ended. Already by mid-1944 the proven success of the new forms of economic planning inspired the nations' leaders to prepare for the huge task of post-war reconstruction.

Bretton Woods: vision and realization, 1944–1991

Whereas the economies of most European countries had been devastated by the war, the powerful US economy had gained in strength, with its gross national product showing a remarkable rise from $209 billion in 1939 to $234 billion in 1947 and to more than $500 billion in 1960. The post-war growth rate at 3½ per cent per annum in real terms 'exceeded by a considerable degree the rate from the beginning of the century to World War II' (Economic Report of the President, January 1961, 48). America was able to make 'the swiftest and most gigantic change-over that any nation has ever made from war to peace', according to the Economic Report of the President, January 1947. By the end of that year the output of civilian goods had already risen above all previous records, a trend of progress which continued, so that by 1965 the actual volume of consumer goods was double that of 1947. In contrast the European picture at the war's end looked grim in the extreme. Out of such devastation, the rebuilding of Europe's economies was a triumph of the human spirit – assisted by Keynesian economics and American wealth skilfully combined and generously distributed. America's buoyant economy supplied vital resources which through the Anglo-American Loan and the generous gift of Marshall Aid gradually helped Europe in the 1950s and 1960s to share with America a long period of unprecedented growth with full employment. This happy outcome exceeded the most optimistic expectations of most of the 730 delegates from forty-four countries who had met at Bretton Woods, New Hampshire, to plan the framework for the post-war system of international trade, payments and investment. Out of their deliberations, with their minds wonderfully concentrated by the war, emerged the most comprehensive and successful group of financial institutions of global scope in world history: the International Monetary Fund and the International Bank for Reconstruction and Development. It will be convenient at this stage to examine briefly the origins and subsequent achievements of these two organizations and to assess their contribution to the smoother working of international payments and to the improved flow of world savings and investment. Plans for a complementary third institution, the International Trade Organization, failed to be ratified by the US Congress, but did at least prepare the way for the General Agreement on Tariffs and Trade, the initial meeting of which was held at Geneva in 1947, and with which the Bretton Woods organizations have liaised closely ever since.

The twin financial institutions were very much, and very naturally, given the military situation, an Anglo-American concept, personally dominated by Keynes and by Harry Dexter White, chief economist at the US Treasury and a lifelong admirer of Keynes. They worked unsparingly to achieve a remarkably successful degree of compromise, despite the strong opposition of ultra-conservatives in the US Congress who were aghast at what they saw as the overliberal, spendthrift and 'socialistic' Keynesian ideas. They both died before seeing the full fruits of their efforts, Keynes in April 1946, and White in August 1948 shortly after he had been arraigned by America's modern version of the Spanish Inquisition, the Committee on Un-American Activities. White scaled down Keynes's ambitious plans for an International Clearing Union with access to at least $26 billion, to what he felt he might be able to get a critical Congress to accept, which was less than a third of Keynes's desired minimum. The twin organizations began operating in May 1947, facing a sea of troubles. By 1951 the fifty members of the Fund had made contributions (apart from a few arrears) of $8.16 billion, payable 25 per cent in gold or dollars and the rest in their own currencies. Exactly one half came from the combined contributions of the USA (34 per cent) and Britain (16 per cent). Third came China (7 per cent), then France (6 per cent) and India (5 per cent). The quotas were based initially on crude assessments of ability to pay, but later incorporated increasingly sophisticated estimates of relative gross national products, with general revisions naturally having to be made, kicking up much dust, every five to six years. Nine general revisions were agreed by 1991.

So clamorous was the initial demand by a hungry world for American goods and services that the Fund's resources were soon seen, as Keynes had predicted, to be woefully inadequate. Consequently demands on the dollars in the Fund had to be strictly rationed according to its 'scarce currency' provisions, so long as the huge 'dollar gap' persisted. This was not, as some prominent pessimists feared, for ever, but only until the 1950s.

Within its politically constrained limits the Fund has achieved some considerable degree of success in pursuing the six objectives laid down in its Articles of Agreement. These were: (a) to promote international monetary co-operation; (b) to facilitate the expansion and balanced growth of international trade . . . promote high levels of employment and real income (at least above what they would otherwise have been); (c) to promote exchange stability and to avoid competitive exchange depreciation (which had wrought such havoc in the 1930s); (d) to assist in the establishment of a multilateral system of payments; (e) to give confidence to members by making the general resources of the Fund available to correct maladjustments in balances of payments; (f) to shorten the duration and lessen the degree of such disequilibrium. For twenty-five years, prosperous beyond pre-war dreams, the IMF helped to hold most of the world's trading nations linked to the US dollar (and hence to gold) at fixed parities that were adjusted from time to time when 'fundamental disequilibria' brought about enforced changes to newly fixed parities, such changes being assisted by the facilities offered by the IMF. The ending of dollar convertibility into gold at the $35 price in 1971 was not the body blow to the IMF that many feared and quite a few hoped. The Fund took to the post-1973 world of floating rates like a duck to water, quickly adapting to the demands of the new regime.

Above all the Fund has not simply sat back patiently awaiting requests for help, but on the contrary has adopted an active, investigatory role vigorously carrying out its mandate, under clause 4 of its articles, to 'exercise firm surveillance over the exchange rate policies of its members'. It has interpreted its mandate widely. Surveillance amounts in reality to detailed inspection through staff consultations with the monetary authorities of its member countries. In the peak year for such investigations, 1985, the IMF carried out as many as 131 official consultations. To its many detractors, including once eager borrowers later burdened with guilt and repayments, the IMF and its full-time staff (1,691 in 1989) are seen as interfering, do-gooding busybodies, yet the skilled, outsider's viewpoint carries an objective value of which Keynes, and Robert Burns doubtless, would have approved:

> O wad some Pow'r the giftie gie us
> To see oursels as others see us!
> It wad frae mony a blunder free us,
> And foolish notion.

Where monetary policies are concerned, the most foolish and costly of notions abound, making the IMF's external and politically neutral advice, as Britain and others discovered in the hyper-inflationary mid 1970s, cheap at the price. Undeterred by its critics, the Fund in September 1989,

> reaffirmed the central role of surveillance in fostering more consistent and disciplined economic policies; noted the contribution of the Fund to the process of policy coordination through its work on key economic indicators and the development of medium-term scenarios . . . and encouraged the Executive Board to continue improving the analytical and empirical framework underlying multilateral surveillance, including the measurement and consequences of international capital flows. (IMF Summary Proceedings 1989, 241–2)

Given his action in resigning from the Versailles Peace Conference in 1919 as a protest against excessive reparations against Germany, Keynes would also have warmly approved the magnanimity with which the USA's Marshall Plan and the resources of the Bretton Woods organizations were made available to Germany and Japan, even though Britain's 'reward for losing a quarter of our national wealth in the common cause' was, according to *The Economist*, 'to pay tribute for half a century to those who have been enriched by the war' (quoted by Brian Johnson in his stimulating study of *The Politics of Money* 1970, 131). The assistance to Germany and Japan came at a most critical time, changing despair into hope and helping to inspire them towards their economic miracles. As the leader of the Japanese delegation to the 44th Annual Meeting of the Fund and Bank has stated:

> At the time it joined the Fund and Bank in 1952 Japan [like Germany] was running chronic trade deficits. The very next year, 1953, and again in 1957, Japan borrowed a total of about $250 million from the Fund to tide it over hard currency shortfalls. Between 1953 and 1966 Japan came to the Bank to borrow $850 million for modern highways, the bullet train and other basic industrial projects. At one point we were the second largest borrowing country from the Bank.

By July 1990 these loans were all fully repaid (Ryutaro Hashimoto, Summary Proceedings, 44th Annual Meeting IMF, September 1989, 29). For most of their history, however, it is in connection with their activities in the so-called Third World that the merits and demerits of the Bretton Woods organizations have mostly been judged, aspects to which we return in chapter 11. All along, whether helping economically advanced or backward countries, it has been the USA that has been the major contributor; and it was largely in connection with its balance of payments problems that a push was given to the adoption of another Keynesian concept, namely that the Fund itself could manufacture gold – or at least 'paper gold' through inventing its 'Special Drawing Rights'.

Keynes had repeatedly proposed from 1943 to 1946 that his 'International Clearing Union' should be authorized to create an international reserve currency, to be called 'Bancor', to tide over countries with balance of payments deficits, and with which countries with surpluses could be credited rather than with gold, thus imposing an added discipline on surplus countries absent in the old gold standard and in the new IMF. Harry White also proposed a similar but much paler version based on a currency he called 'Unitas'. Such notions were however quite unacceptable so long as the USA enjoyed massive balance of payments surpluses, so that it was not until the Dollar Gap had been replaced by a Dollar Glut in the 1960s that the American authorities felt able to support the IMF's belated acceptance of a variant of Keynes's paper gold concept. The phenomenal growth of world trade in the 1960s and 1970s necessitated a much larger pool of international liquidity than could be built on a fixed amount of gold or the volatile supply of dollars. The IMF did periodically manage to increase its members' quotas, which more than doubled between 1959 and 1975, but this was inevitably a lagged response after long and tortuous negotiations. The Fund also received substantial injections of the currencies most in demand, those of the ten major industrial nations, in the form of General Agreements to Borrow, the first of which, amounting to $6 billion, was arranged in 1962. (The ten were Belgium, Canada, France, West Germany, Italy, Japan, the Netherlands, Sweden, UK and, most importantly, the USA.) Other supplements to the Fund's resources include: 'Buffer Stock' and 'Compensatory and Contingency Financing', primarily to assist LDCs to control the stocks and maintain the flows of essential exports and imports; 'Extended Funds Facilities' exist to provide medium-term finance of as long as four years to help members make 'structural adjustments' to their economies; and 'Enhanced Burden Sharing' enables poor members to catch up on their arrears so as not to debar them from the Fund's facilities. The Fund has thus been diligent in developing modern banking skills to find ingenious ways of fulfilling its remit.

All these devices, however admirable, simply redistribute existing reserves more efficiently, but the agreement in 1969 to accept SDRs represented a most significant innovation in world monetary history, for the IMF had, out of nothing, created international reserves which member countries have a right to draw upon in addition to their normal, regular drawing rights, usually when the latter have been used up to their quota limits. All countries had by then learned to dispense with internal gold circulation and to do without gold backing (in almost all cases) for domestic currency. They were now at least beginning to act in the same way with regard to international currency, helping to create and accept collectively what they could not and would not individually, namely abstract or 'fiat' reserves, and to be less dependent on the constraints of an almost fixed supply of gold or on the vagaries of the changing favourites among a small group of national currencies. All the same, as an essential insurance policy the IMF still holds very substantial reserves of gold. These amounted to 3,217,341 kilograms at 30 April 1989, valued at SDR 279.6 billion. Total currency reserves came to SDR 561.8 billion, and this included Fund-created SDRs which amounted to only 21.5 billion, that is less than 4 per cent of total reserves (IMF Annual Report for 1989). The statistics therefore show that as yet international fiat reserve money, although accepted in principle for over twenty years, has been used rather modestly. There is a long, long way to go before the SDR reaches anything like its true potential.

If the fixed-rate–adjustable-peg system established in 1944 could have been maintained indefinitely (i.e. fluctuations limited to 2 per cent bands with parity revisions permissible under specific conditions) then faith in the SDR might well have grown sufficiently to fulfil the Keynesian vision. There are, however, a number of compelling reasons to excuse the relatively poor progress of the SDR. First, bankers, and especially the central bankers whose duty it is to partake in the IMF's activities and to advise their governments, show a marked preference for the practical, tried and tested forms of international currency, and an aversion to theoretical abstractions of academic parentage, which have been on the world stage for only the briefest of periods compared to the many centuries during which gold and some of the national reserve currencies have been in daily use. Secondly, whereas for two decades after 1945 there was a widespread acceptance of the good intentions of planners and bureaucrats and a willingness to give these experts the benefit of the doubt, this amiable but soft characteristic was later replaced by strong, hard scepticism. Neither Whitehall nor Washington (where the IMF was sumptuously installed) really knew best. Most governments could not be trusted to manage money and were too ready to increase liquidity, whether at home or abroad. Thirdly, differences in rates of growth and even more so in inflation caused economies to diverge so widely that previously fixed rates of exchange could no longer be held. The pound was forced to devalue in 1967, while by 1968 the USA was running a deficit in its balance of trade, the first such since 1893. Exchange controls were rapidly strengthened in a number of countries but still speculation continued against the dollar (despite assistance from Germany and Japan), to such an extent that on 15 August 1971 the USA could no longer promise to sell gold to the other central banks at the fixed price of $35. The apparent basis of Bretton Woods had thus been swept away when the anchor of the system had slipped – and the 'adjustable peg' was about to be replaced by a botched repair job, known by its optimistic admirers as the 'crawling peg'.

President Nixon convened an emergency meeting of the ten major trading nations in December 1971 at the Smithsonian Institute in Washington. The result was hailed by Nixon as 'the most significant monetary agreement in the history of the world' – a premature and in retrospect a preposterous statement; and barely plausible at the time, even given the crisis in the world's payments system. A general realignment of currencies was arranged, with the IMF permitting a wider, 4½ per cent band and with the official price of the dollar being raised from $35 to $38, representing a devaluation of around 10 per cent. The new structure began to collapse almost immediately. The

pound was floated in June 1972 amid continuing speculation against
deficit countries, including the USA. In February 1973 the dollar was
again devalued by about 11 per cent, raising the official gold price to
$42.22. By the middle of the year most countries were in fact ignoring
their band limits and were floating. All the pressures of speculation
were now diverted on to the dollar, so that by November 1973 the USA
had also abandoned trying to hold on to a fixed price for gold even in
its official dealings with other central banks.

The IMF, which had been sidelined by these momentous events, had
now to adjust to a world of 'clean' and 'dirty' floating – which it has
done with commendable ease, adroitly changing its philosophy towards
emphasizing market solutions, including privatization of nationalized
industries, wherever possible in LDCs, well before such attitudes
became popular in eastern Europe. In 1991 it succeeded in getting an
increase in quotas of record size, its ninth general review raising the
total by 50 per cent from SDR 99.1 billion to SDR 136.7 billion. Unlike
the Ecu, the SDR is limited to official usage connected directly or
indirectly to balance of payments purposes, and so remains remote
from all retail and normal business usage. No one is ever likely to be
found with an SDR in his pocket. Yet its valuation and rates of interest
are set by market forces, within an official framework. The unit value of
the SDR is determined daily by summing the market value in dollars of
a basket of the currencies of the five countries with the largest exports,
with the base being revised every five years. The percentage weights
based on January 1991 (with the previous base in brackets) were: US
dollar 40 per cent (42); Deutsche Mark 21 per cent (19); yen 17 per cent
(15); pound sterling 11 per cent (12); the French franc also 11 per cent
(12). Thus, to give an example in order to pin the slippery SDR down to
earth, its value on 22 March 1991 was equivalent to $1.37 or DM 2.25
or Y187.16 or £0.76 or Fr.7.66. Similarly the rate of interest on SDRs is
calculated weekly from the weighted average of short-term rates on the
money markets of the same five countries, being for instance 7.86 per
cent on 1 April 1991. Thus SDR rates are less volatile and considerably
lower than hard-pressed borrowers would otherwise be likely to face – a
generally unsung method by which the IMF helps its members.

Despite the medium-term volatility of the dollar, the long-term
dominance of the USA in world trade is obvious from the above figures,
fully justifying the original decision to locate the headquarters of the
Bretton Woods organizations in that country. It may be anomalous that
such financial institutions were placed in the political capital,
Washington, whereas that of the corresponding international political
institution, the United Nations, was placed in the financial capital,

New York. This possibly reflects entrenched American attitudes towards the checks and balances of the Constitution, extended thereby to the international sphere. More direct external American financial involvement is seen in the belated but substantial presence of American banks abroad.

American banks abroad

Although by 1913 the United States had already become the world's largest economy its banks remained inward-looking, leaving the finance of its growing external trade to foreign, mainly British, banks. The insignificant role played by American financial institutions overseas is emphasized by the stark fact that with over 23,000 banks in 1913 only half a dozen banking trusts operated a derisory total of twenty-six branches abroad. This quasi-colonial dependence grew to be a matter of considerable concern in the first decade of the twentieth century, but could be altered only by fundamental changes in the legal basis of banking. As we have seen, strictly speaking, *national* banks were not allowed branches, whether at home or abroad – an opinion specifically confirmed by the Attorney-General in 1911 – while most *State* banks were far too small to contemplate such a step. Yet foreign trade had increased tenfold since the Civil War, and by 1913 the USA had changed from being a net debtor to becoming a substantial net creditor, a position about to be increased yet further during the First World War. The National Monetary Commission of 1911 complained that 'the impediments in the way of the development of our international trade are numerous. Perhaps none of these is more important than the absence of American banking facilities in other countries. We have no American banking institutions in foreign countries. The organisation of such banks is necessary for the development of our trade' (para. 15). The committee also felt that although 'the status of the US as one of the great powers in the political world is now universally recognised, we have yet to secure recognition as an important factor in the financial world'. Commensurate recognition did not arrive until fifty or so years later, but a start was made in dismantling the impediments to the branching of American banks abroad in the Federal Reserve Act of 1913. For 'whereas British banks pushed out all over the world without any encouragement from Parliament, the growth of similar venturing by U.S. concerns had been directly due to legal enactments' (Thorne 1962, 145). Unlike British lawyers, their more numerous American counterparts had, like President Jackson, never forgotten the perilous permissiveness of the South Sea Bubble, and so have been ever ready to shackle their bankers or at least have attempted to confine their activities within strictly defined legal boundaries.

By section 25 of the original Federal Reserve Act member banks with a capital of not less than $1 million could, with the approval of the Federal Reserve Board, set up branches abroad. An amendment passed in September 1916 allowed small banks to club together to establish joint foreign banking corporations, which came to be known as Agreement Corporations. Following pressure by Senator Walter Edge of New Jersey, section 25(a) was added in December 1919 which authorized the Federal Reserve Board to charter corporations with a minimum capital of $2 million 'for the purpose of engaging in international or foreign banking'. The activities of these 'Edge Act Corporations' have since been governed by the board's Regulation K. Provided that they confined themselves to assisting foreign trade, Edge Act Corporations could be set up anywhere, including other States within the USA. Thus banks in the Midwest could open up offices in New York, San Francisco or Miami, greatly facilitating their overseas operations. This marked a breach in the unit banking system and was the first piece of legislation specifically allowing (admittedly limited) interstate branching, a privilege that has continued despite the subsequent passing of the McFadden Act of 1927 which reinforced the traditional prohibition against interstate branching. The Federal Reserve Act also allowed US banks to participate in the 'ownership and control of local institutions in foreign countries', a provision which formed a prudent alternative to setting up branches of American banks 'in localities where economic nationalism or demonstrations against dollar imperialism runs high' (Nzeribe 1966, 12). With the legal impediments thus having been removed between 1913 and 1919, American banks began to expand rapidly abroad, with total branches rising from twenty-six in 1913 to 181 in 1920. This flattering rise, artificially stimulated by the First World War, was reversed in the next few years when half these branches closed, leaving only ninety-one branches abroad in 1924. Gradually the numbers grew again to reach another inter-war peak of 132 in 1933, just before the great bank closures of that year. By 1945 there were still, almost incredibly, only ten US banks operating abroad with a total of just seventy-eight branches. By 1960 mergers had reduced the number of US banks operating abroad to only eight, although the number of their offices abroad had grown to 131, and their total assets to around $4 billion. American dominance in the world economy was still far from being reflected in the rather insignificant part played by American banks abroad.

Attention was drawn in the previous chapter to the Radcliffe Report's short-sighted dismissal of the presence of American banks in Britain as being relatively unimportant in the domestic financial scene in 1959, while in 1961 the Report of the US Commission on Money and Credit completely ignored the subject. During the 1960s the tempo began to change, aided by the liberalization in 1963 of Regulation M by which the Fed governs member banks' foreign operations. By 1965 some thirteen banks operated around 200 branches abroad, and thereafter growth continued almost uninterruptedly until the stock market crash of October 1987.

The total of foreign branches, operated by twenty-nine banks, reached 500 by 1970, 600 branches of thirty-seven banks by 1972, and by 1980 some 200 US banks had opened around 800 branches abroad with representation in all the significant financial centres of the non-communist world. The three largest banks alone had 343 such branches: Citicorp 150, Bank-America 110 and Chase 83. Total assets held in all foreign branches had multiplied by over one hundred times in the twenty years after 1960 to reach over $400 billion. Apart from the rise in offshore banking in the Bahamas and Cayman Islands, most of the reasons for this exodus have already been examined (in the previous chapter). By and large this movement simply represented and reflected American direct investment abroad, a rising tide which alerted the French author Servan-Schreiber to depict it in frighteningly dramatic terms in his most influential work, *The American Challenge*. Looking forward fifteen years from 1968 he feared that 'the world's third greatest industrial power, just after the United States and Russia, will not be Europe, but *American industry in Europe*' (1968, 3). Yet he barely mentions the key role played by the banks in this transatlantic transfer, and also failed to notice the early signs of the reverse flow of European (and Japanese) capital into the USA. This reverse flow later raised blood pressures in the USA. 'The rapid growth of foreign direct investment in the United States during the 1980s has stirred public debate over the desirability of the continued accumulation of US assets by foreigners . . . but no evidence suggests that present or foreseeable levels of foreign ownership of US industry should be troublesome' (*Federal Reserve Bulletin*, May 1990, 277): a confident declaration of the Fed's faith in free trade.

A significant change in geographic distribution accompanied the growing export of American banks in the twenty years from the mid-1960s. Although London remained the principal magnet, high taxation in the UK in the early 1970s and its previous record of sluggish economic growth compared with that of its European neighbours were in large part responsible for diverting much of the growing flood of funds, first to continental Europe and later, much more substantially, to tax havens such as the Bahamas and Cayman Islands. US branches in continental Europe rose from twenty-one in 1965 to seventy-one in 1970. Total deposits in all foreign branches of US banks rose from $30 billion in 1969 to $109 billion in 1973, but in that period the proportion held in the UK fell from over two-thirds (67.3 per cent) to just over a half (50.9 per cent). That held in the rest of Europe grew marginally from 18 per cent to 20 per cent (though substantially in absolute amounts). The really important change was the share held in the Bahamas and Caymans, which trebled in those same four years, rising from 7 to 21 per cent, and continued to grow strongly thereafter as the advantages of these tax havens became more profitably obvious. By 1981 the assets held in the branches of US banks abroad had grown to $460 billion, and while the UK had still managed to attract the largest share, with $160 billion, that of the Bahamas and Caymans had almost grown equal, at $150 billion. Their share on average slightly exceeded that in the UK during the three years from 1986 to 1988. This apparent equality is however grossly misleading, for whereas the Bahamas and Caymans were largely just tax havens, often with little more than 'name-plate' or 'shell' branches, London remained the world's greatest Eurodollar and foreign exchange market providing superlative, if costly, facilities for every type of banking activity. The assets of American banks' foreign branches practically reached a plateau in the 1980s, rising by the comparatively moderate amount of $90 billion in the nine years after 1981 to reach a total of $549 billion in January 1990 with the shares of the UK and of the Bahamas and Caymans groups both claiming around 30 per cent or so of the total, each with $167 billion.

When foreign banks play only a minor role in their host country they benefit from escaping in general the restrictive regulations imposed on indigenous banks, but as they grow in importance so they are forced to conform more or less equally to the rules governing domestic banks. Thus by the International Banking Act of 1978 most of the Federal Reserve and other regulations, such as the keeping of minimum reserves and the limitations on branching, were made applicable to foreign banks' branches – an unmistakable signal of their growing strength. Around the same time the American authorities became concerned about the diversion of funds into the tax havens of the West Indies, with the result that from 1981 'International Banking Facilities' could be established within the US granting similar fiscal and regulatory privileges to those available in the offshore centres of the Bahamas and Caymans. Within a year such IBFs had attracted over $100 billion that would probably otherwise have gone to swell the offshore total. Nevertheless, as in the case of flags of convenience in shipping, tax havens in banking, despite concerted international attempts to widen the application of the Basle rules on capital adequacy, pose dangers to depositors and borrowers arising from the temptations of lax administration. Despite the disappointments and the much publicized heavy losses suffered by some overseas banks in the USA (such as Midland Bank's disastrous experience with Crocker National), assets held by foreign banks within the USA continued to grow in the difficult years of the 1980s, rising from $80 billion in 1984, equivalent to 17 per cent of assets in American banks abroad, to $209 billion in 1990, when they were equivalent to 38 per cent of the total amount held in American banks' foreign branches. A fairer comparison of the relative position of US banks abroad with foreign banks within the US is obtained if the amount held by US banks in the Caribbean tax havens is excluded. Then the assets of foreign banks in the USA in 1990 came to around 55 per cent of the total held by US banks worldwide (excluding the Bahamas and Caymans). Obviously neither the existence of over 13,000 US banks nor the legal minefields had by the 1990s managed to prevent a sizeable penetration of foreign banks into the USA to compensate to a considerable extent for the weight of American banks abroad.

The invasion of foreign banks into previously neglected or protected domestic markets not only reflects the growing integration of the global financial markets but also provides a most powerful illustration of the theory of 'contestable markets' in current practical operation. As US financial institutions expand abroad the demand for reciprocity by foreign bankers will not only increasingly break down the barriers separating countries, and financial sectors within and between countries, but also will in time erode those anachronistic rules which have largely prevented interstate banking within the USA. Ease of entry also helps fundamentally in inhibiting the operation of monopoly power by the large multinational banks. This applies especially to US banks 'because of their central importance in the world banking system, and because they provide a model for the strategic development of banks in other countries' (Coulbeck 1984, xv). Contrary to conventional opinion – particularly in US legal circles – the advantages of scale and scope which favour the giant banks are not incompatible with competitive markets, provided that ease of entry, encouraged as it is by the lever of reciprocity, leads, as it should, to keeping financial markets open and 'contestable', and provided also that these generally overlooked and underestimated free-market controls over monopoly are not thwarted by the well-meaning but often perverse 'anti-monopoly' restrictions beloved by American administrators and their lawyers (Davies and Davies 1984). The belated but massive movement of American banks abroad is thus helping to bring about long-needed, substantial changes within America's domestic financial scene – to which picture we now return.

From accord to deregulation, 1951–1980

The rate of inflation is inescapably one of the main criteria by which the effectiveness of central bank policy should be judged. Whether it should be not simply 'one of the main' but 'the main' or even 'the only' criterion is a subject still being hotly debated by bankers, economists and politicians worldwide in the 1990s. America's inflationary record in the 43-year period from 1950 to 1992, as measured by the annual average change in consumer prices, is given in table 9.3, with figure 9.1 smoothing the annual rates decade by decade. Although American attempts to achieve price stability fall far short of those of countries like West Germany or Switzerland, yet, as a glance at the similar tables given in the previous chapter readily prove, the American record is far better than that of Britain. Like most countries, the USA has experienced almost unbroken and significant degrees of inflation for over half a century with only one year, 1953, showing a fall in prices, and then of only 0.4 per cent. But double-figure inflation has at least been avoided, except, barely, in 1974, with 10.0 per cent, and again, almost, in 1980, with 9.9 per cent; although during the spring quarter of that year the rate frighteningly reached 14.6 per cent. During the post-Second World War period as a whole American inflation was on average not much more than half the rate suffered in Britain. However, what is remarkable is that in both countries the pattern has been surprisingly similar. Since the overt acceptance of monetarist policies inflation has been far worse than when Keynesian policies prevailed. Thus figure 9.1 shows that the average annual rate in the twenty 'Keynesian' years after 1950 was around 2.4 per cent, whereas that of the twenty 'monetarist' years after 1970 was, at 6.3 per cent, well over double the previous rate.

Even if, as extreme monetarists claim, inflation is purely a monetary affair, yet the Fed cannot alone be held responsible either for the moderate degree of inflation experienced from the 1940s to the end of the 1960s nor for the higher inflation of the 1970s and 1980s. In common with the Bank of England and a number of other central banks the Fed found that one of its most important traditional

Table 9.3 Consumer price inflation in the USA, 1950–1990.

Year	Annual average change in price %	Year	Annual average change in price %	Year	Annual average change in price %
1950	4.7	1964	1.5	1978	8.0
1951	2.9	1965	3.0	1979	8.9
1952	2.8	1966	4.1	1980	9.9
1953	−0.4	1967	2.5	1981	8.7
1954	2.7	1968	5.8	1982	5.2
1955	3.4	1969	5.5	1983	3.6
1956	4.0	1970	5.2	1984	3.6
1957	2.8	1971	6.1	1985	3.3
1958	2.0	1972	4.4	1986	1.9
1959	2.3	1973	8.2	1987	4.1
1960	1.3	1974	10.0	1988	4.8
1961	1.3	1975	8.3	1989	5.2
1962	2.5	1976	5.7	1990	5.4
1963	1.2	1977	6.8	1991	3.1
				1992	2.9

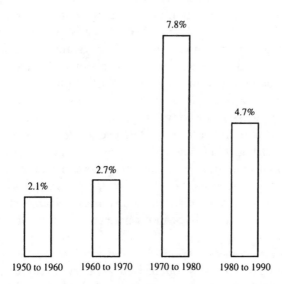

Figure 9.1 Consumer price inflation in USA in decades 1950–1990.*

*Average annual rates
Sources: Federal Reserve Bank of Richmond Review 8, 1 (Spring 1991);
Federal Reserve Bank Bulletin (March 1993).

weapons, the discount rate, was virtually useless for seventeen years before 1951, while ever since 1946 it has been mandated to achieve a number of often incompatible objectives, including especially support for maintaining full or at least maximum possible levels of employment and output. In the period from 1934 to 1941 a frightened world poured its gold into the United States to such an extent that the country's gold stocks rose by a massive $14.9 billion. The banking system therefore enjoyed excess reserves and so had no need to borrow from the Reserve Banks, which in any case laid emphasis on low interest rates to counteract high unemployment. As in the UK, when cheap money ruled, bank rate and discount rate became otiose.

Cheap money was needed to finance the war, from 1941 to 1945, at low cost and so banks were supplied with sufficient reserves to enable them and their customers to purchase government debt, which grew from $58 billion in 1941 (equivalent to 47 per cent of GNP) to $259 billion in 1946 (125 per cent of GNP). To support the Treasury's sales of debt the Fed was required to purchase bonds in the open market. The result of this was to monetize the national debt and, while this policy was fully justified in war, it was conveniently (for the Treasury) continued into the post-war period. This provoked increasing reluctance on the part of the Fed, which was thereby prevented from using discount rate as a weapon of monetary constraint even at a time of inflation. Eventually in March 1951 a famous 'Accord' was reached with the Treasury by which the Fed gave up its automatic support for bonds and confined its open market operations to 'bills only'. This strict policy was modified in February 1961 to 'bills preferably', which allowed the Fed to give the Treasury support on special occasions, such as when large new issues or conversions were being made. The 'Accord' and its amendment indicate the often overlooked burden of a large national debt with its tendency to erode central bank independence and explain the impatiently felt desire and overriding need for the Fed to be free of Treasury restraints in order to carry out monetary policy effectively. From March 1951, after seventeen years on the shelf, discount rate was brought back into operation – but with a significant difference.

When the system was set up in 1913 and for two decades afterwards, discount rate was consciously perceived as a regionally differentiated rate, 'established' separately by each Federal Reserve District Bank according to the economic needs of its own region, although 'subject to review and determination' by the Federal Reserve Board. The wars (Second and Korean) simply accelerated natural market moves towards a nationally determined set of interest rates. As the Commission on

Money and Credit later acknowledged with regard to the powers of the District Banks to set their own interest rates, 'In practice this appearance of a measure of regional autonomy has largely yielded to the national nature of the money market' (CMC Report 1961, 84).

The inflationary overhang of the national debt was not entirely removed by the 'Accord'. The shorter the average age to maturity of the national debt, the greater is its potential liquidity and therefore its potential inflationary pressure. The average maturity of the US national debt fell very substantially from 8.2 years in 1950 to 3.5 years in 1970. This was partly because an unrepealed law passed by Congress in the last year of the First World War to hold down the cost of financing that war laid down a maximum rate of 4½ per cent for bonds in excess of five years – a restraint which was not removed until 1971. Thus fiscal policy had in some form or other inhibited vigorous Federal Reserve action throughout the 'Keynesian' period of relatively low inflation. Probably the most overt and powerful evidence of Keynesian philosophy was in the enactment of the Employment Act of 1946 and in its subsequent amendment in 1978, by which latter date Keynesian concern for full employment was to be joined with Friedmanite measures of the monetary aggregates: two incompatible bed-mates. According to section 2A of the Federal Reserve Act as amended by the Humphrey–Hawkins or Full Employment and Balanced Growth Act of 1978, 'The Board of Governors of the Federal Reserve System and the Federal Open Market Committee shall maintain long-run growth of the monetary and credit aggregates commensurate with the economy's long-run potential to increase production, so as to promote effectively the goals of maximum employment, stable prices, and moderate long-term interest rates.' To achieve full employment, high capacity production, and moderate interest rates through ambitiously hitting long-range, moving monetary targets – all this appears to be another triumph of monetarist hope over practical experience. Furthermore, by setting national levels of employment and production as objectives, the Act yet again increased the central, as opposed to the regional, determination of monetary policy, even if the Federal Reserve District Boards still participate in policy discussions. They talk, but they have little power to act.

Hardly had the ink dried on the Humphrey–Hawkins Act before faith in monetary targeting began to evaporate. M1, the original favourite, became increasingly unreliable despite technical tricks such as being divided into M1A and M1B (to take cognizance of 'NOW' accounts) and then later recombined into a new M1. In 1982 the Fed de-emphasized its former favourite and eventually in 1986 completely gave up setting a target for M1, though continuing to do so for the hitherto less volatile M2 and M3. Hope springs eternal in the monetarist breast. Thus Robert L. Hetzel still argued strongly that if the Fed really stuck to 'an operationally significant target for M2 in the form of a trend line that rises at three per cent per year' then this 'will eliminate inflation' (*Federal Reserve Bank of Richmond Economic Review*, September–October 1989). The Act also set long-term goals for unemployment – of 4 per cent by 1983: it turned out to be nearly 11 per cent. The set target for inflation was 3 per cent by 1983 (almost achieved) and zero by 1988, the latter being yet another example as it happened of wishful thinking. It was, however, with regard to the objective of 'moderate' rates of interest that expectations went most grossly awry. Record rates of interest were being charged and offered involving an increasing variety of monetary instruments and a wider range of institutions in 1979 and 1980 especially. Commercial banks' prime lending rate, which had been as moderately low as 6¼ per cent in May 1977, rose to 11.5 per cent by December 1978 and then shot up through 15 per cent in October 1979 to a record of 21.5 per cent in December 1980.

Such unprecedentedly high rates stimulated an ever wider and ever faster spread of financial innovation, for those institutions that would not or could not join in the new competitive games (because of archaic usury laws, maximum rate ceilings, conservatism or inertia) lost deposits, profits and market shares. Member banks became increasingly irritated by the existing restrictions and so many left the system that the Fed's scope of monetary control, such as it was, grew ever narrower. Eventually the fundamental legal structure of the American banking system was forced to adopt its first major change from the framework laid down in the crisis years of 1933 and 1935. This overdue, market-driven reform, entitled the 'Depository Institutions Deregulation and Monetary Control Act' (DIDMCA), was passed on 31 March 1980 with its provisions phased into the following six to seven years.

The main features of that watershed Act were as follows. First, it directly addressed the erosion of Federal Reserve membership and the narrowing of monetary control by insisting that *all* deposit-taking institutions were to be subject to the Fed's reserve requirements in a phased programme from November 1980 to September 1987 (in effect this allowed former member banks to hold smaller reserves than before while raising those for most of the non-members). Second, in return all depositary institutions were given access to their Federal Reserve District Bank's discount window and similar privileges. Third, all interest rate ceilings on time deposits were to be phased out in stages over the following six years. In other words it was 'goodbye to Regulation Q'. Four, in similar vein Negotiable Order of Withdrawal Accounts were allowed for all depositary institutions nationwide as from the end of 1980. These NOW accounts, which had first been introduced in Massachusetts in 1972, were nominally interest-bearing time accounts but could be switched on demand into checking accounts. The Fed had already authorized the counterpart ATS accounts (automatic transfer from savings accounts) so that the old barriers insisted upon in the crisis-driven laws of the 1930s were broken down. Transactions-money and savings-money intermingled and overlapped, more responsive than ever to changes in interest rates: hence the volatility of poor M1. Five, State usury ceilings for mortgages and for a number of other loans were abolished (but could specifically be reinstated by new State legislation: the dual system could kick back). Six, the insurance limits on deposits in banks and thrifts were raised to $100,000. Whether this last 'reform' was such a good idea became a furiously debated item in the following decade. Before considering why, brief mention should be made of the Garn–St Germain Act of 1982 which, by considerably widening the powers of Savings and Loan Associations, complemented the deregulatory provisions of DIDMCA. This new 'Depositary Institutions Amendment Act' confirmed the right of thrifts to grant consumer loans, allowed the acquisition of a failed bank or thrift by an out-of-state banking organization and authorized deposit accounts 'directly equivalent to and competitive with' the money market mutual fund deposits that had seriously diverted funds away from banks and thrifts over the previous decade. As a result Money Market Deposit Accounts and 'Super-NOW' Accounts (interest-bearing transaction accounts with no rate ceiling) enabled banks and thrifts to claw back a proportion of previously lost deposits. Thrifts began vigorously to diversify their assets – dangerously so, lulled into a false sense of security by their long-suffering deposit insurance system.

Hazardous deposit insurance for thrifts, banks . . . and taxpayers

For most of the post-Second World War period Savings and Loan Associations (S&Ls) enjoyed remarkable success, growing in numbers to around 5,000 and claiming a rising share of assets relative to those of other financial institutions, up from 6 per cent in 1950 to a peak of 16 per cent in 1984. By 1990 however their numbers had halved, mostly from mergers and failures, to around 2,500, with an estimated 20 per cent economically insolvent and with their market share of assets back down to about 11 per cent (Kaufman 1990). Since most of their assets were in mortgages with rates fixed at the low interest rates ruling in the 1950s and 1960s the later substantial rise in rates required to hold on to their deposits inevitably led to more and more thrifts becoming insolvent, squeezed by relatively fixed incomes and unavoidably rising costs. They searched desperately for more profitable (and riskier) business. Their regulatory authority, the Federal Home Loan Bank Board, interpreted DIDMCA liberally and allowed S&Ls to issue credit cards and offer unsecured loans from July 1980. With regard to liberalization it was a case of too late and too much.

Just as the banks were insured from 1934 on by the Federal Deposit Insurance Corporation so were the S&Ls by the Federal Savings and Loan Insurance Corporation, with the maximum limit per account similarly being raised periodically to the $100,000 agreed in 1980. Since the insurance applied to each account rather than to each individual it was possible and profitable for large sums of money to be deposited, commonly via brokers, to seek out the highest returns in separate accounts in any number of S&Ls. The rich and greedy as well as the poor and cautious were equally protected. The depositor was forcing the insurer to accept his bet of 'heads I win, tails you lose'. This in technical jargon is known as 'moral hazard'. Neither the depositors nor the owners (who usually had relatively little capital to lose and who often included the managers) had any incentive to be cautious and every incentive to seek profitable ventures as far as the rules would allow. In 1985 runs on thrifts in Ohio and Maryland led to the insolvency and disappearance of their state-chartered deposit insurance agencies. In 1986 large losses in Texas and elsewhere by federally chartered S&Ls led later in that year to FSLIC itself being officially declared to be insolvent despite having staved off that inglorious débâcle for a number of years by dint of creative accounting. It was kept in existence only by an emergency injection of $10.8 billion provided under the Competitive Equality Banking Act of 1987, which Act nevertheless perversely extended the principle of 'forbearance' (i.e. not closing failed institutions promptly) for savings institutions in depressed areas. The FSLIC still listed 340 S&Ls as insolvent as at January 1989, while its chairman estimated that up to 800 S&Ls with nominal assets of $400 billion needed to be sold, merged or liquidated. Unofficial estimates include that of the prestigious Brookings Institute which conservatively estimated losses exceeding $100 billion or $400 per US citizen (*Blueprint for Restructuring America's Financial Institutions*, May 1989). According to the Wall Street Journal of 22 May 1989 the

Table 9.4 US bank failures and new bank formation, 1977–1992.*

Year	Number failed	New banks	Year	Number failed	New banks
1977	6	154	1985	120	318
1978	7	148	1986	138	248
1979	10	204	1987	184	212
1980	10	206	1988	200	237
1981	10	199	1989	206	193
1982	42	316	1990	168	170
1983	48	366	1991	124	109
1984	79	400	1992	168	74
Total from 1977 to 1992				1610	3590

* These are FDIC Insured Banks and do not include failures of some very small banks.
Sources: Federal Reserve Bulletin, March 1989; FDIC Annual Report 1992. Jennifer J. Johnson, Associate Secretary, Federal Reserve Board, kindly provided me with the most recent figures.

Government's General Accounting Office put the full costs of rescue at $285 billion or $1000 per household. Maximum micro-economic security had led to maximum macro-economic costs. Before looking at congressional action to repair this hopeless situation we turn to examine the frightening increase in bank failures and the impact on the FDIC.

From the start of Federal Deposit Insurance in 1934 until the end of 1992 the total number of failures of insured banks came to 2,015 of which no less than 1,260 or two-thirds have taken place since 1985. The severity of recent failures is even more dramatically illustrated when one considers that the aggregate of deposits in all the banks that failed in the 59-year period from 1934 to 1992 inclusive came to $207.5 billion, of which no less than $158.4 billion or 76 per cent were in banks that failed in just the last five years, from 1988 to 1992 inclusive. In the 32-year period from 1943 to 1974 failures were always below ten annually. Table 9.4 shows how the number of failures began to soar from 1982. In the eight years following 1985 the number of failures has always equalled or exceeded 120 annually with an average of over 160. In many cases failure occurred shortly after the banks had been publicly given a clean bill of health. Auditing and accounting in the USA (as in Britain with the Johnson Matthey and BCCI affairs) have in recent years been exposed as being almost as inexact as the traditional dismal science itself. Of the fifty-six banks that failed between 1959 and 1971, thirty-four had been passed by their supervisor in a 'no problem' category while seventeen were rated as 'excellent'.

Subsequent failures included large banks like the National Bank of San Diego in 1973, Franklin National in 1974 and most frightening of all the near collapse of Continental Illinois Bank which would have failed between 1982 and 1984 had it not been for the intervention of the monetary authorities. Because of the devastating effect which such a failure would probably have had on the banking system as a whole the authorities stepped in with a rescue package, but in doing so their 'Too Big to Fail' philosophy increased the moral hazard throughout the nation's financial industry. The FDIC's list of problem banks rose from 218 in 1980 to 1,600 in 1987, while from the figures already given ratings of 'no problem' and even of 'excellent' among the other 13,000 banks were hardly cast-iron guarantees. By the time the rate of annual failures rose to 200 in 1988 and 206 in the following year FDIC was registering the first annual losses in its history. Faced by such alarming trends, on top of the shambles of the S&Ls, Congress passed the fire-emergency Financial Institutions Reform, Recovery and Enforcement Act in August 1989. Re-regulation was back on the agenda and not a moment too soon.

FIRREA spawned a new regulatory alphabet and gained immediate financial backing with $50 billion being provided as the initial amount for a Resolution Funding Corporation to close or sell insolvent thrifts. It set to work with vigour. By early 1993 it had already disbursed $84.4 billion of taxpayers' money in closing down 653 S&Ls. The 1989 Act replaced the FSLIC with the Savings Association Insurance Fund, hopefully known as SAIF, under the control of FDIC, which was also to run a new Bank Insurance Fund. A new Office of Thrift Supervision directly under the Treasury replaced the old Federal Home Loan Board. More importantly, capital ratios for all banks and thrifts were to be at least 6 per cent by mid-1991 with the 8 per cent risk-capital ratios of the Basle Agreement guidelines as a target for the end of 1992. The Act attempted to push S&Ls back more into their traditional business by giving preferential treatment to a reclassified 'qualified thrift lender' i.e. one with at least 70 per cent of its assets in or closely related to housing. Conversely, it limited the amount of permitted investment in junk bonds and the use of brokered deposits. It attempted to make bank holding companies more responsible for the solvency of each bank subsidiary. Finally FIRREA asked the Treasury with FDIC to make a comprehensive study of the key problems of a viable and efficient system of bank and thrift deposit insurance – an invitation which launched a plethora of papers by bankers, supervisors, economists, politicians and especially lawyers, resulting in intriguing proposals regarding e.g. 'camels' and 'haircuts'. (The 'CAMEL' is a rating given by examiners based on Capital, Asset quality, Management, Earnings and Liquidity. Thus low ratings might be penalized by high premiums. In general, risk-based premia could go very well with risk-based capital ratios. The 'haircut', proposed by the American Bankers Association, would grant depositors only a proportion rather than the whole of their nominal claims, except for the lowest depositors.)

From the 1980s in particular the burden of bank insurance has been shifted cumulatively on to the shoulders of the taxpayers. Angry taxpayers have therefore pushed the authorities not simply to consider scrappy and piecemeal emergency remedies but to face the urgent need for a fundamental reform of the American banking system, including especially the question of nationwide branching. Britain, and more tellingly neighbouring Canada, have had very few failures since they replaced unit banking with nationwide branching a century ago.

From unit banking . . . to balkanized banking

A hundred years ago William Jennings Bryan campaigned against America's being 'crucified on a cross of gold'. Subsequently both gold and his beloved silver have been demonetized: yet America's monetary system remains enchained by centuries-old traditions and outmoded legal prohibitions, around, through, under and over which, at some considerable cost, modern market forces eventually with painful slowness find their way. It is incredibly incongruous when millions of dollars can instantly be transmitted across the globe by satellite that US banks, the main creators of their country's money, may still not be able to open a branch even a few miles away (especially in other States) without quite disproportionate effort, frequently involving numerous committees up to and including the Board of Governors of the Fed to examine the most trivial details. For instance the public is gravely informed that Chairman Greenspan and Governors Johnson, Angell, Kelley and LeWare after due consideration voted on 9 February 1990 against Cedar Vale of Wellington, Kansas becoming a bank holding company through acquiring a bank that 'is the 245th largest banking organisation in Kansas controlling less than one percent of the total banking deposits' of that State, but '10.3 per cent of total deposits in the local market' (*Federal Reserve Bulletin* (April 1990), 257). It is just as difficult to believe that the Board of Governors is subject to being overruled in granting permission for mergers or new branches by the Department of Justice whenever a pseudo-scientific index of monopoly power in local banking districts – the Herfindahl–Hirschman Index – rises above the magical figure of 1800. (Happily in practice the Fed usually refuses to bow down to this false god of numbers: see the note on p. 546 on concentration ratios.)

Despite the legal obstacles, considerable progress has been made in the post-Second World War period in gradually but cumulatively changing from a predominantly unit banking system to one where some form of branch banking is the norm. Even so, because with very few exceptions nationwide branching has been strictly prohibited, compared with other countries the American system of branching is still highly circumscribed. Federal laws restricting branching stem from the National Bank Act of 1864 strengthened by the McFadden Act of 1927, the Banking Act of 1933 and the Douglas Amendment to the Bank Holding Company Act of 1956, the combined effects of which are first to prohibit interstate branching and secondly to concede to the States the authority to determine the degree of intra-State branching, if any, and of BHC subsidiaries that may be allowed. The existence of both federal and State laws, usually euphemized as the 'dual' system, is in fact, as we have already noted, more like a permutation among fifty-one differing varieties as each State copies, modifies or misinterprets the examples of the others. Nevertheless two outstanding general trends have made themselves even more strongly felt in the last few decades: first, the development of nationwide quasi-banking services offered by bank holding companies and 'non-bank' corporations, and, second, the marked liberalization of State laws to permit full banking throughout ever larger geographical areas of their States, and almost full banking with their neighbours.

The main loophole which has been exploited to allow the spread of banking services is the emphasis in the generally accepted legal definitions that a bank necessarily offers *two* kinds of banking services, namely deposit-taking on the one hand plus money-transmission services normally through cheque accounts on the other. Institutions offering limited or specialized services might thus escape branching restrictions. We have already seen how the Edge Act Corporations by simply offering specialized services to encourage international trade were enabled to cross State lines as early as 1919. By the mid-1980s there were 143 interstate Edge offices operated by forty-nine banks. Improved communications and technological innovations have enabled much greater exploitation of this limited banking services principle in recent years by banks, by non-banks and by that uniquely American invention, the 'non-bank bank'. By 1982 forty-four banks were operating 202 single-purpose, self-described 'Loan Production Offices' spread over thirty-four States. An intense and justified irritant to bankers was the fact that non-bank firms such as Merrill Lynch, Sears Roebuck, J. C. Penney, IBM Credit, and the three largest car companies, General Motors, Ford and Chrysler, could compete in the provision of finance right across the USA, whereas the banks were confined within their own metropolitan areas, counties or even, at best, within their own State boundaries. A popular method of hitting back was through the bank holding company.

Until the Bank Holding Company Act of 1956, holding companies doing some limited banking could set up shop anywhere, just like most non-banking companies. That Act brought multi-bank holding companies, i.e. those with two or more banking subsidiaries, within Fed regulations, which included a prohibition of mixing banking with non-banking business. However, by forming 'one-bank' holding companies a way was found around these restrictions, greatly stimulating the formation of these singular forms until Congress was forced to close the loophole in the Bank Holding Company Amendment Act of 1970. This, however, did allow subsidiaries to engage in certain peripheral banking activities provided these were 'bank-related and in the public interest'. Subsequently the Fed increasingly liberalized the kinds of banking activities allowed by subsidiaries so that the momentum to forming bank holding companies continued to roll. Thus by the end of 1973 there were some 1,677 such companies controlling 3,097 banks holding nearly two-thirds of all commercial bank deposits. Because bank holding companies 'share many advantages of a branch system they are especially common in states like Texas where branching is prohibited or restricted' (*Federal Reserve Bank of Kansas Economic Review* (May/June 1990), 55). Not only were the functional boundaries between banks, thrifts, finance companies and so on breaking down, but so also were many of the geographical divisions that had previously characterized the rather atomized American banking system.

One factor leading to fewer unit and more branch banks was the growth in mergers in the banking industry in the 1970s and 1980s. The annual number of mergers grew from 135 in 1976 on a gradually rising trend to 188 in 1980, and thereafter accelerated to 359 in 1981, 422 in 1982, 432 in 1983 and 553 in 1984 before falling slightly to the still very high figure of 472 in 1985 (*Federal Reserve Bulletin*, March 1989). Some mergers were hotly disputed, but few to the degree of that between Manufacturers Trust and Hanover which though approved by the Fed in 1961 was delayed by legal wrangles for five years: the 1992 merger between 'Mannie Hannie' and Chemical Bank turned out to be a much less contested marriage, though far bigger in size, which is illustrative of changing attitudes towards such fusions of power. More than half the 1,610 failed banks shown in table 9.4 were eventually acquired by other banks as part of the 'purchase and assumption' method of disposal commonly arranged by the FDIC. Thus the rise in the number of holding companies, the growth in mergers and the increase in bank failures have all tended to spread the linkages of banks, in some important cases even across previously unbridgeable States. The Garn–St Germain Act permitted the acquisition of failing banks or thrifts by out-of-State banks from October 1982, thus confirming the action taken, with Fed permission, a few weeks earlier when New York's Citicorp stretched across the continent to rescue Fidelity S&L of Oakland, California. Much more important than far distant linkages however has been the spectacular growth of interstate banking, mostly among neighbouring States, which has revolutionized the structure of American banking in the last decade or so. (See also p. 546.)

Although formal branch banking across State boundaries (with very few exceptions) remained forbidden, the situation has been outflanked. States armed with the Douglas Amendment and using the device of the bank holding company have already infiltrated each other's territories to such a degree as to regionalize, and perhaps even to balkanize, the country's banking system. This applied even to many of the States that had been the most stubborn in clinging to America's unit banking traditions. By mid-1990 there were at least 160 'interstate' bank holding companies controlling 465 bank subsidiaries in different States. Since 1975 and up to 1990 every State in the Union, except five (Hawaii, Iowa, Kansas, Montana and North Dakota – hardly the financially most important States) passed interstate banking laws allowing access by other States into their banking markets, most only from neighbouring States but some allowing entry from any part of the country. The crucial matter is that the States can decide from where and in what form such entry will be allowed, mostly on a reciprocal basis. The move to interstate banking began quietly enough in Maine, which in 1975 legalized entry by banking companies headquartered in other States. In 1982 both New York and Massachusetts enacted interstate legislation, but whereas New York allowed entry to all other States provided they did the same for New York's institutions, those of the New England States conferred reciprocity only to banking companies within the New England region, so excluding the much-feared, giant New York banks. The latter duly challenged the New England States for equal rights of entry, only to find that in a key decision in June 1985 the US Supreme Court upheld the New England principle of selective entry.

However, in a complete reversal of previous history, States that had fought tenaciously for around two centuries to keep outsiders – and particularly the big banks – off their banking patches now began to compete vigorously to attract outsiders, even in some important instances, from the main money centres like New York and Chicago. The first State to use the bank holding company as a vehicle to stimulate regional development and employment creation was South Dakota, which in 1980 removed all usury ceilings on credit cards and permitted fees to be charged on such cards. Thereby it enticed New York's Citibank to transfer its lucrative card business to Sioux Falls, South Dakota. By 1987 Citibank had become the largest bank in South Dakota, with domestic assets of $12 billion and providing employment for 3,462 persons. The lesson was quickly learned by other States – and by other banks (even in Britain) which quickly slapped on similar high interest rates and fees for credit cards. From 1980 therefore States felt free to make regional compacts without having to fear that their own banks would necessarily be swamped by the invasion of some of the world's most powerful banks, and knew that if they did allow such entry they could now lay down conditions limiting such entrants to specialized banking that did not compete with the general banking business of their own banks. Thus in much less than a decade the concept of regional banking had become a reality.

In 1913 America's central banking system had been built on the regional principle – but it was not until some seventy years later that the time was ripe for regionalism to become a reality in the life of American commercial banking. Surveying interstate banking developments in February 1987 the *Federal Reserve Bulletin* observed that 'those advocating regional interstate banking laws argue that the development of large regional banks promotes the area's economic growth. The theory is that such banks by understanding and supporting regional industries, will do more for economic growth than the money centre banks would' (p.80). South Dakota has shown how even the money centre banks could be recruited with those same ends in view.

When bank holding companies could thus spread ever more widely it clearly made less sense than ever to cling on to the relics of unit banking including especially the formal but outmoded and outflanked restrictions on branching. It is still – incredibly – the case that at the start of the last decade of the twentieth century neither federal nor State laws (except in Massachusetts) allow banks in general to open branches across State lines nationwide. As for branching within States, the convenient and usual practice is to classify the States into three classes: those allowing State-wide branching, those allowing none, and those which cover the extremely wide range in between. Because somewhere or other in the 'United' States (obviously not yet completely united in terms of banking) lawyers are continually engaged in disputing the extent to which their selection of laws allow branching, the statistics quoted by various authorities sometimes show significant differences; but the general picture is as follows: first, despite occasional backsliding, the long-term trend is unmistakably one-way, towards ever greater geographic freedom and towards a continuous rise both in the absolute number of branches and as a percentage of total banking offices. In 1900 only eighty-seven banks boasted branches, which in total came to 119. By 1929, 764 banks operated 3,533 branches. The number fell in the crisis years of the 1930s but grew slowly thereafter to reach 4,700 branches in 1950. They then more than doubled to 10,200 in 1960, and again to 21,400 in 1970. They reached 38,400 in 1980 and 46,300 in 1987. This average of around three or four branches per bank is still pathetically small compared with that of countries with long-established branch banking systems: yet it clearly marks the end of a centuries-long tradition of unit banking, as does the parallel change in the legal rules governing branching.

In 1929 almost half the States completely prohibited branching. The number of these 'unit' banking States then fell slowly, from the 1929 figure of twenty-three, to fifteen in 1939, and thereafter at an even slower pace, to twelve in 1979. In the 1980s the rate accelerated, leaving only two stubbornly unit States, Colorado and Missouri, in 1990 as remnants of a once solid Midwestern bloc. By that time only twelve States were still in the limited branching category, while the thirty-six remaining States allowed State-wide branching (even though nine of these still restricted this freedom to cases of merger). In effect, however, by 1990 State-wide branching existed practically throughout the nation, though subject to varying conditions and legal interpretations. These legal changes reflected at long last the logic of market forces. Since 1980 especially, technical innovation, the deregulation of interest rates and of functional boundaries between separate financial institutions accompanied and stimulated geographic deregulation despite legal delaying tactics such as the contested merger cases already mentioned. Among the most absurd was the attempt to prevent regional and national networks of Automatic Teller Machines by insisting that ATMs were branches, so that the networks should be confined within branching limits – until 1984 when Marine Midland successfully appealed to the Federal Appeals Court. Thus were the legal Luddites of the third industrial revolution overcome in this particularly significant instance.

The anachronism of an almost complete ban on formal nationwide branching remains, bolstered by constitutional inertia, the entrenched vested interest of most of the existing (and mostly small) banks, and the all-pervading paranoia concerning banking monopolies (see note on p. 546). However, the experience of California, which has allowed State-wide branching for most of this century, shows that fears of monopoly have little substance and proves that small banks can profitably coexist alongside the giants, provided that freedom of entry remains open. In this regard the exclusion of the giant money-centre banks from the newly emerging groupings of States as a result of the bank holding company interstate compacts has given rise to a concern, shared by the Fed's chairman, at the 'balkanization' of American banking, with superregional banks dominating their own region but sheltered from the strong competition which could otherwise be offered by the large money-centre banks. Thus already in 1985 Chairman Volcker publicly expressed his concern regarding such potential balkanization and optimistically 'recommended a federally legislated limit on the number of years that States could maintain a system of regional interstate banking' (*Federal Reserve Bulletin*, February 1987, p.91).

Although there have been a number of other causes for the relative decline in the world ranking of America's money-centre banks in recent years, such as Third World debts and the rise of Japanese banks, there can be little doubt that the balkanization of domestic banking has played its part. In 1970 the ten largest banks in the world were all American. By 1980 only two American banks remained in the top ten, BankAmerica Corp being second and Citicorp being third. In June 1991 according to *The Banker's* list of the world's top twenty banks, ranked by capital, there were no American banks of that size, Citicorp being ranked twenty-first. When ranked by assets Citicorp came eighteenth. The next largest American bank, BankAmerica Corp, was ranked thirty-fourth by capital and forty-third by assets. One can hardly quarrel with that publication's conclusion: 'the absence of full nationwide banking is seen as an obstacle to building global giants' (*The Banker*, June 1991, p.16). On the other hand, compensating for the disappearance of American banks from the world's top twenty and highlighting the preponderant weight of American banking in world terms is the fact that, in *The Banker's* list of the top 1,000 banks in the world (July 1991), there were far more banks from the USA, at 203, than from any other country. Japan had 109 (with six in the top ten); Italy had 103 (none in the top ten); Germany 84 (none in the top ten); Spain 36 (none in the top ten); the UK 35 (two in the top ten); Switzerland was strongly represented for such a small country, with 32 (one in the top ten); while France had 24 (also with one in the top ten).

Furthermore despite the rise in the failure rate of US banks the continuing vigour of its banking industry and the 'animal spirits' of its financial entrepreneurs are evident from the bottom line of table 9.4, which shows that, in the sixteen years from 1977 to 1992 inclusive, 3,590 new banks were formed – that is about six times the number of *existing* authorized banking institutions in the United Kingdom. As many as 400 new banks were formed in the USA in the one year, 1984, with an annual average of over 224 for the sixteen years shown. The birth rate of American banking – in terms of numbers of course, not size – vastly exceeded the death rate, speaking volumes not only for ease of entry as a weapon for contesting monopoly but also for the persistently optimistic belief, despite gloom, doom and losses all round, that banking is still seen as a licence to print money – for the proprietors as well as for the general public.

Summary and conclusion: from beads to banks without barriers

For the first three-quarters of the eighteenth century America's monetary development was kept on such a taut lead by England that it was forced to make indigenous products like wampum, furs, maize and tobacco into limited legal tender. In such circumstances the drain of precious metals to pay taxes was felt so keenly as to play its part in the Revolution. Freedom to print the paper money with which the Revolutionary War was financed was carried to excess as, with the debauchery of the 'Continentals', America first experienced runaway inflation, causing the States to concede to central government the right 'to coin money and regulate the value thereof'. The States were left with rights over the unofficial types of bank-issued moneys, thereby giving rise to the dual system which has, on balance, plagued its monetary development thereafter. State–federal rivalry destroyed the First and Second 'Central' Banks and left the American banking system rudderless against the violent storms of the nineteenth century. During the Civil War while the lax financial policies of the South led again to runaway inflation, the North through greater fiscal and financial rectitude experienced only moderate inflation. During most of the nineteenth century the obvious benefits of sound money were achieved by *de facto* adherence to the gold standard just when, luckily, supplies of newly mined gold were increasing. The USA avoided, but only just, becoming ensnared in the irrelevance of bimetallism, though not until 1900 was the gold standard enshrined in law. Unfortunately without a central bank even the gold standard failed to provide enough 'elasticity' to the money supply. It was in order to supply such elasticity that the Fed was finally established in 1913, adopting a regional structure for that purpose just when modern communications were bringing about a potential nationwide market for money.

America's fatal attachment to unit banking, coupled with the Fed's restrictive monetary stance, intensified the world's biggest slump in the 1930s and fatally weakened a third of America's banks. The reforms then introduced, separating investment from commercial banking and establishing an exemplary deposit insurance system, seemed justified by thirty post-war years of safe and expanding banking at home and abroad, marred only, it seemed, by moderate inflation. Eventually rising inflation and ingenious innovation broke down a system basically dependent on usury laws and legal barriers, forcing officialdom to accept widespread functional deregulation and some forms of interstate and regional banking in preference to traditional unit banks. Deregulation accompanied and was followed by (without necessarily implying a causal connection) an alarming rise in bank and thrift failures, prompting a rising chorus of calls for fundamental reform in the 1990s.

The complexity of the American financial system has provided a paradise for lawyers, while the Byzantine supervisory structure has imposed heavy annual operating costs, currently of over a billion dollars, which have to be carried by banks and their customers, quite apart from the periodic massive reconstruction costs borne impatiently by the taxpayers.

America in 1991 boasted 362 large 'billion-dollar' banks, yet most of the other 12,000 banks were quite small by international standards, protected from competition by an irrational fear of monopoly and by the one large remaining physical barrier prohibiting nationwide branching. This will surely be further undermined if not removed – possibly by allowing branching throughout each Federal Reserve District, as a stage on the way to ultimate geographic freedom nationwide. Consequently it is not unlikely that as the twentieth century comes to a close the USA will experience the biggest merger boom in world banking history as 12,000 banks furiously coalesce, eventually towards a few thousand or even less in a nation at last without banking barriers.

Although America has officially enjoyed a single currency since 1790 it has not yet achieved a single banking market. It is one of history's exquisite ironies that Europe, or most of it, reached the goal of a single market by 1992. A single currency for most of Europe by the year 2,000, as already planned on paper, appears highly doubtful.

Note

Bank Concentration Ratios The two most popular measures of banking monopoly in the USA are: (a) the 'Three-Bank Concentration Ratio' (3BC) which simply adds the percentage share of the three largest banks within a defined geographic banking area; and (b) the Herfindahl–Hirschman Index (HHI) which is the sum of the squares of the market shares of all the banks within that defined area. An example will illustrate why HHI is preferred by the Department of Justice and the Fed in cases like merger or *de novo* entry.

The Banksville area boasts eleven unit banks, of which three are large, each with a market share of 20 per cent, while the other eight banks are small, each with only 5 per cent of the market.

(a) 3BC = 20 + 20 + 20 = 60%
(b) HHI = $3(20^2) + 8(5^2) = 1,400$

Now suppose there is a merger between two of the large banks:

(a) 3BC = 40 + 20 + 5 = 65%
apparently indicating only a small increase in monopoly power. On the other hand:

(b) HHI = $40^2 + 20^2 + 8(5^2) = 2,200$ *indicating such a large increase, of 800 points, that would cause the authorities to reach for their revolvers.*

Thus, according to the official notification of the legal results of an investigation of possibly excessive monopoly in 1990, the *Federal Reserve Bulletin* of April 1990 states: 'Under the revised Department of Justice Merger Guidelines a market in which the post-merger HHI is above 1,800 is considered highly concentrated. In such markets, the Department of Justice is likely to challenge a merger that increases the HHI by more than 50 points' (p.249).

Dangerously Hidden Cost of Legal Constraints Despite legal rearguard actions, the rising tide of mergers has continued relentlessly to sweep away traditional barriers and to expose the naïvety of conventional anti-monopolistic attitudes. Outstanding examples during 1995–6 included the marriage of Chase Manhattan and Chemical in New York City to form America's largest bank; and the inter-state merger of First Chicago with NBD of Detroit. Reluctantly, step after grudging step, the legal authorities have been forced to recognize the economic logic of the domestic and international financial markets. Such needless delays impose a considerable hidden cost in holding back the long-term growth of America's huge gross national product below its potential rate.

10

Aspects of Monetary Development in Europe and Japan

Introduction: banking expertise shifts northward

Only the briefest glimpse can be given here of some of the salient features of the development of money and banking in parts of continental Europe since about 1600 and in Japan during the nineteenth and twentieth centuries. Special emphasis will be given to the close attention which the banks and the monetary authorities have continued to give to industrial and regional development when compared with the situation elsewhere, and in particular the United Kingdom. One of the most persistent and intrusive factors influencing the growth of monetary institutions, instruments and policies over most of Europe, which tended to bring some degree of similarity to its almost infinite regional variety, came from outside Europe. International trade provided the resources for which European nations and city-states competed vigorously by economic and military means, for at that time, war – to modify Clausewitz – was the continuation of monetary policy by other means. 'Nowadays that prince who can best find money to pay his army is surest of success' (Davenant 1771, 348). 'There is no question', wrote Professor Lipson 'that the mercantilists attached importance to the precious metals largely as an instrument of war' while 'the imperfect development of credit instruments gave greater prominence to precious metals' (1956, III, 67–8). The great geographical discoveries and their associated military conquests, as noted in chapter 5, moved the centre of gravity of banking expertise northwards from the Mediterranean, and especially from its Italian cradle, to France, the Germanic states and to those persistent rivals in the search for and control of the spice trade, England and Holland. By the end of the seventeenth century the latter two countries had become the most financially advanced and were 'the only countries where anything except coined money made a really significant contribution to the internal money supply outside the few favored cities' (Spufford 1988, 396). Although most trade was local and based on silver coins it was from wholesale and external trade carried on by merchants assisted by merchant bankers using gold, bills of exchange and other forms of credit, that the impetus to financial innovation was in the main derived.

The rise of Dutch finance

The importance of the Bank of Amsterdam

Between 1585 and 1650 the increasing involvement of western Europe in overseas trade led to a rising trend of prosperous economic activity in Holland, with Amsterdam taking over the key trading position previously occupied by Antwerp. Amsterdam became the chief commercial emporium of Europe. Its stock exchange quoted a list of prices as early as 1585. Important new companies, such as the Dutch East India Company of 1602 and the West India Company of 1621, provided the financial backing for Dutch political and economic competition with England in the Far East and in the New World, involving the control of the spice trade in the former area and of the town and colony of New York in the latter. A Dutch 'corner' in pepper raised its price in London from 3s. to 8s. per lb in the first decade of the seventeenth century, and only strenuous action by the English East India Company managed to bring the price back down to 2s. by 1615. Although trade in exotic products was thus subject to strong monopolistic elements, when it came to currencies and the precious metals Holland led the world in providing the clearest example of the benefits of free trade.

The Dutch authorities produced two forms of currency: an internal, inferior (slightly) but perfectly acceptable form designed purely for domestic use with a silver content made lower than its face value to discourage export; and secondly 'trade coins' of such a high intrinsic quality that they were eagerly accepted as a most popular international commodity money. 'Just as the Florentine florin and the Venetian Ducat are said to have been the dollars of the Middle Ages, it could be said that Dutch currency became the dollar of the seventeenth century' (Vilar 1976, 205.). Early in that century fourteen mints operated in Holland to supply such currencies, later merging into eight. Trade was vitally dependent on the fast and efficient handling of the foreign exchanges of coins and of bullion, and it was for this reason above all others that the public Bank of Amsterdam was established in 1609 to give a superior and more controlled service than was available from the host of private exchangers and 'bankers' that had been springing up over much of north-west Europe. It soon developed an international reputation, not only as an exchange bank but also as a deposit bank, though such deposits were of a wholesale size, suited to the needs of the rich merchants, states and municipalities that were its customers. It was not a bank of discount, nor in its early years did it make loans to the general public, though, exceptionally, it did grant loans to the East India Company and to the larger Dutch municipalities. We have seen how its example led to the establishment of the Bank of England, which gradually gained international precedence. All the same, Adam Smith was constrained to sing the Dutch bank's praises in his famous Digression in his *Wealth of Nations* on 'Banks of Deposit, Particularly that of Amsterdam'. Smith's views of the fundamental role played by the Bank of Amsterdam in modern monetary development are confirmed by recent writers.

Smith showed how the Amsterdam bank 'gave a credit in its books' for deposits of coin, whether domestic or foreign. 'This credit was called "bank money" which, as it represented money exactly according to the standard of the mint, was always of the same real value, and intrinsically worth more than current money', which was subject to fair and unfair wear and tear (1776, Book IV, 422). He went on to say that such 'bank money' carried a premium or *agio* over coinage and was far more convenient than bullion for most purposes: 'The Bank of Amsterdam has for these many years past been the great warehouse of Europe for bullion' (p.427). Vilar similarly, in his stimulating *Gold and Money* devoted a chapter to 'The Monetary Role of the Bank of Amsterdam', and concluded that the bank 'was for a long time an essential part of the monetary system of Europe and indeed of the world' (1976, 210). The Dutch were teachers of banking and of business to the seventeenth-century world. In Holland, said Smith, 'it is unfashionable not to be a man of business' (Book I, 86). Nevertheless it is ironically apt that the Dutch also supplied the modern world with its first example of widespread business mania.

The Dutch tulip mania, 1634–1637

Futures markets in exotic products like tea and pepper had become firmly established in Holland during the first quarter of the seventeenth century. It was however in connection with the domestic production of a previously exotic import – the tulip – that the world's first nationwide mania, based on bulb futures, took place in the 1630s. The first shipment of tulips to arrive in the Low Countries was brought into Antwerp from Constantinople in 1562 and soon formed the basis for the later development of the enormously lucrative bulb industry of that region. Rarity naturally led to high prices for distinctive varieties, especially after the blooms had become highly fashionable in Paris society in the early 1630s. Particularly esteemed were the flamed, double-coloured and striped blooms. These striata or 'sports' were (as we now know) caused by a virus carried in the bulb and its excrescences or 'buds', but not in the seeds. This limited the extent to which supply could respond to a particular surge in demand. Whereas other futures markets were generally limited to experts and specialists, futures in bulbs and their 'buds' were comprehensible and available to the common man, in fact anyone with a few square yards of ground. Professor Posthumus, one of the few economists to have made a thorough study of the tulip mania, states that 'the proximity of Amsterdam, with its commercial and speculative spirit, to Europe's main bulb-growing region was certainly a very powerful stimulant' for the rising speculation which grew from 1634 onwards to the climax of 1636–7 (Posthumus 1929, 435).

Cycles of rising and falling prices for bulbs have continued ever since, as has recently been painstakingly demonstrated by Peter M. Garber in what is claimed to be 'the first serious effort to investigate the market fundamentals that might have driven the tulip speculation' (1989, 535). Professor Garber even raises the question 'Was this episode a "Tulipmania"' (p.555). On balance however there is no escaping Posthumus's conclusion that 'this fluctuation would do very well as an example of the "psychological" theory of business cycles' (p.449). Holland was enjoying a period of considerable prosperity in the 1630s. The tulip offered a timely outlet for the general financial euphoria, in which from 1634 onwards the ordinary person could add his demand, so greatly swelling the normal speculative wave. Even the poor could join the tulip craze, which needed 'none of the involved and, to them, awe-inspiring technical and financial complications which accompanied a deal in spices or in shares of the East India Company' (p.449). The volume and speed of bargains increased rapidly. Whereas the expert bulb growers customarily drew up legal contracts, signed by notaries, regarding prices, payment and delivery dates, the non-experts arranged markets called 'colleges' in inns and taverns, drawing up their own laxer rules regarding such matters. Payments were often a mixture of cash, credit and payment in kind including cattle, wheat, housing, paintings, silver ornaments, barrels of beer and so on. The public's appetite was whetted by well-publicized examples of bulb prices increasing twenty times during the short auction season, with a few cases recording a two-hundredfold increase. Total sales in just one town were valued at ten million florins. In an inflationary age like ours it is not possible to give exact valuations in current money of the astronomic heights to which certain bulbs, including common strains, rose (on paper, mostly) at the height of the mania. The 'degeneration of speculation into a pure craze may be placed', according to Posthumus, 'in the autumn of 1636' (p.443). Garber more precisely dates what he calls the 'potential bubble' to 'the period from January 2 1637 to February 5 1637' (1989, 555). Professor Kindleberger gives the highest price for a single bulb as the equivalent of £20,000, quoting a 1927 source – probably a very considerable underestimation on current prices (1984, 215). Professor Garber in his serious, factual study dismisses as illogical the droll story of the hungry seaman, who mistaking a valuable (but unguarded) tulip for an onion, indulges himself in the world's most expensive snack. History however laughs at logic, so that the Dutch mania cannot thus escape the possible operation of Murphy's law.

If this was not 'mania', there never has been any. It remains as clear as day that the Dutch experience certainly justifies Posthumus's 'psychological' interpretation. Just a week after the frenzied peak reached in the first week of February 1637 the bubble suddenly burst, confidence vanished and prices plunged to one-twentieth or less of those recorded a few days earlier. The abrupt ending of the boom was followed by a long period of a year or more of adjustment, when a series of voluntary agreements were made, with municipal guidance, to limit the damage. Doubt was cast on the legality of many of the dealings, which being interpreted as gambling were not strictly enforceable in the courts. Many could no longer raise the credit which had grossly inflated nominal debts. Mutual debt cancellations were arranged, with, typically, cash payments of 3.5 per cent of peak nominal values being commonly accepted in final settlement. The modern world's first financial mania, based on a sound and growing industry, and liberally supplied with plentiful and new kinds of credit, thus subsided with surprisingly little economic damage. It had encouraged participation by a larger proportion of the ordinary population of a nation than any other mania up to the Wall Street boom of 1929. Finally it showed the world that the much admired financial sophistication of the Dutch could be carried to excess – a lesson almost every generation has subsequently needed to relearn for itself, ever since 'bank money' greatly expanded man's ambitions.

Other early public banks

Although Britain and Holland, as eager apprentices of Italian financiers, led the way in the development of modern banking in the seventeenth and eighteenth centuries, similar developments were spreading throughout the most of Europe, even in areas previously financially backward. In the same year as the Bank of Amsterdam was formed a similar public bank was formed in Barcelona (1609). Other Dutch banks were set up shortly afterwards including those of Middelburg (1616), Delft (1621) and Rotterdam (1635). Meanwhile the Hamburg Girobank (1619) and the Bank of Nuremberg (1621) showed how the trend towards publicly owned banks was spreading to complement the older private banks, such as those of the Fuggers, first set up in Augsburg in 1487. Of particular interest is the Bank of Sweden, granted a most liberal charter in 1656. This authorized it to accept deposits, to grant loans and mortgages and to issue bills of exchange. It became the first chartered bank in Europe to issue notes, which it began in 1661. However, in 1668 it ran into difficulties, but had already become recognized as so important that it was rescued and reorganized as the Riksens Ständers Bank, later called more simply the Riksbank or Bank of Sweden. It then became the world's first central bank and a partial model for later note-issuing central banks (notably the Bank of England). It remains the world's oldest existing public bank. By the end of the seventeenth century there were at least twenty-five public or semi-public banks offering an increasing range of services in various parts of Europe including areas previously dependent on foreign agents or private quasi-banking institutions. According to an exceptionally widely experienced banker of that period, Sir Theodore Janssen, one of the founders and a director of the Bank of England, such banks arose from a mixture of motives, including 'Safety, Conveniency and Income' (Heckscher, in Dillen 1934, 169). Convenience, security and profit have remained the main motives in different mixtures for setting up banks ever since.

In time the early public banks were vastly outnumbered by the relatively unsung private banking institutions which grew to be far more important in terms of their influence on the economic development of their communities than the public banks, particularly in supplying the credit demands of the business community. In general it may be said that the private banks were the main agents responsible for the increase in the quantity, whereas the public banks were more concerned with maintaining or enhancing the quality, of money. The public banks were much larger, gained greater prestige and were more involved with governmental and municipal loans, i.e. with public debt, than most private banks. A number of public banks were set up from their commencement to carry out what were later considered to be essentially central banking functions, while others eventually acquired such functions, some very belatedly. Russia's two first public banks, both banks of issue, were formed by Catherine the Great in 1768 to finance her wars with Turkey. The Russian State Bank, with wider functions, was not set up until 1860, while in countries like Germany and Italy central banking had to await political unification in the 1870s. Even in France, the largest and most politically powerful European state of the eighteenth century, not only public banking, but almost all modern types of banking, suffered from painfully slow and weak development, especially when compared with that of Britain and Holland.

France's hesitant banking progress

France's first venture into public banking was instigated by John Law (1671–1729). He was born in Edinburgh, where his father was a goldsmith and banker. The son showed an early proficiency in mathematics and worked in his father's bank from the age of fourteen until seventeen, when his father died. He then moved to London and got involved in a duel with a certain Mr Wilson, whom he killed. He escaped from prison by fleeing abroad, living in France, Holland, Germany, Italy and Hungary, profiting from his gifts for speculation and gambling, but also making a serious study of money and banking. After some ten years' absence he returned to Scotland where in 1705 he published his unconventional but inspiring ideas in a book entitled *Money and Trade Considered: With a Proposal for Supplying the Nation with Money*. Metallic money was unreliable in quantity and quality, often inflicting restraints on trade. Banknotes, issued and managed by a public bank, were superior and would remove the harsh brakes imposed by an insufficient supply of precious metals. 'National Power and Wealth', he wrote 'consists in numbers of people and [stores] of Home and Foreign Goods', which stores of goods in turn 'depend on Trade and Trade depends on Money'. But only banker-created money ensures a sufficiently active supply. 'By this Money,' he explained, 'the People may be employed, the Country improved, Manufacture advanced, Trade Domestic and Foreign be carried on, and Wealth and Power attained' (Vilar 1976, 249–50). His ideas were rejected in his own country but, after he returned to France in 1713 and gained the ear of the Duke of Orleans, were eventually put into practice, largely because of the parlous state of French public finance.

Despite the fiscal reforms of Richelieu, Mazarin and Colbert, the costly wars and conspicuous extravagance of Louis XIV and his court had by the time of the king's death in 1715 crippled the nation's finances and placed the duke, newly created Regent of France, in an impossible position. The government's annual expenditure was running at more than twice its annual revenue, while the vested interests and tardy procedures of the tax farmers caused the gap between expenditure and revenue to widen. Attempts to gain immediate funds were made by the issue of state promissory notes (*billets d'État*) but these fell to one-quarter of their face value within the year. In desperation the Duke of Orleans turned to Law. 'No other "Keynesian" ever had such a golden opportunity' (Kindleberger 1984, 97).

Law's first step was to economize on the use of precious metals by establishing a note-issuing bank. Law & Co., or the Banque Générale as it became known, France's first public bank, began operations in June 1716. At first it was a great success. In contrast to the state's short-term paper, Law's banknotes actually appreciated, by 15 per cent by 1717. To mark its success (and to be able to place these lucrative note issues more directly under his own influence) the Regent reorganized Law's bank into a newly chartered Banque Royale in 1718. The temptation to overissue, held in check for a while, was later to become only too apparent. However, the state was now much less dependent on the Tax Farmers who, resenting the loss of their influence and even more of their income, bided their time to wreak vengeance on Law. As well as establishing a bank and solving, temporarily at least, the state's fiscal problem, Law's 'system' had a third vital element, namely the sale of shares in a company to tap the seemingly limitless wealth of the French colonies, especially those of the Mississippi basin or Louisiana. Frenchmen and foreigners clamoured to buy shares in the Mississippi Company, which was inaugurated in August 1717. In 1719 it was also given the monopoly of trade with the East Indies and China and was merged with the French East India Company, which had been formed by Colbert in 1664. Law's 'system' thus became in effect a vast state trust controlling banking, the national debt and a great part of the country's foreign trade. For a while the system worked with startling success and the nation, as well as the speculators, prospered. Law himself made a fortune, and after conversion to Roman Catholicism was made Minister of Finance. However by the spring of 1720 the overissue of notes, combined with excessive speculation in the shares of the new companies, led to a drain of precious metals from France to London and Amsterdam. On Law's advice the Regent attempted to stem the tide by enforcing payments in notes only, while maximum personal holdings of coin were to be limited to 500 livres. These were totally unworkable controls. The tax farmers saw their opportunity and forced the Regent to dismiss Law on 27 May 1720. On the same day the Banque Royale stopped payment. The Mississippi Bubble had burst and Law's system had gone into reverse. Law left France and nine years later died in poverty in Venice. Thus ended, in Adam Smith's judgement 'the most extravagant project both of banking and of stock-jobbing that, perhaps, the world ever saw' (1776, Book II, 283). The world's appetite for such spectacles has sadly remained insatiable; but Frenchmen turned away from banking, not only in name but to a large part also in substance, for a hundred years or more – with just one important exception, the Bank of France.

It was not until fifty-six years after the failure of Law's venture that Parisians dared contemplate another public note-issuing bank, and even then the lead was given by two foreigners, Panchaud, a Swiss, and Clouard a French-sounding Scot. Their Caisse d'Escompte was formed in 1776 and, after enjoying ten successful years, began treading the slippery slope of granting too many loans to the government, accompanied by excessive note issues, until it was forced into liquidation in 1793. Two other stop-gap banking institutions followed in 1796 and 1797, the Caisse des Comptes Courants and the Caisse d'Escompte de Commerce, with similarly short careers until they were absorbed by the Bank of France in 1800 and 1803 respectively. The bills of these public discounting houses and of the many private houses supplemented a growing flood of state paper issued by the hard-pressed revolutionary governments in the eleven years from 1789 to 1800. The most notorious of such issues were those of the *assignats*. One of the first acts of the revolutionary government in November 1789 was to take over the ownership of Church lands, and on the basis of this security to issue bonds carrying 5 per cent interest, with purchasers being 'assigned' on redemption a portion of land to the value of the bond. The idea of land being sound security for bond and note issues was not new – as we saw in the many rival schemes when the Bank of England was set up. But the French government's pretence of allocating the ownership of particular plots of land, together with the privilege of 5 per cent interest was soon abandoned, and the *assignats* simply became state-issued, inconvertible fiduciary notes.

At the same time as the total issues mushroomed, the denominations of individual notes were widened from the original typical 1,000-livre note of 1790 down to notes as small as 5 livres by the following year. There followed the usual consequences: inflation, dual pricing (with note payers forced to give more than coin payers), the hoarding and practical disappearance of coins, the flight of capital abroad, followed by even greater issues of *assignats* in a vicious spiral. The original issue of 800 million livres in December 1790 climbed rapidly through an estimated circulation of 8 billion livres in December 1794 to a peak of 20 billion officially estimated on 23 October 1795, by which time the nominal 100-livre or newly designated 100-franc notes could be exchanged, if at all, for only 15 sous in coin. The Paris riots of April and May 1795 paved the way for the rise of Napoleon – and for his Bank of France as an essential agent for re-establishing sound finance. The inflationary trauma of the *assignats* reinforced the French public's painful memories of Law's banking experiments, strengthened their atavistic attachment to silver and gold, and with good reason confirmed their primitively cautious and conservative attitudes towards paper money and the banks that issued it. However, with its belated foundation in 1800 the Bank of France at last supplied the nation with the kind of public financial institution that its neighbours in England, Holland and Sweden had been enjoying for a century or more.

The Bank of France's monopoly of note issue was confined to the Paris region until 1848. The rest of the country was in the main forced to depend on the note issues and bill discounting of local banks, most of them weak, unit banks, with all of their eggs in their local basket. The Bank of France and the government between them followed a vacillating policy, sometimes supporting and at other times opposing local note-issuing banks. Most local notes were unacceptable outside their own districts. Large numbers of local banks failed in the crisis year of 1847 and in the revolutionary year of 1848. To fill the gap the Bank of France was given a complete, nationwide monopoly of note issue in 1848 and also began to expand its branch numbers, which grew to thirty by 1852 and to fifty-four by 1867. The late 1890s saw a renewed surge, so that by 1900 the Bank of France had some sort of office representation in 411 towns throughout France, with as many as 120 being full branches – compared with just eight Bank of England branches in Britain. As François Caron explains, 'by the beginning of the twentieth century the role played by the Bank of France in the banking and monetary system was relatively more important than that of the Bank of England'; and then, more revealingly still, he adds, 'or to put it differently, the role of the other banks was much less important than that of comparable institutions in England' (1979, 50–1). This view as to the comparative dominance of the Bank of France is authoritatively confirmed by the researches of Jean-Pierre Patat and Michel Lutfalla who show that 'the French banks experienced a less vigorous development than their English or German counterparts' being more dependent on their central bank than was the case in other countries' (1990, 14). From being a gap-filler, the Bank of France had become a cuckoo in the regional nests.

Because nineteenth-century France exhibited the wide contrasts typical of a dual economy (i.e. with selected areas and cities enjoying relatively advanced facilities when other areas, many of them quite large, remained backward) it has been common for different authorities to paint starkly contrasting pictures of French economic development. An official report of 1840 described French agriculture (by far its main employer) as 'stagnant, backward, even primitive'. 'French agriculture in 1850 in most regions was still producing for self-subsistence' (R. Price 1981, 48, 61). Further proof of the duality of the financial system is shown by the fact that, until the 1850s, credit in Paris could fairly readily be had at 2.5 or 3.0 per cent, whereas credit in the countryside, much of it still supplied by the country's 10,000 notaries, cost between 7 and 9 per cent. According to Professor Caron 'even up to the 1860s large areas of France were still deserts as far as money was concerned' (1979, 54), while he goes on to conclude that 'the duality of French growth in the first two-thirds of the nineteenth century is clear' (p.136). Even when local banks were supplemented by branches of the Bank of France their notes were of little or no use to the vast majority, who clung tenaciously to their precious coins. Until 1846 the minimum legal denomination for banknotes was 250 francs, equal to more than a month's wage for the average worker. Although the minimum was very gradually reduced, it was as slow and difficult a process to wean the public from coins to notes, as it was to wean the businessmen from notes to bank deposits and cheques. Not until 1865 was the law on the use of cheques simplified enough to encourage more widespread use. Consequently reliance on coinage and banknotes remained far higher in France than in Britain, Germany or the USA, with the Bank of France having to amass large quantities of gold in its sterile reserves to back up its vast note issue. As late as 1903 total bank deposits came to only about one billion francs, i.e only one-tenth of the money supply, compared with a circulation of over five billion in coins. Little wonder that France used its love of gold and silver to lead world opinion in the bimetallist fallacy and to push through the Latin Union from 1865 (as shown in the previous chapter).

Professors Patat and Lutfala demonstrate the extent to which France had an 'outmoded monetary structure' when compared with that of the UK or Germany, in which countries bank deposits were respectively five times and twice as large as the total in French banks. Banknote circulation in France at the end of the nineteenth century was eight times larger than the Bank of England's fiduciary issue and twice that of Germany, and while the Bank of England's gold reserves, despite having to back the role of sterling as a world currency, were relatively very small, those of the Bank of France typically exceeded even its vast total of note issues. In France gold was needed to support its hand-to-hand currency rather than to furnish the foundation for a multiple expansion of bank credit. Whereas Britain had erected an inverted pyramid of bank credit upon a small gold base, with open market operations and bank rate impinging on the bank multiplier to bring about the desired variations in the quantity and price of credit, France built a more stolid, columnar structure resting on a broad base of gold, with far less use of open market operations or of variations in the rate of discount. The Bank of France hardly ever changed its discount rate in the first half of the nineteenth century, being fixed at 4 per cent from 1817 to 1852, except for the revolutionary period in 1848. Even at the turn of the century it remained far less flexible than elsewhere. Between 1898 and 1913 the Bank of England's rate was changed seventy-nine times, and that of Germany on sixty-two occasions, while that of the Bank of France was changed only fourteen times and then only within the narrow range of 2 to 4 per cent. Because the French monetary and banking system thus differed considerably from that of Britain the use of central banking's two traditional weapons was obviously less appropriate. However, the Bank of France, with its preponderant weight and usually with the co-operation of the big Parisian banks, could and did frequently intervene directly to select the sectors and areas where it felt help was needed.

Turning now to the commercial banking scene, it is apparent that, particularly in the first half of the nineteenth century, French industrial development, with few exceptions, received little support from its banking system, not only from a lack of long-term loans but also from a dire shortage of working capital. This situation began to change substantially for the better in the third quarter of the nineteenth century. France's first, effective, major bank specially set up to provide investment funds for industry and the infrastructure was the Crédit Mobilier, formed by the brothers Émile and Isaac Péreire and a group of other bankers, with a large initial capital of 60 million francs, which began operations in December 1852. There had been a few earlier, weaker, attempts to create such a bank, modelled partly on existing banks, like Rothschilds (for whom Émile Péreire had previously worked), and partly on the Belgian Société Générale, which had been founded in 1822 and had played a vigorous role in Belgium's industrial revolution – the first on the European mainland. Another predecessor was the Caisse Générale du Commerce et de l'Industrie, displaying its objectives in the title. It led a troubled life from 1838 until its demise ten years later. Although the Crédit Mobilier was also destined for a short life of fifteen eventful years, from 1852 to 1867, it symbolized a dramatic change in French banking history.

During this third quarter of the nineteenth century the French people's considerable savings were channelled far more effectively than ever before into essential investments in transport, communications, agriculture and industry by means of a whole host of new financial intermediaries. As well as the Crédit Mobilier these included: the forerunner of the Comptoir Nationale d'Escompte de Paris, originally one of sixty-six emergency discount offices set up by the government during the crisis of 1848; the Crédit Foncier (1852) to supply mortgage finance to support the building boom of the Second Empire; the Crédit Industriel et Commercial (1859); the Crédit Agricole (1860); the Crédit Lyonnais (1863), the largest of the regional banks; the Société Générale pour Favoriser le Développment du Commerce et de l'Industrie en France (1864) – again no doubt about its objectives – and the Banque de Paris et des Pays-Bas, formed with Dutch assistance in 1872. These now supplemented and competed with the old private 'Haute Banque', mostly Jewish merchant banks like Rothschilds, Lazards and Banque Worms, in financing the growth of heavy industry, in the building of ports and harbours and above all in the construction of the railway system. As Roger Price shows, 'the most significant investment activity of the banks was undoubtedly railway finance . . . closely associated with investment in, and continuous short-term loans to, heavy industry' which involved 'the interlocking directorates of a whole series of major banking, railway and heavy industrial companies' (1981, 156). By the development of the railway and the telegraph, the Parisian and regional banks were enabled to expand their branch networks so that the previously fragmented, separate local economies could now begin to operate as a truly national market, a fact signalized by the opening of the Paris Clearing House in 1872 – one hundred years later than that of the London Bankers' Clearing House. Professor Kindleberger, having carefully considered recent views to the contrary, is in no doubt that, in matters of money, banking and finance, France was in general a hundred years behind Britain, and that this had significantly held back its economic development (1984, 115).

We have seen, in chapters 7 and 8, that, contrary to conventional opinion, British banks played an important investment role in the first industrial revolution through supporting the local, small-scale industrial firms typical of that period by granting what were in effect medium- and long-term loans through customarily renewing nominally short-term loans. However, just when the banks in France, and even more so in Germany, were forging their close links with industry and strengthening the regional bases of their financial institutions, the British banks were loosening their ties with local industry, strictly avoiding becoming entangled in medium- and long-term lending, and began centralizing financial flows and decision-making in London. Partly as a consequence the failure rate of the British banks declined – as did the growth rate of British industry together with Britain's long-held lead, economically and financially, over its continental rivals. In France the failure of banks like the Crédit Mobilier, which took in short-term deposits and lent out as long-term, led to a tendency for deposit-taking banks to separate themselves from the 'banques d'affaires' or investment banks, although it was not until after the Second World War that this distinction was, as a seemingly sensible safety measure, legally enforced. One complaint commonly heard in France under the term 'drainage' was the diversion of domestic savings away from internal investment in industry towards government funds and foreign investment, increasingly so in the period from 1870 to 1914 – a faint echo of the much stronger diversionary flows in Britain.

There are two outstanding areas of finance where French institutions gave a lead to Britain and grew in the twentieth century to become the largest, or among the largest, in the world, namely agricultural credit and postal money transmission. The old Crédit Agricole, first formed in 1860 as an off-shoot of the Crédit Foncier, was radically reconstructed in 1894 into a three-tiered system. First came thousands of local institutions, the Caisses Locales, each of which was linked to the second tier, the Caisses Régionales, of which there were originally about one hundred, though the numbers fell with interregional amalgamations. Finally these were joined to the Caisse Nationale de Crédit Agricole which still has a million or more customers despite the drastic decline of the total numbers working in agriculture. During the early 1980s the Crédit Agricole was classed as the world's largest bank. The annual ranking given by The Banker of July 1991 places only four European banks in the top ten (the other six being Japanese). Crédit Agricole came sixth, just behind the Union Bank of Switzerland, compared with Barclays in eighth position and National Westminster in tenth. French farmers are thus backed by the world's largest 'agricultural' bank. The supply of short-, medium- and long-term funds has thus for generations been made readily available on reasonably favourable conditions for French farming communities, the designation 'farming' being widely interpreted, providing a financial dimension to reinforce France's stubbornly strong political support for the EC's Common Agricultural Policy, which French politicians had played so large a part in formulating.

Given the relatively small use made of cheque payments in France compared with Britain, it was natural that France should have been more strongly attracted to the advantages demonstrated by Austria's original postal giro system. Whereas Britain's belated National Giro was not set up until 1968, that of France was established fifty years earlier. By the time Britain's giro began, that of France had already grown to be by far the world's largest, relieving the French commercial banking system of a heavy burden of costs and supplying a simple payment system, especially beneficial to poorer persons without bank accounts, spread throughout the country. Compared with the UK giro's 467,000 accounts in 1972, Western Germany's postal giro, the world's second largest, had 3,369,000 accounts, while France's postal giro was easily the world's largest with 7,156,000 accounts, twice that of Germany and over fifteen times as large as that of Britain – which latter, as we saw, was still small enough to be swallowed by a building society in July 1990 (Davies 1973, 195). By 1992 Britain had 2.5 million Girobank accounts, but France with 8.5 million equivalent accounts was still, in absolute terms, the world's biggest, though in *per capita* terms Holland remained by far the world's most intensive user of postal giro banking (Bridge and Pegg 1993, 9).

Turning now to review certain salient features of macro-economic policy closely relevant to financial development, reference might first be made to the ease with which the plentiful savings of the French nation were mobilized to pay off the large indemnity of five billion francs demanded by Germany after the war of 1870. The Thiers government loan raised for this purpose was more than ten times oversubscribed, enabling the indemnity to be repaid within three years – a remarkable tribute to the financial strength of the French economy. This experience goes some way to excuse both the tendency of the French government to rely excessively on borrowing to finance the First World War and French insistence, despite the eloquent warnings of Keynes and the more taciturn opposition of Montagu Norman, that Germany could and should pay the massive reparations demanded at the Versailles Peace Conference of 1919. Overborrowing at short term and excessive reparations had important consequences for European monetary and banking development. No system of income tax was imposed in France until the First World War, and then in a most hesitant and piecemeal fashion, 'In France,' said Keynes 'the failure to impose taxation is notorious' (1920, 230), thus forcing greater reliance on borrowing. The external deficit on the balance of payments was met largely by loans from Britain and America, while the internal, budgetary deficit was met by a combination of internal borrowing and expansion of the note issue. By 1919 note circulation at 34.7 billion francs had grown to more than six times larger than even its already bloated pre-war circulation of 5.7 billion. The French national debt rose from about 28 billion francs in 1914 to 151 billion francs in 1918, with half of it in the form of floating debt. Nevertheless, despite the massive economic and human losses suffered by France, including 1.3 million dead, the immediate post-war period was characterized by inflationary euphoria, based on the belief that Germany would pay the full costs of reconstruction.

The euphoria soon gave way to reluctant acceptance of the grim realities of the inter-war period. The 1920s saw an international scramble for gold to re-establish national gold standards, while the next decade showed the opposite folly of competitive devaluations as country after country was forced to abandon fixed prices for gold. Despite amassing vast amounts of gold, it took the French government until 1928 to achieve its form of gold standard. During most of the period from 1914 to 1918 the franc had been held, with British and American assistance, close to the ratio of 5 francs to $1, but by 1924 it had fallen to 18:1 and by July 1926 it touched as low as 49:1. Raymond Poincaré, during his second premiership form 1926 to 1929, managed to stabilize the franc by the second half of 1926 and to establish a form of gold standard within two years of taking office. By mid-1928 the country's gold reserves had been built up to 29 billion francs, and with the franc then worth 1/25 of a dollar again, it seemed strong enough to go back to gold convertibility. By the Monetary Law of 25 June 1928 a form of gold standard was reintroduced (at the equivalent franc/dollar ratio of 25:1) but with the convertibility of Bank of France notes limited to wholesale transactions of a minimum of 215,000 francs. Silver convertibility was no longer guaranteed, finally ending France's long, lingering attachment to bimetallism. Note issues were to be backed by a gold reserve of at least 35 per cent. At first this posed no problem for France, though it did to Britain and later boomeranged on France itself. By September 1931, having withdrawn £200 million from London in the previous six weeks, the USA and France between them had squirrelled away 75 per cent of the world's gold stock. By mid-1932 the official French gold stock (not counting unknown private hoards) had risen to 89 billion francs, treble its size on the inception of its gold standard.

The government's policy in favour of a strong franc lasted in all for ten years, from 1926 to 1936, but was undermined by competitive devaluation. The strong franc was good for prestige but bad for French exports and for the exports of the Gold Bloc countries that had allied their currencies to the French franc, including Belgium, the Netherlands, Switzerland and Italy – a pale reminder of the old Latin Union of 1865. With the devaluation of the pound in September 1931 and the dollar in April 1933 the pressures on the Gold Bloc mounted. The devaluation of the Belga in 1935 signalled the imminent break-up of the bloc. French official gold reserves fell by some thirty billion francs during the first six months of 1936, lost partly to other countries and partly to internal hoarding. In September 1936 the gold standard was abandoned, the franc being devalued by 25 per cent, followed by a Dutch devaluation by 25 per cent and a Swiss devaluation by 30 per cent. Later that same month France joined the USA and Britain in their Tripartite Agreement to stabilize their exchange rates and so begin a new short-lived period of international managed money until the cataclysm of the Second World War.

Despite the vastly different military situation facing France in the two World Wars, the monetary developments were remarkably similar, with the total money supply in both cases rising by about 300 per cent, coupled with a relatively greater increase in the supply of banknotes, which between 1940 and 1945 increased more than fourfold. At the same time the supply of goods was drastically curtailed as enforced exports left few goods domestically available to face the expanded money supply. Nevertheless the rise in inflation was suppressed not only by a severe wage freeze and by the administrative control of the Vichy and German governments, but also by a reduction in the velocity of the circulation of banknotes. With the step-by-step removal of controls after the Liberation in August 1944 the suppressed inflation was released, first in a stream and then in a torrent, despite the wholesale monetary reforms of 1945. Before considering these reforms, an overview of the growth of the money supply as a whole during the first three-quarters of the twentieth century is most revealing. Apart from a few interludes of moderation, as in the Poincaré years, French money supply grew at an almost incredible pace. The researches of Patat and Lutfalla show that total money supply (M2) in France increased between 1900 and 1973 by no less than 4,515 times! They highlighted a most important difference in that 'before the Second World War monetary growth was for most of the time passive and ineffective, after 1945 it was conscious and its role as a stimulus to the economy was obvious' (Patat and Lutfalla 1990, 220–3).

By the legislation of December 1945 the Bank of France and the four largest deposit banks were nationalized, a National Credit Council was set up and a rigid separation was enforced between deposit and investment banks. Given the dominant size of the Bank of France and its ubiquitous branch penetration, its nationalization, together with that of the Crédit Lyonnais, the Société Générale, the Banque Nationale pour le Commerce et l'Industrie and the Comptoir National d'Escompte de Paris, supplied French planning with a most effective strong right arm. The National Credit Council, apart from mundane duties such as controlling the opening of new banks and branches, supplied a continuous strategic overview of financial developments and was in a key position to see that its advisory recommendations secured influential attention. The separation of deposit from investment banking was a backward move, reflecting the bank failures of the 1930s and, fortunately for French industrial development, had to be reversed later. As the pace of post-war inflation grew to crisis levels in the late 1950s the conservative monetary economist Jacques Rueff was asked to chair a committee which produced its Report on the Financial Situation in December 1958, coincident with the election of General de Gaulle as President and with the end of the first year of Europe's boldest experiment, the founding of the EEC. It was not until 1 January 1960 that the Rueff Committee's main recommendation was carried out, namely the substitution of a new 'heavy' franc, equivalent to one Deutsche Mark, for one hundred old francs.

Following the reform of the currency in 1960 further thoroughgoing improvements were made in the financial system in 1965–7. By a series of laws the financial markets were liberalized. The rigid barriers between deposit and investment banking were broken down as both types of banks began to compete in deposit and lending business over a much wider range than before. De-regulation was in full swing. The opening of bank branches was allowed without prior reference to the National Credit Council and freedom was given for the leasing of capital goods on hire purchase, while the capital markets were similarly freed from a number of previous restrictions. New incentives were provided for personal savings particularly when associated with equity investments. The life of medium-term paper for business loans, acceptable for refinancing at the Bank of France, was extended from five to seven years. Private enterprise became eager to take up these new supplies of credit as France began to change dramatically into an 'économie d'endettement', an 'overdraft economy'. These financial changes showed concrete results as France enjoyed a long period of growth and prosperity amounting to an economic miracle of almost Germanic proportions and clearly overtaking Britain by around 1970. Almost two decades later the picture remained similar. Thus the neutral World Bank Atlas of 1987 gave the following statistics for GNP per head: UK $8,390; France $9,950; West Germany $10,940; Japan $11,330; and USA $16,400. Apart from the similar examples of Germany and Japan there can be few more powerful illustrations in world history than French experience in demonstrating the positive role that banking improvements can make to economic growth when they form part of a clear-sighted long-range policy of stimulating savings and steering them skilfully into productive investment. Although there were other causes for French economic backwardness during much of the nineteenth century, there can be little doubt that a relatively undeveloped banking system played a major part. Conversely, although other factors helped France achieve her economic miracle, there can be equally little doubt that the improvement in financial institutions and practices played a key role.

German monetary development: from insignificance to cornerstone of the EMS

In no other country in the world have money and banking played a more crucial role than in Germany, its experience illustrating money at its best and at its worst, and for that very reason providing an outstanding example, of interest not only to monetary theorists but, much more importantly, of practical value to politicians and monetary authorities everywhere. Because Germans for two periods within living memory have suffered the devastating economic, social and political effects that followed from the complete breakdown of their monetary system, the people in general have become highly sensitive to the dangers of inflation and have therefore accepted, not with evasion or reluctance, but with ready co-operation, the disciplines imposed by their central bank to ensure the stability of the currency. Decades of rising productivity, moderation in wage claims and monetary discipline worked together to raise the prestige of the Deutsche Mark and the Bundesbank to the position where they have been able to act as model and cornerstone of the developing European Monetary System during the last two decades of the twentieth century. German monetary history is of pressing topical significance for the western world's largest economic community – of well over 300 million people. Little wonder that David Marsh, with pardonable, pointed exaggeration, subtitled his incisive study of the Bundesbank 'The Bank that Rules Europe' (Marsh 1992).

The most typical and important type of German commercial bank, economically speaking, is the 'universal' bank with its special emphasis on and relation with industrial finance. This type of bank did not emerge until the second half of the nineteenth century. Such developments were if anything more belated than in France, but, once started, proceeded apace. Before then the various German states were dependent upon private banking houses supplemented by state-sponsored companies which carried out various kinds of banking operations usually alongside other trades. First and foremost among such state banks was the Royal Prussian Seehandlung, founded by Frederick William I in 1722 to stimulate foreign trade. As well as acting as a merchant bank it granted credit – in large amounts – to the Prussian state government, and from the 1770s it also issued notes. Despite many vicissitudes it became the most powerful credit institution in Prussia in the first half of the nineteenth century (Born 1983, 28). A number of agricultural credit institutions grew up in the 1770s and 1780s in the form of state co-operatives which granted mortgages and other credit based on land, mostly to large landowners to improve their properties and farming operations. The first of these *Landschaften* was set up in Silesia in 1771. Other state-sponsored banks with less restricted aims were the Leyhaus Bank of Brunswick (1765) and the Royal Giro and Loan Bank founded by Frederick the Great in the same year. This was Germany's first note-issuing bank, later in 1846, becoming known as the Bank of Prussia, and in turn in 1875 the Reichsbank.

Outside Prussia the most important banking institutions were the private houses led by the Rothschilds of Frankfurt, which also boasted the banking houses of Bethmann Brothers and of Metzlers, making it even then the foremost banking centre in Germany. Secondly came Cologne with Herstatt (founded in 1727), Oppenheim (1789), quickly followed by Stein and Schaaffenhausen, both founded in 1790. Third in general importance but first in terms of the finance of international trade came the Hamburg houses led by the Englishman John Parish, with native houses like those of Donner, Heine and Warburg. Most of these houses became very active participants in financing the building of the railways not only in Germany but throughout central and eastern Europe. Despite the qualified successes of the state banking and credit institutions and the more obvious strengths of the private banks, new and larger sources of industrial finance were becoming increasingly essential as the nineteenth century progressed, with fundamental constitutional and fiscal changes, particularly the Zollverein of 1834 and the Münzverein of 1857, adding to the stimulation given to economic growth by improved communications.

At the beginning of the nineteenth century Germany still consisted of a mosaic of mostly petty states, dukedoms and municipalities each claiming some degree of sovereignty, the farcical remnants of what Voltaire had lampooned as 'neither Holy, nor Roman, nor an Empire'. Around 1,800 different custom barriers hindered the flow of trade, there being sixty-seven different local tariffs within Prussia alone. In the Germanic territories as a whole there were 314 sovereign regions with some 1,475 imperial knights legally entitled to some degree of fiscal authority over their manors. Even after the post-Napoleonic settlement of 1815 had reduced the number of states to thirty-nine, it was obvious to most, and most obvious to Prussia, that economic progress required much greater unity. Prussia led the way by abolishing all its internal customs between 1816 and 1818. Other states, with differing speeds, followed its example. By 1833 agreement was reached with nearly all the states to begin a full customs union (Zollverein) as from 1 January 1834. This formed the basis for a much more rapid industrialization of the German economy than would have been otherwise possible. According to Helmut Böhme, the founding of the first Kreditbanken 'was an expression of the extent to which the Customs union had participated in the economic boom between 1850 and 1857' (1978, 34). Despite the overwhelming strength of this traditional view recent researchers have attempted to play down the benefits of the customs union, e.g. R. H. Dumke considers the 'welfare gains' to have been 'relatively small', adding that German trade had already been expanding from the 1820s while British demand for German goods provided 'a greater stimulus' to the German economy 'than the Zollverein' (in W. R. Lee 1991, chapter 3).

Along with a variety of regional weights and measures the German people had to put up with a confusing plethora of coinages, currencies and units of account, foreign as well as native. The agreement on the customs union in 1833 had suggested larger regional groupings for common currencies arranged around the mark, the thaler, the gulden or the florin (the latter two usually but not always being the same value). In 1838 a convention at Dresden established fixed rates of exchange between the Prussian thaler, used mostly in northern Germany, and the gulden, widely used in the south, but at the awkward rate of 4 to 7. Further limited progress towards wider acceptance of the different currencies followed the grandiosely-named Münzverein or coinage union of 1857. German businessmen pressed for the logical solution – a single, common currency (a telling pointer to arguments in the 1990s regarding a single currency for the EEC). Eventually – but significantly not until political union had been achieved – the new Reich of 1871 adopted the gold standard with the mark as its single currency. To complete the process of monetary union the Bank of Prussia was reformed as the Reichsbank in 1875, rapidly absorbing the note issues of some thirty other state banks and replacing them with its own notes. A single kingdom, a single currency, a single note issue and a single central bank had in three-quarters of a century replaced the previously chaotic, trade-inhibiting structure, providing a springboard for German industry and banking.

The rise of German joint-stock banking may be dated from the year of European revolutions, 1848, when the difficulties of that year forced the banking house of Schaaffenhausen in Cologne to be reconstituted, with state help, as a public joint-stock company. The prompt help of the Prussian state was provided not so much to rescue the owners but rather to save its industrial customers in the Rhineland from the consequences of the bank's failure. This provides a striking early example of the close links between banking, industry and the state. The objective of stimulating industrial development is seen even more clearly in the formulation of the next joint-stock bank, the Bank für Handel und Industrie, established by a group of bankers, most of them directors of the Schaaffenhausen bank, in 1853 in the somewhat unlikely base of Darmstadt after the influence of the Rothschilds had ruled out the preferred choices of Frankfurt or Berlin (the bank being commonly thereafter also known as the Darmstädter Bank). Its original statutes empowered it 'to bring about or participate in the promotion of new companies . . . and to issue or take over the shares and debentures of such companies . . . to participate in the financial transactions and investments of governments and to carry on all banking transactions'. Its first annual report further described its aims as to 'facilitate the export trade and the thousand other relations between German industry and the money market' (Whale 1930, 12–14). The bank thus foreshadowed two of the basic characteristics which later flourished into creative fullness in the German banking system as a whole, namely industrial banking as a special feature of universal banking. These banks imitated but took to more effective lengths the basic principles of the French Crédit Mobilier by channelling the growing savings of their regions so as to speed up the industrialization preferably of their own regions, but failing that, of Germany as a whole.

A number of similar banks sprang up in the 1850s although many were soon weeded out by the economic storms of 1857, which thus provided a sharp early lesson of the risks associated with industrial banking. Among the important survivors were two Berlin banks, both formed in 1856, the Disconto-Gesellschaft, which had previously operated narrowly as a credit co-operative, and the Berliner Handels-Gesellschaft. A period of steady consolidation in the 1860s was followed by a rapid surge of joint-stock company formation, including banks, in the early 1870s, caused by three factors. First came a much more liberal company law in June 1870, secondly came the euphoria surrounding German unification in 1871, followed, thirdly by the war bounty of the French reparation payments. A veritable banking mania led to the formation of 107 joint-stock banks between 1870 and 1872. Many of these failed to withstand the 1873 crisis, but among those which did there were three which quickly grew to be among the largest and most successful of German banks: the Commerz und Disconto formed in Hamburg in March 1870, the Deutsche Bank formed in Berlin at the same time, and the Dresdner Bank formed from a previously private banking house in 1872. The two latter banks soon became household names, being linked with the older Darmstädter and the Disconto-Gesellschaft as the 'Big Four D-banks', although they never quite attained the predominant position that the 'Big Five' (later four) obtained in Britain. While the Dresdner Bank followed the traditional Crédit Mobilier route, the other two new banks followed the example of the English banks in specializing in the finance of international trade and in gathering deposits largely for that purpose, at least for the first decade or so. For a time it seemed as if German banks, like the French, were dividing themselves into either deposit banks or investment banks; but that division was never clear-cut and did not last long, with all the large banks from the 1880s emphasizing their close and continuing links with German industry as an essential part of their many-sided financial activities.

German banks usually not only retained sufficient shares of the companies they promoted to justify representation on the supervisory boards of such companies, but they also gained further representative powers on behalf of company shares deposited in their banks by their own customers. When German banks made – or make – loans to industry they have the benefit of continuously up-to-date inside information. P. Barrett Whale shows that as early as 1911 the six biggest German banks together held a total of 825 supervisory directorships widely spread among all the major sectors of manufacturing, commercial, financial and transport business (1930, 50). More recently Professor Born in his fascinating and comprehensive account of international banking gives many pages of detailed reference to the 'close and lasting links forged between individual credit institutions and certain major industrial and transport enterprises' (1983, 89). Furthermore as George T. Edwards has pointed out in his fiery polemic on *The Role of Banks in Economic Development,* holders of 25.1 per cent or more of a company's shares have certain legal powers of veto – a figure widely reached by the banks. Hence, adds Edwards, 'although German industry only appears to be 10 per cent owned by the banks, their actual power over companies is immense' (1987, 99).

The structure of German industry was influenced by the fact that German bankers particularly disliked seeing cutthroat competition among their customers, and so actively encouraged the process of cartelization in industry before the First World War. In the same spirit take-overs and mergers among the banks themselves led to each of the Big Four D-Banks being 'surrounded by a group of provincial banks working in harmony with it and more or less under its control' (Whale 1930, 29). The provincial banks however, as we shall see, were never practically extinguished as they were in England and Wales. Before switching the focus of our attention back to the currency, two other related aspects require to be noted, namely the importance of savings and co-operative banks, and the continued emphasis in policy and practice placed upon the regional factor in financial and general economic development in what has remained, whether imperial or republican, a country with a meaningful federal constitution.

One of Europe's earliest savings banks was founded in Hamburg in 1778, giving rise to a handful of similar banks in north Germany by the end of the eighteenth century. The return of peace in 1815 saw a quickened pace, with 280 savings banks formed by 1836. Thereafter the savings movement gathered an even stronger momentum, so that by 1850 there were more than 1,200 such banks. By 1913 the savings banks numbered 3,133, and had amassed assets totalling no less than 21 billion marks, or more than double the total assets of the nation's commercial banks, which stood at 9.6 billion. The local savings banks had by then become integrated in a series of regional Girozentralen, the system culminating in the Deutsche Girozentralen or the Central Bank for Savings Banks established in Berlin in 1918. Other important working-class financial institutions included two main types of credit co-operatives. The rural credit co-operatives set up by Friedrich Wilhelm Raffeisen from around 1846 were at first very modest affairs but soon mushroomed to reach 17,000 by 1914. The more urban areas similarly saw a contemporaneous rise of industrial credit co-operatives from around 1850 inspired by Herman Schultze-Delitzsch. Almost every town of any size had one or more such institutions, the total reaching 1,500 by 1913, with well over 800,000 individual members and with outstanding credits of over 1.5 billion marks. By 1930 the total number of credit co-operatives of all kinds came to around 21,500. Thereafter amalgamation strengthened the local societies but drastically reduced their numbers – from 11,795 in West Germany in

1957 to 3,042 in 1990, or to 3,380 in reunited Germany as a whole (Deutsche Bundesbank, monthly report, September 1991, Stat. 45).

As in England, the savings banks were originally intended to be simply vehicles for the exercise of thrift by the poor, and certainly not meant to encourage borrowing; but the competition of the credit co-operatives eventually led the savings banks also to grant similar facilities. Thus, quite unlike the situation in Britain where the POSB (and the TSBs until comparatively recently) syphoned local savings exclusively into government coffers and did not supply credit at all, the German working-class financial institutions increasingly became vehicles for the agricultural and industrial development of their regions, to such an extent that even by 1930 'they had become universal banks in the full sense of that term' (Born 1983, 248). Many of the larger municipal and regional savings banks competed successfully with the big nationwide universal banks to gain substantial stakes in industry, and had thus liberated their activities to a far greater extent already by the first quarter of the twentieth century than the various British savings banks had dared to dream about even by the last decade of this century. As the present writer emphasized (to the Wilson Committee), 'there is considerable justification for the view that the inadequacy of bank support (in Britain) for industry extends far back to the early days of the twentieth century' (quoted in Edwards 1987, 31). In every locality in Germany local, regional and nationwide banks compete to supply local industrialists with their particular requirements. Another example of the strength of the centrifugal pull of the regions in Germany is seen in the case of the branches of the central bank. Whereas by 1914, within forty years of its establishment, the Reichsbank had over a hundred main branches and 4,000 sub-offices, the Bank of England did not open a single branch during its first 132 years and has never had more than ten (and mostly not more than eight) branches.

German history from 1850 to 1914 thus appears to afford a striking example of the special role played by all the main sectors of the banking industry in speeding up the growth of a previously backward economy, and so, despite writings old and new to the contrary, seems to give strong confirmation of Alexander Gerschenkron's thesis on *Economic Backwardness in Historical Perspective* (1962). A recent instance of the contrary view is given by Dr Feldenkirchen who points to a number of cases where companies grew without help from their banks, or in other cases where the banks deliberately ignored wealthy customers. (Given millions of customers and thousands of banks, such micro examples do little to dent the macro-economic generalization.)

Even Dr Feldenkirchen is forced to concede that instead of speaking of a 'dependence of industrial enterprises on the banks' – which he tries to dispute – we should speak 'rather of a mutual interdependence' (1991, 135). It was this special relationship between banks and industry that helped Germany to achieve such spectacular growth in the half-century up to 1914, by which time it had overtaken England to become 'the most populated (68 million), richest and most powerful trading country in Europe' and so well equipped financially, industrially and militarily to embark confidently upon the disastrous voyage of the First World War (Böhme 1978, 87).

German fiscal policy during the war relied, like that of France, more on borrowing, particularly short-term, and less on taxation than was the case in Britain. Consequently it was basically more inflationary. With the breakdown of the international gold standard from 1914 it was the differences in relative inflation that were seen to be the major determinant of foreign exchange rates. The theory linking the internal and external value of money was most fully developed at this time by the Swedish economist, Gustav Cassell, in the form of his 'Purchasing Power Parity Theory of Money and the Foreign Exchanges'. He argued that 'Our valuation of a foreign currency in terms of our own mainly depends . . . on their relative purchasing power in their respective countries', so that when the two countries have undergone inflation 'the (new) rate will be equal to the old rate multiplied by the quotient of their relative inflation.' This provides 'the new parity, the point of balance towards which the exchange rates will always tend' (Cassell 1922, 138–40). Despite its many weaknesses, such as insufficient weight given to capital movements including reparations, and the assumption of relatively free markets, it shed a useful light at a time when international trade had grown to play so large a role in Europe's economies. Because the dollar was the least adversely affected currency of the major economies the two most commonly used indicators of the extent of the German inflation of 1914 to 1923 are the dollar rate and the note issues of the Reichsbank.

The German inflation of 1913 to 1923, and especially the hyper-inflation of 1922–3 have become for economists, historians and politicians, the classic example of all time, appropriately generating a plethora of books and papers. Fascinating and important as many of these are, only a brief look at some of the essentials can be given here. As table 10.1 shows, the external value of the mark fell by only a half in the period from 1913 to 1918 – when trade was severely controlled – despite the fact that note circulation had increased by 8.5 times. However, with the return of freer markets after the war the exchange

Table 10.1 German inflation 1913 to 1923.[1]

Year end	Reichsbank note issue	Value of one US $ in marks
1913	2593 m.	4.2
1918	22188 m.	8.0
1921	113640 m.	184.0
1922	1280100 m.	7350.0
18 Nov. 1923	92844720.7 billion[2]	4.2 billion[2]

Notes: [1] A fuller table, on which the above is based, is given in Whale 1930, 210.
[2] 'Billion' here means a million million.

rate changed from a lagged to a leading indicator as operators on the foreign exchange began to expect tomorrow's mark to be worth less than today's. The internal equivalent of such expectations led to the velocity of circulation increasing so rapidly that there was paradoxically a dire shortage of notes despite all the Reichsbank's printing works being used flat out. From August 1923 prices soared astronomically. With common necessities such as a loaf of bread or a local postage stamp costing one hundred thousand million marks, daily wage negotiations preceded work, wages were paid twice a day and promptly and completely spent within the hour. Large sections of society, including the middle classes, became impoverished; food riots were common; there was a complete flight from money, which had plainly become worthless to hold.

The explanation as to why the German authorities acted so as to generate such an inflationary spiral is, in retrospect, readily discernible. First was the fact that, initially, the economy as a whole seemed to benefit, thus setting the country on the slippery slope. Then came the realization that certain influential sectors benefited enormously to the very end or nearly so. Such favoured groups included farmers and industrialists with mortgages, all net debtors, including the provincial states and the central government, helped by the hugely negative real rates of interest. Borrowing was rewarded and reconstruction received a strong boost. Registered unemployment in Germany in October 1922 was only 1.4 per cent, compared with 14 per cent in Britain and over 15 per cent in 'neutral' Sweden (Born 1983, 219). France was convinced that the inflation was a trick to escape the burdens of reparations and so sent its army, with that of the Belgians, into the Ruhr in January 1923. A general strike ensued, leading to a drastic fall not only in coal production but also in coal exports in which reparations were partly paid. In retaliation the French blocked fiscal payments from the occupied territories to the Reich government, substantially increasing the budgetary deficit, which in turn was met by merrily printing still more money. Inflation seemed to provide an easy way out of the difficulties facing the weak Weimar Republic.

Nevertheless as 1923 wore on, the beguiling short-term advantages of inflation became submerged by the harsh realities of social and economic chaos, the return of barter and the dangers of civil war. On 15 November 1923 the old currency was replaced by a new, temporary, currency, the Rentenmark. This transitional currency was secured on mortgages on land and industrial property, and more importantly was limited to a total issue of 3.2 milliard marks. The necessary discipline was reinforced when Dr Hjalmar Schacht became president of the Reichsbank in December 1923. In the next few months the Dawes Plan was drawn up to provide a solution to the reparations problem and to lead Germany back to the gold standard. As from 1 September 1924 Germany returned to the gold standard though, as was to become customary, without internal gold coin circulation. The new currency, the Reichsmark, equivalent to the pre-war gold mark, had to carry a reserve of 40 per cent, of which at least three-quarters was to be in gold. Furthermore the London Agreement (which ratified the Dawes Plan) insisted upon the independence of the Reichsbank, and strictly limited the maximum loans which the bank could make to the government. Germany's monetary ills appeared for a while to have been cured, but renewed financial difficulties in the early 1930s paved the way for the rise of Hitler and the loss once more by the Reichsbank of its hard-won but short-lived independence. It is worth repeating here that the price of monetary – and therefore of other – liberties is eternal vigilance.

The recurring financial crisis of 1929–33 had two underlying elements; the vast size and volatility of international liquid, short-term assets on the one hand and the marked decline in the value of medium- and long-term loans and shares in the portfolios of banks on the other. British banks were worried chiefly by the former, for it was that volatility that led to sterling's departure from gold in September 1931: the banks in Britain had remained solid and secure. German and Austrian banks suffered from both features, including not only the withdrawal by American and other foreign investors of liquid deposits, 'hot money' in flight for political as well as economic reasons, but also were extremely vulnerable to the sharp decline in the value of their medium- and long-term loans to and shares in shaky industrial customers. The first to collapse was the Creditanstalt, Austria's largest bank, which closed its doors on 11 May 1931. The panic spread quickly to involve the big German banks, the most vulnerable of which, the Darmstädter and National Bank (the 'Danat'), closed on 13 July 1931. The Austrian bank was reopened only after an international rescue operation had been arranged by Montagu Norman. To forestall a run on the other German banks an extended Bank Holiday was announced, lasting for a fortnight, with the German banks eventually opening again on 5 August. In the mean time an international financial conference was held in London from 21 to 23 July, at which US President Hoover proposed a one-year moratorium on international political debts, including German reparations. Despite strong French reluctance (since they rightly, if prematurely, feared a German–Austrian 'Anschluss'), this was accepted, providing a basis for the almost-final settlement of reparations and inter-Allied war debts and giving time for the German authorities to prepare plans for strengthening their perilous banking system.

As part of this process the Danat was merged with the Dresdner Bank, with the state taking up about 90 per cent of the shares. Similar capital restructuring saw 70 per cent of the shares of the Commerzbank and over 33 per cent of the capital of the Deutsche Bank being owned – temporarily – by the state, although these share holdings were reprivatized by 1936. A more permanent reform was provided by the Banking Act of 1934. This set up, for the first time a national Banking Supervisory Board, authorized to license every bank and to receive monthly reports from all the banks in which details of all loans of RM 1 million or more had to be provided. As a result of the crisis the banks reined back on their previously aggressive lending policies, the new restrictions helping to push German unemployment to over five million by mid-1932. After the social turmoil of the next six months Hitler was installed as Chancellor in January 1933. From then onwards the financial system and the economy in general were geared to rearmament. Reichsbank President Schacht introduced rigid exchange controls with an effective range of multiple exchange rates which not only helped limit balance of payment deficits but also assisted the drive for 'autarky' or self-sufficiency by reducing reliance on key imports.

The early victories gained by Germany in the war of 1939–45 generously supplied her with greatly enlarged resources to add to those coming from a much improved fiscal regime, compared with that of 1914–18, including high-yielding income and other taxes. Thus whereas only 13 per cent of government expenditure in the First World War came from taxation, in the Second this percentage rose to 48. Such measures, together with a compulsory price freeze, enabled the German authorities very effectively to suppress inflation until near the war's end in May 1945. By then, with devastation all around, the economy as a whole as well as its monetary sector virtually ceased to function. In the official markets ration cards and permits were far more important than currency, while in the black market, as any old soldier in the invading armies will recall, cigarettes, soap, bully beef and chocolate became preferred items of currency. The Allied occupation powers initially enforced their divide-and-rule policies with regard to German industrial and financial combines. This 'decartelization policy' was applied both to the big commercial banks and to the central banking system. The Deutsche, the Dresdner and Commerz banks were each split up into legally separate entities in each of the German provinces, while no bank was allowed to own branches outside its own province, thus reflecting American banking theories and practices. This divisive policy began to be reversed in the three western zones as Allied co-operation with Russia changed into the Cold War, with West Germany joining the European Recovery Programme by October 1949 and so benefiting from the precious dollars of the Marshall Plan. As for the legally separated big banks, each of their divisions in practice began acting increasingly in a co-ordinated fashion, Gradually the law caught up with practice. In 1952 the Law on the Regional Scope of Credit Institutions divided the Federal Republic into three banking zones, within each of which branching was allowed to spread until finally in December 1956 the Act to Terminate the Restriction on the Regional Scope of Credit Institutions again allowed nationwide freedom, so far as West Germany was concerned, with East Germany included after July 1990.

With regard to central banking, the modifications significantly retained and in some ways reinforced the regional element because this conformed both to American and German federal tendencies. The former Reichsbank was at first in 1948 replaced by a legally autonomous 'Landesbank' in each province, with the necessary degree of co-ordination being supplied by the Bank Deutscher Länder in Frankfurt. This system was easily modified by the Banking Act 1957 setting up the Deutsche Bundesbank with its head office still in Frankfurt and with its eleven Länder central banks each with its own branch system, the largest, North-Rhine-Westphalia, having as many as fifty branches.

Having twice suffered the worst evils of inflation within a single generation the German people were fully behind the government in conceding such a high degree of autonomy to the Bundesbank as to make it the most independent central bank in the world, considerably more so than the US Fed that had been its original model. Its constitution granted its president a normally secure eight-year period of office and specifically stated that the bank was to be 'independent of instructions of the federal government' although being 'bound in so far as is consistent with its functions, to support the general economic policy of the federal government'. Its one simple, clear objective is given in the Bundesbank Act as 'regulating the amount of money in circulation and of credit supplied to the economy, using the powers conferred on it by this Act with the aim of safeguarding the currency'. There was no misconstrued Keynesian nonsense here – as was shown in the almost contemporary Radcliffe Report in Britain – regarding the unimportance of the money supply or of the exaggerated difficulties in measuring, let alone controlling, it, nor of the acquiescence in rubber-stamping the inflationary demands of government. On the contrary, it has been the success of the Bank Deutscher Länder and of the Bundesbank in safeguarding the currency during the second half of the twentieth century, when so many other central banks have dismally failed in that duty, that has made the German central bank a model for international imitation, and especially in formulating current plans of a European central bank – at least until the European slump of 1990–3.

The German central banking system could not have achieved such an enviable record had it not been provided right from the start with a reformed currency in a free market economy. The currency reform of 1948 has been adjudged by Professor Kindleberger as 'one of the great feats of social engineering of all time' (1984, 418). On Sunday 20 June 1948 the Reichsmark was replaced by the Deutsche Mark at a ratio of 10:1, except for an initial personal allowance of DM 40 at a rate of one-for-one. Simultaneously the economics minister, Ludwig Erhard, announced the ending of most of the previous restrictions, such as the freeze on prices and wages and most of the rationing system. The resultant economic miracle was 'the miracle of a free market' (Friedman and Friedman 1980, 79). The ability to exchange goods into worthwhile money that retained its value proved to be an enormous incentive, bringing goods out of hiding into the open market and providing the savings for a prolonged investment drive, not into welfare services, which would then have seemed unjustifiable extravagance, but into more directly productive manufacturing industry and basic infrastructure. The West German currency and economic reforms of 1948 thus provide a pertinent and topical lesson for the former communist, command economies of eastern Europe and the USSR.

It is interesting to see that when, as a special part of this process, the Federal Republic and the German Democratic Republic decided on economic, social and monetary union by the Treaty of 1 July 1990, it was the view of Chancellor Helmut Kohl that prevailed against that of the Bundesbank's President Otto Pöhl, who had previously publicly decried as 'fantastic' the very idea of one-for-one exchange rate between the West and East German marks. Although a general (and still generous) rate of DM 1:OM 2 was applied to all business and to large personal holdings, a personal preferential rate was conceded at one-for-one to a maximum limit of 2,000 marks for children below fourteen years; a maximum of 4,000 for persons from fourteen to fifty-nine and a maximum of 6,000 for older persons. Thus, says Professor Ellen Kennedy, in her illuminating study, *The Bundesbank*, 'the Bank lost on the issue of a currency union between two very different economies' (1991, 109). Chancellor Kohl's gamble (giving the small person, i.e. most of the voters, a bonus) appeared initially to have worked well, for claimed the Bundesbank, with premature optimism, 'since the monetary union the West German economy has grown much more strongly than before . . . and in 1990 experienced its eighth successive year of economic upswing' (Deutsche Bundesbank Monthly Report, October 1991, 14). The state bank system of East Germany was modified to fit the western system while the Bundesbank formally assumed responsibility for domestic and external monetary policy over the whole of the reunited country.

In concluding this outline of German monetary and banking development it is necessary to point out that despite considerable apparent concentration in banking since 1957, Germany remains a country where the big three commercial banks, the Deutsche, Dresdner and Commerz, ranked eleventh, twenty-fifth and thirty-sixth in the world, (*The Banker*, July 1991) are still faced with strong competition from over 4,000 other banking institutions, a large number of which offer universal banking just like the big banks and with 335 being classed as 'commercial banks'. In addition, as in most continental countries, Germany's Postbank provides a widely used payments system, with 4.8 million giro accounts in 1990. Thus the structural complexity of the German banking system allows local, regional and nationwide banks to overlap and enjoy a lively competitive co-existence. Such competition has been particularly effective in stimulating Germany's consistently high personal savings ratio, which, according to the Bundesbank, was a significant factor in raising West Germany's per capita income to one-third above the EC average (Monthly Report, October 1993). The structural picture is summarized in table 10.2, showing a marked decline in bank numbers together with a corresponding strong increase in branches. Most of the concentration took place between 1957 and 1977, during which the number of banks

Table 10.2 Number of banks and branches in Germany 1957–1990.

Year	No. of banks	No. of branches	Total offices
1957	13359	12974	26333
1967	10859	26285	37144
1977	5997	37764	43761
1987	4543	39913	44456
1990a	4170	39807	43977
1990b*	4711	43559	48270
1991	4451	44862	49313
1992	4191	48645	52836

Source: Bundesbank Monthly Report, August 1993, table 23.
*Figures from 1990b onwards include East Germany, all previous figures being for West Germany only.

fell to less than half their former number whereas total branch numbers practically trebled. Thereafter the number of banks fell only very gradually so that, making allowance for reunification, there has been a remarkable stability in the number of branches and in total offices. The stability of the currency has thus been matched by aggregate stability in the banking system as a whole, (until the monetary union), a stability which masks the dynamism of its individual components.

It was however to Germany's central banking system, working within an economy with rising productivity supplied by industry-wide unions, that the inflation-weary eyes of the rest of the world turned with much admiration and yearning, as providing an anchor for Europe's Exchange Rate Mechanism and a model for a European central bank which in due course was confidently expected to become the centre of gravity of a European System of (Independent) Central Banks. The real cost of reunion to West Germany and, indirectly to the rest of the EC, was soon seen to be much heavier than originally anticipated, in that it helped to increase inflationary pressures in Germany just when unemployment was rising there and elsewhere. There were already nearly eighteen million unemployed in the Community by 1992, and it was feared that this would rise to twenty million if interest rates were not quickly and substantially reduced. Such high rates of unemployment were incompatible with the high rates of interest needed to keep EC currencies on track towards a single currency anchored to the Deutsche Mark. Hence came the monetary crises of 1992–3 which led to the virtual disruption of the Exchange Rate Mechanism. The history of the 1930s was being repeated in the 1990s. Other countries should not however blame the Bundesbank for the results of their own previous monetary mismanagement. From being a long-run ideal, the Bundesbank was turned into a temporary scapegoat with Dr Helmut Schlesinger, like Montagu Norman sixty-seven years earlier, taking the role of unemployment-raising, sound-money villain. Nevertheless, the European Union's long-run commitment to financial rectitude was reaffirmed in October 1993 by the decision to site the European Monetary Institute, and hence eventually the European Central Bank, in Frankfurt, thus giving greater credibility to the expectation that the Ecu will graft itself on to the well-rooted reputation of the Deutsche Mark.

The monetary development of Japan since 1868

Introduction: the significance of banks in Japanese development

No major country in the world has managed to achieve such a remarkably sustained record of economic growth as that attained, with few interruptions by Japan, in comparison with which even the German post-1950 economic miracle falls very much into second place. It is no coincidence that in no other country has support for industry from the banks, together with the active encouragement of government, been so strong and continuous. Long-term perspectives tend to predominate over short-term expediency both in industry and in banking. Japanese banks have long discovered that the best way of helping themselves has been to aid industrial growth through medium- and long-term lending as well as by short-term, operational loans. While the Japanese economy has overtaken the rest of the world to come second only to the USA, her banks have grown without any doubt into the world's largest. In 1990 no US bank appeared in the world's top twenty, whereas Japan had no less than nine banks in the top twenty, and as many as six in the top ten (*The Banker*, July 1991). The four biggest banks in the world, all Japanese, together owned assets in 1990 totalling $1,634,548 million, a total not reached even by the sum of the assets of America's thirty biggest banks.

Furthermore it is not as if the Japanese banking system is so highly concentrated that the giants have inhibited the growth of other large and medium-sized competitive banks. On the contrary, so vigorous has been the growth of large and medium-sized banks that altogether Japan has 109 banks listed in the world's top thousand. British banks, despite their greater concentration, have only thirty-five in the top thousand, while the assets of these thirty-five together come to only 70 per cent of the total held by the four biggest Japanese banks. Neither is it the case that Japanese banks have grown only because of their naturally privileged position inside the successful Japanese economy – though that has been the foundation factor and remains the major reason for their robust strength. Nevertheless when tested outside their home base, for example in the highly competitive 'neutral' market of London, Japanese banks (as detailed in chapter 8) have come to hold by far the largest share of assets among foreign banks, the Japanese total being £252,754 million in June 1990, around twice the total held by American banks, at £128,507 million (*BEQB* August 1991).

It is abundantly clear from the Japanese example that the close involvement of banks in industry, if properly developed, does not, as feared in Britain, inhibit or endanger the growth of the banking industry – a fear once more strongly but falsely paraded during the 1990–2 recession. (It was not lending long to British industry but rather to property companies and Third World countries that led to the large banking losses in Britain and America, even though domestic industries were punished by heavier costs and restricted lending as if they were the guilty parties.) Japanese history provides the world's most powerful demonstration of the mutual benefits that the banks as well as their industrial customers gain from their close interrelationship, and at the same time exposes the myth, nurtured for a century by conventional British bankers and complacent governments, that only through their cold and cautious avoidance of long-term commitments to industry can British banks avoid failure. It is this glaring contrast in banking philosophy that gives the Japanese experience of banking development its special significance. This development may now be conveniently traced in three periods from the Meiji restoration in 1868 up to the end of the First World War, then from 1918 to 1948 and finally the subsequent period to the present, encompassing the world's greatest economic miracle.

Westernization and adaptation, 1868–1918
Modern banking in Japan first started with the Meiji restoration of 1868, which ended the barren isolationist policy previously pursued and which began deliberately fostering the modernization of its economy through first imitating and then adapting western models to its own particular requirements. Perceptive adaptation was equally, if not more important than eager imitation in explaining the speed with which Japan caught up with the West. Although a few pre-Meiji rudimentary banking organizations had been developed by the Zaibatsu baronial family groups to provide financial services for their trading enterprises, mostly in the form of exchange offices, these were completely inadequate to meet the needs of liberalized trade after 1868. The pre-

Meiji regime had left the monetary system in such a state of chaos that a reformed currency was urgently needed, together with a completely novel banknote circulation, which in turn required the rapid establishment of banks of issue. The 1871 Currency Act established the national Mint at Osaka, introduced the decimal system of yen and sen, and indicated the government's intention to change from its traditional silver standard to the increasingly fashionable gold standard, although it was not until the successful conclusion of the Sino-Japanese war of 1894–5 had provided Japan with sufficient gold reserves that eventually in 1897 the gold standard was officially adopted.

Meanwhile the Japanese authorities had turned to America to provide the model for its commercial banks, and to Belgium for the constitution of its central bank. Leading the way as the first bank to be established under the American-like rules of the National Bank Act of 1872 was the Dai-Ichi Bank set up in 1873 by the government with the support of some of the larger Zaibatsu banks. However the regulations of that Act were soon seen to be inappropriate to Japanese conditions, and only three other banks were formed until the Act was modified in 1876. Thereafter there was a surge in bank formation, with the numbers increasing rapidly to reach 153 by 1879. A further pointer to Japanese adaptability was the tacit permission to allow unofficial quasi-banks to operate alongside the official banks in carrying out financial operations, including note issue. However, the plethora of local note issues was confusing and unreliable, thus adding to the pressures leading to the setting up of a central bank with a centralized, and eventually single and uniform, note issue.

The Bank of Japan was established in 1882 following an investigative visit by the minister of finance to Europe in the previous year. He took as his model the National Bank of Belgium for, after all, the Americans had no central bank and the Bank of England no written constitution. The National Bank of Belgium, a country which had closely followed Britain in industrialization, possessed a written constitution and had been formed in the relatively recent past, in 1850. As the Japanese Prime Minister later explained: 'After careful study and comparison of the central banking system of Europe we found the Bank of Belgium was peerless . . . consequently it was decided to adopt the Belgian system' (Goodhart 1985, 144). Gradually the Bank of Japan expanded its own note issues to replace those of other banks, a process completed by 1899, when all other notes ceased to be legal tender and Bank of Japan notes were fully convertible into gold. The goal of an efficient currency system had thus been finally achieved by the end of the century, by which time the Bank of Japan had become not only 'the central feature in the consolidation of the monetary, banking and credit systems' but also 'the cornerstone of the modernisation of the Japanese economy and of the development of modern industries' (Pressnell 1973, 10). Two of the main methods by which the Bank of Japan had achieved these results were by its consistent downward pressure on interest rates for privileged purposes and its encouragement of special banks set up to provide long-term loans to industry.

By 1901 the number of banks had reached its peak of 1,867. Thereafter amalgamation and merger reduced the numbers, especially of the weaker banks, and so increased the average size and strength of the banks. Among the most powerful of such banks were those established by the Zaibatsu. Thus the Mitsui family managed to upgrade their exchange bureau into the Mitsui Bank in 1876, followed by the Mitsubishi Bank and the Yasuda Bank, both formed in Tokyo in 1880. In 1895 the Sumitomo Bank was established in Osaka. Having been built on widespread family trading empires that in some cases stretched back for centuries, the Zaibatsu banks were from the beginning much larger and stronger than most of the other banks and grew to absorb many of these; e.g. the Yasuda Bank had absorbed seventeen other banks by 1912. The Zaibatsu banks have concentrated mainly but not exclusively on accommodating the needs of their own industrial, commercial and financial combines particularly in granting long-term finance, a selective and preferential policy justified to the extent that the lending bank has a very close knowledge of the assisted firm and they both have a long-lasting mutual commitment to each other. Short-term operational finance was more widely and readily supplied even to companies outside their empire. Thus in their long-term lending they mirrored the German banks, while in their deposit-gathering and short-term business lending they imitated traditional English banking. In this way the Zaibatsu banks paved the way for the general adoption of 'universal'-type banking by the Japanese commercial banks.

Other important types of banks also emerged in the Meiji period (1868–1912). These include the savings banks, whose number had risen to 441 by 1901, having increased twentyfold from a mere score of such banks ten years earlier. Wherever the government perceived special needs or gaps in the financial system it stepped in to meet the need or fill the gap itself or prodded others to, rather than adopting a *laissez-faire* attitude and allowing the market to do so in its leisurely way, if ever. In particular the government helped to establish special banks to assist the growth of the export trade and to supply long-term loans to large and small industrial companies. The earliest of such special banks was the Yokohama Specie Bank, privately founded in 1880 but with a third of its capital supplied by the government, which took a guiding interest in its activities. Its first task was to replace the control exerted by foreign banks and merchants over the financing of Japanese overseas trade. It co-operated closely with the Bank of Japan in financing exports and in channelling the proceeds into the reserves of the Bank of Japan, the Japanese exporters gaining through being given immediate credit or fully convertible notes rather than having to wait until the foreigner's bank paid up or discounted, at a not particularly favourable rate, their bills of exchange. In favourable contrast, the Bank of Japan provided finance to discount trade bills at the cheap rate of 2 per cent, most of it via the Yokohama Specie Bank. This latter bank was granted a virtual monopoly in the financing of Japanese trade, and for this purpose found it convenient to establish at an early date branches in places like London, San Francisco and New York.

The Hypothec banking law of 1896 provided umbrella legislation under which a number of different kinds of specially favoured industrial and agricultural banks were set up. First came the Hypothec Bank of Japan, established in 1897 to provide the larger farmers and entrepreneurs with long-term loans. Under the same law the government gave subsidies for the establishment in each of Japan's forty-six prefectures of banks to supply similar long-term loans, but tailored to the small-scale requirements of the local communities concerned. Still more regionally orientated finance was provided by the Hokkaido Colonial Bank, set up in 1899 for strengthening the economy of this remote northern province. In addition, the Industrial Bank of Japan was established in 1900 to provide long-term loans and debentures to assist the development in particular of the mining and metallurgical industries. In 1906 Japan became, with Switzerland, the first country to follow Austria's lead in developing the postal giro system. According to Britain's Fabian Society the Japanese postal service was by 1916 'more up to date than our own country' (Davies 1973, 79).

Certainly in terms of military power (perhaps the main motive behind the drive to industrialize) Japan was already catching up with the West, as was clearly demonstrated by her victory in the war with Russia in 1904–5. The First World War greatly stimulated Japanese industry, shipping and shipbuilding, so that by 1918 another milestone in her economic progress had been passed, as she turned from being a debtor into a creditor country.

Depression, recovery and disaster, 1918–1948
In contrast to the previous period when economic trends pointed strongly upwards and the banks, despite occasional and relatively minor failures, generally prospered and expanded at a rapid rate, the thirty years from 1918 unfortunately contained only a few bright spots separated by long intervals of gloom, failure and difficulty, culminating in the disastrous results of the Second World War. By 1920 the boom generated by the First World War had petered out, ushering in a chronic depression. The economy had by no means recovered when on 1 September 1923 Tokyo with its port of Yokohama, the country's economic and financial centre, was hit by an earthquake which killed around 140,000 people and devastated large areas of the city (see *The Economist*, 7 December 1991).* The government imposed a one-month moratorium, while the Bank of Japan co-ordinated the activities of all the main banks to finance the massive programme of reconstruction that was urgently required. The country had barely recovered from this natural disaster when in March 1927 another financial crisis began with a run on the Bank of Taiwan (Taiwan had been a colony of Japan since 1895). A number of that Bank's important customers, including the large Suzuki conglomerate, then under suspicion, had also been granted long-term loans by other banks in Tokyo and Osaka. Consequently the banking panic in Taiwan quickly spread to the banks in these two centres, forcing the closure of a number of banks there. Eventually as many as thirty-seven banks were closed, at least temporarily. To meet the immediate difficulties, the government resorted to its usual device of a moratorium, which lasted for three weeks during which the Bank of Japan organized a programme of assistance. The depth of the crisis had however made it quite clear that fundamental changes were required to re-establish a sound banking system. The 1920s had exposed the vulnerable side of an industrial banking system – although it must be stressed that the Zaibatsu banks remained strong and, as we shall see, became even stronger through picking up the pieces after the débâcle. It was not industrial banking as such that was to blame but rather the dangers of lending too much too long to weak businesses by banks with insufficient capital and poor management.

To meet these dangers the Bank Act of 1927 was passed, stipulating, first, that the designation 'bank' was to be more strictly defined, thus diverting business away from some of the quasi-banks to institutions where their business was likely to be more carefully examined before loans were granted. Secondly, the designated banks were to be prohibited from engaging in non-banking activities: in other words they had to concentrate on being simply banks. Thirdly, a stronger system of

*Contrast the effects of the Kobe earthquake of 17 January 1995 – see pp. 665 and 670.

bank supervision was laid down. Fourthly, limitations were placed on the freedom to open branches. Fifthly, and possibly most important of all, minimum capital requirements were substantially raised, increasing with the size of the town in which the bank's head office was situated. This latter measure alone disqualified more than half the number of banks then in existence. The already marked trend towards amalgamation was thus greatly speeded up, with the number of banks falling from 1,400 in 1926 to 683 by 1932 and to 418 by 1937. In contrast the Zaibatsu banks, as indicated, greatly increased their relative importance, with the five biggest banks increasing their share of total deposits from 24 per cent in 1926 to 37 per cent in 1930 (Pressnell 1973, 26). Amalgamation similarly led to a dramatic reduction in the number of savings banks from 636 in 1921 to 124 in 1926, and down to just seventy-two in 1936. By then military adventures were beginning to dictate economic policy and financial priorities. Having become a great international trading nation Japan was at first deeply affected by the Wall Street crash and the subsequent world slump; but with a remarkable resilience, largely overlooked by western economists, Japan rapidly recovered from this greatest of all world depressions.

It managed to cling on to the gold standard for some months after sterling left gold in September 1931, until, following an alarming loss of reserves, the yen too went off gold on 17 December 1931. In Japan's case there was an additional reason in that her military actions along Manchuria's border with China on 18 September 1931 had frightened foreign creditors into accelerating their withdrawals of gold from Japan. Thereafter, inspired by the finance minister, Korekiyo Takahashi, Japan embarked on an external policy of manipulated exchange rates and an internal policy of controlled inflation, a striking combination of Schachtian and Keynesian economics that was particularly effective. Reflation and competitive devaluation stimulated production and exports (leading to loud complaints of 'dumping' from the USA and Britain) and enabled Japan to devote increasing resources to rearmament in the years leading to its entry into the Second World War on 7 December 1941. It was by means of 'Takahashi finance', wrote Professor Takafusa Nakamura that 'Japan climbed out of the depression even as other countries remained mired in it, enjoying an expansion that calls to mind the high-growth period of the post-war years' – as is shown in figure 10.1 (1989, 6).

Only three aspects of war finance need to be noted: first, the complete priority by which the banks financed the borrowing requirements of the munitions industries; secondly, the support which all the banks gave to government bond issues; and thirdly, the impetus

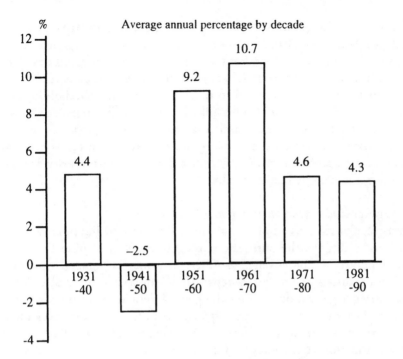

Source: Takafusa Nakamura, *Economic Eye*, Tokyo Summer 1989 and 1990.
Figure 10.1 Real economic growth rates in Japan, 1931–1990.

towards amalgamation. Between 1936 and 1945 total lending by the commercial banks increased eightfold, but the number of banks fell from 418 to 61. The fall in the number of savings banks was even more dramatic, from sixty-nine in 1940 to only four in 1945. Many of these savings banks were absorbed by the big commercial banks for, in order to provide further assistance to war financing, the regulations were modified to allow the commercial banks to open savings accounts. Amalgamation among some of the big banks also took place, such as that between the Mitsui and the Dai-Ichi banks. In such ways, with the financial, administrative and industrial powers of the Zaibatsu being still further strengthened during the war, they were seen as the economic heart of the military machine.

Not surprisingly, therefore, as soon as the war ended, one of the first economic policy decisions of the American occupying forces was to pass anti-monopoly and de-centralization laws in an effort to break up the Zaibatsu and to separate their banking activities from their industrial bases. In a series of directives between September 1945 and the middle of 1948 the Allied authorities closed down a number of the

Japanese special banks such as the Yokohama Specie Bank and the Bank of Taiwan (although the former was later reopened as a commercial bank called the Bank of Tokyo). As in American practice, the authorities insisted on the separation between 'commercial' and 'investment' banking and tried to reduce inter-group shareholdings. It seemed as if the traditional close links between the big Japanese banks and their basic industries, a link that had enabled Japan to rise so rapidly into a first-class economic – and military – power, were to be permanently severed. However, within the space of just a few years the picture again changed dramatically.

Resurgence and financial supremacy, 1948–1990
It was fear of the spread of communism and the growing international tensions leading to the outbreak of the Korean War in June 1950 that brought about a rapid reversal of American policy in Japan. The former policy of insisting on harsh reparations, breaking up viable large enterprises, rigid rationing, huge budgetary deficits, multiple exchange rates and so on, was replaced by American aid for reconstruction and a drive towards free markets as the economic counterpart of democratization. The initiator of this new approach was Joseph Dodge, a Detroit banker. Under his guidance the 1949 budget was balanced, rationing abolished, runaway inflation was brought under control and a single rate of exchange established, at 360 yen to the US dollar, which was to last unchanged for twenty-two years. From mid-1950 Japan benefited very considerably from being the main Asiatic base for the supplies needed for the Korean War, its services in this way bringing in a bounty averaging $800 million each year between 1951 and 1953, all the more welcome for coming at a time of world dollar shortage. These precious dollars reinforced the Dodge free-market policy, together playing a crucial role in setting Japan's reindustrialization in motion.

Special banks were again set up wherever any gaps were perceived, e.g. to assist in financing exports and to grant long-term loans for industrial and regional development. Among these were the Export Bank founded in 1950 (and becoming the Export-Import Bank in 1952); the Japan Development Bank (1951) and the Small Business Finance Corporation (1953). Local co-operation and savings banks were permitted to resume with greater freedom than before. The Zaibatsu re-emerged, all the more quickly because, unlike the situation in Germany where the Big Three Banks as well as the cartels were broken up, in Japan by contrast the Zaibatsu banks had been kept intact and simply cut off from the rest of the group business. The leaders of the Mitsui, Mitsubishi and Sumitomo Zaibatsu had continued their habit of regular weekly meetings, so that as soon as the Peace Treaty of 1952 returned governmental authority to the Japanese, the American-type anti-trust laws were repealed and the Zaibatsu, complete with their core banks, were rapidly reconstituted. Moreover a number of other industrial groupings sprang up, each with their own favoured and partly owned bank at its centre. These are the 'Keiretsu' of horizontally and/or vertically integrated groups, whose councils, consisting mainly of the group's directors and chief executives – an effective blend of seniority and meritocracy – hold regular meetings. These afford opportunities to discuss matters such as key staff appointments and the broad outlines of the group's long-term policies in a leisurely and confidential manner. By common consent the monetary, industrial and trade policies of the Bank of Japan, the Ministry of Finance and of MITI (the Ministry of International Trade and Industry) are digested, co-ordinated and more effectively applied because of the existence of such 'Keiretsu' and the spirit of consensus which they engender. The central role of the banks is obvious in this group network.

The most internationally visible sign of the recovery of Japan's basic industries was seen when in 1956 it had achieved first place in world shipbuilding. Thereafter, through meticulous long-term planning based on the near-certainty of sufficient supplies of long-term finance at relatively low rates of interest, a number of other specific industrial sectors were targeted, including motor-cycles, cars, electronic equipment and heavy earth-moving vehicles. As well as long-term bank loans, much of the equity finance was provided by the industrial groups related to the target industry with a commitment to its success, proving to be stable rather than volatile investors, accustomed to taking a long-term perspective. These are just a few examples of the industrial sectors contributing to the export-led growth of the Japanese economy. In every case, though far from being the only factor, the financial aspects were of central importance to the success of the Japanese economic miracle, the most substantial and sustained example of economic resurgence in world history, the remarkable extent of which is illustrated over the long term in figure 10.1 and, in its most recent, more modest but still impressive performance, in table 10.3.

In the 1950s a young Keynesian economist, Osamu Shimomura, persuaded the authorities to endorse a startlingly ambitious plan intended to double the average income in a decade, i.e. requiring a growth rate of 7.2 per cent each year. In fact the actual average annual growth rate in the 1950s came to 9.2 per cent, and in the 1960s to an astonishing 10.7 per cent. These are not freak results obtained as an aberration in the odd year but substantial averages of around 10 per

Table 10.3 Selected economic and financial indicators, Japan 1983–1989.

Year	1983	1984	1985	1986	1987	1988	1989
Real GNP growth %	3.2	5.1	4.9	2.5	4.5	5.7	4.9
Retail prices increases %	1.9	2.3	2.0	0.6	0.1	0.7	2.3
Unemployment %	2.6	2.7	2.6	2.8	2.8	2.5	2.3
Money supply M2 & CDs %	7.4	7.8	8.4	8.7	10.4	11.2	9.9
Balance of payments surplus, current a/c, US $ million	20799	35003	49169	85845	87015	79631	57157
Gold & foreign exchange reserves, US $ million	23262	24498	26510	42239	81479	87662	84895
Yen per US $ average annual rate*	237.53	238.58	238.54	168.51	144.62	128.15	137.96

* The rate of 360 was fixed in 1949 and lasted unchanged until August 1971.
Source: Economic Eye (winter 1989 and summer 1990).

cent for the two decades between 1950 and 1970. To a country as heavily dependent on imported fuel as Japan, the oil shock of 1973 initially had a tremendous impact, helping to push up retail prices by 23 per cent in 1974. However, the necessary adjustments were quickly made, and although the growth of the earlier 'miracle' years has never been regained, the subsequent average of around 4.5 per cent for the years from 1970 to 1990, built upon a higher base, is still significantly higher than that of other major economies.

By the mid-1970s Japan had overtaken the USA in average income per head, at least according to Japanese official statistics. For the five major non-communist economies the comparative per capita income figures, in descending order, for 1988 were as follows; Japan $23,382; USA $19,813; West Germany $19,741; France $16,962; UK $14,658 (Institute of Social and Economic Affairs, Statistical Abstract, Tokyo, October 1991, 12). Based on the secure backing of a large and growing home market, Japanese exports soared to give it the highest balance of payments surpluses ever earned by any country in absolute terms, reaching $87 billion in 1987 and giving an annual average of around $60 billion for the five-year period to 1989 (table 10.3). These export earnings have been shared among increases in Japan's holdings of gold and foreign exchange reserves, aid to Third World countries, and above all in the form of direct and portfolio investment abroad. They also led to a substantial reduction in Japanese import tariffs and to continuing attempts to reduce Japan's many subtle forms of 'invisible' import barriers. The external flow of capital has been strongly supplemented by the diversion of domestic savings from Japan to benefit from the much higher rates of interest available in the USA. Japan has been exporting its goods, its savings and, as a method of getting around quota restrictions, its factories also, in the form of direct investment abroad. Most of the Japanese investment has naturally gone to the USA, its largest export market, while substantial amounts have also been invested in Britain as a gateway to the EC, bringing significant benefits in reducing regional unemployment. Thus in the mid-1970s the present writer commented that 'Japanese firms, from what is still likely to be the world's fastest growing economy, are already evident in Wales and will probably become an increasingly important source of overseas investment' (Davies and Thomas 1976, 198). Despite occasional carping criticism of Japanese purchases of highly visible investments like the Rockefeller Centre in New York or the former *Financial Times* building in London, most Japanese investment has had positive effects on the recipient countries, whether backward or advanced. The USA's double deficits have been substantially financed by Japanese investments, without which US interest rates would have been higher, with greater braking effects on US growth. Japan, even more than Germany, has thus from time to time acted as the locomotive pulling other economies along.

It is a well-researched thesis that the total value of financial institutions rises faster than national wealth, a feature known to economists ever since the pioneering work of Professor Goldsmith as the 'Financial Inter-Relations Ratio' or FIR (Goldsmith 1969). It should therefore come as no surprise to note that whereas Japan's economy in absolute terms is the non-communist world's second largest, after the USA, when reckoned in terms of the total value of its financial institutions Japan has for some years been far and away the world's largest. Thus Yaichi Shinka, professor of economics at Osaka University, in an illuminating article on 'Japan's Positive Role as the World's Banker', points out that 'People tend to think of Japan as an *economic* superpower, but its financial presence . . . more than anything else Japan is a *Financial* superpower' (1990, 22). One of the conventional conclusions of FIR theory, namely that the role of banks eventually diminishes as that of other financial institutions increases, may not follow in countries which like Germany and Japan practise universal banking or include a very wide functional range of institutions under the designation of 'banks'. Consequently Japan's premier position, in terms of total bank assets, is unlikely to be overtaken in the foreseeable future – nor is its successful record in integrated long-term industrial lending likely to be challenged.

In conclusion it should be stressed that while there are many other reasons for Japan's amazing record of economic growth combined with low unemployment, paramount among them are the financial factors. How else could Japan have become the world's financial superpower? Among these financial factors are relatively stable prices, high savings, and perhaps most important of all, a banking system which consistently, skilfully and sympathetically stands ready to supply substantial sums of long-term credit at low rates of interest to support industrial, commercial and regional development. Just as Japan carefully studied, imitated and adapted British and American models, so these latter countries could surely profit from applying the powerful lessons of recent Japanese economic and financial history.*

---

* But note Japan's banking problems of the mid-1990s, p.670.

11

Third World Money and Debt in the Twentieth Century

Introduction: Third World poverty in perspective

Although there are hundreds of millions of relatively well-to-do people in the world today, far more than ever before, yet at the same time it is also true to say that most of the world's inhabitants remain desperately poor. The relatively rich, lucky to be born in industrialized countries, form a substantial and powerful global minority, whereas the majority of the world's population, concentrated mostly in what has come to be called the Third World, suffers from chronic poverty. Individuals and even certain countries may rise above such poverty, but up to now these are rather exceptional. The general rule is that while most of the inhabitants of the western industrialized nations have risen well above abject poverty, most countries of the Third World appear to be caught in a monstrous poverty trap. Economics is now more than ever before a study not only of the wealth of nations but also of the poverty of nations. With the ending of the Cold War in the 1990s, greater opportunities exist to help deal with what has become the major problem facing mankind, namely of enabling millions of the world's poorest men and women to earn a decent living for themselves. Although 'development' means more than just economic growth, the latter provides the essential fundamental basis for the wider enhancement of life.

The term 'Third World' is so vague, variable and elastic that its use in economic analysis should always be qualified. The term originated from the post-1950 international political agenda as indicating those countries, mostly in Africa and Asia, which were non-aligned as

Table 11.1 National contrasts in income (1975 and 1985) and growth (1973–1985).

	1975	US dollars per head (% USA)	1985	(% USA)	Real annual growth rate % 1973–85
Mali	90	(1.27)	140	(0.09)	1.0
India	150	(2.12)	250	(1.52)	2.0
Nigeria	310	(4.39)	760	(4.63)	-2.5
China	350	(4.96)	1440	(8.78)	5.6
Algeria	780	(11.0)	2530	(15.43)	2.6
South Africa	1320	(18.7)	2010	(12.26)	0.0
Greece	2360	(33.4)	3550	(21.65)	1.4
United Kingdom	3840	(54.4)	8390	(51.20)	1.1
Libya	5080	(72.0)	7500	(36.40)	-2.6
France	5760	(81.6)	9550	(58.23)	1.6
West Germany	6610	(93.6)	10940	(66.71)	2.1
USA	7060	(100.0)	16400	(100.00)	1.4
Sweden	7880	(111.6)	11890	(72.50)	1.0
Switzerland	8050	(114.0)	16380	(99.88)	1.0
Kuwait	11510	(163.0)	14270	(87.01)	0.3

Source: World Bank Atlases 1977 and 1987.

between, first, the capitalistic western world, which looked to the USA as its leader, and second the communist countries, which looked to the USSR for leadership. Because policies which affected everybody were in fact being decided by the two superpowers and their supporters, in the northern hemisphere mostly, those countries to the south of these two blocs attempted to adopt common 'Third World' policies and attitudes to look after their own interests. Belief in such countervailing power was given an exaggerated boost when OPEC, whose numbers had grown from the original five countries of 1960 (four Gulf states plus Venezuela) into a dozen in 1973, had grown sufficiently powerful to enable them to force a quadrupling of the price of oil within the following year. However, as well as damaging the West, it was the non-oil 'less developed countries' (LDCs) that were hardest hit. This triggered a special session of the UN General Assembly in 1974 to call for the implementation of a 'new international economic order'. However, just as the coming of political independence to the former colonies did not bring with it economic independence, so the progress of the Third World countries has failed to live up to the earlier expectations of catching up with the West, while their inability to service their vast international debts put a brake on their growth. Some idea of the extent of the task required to catch up with the West is given in table 11.1 which selects fifteen countries, ranging from the poorest to the richest, from the 184 countries detailed in the World Bank's Atlas for 1987.

It should be emphasized that figures such as those in table 11.1 should be used only to convey rough orders of magnitude rather than precise differences. Statistics in a number of LDCs are notoriously unreliable (though the IBRD and IMF have over many years struggled to improve them and their overall comparability). Secondly, the US dollar, used as the common denominator, has fluctuated so much in the foreign exchange markets that one is forced to rely on a rather elastic ruler. GNPs are simply one component in the assessment of living standards, and because of the high degree of self-subsistence in many LDCs, their low figures, and therefore the degree of superiority of western countries, tend to be considerably exaggerated. Nevertheless when all allowances have been made for these and similar limitations, the contrasts in living standards are startling. Table 11.1 shows that the average income per head in 1975 in Kuwait, at $11,510, was over 120 times as high as that of the poorest, Mali, and 100 times as high in 1985. When oil prices were relatively higher and the exchange rate of the dollar lower, as in 1980, the then richest country, the United Arab Emirates, enjoyed a per capita income over 400 times that of the then poorest, Laos, and over 200 times as large as that of Bangladesh, with $130. In order to overcome the volatility of comparisons with the richest oil exporters, table 11.1 provides percentage comparisons with the USA, which for example show Mali's average per capita income at around 1 per cent of that of the USA. Alternative measures based on purchasing power parity have been produced by the UN which in the case of some LDCs reduce the per capita differences by factors of between 1.5 and 3.5. All the same the differences remain vast. It has been well said that 'the main effect of better statistics is not to make us change our views about the extent of poverty in the underdeveloped countries, but rather to make us attach different numbers to the scale of poverty and wealth' (D. Usher 1966, 40). It does not make much difference to a drowning man whether he is 10 feet or 30 feet under the water: particularly if the lifeguards confine their energies to disputing their measurements.

Data for aggregating countries' GNPs into total world annual production are not available, but the World Bank does provide such statistics for 151 countries comprising around 85 per cent of the world's population. The figures for 1985 show that the thirty-five poorest countries, with a total population of 2,318,000,000, had an average income per head of only $280. Their share of the total product of the 151 countries listed came to only 19 per cent. On the other hand the richest forty-eight countries with a total population of 776 million (18 per cent of the total of the 151 countries) enjoyed an average income per head of $11,630, or forty times that of the former group, and produced 81 per cent of the aggregate annual product of the 151 listed countries (World Bank Atlas 1987, 16). In plain terms, a fifth of the world's population, situated in the industrial countries, produces around 80 per cent of the world's income, while over four billion people, mostly in the Third World, are able to produce between them only about a fifth of the world's gross annual product.

Although it is legitimate, and indeed essential, to use such contrasts (bearing in mind their limitations) to place Third World poverty in perspective, and to draw attention to the massive nature of the economic problem facing the world at the end of the twentieth century, the polarization between 'developed' and 'undeveloped' countries should not lead us into the mistaken but common belief that there is an unbridgeable gap between rich and poor countries. On the contrary, as is hinted in the range shown in table 11.1, if all the countries of the world were arranged in ascending order there would be a continuous gradation from the poorest to the richest without any perceptible gap – more like beads on a string rather than uneven, shaky stepping stones across a stormy river. This important fact, plus the successful experience of a number of quite different countries that have been able to achieve high rates of growth over a considerable period, offers sound prospects for sober optimism, even among economists. The variable picture of growth and decline in the period 1973–85 given in table 11.1 is supplemented in table 11.2, where the record of the ten most successful countries, in terms of economic development, during the same thirteen-year period is given.

Of the 184 countries listed only ten had growth rates, allowing for inflation and the growth of population, of over 5 per cent annually over the thirteen-year period from 1973 to 1985 (or eleven if Montserrat with a population of only 12,000, and a growth rate of just 5.1 per cent, is included). These countries were spread among the poor to middle-income groups. None came from the industrialized countries and none was blessed with significant oil deposits. For example the corresponding growth rate for Japan was 4.5 per cent and for Saudi Arabia 1.7 per cent. It is interesting to see that these ten fast-growing economies were spread among small countries like Tonga, medium-

Table 11.2 The ten fastest-growing economies, 1973–85.

	Population 1985 (millions)	Real annual growth rate % GNP per capita
Malta	0.36	6.7
Singapore	2.55	6.5
Tonga	0.097	6.4
Botswana	1.07	6.4
Hong Kong	5.43	6.3
Netherlands Antilles	0.26	6.2
China	1041.00	5.6
S.Korea	40.65	5.5
Egypt	47.11	5.4
Jordan	3.51	5.2

Source: World Bank Atlas 1987, 'Statistics on 184 Countries'.

sized countries like South Korea's 40 million and Egypt's 47 million, up to, above all, China's one billion. Significantly, excluding Kiribati (which has a population of just 64,000), only one of the 184 countries registered a fall of over 5 per cent in growth during the period 1973–85. That was one of the world's wealthiest, Qatar, with −8.5 per cent. This fall, from a very high base, nevertheless illustrates the oil producers' fears, most prominent among those with low reserves, but universally noticeable, that their drive to full industrialization might be aborted because of the uncertainty of future energy prices. It is still largely true, as Robert Stephens concluded in his study of *The Arabs' New Frontier*, that 'The Arab states, like most countries of the developing world, seem uninhibitedly committed to following as far as possible the path of "modernisation" which the industrial countries have already trodden' (1976, 262). Although a flood of petro-dollars has undoubtedly eased the path of OPEC's development, the example of the ten fastest-growing economies suggests that the balance between the role of finance and of other factors is a complex one. We shall now examine some of the changing views regarding the part played by financial factors in the development of former colonies during the twentieth century as decisions on monetary policies moved from foreign to indigenous hands.

Stages in the drive for financial independence

The former colonies and dominions in the Third World, with those of Britain providing the main examples, have gone through four distinct stages, which though varying in degree and timing from place to place exhibit certain common characteristics. In the first stage, already in being at the beginning of the twentieth century, parts of the British currency system together with British-based commercial banking were extended piecemeal to the colonies to answer the demands of trade with the 'mother' country. These movements included the spread of branches of British banks, mostly to the main ports of the colonies, to assist exports to and imports from Britain, and the establishment of Currency Boards in East and West Africa, Malaysia and the West Indies. Free trade and *laissez-faire* shielded by the Pax Britannica and still inspired by Adam Smith, ruled international trade, most of which was conducted in sterling. Internal, indigenous development in the colonies was a tangential by-product of overseas trade. In small colonies like Singapore and Hong Kong, where overseas trade exceeded domestic, international trade was a powerful spur for domestic growth. In large countries like India and Nigeria overseas trade was too small and too distorting to have much impact on indigenous economic development within the vast interiors where most of the population lived. Expatriate currency and banking in the case of such large countries seemed at best irrelevant and at worst diverted finance from internal projects. Such complaints were of modest dimensions during this first stage, which lasted from about 1880 to 1931.

The second stage began with the emergence of the 'sterling area' when Britain went off the gold standard in 1931, followed by the ending of free trade and a corresponding increase in imperial preference from 1932 onwards. This second stage also saw the substantial growth of sterling assets credited to the colonies and dominions during and for some years after the Second World War. The traditional pattern of indebtedness as between Britain and the Commonwealth had gone into reverse, while the reduction in the dollar value of the sterling balances through the unilateral decision to devalue sterling in 1949 forced the pace of change towards financial and political independence in the remaining colonies, following the prior examples of India and Pakistan in 1947. Quite apart from any direct influence, positive or negative, that financial factors had over economic growth, it became clear that they played a key role in the pace of political independence, which latter was confidently expected to remove the shackles of 'imperial exploitation' from indigenous enterprise.

The third stage, from about 1951 to 1973, thus brought with it political independence, indigenous central banks and the apparent ability to decide one's own monetary policy as part of a centralized planning process. Significantly, these changes coincided with the zenith of belief in a powerful blend of Keynesian and Rostovian ideas. The new governments eagerly welcomed these timely twin concepts in political economy which promised so much for the ambitious medium-term plans enthusiastically produced by and for the ex-colonial countries. Some fortunate newly industrializing countries, (NICs) even achieved their own economic 'miracles'. By the early 1970s, however, most LDCs were beginning to realize that neither independence nor planning were guarantors of growth, while any remaining euphoria was abruptly ended (except of course in the oil-producing countries themselves) with the quadrupling of oil prices in October 1973.

The fourth and final stage, after 1973 has seen a gradual return to economic realism for most countries with a greater emphasis on free markets, thus giving financial institutions a higher profile than in the previous stage. As confidence in central planning and in Keynesian–Rostovian ideas evaporated, so there arose a greater acceptance in theory and in practice of the concepts of Professor R. I. McKinnon concerning the importance of 'financial deepening'. This involved in particular the removal of controls over interest in order to stimulate savings and to enforce market disciplines on lenders and borrowers. However in a few countries independence meant movement in the opposite direction, allowing even greater controls and preventing most customary forms of interest payments. These experiments in Islamic banking have been exceptions to the more general rule of a worldwide move towards greater financial and commercial freedom embracing, from the late 1980s, even most of the former communist countries (Elzubeir 1984). Freer markets in goods and money are seen as essential ingredients of growth. Thus towards the end of the century, as at its beginning, the ideas of Adam Smith rather than those of Karl Marx are in the ascendant. It was in this last period that overborrowing, stimulated during the euphoric third stage, inevitably matured into the crippling burden of Third World debt – a problem which because of its special importance will be examined as a separate topic later in this chapter. In the mean time some specific examples of the problems associated with the development of financial institutions and policies in some of the former colonies will be analysed within the pattern of the general stages already outlined, concentrating first on the monetary history of colonial Africa.

Stage 1: Laissez-faire and the Currency Board System, c.1880–1931

Within a remarkably short space of time much of Africa has traversed the whole span of monetary development from substantial reliance on primitive money to the establishment of sophisticated indigenous banks and other financial institutions, using expatriate currency and banking systems as an essential bridge between these two extremes. Trade followed the flag, and banking followed in the wake of trade. Demand therefore preceded supply, with the important corollary that banking profits were more likely to arise than when, in later stages, artificially contrived opening of branches in places where actual demand lagged woefully behind anticipated, 'potential' demand brought about such heavy losses as to cause the overbranched banks to fail. In any case, as is shown in chapter 2, primitive forms of money such as cowries and manillas continued to be in widespread use in parts of West Africa right up to the 1960s; while the records of the United Africa Co. show that it still found it essential to trade in manillas (imported from the manufacturers in Birmingham) for some years after the Second World War. In this connection it is worth noting that both these main kinds of primitive moneys were imported; therefore increases in domestic money supply depended almost entirely on achieving export surpluses – a feature preceding the advent of foreign banks. That such moneys could be obtained only externally helped to keep up their value and hence their attractiveness. External trade was and remained the key to monetary development.

The first rudimentary banking operations were carried out by trading companies like the Royal Niger Co. (chartered in London in 1886), John Holt & Co., the United Africa Co., Elder Dempster & Co. and so on. Banking proper came late to West Africa, but by the 1890s the ancillary financial activities of the trading companies had grown sufficiently large to justify hiving off such operations on to fully fledged banks. Import and export trade between West Africa and Britain, which had remained rather stagnant for fifty years from 1840 to 1890, then began to accelerate from an average annual value of £2.7 million over the five-year period 1886–90, to £6.3 million in 1896–1900 and to £16.3 million in 1906–10. Bearing in mind the relatively stable prices of that period, this was a sixfold increase in real terms in just twenty years, supplying a springboard for financial development (Fry 1976, 32). The chief executive and largest shareholder in Elder Dempster, Alfred Jones, was about to begin forming a bank in Lagos when he was made aware of the decision of the directors of the African Banking Corporation, based in Cape Town, to open a branch in West Africa. Thus, when this first West

African bank opened in 1892, it operated from Elder Dempster's office in Lagos with Elder Dempster's agent, George Neville, as its first manager. Mr Jones right from the start considered it as his own bank and soon persuaded the African Banking Corporation to concentrate its activities in southern Africa while he with Mr Neville took the lead in forming the Bank of British West Africa, which began operations from the same Lagos office in March 1894. It opened a branch in Accra on the Gold Coast in 1896 and in Freetown, Sierra Leone, in 1898. A rival institution, the Anglo-African Bank, sponsored by the Royal Niger Co., was set up in Calabar in 1899, encroaching on the business of BBWA, with expatriate traders especially benefiting from the cutthroat competition, at least until the competitor – which had been called the Bank of Nigeria from 1905 – was absorbed into BBWA in 1912. Although the great majority of the bank's customers were drawn from expatriate traders, government agents and the military and did not *directly* include many West Africans, yet there is some justification for the view given in the Lagos Government Report for 1896 which stated that BBWA had 'benefited the Colony in many ways and supplies a want which was much felt in the past' (Fry 1976, 29). One great boon in which the banks had given assistance was in the introduction and development of the cocoa industry to supplement previous overdependence on palm oil. Exports of cocoa began in 1891 with a mere 80 lb but rose rapidly to 10,000 tons by 1906 and to 50,000 tons in 1913. Finance to cover the seven years from planting to harvesting was in part supplied by the banks. Similar efforts with rubber came to naught. The banks were not invariably overcautious and short-sighted.

The sixfold growth in external trade was more than matched by a spectacular rise in the import of the kind of money strongly preferred by the indigenous traders, namely cash, predominantly in the form of sterling silver coins. This love of silver was also in line with long-established British government policy, for as early as 1825 it was made clear by an Order in Council that 'both on grounds of policy and expediency . . . it was desirable to introduce British silver coins into the circulation of the Colonies' (Greaves 1953, 10). Henceforth, according to Lord Chalmers's *History of Currency in the British Colonies*, 'the shilling was to circulate wherever the British drum was heard' (Chalmers 1893, 40). It must have been deafening in West Africa at the turn of the century. The annual amount of silver issued for West Africa rose from an average of £24,426 in the five years to 1890 to reach £847,850 by 1911, a rate which 'actually exceeded the amount issued for use in the UK' (Fry 1976, 70). Trade had increased sixfold: the cash required to support it had increased by over thirty times.

Furthermore when the colonial banks returned silver coin deposits to Britain, these were in practice accepted at par even for large amounts and so were virtually convertible into gold. Thus whereas silver was only of limited legal tender in the UK, this was not strictly the case for colonial banks' silver holdings. When colonial holdings were low this was no problem, but by 1911 the matter had become of such major concern that the government appointed an official committee to make a thorough investigation of the colonial monetary system. The Emmott Committee Report (Cd 6426) was issued in June 1912 and on its recommendations the Currency Board System was established in stages throughout the colonies – until they obtained their political independence. This was some fifty or so years later in the case of the West African colonies of the Gold Coast, or Ghana, and Nigeria. The two essential features of the Currency Board system were, first, that the British government formally assumed responsibility for the issue of the appropriate currency in each of a number of geographically contiguous regions of the colonial empire; and secondly the UK government guaranteed that the values of these currencies were exactly the same as that of sterling. Dr Ida Greaves put the point lucidly as follows: 'while the currency Authorities in various colonies have issued the types and denominations which local custom required, every colonial currency is really sterling in a different place from the United Kingdom' (1953, 10). In some respects there was therefore a logical similarity in principle with the later development of the Eurodollar, in both being convertible currencies held outside the home country, although in the case of the colonies all the decisions regarding convertibility remained in London.

Appropriately enough, since it was that region that had imposed the biggest drain on sterling coins, it was the West African Currency Board (WACB) that was the first to be set up, hurriedly in 1912, covering Nigeria, the Gold Coast, Gambia, Togoland and the British Cameroons. It became the prototype for all the others set up later, such as that for East Africa in 1919, for Central Africa a decade later, and for the last to be formed, the short-lived Malayan Currency Board, in 1938. Similar but less formal systems ruled in Fiji, Gibraltar, Malta and in the West Indies, in which latter area Canadian banks and some US banks competed strongly with those from Britain. The operations of the Currency Board system lasted longest and were most clearly seen in Africa, because there more than elsewhere the preference for sterling silver coins was strongest, forcing the banks to maintain much higher (and costlier) cash-to-deposit ratios than in other colonial areas. From 1917 onwards, to supplement its own coinage (produced by the Royal Mint in London) the WACB issued its own banknotes. These, however, like the local bank cheques, were used mostly by traders and government agents. In that same year the Colonial Bank, which had been formed in 1836 in London, opened its first branch in West Africa: it was absorbed into Barclays Dominion, Colonial and Overseas in 1925.

Adding to the burden of excessive reliance on silver coins was the West African aversion to using gold for monetary purposes. Gold coins quickly vanished to reappear as ornaments. Love of silver coins thus imposed a huge and costly physical burden on banks and traders. Even as late as 1949 the United Africa Co. complained of the heavy costs, made worse by the poor state of the roads, of hauling several million pounds' worth of silver to pay for the purchase of palm oil, cocoa and other 'cash crops', bearing in mind that a three-ton truck could carry only £10,000 in silver coins (*Statistical and Economic Review*, March 1949). When allowance is made for such down-to-earth practicalities, then the monopoly granted to the BBWA from 1894 to 1912 of being the sole importer of silver, and from 1912 to 1962 of being the sole agent for the WACB, though doubtless a prestigious privilege, was not the blank cheque it might at first seem. The agency fee, fixed at £4,000 p.a. in 1927, remained ridiculously low considering inflation and the vast increase in the board's currency circulation, which at its peak in 1956 had risen to £125 million (Loynes 1974).

Any sizeable credit accruing to banks, companies, government departments or agencies which was surplus to their immediate requirements locally, was transferred for deposit in the London money market, for there were no local avenues for safely earning a return on liquid funds. The London money market was thus the intermediary for colonial banks and businesses just as it was for such institutions within the UK. The Currency Boards and the colonial governments themselves were legally obliged to invest in UK and other Commonwealth government stock. The counterpart was the privilege of trustee status conferred by the Colonial Stock Act of 1900 (and its amendments) on the London issues made by or for the colonies and dominions. This greatly added to the value and marketability of colonial issues. In 1929 a Joint Colonial Fund was formed in London to pool the surpluses from the various colonial sources so as to earn better returns than could be obtained from the smaller, separate sums. Short-term funds from the colonies were profitably and safely invested in London in readily realizable forms, while London provided long-term funds for capital investment in the colonies and dominions. In general the system worked well. If the colonies were to benefit from a fully convertible currency of the type they seemed to prefer, and also to enjoy some of the benefits supplied by modern, viable and reliable banks, then the combination of the Currency Board system with expatriate banking was justified by results. But this symbiotic situation began to change from the 1930s onward.

Stage 2: The sterling area and the sterling balances, 1931–1951

Free trade and *laissez-faire* were largely discredited and therefore discarded when the international gold standard broke up in the 1930s. Nevertheless external trade and payments continued to exert their customary force as key factors in colonial monetary development at a time when the world split up into two main monetary blocs, the sterling area and the dollar area. Managed trade and managed finance were two sides of the same coin. Controls on trade and finance increased during the 1930s, rose very naturally to their zenith during the Second World War, but then were maintained at quite a high level in the sterling area for a surprisingly long period thereafter. The sterling area comprised all those countries between which payments were mainly or entirely made in sterling, which therefore kept their reserves in sterling and which found it convenient or imperative to rely on the financial services of the City of London, which had long been (and still remains) the largest foreign exchange market in the world. At a time of growing restrictions on international trade and payments, the sterling area remained the largest area in the world within which payments could freely be made in what in the 1930s was still the most widely accepted currency. In Sayers's well-known phrase, 'sterling was always useful and sterling was always available' (1953, 148). Because the trade of sterling area members was mostly with each other and especially with the UK, it followed that when sterling went off the gold standard in September 1931, and thus forced countries to make a choice, all the independent dominions (except Canada, which was drawn to the United States) chose to cling to sterling, as did a number of non-Commonwealth countries such as Portugal, the Scandinavian countries, Egypt, Iraq, Jordan, Argentina and for a time even Japan. The colonies had no choice in the matter, but even if they had, their existing trade and financial links would have made any other course extremely unlikely. All members kept their currencies fixed to sterling and kept their exchange reserves entirely, or almost so, in the form of sterling balances in London.

The massive depression of the 1930s – which was the basic cause of the break-up of the gold standard – was in fact substantially less severe in Britain than in the USA. Thus, as an American authority on the sterling area has pointed out, US national income fell by no less than 50 per cent from 1929 to 1932, compared with a fall of 15 per cent in Britain. Furthermore Britain's initiative in strengthening Commonwealth Preference by the Ottawa Agreement of 1932 provided a more stable basis for trade arrangements than could be obtained elsewhere at the time. 'Greater stability of British imports than those of other major industrial countries, and of the US in particular' was 'a significant attraction of sterling area membership' (Bell 1956, 334). By an Order in Council of 3 September 1939 the sterling area system of controls was tightened so as to make it in effect an instrument of war. Although most current payments within the area remained free, controls on capital were brought in while all payments beyond the sterling area were strictly controlled. All dollars and other 'hard' currency receipts were centralized in London's 'dollar pool' with disbursements requiring Treasury authority exercised by its agent, the Bank of England. The need for such pooling may be gauged by the fact that at their lowest point, in April 1941, Britain's gold and dollar reserves fell to only £3 million.

While the war drastically curtailed Britain's export earnings, those of the rest of the sterling area (RSA) grew enormously. In addition to the UK's normal expenditure on food and raw material from RSA, there were the vast new current expenditures on supplies of all kinds for the military forces together with emergency capital spending on harbours, roads, railways, airfields, barracks and so on around the world, mostly within the sterling area. Because British manufacturing capacity was reserved for war purposes, as was shipping capacity, the swollen incomes of RSA could not be spent on customary British manufactured exports. As a result RSA's 'unrequited' export earnings were increasingly accumulated in London as 'sterling balances'. These grew to such an extent that not only was much of the RSA's previous indebtedness to the UK repaid but also resulted in the RSA becoming substantial short-term creditors, and as time went on, in the medium term also. London-held sterling balances, largely in the form of Treasury bills and other short-term instruments, rose by almost £3 billion between 1938 and 1945, by the end of which year they stood at £3,547 million. Despite some significant changes in composition, they stood at around that same level over the following twenty years. This fundamental change in Britain's position from being a large creditor into becoming a large debtor – and to poorer countries at that – had important consequences for her and for the Commonwealth.

The debts could, of course, like those of a number of other nations in similar circumstances, have been repudiated, cancelled or at least written down. They represented part of Britain's huge war effort on behalf of the RSA as well as for herself. But this was not the British attitude to debts, as was plainly stated by the Chancellor of the Exchequer, Sir Stafford Cripps, in Parliament (*Hansard*, 19 November 1949). Agreements were reached to prevent the balances from being run down too rapidly, and particularly to prevent the draining of the dollar pool, despite the strong desires on the part of the RSA to purchase American capital goods to speed up their own economic development. Although the sterling balances were not written down, their value was eroded by inflation, unconsciously perhaps, and also by the deliberate, and unavoidable, sudden, decision of the British government to devalue sterling by around 30 per cent, in terms of the dollar in September 1949. The colonies could have no say in the matter while 'there were evidences in almost every monetarily-independent sterling area country of dissatisfaction with the impact of sterling devaluation on the position of overseas members' (Bell 1956, 425). Furthermore Britain's cheap money policy from 1932 to 1951 meant that the interest earned on sterling balances, which had previously been a highly attractive feature in pulling RSA funds to London, had become so low that a strong stimulus was given to the development of money markets in the dominions to supplement the effectiveness of their new central banks. These same attitudes and pressures were to lead a decade or two later to similar, if weaker, results in the colonies.

Whereas the dominions had managed to reduce their blocked London balances by 1951, those of the colonies rose year on year to reach over £1,000 million by then. In a parliamentary debate in November 1951 the Secretary of State for the Colonies spoke of 'the alarming growth of the sterling balances of the Colonies', adding that 'a system of colonial development which leaves the Colonies to finance the Mother Country to the extent of £1,000 million cannot continue unchecked' (Greaves 1953, 82). The well-known development expert, Professor W. A. Lewis, published his opinion, in the *Financial Times* of 18 January 1952, that 'Britain talks of colonial development but on the contrary it is African and Malayan peasants who are putting capital into Britain. For the first time since free trade was adopted in the middle of the nineteenth century, the British colonial system has become a major means of economic exploitation.' Similarly *The Economist* of 21 April 1951 after pointing out that 'Many of the largest accumulators [of sterling balances] are colonial territories whose policy is determined in London' went on to say, 'The momentum of past habits will still make it possible for the welfare state and cosseted economy of Britain to be maintained on the backs of other, and in many cases, poorer countries' (quoted by Greaves 1953, 822).

THIRD WORLD MONEY AND DEBT IN THE TWENTIETH CENTURY   607

Thus the early 1950s marked a turning-point in that it came to be widely recognized that no longer could the economic development of the colonies be left to occur as a by-product of expatriate banking, nor could the monetary policies of the colonies be uniformly and unilaterally decided by the Treasury and Bank of England where the economic interests of the UK would most likely and most naturally be the predominant consideration. The economic and financial complementarity of the pre-war Commonwealth had been drastically altered by a war which had accelerated the political, economic and financial motives for independence.

Stage 3: Independence, planning euphoria and banking mania, 1951–1973

Summarizing the results of an international conference on National Economic Planning convened by the US National Bureau for Economic Research held at Princeton in 1964, Professor Millikan recalled that from the early 1950s 'the idea of economic planning was beginning to gain wide popularity (in LDCs) as a necessary and sometimes sufficient condition for economic growth' and that, having just gained political independence, the new leaders of the former colonies 'turned naturally to economic planning as a tool' because 'the emerging theories of economic development being spawned by economists suggested that only through conscious and determined government policy could those countries escape from the low-income trap in which they found themselves' (Millikan 1967, 3–4). These theories were a blend of Keynesian concepts on macro-economics and national income accounting (supplemented with Tinbergen's input-output matrices where data were optimistically believed to be adequate) plus Professor W. W. Rostow's theory of the stages of economic development which seemed to promise that, given adequate and properly developed investment programmes, the LDCs could 'take off into self-sustaining growth'. During the period 1952–73 almost all British colonial territories became politically independent, following the examples of India and Pakistan in 1947. The establishment and nurture of their own central and commercial banking systems followed by their own money and capital markets were seen as vital parts of this planned process of economic development. Nigeria affords one of the best examples of this process, first because it was the largest, and secondly and more importantly, because in no other colony have indigenous writers published their own insights more than in the case of Nigeria, with e.g.

the most authoritative, clear, controversial and prolific of these being Professor G. O. Nwankwo, whose personal experience has spanned the monetary spectrum from using cowrie shells as a boy to becoming an executive director of the Central Bank of Nigeria and chairman of one of its largest commercial banks.

The main features which require to be examined in assessing the remarkable development of Nigerian banking and finance from around 1951 to 1973 include, first, the struggle to gain a central bank; secondly, the effectiveness of the indigenization of expatriate banking; and thirdly, the causes and consequences of 'boom and bust' in indigenous commercial banking. With regard to central banking in LDCs, two theories came strongly into contention at this time: the conservative, traditional view, which may be called the 'coping-stone' theory, versus the newer, progressive 'cornerstone' theory. The coping-stone theory, maintained that the erection of a central bank should be undertaken only *after* the financial system of banks and money markets had already been built up to a substantial degree. A central bank's two main weapons, bank rate and open market operations, would be useless in undeveloped financial systems, leaving the central banker and his staff with nothing to do but twiddle their thumbs. In such circumstances a central bank would be a white elephant, an ostentatious, costly, unnecessary, empty symbol. Worse still, in order to get indigenous staff it would have to divert to itself and find artificial work for the very kind of skilled labour that was especially scarce in LDCs. These scarce, skilled resources would be much more productively employed in building up the banking system in the challenging rural areas instead of being cosseted in the capital city. The opposing cornerstone (or foundation-stone) theory saw, as an urgent necessity, a positive role for a central bank as a catalyst for development, training other bankers, instituting an independent monetary policy more appropriate to indigenous needs, assisting the government in its economic planning and so on, rather than being simply or mainly an instrument of economic stabilization. These competing views are admirably illustrated in the seven-year struggle from 1952 to 1958 inclusive to set up Nigeria's central bank.

Financial planning was only loosely integrated into the series of macro-economic plans busily produced in West Africa during this period. The first for any West African country was the 'Ten Year Plan for Development and Welfare' produced by the colonial office for Nigeria in 1946. This was followed, after Nigerian independence in 1960, by sequential five- to six-year plans doggedly produced despite massive disruptions, negative or positive, such as the civil war (1967–70) and the oil crisis of 1973. Among the most important of a plethora of investigations into monetary and banking conditions in West Africa were the Paton Report (1948), the Trevor and Fisher Reports (both in 1952), the World Bank Report (1954), the Loynes Report (1957) and the Coker Report (1962). The first of these deals mainly with commercial banking, and so will be noted later. The main recommendation of the Trevor Report on 'Banking Conditions on the Gold Coast and the Question of Setting up a National Bank' was immediately implemented when the Bank of the Gold Coast, that country's first indigenous bank, was established. In 1957 when the country became independent, the bank was split into two, with the Bank of Ghana becoming a bank of issue and eventually taking on all the duties of a central bank, while the other half, now known as the Ghana Commercial Bank, still 100 per cent government-owned, carried on with its commercial functions. Thus was overcome the widespread fear expressed by Dr Kwame Nkrumah in his autobiography: 'Our political independence will be worthless unless we use it to obtain economic and financial self-government' (1961, 111).

In Nigeria financial independence took a little longer to arrive. In 1952 Mr J. L. Fisher, adviser to the Bank of England, was asked to report on 'the desirability and practicability of establishing a central bank in Nigeria for promoting the economic development of the country'. He soon made it painfully plain that he thought the whole idea to be undesirable, impractical and in any case premature. 'In his orthodox approach to monetary problems, Fisher argued that it was better to build the financial structure from the base upwards rather from the top downwards' (Ajayi and Ojo 1981, 86). 'I conclude,' said Mr Fisher with brutal frankness 'that it would be inadvisable to contemplate the establishment of a central bank at the moment . . . Moreover it is hard to see how a central bank could function as an instrument to promote economic development' though it might be considered 'in due course' (Nwankwo 1980, 4). The World Bank Report of 1954 was rather less negative and gave some hope by suggesting the formation of a State Bank of Nigeria as a halfway house in the direction of central banking. This compromise was rejected and instead, as soon as Nigeria was granted autonomy in internal matters in 1957, another Bank of England official, Mr J. B. Loynes, was asked to give his advice on how best to go about setting up a proper central bank. His 'Report on the Establishment of a Nigerian Central Bank and the Introduction of a Nigerian Currency' (1957) was quickly adopted and the Central Bank of Nigeria began operations on 1 July 1959. The West African Currency Board ceased to exist in 1962 as the new central banks in

Ghana and Nigeria carried out their exciting new roles of tailoring central banking operations to the needs of indigenous development so as to demonstrate in practice the victory the cornerstone theory had won over its old coping-stone rival.

Expatriate banks in the post-1951 period began participating much more fully than ever before in the economic development of their host countries, which nevertheless considered their actions to be far too little and much too late. Names were changed to reflect decolonization, the number of bank branches was considerably increased and local boards of directors were set up with a few native directors. The BBWA dropped 'British' from its title in 1957, and in 1965 merged with the Standard Bank (previously appended by 'of South Africa'); the renamed Barclays DCO similarly de-emphasized its 'Colonial' title; the British and French Bank, formed in 1948, became the United Bank for Africa in 1961, and so on. But an expatriate bank by any other name was still resented as foreign. Criticism was made of the slow process of Africanization in the expatriate banks' staff, although, because of the huge increase in the native civil service in the run-up to independence, these banks had many of their best staff poached. The Bank of (British) West Africa increased the total of its branches from thirty in 1945 to fifty-one in 1954, and up to 118 by 1963. Over many years such branches had been managed largely by British staff; for instance, many Scots bankers when they completed their training were attracted to the British overseas banks because far more were trained than could find suitable posts in Britain (Gaskin 1965, 51). The work of the Institute of Bankers deserves notice for its key role in preparing the groundwork for indigenous control of banking. By 1970 its overseas membership had risen to 13,000. The Lagos institute was set up in 1963, and by 1970 when the Nigerian Institute of Bankers was formed the Lagos branch itself boasted 5,000 members (Green 1979, 171). Expatriate banks (and the trading companies) also assisted indispensably in the early stages of the development of local money and capital markets. Thus BBWA tendered substantially for the first issue of Treasury bills made by the Gold Coast administration in 1954; in 1958 it granted the Nigerian government a ten-year loan of $1 million in participation with the World Bank's loan of $28 million to improve Nigerian railways; in the same year it subscribed £50,000 towards the original capital of the Development Corporation of Nigeria; in 1963 it loaned £1 million for road building in Ghana, and for a number of years helped to finance the early growth of Nigeria's oil industry. However, such concrete evidence of expatriate involvement in internal development simply spurred on the drive for financial independence, particularly with regard to the needs of the vast numbers of small indigenous entrepreneurs.

According to research carried out for the Central Bank of Nigeria over 80 per cent of the loans made by expatriate banks during the period 1963–8 matured (nominally at least) within three months, and 95 per cent within twelve months. In 1970 just over half of their loans went to purely expatriate enterprises with just a third to Nigerian borrowers, the rest going to enterprises of mixed ownership (Nwankwo 1980, 75). Although the total lending by indigenous banks was very small compared with that of the expatriates, the bulk of their lending was to Nigerians (77 per cent), while 21 per cent of their lending was for terms over twelve months. There had long been some substance behind the vociferous case for indigenization. However, before we attempt to assess the results of financial indigenization a brief glance needs to be cast on the rise and fall of indigenous banking and on the new money and capital markets.

Only three indigenous banks had been formed in Nigeria before 1945, one of which failed within a year of formation, another struggled on for five years before failing, leaving only the original one, the National Bank of Nigeria formed in 1933, to survive. Compared with what was to come this ratio has to be considered a great success. A native banking boom began in 1945 and rose to a veritable mania by 1952. The actual number of 'banks' so called remains a matter of some dispute among the authorities because registration did not always result in active banking operations; but there is no doubting the strength of the boom. Between 1945 and 1948 some 145 banks were registered, followed by a similar number in the subsequent four years. There were no banking laws of any kind to attempt to regulate this flood. Concerns about the dangers of such an uncontrolled rush, together with the adverse publicity accompanying the losses suffered by depositors of the Nigerian Penny Bank, which failed just a year after it had been set up in 1945, led to a commission of inquiry being set up in 1948 chaired by Mr G. D. Paton of the Bank of England. His report's recommendations, after four years' delay, resulted eventually in Nigeria's first law passed to regulate the formation and operation of banking. All banks were to be licensed. Minimum capital requirements, of 25,000 naira for indigenous banks and 200,000 for expatriate banks, were demanded, and later raised to take account of inflation. In the mean time, between 1945 and 1955, when the new rules were to come fully into operation, the mushroom banks had enjoyed complete freedom of operation and were managed by persons with little or no experience of banking. Euphoria, incompetence, nepotism, corruption and widespread fraud (vices not uncommon in the early stages of banking in the UK or USA) made wholesale failure inevitable. By 1955 all these indigenous banks, except for only three, had failed. Although post-war booms and failures had occurred elsewhere, the Nigerian example stands out as a classic case of its type. By the mid-1950s the banking flood had become a trickle. The public lost faith in indigenous banks unless, as was later the case, they were either sponsored by or owned by one of the nineteen State governments.

Immediately following the decision to set up a central bank a committee under Professor R. H. Barback was asked to make recommendations on setting up a stock exchange. As a result the Lagos stock exchange was formed in 1960 and began operations the following year. The first major step in the establishment of a money market was also taken at this time when, in April 1960, the government made its first issue of Treasury bills. The market was broadened when, from 1968 onwards, the Central Bank began issuing Treasury certificates of one- and two-year maturities. As we have seen, the expatriate banks strongly supported these moves, but the fact that the bulk of their business had still not penetrated to meet the needs of the small- and medium-sized native enterprises made the Nigerian government decide to take further steps to 'command the strategic heights of the economy'. In 1972, as part of its general indigenization programme, the government took up 40 per cent of the equity of the Big Three expatriate banks (Barclays DCO, Standard and United), and just four years later increased its ownership, this time of all expatriate banks along with other strategic expatriate industries, to 60 per cent. The effect of the expansion of dealing in the stock market was dramatic. The total annual value of transactions on the Lagos stock exchange rose from 1.5 billion naira in 1961 to 18 billion in 1971. It then shot up to over 92 billion in 1973, and to 180 billion naira in 1977.

Despite the successes achieved in setting up and developing the appropriate instruments and policies for the central bank and for the money and capital markets, the process of indigenization of commercial banking, which is a vital element in development, had fallen far short of reaching the degree of success anticipated by its protagonists. Indeed, one of the most influential of these, Professor Nwankwo, devoted a chapter of his book on *The Nigerian Financial System* to what he roundly calls 'The Failure of the Indigenization of Nigerian Commercial Banking'. Among his many recommendations for improvement is his belief that the government 'should upgrade its participation in the expatriate banks to 100 per cent and assume 100 per cent control and management of the banks' (1980, 86). By the mid-1970s, however, opinion in general was moving away from such faith in the power of government controls and being replaced by considerable doubt as to whether the take-off into self-sustaining growth could be guaranteed by seizing the commanding financial heights. A much more pragmatic approach seemed to be more appropriate.

Stage 4: Market realism and financial deepening, 1973–1993

The Nigerian experience

Disillusionment over the painfully obvious lack of progress in the development of indigenous commercial banking was part of a wider pessimism concerning the growth of LDCs, which had confidently been expected to have made much faster progress once they had achieved political independence. The pessimism of the 1970s, symbolized by the Rome 'doom' thesis on the 'limits to growth', extended into the 'lost decade' of the 1980s. This pervading sense of failure was well summarized by the then head of the Nigerian government, Lt.-Gen. Obasanjo: 'We have got caught up in the conflict of cultures, of trying to graft the so-called sophistication of European society to our African society. We are betwixt and between' (*Financial Times*), 30 August 1978). It is, however, inherent in the nature of most LDCs that they are 'betwixt and between', for typically they are 'dual economies' with a very substantial, if not the greater, part of their population existing in rural poverty despite the considerable and sometimes spectacular advances achieved in their more industrialized sectors situated mostly in their rapidly growing urbanized and westernized areas. The fashionable growth models copied from the West ignored this duality. 'The success of the Marshall Plan led many to believe that a similar transfer of capital to developing countries would achieve similar results . . . The early model of development therefore placed nearly total emphasis on increasing physical capital to raise production', particularly in industry. 'Agriculture was largely neglected' (World Bank Development Report 1985, 97–8). Neither Keynesian–Rostovian theories, imitative Marshall-type planning nor financial indigenization, so long as these were based on western, mainly British, modes of practice, seemed to work.

Growth had failed to 'trickle down' to the poor, nor had investment in infrastructure and in industry 'spread out' to stimulate the dual economy in general. For nearly two decades most of the sub-Saharan countries had seen their per capita incomes actually fall, some drastically. Even Nigeria, despite its oil, saw per capita income fall by an average annual rate of 2.5 per cent from 1973 to 1985 (table 11.1), her rising GNP cut down by an even faster-rising population. Nigeria's population, roughly estimated at 55 million in 1970, had already doubled to 110 million by 1989 and was then expected to rise to 160 million by the year 2000 and to 302 million by 2025 (World Development Report, 1990). The task of raising per capita income therefore demands a most formidable effort in which the banking system is being modified to play a more effective role than before. Professor E. C. Edozien, economic adviser to the Nigerian president, has placed on record his view that 'the banking system has played a significantly less important role in promoting Nigeria's development' than is suggested by 'its dominance of the financial sector' (1983, 110). The banks needed to be dragged, kicking and screaming, into the rural interior to provide the kinds of service in the imaginative forms required to stimulate more rapid and more widespread development in the lower section of the dual economy.

Turning first to the number and distribution of bank branches, Professor Newlyn gave the total number of branches in West Africa in 1951 as being only fifty, of which twenty-nine were in Nigeria, almost all being situated in the seaports (Sayers 1952, 437). By 1967 Nigeria's eighteen commercial banks had sprouted 445 branches, a tenfold increase. There was still a marked concentration in the large towns, with Lagos State holding ninety-four branches, whereas four States had on average only six branches each to cover the whole of their State; 70 per cent of the rural population had no access to banks (Ajayi and Ojo 1981, 22). Such continued rural paucity spurred the government in 1977 to embark vigorously on the 'rural banking initiative'. In the space of the following five years the number of branches doubled to more than 950, of which over 270 were located in the formerly neglected rural areas. Although this represents a bank density of only one branch on average for 100,000 persons, compared with one branch for 2,300 in the UK, it still marked a striking improvement by providing a bare framework for a nationwide penetration by the banks. It took strong pressure by the government and stern guidance by the Central Bank of Nigeria to persuade the banks to take these steps into the interior. The heavy costs of rural branches, which tend to rise with remoteness, were also, perversely, felt more keenly by the newer and smaller indigenous banks than by the larger, long-established former expatriate banks. Even one of the Big Three, the United Bank for Africa, thought it 'pertinent to mention that all the rural branches opened so far are incurring losses and the prospects of a majority of them ever becoming profitable are very slim' (UBA annual report, 1981). In the view of the authorities, rural development was worth being subsidized initially by the profits of the banks' urban branches, while the viability of rural branches could be speeded up if appropriate practices were followed. The Central Bank tried to educate the commercial bankers to get them to lengthen the terms of their loans; to make moderately large loans to rural co-operatives and other village groups for on-lending rather than be faced with granting uneconomic, tiny loans to previously unbanked individuals; to modify their rules regarding collateral away from individual titles to land, insurance policies and such traditional items, and to accept instead less conventional forms of security more appropriate to rural communities, and so on. It has been the World Bank's experience, in Africa and elsewhere, that 'costs can be reduced when there are procedures especially tailored to facilitate lending to small producers' ('Integrated rural development projects' *Finance and Development*, March 1977, 18).

As well as pushing the commercial banks to modify their lending, the authorities encouraged them to tap into what were believed to be the considerable savings hidden away in local nooks and crannies such as those kept by the traditional village co-operatives. The numerous, relatively small and generally passive and fragmented pockets of savings, which in any case were usually wastefully spent on conspicuous consumption, could instead be channelled into productive investment. The integration of these informal credit markets into the commercial banking system was, however, a disappointingly slow process. The devastating civil war of 1967–9 could carry only part of the blame for this. In the event, any shortage of savings as a constraint on development seemed suddenly to have been removed by the quadrupling of oil prices in 1973. By the end of the 1970s Nigerian oil accounted for 98 per cent of its export earnings and 80 per cent of the government's revenue. The oil boom was not an unmixed blessing. Among its less welcome results were 'a drift from rural to urban areas, neglect of agriculture and a gigantic appetite for imported consumer goods to the detriment of local industries' (Ojomo 1983, 235). The formal financial system was greatly stimulated by the oil boom. All the same, in Professor Edozien's view, whereas 'the growth and financial deepening of the banking system followed the expected patterns' yet the 'rapid growth of the banking system' did not have 'the corresponding impact on the economy normally associated with such impressive growth elsewhere'. The financial deepening was more apparent than real, a 'camouflage concealing a high degree of under-development' (pp.107–9). It should however be remembered that Nigeria started from a very low base, with by far the lowest banking density of all the twenty-five colonies analysed by Professor Newlyn in 1952. Before looking at other, more favourable examples of 'financial deepening' the significance of the term itself needs further examination.

Impact of the Shaw–McKinnon thesis

In 1973 two Stanford economists, Professors E. E. Shaw and R. I. McKinnon, each published a book crystallizing their previous researches, which together marked a turning-point in the economic theorizing underlying the appropriate policies for faster and more sustainable growth in the standards of living in LDCs. Although differing in detail, their main concepts reinforce each other. Their contribution may be – very baldly – summarized in the following six points. First, they wished to alter the balance between government planning and reliance on market forces in favour of the latter. In itself there was little new in this, for a number of writers had for years been questioning whether governments, in LDCs especially, were equipped to carry their plans into practice. Among these critics none was more consistent than Professor P. T. Bauer, who as early as 1958 had written: 'The adequate performance of these (planned) functions exceeds the resources of all undeveloped countries . . . we are faced with the paradoxical situation that governments engage on ambitious tasks when they are unable to fulfill even the elementary and necessary functions of government '(quoted in World Development Report, 1991, 34).

Shaw–McKinnon, however, focused this general criticism on to money, banking and finance, the one key sector where reform was seen to be an essential feature without which all the other market-orientated reforms would fail to reach their potential. Their second and vital contribution therefore was to advance monetary factors to the centre of the stage. 'The theme of this book,' says Professor Shaw 'is that the financial sector of an economy does matter in economic development' (p.3). Money was neither neutral nor passive in economic development and furthermore relative prices mattered as signals for all economic units and should not be obscured by rationing, subsidies and so on. Thirdly, the 'shallow' and 'fragmented' financial systems of LDCs need to be liberalized in order for price signalling to be effective. 'Liberalisation opens the way to superior allocations of savings by widening and diversifying the financial markets', while the 'local capital markets can be integrated into a common market' so that 'new opportunities for pooling savings and specialising in investment are created' (Shaw 1973, 10). Similarly McKinnon writes that 'the unification of the capital market sharply increases rates of return to domestic savers, widens investment opportunities' and 'is essential for eliminating other forms of fragmentation' (1973, 9).

Fourthly, Shaw and McKinnon declare war on manipulated interest rates. Because money pervades the economy (or should be made to do so), liberalization of the price(s) of money was the most important market freedom. The control of rates of interest such as low rates for certain selected and highly privileged sectors, together with the attempts to enforce severe anti-usury laws – both common practices in LDCs – were especially pernicious in their effects, causing gross misallocation of investment and holding back total savings to such a degree as to raise rather than to reduce real rates of interest for the vast majority of borrowers. Despite political independence, the old colonial banking system has been generally replaced with very similar systems which allow privileged borrowers the lion's share of available finance at low real rates while depriving the vast majority of indigenous farmers and industrialists of the finance they need. Professor McKinnon gives examples from Ethiopia of moneylenders charging rates of interest of from 100 to 200 per cent in the rural areas while in the urban areas banks were charging importers 6 per cent and manufacturers 8 or 9 per cent. This 'disparity between rates charged in urban enclaves and those in rural areas – the latter containing 90% of the population – is startling if not uncommon' (McKinnon 1973, 71).

Fifthly, although insisting that the liberalization of financial markets is of central importance, Shaw and McKinnon believe that this should be accompanied by more general liberalization. This process of liberalization should not be in a slow series of steps, each one being consolidated before the next, but rather should be a rapid advance on a wide front. Although the context is different, the approach is similar to the later acceptance of the 'Big Bang' method of reforming the City of London in 1986 or the continuing debate in the 1990s of how best to introduce the free-market systems into the centrally planned economies. Sixthly and finally, the Shaw–McKinnon thesis gives support to the 'trade not aid' and 'bootstrap' approaches to development. The authors show that much (though not all) aid is perverse in its results, being in unreformed LDCs subject to the same distorting effects as other forms of finance, while tempting governments to postpone essential, if painful, reforms. Lending by international agencies at preferential rates to unreformed LDCs may similarly prop up inefficient systems. Thus 'experience suggests that foreign funds may be managed no more rationally than funds of domestic origin' and 'bear no relationship to the scarcity price of capital' (McKinnon 1973, 171). The truth of this fear was to be dramatically illustrated by the problems of Third World debt, which will shortly be examined. Shaw and McKinnon's thesis goes far to explain why LDCs must rely chiefly on their own efforts if they are to raise their populations above abject poverty.

In view of the above authors' endorsement of free markets in general and of their emphasis on financial markets in particular, their theories appeared to combine the classical economics of free trade with certain aspects of monetarism. Yet, as Shaw and McKinnon emphasize, neither Keynesian nor monetarist policies can be applied uncritically to LDCs, which typically have fragmented markets. Because the newly independent economies had naïvely adopted Keynesian ideas as essential parts of their planning, both Keynesianism and planning were legitimate targets to be aimed at and, largely, destroyed, at least in their generally accepted forms. It was not simply that Keynesian (and monetarist) doctrine was irrelevant to LDCs; it was harmful. One important area where the Shaw–McKinnon view was radically opposed to that of Keynes was with regard to the latter's lenient attitude towards laws against usury. On the evidence of history, Keynes had argued that 'it was inevitable that the rate of interest, unless it was curbed by every instrument at the disposal of society, would rise too high to permit of an adequate inducement to invest' (1936, 351). We have seen how effectively Shaw and McKinnon exposed that commonly held fallacy. The thrust of the Shaw–McKinnon thesis was therefore anti-Keynesian leading to a rejection of the pernicious alliance between Keynesianism and planning that had worked to the detriment of the development of many LDCs in the period from about 1945 to the early 1980s.

The Shaw–McKinnon doctrines – perhaps attitudes would be a better description – have spread with remarkable speed through the usual channels of seminars, doctoral theses, articles and textbooks to gain a considerable degree of acceptance by LDC governments themselves and by the international agencies. Thus Barber B. Conable, president of the World Bank, introducing the World Bank's Development Report 1991, claims: 'This Report describes a market-friendly approach. Experience shows that success in promoting economic growth and poverty reduction is most likely when governments complement markets; dramatic failures when they conflict.' Similarly M. Camdessus, managing director of the IMF, has welcomed the 'silent revolution' spreading through the LDCs, 'giving greater scope to market forces and reducing the role of government'. In answer to his own rhetorical question 'Why are more countries adopting this approach?' he answered, 'Because it has worked and the alternatives have not' (IMF Summary Proceedings 1989, 201). At the same IMF meeting the Governor of the Bank of Malta spoke of 'a new emphasis on market forces and private initiative . . . a clear commitment to reduce the role of the public sector . . . Policies which boost domestic savings and encourage investment are being introduced together with trade liberalisation' (p.189). The Shaw–McKinnon thesis, pragmatically modified as necessary, was being widely put into practice.

Contrasts in financial deepening

The modern monetary and banking systems exported from Europe by its bankers in order to finance the growing trade in palm oil, cocoa, coffee, jute, tea, rubber, tin and so on were superimposed on a number of vastly different indigenous financial foundations, ranging from the predominantly primitive monetary economies of much of Africa and the West Indies to the much more complex and long-established financial practices of India, China and South-East Asia. The colonial powers succeeded in imposing a considerable degree of uniformity in the various countries with regard to currency systems and monetary policies before independence allowed each of the new governments to make its own choices. By that time the expatriate banks had established themselves as by far the strongest and most reliable banks and formed the pattern to be imitated by the indigenous banks. Similarly when the new central banks were set up, the model mostly copied was the Bank of England, whose officials usually helped in drawing up the new banks' constitutions with some of the Bank of England's officials generally being seconded to help during the formative years. There were some exceptions – Ceylon imitated the United States' Federal Reserve System, an equally if not more irrelevant model. The first phase of financial indigenization after independence therefore remained neo-colonial in essence and operational practice for twenty years or so.

The second phase of decolonization so far as financial developments are concerned led to sustained attempts to integrate the fragmented markets of the dual economies by extending the mainly urban modern banks into the rural areas, and secondly to stimulate the growth of money and capital markets together with appropriate credit instruments, that is by 'deepening' the financial system. The two methods overlap and complement each other and in practice have reflected a mixture of 'planning' and 'liberalization' policies applied in considerably different proportions in, for example, West Africa, India and South-East Asia. We have already noted some of the problems associated with the extension of bank branches in West Africa, and it will be convenient to look very briefly at the progress made in trying to establish effective money and capital markets in that area before turning elsewhere. The first attempt at setting up a money market in West Africa was that made in the Gold Coast in 1954, when the government issued its first tranche of ninety-day Treasury bills. The whole of the issue was taken up by just a few purchasers, comprising mainly the United Africa Co. plus two British banks. Later such issues in Ghana and Nigeria were similarly purchased (and held) by a few large expatriate firms and banks and by the Marketing Boards. The money markets were dominated by government paper purchased, and mostly held to maturity, by a handful of government agencies and expatriate firms. A few large swallows do not make a money market.

Similarly, when the Lagos Stock Exchange first began operating in 1961 it dealt in only nineteen securities. Having extended to three other branches the Nigerian Stock Exchange dealt in thirty-five securities in 1972. Thereafter the total number of securities grew more rapidly to reach 168 in 1983, mainly because of the artificial boost given by the company indigenization programme. By that year the number of shareholders exceeded 700,000, and there were seven issuing houses, seven merchant banks and twelve stockbroking firms doing business. Even so, according to Mr A. O. Fadina, the head of the investment department of the Nigerian stock exchange, 'the volume of trading on equity has remained low due to the behaviour of Nigerians in holding on to their securities, while speculation in securities is non-existent' (1983, 197). In some ways the oil boom worked to depress the growth of the money and capital markets, for by the end of the 1970s oil supplied 80 per cent of government revenue. The effect was to reduce, for most of that decade, the need for the government to borrow, and so reduced drastically the volume of Treasury bills, and federal and State loan stock etc. on the markets. It is clear that institutional provision is a necessary but insufficient condition for true financial deepening. Nevertheless considering the initially 'empty' state of these markets, the Nigerians should not be too self-deprecating about the degree of progress made in developing their financial markets within a single generation.

The indigenous monetary scene in India was glaringly different from that of the much more primitive picture which faced European traders in much of Africa. Silver and copper coins had been in use in India for 1,000 years, while for hundreds of years special castes or family communities of moneylenders had provided credit, collected deposits and arranged trading deals through bills of exchange or 'hundi'. In addition there had existed from time immemorial the resident village moneylenders. A few examples taken from this mosaic of indigenous financiers must suffice. The Multanis comprised a caste specializing purely in banking, mostly in urban areas where they could be relied upon to arrange quite large loans for their selected customers. They neither speculated themselves nor did they lend funds for speculative purposes. The Marwari were merchants as well as bankers; they engaged in a wider variety of banking activities than did the Multanis. The Marwari speculated themselves and frequently lent support to what they considered to be justifiable speculation by their customers. Like the Multanis, they were capable of providing large loans. In contrast were the large numbers of different kinds of moneylenders who concentrated on lending small sums to the poorer sections of society. Prominent among such lenders were the itinerant Pathans who were to be found throughout the Indian subcontinent in both the urban and rural areas, providing sporadic competition to the local village moneylender. The indigenous financial system was thus composed of various kinds of moneylenders (i.e. those who lent mainly their own money), and informal bankers (i.e. who lent mainly other people's money), though, with so many categories, the distinction between them was blurred. Some moneylenders supplemented their own funds by borrowing elsewhere for on-lending like the banking intermediaries, while the informal bankers were often well supplied with their own surplus funds. The categories overlapped, and between them they covered, in their informal and haphazard fashion, the whole range from lending petty amounts to impoverished peasants to carrying on business deals of a size and complexity not infrequently exceeding those carried out by the formal banks.

The formal, joint-stock banks included British-based banks such as Lloyds, Grindlays, the Chartered Bank of India, Australia and China, together with those of mixed parentage. They grew up in the nineteenth century to facilitate the trade in 'colonial' goods. In general, in their formation and development they closely resembled those already described for West Africa, and their story will not be repeated here. (A fascinating account of the Chartered Bank is given by Sir Compton Mackenzie in his *Realms of Silver*, 1954). Among the significant differences which do require examination are the three related matters of the currency system, the establishment of central banking and the integration of the long-established indigenous financial system into the modern formal financial system as a vital part of government planning to give India the best of both worlds – the indigenous and the modern, westernized system. Unlike West Africa, India had no need to import British coins, but it had a voracious and persistent appetite for silver and gold from any quarter. There was a pressing need to finance the growing trade with India and to maintain as much stability as possible between sterling in all its forms (whether in coins, notes or bills of exchange) and the rupee in all its many varieties. The most important of the formal banks set up to supplement the internal money supply were the three 'Presidential Banks' – the Bank of Bengal, established in

1806, the Bank of Bombay (1840) and the Bank of Madras (1843). The 'Exchange Banks', such as the Oriental Bank (1842) and the Chartered Bank (1843) looked after the business of financing external trade and foreign exchange from which the Presidency banks were debarred by their charters.

The fact that Indian currency was based entirely on silver, whereas Britain, followed later by others, was on the gold standard, caused recurring problems. Difficulties caused by the existence of twenty-five varieties of indigenous issues of rupees were largely overcome when in 1835 the East India Company was given authority to issue its own rupee, which came to be accepted as the standard throughout India and beyond. At the same time the silver rupee was given legal tender status, while any gold coins lost that privilege. With its currency thus based firmly on silver (as was that of China and Japan and much of South-East Asia) the vast increases in the supply of silver coming on to the world markets from around 1870 onwards – as a result of plentiful new mines and even more from the demonetization of silver as Germany, Scandinavia and others went on to the gold standard – brought about dramatic changes in India's terms of trade, inevitably reflected in the fall in the value of the rupee. For forty years before 1873 the value of the rupee had been maintained, with only very narrow fluctuations, at or near to 2s. By 1893 it had fallen to 1s. 3d. and, it was feared, was about to fall to only 1s. The authorities were forced to take action. Such a fall in the value of the legal and undebased coinage of a large group of countries comprising more than half the world's population was without precedent – a neglected aspect of the costs of the international gold standard and of the supremacy of sterling.

One of the Indian government's first actions was to set up the Herschell Committee, on whose recommendations the government suddenly closed the Indian mints to the free coinage of silver from June 1893. The resulting reduction in the circulation of rupees soon had the intended effect of raising the exchange value to its target rate of 1s.4d. at which level it was to be stabilized. This rate was commercially and administratively convenient, equating the anna with the penny and making fifteen rupees exactly equivalent to the gold sovereign, thus preparing the way for a fuller transfer to the 'ideal' of the gold standard. The reduction in the circulation of rupees and the high rates of interest required to sustain its higher exchange value led to widespread complaints of trade being strangled. In a further attempt to resolve matters another committee, this time under Sir Henry Fowler, was appointed in 1898. It endorsed and strengthened the previous commitment towards the gold standard, recommending a larger gold reserve to support the rupee, and renewed issues of gold sovereigns and half-sovereigns, which were again given unlimited legal tender status. The attempt to prop up India's limping bimetallism with the insertion of these gold coins was a failure. In any case, too much attention was being paid to mere coinage at a time when in India, as in the rest of the world, notes and bank deposits were more vital ingredients of the money supply. It was these wider financial matters which were at last faced by the Royal Commission on Indian Currency and Finance set up in 1912, chaired by Austin Chamberlain and enlivened by the brilliant unorthodoxy of its youngest member, a Mr J. M. Keynes.

Keynes's view, presented briefly in a memorandum in the Chamberlain Report (1913), were expounded more fully in his first book, *Indian Currency and Finance*, published later that year. In it he attacked the previous orthodox opinions of the Fowler Report and its insistence on trying to force all the trappings of a full gold standard, including gold coinage, on to the Indian economy. Keynes argued that there was no need for an internal gold circulation and that the gold saved from that purpose would be much better used to form part of a much enlarged gold reserve for a possible state bank which would be able not only to support the external value of the rupee but might well take over the responsibility for the note issue and assume at least some of the essential functions of a central bank. He pointed to the deflationary dangers, to Europe as well as to India, which arose from India's strong habits of acting as a 'sink of the precious metals' and of hoarding a considerable proportion of the metals she attracted from the rest of the world. The world should not leave 'the most intimate adjustment of our economic organism at the mercy of a lucky prospector, a new chemical process, or a change of ideas in Asia' (1913, 101). It was Indian hoarding that triggered Keynes's mind towards his later discoveries of the fundamental macro-economic relationships between savings and investment which culminated in his *General Theory*. His *Indian Currency and Finance* paved the way for what would later be recognized as the Gold Exchange Standard and also started the series of steps by which India established its own central bank. Keynes learned a lot from India; and the world learned a lot from Keynes. Little wonder that independent India eagerly imbibed Keynesian monetary and fiscal policies and combined them with an idealized faith in its five-year plans probably to a greater extent than any other LDC.

After the delays associated with the 1914–18 war, the recommendations of the Chamberlain Report were in part put into effect in 1921 when the three Presidency banks were amalgamated to form the Imperial Bank, a halfway house towards a central bank. The Imperial Bank dominated the formal banking scene in the inter-war period. It acted as the bankers' bank, it rediscounted bank and trade bills, it kept other banks' cash reserves and clearing balances, and came to their assistance in times of difficulty. It was not, however, allowed to deal in foreign exchange or to issue notes. Note issue had been a government monopoly ever since 1861. Thus, with only some of the essential functions of a central bank having been granted, Indian opinion clamoured for a proper central bank. As a result of yet further examination, led by the Central Banking Enquiry Committee, which reported in 1931, the Reserve Bank of India at last began its operations in 1935. Naturally it was modelled on the Bank of England.

After independence in 1947, the banking system was remodelled to fit its Indian environment. In 1948 the Reserve Bank was nationalized, a clear signal that banking was to be directed towards the objectives laid down by the government. The Reserve Bank was largely responsible for the establishment in 1948 of the Industrial Finance Corporation to provide medium- and long-term finance to industrialists unable to get such funds from normal banking services. The corporation was therefore intended to fill India's enormous 'Macmillan gap'. In 1952 the Reserve Bank made considerable improvements to the structure and operation of its formal money markets by creating a bill market in which the larger banks were actively engaged. In 1955 the Imperial Bank was at last re-formed as the State Bank of India; its few remaining central banking functions were taken over by the Reserve Bank, leaving it to concentrate on its commercial business, but with its duty to promote an active branching policy re-emphasized. The monetary authorities also encouraged mergers and amalgamation among the smaller banks in order to strengthen the banking system (for the smaller banks had a higher failure rate). Thus the number of 'reporting banks', which stood at 517 in 1952, fell rapidly to 154 by 1964 and then more slowly to reach its low point of ninety in 1967. In 1969 the fourteen largest private banks were nationalized, a process later extended to other private Indian banks, but not to the foreign banks.

One perverse result of the government's attempts to 'socialize' and control the rural moneylenders is instructive. Annual licensing, formal written contracts, maximum interest rates and so on had the effect of driving the moneylenders underground. There resulted such a shortage of credit in many villages that agricultural output fell. Desperate villagers were either denied credit altogether or had to pay even higher rates to compensate the moneylenders for the higher risks associated with their 'illegal' activities. The authorities reacted to this situation by trying hard to fill the rural vacuum by stimulating the growth of co-operatives and by a sustained drive to extend commercial bank branches into the villages. The number of banking offices rose from 1,951 in 1939 to 4,819 in 1947, and to 8,262 in 1969. Thereafter the pace hotted up to reach 30,202 in 1979 and 42,016 in 1983 (Nwankwo 1980, 47; J. S. G. Wilson 1986, 145). Thus, despite the rapid increase in population, banking density has been improved to a remarkable extent, e.g. from 1:65,000 in 1969 to 1:16,000 in 1983. A *laissez-faire* policy would not have brought about such an impressive degree of rural penetration. Much has therefore been done to extend and integrate the formal and informal financial systems within India's dual economy. The efficacy of these and similar measures is however held back by a number of considerable weaknesses, including the key factor of illiteracy, which in 1985 was still 57 per cent for male adults and 75 per cent for female adults. With per capita income of only $340 in 1988, India seemed fixed among the poorest group of countries, yet its neighbour, Bangladesh had a per capita income of only half that low figure. In an attempt to raise its growth rate, India from the late 1980s embarked on more liberal policies, no doubt influenced by the startlingly more successful results achieved in South Korea, Taiwan and in the two city-states of Singapore and Hong Kong, to which latter two examples we now turn.

The colonial territories to the east and south-east of India used a motley of different moneys; they shared their formal banking business among the British, Dutch and Indian banks, while their considerable informal banking was carried out by financial middlemen, such as the Indian Chettiars, and by a growing number of small indigenous local banks which arose to meet mainly the needs of their particular ethnic groups. The main links between the informal market and the more formal were supplied by the Chettiars. In the Malayan peninsula a varied mixture of media of accounts and means of payment provided the 'exchange' banks with ample justification for their generic title. During most of the nineteenth century the official currency in British Malaya was Indian, i.e. the government of the Straits Settlement kept its accounts in rupees and annas, although the general public kept their accounts and made most of their payments in dollars and cents, including their taxes. In this region, where the traders of East and West converged, the repeated official attempts to gain uniformity by insisting on the rule of the rupee were long doomed to failure. The public's revealed preferences were recognized when in 1867 dollars coined by the Hong Kong mint together with the highly favoured Mexican dollar and those of Bolivia and Peru were officially accepted as legal tender. In

1874 the same privilege was extended to the Japanese yen and the US dollar. Subsequently most of the former British colonies have retained the dollar designation, although until the late 1960s they were linked with sterling rather than the US dollar. With floating currencies internationally widespread from the 1970s these regions have all adopted managed floating to suit their own circumstances. In retrospect 'it seems fantastic that great British centres of commerce like Singapore and Hong Kong should have depended on foreign coinage' for so long, wrote Sir Compton Mackenzie, who goes on to explain that from 1894 a British dollar was at last specially minted for use in the East, being minted chiefly in Bombay (Mackenzie 1954, 114). In 1902 a Straits Settlement dollar was introduced, and in 1904 the Mexican and other dollars were demonetized, greatly simplifying transactions in communities which were still highly cash-conscious.

In much the same way there was no uniformity in paper money either. Official government notes were not issued in most of this region until the middle of the twentieth century, and had not by 1994 arrived in Hong Kong. During most of these two centuries the areas relied on the licensed privileges granted to just a few of the large commercial banks. The first of these note-issuing banks to operate in Singapore and Malaysia was the London-registered Mercantile Bank, which had spread south from its Indian base in 1856. Its issues were soon overtaken by those of the Chartered Bank, which saw the total circulation of its notes issued by its Singapore branch rise to over $300,000 in 1872 and then almost treble to $874,000 by 1880, faithfully reflecting the rise in trade and the growth of the banking habit. In the absence of either a central bank or of a Currency Board, these exchange banks filled the gap by profitably providing a reliable currency in the form of their own banknotes for a period of from eighty to a hundred years. In Hong Kong, the Hong Kong and Shanghai Bank has acted continuously since its formation in the colony in 1865 as the main bank of issue. In the 1980s it was still responsible for around 80 per cent of the Crown Colony's note circulation, the other 20 per cent being supplied by the notes of the Chartered Bank.

Although these exchange banks were originally established in the East to finance the local trading houses which dealt in tea, coffee, rubber, tin and so on, they soon diversified and in time spread far beyond their eastern bases, reaching back to absorb other banks in the Middle East, Europe and America, and developed a network of international branches. It is a tribute to the strength of their eastern bases that they were able to re-export their financial services in this way. Already by the end of the nineteenth century the HKSB had established branches in London, New York, San Francisco, Hamburg and Lyons. Its expansionary ambitions became especially aggressive in the second half of the twentieth century. In 1959 it acquired two London-registered banks, the Mercantile Bank (of India) and the British Bank of the Middle East. In 1965 it took a majority holding in its local Hang Seng Bank. In 1980 it obtained full control over the London merchant bank, Antony Gibbs, and also acquired a 51 per cent stake in Marine Midland Bank of New York. In 1982, it was, however, thwarted in its bid for the Royal Bank of Scotland, that country's largest bank, after investigation by the Monopolies Commission and adverse comments by the Bank of England for not heeding its advice (Report of the Monopolies and Mergers Commission, January 1982). By 1990 the Hong Kong Banking Group was ranked the thirtieth largest in the world; it had over 1,300 branches, of which 433 were in the USA, 409 in Hong Kong, 124 in Cyprus, 43 in Malaya, 39 in Saudi Arabia, 29 in the UK and 25 in Singapore. In 1992 it took a controlling interest in Britain's Midland Bank – a sort of reverse colonialism. As we have previously noted, the Chartered Bank followed a similar course. After its amalgamation with the Standard Bank, the enlarged bank successfully took over the Hodge group to provide itself with a regional spread of branches within Britain. In 1990 it had grown to achieve ninth place in the UK and a world ranking of 127th. As an indication of the vigour of the commercial banks of the two city-states, Singapore with a population of 2.6 million had five banks in the world's top thousand; Hong Kong with a population of 5.7 million had nine such banks; India with a population of 815.6 million had just eight, while Nigeria had none (*The Banker*, July 1991). A similar success story is seen in other aspects of financial deepening in these territories.

The increase in the number, size and range of activities of the commercial banks in Singapore and Hong Kong has been supplemented by the rise of other financial institutions and the development of their money and capital markets. The encouragement given to indigenous enterprises has not been at the expense of foreign financial institutions for both countries, heavily dependent as they are on international trade, have adopted liberal, open-door policies. Thus in Hong Kong, seventy-nine of its 113 licensed banks are foreign, while of its total of 283 deposit-taking companies, some 150 are either subsidiaries of foreign companies or are joint ventures with Hong Kong partners. Professors Lee and Jao, in their authoritative account of *Financial Structures and Monetary Policies in South-East Asia* consider that 'on this count Hong Kong is probably next only to London and New York in having the largest number of foreign banking and near-banking institutions' (1982, 9).

Similarly in Singapore twenty-four of its thirty-seven fully licensed banks are foreign, with their assets comprising 73 per cent of the total. Singapore's merchant banks grew from only two in 1970 to thirty-seven in 1980, most of them being joint ventures. The largest banking institutions in both countries, blessed with their international network of branches, have not only been active participants in the Euro-dollar market but have also strongly supported the development of an active Asian dollar market and an, as yet modest, Asian bond market. Hong Kong has the largest stock market in South-East Asia with a wide dispersion of ownership of shares among most income groups and with a large international clientele. With regard to financial securities, the rapid growth of this sector in Hong Kong may be illustrated by the growth in the number of professional dealers, advisers and representatives – from less than a hundred in 1967 to 2,204 in 1979.

Both countries have thus followed liberal, market-driven policies – but with significant exceptions seen for instance in Singapore's official discouragement of low-wage 'screw-driver' factories and its insistence on high-wage, high value-added products requiring skilled labour. Just two illustrations of financial 'dirigisme' may be given. The first concerns the Development Bank of Singapore which was set up in 1968 to provide long-term finance for industry and to serve generally as an instrument of government policy as a channel to support the government's chosen priority sectors. The DBS has collaborated closely with British, US and Japanese financial institutions in supporting a number of important industrial projects and in the development of the capital market by its own equity involvement and by acting as an issuing house for the shares and debentures of other companies. It similarly assisted the growth of the money market by helping to establish the National Discount Company in 1972. It has thus acted on a significant scale in a threefold capacity as a commercial bank, a development bank and a merchant bank. The second example concerns the Post Office Savings Bank, which in 1971 was separated from the Post Office of Singapore. Whereas the old colonial POSB, like its British parent, had to invest only in government securities and paid out only low and mean rates of interest, the new POSB gave tax-free interest and invested the resulting increased funds in priority projects such as public transport, shipping and aviation, including Changi Airport. As a result of this change of policy the number of POSB branches rose from forty-four in 1971 to ninety-eight in 1979 while the total of savings deposits increased by an astonishing twenty-eight times (S. Y. Lee, in Skully 1982, 63–4). Naturally this angered the other banks and led to a few modifications; yet it forms a brilliantly successful contrast to the overcautious and stodgy policies in connection with Britain's NSB and Giro as described earlier.

Liberal markets and financial deepening have worked together to provide an essential part of the foundation on which the successful growth of the two city-states has been built. Although it is much easier to raise the standard of living of small regions than of vast, highly populated countries like India or Nigeria, yet even when every allowance is made for such factors, the marked differences in the relative degrees of free markets and in their progress in financial deepening combine to tell a convincing story. Part of the difference for these contrasts lies in the extent to which Nigeria and India, together with a depressing number of other LDCs, have become increasingly indebted to their overseas creditors.

Third World debt and development: evolution of the crisis

Adam Smith, foreshadowing Rostow by three centuries, emphasized the crucial role of capital in development as follows:

> Every increase or diminution of capital tends to increase or diminish the real quantity of industry, the number of productive hands, and consequently the exchangeable value of the annual produce of the land and labour of the country, the real wealth and revenue of all its inhabitants.

Smith also succinctly encapsulated the later prolix preaching of the IMF and World Bank when he went on to warn that 'Capitals are increased by parsimony, and diminished by prodigality and misconduct' (*Wealth of Nations*, Book II, 'On the Accumulation of Capital' 301). However, for capital investment to take place at all, someone, somewhere has to save, a habit which the rich individual or nation finds much easier to foster than the poor, resulting in relatively and absolutely greater savings and investment potential in the richer countries. There is no doubt that the total psychic cost of saving is reduced by the transference of savings from the richer to the poorer countries – but this situation, if a true loan and not a gift, can continue only so long as the benefits from the proceeds of the resulting investment in the poor country exceed the repayment costs. Otherwise the savings of the poor are transferred to the rich, or the debt is repudiated, cutting off further supplies, a situation which has arisen not infrequently in practice in the past and underlines the world debt crisis of the last two decades of the twentieth century.

To the extent that freedom of money and capital markets exist, then savings tend to flow to the regions containing those sectors promising the highest net returns – those, in the Keynesian jargon, where the marginal efficiency of capital is greatest. In practice, political risks and incentives are added to economic uncertainty so as to interrupt and divert the flows of capital. All the same, there would seem to be a natural bias for investment funds to flow between and towards (rather than away from) the already industrialized countries with their well-established money and capital markets, where research and development activities breed new products and reduce costs, and where political structures provide more stable environments for investment than are generally found in LDCs. Thus over the long period the terms of trade tend to favour the rich countries, although there are frequent deviations from this trend strong enough and long enough to give particular groups of LDCs short- to medium-term advantages. Furthermore the degree of superiority in the productive powers of the rich countries over those of the poor is not the same in every sector. Thus profitable investment opportunities can arise in LDCs for their export trades in addition to their natural advantages in their domestic economies. However, while it is true that the workings of the law of comparative costs may provide opportunities for exportable goods lucrative enough to repay indebtedness, there can be no reasonable guarantee as to the broadness or duration of such opportunities. In the indefinite long run, the poorest LDCs are always trailing further behind the rich countries.

The long-run advantages in the terms of trade enjoyed by the richer countries are especially noticeable with regard to their greater bargaining power in the setting of international rates of interest and in determining debt repayment terms. The borrower and the creditor are rarely equal partners: as the proverb more crudely puts it, beggars can't be choosers. Keynes, in a section of his *Treatise* dealing with 'Methods of Regulating the Rate of Foreign Lending' showed how 'during the latter half of the nineteenth century the influence of London on credit conditions throughout the world was so predominant that the Bank of England could almost have claimed to be the conductor of the international orchestra' (1930, 306–7). The baton was passed to the USA in the 1930s while after 1945 a larger group of industrial powers including Germany and Japan, together with the IMF and the World Bank, have been the main determinants of international rates of interest. In such matters the LDCs may try to persuade (sometimes with success) but they cannot be decisive. Little wonder then that difficulties regarding LDC debt repayment have been endemic, though by and large manageable. Special circumstances since the mid-1970s magnified these

Table 11.3 Burdens of the twenty most indebted LDCs in 1988 compared with 1970.

	Rank	Total debt 1988 $m	Debt as % GNP 1970	Debt as % GNP 1988	Debt service as % exports 1970	Debt service as % exports 1988
Brazil	1	101356	12.2	29.6	21.8	42.0
Mexico	2	88665	16.2	52.4	44.3	43.5
India	3	51168	13.9	19.3	23.7	24.9
Argentina	4	49544	23.8	58.6	51.7	36.0
Indonesia	5	45655	30.0	61.7	13.9	39.6
Egypt	6	43259	22.5	126.7	16.6	38.0
Poland	7	33661	n.a	51.1	n.a	10.0
China	8	32196	n.a	8.7	n.a	6.9
Turkey	9	31589	15.0	46.1	22.6	35.2
Venezuela	10	30296	7.5	49.0	4.2	39.7
Nigeria	11	28967	4.3	102.5	7.1	25.7
S. Korea	12	27376	22.3	16.2	20.4	11.5
Philippines	13	24467	21.8	62.6	23.0	27.7
Algeria	14	23229	19.8	46.6	4.0	77.0
Yugoslavia	15	19341	15.0	38.9	19.7	17.6
Greece	16	18797	12.7	35.9	14.7	32.1
Morocco	17	18767	18.6	89.8	9.2	25.1
Malaysia	18	18441	10.8	56.3	4.5	22.3
Thailand	19	16905	10.2	29.7	14.0	15.7
Chile	20	16121	32.1	79.3	24.5	19.1

Total debt 20 LDCs = $719,800 million = 74 per cent total debt of all 89 LDCs in WDR.

difficulties into a world debt crisis of unprecedented degree and which seemed of almost unmanageable proportions.

Most LDC external trade is naturally with the rich, industrialized countries, so that the unprecedented strength and persistence of economic growth in the industrialized countries from 1950 into the early 1970s, despite minor setbacks, enabled the LDCs to borrow readily and to repay without insuperable difficulty. The amount of such borrowing increased substantially throughout the 1960s and into the 1970s without arousing international concern. Already by 1970, as is shown in table 11.3, a number of countries had built up very considerable amounts of long-term debt: e.g. Indonesia's debt was equal to 30 per cent of its GNP, Argentina's debt-servicing requirements took 51.7 per cent of the value of its exports, while Mexico's debt servicing was equivalent to 44.3 per cent of its export earnings. Such

Table 11.4 LDCs where external debt exceeded GNP in 1988.

	Rank	Debt as % GNP		Rank	Debt as % GNP
Mozambique	1	399.7	Tanzania	8	149.7
Congo	2	205.0	Côte d'Ivoire	9	135.1
Yemen	3	199.4	Jamaica	10	127.2
Mauretania	4	196.2	Egypt	11	126.7
Madagascar	5	192.7	Zaire	12	118.0
Somalia	6	185.2	Zambia	13	116.7
Laos*	7	153.5	Nigeria	14	102.5
			Mali	15	100.8

* Laos also had by far the highest debt service as % of exports (143.5).
Source: World Development Report, 1990, 222–3.

debts continued to grow without engendering any sense of impending doom until more than ten years later. It was not until August 1982, when Mexico failed to meet its contractual interest repayments, that the world debt crisis emerged into prominence to pose a danger to the development prospects of a number of LDCs during the remainder of the twentieth century.

The causes of the crisis were laid in the 1970s. The quadrupling of oil prices in October 1973 helped drastically to reduce the normal increase in the volume of world trade in general. The annual growth of world trade, which had been at the buoyant rate of 9 per cent between 1965 and 1973 fell to 4 per cent between 1973 and 1977. Higher oil prices transferred incomes, which would have been spent, to OPEC countries, whose powers of absorption were low and whose savings were high, a large proportion being kept as bank deposits in the western world. As a result there was downward pressure on world output and on international interest rates, which in real terms turned negative for several years. The scenario for a massive 'recycling' of petro-dollars via the banking system was thus laid in place, so that, after an initial hiccup, LDC borrowing was raised to an even higher level. Bank presidents travelled the world peddling their loans at bargain prices, with those of the larger American banks leading the way. By 1975 some 38 per cent of commercial bank lending (including short-term) to LDCs was by banks from the USA, with even many of the relatively small regional banks prominent in lending to their oil-producing neighbour, Mexico (Amex Bank Review January 1985).

The nature of much of the new borrowing, with relatively more coming from the commercial banks and less from governments and the international agencies such as the World Bank, made the LDCs much more vulnerable than previously. Compared with official sources, more commercial bank lending was at variable rather than at fixed rates and for shorter terms. When the industrialized world felt constrained to turn to monetarist policies to cure inflation, its imports (including those from LDCs) fell, rates of interest rose substantially, and aid programmes to LDCs were reduced to half or less of the 0.7 per cent of GNP, which had been accepted as a target by the UN in 1970. The monetarist fervour of the North cost the South dearly. The initially very attractive low or negative real interest rates had allowed the LDCs to embark on ambitious projects with low returns, including many that showed little or no potential for securing export earnings. Debts mounted and medium-term loans had to be renewed at higher rates, while export earnings to repay such debts failed to rise correspondingly. The swing from euphoria to panic, when it eventually came, was remarkably swift and all the more severe from having been delayed so long. The monetary pendulum applies to long-term and medium- as well as to short-term credit.

The second oil price shock, which led to a doubling of oil prices between 1978 and 1980, again helped to raise international interest rates and, combined with other causes, pushed the industrial countries into a deep recession, although the higher oil prices at first benefited some of the major debtors, such as the oil-producing countries like Mexico, Nigeria and Venezuela, thus postponing their day of reckoning. The first, but unheeded warning of imminent crisis came from an unexpected quarter when, in late 1980, Poland declared itself unable to meet its debt obligations. A mutually acceptable rescheduling programme was quickly agreed among the creditors. Poland's difficulties did, however, react on her neighbours in eastern Europe as western bankers, previously eager to lend, rapidly withdrew their funds. These two aspects of the Polish crisis – the 'regionalization syndrome' and the rapid reversal of bank funds – were soon to show themselves on a much vaster scale, but because the Polish situation was believed to be the unique result of its particular political disturbances, its warning signs were ignored by the world debt markets. It was the Mexican débâcle in August 1982 which led to a sudden and worldwide recognition of the unstable and untenable state of LDC indebtedness.

The Mexican crisis was triggered by a massive flight of capital to the USA in the late summer of 1982. The US government came immediately to Mexico's aid by making an advance payment of $1 billion for future oil receipts, while the New York Federal Bank together with the IMF and the Bank for International Settlements quickly arranged a package of bridging loans and credits of about $5 billion. The Mexican crisis immediately produced a 'regionalization syndrome' in Latin America, with flights of capital from heavy borrowers such as Argentina, Brazil and Venezuela. The effects quickly spread to reduce the borrowing powers of LDCs elsewhere, so that by the spring of 1983 some twenty-five LDCs with debts comprising two-thirds of the LDC total had been forced to enter rescheduling negotiations with their bankers, while many of them were completely cut off from new banking funds. 'It is not easy to escape the conclusion,' said the Bank for International Settlements, 'that international borrowing since 1974 has not been very advantageous to the debtor countries, although a good part of it was an inevitable product of two major rounds of oil price increases' (BIS Annual Report, 1983, 130). The lending bankers found their balance sheets under strains of unaccustomed severity, but *sauve qui peut* attitudes would only make things worse for other bankers as well as for the borrowers. Consequently in the ten years following the Mexican crisis a whole series of co-operative ventures were arranged, involving the debtor governments, the international agencies (IMF and World Bank etc.) plus the governments of the industrial countries and the lending bankers. Because of the prominence of American interests, the lead in such negotiations was first given by the US Treasury Secretary, James Baker, in October 1985, followed up by a modified and improved version by his successor, Nicholas Brady, in March 1989. While the details of these various initiatives differ, they offered combinations of debt forgiveness, debt lengthening, interest-free interludes, equity swaps, sales of discounted debt on secondary markets and so on. Of vital importance have been the structural adjustment programmes designed with the help of teams of experts from and engaged by the IMF and World Bank and tailored to the special requirements of each co-operating debtor – an essential factor in improving the debtor's prospects and one which the commercial bankers on their own would be quite unable to accomplish.

An indication of the size of the problem which still remained in the mid-1990s is given in tables 11.3 and 11.4. In terms of absolute size, LDC indebtedness is concentrated in a group of about twenty countries, with Latin America being prominently represented. In 1988 three-quarters of the total debt of all the eighty-nine LDCs listed in the World Bank's debt statistics was owed by the twenty countries shown, with Brazil and Mexico still the leading debtors and with 40 per cent of the debt of this most indebted group incurred by Latin American countries. In the 1980s the net flow of real resources has been away from most of these countries to the creditor countries. Debts and credits are born together as non-identical twins; hence debtors and creditors must share the blame for the 'lost decade' of the 1980s, but not necessarily in equal proportions. In this connection it might be appropriate to reflect on some of the views given by the financial leaders of heavily indebted LDCs at the annual meeting of the IMF and World Bank held in Washington in September 1990. The representative of India, the Third World's third largest borrower, stated: 'Our mandate must be to ensure the transfer of real resources to developing countries: we seem to be accomplishing quite the opposite' (IMF Summary Proceedings, 1990, 89). The Brazilian delegate, speaking on behalf of a group of twenty-three countries, mostly Latin American, was more specific:

> The debt problem is one of the most significant factors explaining the economic stagnation of the 1980s. Since the beginning of the debt crisis Latin America has transferred roughly $250 billion to creditor countries whereas it has received only $50 billion in financial resources. The figures are eloquent enough: the region exported resources in amounts several times greater than those in the Marshall Plan. (Proceedings, 1990, 93–4)

If the debt burden is measured not in absolute size but as a percentage of GNP then the plight of the very poorest countries is made plain, as is the near-impossibility of their being able on their own to repay their debts on the originally contracted terms. Table 11.4 shows that, of the fifteen countries whose external debt is greater than their national income, twelve are in Africa, including Congo with a ratio of debt to GNP of 205 per cent and the extreme case of Mozambique, whose debt is four times its national income. At the IMF meeting already mentioned the chairman of the Board of Governors, speaking on developments in sub-Saharan Africa, stressed the dangers of borrowing not only money but the package of ideas which came with them: 'We cannot afford to borrow foreign ideologies and models for our own development' (Proceedings, 1990, 80).

The 1990s opened with a new challenge to the South, sharply perceived by Governor Sumalin of Indonesia, the fifth most indebted LDC: 'Restructuring Eastern Europe is likely to require heavy infusions of capital, creating a new and sizeable claim on international financial resources that will compete with both the investment needs of the industrial countries and the development and debt alleviation needs of the developing countries' (Proceedings, 1990, 36). This argument, while having some short-run validity, smacks too much of the 'fixed sum of capital' fallacy or the false assumption of a zero-sum game, forgetting the long run, in which Keynes's ideas are not all dead. As part of the swing of the pendulum, Keynes is no longer king; but his insight into the relationship between saving and investment taught us that saving is not a fixed sum determining investment – but rather that investment (if efficient, as we have now learned), enlarges the global income so as to provide the higher savings required. Governor Sumalin also made a point, which would have been deeply appreciated by the prodigal son's elder brother, that heavily indebted but performing countries should not be forgotten. Prominent among such performers was his own, oil-producing country and non-oil-producing South Korea. Korea's debt was in 1988 about the same size as Nigeria's but represented far less of a burden in that Korea's debt was only a sixth of its GNP, while oil-producing Nigeria's was fully as large as its GNP. Korea and the other NICs of Taiwan, Singapore and Hong Kong have provided powerful examples to the remaining LDCs, showing that borrowing can be a springboard rather than a millstone.

A further hopeful feature for the Third World is the growing universal awareness in the last decade of the twentieth century of environmental issues, of which the IMF/World Bank's Global Financial Facility is but a starting point. While the Third World must not be made a dumping ground for northern pollution, there can be plenty of room for acceptable trade-offs in return for debt reduction and in 'swap for nature' deals of a thousand and one kinds – given only the vision. Where there is no vision the people perish.

Conclusion: reanchoring the runaway currencies

People who cannot look after their own money are unlikely to make a good job of managing other people's money, and so with countries. Inefficient investment of externally borrowed funds is more likely to occur where the domestic economy is highly inflationary, so that price signals cannot perform their allocative functions properly. Unfortunately, many of the highly indebted countries suffer chronic inflation to an almost incredible degree. During the 1980s the average annual rate of inflation for the severely indebted countries exceeded 100 per cent, compared with just under 5 per cent for the high-income economies. Table 11.5 indicates the severity of the inflationary disease among the poorer countries.

All but one of these twenty countries come from low or middle-income economies. The exception, Israel, relies to an extraordinary degree on indexing prices and incomes to the US dollar. Such devices are palliatives rather than cures. As Professor Patinkin of the University of Jerusalem emphasizes, the Israeli experience shows that 'an economy

Table 11.5 The twenty most inflationary countries, 1980–1988.*

	Rank	Annual average % price rise		Rank	Annual average % price rise
Bolivia	1	488.8	Zaire	11	56.1
Argentina	2	290.5	Ghana	12	46.1
Brazil	3	188.7	Turkey	13	39.3
Israel	4	136.6	Somalia	14	38.4
Peru	5	119.1	Mozambique	15	33.6
Uganda	6	100.7	Sudan	16	33.5
Nicaragua	7	86.6	Zambia	16	33.5
Mexico	8	73.8	Ecuador	18	31.2
Yugoslavia	9	66.9	Poland	19	30.5
Uruguay	10	57.0	Costa Rica	20	26.9

Source: World Development Report, 1990, 178–9.

whose money supply is indexed will generate a frictionless inflationary process which will accordingly continue indefinitely at indeterminate rates' (Patinkin 1993, 26). Seven of the leading ten inflationary countries come from heavily indebted Latin America. Bolivia leads this inglorious list with average annual inflation rates of around 500 per cent for the 1980s with Argentina averaging around 300 per cent and Brazil nearly 200 per cent. These averages mask the destructive power of inflation during its extreme ranges. Of all LDCs inflation appears to have become most endemic in Latin America, the extent and continued extreme severity of which is further illustrated in table 11.6. Peru's spectacular rate of 7,482 per cent fell in the three years 1990–2 to 'only' 73.5 per cent; similarly Brazil's from 3,118 per cent to 'only' 982 per cent. In view of such experience it would appear highly doubtful whether the patchy progress in reducing inflation between 1990 and 1992 is at all sustainable.

Some LDCs have, however, managed remarkably well in controlling inflation. India, though partly through rigid price controls, quotas and directives, has held down its inflation rate to an annual fairly respectable average of 7.5 per cent for twenty-five years. The true test is to be seen as it frees its markets. Indonesia reduced its average annual inflation rate from 34.2 per cent in 1965–80 to 8.5 per cent from 1980–8. Korea, another 'performing' debt repayer, similarly reduced its rates during that period from 18.7 per cent to 5.0 per cent. Inflation is not ineradicable even for LDCs.

For a hundred years up to about 1950 colonialism provided currencies of good quality and sound banks though constraining internal monetary

*For inflation in the 1990s see pp.667–72 below.

Table 11.6 Latin America's inflationary record, 1984–1992.

	Consumer prices % rises			
	1984–9 average	*1990*	*1991*	*1992*
Argentina	444.5	2314.0	171.1	25.0
Brazil	391.5	3118.0	428.0	982.0
Chile	20.5	26.0	21.8	15.5
Mexico	77.3	26.7	22.7	15.5
Peru	371.5	7482.0	409.5	73.5
Venezuela	30.5	40.8	34.2	31.5

Source: BIS 63rd Annual Report, June 1993, p.55.

growth and diverting development excessively into exports. Fifty years of subsequent independence has led to the other extreme of hyper-inflation which also strongly distorts development. Admittedly inflation during the second half of the twentieth century has been worldwide but with an enormous difference of degree between most advanced countries and most of the LDCs. Efficient spending, saving and investment decisions require reductions in inflation globally but most of all in the Third World and in the former command economies of the ex-communist countries. If the LDCs, in an effort to swing the secular monetary pendulum away from its inflationary extreme, were to anchor their currencies firmly once again to one or other of the northern currency blocs – the US dollar, the Japanese Yen, or one of the strong European currencies, it would be an act, not of neo-colonialism, but of plain commonsense, soundly based on the hard-learned lessons of their own experience. Reanchoring their runaway currencies is a prerequisite for development to reach its true, more equitable, long-run potential.

12

Global Money in Historical Perspective

Long-term swings in the quality/quantity pendulum

From early times when money first began to be used for a variety of purposes up to around the second half of the seventeenth century some form of physical commodity supplied either the only or the main form of money. In general, therefore, during that very long earlier period the limits within which money could become relatively scarce or plentiful were closer than have subsequently been the case. Even so, quite wide swings did occur from time to time in the relative quantities and velocities of circulation of money despite communities being reliant solely or mainly on commodity moneys. To some degree the alternations between inflationary and deflationary pressures are as old as money itself, although it is only after the development of modern forms of fiat money and of banking that the speed and extent of such fluctuations were able to increase without apparent limit. Modern fluctuations in the value of money are therefore simply differences of degree, not of kind, from those occurring in earlier periods, because money itself has a built-in pendulum to which extraneous forces ceaselessly add their own powerful pressures. Money is not an inert object, but a creature responsive to society's demands.

Our distant forebears yielded to temptation and returned chastized from their more modest backslidings to yield valuable lessons to modern generations, for money is among the most long-rooted of human institutions. Among the key characteristics which have given money its uniquely desirable qualities is scarcity relative to the demands made upon it for spending and saving (including conspicuous consumption and ornamentation). Such scarcity arose either from the difficulties of growing crops or rearing animals, catching fish, dredging, quarrying, digging mines and so on to provide supplies of the preferred type of money – or from the exercise of monopoly power by the main source or arbiter of the thing used as money. All these brakes on the money supply, whether natural or state-imposed, slipped from time to time. We have seen that where a state has a monopoly over money, it is extremely likely that, when pressed, it will seek salvation by such devices as printing more money, or in former times, by debasing the coinage, a process commonly carried to such an extreme that money became valueless, and a new scarce money of high quality had to be reintroduced. Such processes were invariably accompanied by and reinforced first by increases and then by decreases in the velocity of circulation. From the many examples already given just a few are reproduced here in this summary chapter to illustrate such pendular swings.

Examples are given in chapter 2 of the five-hundredfold depreciation in the value of the cowrie shell in Uganda following the wholesale importation of such shells in the mid-nineteenth century, and of a similar though not quite so drastic fall in the value of wampum in the USA following the introduction of mechanized drilling and factory assembly of wampum in New Jersey in 1760. We also noted in our study of primitive money that many communities used a number of commodities as money at the same time, thus providing an insurance when one of these types dropped in value. A positive and long-sustained increase in both the quantity and quality of money accompanied by similarly sustained increases in trade and mercenary military activity followed the invention of coinage in Lydia and the growth of mints around the eastern Mediterranean. The Greek city-states vied to produce the finest coins, with Greek bankers becoming the civilized world's most experienced money-changers. A further enormous stimulus to trade was later provided when Alexander the Great monetized the previously stagnant, huge gold stocks of the Persian empire, much of which gold was added to the silver stocks of the Greek bankers, so bringing down the gold–silver ratio from over 13:1 to a round and convenient 10:1. As was suggested in chapter 3, the London goldsmith-bankers would readily have recognized the Greek bankers as their close relatives; both were aware of the working of Gresham's Law in practice, and of the fundamentals of the bullionist theory of value.

For the ancient world's greatest example, by far, of excessive inflation we have to remind ourselves of the great debasement of the Roman coinage in the second half of the third century AD. By AD 270 the silver content of the denarius had fallen to 4 per cent, from 50 per cent twenty years earlier. By the end of the century the prices of the main goods were over fifty times higher than during the first century AD. This runaway inflation caused Diocletian to issue his famous Edict of Prices of 301, to institute a thorough reform of the currency and to support these measures by a strong fiscal policy in the shape of the world's first annual budget. Rome produced rubbishy metallic flakes for the impecunious together with gold coins for the rich. Roman experience clearly demonstrated excessive swings from monetary scarcity to monetary oversupply, and also the possibility of carrying on simultaneously with a two-tier monetary system – just as we today have relatively good currencies in most of the rich countries and bad currencies in most of the poor countries. Similarly, just as economists differ about the causes and cures of present inflationary and other ailments, so the ancient world still provides an exciting academic battleground for modernist, Marxist and primitivist historians (see Garnsey, Hopkins and Whittaker, 1983).

After the fall of Rome Britain showed the unique spectacle of being the only former Roman province to withdraw completely from minting money, and even refrained from using coined money for nearly 200 years. The velocity of money fell quickly after AD 410, as is indicated by the increase in the number of hoards found in the following few decades. Velocity, even including 'foreign' coins, probably fell to zero within a generation. In Britain the Dark Ages were particularly sombre so far as money was concerned (Grierson and Blackburn 1986, 4). The absence of money reflected and intensified the breakdown of civilized living and trading. When foreign gold coins did return to Britain from the Continent they were initially held to be too valuable for common currency and so were used mainly as ornament. Trade and velocity of monetary circulation increased together, recreating a demand for indigenous mints in Britain, so that by about the year 1000 some thirty mints were producing millions of silver pennies for trade and tribute in the form of Danegeld. The reminting of the coinage provided some of the early English kings with a rich source of income and a convenient alternative to taxes, a process which led to a more or less regular cycle of complete recoinage every few years, inevitably producing alternate shortages and surpluses of money. The value of medieval money in Europe depended crucially on securing a sufficient supply of bullion, whether from its own mines (in the case of silver) or from Africa (in the case of gold), especially when gold coins began increasingly to supplement its previously monometallic silver coinages.

The commercial revolution of the long thirteenth century (from around 1160 to 1330) was stimulated by increased supplies of both silver and gold, enabling the creation of multi-denominational currencies, comprising gold coins for very large payments with silver and copper (mostly silver) being used for the medium and small transactions which made up the vast majority of payments. A much more economically significant increase in the money supplies from this time onwards came from the development of banking and the use of bills of exchange, spreading from the leading centre of Lombardy to France, Spain, the Low Countries and then to London. The Black Death of the mid-fourteenth century illustrated the rare case where, although the absolute money stock in general remained unchanged, its relative supply was greatly increased. Even so, the inflationary effects, though patchily present, were compensated to a considerable degree by a drastic decline in the velocity of circulation.

The plentiful supplies of money in the long thirteenth century gave way to recurring bullion famines in the later Middle Ages, e.g. in the first decade of the fifteenth century, even more severely from 1440 to 1460, and again in the first half of the sixteenth century. To overcome such shortages monarchs resorted to debasement, especially on the Continent, while the Tudors also made use of other devices such as the dissolution of the monasteries, with the Church's silver plate adding to the proceeds of the sale of monastic lands. Such devices were rendered less necessary by the influx of precious metals into Europe from the Americas, and by the simultaneous rise in the acceptance and circulation of banknotes. Printed money supplemented minted money, moderately at first when linked together through the principle and practice of 'convertibility', but later without limit when governments found it expedient to abandon convertibility despite the inflation which inevitably followed, and which in turn could be cured only by relinking paper money to gold or silver or some combination of both. Numerous examples of such alternations, under modern conditions, of monetary excesses and reforms have been detailed in the previous chapters, with the extremes of astronomical price increases followed by complete monetary breakdowns occurring more frequently and becoming more geographically widespread since the 1920s than ever before. Warnings of the repeated tendency of the quality of money to deteriorate through excess supplies exceed the span of recorded history, from the fable of the Midas touch down to the annual reports of almost every central bank in the last two decades of the twentieth century. It should be abundantly clear that the need to understand and to control money is consequently also greater today than ever before.

The military and developmental money-ratchets

Although it has been possible to achieve long periods of reasonably stable prices in times of peace, wars have almost always brought with them rising prices, for two main reasons: first, government expenditures grow during wars, while productive factors are diverted into non-productive channels and, secondly, the government's normal powers to borrow and to create money are greatly stimulated by the imperatives of war. Even when, in post-war periods, resources return to productive uses, the inflated money supplies tend to remain in existence to form a new, higher base on which the economy operates. The military ratchet was the most important single influence in raising prices and in reducing the value of money in the past 1,000 years, and for most of that time debasement was the most common, but not the only, way of strengthening the 'sinews of war'. Supplementing the periodic bouts of official debasement were the more continuous practices of counterfeiting, clipping and forgery carried out on a considerable scale to supplement the official money supply, despite being subject to the harshest punishment, including the death penalty. However morally reprehensible, such practices when widespread pointed to the demand for money exceeding the supply, leading to attempts by the more entrepreneurial elements to overcome the constraints of a money supply wherever the incentives were sufficiently profitable. Bad money did not always drive all good money out of use but usually supplemented rather than supplanted good money, the latter being kept selectively for high-priority purposes, e.g. for export or for the payment of taxes. Gresham's Law at first worked to increase both the quantity and velocity of circulation, but if carried to extremes went into reverse, as coins became of such poor quality that they were no longer readily accepted, while holders of good coin would no longer part with them. Thus the various forms of official and unofficial debasement were accompanied by hoarding and dishoarding and so widened the swing of the monetary pendulum.

Given the ultimate disadvantages which inevitably followed the initial beneficial results of debasement, it is easy to see that in the long run increased supplies of specie obtained through trade or new mines, though of uncertain or accidental occurrence, were the best way of removing constraints on the growth of the economy. Long-run trends in depression and prosperity correlate extremely well with the specie famines and surpluses of the Middle Ages, as has been clearly demonstrated in the incomparable survey of money during this period made by Dr Spufford. Furthermore it was to the most prosperous areas of Europe, e.g. the towns of north Italy, that the increased supplies of gold and silver were in the main attracted, so encouraging the growth of new forms of money such as bank deposits, public debt instruments, bills of exchange and cheques. These paper additions to commodity money eventually widened the swing of the money pendulum to greater extremes than would otherwise have been the case. During this period the pound sterling gained considerable prestige by being less frequently and less drastically debased than most continental currencies. In this connection, however, we should remind ourselves of the point emphasized in chapter 4, that the countries which experienced the greatest economic growth were also those which had indulged in the most severe debasement. A 'sound money' such as sterling was in part purchased at the cost of crucifying the economy on the silver-cross penny or its later equivalents.

When modern paper money released prices from their metallic anchors, the military inflation ratchet began to be seen at its most powerful. The first extensive use of state paper issues (outside China) occurred in America, whose colonial governments, in a reaction to the extreme scarcity of sterling imposed by the British home government, began issuing their own notes. The 'Continentals' of the new USA fell in value by the end of the Revolutionary War to one-thousandth of their nominal value, a process repeated by the Confederate paper which similarly became worthless by the end of the Civil War. The *assignats* of the French Revolution and the hyper-inflation of the German mark between 1918 and 1924 are simply among the best-known of hundreds of examples of war-induced inflation.

Second only to war as an engine of inflation is the general acceptance of the need for an ever-expanding supply of money in order to facilitate economic development, a belief which in a weaker and vaguer form long preceded the Keynesian revolution, though it was the Keynesian ratchet which acted as a strong causative factor in the unusually high peacetime inflations of the second half of the twentieth century. The seventeenth-century writers on Political Arithmetic waxed lyrical on the positive powers of money to create national wealth. Sir William Petty, for instance, was convinced that, properly set up, a new public bank could 'drive the Trade of the whole Commercial World' (see chapter 6). John Law, the Keynes of the early eighteenth century, published a *Proposal for Supplying the Nation with Money* virtually anticipating the 'multiplier', and which when first put into effect in France producing beneficial results before leading on to the fiasco of the Mississippi Bubble. This failure pushed

French opinion back to the other extreme of opposing for more than a century the kind of banking system the country needed – another example of extremes in one direction leading to equally if not more damaging extremes in the other direction. France provides one of the best examples in history of belated industrial development being to a large extent caused by delay in adopting a modern banking system.

It would therefore be difficult to quarrel with the conclusion reached by Professor Rondo Cameron in his study of *Banking in the Early Stages of Industrialisation* that 'both theoretical reasoning and the historical evidence suggest that the banking system can play a positive "growth-inducing" role' (1967, 291). That was the attitude of the appropriately named 'Banking School' of the mid-nineteenth century in opposition to the 'Currency School', which latter emphasized the need to maintain the quality of money by restricting banking through tying note issue strictly to variations in the amount of gold. Similar polarization of views had been put forward by the anti-bullionists and the bullionists in the previous generation. Given the pendular motion of actual money supplies over time, it is no surprise to discover that most writers on money fall into one or other of these variants of the expansionist or the restrictionist schools. It was the *special* circumstances of the 1930s which gave rise to Keynes's so-called *General* Theory. Writing in the depth of the depression in 1933, Keynes pointed out that 'the first necessity is that bank credit should be cheap and abundant', but he also advocated the urgent need for 'large-scale government loan-expenditure'. 'Hitherto war has been the only object of governmental loan-expenditure on a large scale which governments have considered respectable' (1933, 20–2). Thus was the Keynesian ratchet invented. Later it was eagerly applied worldwide, especially by the newly independent nations of the post-colonial regions. However much the Keynesian revolution may be condemned for its long-run consequences of high and stubborn inflation, Keynes's enormous successes in providing cheap finance for the Second World War and in being largely responsible for the inestimable benefits of full employment for the first post-war generation, i.e. for its short- and medium-term benefits, should not be forgotten. Given its long-run drawbacks, the pendulum inevitably swung away from Keynesian expansionism back to a re-emphasis of *laissez-faire*, to monetarist restrictions on the money supply in particular and against government intervention and 'planning' in general. The slump of 1991–3 began to push the pendulum back away from monetarism towards new variants of Keynesianism.

Free trade in money in a global cashless society?

Technical improvements in media of exchange have been made for more than a millennium. Mostly they have been of a minor nature, but exceptionally there have been two major changes, the first at the end of the Middle Ages when the printing of paper money began to supplement the minting of coins, and the second in our own time when electronic money transfer was invented. ('Electronic funds transfer' is only one of a number of major improvements in communications which include the development of lasers, the use of satellites and so on, and is used here simply as a shorthand reference to the whole range of such inventions relevant to banking and finance.) Such major economies in the production of the monetary media have considerable macro-economic effects. The first stimulated the rise of banking, while the second is opening the way towards universal and instantaneous money transfer in the global village of the twenty-first century. It is hard to improve on Adam Smith's description of the revolution caused by the introduction of paper money – an invention more readily adopted in his own country than in the rest of Great Britain. 'The substitution of paper in the room of gold and silver money replaces a very expensive instrument of commerce with one much less costly, and sometimes equally convenient. Circulation comes to be carried on by a new wheel, which it costs less both to erect and to maintain than the old one' (1776, Book II, 257).

One of the most significant but insufficiently noted results of these two major kinds of invention is the fundamental reduction they bring about in the degree of governmental monopoly power over money. When coins were the dominant form of money, monarchs were jealous of their sovereign power over their royal mints. Paper money allowed banks to become increasingly competitive sources of money, a development which led not only to significant macro-economic changes but also facilitated contemporary revolutionary constitutional changes (as outlined in chapter 6). It was no accident that the Whigs, who supported the limited constitutional monarchy of William and Mary, were prominent in promoting the Bank of England. Similarly in the era of electronic banking 'national' moneys are becoming increasingly anachronistic as millions of customers, irrespective of their country of domicile, are eagerly offered a variety of demand and savings accounts by a multitude of competing financial institutions in a variety of competing currencies. They are spoiled for choice – and national money monopolies are thereby also being 'spoiled', in the sense of being reduced in effectiveness. The monetary authorities always try to reassert their monopolistic power – in economic jargon, to make sure that money is exogenously created – as opposed to money supplies produced elsewhere by the working of market forces – or 'endogeneously' as the economists describe the process. Just as the effective working of the international gold standard at the beginning of the twentieth century was dependent on the activities of the Bank of England, so the evolving European Monetary System in the last decade of this century has been dependent on the discipline imposed by the German Bundesbank, which was readily accepted by a German population that has remained painfully aware of the hyper-inflations it suffered after each of the two world wars. Twice bitten, thrice shy.

It was not until the UK experienced a frightening annual inflation rate of 27 per cent in the mid-1970s, when the trade unions rather than the Governor of the Bank of England were the real controllers of the money supply, that the Keynesian ratchet was thrown away and replaced by the monetarist policies that had long and consistently been proposed by Milton Friedman. He saw government restriction of the money supply as being by far the most important if not quite the only method of controlling inflation. However, another lifelong opponent of Keynesianism, Friedrich Hayek (1899–1992), proposed a strikingly different solution, based less on the power of government and more on the strength of the market led by consumer choice over the kinds of money to be used, with consumer sovereignty rather than government monopoly being the best guarantor of the value of money. It was in the UK's inflationary peak year of 1976 that Hayek published his two Hobart Papers of *Choice in Currency* and the *Denationalisation of Money*, updated in his book on *Economic Freedom* (1991). He lived to see the reversal of Keynesianism and the almost global triumph of the market over Marxism which he had prophesied. He advocated a Free Money Movement similar to the Free Trade Movement of the nineteenth century with 'the prompt removal of all the legal obstacles which have for two thousand years blocked the way for an evolution which is bound to throw up beneficial results which we cannot now foresee' (Hayek 1991, 220). Unfortunately the unforeseeability detracted from the acceptability of this part of his proposals. Wider credibility was given to his proposal to allow people to trade in dollars, pounds, marks etc., in the High Street but rather less to his suggestion that they should also have the right to claim their wages and so on in the currency of their preference. Echoes of this idea resurfaced in the British government's proposal of the 'hard Ecu' to compete with the other EC currencies. Retail choice of currency would replicate what had long been possible at the wholesale level in the foreign exchange markets.

This choice could include the use of gold coins, though Hayek was forced (reluctantly) to acknowledge that a return to the gold standard was impractical, since the very attempt to do so would cause huge and destabilizing fluctuations in the price of gold. Before returning to the implications of Hayek's concepts for the future of multinational currencies it is convenient here to consider briefly to what extent payments, in whatever currency, might come to be made in cashless form.

With regard to the technology of money transfer there is probably much truth in the paradox that the peaks of the longer-term future are easier to perceive than the misty low ground which comes within the compass of our more immediate vision. There is general agreement with regard to the long-term development of versatile, economic and ubiquitous money transfer systems, so that payment and credit facilities operated by the individual at home through video terminal or telephone, by the executive at the office or by the customer at the shop, all linked directly to a central computer, will at some future date be virtually on tap, enabling immediate validation and payment within agreed limits for practically everyone in western society, and probably also to the richer persons in the urban areas of the less developed countries. Disagreement arises as to exactly when this picture of a universal, direct credit-and-debit system will largely replace rather than merely supplement existing cash and paper transfer systems: it merely requires the extension of practices already in existence at the wholesale level downwards into the retail trade and greater co-ordination across regional currency systems similar to that anticipated by Hayek. A comparison with the history of development of the steamship is relevant here in that the threat of steam brought about such a remarkable improvement in the quality of sailing ships that this apparently obsolete mode of transport was extended for considerably longer than had seemed at all probable. This 'sailing-ship effect' is very much in evidence in the present paper transfer systems supplemented by electronic devices – improvements which have postponed the advent of the impatiently awaited cashless society to a rather more distant future than was anticipated only a few years ago. Cash, when compared with other forms of payment, still has many virtues, including that of anonymity, obligatory for the poor and yet also much appreciated by the rich criminal (as was demonstrated in the frauds that helped to bring about the failure of the Bank of Credit and Commerce International in 1991). Thus although cash will continue its present trend in becoming *relatively* less and less important in the industrialized world (despite some nostalgic attempts to revive a few prestigious gold and silver coins), it will remain of considerable importance for the greater part of the world's population. Real choice in currency, as in means of payment, is an option possible only in affluent societies, where traditional boundaries between currencies, banks and other financial institutions are dissolving. Hitler was a little premature in saying that there were no longer any islands: the smart card and the satellite have made most geographical boundaries obsolete insofar as the movement of money is concerned. Even multinational action by the monetary authorities can fail to control this flood on those occasions when the global, instantly mobilized army of speculators decides to strike.

Independent multi-state central banking

It might at first sight seem that the reference to Hitler is irrelevant. It certainly is not. It was his legacy of war and inflation which gave rise not only to the Schuman Coal and Steel Community so as to make future European wars much less likely, but also to the historic decision to grant the German central bank an unusually high degree of independence. The Schuman Plan led on to the Common Market, and from the beginning of 1993 to the Single Market. This in turn leads on in plain and painful logic to the concept of a Single Currency. In the same line of argument (as shown in chapter 8) Keynes's post-war policies would not have been adopted had he not demonstrated in *How to Pay for the War* his novel method of financing the most expensive war in history at rates of interest lower than ever before. His ideas were taken to extremes in the two decades following the Radcliffe Report, according to which money did not matter very much, and so economic discipline in Britain was drowned in a sea of liquidity. Thus the new-forged Keynesian inflation ratchet took over in peacetime from the age-old military ratchet. The slow, tide-like convergence in European inflation rates since discarding Keynesianism has been reflected in the attempts to narrow their exchange rates on the planned path towards irrevocably fixed rates of exchange, which by definition means a single currency, whether the different countries retain their old currency names or not.

A draft treaty on European Union was signed, with varying degrees of reluctance and euphoria, by EC heads of state in Maastricht in February 1992 in which the proposals for Economic and Monetary Union (EMU) were of special significance, outlining in confident detail the path towards a system of independent multi-state central banking for controlling monetary policy throughout the EC. By the end of 1993, after much political turmoil, the treaty had in general been accepted by the member states. In the mean time the speculative storms of September 1992 and July 1993 practically destroyed the Exchange Rate Mechanism and so greatly strengthened the hands of the opponents of the treaty that some considerable delay in implementing the original programme is almost inevitable, with only an inner core of, say, Germany, Benelux, France and perhaps Denmark pressing ahead with a modified plan. The prospect appears uncertain. The best-laid plans of bankers and bureaucrats gang aft agley. However, if the fundamentals of the treaty are eventually put into practice, then early in the twenty-first century a European Central Bank is likely to be fully operational, which together with the central banks of the participating member countries will comprise the European System of Central Banks (ESCB). In a radical departure from the traditions of a number of EC countries, ESCB will be guaranteed political independence.

Despite the opposition of those who, with some justice, decry such developments as being irreversible surrenders of national sovereignty to unelected and therefore democratically unaccountable bureaucrats, there would appear to be sufficient momentum already built up to carry at least the inner core of member countries towards the 'convergence' required to progress eventually through the various stages on to the climax of the final stage when a single currency, the Ecu (symbolically combining a medieval French currency with the reality of the modern German mark), is to become the sole legal tender of the participants.* After all, for hundreds of years in the Middle Ages, an abstract, fictitious unit of account, the *écu de marc*, was used in foreign exchange to circumvent the much more numerous national and regional boundaries of that period (Einzig, 1970, 71). Thus the future, in fact though not now in name, as is especially typical of monetary history, will be repeating the half-forgotten experiences of the distant past.

Neither Britain's proposal of a thirteenth currency, the 'hard Ecu', nor Hayek's free choice in currencies stand much practical chance of widespread adoption. The maintenance of multiple currencies would deprive EMU of one of its main advantages, namely the removal of exchange costs. According to a European Commission report entitled *One Market, One Money*, a single currency would remove transaction and exchange costs worth up to 1 per cent of GDP annually for the smaller state and around 0.5 per cent for the larger states. There would also be a saving of around Ecu 160 billion in the EC's foreign currency reserves. Such savings would not simply be of a once-for-all nature but would, dynamically, allow a higher sustainable rate of growth to be achieved (European Commission, Luxemburg, October 1990) – a consideration meriting close study by those who ask 'What price

---

* See pp. 658 and 662–3, where 'Euro' not 'Ecu' becomes the new name for the single currency.

sovereignty?' In any case, single sovereignty facing a financially and economically integrated Europe differs greatly from what existed previously. Either way, positively through entry or negatively through refusal, some sacrifice in traditional financial sovereignty is inevitable except, in the latter case, the sovereign right to inflate, a dubious benefit.

The worldwide swing of opinion and policy in favour of removing inflation at almost any cost has exhibited common features which have been enthusiastically adopted by a range of monetary authorities of differing political colours such as New Zealand, Australia, Chile and Canada, and have been incorporated into the EC's financial programmes. These include the setting of specific targets for inflation, the strengthening of the legal independence of the central banks, and the imposition of ceilings on government deficits. Spendthrift governments are to be pilloried. The annual report of the Bank of Canada may be taken as a typical example of the new fashion of setting out a published profile for the reduction of inflation over the medium term, not simply in a wishful vague declaration but in specific figures.

In February 1991 the Bank of Canada and the Government jointly announced targets for reducing inflation. The specific targets are to reduce the year-over-year rate of increase in the consumer price index to 3 per cent by the end of 1992; 2½ per cent by the middle of 1994; 2 per cent by the end of 1995. Thereafter the objective would be further reductions until price stability was achieved. (Ottawa, 28 February 1992)

In October 1992 the UK similarly adopted an inflation target, of 1 per cent to 4 per cent, with the Bank of England given the task of publishing each quarter its own independent assessment of progress.

Because of the inherent imperfections of almost all retail price indexes (e.g. in not being able to make allowance for the stream of new goods that feature heavily in modern consumer expenditures and in not allowing sufficiently for the increased quality of the 'same' goods) a nominal inflation of about 2 per cent is held by many authorities to be roughly equivalent to stable real prices. Attempts to go below that might well bring disproportionately greater costs. Thereafter competitive disinflation might have similar effects to the 'exporting' of unemployment by the competitive devaluations of the 1930s, or at least might depress the growth of world trade below its trend potential, causing a substantial and irrecoverable loss. On the other hand, unless the authorities are seen to make a really strong case for price 'stability' their loss of credibility might make its attainment impossible. It is in this connection that the case has arisen not only for the greater independence of central banks but also for giving to central banks the overriding priority for the achievement and maintenance of price stability. To give central banks a number of objectives which experience has shown to be incompatible leads to impotence where it really matters – the value of money (Roll, 1993).

Thus the ESCB is to be explicitly committed to the primary objective of price stability, and while it has to support the general economic policy of the Community, this must be only to the extent that it does not conflict with its primary objective. Its political independence is strengthened by a number of practical measures such as guaranteeing adequate finance for its operations, stipulating long-term appointments for its board (for eight years) and so on. The bank will not be allowed to make loans to public bodies, thus denying governments their easiest access to finance and blocking off a traditional road to inflation. The ESCB's statutory advisory duties regarding member countries' economic policies, such as the exchange rates with non-EC countries and fiscal policies – particularly the size of balance of payments or budgetary deficits – will reflect its primary commitment to monetary stability. ESCB has anti-inflation built into its constitution, an essential safeguard against the power of vested interests to push governments into excessive expenditure. For two generations inflation has been an almost permanent, though disguised and arbitrary, tax on the consumer. ESCB represents the consumers' response, a modern version of the revolting American colonists' cry of 'no taxation without representation', a democracy of the money box which is less inflationary than the ballot box.

Conclusion: 'Money is coined liberty'

The omens look promising for an era of much lower inflation in the richer countries from the mid 1990s. *The Economist* boldly sees zero inflation rather than merely low inflation as a distinct possibility for OECD countries which, having suffered high unemployment and low growth in the early 1990s in order to bring down the rate of inflation, would not wish this sacrifice to have been in vain (22 February 1992). The lesson has been learned worldwide, though at great cost, that it is countries with low inflation that have achieved high growth and therefore low unemployment. Thus, as detailed in chapter 11, the LDCs have learned the virtues of 'financial deepening', which could be obtained only through turning from Keynesian-type government planning towards allowing instead much greater freedom for market forces in general and financial liberation in particular. Even in the leading industrial countries inflation had appeared to be unstoppable for the whole of a long sixty-year period since 1933, during which the cumulative effect on the level of retail prices has been enormous, equivalent to 4,000 per cent in the UK and 950 per cent in the USA: others were far worse.

Attention has been drawn in earlier chapters to the paradox that in Britain and the USA inflation *increased* after the change in the mid 1970s from Keynesian to monetarist policies. This was for two reasons. First, the introduction of monetarism coincided with and complemented extensive financial deregulation. Secondly, and more importantly, inflation had become so embedded in Anglo-American society that its potential momentum, which had been suppressed by the planning controls associated with Keynesianism, was suddenly released. The frustrated inflationary horse had been given its head: it took a long time to bring its gallop to an end.

It has taken two generations for the truth finally to be fully accepted by the general public and by the political decision makers – first, that the apparent short-term benefits of inflation are outweighed by its long-term costs; secondly, that inescapably one of the keys to a successful economy is control of the money supply in its changing forms; and, thirdly, that this can be achieved only by limiting national governments' sovereignty through setting up independent central banking systems. In time the patient optimism of Lord Robbins, one of the few British economists to oppose Keynesianism when it was in full flood, has been justified: 'It really should not be beyond the wit of man to maintain control over the effective supply of money; and, as I conceive matters, eventually little less than the future of free societies may very well depend on our doing so' (Robbins 1971, 119). Thus it would appear that in the long run Keynesianism has been killed.

However, if the concept of the long-term pendulum is correct, then the monetarists' claims regarding the death of Keynesianism are exaggerated, for, as has been repeatedly demonstrated by past experience, theories and practices favouring financial restraint tend in the course of time to give way to precisely the opposite. This comes about in part because of social amnesia, in part because constraints, if long imposed, become increasingly irksome, unfair and patchy in coverage as privileged or ingenious persons find ways around the constraints and invent acceptable money-substitutes. Perhaps the strongest force undermining monetary restrictions in the long term is the common complaint of output forgone, as shown in the various versions of countries being 'crucified on a cross of gold', or 'held to ransom by money monopolists' or being 'made bankrupt by high interest rates' and so on. Opinion begins to turn again in favour of less restrictive – and eventually, of clearly expansive – monetary policies.

Furthermore when prices have remained relatively stable for some years, so that inflationary expectations have evaporated, then Keynesian-type policies really can work again, provided that they are believed to be genuinely short- to medium-term in duration and/or restricted to particular regions, or for clearly exceptional purposes.

German reunification provides a powerful example of how a country which has had an excellent long-run post-1950 record (compared with most others) in controlling inflation, has consequently been able to put Keynesian-type policies to work with good effect, deliberately seeking unbalanced budgets and running down its customarily large balance of payments surplus into a significant deficit, as a result of making huge financial transfers from West to East Germany, which in 1992 were, at DM 180 billion, equivalent to 6.5 per cent of West Germany's GNP (see 'Massive support for the new Länder' in Deutsche Bundesbank Monthly Report, March 1992, 15 ff.). The conversion rate for the merging of the marks, as explained in chapter 10, was certainly not chosen by the free market, nor, despite its blustering, by the Bundesbank, but was most definitely a political decision boldly taken by Chancellor Kohl. The balance of benefit to Germany was clear, despite some increase in inflation and in interest rates which turned out to be acceptably moderate in Germany, but unfortunately extremely awkward for the rest of the EC, forcing their rates up at a time of rising unemployment, when naturally they would have wished to reduce them. Policy synchronization in a multi-state system poses considerable difficulty for the future ESCB. In the case of countries such as Britain and the USA which had not been able to control inflation, Keynesian policies worked perversely, making matters much worse and so contributed to a considerable degree to a debilitating process of deindustrialization. Only after the conquest of inflation can Keynesian-type weapons become again available for re-industrialization and regional stimulation, and then only for a limited, medium-term period.

In most countries the current anti-expansionist monetary pendulum probably still has until around the turn of the century before the movement back in favour of Keynesian expansion reasserts itself. Mounting, if belated, concern about the vast increase in population occurring mainly in the poorest countries, the depletion of finite resources, the problem of global pollution and other environmental concerns are at best only partially amenable to free-market solutions. The market gives no priority to posterity or the poor: silent majorities. As the costs of market failure become more obvious, so will the need for increased co-operative governmental intervention. (Perhaps concern about global warming and the ozone layer might even replicate the 'sun-spot' theories of the nineteenth century as contributory causes of economic disequilibrium.) The wide, long-term oscillations to which monetary policies are prone are brought about not only by the obviously strong destabilizing forces of wars, famines, inventions and so on, but also because money itself frequently exerts its own inherent instability. While it is readily conceded that 'real' factors can push demand and supply so much out of balance that cumulative disequilibrium may follow, it is not sufficiently emphasized that money contains within its many-sided nature dynamic features that also can be destabilizing. More notice is usually given to the other functions of money, in facilitating the myriad exchanges of daily commerce, where money is the indispensable equilibrator, a cybernetic mechanism of immense power and delicacy: but it is not infallible.

We have seen that most theories of money tend to fall into one of two contrasting groups which, however, given a long-term perspective, are complementary. Writers of the first group emphasize the importance of limiting the quantity of money in order to enhance or maintain its value or quality. The second group of writers are more concerned with allowing or encouraging an expansion in the effective quantity of money so as to stimulate economic growth or at least to remove any brake on such growth, notwithstanding the decline in the quality of money which might result from such expansion. Among this latter group, Schumpeter and Keynes were in agreement that it was the entrepreneurs with their 'animal spirits' that disturbed the 'status quo' which economists call equilibrium. In borrowing to fulfil their ambitions, the entrepreneurs alter the previous flows of saving, investment and income in ways which not uncommonly become cumulatively destabilizing. Briefly, then, the money pendulum is likely to be set in motion even when there are no external shocks, but its amplitude tends to be increased by the frequent though random appearance of such shocks.

In the normal course of events money is rarely 'passive' or 'neutral', while the safe haven of equilibrium on which so much economists' ink has been spilled and which still appears to inspire the dangerous, earth-flattening zeal of the Brussels bureaucracy, is equally rarely attained. An assumption, possibly unconscious, of some ideal equilibrium may lie behind Euro-planners' enthusiasm for 'level playing fields' for all the Community's financial and other economic units, and so carries the danger of imposing a far too restrictive network of rules and regulations with regard to fiscal, financial and industrial policies. In this connection Lord Robbins's view is even more relevant now than when he first produced his masterly analysis over fifty years ago: 'There is no penumbra of approbation round the theory of equilibrium. Equilibrium is just equilibrium' (1940, 143). Sir Gordon Richardson, when Governor of the Bank of England, wrote of his experience as follows:

> I regret to say that I have little direct experience with economic equilibrium – indeed, so far as I am aware, none at all. I sometimes see suggestions that we shall be moving towards equilibrium next year or perhaps the year after: but somehow this equilibrium remains firmly in the offing. In the mean time, governments and central banks are likely to be faced with a series of difficulties which have to be addressed. (IMF Essay on 'The Pursuit of Equilibrium', Euromoney, October 1979)

While the swings of the pendulum cannot thus be held fixed at mid-point, the art of monetary policy consists of moderating their amplitude rather than seeking to achieve some unobtainable, unreal, theoretic goal of equilibrium.

There is ample evidence to show that monetary policies, whether expansive or restrictive, can when appropriately applied and supported, work remarkably well – but only for a limited short- to medium-term period, without having to be radically readjusted. If pushed too far or carried out for too long, as happens when policy-makers become convinced of the eternal verities of the scribblings of some transient economist, then both kinds of policy suffer from a pernicious form of macro-economic diminishing returns. Sound money, in the sense of an optimally adjusted supply, is the foundation both of capitalism and of freedom. It is therefore fitting and timely that the last two comments on the fundamental importance of money should be ascribed to two famous Russian writers. 'Lenin is said to have declared that the best way to destroy the Capitalist System was to debauch the currency' (Keynes 1920, 220). Dostoevsky's comment is more concise and positive:

Money is coined Liberty.

Postscript: The View from 1996

1. More *coins in an increasingly cashless society*

Historians need to put in a good word for numismatists for they help to bring the past vividly to life. A brilliant instance of this took place at an auction by Sotheby's on 5 July 1995 of some two hundred ancient coins, estimated to fetch £1½ million but actually realizing £2,099,295. The collection, reckoned to be the most important of its type to be auctioned in London for over fifty years, included a selection of electrum, gold and silver coins spanning a thousand years. An aureus of Maxentius Aurelius, AD 306–12, was sold for £71,500, with the highest price, £132,000, being reached for a tetradrachm of Naxos, Sicily, of around 460 BC. These costly examples eloquently remind us that for most of the last 2,700 years coins have been by far the most important form of money. At the end of the twentieth century it is, surprisingly, still true that more coins are being produced and put into daily use by more people around the world than ever before, despite the fact that during the past three or four centuries paper money has grown first to supplement and then practically to supplant coins in terms of their relative values. As we approach the new millennium the rapid rise of completely new forms of money substitutes in the shape of plastic and electronic money finally threaten to accelerate the apparent terminal decline of the longest-lived, most tried and tested kind of money known to civilized society. Are coins, which have been dismally neglected by most economists for seventy years or more, finally to disappear into the dustbin of history, to be treasured only by numismatists and the occasional aberrant economic historian?

Far from dying, however, a new exuberant florescence of recoinage is about to spring forth, fed by three powerful stimuli: the frantic search for a Single Currency which – if the European Commission's projections are followed – will require a new series of Euro-coins to replace the many existing varieties from the year 2000 onwards; similar replacements for the new democracies of the former Soviet Union and its satellites; and, much the greatest, the demands of the growing poor multitudes in the Third World. For the poor are always with us, more so in the years ahead, and so also for the foreseeable future will be the necessity for hard cash, the poor man's credit card. (Popular slogans, as in this case, often out-perform expert predictions.) Even before such impending demands arise, confirmation that the actual amounts of currency being produced in recent years is at record, best-ever levels is proven by the figures available from the annual reports of the Royal Mint for the years 1993 to 1995 and from a special study by P. B. Kenny on behalf of the Mint: 'The Number of Coins in Circulation', the first such study since the preparations for decimalization in 1971 (*Economic Trends* No. 495, Jan. 1995). The Mint's report for 1993–94 shows that 'the production of blanks and coins [at nearly 3.5 billion], operating profit and export sales [to seventy countries] were all substantially in excess of the best achieved in its long history' of over a thousand years. Furthermore, 'the number of UK circulating coins issued, at 1,366 million, was a 21 per cent increase on 1992–93'. Table PS 1a (see p. 660 below) shows that the number of coins in circulation in the UK in December 1994 was well over 17 billion with a total value of nearly £2 billion. It also indicates that, with the sole exception of the unloved 50p. piece, there is, just as one would expect, an inverse relationship between the values and the volumes of each denomination.

Further confirmation of the continuing popularity of cash, i.e. coins plus notes, is given by Susan Bevan in an article entitled 'Cash is Still King', where she comments: 'The cashless society, with clumsy and expensive to handle coins and notes replaced by efficient electronic payment messages, is a dream cherished by banks, but the British public remains firmly attached to the traditional way to pay' (*Banking World*, Oct. 1994, 16). Cash transactions actually increased in 1993, probably a temporary regression because of the recession, and accounted for 63 per cent of all the 26.7 billion transactions of more than £1 in value made in that year. The recent increase in output by the Royal Mint is likely to be far exceeded by the enormous potential demand for new 'Euro' coins which the European Monetary Institute predicts will be required by 2002. Even allowing for considerable slippage in timing and in the number of core countries participating, the prospect emerges of an unprecedentedly large, contemporaneous demand for up to 370 million customers during the first decade or so of the new millennium. Politics, not economics, will be the decisive factor determining the pace and extent of these monetary changes in the EU and the former command economies of the Soviets and satellites – but that, as has been amply demonstrated above, is nothing new. Between 1993 and 1995 the Royal Mint had already found customers in Estonia, Mongolia, Turkmenistan, Croatia and the Czech Republic.

The market for coins in the so-called Third World is likely to be even larger for a number of reasons which can only be hinted at here. First, above a certain very low threshold, the demand for coins by the poor is proportionately, and in many cases absolutely, higher than that by richer persons, who have easy recourse to other forms of payment denied to, or made difficult for, the poor. To the economist coins are not merely 'inferior goods' but exhibit 'Giffen' tendencies where an individual's demand for coin actually falls when his income rises to a higher level. (To the numismatist, in contrast, for those rich people who can afford to purchase the kind of coins auctioned at Sotheby's, such coins are 'superior goods', prized for the high prices they command and are typical of what the US economist Thorstein Veblen first called 'conspicuous consumption'.) Thirdly, allied to the above factors, is the remarkably young age distribution in most Third World countries. Fourthly, the size and growth of population in the poor countries greatly exceeds that in the rich. Fifthly, the infrastructural assets, such as telecommunications, essential for the development of non-cash systems are not as available or reliable as in rich countries. Finally inflation in poor countries generally greatly exceeds that in the advanced nations – and inflation feeds the need for repeated recoinages for a rapidly growing money supply.

When we turn to examine the total values rather the volume of transactions, then the picture changes dramatically and a clear explanation emerges to account for the paradox of coinage, namely its rising absolute production combined with its falling relative economic significance, as is illustrated by the figures given below. Table PS 1b shows that the total value of coins in circulation in UK in December 1994 was just one-tenth of notes and only one-three-hundredth part of the total broad money supply, M4. Obviously there is no gainsaying, even when every allowance is made for velocity of circulation, that coins are more than ever merely the very small change of a modern country's money supply. Nevertheless, everywhere around the world they remain stubbornly indispensable, a vigorous anachronism, surprisingly but indisputably likely to grow substantially in absolute volume for decades

The paradox of coin: rising production – falling significance

Table PS 1a. Coins in Circulation in UK, Dec. 1994:
Values and Numbers (million).

Denomination	£ million	%	Number	%
1p	64	3.2	6,400	37.0
2p	78	4.0	3,900	22.6
5p	133	6.8	2,660	15.4
10p	134	6.8	1,340	7.8
20p	297	15.2	1,485	8.6
50p	240	12.3	480	2.8
£1	1,012	51.7	1,012	5.8
Total	1,958		17,277	100.0

Table PS 1b. Narrow and Broad Money Supply in UK, Dec. 1994
(£ million).

Coin	1,958	% M4 = 0.3%	⎫ 'cash' 21,849 (3.9%)
Notes	19,891	3.6	⎭

		%
Banks' operational balances B of E	175	0.03
Narrow Money (MO)	22,024	4.0
Bank & Building Soc. Deposits	546,411	96.0
Broad Money (M4)	568,435	100.0

NB Coins = 1/10th of 'Cash' and only 1/300th of total money supply.

Sources: Royal Mint; *BEQB*, Feb. 1995, and Bank of England Monetary Statistics, Feb. 1995.

to come. Despite the fact that we all learn our first monetary lessons through coins – lessons which we might well think would therefore be indelible – the true influence of coins on modern social, economic and political history has been grossly underestimated. A challenging exception to this general neglect is to be found in the recent stimulating researches of Professor Angela Redish of the University of British Columbia – for example in assessing the relationship between Britain's improved token coinage and its early formal adoption of the gold standard; and the contrasting picture in France and the Latin Monetary

Union where bimetallism belatedly persisted. A pale reminder of nineteenth-century bimetallism now being introduced in many mints is the production of bi-coloured coins for high-value denominations (thus partly replacing low-value banknotes). These increase the 'grasp' of coins up the income chain: and that, as we have seen, was the original meaning of 'drachma' when coinage began its not-yet-ended Odyssey.

Turning to the economically dominant non-cash payments, according to the latest assessments of Britain's Association for Payment Clearing Services (APACS), over 90 per cent of adults in UK hold a bank or building society account, over 75 per cent possess a plastic debit or credit card, while over 75 per cent of the workforce are paid through Bankers' Automated Clearing Services (BACS). Paper-based systems, mostly cheques, peaked in use in 1990, their subsequent fall more than being made up by the rise in plastic card and other forms of automated payment. In terms of volume, around nine million cheques were still being cleared through the Cheque and Credit Clearing Company on average every day in 1994. One small but interesting page of history was turned when the old Town Clearing, first set up in 1773, was closed in February 1995. High value payments were normally cleared 'same day' through the Clearing House Automated Payment Scheme (CHAPS) and totalled well over 90 per cent of the value of all average daily clearings. As a result of co-operation between the Bank of England, CHAPS and APACS, the speed and security of large value payments will be still further improved by the introduction of a 'Real Time Gross Settlement System' from mid-1996.

The picture in other major economies is roughly comparable. Thus in the USA 'based on value, over 90% of all transactions are now made electronically. Based on volume, over 90% are still made by cash or check' (*Federal Reserve Board Review*, Kansas, 3rd. Quarter, 1995). It is the disproportionately high costs, especially in high income countries, of providing cheques and coin payments which has acted as the main spur for banks in their efforts to extend electronic payment systems more widely at the retail level. Of the costs of providing payment services as a whole in the UK in 1993, assessed by APACS at £4.5 billion, by far the greater part is attributable to cheques and coins. Interbank competition holds back attempts to charge customers directly anything near the full cost of providing paper services: customers pay when buying other services, thus distorting resource allocation. Similarly the public's atavistic attachment to coins acts as a brake on any rapid development of electronic cash at the retail level. Nevertheless, trials of such systems are being undertaken in a number of countries. In the UK a multifunctional card or 'purse', optimistically called Mondex, was introduced in Swindon in July 1995. NatWest, its parent, together with Midland and Bank of Scotland are co-operating in its further extension. The franchise for the Far East has been bought by the Hong Kong Bank, while the Royal Bank of Canada and the Imperial plan to cover Canada. In November 1995 the Mark Twain Bank of St Louis, Missouri, introduced a new form of digital currency developed by David Chaum, one of the world's leading experts on computerized currency.

Now that wholesale payments have been caught in the full tide of the electronic revolution, traditional commercial banks will face stronger competition from non-banks and from 'dis-intermediation' as lenders and borrowers can deal more easily directly with each other without needing a financial intermediary. Central bankers' tasks in attempting to define, measure, monitor, control and supervise their own countries' changing forms of money and monetary institutions, will become much more complex as the old boundaries between national and regional monetary domains will be broken down by new forms of competitive currencies. Wholesale systems, despite the obvious security problems, seem technically capable of being adapted to deliver some kind of global 'single currency' early in the new century, possibly before Europe's single currency is firmly and widely adopted (see Keating, G., *Financial Times*, 2 Nov. 1995, 15).

The European Commission's plans for 'One Currency for Europe', published as a Green Paper in May 1995, together with the Cees Maas Report of the 'Expert Group on the Changeover to the Single Currency', still spoke in confident tones, but with hints of desperate urgency. The Green Paper boldly began: 'By the end of the century, Europe will have a single currency. This was the wish of its peoples and leaders in signing and then ratifying the Treaty of European Union' (p.3). The vigour of both statements appears overdone. Furthermore: 'Establishment of the single currency will be completed only with the introduction of the ecu as the single currency in all its aspects, including notes and coins' (p.4). With regard to large value payments it goes on to say: 'The advent of a single monetary policy' will 'require the establishment of a European system of real time gross settlement. TARGET (Trans-European Automated Real time Gross settlement Express Transfer) will be the payments system for the implementation of the monetary policy of the ESCB in ECU' (p.40). Similarly, the Maas Report predicted that 'at the end of 1999, the old currencies will be exchanged for the new currency over a brief period whereupon the new currency will be the only legal tender in EMU countries. The rapid introduction of the ECU as the single currency will then be a reality' and 'there will be no need to continue with the current basket ECU' (p.10). In December 1995 at the Madrid Summit Meeting, it was agreed, unanimously but unenthusiastically, to call the new currency, the 'Euro', a name apparently uncontaminated with national or historical connections. A new Babel looms large (see Connolly (1995) and *The Economist* (3 Feb. 1996).)

In any event, as far as retail, small payment systems are concerned, coins have clearly demonstrated their indestructibility and seem able to survive and indeed to thrive alongside any kind of competitor. Even in the long run they are not dead.

2. The death of the Treasury tallies, 1782–1834

One ancient and long-lived form of quasi-money that did eventually die an intriguing death was the tally. We saw (p.147 ff. above) that wooden tallies, the world's oldest accounting system, came to be used by the English Treasury as a versatile credit instrument to an extent much greater than elsewhere. By the second half of the eighteenth century it was becoming painfully obvious to everyone outside the Treasury that their day was over. At last an Act of 1783 decided on their abolition – but this was not to take place until the death of the last of the officials operating the system, the Exchequer Chamberlains, which event did not occur until 1826. By that time the tallies had become increasingly ridiculed, public opinion being most vividly expressed by Charles Dickens. He attacked the Treasury's 'obstinate adherence to an obsolete custom' as if these notched sticks were 'pillars of the constitution'. In a way that could not have been imagined by Dickens or anyone else, their connection with the constitution even in their final days turned out to be surprisingly close. After 1826 the redundant tallies were returned to Westminster where the old Star Chamber and other parts of the House of Commons became jam-packed with these wooden relics. In 1834, in order to save space and economize on fuel it was decided that they should be thrown into the heating stoves of the House of Commons. 'So excessive was the zeal of the stokers that the historic Parliament buildings were set on fire and razed to the ground. The tallies perished in a blaze of defiant glory' (Robert, R. 1956, 76). This backward glance is a further timely reminder that fundamental monetary changes rarely leave the political constitution unmoved. Technical progress made the tally redundant: perhaps the computer will chip away what remains of Parliamentary sovereignty in matters of finance.

3. Derivatives and the new Barings crisis of 1995

With a gap of a century since the infamous crisis of 1890, history repeated itself with a fatal vengeance when Barings, Britain's oldest and one of the most prestigious merchant banks, finally failed in February 1995. What was amazing about the new crisis was the ability of one person, relatively inexperienced and acting alone, to incur losses, undetected, of £860 million, so far exceeding Barings total capital as to put the bank beyond rescue. The sorry tale is summarized in a few words: old-fashioned greed, fraud, and woefully inadequate supervision, combined with modern 'derivatives'. Mr Nicholas Leeson was recruited to work in Barings 'back office' in London in 1989. In April 1992 he was appointed to be in charge of the back office, dealing in humdrum settlement business, in Singapore, but very soon afterwards he also took over the 'front office' business, dealing on the Singapore International Monetary Exchange ('SIMEX'). To be allowed to operate this dual position seems inexcusable, but the offices were new and Barings management structure was being altered. A tug-of-war was taking place between the traditionalists, wedded to corporate and investment banking, the profits from which were based on a long-term horizon, and on the other hand the new managers, pushing for an extension of the fashionable trading in equities, options and derivatives, yielding rapid results: two vastly different cultures which did not mix well. Leeson profited from this division. At first he dealt only in 'agency business' acting on behalf of Barings' customers (which earned modest commissions), but soon began 'proprietory' trading, that is using Barings' own funds with the chance of gaining much higher profits. Any losses were shovelled by Leeson into a seemingly innocuous 'Error Account' which he opened as early as 3 July 1992. This account, No. 88888, became a black hole into which huge losses disappeared unseen while all the time his apparent, but fictitious, profits mushroomed.

Derivatives are financial instruments which derive their value from a price, or an index of prices, in some underlying market. They are widely used to speculate, or to alter market exposure cheaply and quickly, in currency, bond and equity markets. Derivatives developed out of traditional hedging and forward trading. There are two main categories of derivatives. The first involves actually purchasing or selling assets at a particular time or within a certain period, while the second broad category simply deals in options, i.e. conferring the right, but not the obligation, to buy (call option) or sell (put option). They range in complexity and may involve floors, ceilings, caps, collars, swaps, swaptions and even options on options. Leeson's activities were technically rather straightforward, and it was assumed, but not checked, by Barings that his contracts were fully hedged by matching positions. In fact they were not, thus exposing Barings to huge losses from even small market fluctuations. Computerization enabled small price differences to be spotted and acted upon immediately, with large volume operations enabling skilled traders to earn sizeable profits even from such small price differences, although such large amounts, as is the essential nature of arbitrage, narrow and erode the original difference in prices. Leeson operated mainly by taking advantage of small differences in financial futures between the markets in Singapore (SIMEX), the Osaka Securities Exchange and the Tokyo Stock Exchange, based on the Nikkei 225 index of leading Japanese company shares, the ten-year Japanese Government Bond and the three-month Euroyen.

Leeson's strategy was based on a firm belief that the Nikkei 225 would not move materially from its normal trading range, an obsession rudely shattered by the devastating Kobe earthquake of 17 January 1995. Leeson's days of ever wilder speculation were numbered and the incompetently managed Barings Group went into the administrator's hands as bankrupt in London on 26 February 1995 and in Singapore one day later. Within ten more days, with losses then reckoned at £860 million, Barings was taken over by Internationale Nederland Groupe, a large, expanding 'bancassurance' institution which had been formed in 1991 when NMB Postbank, Holland's third largest bank, merged with Nationale-Nederland, its largest insurance company. Meanwhile Leeson was arrested in Frankfurt and after some six months in jail was extradited back to Singapore. There the courts, with commendable speed, sentenced Leeson on 2 December 1995 to jail for six and a half years.

The financial world has been busily seeking to learn the appropriate lessons from Barings' ignominious fall, particularly with regard to banking supervision and compliance control. In sharp contrast to the praise heaped on the Bank of England in 1890, this time it has incurred strong and widespread criticism, especially from the financial authorities in Singapore. The main criticism made in the official Board of Banking Supervision Inquiry, chaired by Governor Eddie George, was its laxity in enforcing the legal rules on 'requiring any UK authorised institution to notify the Bank before incurring an exposure of over 25% of its capital base'. The Bank had granted Barings an 'informal concession' to bring its over-exposure – which had on occasion exceeded 75 per cent of Baring's capital – into line in due course. What this report also brings out is the danger arising from a

payment structure heavily dependent on bonuses, that for Leeson rising
from £35,746 in 1992 to a proposed bonus, based on his reported
profits, of £450,000 in 1994 (which he did not receive). The proposed
bonuses for three Barings directors for 1994 together amounted to
£3,650,000. The flavour of the *Report of the Inspectors of Baring
Futures (Singapore) Pte. Ltd* (1995) is shown in these extracts: 'Mr
Leeson's product managers accepted the reports of his considerable
profitability with admiration rather than scepticism' (para. 14). With
regard to gross breeches of the large exposure limit: 'This did not evoke
a strong reaction from either the Bank of England or the Barings
Group's senior management' (para. 16). The report 'does not accept the
contention that account 88888 was an unauthorised account that they
had no knowledge of' (para. 17), but if that were so, then 'key
individuals of the Barings Group management were grossly negligent,
or wilfully blind and reckless to the truth' (para. 18).

The Bank of England was undoubtedly right in its contention that
the Barings crisis would not lead to systemic failure nor frighten
business away from the City. The fourth triennial survey co-ordinated
by the Bank for International Settlements in April 1995 showed that
London had again consolidated its position as the world's largest centre
for foreign exchange business. Its daily turnover averaged $464 billion,
60 per cent up on the $290 billion of 1992. This compared with New
York's daily turnover of $244 billion, up 46 per cent on 1992, and
Tokyo's $167 billion, up 34 per cent on 1992 (*BEQB* Nov. 1995, 361–3;
see also p. 447 above). There is little doubt however that the Barings
fiasco spurred the world's monetary authorities into giving greater
urgency to the studies they were already engaged in with regard to the
size, nature and potential dangers associated with the huge rise in the
use of derivatives. Consequently, in April 1995 a survey, again co-
ordinated by the BIS and intended to run alongside its triennial 'forex'
survey, involved twenty-six central banks in the collection of
information on derivatives, to cover not only the trades conducted
through the registered foreign exchange markets but also derivative
trading carried on outside, on 'over the counter' markets. Finally, Mr
Leeson, in what may possibly turn out to be his most profitable deal yet,
brazenly made while still in prison, tells his insider's story in his aptly
titled *Rogue Trader* (1996).

4. The end of inflation?

Well over 90 per cent of the world's current population have spent all
their lives in an age of inflation, open or suppressed, unprecedented in
degree, extent and duration. For millions of people, hyper-inflation has
been the norm rather than the exception; and they, including many in
the advanced countries, have had to learn to live with price rises which
previously would have been considered impossible in peace time and
barely tolerable at any time. Even countries which have been among the
most successful in fighting inflation, like Switzerland, West Germany
and the Netherlands, have experienced rates which in the previous
century would have been a cause for concern rather than congratulation.
For most of the last fifty years, falling price levels – as distinct from

Table PS 2a. Twenty Countries with Severe Inflation 1990–1994.
(percentage increase in consumer prices over previous year)

	1991	1992	1993	1994
Argentina	277.5	79.1	35.4	28.8 to Q3
Brazil	380.6	744.9	1,584.4	5,329.8 pre reform
Nicaragua	3,726.0	53.0	-1.0	13.0
Mexico	91.6	70.3	17.3	10.9
Peru	476.4	78.2	76.5	30.7
Uruguay	104.0	93.0	64.5	38.4
Venezuela	52.7	26.5	-2.5	101.4
Guinea-Bissau	59.3	50.8	42.7	46.7
Kenya	16.6	29.7	37.4	18.0 (estimated)
Zimbabwe	34.5	11.7	40.0	55.3
Zaïre	1,083.0	5,498.0	1,658.0	8,377.0
China	25.5	31.6	27.9	n.a.
India	17.5	20.2	10.1	21.5
Pakistan	19.0	20.0	8.2	10.9
Korea	19.7	35.6	18.4	9.8
Turkey	45.9	59.2	78.4	72.4
Israel	26.5	22.8	25.8	19.7
Poland	65.7	31.4	31.8	35.6
Estonia	n.a.	291.5	133.2	40.3
*Russian Federation	n.a.	1,533.2	883.3	302.9

n.a. = not available or not applicable.
Source: IMF 'International Financial Statistics', Nov. 1995.
　　*BIS 65th Annual Report, June 1995, p.31.

Table PS 2b. Twenty Countries with Low to Moderate Inflation 1983–1995, Q1.
(annual average increase in consumer prices)

	1983–92	1993	1994	1995 Q1
Japan	1.8	1.3	0.7	0.1
Netherlands	1.8	2.6	2.8	2.4
(West) Germany	2.2	4.1	3.0	2.3
Austria	3.0	3.6	3.0	2.5
Switzerland	3.2	3.3	0.9	1.4
Belgium	3.5	2.8	2.4	1.8
USA	3.8	3.0	2.6	2.8
Denmark	4.2	1.3	2.0	2.4
Canada	4.3	1.8	0.2	1.6
France	4.4	2.1	1.7	1.7
Finland	5.3	2.2	1.1	1.8
United Kingdom	5.5	1.6	2.5	3.4
Norway	5.7	2.3	1.4	2.6
Australia	6.4	1.8	1.9	3.9
Sweden	6.7	4.6	2.2	2.6
Italy	7.4	4.2	3.9	4.4
Spain	7.6	4.6	4.7	4.8
New Zealand	7.9	1.3	1.8	4.0
Portugal	14.9	6.5	5.2	4.5
Greece*	18.0	14.4	10.9	10.6

*Exceptionally high still for a member of EU.
Source: Bank for International Settlements, 65th Annual Report, June 1995.

reductions in the rate of inflation – have been as rare as snowballs in the Sahara, as the comprehensive 'International Financial Statistics' published by the IMF and covering some 157 countries convincingly prove. Figures from forty countries' recent experience of inflation are given in the tables above, the first set comprising those generally suffering hyper-inflation, while the second group contains by contrast a number of those which have been among the most successful in controlling inflation. Both sets of statistics throw up a few markers giving grounds for optimism while still indicating how strongly inflation has embedded itself into the foundations of the world's economies and stubbornly persists almost everywhere, despite the ritual official protestations repeated loudly every year that the reduction, if not the eradication, of inflation was being given the highest priority. Political rhetoric and economic reality have displayed their contrasting roles on a grand, global scale.

During the 1990s valiant attempts have been made and pressed home more strongly than before to control inflation. Table PS 2a includes seven countries from Central and South America, notorious as the world's most inflation-prone area. In 1993–4 Argentina and Brazil tied their currencies to the US dollar and introduced a series of supporting measures to reduce their external and internal deficits. In July 1994 Brazil's dollar-linking arrangements were confirmed by the issue of a new currency, the cruzeiro real, whereupon Brazil's inflation rate plunged from over 40 per cent per month to around $1\frac{1}{2}$ per cent. Similarly, in the year following reform in Argentina the annual rate fell to 4.2 per cent. Nicaragua's spectacular inflation, of over 3,700 per cent in 1991, fell to minus 1 in 1993 and remained moderate at 10.9 per cent in 1994. Much greater back-sliding was shown by Venezuela whose apparent success in 1993 was spoiled by a return of over 100 per cent in 1994, being a pointer to the enormous difficulties of turning temporary success into sustainable, low inflation in countries inured to hyper-inflation.

The problem of Third World indebtedness, which had erupted into the financial headlines after the Mexican crisis of 1982, (and which was, with ominous optimism, pronounced by the World Bank as 'more or less over by 1994')[*] was again highlighted in December 1994 by a second Mexican crisis. However, the swiftly arranged credit of $50 billion by the United States and the IMF successfully prevented this second Mexican crisis from leading to the threatened complete breakdown of credit flows to the Third World, but has raised the dangers of 'moral hazard' to international proportions. Among the African countries shown in the table, Zaïre's painful record stands out, its ramshackle economy showing an inflation rate of well over 8,000 per cent in 1994. The other three countries are rather typical of most of Africa with rates averaging around 40 per cent. The four Asian countries selected, with a total population of well over two billion, show that they can live (and some even thrive) with rates averaging around 20 per cent. Israel and Turkey are examples of relatively advanced countries with very poor inflation records. The final group in this table testify to the varied success experienced by former command economies in their transition towards free markets. Poland and Estonia show encouraging signs of progress but in contrast the Russian Federation still suffers from the monetary debauchery which Lenin had associated with capitalism.

With the exception of Greece, all the statistics for the twenty countries in Table PS 2b show an encouragingly successful picture, led by Japan, whose recent anti-inflation record betters that of the

*See the prophetic comments by Pringle, R. in Kynaston, K. (1994, 146).

Netherlands, Germany, Austria and Switzerland. Japan appears virtually to have conquered inflation. Among the positive factors behind this success are: the strong yen, which kept import prices low; Japan's ability to produce its way out of inflation; its high personal savings ratio and its similarly high rate of investment. Certain negative factors also helped in deflating the 'bubble economy' of the 1980s which had hugely inflated property and equity prices. As the bubble burst so an increasing mountain of bad debts held by the banks were reluctantly disclosed in the bank reports from 1993 onwards. At first the concern was confined to the smaller financial institutions such as the two Tokyo-based credit unions, Kyowa Credit and Anzen Credit which were baled out by the Ministry of Finance and the central bank, the first rescue operation of this kind made by the central bank since 1927. In October 1994 Nippon Trust Bank was saved when taken over by Mitsubishi Bank. Sumitomo Bank, Japan's – and the world's – largest bank disclosed a post-tax loss for 1994, the first such declared loss for the county's biggest banks for fifty years. Official funds were extended to the Bank of Kobe, a large regional bank, following the devastation of that region by the earthquake of 17 January 1995 (though the strength of the real economy has saved the country from the massive deflationary effects which followed the Tokyo earthquake of 1923). The international standing and credit ratings of Japan's banks were further adversely affected when news was belatedly and reluctantly released concerning the activities in Daiwa Bank's branch in New York of a certain Toshihide Iguchi. He had for a period of eleven years been dealing fraudulently in US Bonds and Bills with accumulated losses, skilfully hidden, of $1.1 billion – second only to that of Nicholas Leeson's $1.4 billion. All of the above factors have contributed to reducing inflation and inflationary expectations in Japan. As for the future outlook, Japan's widely based economic strengths and its unique policy combination of paternalism, rationalization and competition, are likely to continue to provide a firm foundation for its banking system which, despite current difficulties, still boasts the six biggest, and eleven of the top twenty-five, banks in the world (*The Banker*, July, 1995).

Japan's achievement in conquering inflation in recent years was, as we have seen, outshone by Germany over a longer time period. Germany has also successfully absorbed its eastern provinces without rekindling any substantial degree of inflation. It has preserved the prestige of the Deutschemark and supported the 'strong franc' policy of France, though at some cost in higher rates of interest and of unemployment in those countries and elsewhere in Europe. It has thus drawn some (but still insufficient) attention to the problems of convergence given the asymmetry in the business cycles of the fifteen members of the European Union. The experience of the United States points to inflationary pressures having been much less than expected, after three years of recovery, compared with earlier cycles. Denmark, Canada, New Zealand, UK – indeed almost all the twenty countries shown in the table, have achieved during the last three years or so rates of inflation averaging barely half the average levels experienced in the previous thirteen years from 1983 to 1992.

Furthermore, there is general agreement that the statistics have tended to overstate actual inflation with regard to the relationship between consumer price levels and the real standard of living. Two examples must suffice. In September 1995 Germany's Federal Statistical Office introduced a new cost-of-living index which showed that previous rates were overstated by 0.3 per cent. (*Deutsche Bundesbank Monthly Bulletin*, September 1995, 59). More startling differences emerge from the USA, where the Senate Finance Committee set up an investigation chaired by Professor Michael Boskin of Stanford University. Their interim report, *Towards an Accurate Measure of the Cost of Living*, published in September 1995, concluded that in recent times the consumer price index had overstated inflation by about 1.5 percentage points. Such matters are not mere academic quibbles, particularly given the extent to which wage rates and welfare payments are index-linked or used as basic reference points in modern economies. Hence there has been a general move towards policies of 'low' inflation rather than the appealingly simple but misleading and excessively costly goal of zero inflation.

Associated with and in part responsible for the marked reduction in inflation in recent years has been the greater degree of independence granted in practice to a number of central banks and a general consensus that they should concentrate single-mindedly on the supreme goal of price stability. The means by which the monetary authorities strive to achieve such stability must remain flexibly adapted to the differing social demands and institutional patterns of the countries concerned. In countries like Switzerland and Germany where long-term public support for strict monetary policies has been evident, the policy of targeting some measure of the money supply has proved itself to be effective. An increasing number of other countries, where the social and economic environment has been less supportive, have moved towards targeting inflation more directly. New Zealand's lead in 1990 was followed by Canada (1991), UK (1992), Sweden and Finland (1993) and Spain and Mexico in 1993 (see p.651). In pursuing an inflation target the monetary authorities are required to look at money in a very broad context (a salutary acceptance of one of the abiding lessons of history) – what Andrew Haldane, of the Bank of England's Monetary Assessment and Strategy Division, has dubbed a 'look at everything' approach (see his excellent article on 'Inflation Targets', *BEQB*, August 1995). One of the key non-monetary assets rightfully given prominence is that for house prices, which were a major causative factor in the inflationary surge of the late 1980s but, acting in reverse, have helped very significantly in the toning down of Britain's inflation psychosis in the 1990s. The euphoria of equity withdrawal has been replaced by the harsh pain of negative equity as house prices have fallen below mortgage obligations, particularly in London and the south-east. Significantly, the pain caused by such falls in asset prices no longer acts with its previous force to inhibit anti-inflation policies. The folk-memory of deflation, debilitatingly present in the minds of those occupying positions of power and influence in the three or four decades after 1945, has now faded away, allowing more ruthless and effective disinflationary policies to be adopted and sustained.

In theory and practice the monetary pendulum has obviously been swinging widely in recent decades, but with the distinct promise of a narrowing range, at least for most of the world's advanced economies, as we approach the turn of the millennium. Consumer sovereignty can best be exercised given a situation of reasonable price stability, where, in the words of Alan Greenspan, Chairman of the Federal Reserve System, 'expected changes in the average price level are small enough and gradual enough that they do not materially enter business and household decisions'. However, the liberty conferred by stable money requires eternal vigilance on the part of the monetary authorities, especially by the Federal Reserve System, the Bank of Japan and the new European Central Bank as they co-operate with the other 150 or so central bankers in ridding the advanced countries of the scourge of inflation and in providing a firm anchor to limit the slippage in the value of other currencies.

Billions of fingers, at the touch of a button in a borderless world, will keep the august monetary authorities on their toes, as new definitions of money, of monetary sovereignty and control will be dictated by the as yet unknown demands of the electronic age. For the computer chip with its phenomenal memory enables us practically to turn Blake's poetic vision into virtual reality:

> To see a World in a Grain of Sand . . .
> Hold Infinity in the palm of your hand
> And Eternity in an hour.

Bibliography

Articles, books, papers and theses

Adekanye, F. (1983) ed. *Banks and the Nigerian Economy* (Lagos).

Ajayi, S. I. and Ojo, O. O. (1981). *Money and Banking in the Nigerian Context* (London).

Allen, D. F. (1980). *Coins of the Ancient Celts* (Edinburgh).

Alsop, J. D. (1982). 'The theory and practice of Tudor taxation', *English Historical Review*.

—— (1984).'Innovation in Tudor taxation', *English Historical Review*.

Amex Bank Review (various).

Anderson, B. L. and Cottrell, P. L. (1975). 'Another Victorian capital market: a study of banking and bank investors on Merseyside', *Economic History Review*, XXVIII, 4.

Andreades, A. M. (1933). *History of Greek Public Finance* (Cambridge, Mass.).

—— (1966). *History of the Bank of England* (London; 1st edn 1909).

Andrewes, A. (1967). *The Greeks* (London).

Andrews, J. (1980). *Exeter Coinage* (Exeter).

Andrews, K. R. (1984). *Trade, Plunder and Settlement* (Cambridge).

Aristophanes (1912). *Comedies*, tr. Athenian Society (London).

Atwell, W. A. (1982). 'International bullion flows and the Chinese economy 1530–1650', *Past and Present*, 95.

Austin, N. M. and Vidal-Naquet, P. (1977). *Economic and Social History of Ancient Greece* (London).

Bagehot, W. (1873). *Lombard Street* (London).

Bank for International Settlements, Basle (various).

Bank of England Quarterly Bulletin (BEQB) (various).

Bankers' Magazine, London (various).

Banking World, London (various).

Baring Brothers (1970). *Merchant Banking Today* (London).

Barnett, Corelli (1986). *The Audit of War: The Illusion of Britain as a Great Nation* (London).

Basu, R. S. (1978). *Central Banking in a Planned Economy: The Indian Experiment* (New Delhi).

Bauer, P. T. (1984). *Reality and Rhetoric: Studies in the Economics of Development* (London).

Beales, H. L. (1954). 'The Great Depression in industry and trade', in E. M. Carus-Wilson.

Bell, P. W. (1956). *The Sterling Area in the Post-War World* (Oxford).

Bevan, S. (1994). 'Cash is still King', *Banking World*, (October).

Blackburn, M. (1986). *Medieval European Coinage* (Cambridge).

Blunden, Sir George (1976). Speech on 'Recent Developments in British Banking', Cardiff Business Club, 25 October.

Blunt, C. E. (1961). 'The coinage of Offa', in R. H. M. Dolley.

Bodin, J. (1568) *La Réponse de Jean Bodin a M. de Malestroit* (Paris, reprint 1932).

Bogart, E. L. (1930). *Economic History of the American People* (New York).

Böhme, H. (1978). *Social and Economic History of Germany* (Oxford).

Bordo, M. and Capie, F. (eds.) (1993). *Monetary Régimes in Transition* (Cambridge).

Born, K. E. (1983). *International Banking in the Nineteenth and Twentieth Centuries* (London).

Boswell, J. (1791). *Life of Johnson* (London).

Boyle, A. (1967). *Montagu Norman* (London).

Boyle, J. A. (1968). *The Cambridge History of Iran* (Cambridge).

Brandt, W. (1980). *North–South: A Programme for Survival* (London).

—— (1983). *The Brandt Commission: Common Crisis* (London).

Breasted, J. H. (1920). *Ancient Times* (Chicago).

Bridge, T. D. and Pegg, J. J. (1993) *Post Giro Banking in Europe* (Tavistock).

Briggs, A. (1958) ed. *Self-Help* (by Samuel Smiles, Centenary edn) (London).

Bronowski, J. (1973). *The Ascent of Man* (London).

Brookings Institute (1989). *Blueprint for Restructuring America's Financial Institutions* (Washington).

Brown, D. (1978). *Anglo-Saxon England* (London).

Bundesbank, Frankfurt-am-Main (various).

Burnett, A. (1980). 'Rome and the Hellenistic world', in M. J. Price.

Cairncross, A. K. (1953). *Home and Foreign Investment 1870–1913* (Cambridge).

—— (1958). 'The English capital market before 1914', *Economica*, London (May).

Callaghan, James (1987). *Time and Chance* (London).

Cameron, A. (1995). *Bank of Scotland 1695–1995* (Edinburgh).

Cameron, R. (1967). *Banking in the Early Stages of Industrialisation: A Study in Comparative Economic History* (Oxford).

Cannan, E. (1919). *The Paper Pound* (London).

Capie, F. (ed.) (1993) *History of Banking 1650–1850* (London).

Capie, F., Goodhart, C. A. E., Fischer, S. and Schnadt, N. (1994). *The Future of Central Banking* (Cambridge),

Caron, F. (1979). *An Economic History of Modern France* (London).

Carosso, V. P. (1987). *The Morgans: Private International Bankers* (Cambridge, Mass.).

Carus-Wilson, E. M. (1954). 'An industrial revolution in the thirteenth century', in idem, ed., *Essays in Economic History* (London).

Cassel, G. (1922). *Money and the Foreign Exchanges after 1914* (London).

Cassis, Y. (1994). *City Bankers, 1890–1914* (Cambridge).

Cecco, M. (1984). *The International Gold Standard: Money and Empire* (London).

Challis, C. E. (1978). *The Tudor Coinage* (Manchester).

Chalmers, R. (1893). *History of the Currency in the British Colonies* (London).

Chandaman, C. D. (1975). *The English Public Revenue 1660–1688* (Oxford).

Chandler, L. V. (1958). *Benjamin Strong: Central Banker* (Washington).

—— (1981). *The Economics of Money and Banking* (New York).

Chapman, S. (1984). *The Rise of Merchant Banking* (London).

Checkland, S. G. (1975). *Scottish Banking: A History, 1695–1973* (Glasgow).

Chrimes, S. B. (1966). *Administrative History of Medieval England* (Oxford).

—— (1972). ed. *Fifteenth century England* (Manchester).

Chrystal, K. A. (1992). 'The fall and rise of saving', *Natwest Bank Review* (February).

Cipolla, C. M. (1981). *Before the Industrial Revolution: European Society and Economy, 1000–1700* (London).

Clapham, Sir John (1970). *The Bank of England: A History* (Cambridge).

Clark, D. M. (1960). *The Rise of the British Treasury: Colonial Administration in the Eighteenth Century* (New Haven).

Clark, K. (1969). *Civilisation* (London).

Clay, H. (1957). *Lord Norman* (London).

Clower, R. W. (1969) ed. *Monetary Theory* (London).

Cochran, J. A. (1967). *Money and Banking in the Economy* (New York).

Colander, D. C. (1979). 'Rationality, expectations and functional finance', in Gapinski, J. H. and Rookwood, C. E., eds., *Essays in Post-Keynesian Inflation* (Cambridge, Mass.).

Coleman, D. C. (1977). *The Economy of England 1450–1750* (Oxford).

Congdon, Minford, Pepper et al. (1990). Letter to *The Times*, 28 September.

Connolly, B. (1995). *The Rotten Heart of Europe: the Dirty War for Europe's Money* (London).

Corti, C. (1928). *The Rise of the House of Rothschild* (London).

Coulbeck, N. (1984). *The Multinational Banking Industry* (London).

Cox, N. and Cox, A. (1994). *The Tokens, Checks, Metallic Tickets and Tallies of Wales, 1880–1993: Two Hundred Years of Paranumismatic History* (Cardiff).

Craig, J. (1953). *The Mint: A History of the London Mint from* AD 287 *to 1948* (Cambridge).

Cribb, J. (1979). 'An historical survey of the precious metal currencies in China', *Numismatic Chronicle* XIX, 185.

—— (1980) 'The Far East' in M. J. Price.

Crick, W. F. and Wadsworth, J. E. (1936). *A Hundred Years of Joint-Stock Banking* (London).

Crowther, G. (1940). *An Outline of Money* (London).

Cule, J. E. (1935). 'The Financial History of Matthew Boulton, 1759–1809' (unpublished M.Com. thesis, Birmingham).

Cunningham, W. (1938). *The Growth of English Industry and Commerce* (London).

Dalton, G. (1967). *Tribal and Peasant Economies* (New York).

Dalton, R. (1922). *The Silver Token Coinage 1811–1812* (London).

Davenant, C. (1771). *Works* (London).

Davies, Glyn (1971). 'Inflation and the integration of an expanding monetary system', *Euromoney*. (March).

—— (1973). *National Giro: Modern Money Transfer* (London).

—— (1974) ed. *European Finance for Development* (Cardiff).

—— (1981). *Building Societies and their Branches: A Regional Economic Survey* (London).

—— and Davies, J. E. (1984). 'The revolution in monopoly theory', *Lloyds Bank Review* (July).

—— and Evans, J. Wynne (1983). 'Employment and profitability in U.K. financial services', *Services Industries Journal*. (November).

—— and Thomas, I. I. (1976) *Overseas Investment in Wales* (Cardiff).

Davies, M. (1993). *The Origins and Development of Cartelisation in British Banking* (Bangor).

Day, J. (1978). 'The great bullion famine of the fifteenth century', *Past and Present*, 79.

Defoe, D. (1960). *Essay on Projects* (London).

Dent, J. M. (1908) ed. *The Travels of Marco Polo* (London).

Diamond, D. E. and Guilfoil, J. D. (1973) *United States Economic History* (New York).

Dickson, P. G. M. (1967). *The Financial Revolution in England: A Study in the Development of Public Credit 1688–1756* (London).

Dietz, F. C. (1932). *English Public Finance 1588–1641* (New York).

Dillen, J. G. (1934) ed. *A History of the Principal Public Banks* (London).

Dolley, R. H. M. (1961). *Anglo-Saxon Coins* (London).

—— (1966). *The Norman Conquest and the English Coinage* (London).

Drummond, I. M. (1987). *The Gold Standard and the International Monetary System 1900–39* (London).

Dubois, A. B. (1938). *The English Business Company after the Bubble Act 1720–1800* (New York).

Duesenberry, J. S. (1958). *Business Cycles and Economic Growth* (Cambridge, Mass.).

—— (1967). *Income, Saving and the Theory of Consumer Behaviour* (Cambridge, Mass.).

Dumke, R. H. (1991). *Tariffs and Market Structure: the Zollverein as a model of Economic Integration* in W. R. Lee.

Duncan-Jones, R. (1982). *The Economy of the Roman Empire* (Cambridge).

Edgeworth, F. Y. (1895). 'Thoughts on monetary reform', *Economic Journal* (September).

Edozien, E. C. (1983), 'A Critical Assessment of the Role of Banks in the Nigerian Economy' in F. Adekanye.

Edwards, G. T. (1987). *The Role of Banks in Economic Development: the Economics of Industrial Resurgence* (London).

Eichengreen, B. (1985). *The Gold Standard in Theory and History* (London).

—— (1990). *Elusive Stability: Essays in the History of International Finance, 1919–1931* (Cambridge).

—— (1992). *Golden Fetters: the Gold Standard and the Great Depression, 1919–1939* (New York).

Einzig, P. (1956). 'The dynamics of hire purchase credit', *Economic Journal*.

—— (1966). *Primitive Money*, 2nd edn. (Oxford).

—— (1970). *The History of Foreign Exchange* (London).

Elton, G. R. (1969). *England 1200–1640: The Sources of History* (London).

Elzubeir, E. (1984). 'The Marketing of Islamic Banking' (unpublished Ph.D. thesis, University of Wales, Cardiff).

Evans, J. Wynne (1985). 'William Paterson: a biography', *Scottish Bankers' Magazine* (May).

Exchange and Mart, 30 June 1983.

Fadina, A. O. (1983). 'The Increasing Role of the Capital Market in the Economy' in F. Adekanye.

Farson, N. (1940). *Behind God's Back* (London).

Fay, C. R. (1928, 1948). *England from Adam Smith to the Present Day* (London).

Feavearyear, A. (1963). *The Pound Sterling*, 2nd edn. (Oxford).

Federal Reserve Bulletins, Washington (various).

Feinstein, C. H. (1990). 'What really happened to real wages? Trends in Wages, prices and productivity in U.K. 1880–1913', *Economic History Review* (August).

Feldenkirchen, W. (1991) 'Banking and economic growth: banks and industry in Germany in the 19th and 20th centuries' in W. R. Lee.

Fetter, F. W. (1965). *Development of British Monetary Orthodoxy, 1797–1875* (Cambridge).

Finley, M. (1975). *The Ancient Economy* (London).

Fisher, F. J. (1940). 'Commercial trends and policy in sixteenth century England', *Economic History Review*, X, 2.

—— (1954). 'The London food market 1540–1640', in E. M. Carus-Wilson.

Fisher, I. (1911). *The Purchasing Power of Money* (New Haven).

Fite, G. C. and Reese, J. E. (1973). *Economic History of the United States* (Boston).

Fox, R. L. (1973). *Alexander the Great* (London).

Francis, J. (1848, 1862). *A History of the Bank of England* (London).

Franklin, Benjamin (1729). *A Modest Enquiry into the Nature and Necessity of a Paper Currency* (Philadelphia).

Fryde, E. B. (1981). Introduction to C. Oman, *The Great Revolt of 1381* (originally published 1906) (London).

Friedman, M (1953). 'The case for flexible exchange rates', in *Essays in Positive Economics* (Chicago).

—— (1956). *A Restatement of the Quantity Theory of Money* (Chicago).

—— (1962). *Capitalism and Freedom* (Chicago).

—— (1990). 'Bimetallism revisited', *Journal of Economic Perspectives*, Chicago (Fall).

—— and Friedman, Rose (1980). *Free to Choose* (New York).

—— and Schwartz, A. (1963). *A Monetary History of the United States* (Princeton).

Fry, R. (1976). *Bankers in West Africa: The History of the Bank of British West Africa* (London).

Fullarton, J. (1845). *On the Regulation of Currencies* (London).

Furness, E. (1975) *Money and Credit in Developing Africa* (London).

Galbraith, J. K. (1955). *The Great Crash 1929* (London).

—— (1975). *Money: Whence it Came and Where it Went* (London).

Garber, P. M. (1989). 'Tulipmania?' *Journal of Political Economy*, Chicago, (vol. 97, no.3).

Garnsey, P., Hopkins, K., and Whittaker, C. R., eds. (1983). *Trade in the Ancient Economy* (London).

Gaskin, M. (1960). 'Anglo-Scottish banking conflicts, 1874–81', *Economic History Review* (May).

—— (1965). *The Scottish Banks: A Modern Survey* (London).

Gerschenkron, A. (1962). *Economic Backwardness in Historical Perspective* (Cambridge, Mass.).

Gibbon, E. (1788). *The History of the Decline and Fall of the Roman Empire* (London).

Gilmour, Sir Ian (1983). *Britain Can Work* (Oxford).

Giuseppi, J. (1966). *The Bank of England* (London).

Goldfield, S. M. and Chandler, L. V. (1981). *The Economics of Money and Banking* (New York).

Goldsmith, R. W. (1969). *Financial Structure and Development* (New Haven).

Goodhart, C. A. E. (1972). *The Business of Banking, 1891–1914* (London).

—— (1985). *The Evolution of Central Banks* (London).

—— (1987). *Money, Information and Uncertainty* (London).

Goodrich, L. C. (1957) *A Short History of the Chinese People* (London).

Gordon, B. (1975). *Economic Analysis before Adam Smith* (London).

Gould, J. D. (1970). *The Great Debasement* (Oxford).

Grant, M. (1968). *Roman History from Coins: Some Uses of Imperial Coinage to the Historian* (Cambridge).

Greaves, I. (1953). *Colonial Monetary Conditions* (London).

Green, E. (1979). *Debtors to their Profession* (London).

Gregg, P. (1976). *Black Death to Industrial Revolution* (London).

Grierson, P. (1975). *Numismatics* (Oxford).

—— (1977). *The Origins of Money* (London).

—— (1979). *Dark Age Numismatics* (London).

—— (1986). *Medieval European Coinage* (Cambridge).

Habakkuk, J. (1940). *Cambridge History of the British Empire* (Cambridge).

Hailey, Lord (1938). *African Survey* (London).

Haldane, A. (1995). 'Inflation Targets', *BEQB* (August).

Hall, A. R. (1957). 'A note on the English capital market as a source for funds for home investment before 1914', *Economica*, London (February).

Hamilton, A. (1790). *Report on the Public Credit* and *Report on a National Bank* (Philadelphia).

Hamilton, E. J. (1934). *American Treasure and the Price Revolution in Spain, 1501–1650* (Cambridge, Mass.).

Hammond, B. (1976). *Banks and Politics in America* (Princeton).

Hammond, N. G. L. (1981). *Alexander the Great* (London).

Hargreaves, E. L. (1966). *The National Debt* (London).

Hartwell, R. M. (1971). *The Industrial Revolution and Economic Growth* (London).

Hasebroek, J. (1928). *Trade and Politics in Ancient Greece* (Tübingen), (London 1933).

Hatcher, J. (1977). *Plague, Population and the English Economy 1348–1530* (London).

Hawtrey, R. G. (1938). *A Century of Bank Rate* (London).

Hayek, A. F. (1944). *The Road to Serfdom* (London).

—— (1976). *Choice in Currency: The Denationalisation of Currency* (London).

—— (1991). *Economic Freedom* (London).

Heckscher, E. F. (1934). 'The Riksbank of Sweden', in J. G. Dillen.

—— (1955). *Mercantilism* (London).

Heichelheim, F. M. (1958). *An Ancient Economic History* (Leiden).

Hetzel, R. L. (1989) 'M2 and monetary policy' in *Federal Reserve Bank of Richmond Economic Review* (September/October).

—— (1990). 'Free Enterprise and Central Banking in formerly Communist Countries', *Federal Reserve Bank of Richmond Economic Review*, (May/June).

Hession, C. H. and Sardy, H. (1969). *Ascent to Affluence* (Boston).

Hobbes, T. (1651). *Leviathan* (London).

Hobsbawm, E. J. (1968) *Industry and Empire* (London).

Hodges, T. M. (1948). 'Early Banking in Cardiff', *Economic History Review*, 2.

Hodgson, R. A. (1976). 'The economics of English country banking', *The Banker* (January).

Holden, J. M. (1955). *History of Negotiable Instruments in English Law* (London).

Hopkins, K. (1980). 'Taxes and trade in the Roman empire', *Journal of Roman Studies*, 70.

—— and with Garnsey, P. and Whittaker, C. R.(1983). *Trade in the Ancient Economy* (London).

Horne, O. (1947). *The Savings Banks* (London).

Horsefield, J. K. (1960). *British Monetary Experiments, 1650–1710* (London).

—— (1982). 'Stop of the Exchequer re-visited', *Economic History Review*, XXXV, 4.

Howson, S. (1993). *British Monetary Policy 1945–51* (Oxford).

Humphrey, T. M. (1989), 'Lender of Last Resort: the concept in history', in *Federal Reserve Bank of Richmond Review* (March).

International Monetary Fund, Washington (various).

Jevons, W. S. (1875 and 1910). *Money and the Mechanism of Exchange* (London).

John, A. H. (1950). *The Industrial Development of South Wales 1750–1850* (Cardiff).

Johnson, B. (1970). *The Politics of Money* (London).

Johnson, E. A. J. (1965). *Predecessors of Adam Smith* (New York).

Jones, D. W. (1988). *War and Economy in the Age of Marlborough* (Oxford).

Jones, F. S. (1976). 'Government, currency and country banks in England 1770–1797', *South African Journal of Economics*, 44, 3.

Jones, G. (1991) ed. *Banks and Money: International Competitive Finance in History* (London).

Jones, G. D. B. (1980). 'The Roman mines at Rio Tinto', *Journal of Roman Studies*, Vol.LXX, 146.

Kaldor, N. (1970). 'The new monetarism', *Lloyds Bank Review* (July).

Kaufman, G. G. (1990), 'Crisis in the "S and Ls"', *Chicago Fed Letter* (December).

Kennedy, E. (1991). *The Bundesbank: Germany's Central Bank in the International Monetary System* (London).

Kennedy, W. P. (1982). 'Economic growth and structural change in U.K. 1870–1914', *Journal of Economic History* (March).

Kenny, P. B. (1995). 'The Number of Coins in Circulation', *Economic Trends* No. 495 (January).

Kent, J. (1980). 'From the classical to the medieval world 300–700', in M. J. Price.

Kerridge, E. (1953). 'The movement of rent 1540–1640', *Economic History Review*, VI, 3.

Keynes, J. M. (1913). *Indian Currency and Finance* (London).

—— (1920). *The Economic Consequences of the Peace* (London).

—— (1925a). 'Is the pound over-valued' *New Republic*, New York, 6 May.

—— (1925b). *The Economic Consequences of Mr Churchill* (London).

—— (1930). *A Treatise on Money* (London).

—— (1933a). *The Means of Prosperity* (London).

—— (1933b). *Essays in Biography* (London).

—— (1936). *The General Theory of Employment, Interest and Money* (London).

Kindleberger, C. P. (1978). *Mergers, Panics and Crashes* (London).

—— (1984). *A Financial History of Western Europe* (London).

—— (1985). *Keynesianism vs. Monetarism and Other Essays in Financial History* (London).

King, C. E. (1981). 'Late Roman silver hoards in Britain', *British Numismatic Journal*, LI, 5.

King, E. (1979). *England 1175–1425* (London).

King, F. H. H. (1988). *The History of the Hong Kong and Shanghai Banking Corporation* (Cambridge).

King, M. (1993). 'The Bundesbank: a view from the Bank of England', *BEQB* (May).

King, W. T. C. (1936). *History of the London Discount Market* (London).

Kirkland, E. C. (1946). *A History of American Economic Life* (New York).

Kirschner, J. (1974). *Business, Banking and Economic Thought* (Chicago).

Klingman, L. and Green, G. (1952). *His Majesty O'Keefe* (London).

Knapp, G. F. (1924). *The State Theory of Money*, English edn. (London).

Kynaston, D. (1994). *The City of London: a World of its Own* (London).

Laffer, A. and Meiselman, D. (1975). *The Phenomenon of World Inflation* (Washington).

Law, J. (1705). *Money and Trade Considered* (Edinburgh).

Lawson, N. (1984). The Fifth Mais Lecutre, London, 18 June.

Leamer, E. E. (1983). 'Let's take the con out of econometrics', *American Economic Review*, 73, no.1.

Lee, S. Y. and Jao, J. C. (1982). *Financial Structures and Monetary Policies in South-East Asia* (London).

Lee, W. R. (1991) ed. *German Industry and German Industrialisation* (London).

Leeson, N. (1996). *Rogue Trader* (London).

Leiderman, L. and Svensson, L., (eds.) (1995). *Inflation Targets* (London).

Lewis, W. A. (1952). 'The colonial sterling balances', in *Financial Times*, 18 January.

Lindgren, H. C. (1980). *Great Expectations: The Psychology of Money* (New York).

Lipson, E. (1956). *The Economic History of England*, 6th edn. (London).

Lloyd George, D. (1930). *War Memoirs* (London).

Lockhart, J. H. S. (1907). *Collection of Chinese Copper Coins* (London).

Loyn, H. R. (1977). *The Vikings in Britain* (London).

Loynes, J. B. (1974). *History of the West African Currency Board 1912–1962* (London).

McCloskey, D. N. (1970). 'Did Victorian Britain fail?' *Economic History Review*, XXIII, 3.

Mackenzie, C. (1954). *Realms of Silver: One Hundred Years of Banking in the East* (London).

McKinnon, R. I. (1973). *Money and Capital in Economic Development* (Washington).

Mann, J. C. (1979). 'Power, force and the frontiers of empire', *Journal of Roman Studies*.

Marsh, D. (1992). *The Bundesbank: The Bank that Rules Europe* (London).

Masefield, G. B. (1967). 'Crops and Livestock' in *Cambridge Economic History of Europe*, IV, ed. E. E. Rich and C. H. Wilson (Cambridge).

Matthias, P. (1962). *English Trade Tokens: The Industrial Revolution Illustrated* (London).

Mattingly, H. (1960). *Roman Coins from Earliest Times to the End of the Western Empire* (London).

Mayer, H. E. (1982). 'Henry II of England and the Holy Land', *English Historical Review* (October).

Maynard, G. (1962). *Economic Development and the Price Level* (London).

Menninger, K. (1969). *Number Words and Number Symbols* (London).

Metcalf, D. M. (1980). 'Continuity and change in English monetary history 973–1086', *British Numismatic Journal*, XLX, 73.

Michell, H. (1957). *The Economics of Ancient Greece* (Cambridge).

Millikan, M. F. (1967). *National Economic Planning* (New York).

Milne, J. G. (1931). *Greek Coinage* (Oxford).

Mitchell, S. K. (1951). *Taxation in medieval England* (New Haven).

Moggridge, D. E. (1969). *The Return to Gold 1925* (Cambridge).

—— (1972). *British Monetary Policy 1924–31: The Norman Conquest of $4.86* (Cambridge).

Moody, J. (1906). *The Truth about the Trusts* (New York).

More, T. (1516). *Utopia* (London).

Morgan Guarantee Survey (1978). 'Barter and counter-trade: a new upsurge' (October)

Morley, J. (1911). *Life of Gladstone* (London).

Morton, F. (1963). *The Rothschilds: A Family Portrait* (London).

Moss, D. J. (1992). 'The Bank of England and the establishment of a branch system, 1826–1829' *Canadian Journal of History*, No. 27.

Muellbauer, J. (1990). *The Great British Housing Disaster and Economic Policy* (London).

Muir, R. (1947). *A Short History of the British Commonwealth*, 6th edn (London).

Murray, O. (1980). *Early Greece* (London).

Myers, M. G. (1970). *A Financial History of the United States* (New York).

Nakamura, T. (1989). 'An economic history of the Showa era', *Economic Eye*, Tokyo (Summer).

Nash, D. (1980). 'The Celts' in M. J. Price.

Needham, J. (1971). *Science and Civilisation in China* (Cambridge).

Nef, J. U. (1954). 'Prices and industrial capitalism in France and England 1540–1640', in E. M. Carus-Wilson.

Nevin, E. (1953). 'The origins of cheap money', *Economica*, (September).

—— (1955). *The Mechanism of Cheap Money: A Study of British Monetary Policy 1931–39* (London).

Nishimura, S. (1971). *The Decline of Inland Bills and the Mechanism of Exchange in the London Money Market 1855–1913* (Cambridge).

Nkrumah, K. (1961). *I speak of Freedom* (London).

Nugent, W. T. K. (1968). *Money and American Society 1865–1880* (New York).

Nwankwo, G. O. (1980). *The Nigerian Financial System* (London).

Nzeribe, A. J. (1966). 'The American Banks in London: Their Role in the London Money Market since 1945' (unpublished MA (Econ.) thesis, University of Strathclyde, Glasgow).

Oates, J. (1979). *Babylon* (London).

Ojomo, M. A. (1983). *Banks in the Nigerian Economy* (Lagos).

Oman, C. (1910). *England before the Norman Conquest* (London).

—— (1931). *Coinage of England* (Oxford).

—— (1981). *The Great Revolt of 1381*, with introduction by E. B. Fryde (Oxford).

OPEC *Bulletins*, Vienna (various).

Orsingher, R. (1964). *Banks of the World: A History and Analysis* (Paris).

Outhwaite, R. B. (1982). *Inflation in Tudor and Early Stuart England* (Cambridge).

Owen, F. (1954). *Tempestuous Journey: Lloyd-George, his Life and Times* (London).

Paine, T. (1776). *Common Sense* (Philadelphia).

Petty, W. (1682). *Quantulumcunque Concerning Money* (London).

Parkin, M. (ed.), (1994). *The Theory of Inflation* (London).

Patat, J. P. and Lutfalla, M. (1990). *A Monetary History of France in the Twentieth Century*, English edn (London).

Patinkin, D. (1993). 'Irving Fisher and his compensated dollar plan', *Federal Reserve Bank of Richmond Quarterly Review*, 3.

Phillips, M. (1894). *Banks, Bankers and Banking in Northumberland, Durham and North Yorkshire* (London).

Platt, D. C. M. (1984). *Foreign Finance in Continental Europe and USA 1815–70* (London).

—— (1986). *Britain's Investment Overseas on the Eve of the First World War* (London).

Plumptre, A. F. W. (1940). *Central Banking in the British Dominions* (Toronto).

Pöhl, K. O. (1990). Speech at London School of Economics, November.

Pollard, S. (1970) ed. *The Gold Standard and Employment Policies between the Wars* (London).

—— (1989). *Britain's Prime and Britain's Decline 1870–1914. (London).*

Porteous, J. (1969). *Coins in History* (London).

—— (1980). 'The nature of coinage', in M. J. Price.

Postan, M. M. (1954). 'Credit in medieval trade', in E. M. Carus-Wilson.

—— (1966). 'Medieval agrarian society in its prime: England', in *Cambridge Economic History of Europe* (Cambridge).

—— (1972). *The Medieval Economy and Society (London).*

Posthumus, N. W. (1929). 'The tulip mania in Holland', *Journal of Economic and Business History* (May).

Priesigke, F. (1910). *Girowesen in griechischen Aegypten* (Strasbourg).

Pressnell, L. S. (1956). *Country Banking in the Industrial Revolution* (Oxford).

—— (1973) ed. *Money and Banking in Japan* (London; original Japanese edn published by Bank of Japan).

Price, J. S. (1958). *Building Societies: Their Origin and History* (London).

Price, M. J. (1980). 'The first three centuries of coinage', in idem, ed. *Coins from 650 BC to the Present Day* (London).

Price, R. (1981). *An Economic History of Modern France 1730–1914* (London).

Pugh, T. B. (1972). 'Magnates, knights and gentry' in S. B. Chrimes.

Quiggin, A. H. (1949). *Primitive Money* (London).

Radford, R. A. (1945). 'The economic organisation in a P.O.W. camp', *Economica*, 12.

Rae, G. (1885). *The Country Banker* (London).

Rait, R. S. (1930). *The History of the Union Bank of Scotland* (Glasgow).

Ramsey, P. (1956). 'Some Tudor merchants' accounts', in A. C. Littleton and B. S. Yamey, eds., *Studies in the History of Accounting* (London).

Redish, A. (1990). 'The evolution of the gold standard in England', *Journal of Economic History.*

—— (1993). 'The Latin Monetary Union and emergence of the international gold standard' in M. Bordo and F. Capie (eds.).

—— (1995). 'The persistence of bimetallism in nineteenth-century France', *Economic History Review*, XLVIII, 4.

Rees, J. F. (1921). *A Short Fiscal and Financial History of England* (London).

Reid, M. (1982). *The Secondary Banking Crisis 1973–75* (London).

Richards, R. D. (1929). *The Early History of Banking in England* (London).

Richardson, G. (1979). 'The pursuit of equilibrium', *Euromoney*, (October).

Richardson, H. W. (1979). *Economic Recovery in Britain 1932–39* (London).

Riley, B. (1990). 'The booming house-mortgage market' in *Financial Times*, 14 October.

Riley-Smith, J. (1982), 'The Crusades', in *History Today* (April).

Robbins, L. (1940). *The Nature and Significance of Economic Science* (London).

—— (1971) *Money, Trade and International Relations* (London).

Robert, R. (1952). 'A short history of tallies', *Accounting research*, (July).

Roberts, R. and Kynaston, D. (1995). *The Bank of England: Money, Power and Influence, 1694–1994* (Oxford).

Robertson, C. H. (1988). 'Pre-banking financial arrangements in Scotland', *Royal Bank of Scotland Review* (June).

Robinson, E. A. G. (1938). *African Survey* (London).

Robinson, E. S. G. (1956). 'The date of the earliest coins', *Numismatic Chronicle*, VI, 137.

Robinson, J. (1933, 1963). *Imperfect Competition* (Cambridge).

Robinson, W. C. (1959). 'Money, population and economic change in late medieval Europe', *Economic History Review*, XII(1).

Roll, E. (1993). *Independent and Accountable: a New Mandate for the Bank of England* (London).

Rostovtzeff, M. (1941). *The Social and Economic History of the Hellenistic World* (Oxford).

Rostow, W. W. (1960, 1971). *The Stages of Economic Growth: A Non-Communist Manifesto* (Cambridge).

Royal Mint, Annual Reports.

Ruding, R. (1819, 1840). *Annals of the Coinage of Great Britain and its Dependencies* (London).

Rueff, J. (1958). *Report on the Financial Situation* (Paris).

Samuelson, P. A. (1969), quoted in Clower.

Sardy, H, and Hession, C. H. (1969). *Ascent to Affluence* (Boston).

Sarton, G. (1948). *Science and Learning in the Fourteenth Century*, vol. II of *The History of Science* (Baltimore).

Sawyer, P. H. (1978). *From Roman Britain to Norman Britain* (London).

Sayers, R. S. (1936). *Bank of England Operations 1890–1914* (London).

—— (1952) ed. *Banking in the British Commonwealth* (Oxford).

—— (1956). *History of the Second World War: Financial Policy* (London).

—— (1957). *Lloyds Bank in the History of English Banking* (Oxford).

—— (1962) ed. *Banking in Western Europe* (Oxford).

—— (1968). *Gilletts in the London Money Market* (Oxford).

—— (1976). *The Bank of England 1891–1944* (Cambridge).

Scammell, M. W. (1968). *The London Discount Market* (London).

Scott, P. H. (1981), ed. *The Letters of Malachi Malagrowther* (Edinburgh).

Seaby, P. and Purvey, P. F. (1982). *Coins of England*, 19th edn. (London).

Seldon, A. (1960). *Not Unanimous: A Rival to Radcliffe on Money* (London).

Servan-Schreiber, J. J. (1968). *The American Challenge* (London).

Shannon, H. A. (1954). 'The coming of general limited liability', in E. M. Carus-Wilson.

Shaw, E. S. (1973). *Financial Deepening in Economic Development* (Oxford).

Shinka, Y. (1990). 'Japan's positive role as world banker', *Economic Eye*, Tokyo.

Skully, M. T. (1982) ed. *Financial Institutions and Markets in South East Asia* (London).

Smith, Adam (1776; Dent edn 1933). *An Enquiry into the Nature and Causes of the Wealth of Nations* (London).

Smith, Adrian (1981). 'The informal economy', *Lloyds Bank Review* (July).

Smith, Sidney (1820), in *Edinburgh Review* (January), reprinted *Works* (1839).

Sombart, W. (1924). *Der Moderne Capitalismus* (Munich).

Spooner, C. F. (1968). 'The Economy of Europe 1559–1609' in Wernham, R. B. (ed.), *The New Cambridge Modern History* Vol. III, (Cambridge).

Spradley, J. P. (1972). *Guests Never Leave Hungry: The Autobiography of James Sewid* (Montreal).

Spufford, P. (1988). *Money and its Use in Medieval Euope* (Cambridge).

Steel, A. (1954). *The Receipt of the Exchequer 1377–1485* (Cambridge).

Stenton, F. M. (1946). *Anglo-Saxon England* (Oxford).

Stephens, R. (1976). *The Arabs' New Frontier* (London).

Strasser, D. (1980). *The Finances of Europe* (Brussels).

Sutherland, C. H. V. (1973). *English Coinage 600–1900* (London).

Swift, J. (1724). *Drapier's Letters* (Dublin).

Sykes, J. (1926). *The Amalgamation Movement in English Banking* (London).

Tallman, E. (1988). 'The role of the Regional Clearing Houses', *Federal Reserve Bank of Atlanta Economic Review* (December).

Tawney, R. H. (1954). 'The rise of the gentry' in E. M. Carus-Wilson.

Thomas, I. I. (1976). 'The Expansion of American Banks from London to the Regions' (unpublished Ph.D. thesis, University of Wales, Cardiff).

Thompson, J. D. A. (1956). *Inventory of British Coin Hoards* AD 600–1500 (Oxford).

Thorne, W. J. (1962), *Banking* (London).

Tooke, T. and Newmarch W. (1857). *A History of Prices and of the State of the Circulation from 1792 to 1856* (London).

Toynbee, A. J. (1960). *A Study of History* (Oxford).

Trevelyan, G. M. (1938). *The English Revolution 1688–9* (London).

Trued, M. N. and Mikesell, R. F. (1955). 'Post-war bilateral payments agreements', *Princeton Studies in International Finance*, 4 (April).

Unwin, G. (1927). *Studies in Economic History* (London).

Usher, A. P. (1962). *A History of Mechanical Inventions* (Cambridge, Mass.).

Usher, D. (1966). *Rich and Poor Countries: A Study of the Problems of Comparisons of Real Incomes* (London).

Veblen, T. (1899). *Theory of the Leisure Class* (Chicago).

Vilar, P. (1976). *A History of Gold and Money 1450–1920*, English edn. (London).

Viner, J. (1937). *Studies in the Theory of International Trade* (London).

Whale, P. B. (1930, 1968). *Joint-Stock Banking in Germany* (London).

White, L. (1984). *Free Banking in Britain, 1800–1845* (Cambridge).

Wiebe, G. (1895). *Zur Geschichte der Preisrevolution des xvi und xvii Jahrhunderts* (Leipzig).

Wilson, C. (1965). *England's Apprenticeship 1603–1765* (London).

Wilson, J. S. G. (1986). *Banking Policy and Structure: A Comparative Analysis* (London).

Withers, H. (1909). *The Meaning of Money* (London).

Woodward, G. W. O. (1966). *The Dissolution of the Monasteries* (London).

Yamey, B. S. (1982). *Further Essays in the History of Accounting* (London).

Yang, Lein Sheng (1952). *Money and Credit in China* (Cambridge, Mass.).

Yeager, L. B. (1975). *International Monetary Relations in Theory, History and Practice* (New York).

Youings, J. (1984). *Sixteenth-Century England* (London).

Yule, H. (1914, 1967). *Cathay and the Way Thither*, Hakluyt Society (Liechtenstein).

Ziegler, D. (1990). *Central Bank, Peripheral Industry: the Bank of England in the Provinces, 1826–1913* (Leicester).

Ziegler, P. (1988). *The Sixth Great Power: Barings 1762–1929* (London).

Zimmern, A. (1961). *The Greek Commonwealth* (Oxford).

Reviews and reports by banks and other financial institutions in the private sector, some published for the best part of a century, provide an invaluable source of information, especially for financial aspects of developments in the twentieth century.

Official reports and publications

These are arranged chronologically from 1717. The place of publication, except where otherwise indicated, is Great Britain.

1 Gold and Silver Coin: Report of Sir Isaac Newton to the House of Commons, 1717.

2 Report on Public Credit, Alexander Hamilton, USA, 1790.

3 Report on a National Bank, Alexander Hamilton, USA, 1790.

4 Commercial Credit: Select Committee Report, 1793.

5 The High Price of Gold Bullion: Select Committee Report, 1810.

6 Report on the State of the Coin: House of Commons, 1816.

7 Report of the House of Lords Committee on Promissory Notes under £5, 1826–7.

8 Joint Stock Banks: Select Committee Report, 1837–8.

9 Banks of Issue: Select Committee Report, 1840.

10 Bank Act of 1844 . . . and the Causes of the Recent Commercial Distress: Select Committee Report, 1857–8.

11 Report of the Treasury Committee into the Money Order System and the Proposed Scheme of Post Office Notes, 1876.

12 Royal Commission on the Relative Values of the Precious Metals: 1st, 2nd and 3rd Reports, 1887–8.

13 Report on Indian Coinage and Exchanges (Herschell Report), 1893.

14 Report on Indian Coinage and Exchanges (Fowler Report), 1898.

15 National Monetary Commission Reports USA (N. W. Aldrich et al.) 1908–12.

16 Report of the Committee on Currency in British Colonial Africa (Emmott Report), 1912.

17 Report on Money Trusts (Pujo Report), USA, 1913.

18 Royal Commission on Indian Currency and Finance (Chamberlain Report), 1913.

19 Report of the Committee of the Treasury on Bank Amalgamations (Colwyn Report, Cd 9052), 1918.

20 Interim Report of the Committee on Currency and Foreign Exchanges (Cunliffe, Cd 9182), 1918.

21 Final Report of the Committee on Currency and Foreign Exchanges (Cunliffe, Cmd 464) 1919.

22 Report of the Committee of the Treasury on the Currency and Bank of England Note Issues (Cmd 2393), 1925.

23 Report on National Debt and Taxation (Colwyn Report, Cmd 2800), 1927.

24 Report on Finance and Industry (Macmillan Report, Cmd 3897), 1931.

25 Report of the Royal Commission on the Geographical Distribution of the Industrial Population (Barlow Report, Cmd 6153), 1940.

26 International Currency Experience: Lessons of the Interwar Period, League of Nations, Geneva, 1944.

27 Report on Banking in Nigeria (Paton Report), 1948.

28 Banking Conditions in the Gold Coast and the Question of Setting up a Central Bank (Trevor Report), 1952.

29 Enquiry Concerning Setting up a Central Bank in Nigeria (Fisher Report), 1953.

30 The Sterling Area: Bank for International Settlements, Basle, 1953.

31 Proposals for a Nigerian Central Bank (Loynes Report), 1957.

32 Report on the Financial Situation (Rueff Report), Paris, 1958.

33 First and Second Reports of the Council on Prices, Productivity and Incomes, 1958.

34 Report on the Establishment of a Stock Exchange in Nigeria (Barback Report), Lagos, 1959.

35 Third Report of the Council on Prices, Productivity and Incomes, 1959: (see also Fourth Report, 1961).

36 Report on the Working of the Monetary System (Radcliffe Report, Cmnd 827), 1959.

37 Commission on Money and Credit: Their Influence on Jobs, Prices and Incomes, New Jersey, 1961.

38 Commission on Money and Credit: Stabilisation Policies, New Jersey, 1963.

39 Report of the Committee of Enquiry into Decimal Currency (Halsbury Report, Cmnd 2145), 1963.

40 Report on the Rate of Interest on Building Society Mortgages (Cmnd 3136), 1966.

41 Report on Bank Interest Rates (Cmnd 499), Belfast, 1966.

42 Report on Bank Charges (Cmnd 3292), 1967.

43 Capital Markets Study: Committee for Invisible Transactions (sic), OECD, Paris, 1967.

44 The Basle Facility and the Sterling Area (Cmnd 3787), 1968.

45 Barclays Bank Ltd, Lloyds Bank Ltd, Martins Bank Ltd: A Report on the Proposed Merger, Monopolies Commission, 1968.

46 First Report from the Select Committee on Nationalised Industries: Bank of England, 1970.

47 Report on the Realisation by Stages of European Economic and Monetary Union (Werner Report), Luxembourg, 1970.

48 Report of the Committee on the Financial Facilities for Small Firms (Economists' Advisory Group), 1971.

49 Report of the Committee of Inquiry on Small Firms (Bolton Report, Cmnd 4811), 1971.

50 Report of the Committee on Consumer Credit (Crowther Report, Cmnd 4596), 1971.

51 Competition and Credit Control, Bank of England, 1971.

52 Report of the Committee to Review National Savings (Page Report, Cmnd 5273), 1973.

53 Public Expenditure, Inflation and the Balance of Payments: Ninth Report of the Expenditure Committee (HC 328), 1974.

54 The Attack on Inflation (Cmnd 6151), 1975.

55 The Licensing and Supervision of Deposit-Taking Institutions (Cmnd 6584), 1976.
56 Monetary Control (Cmnd 7858), 1980.
57 Report of the Committeee to Review the Functioning of Financial Institutions (Wilson Report, Cmnd 7937), 1980.
58 Monetary Policy: Third Report from the Treasury and Civil Service Committee (3 vols.), 1981.
59 *Global 2000*: United Nations, 1982.
60 The Hong Kong and Shanghai Banking Corporation, the Standard Chartered Bank Ltd, the Royal Bank of Scotland Group Ltd: Report on the Proposed Mergers, Monopolies and Mergers Commission, 1982.
61 The European Monetary System: Report of the Select Committee of the House of Lords, 1983.
62 Report of the Committee to Consider the System of Banking Supervision (Leigh-Pemberton Report, Cmnd 9550), 1985.
63 Report of the Committee on Economic and Monetary Union in the European Community (Delors Report), Brussels, 1989.
64 Report of the Committee on Banking Services: Law and Practice (Jack Report, Cm 622), 1989.
65 The European Financial Common Market: Report for the European Parliament, Luxembourg 1989.
66 Report of the House of Lords Select Committee on European Monetary and Political Union (Aldington Report), 1990.
67 *One Market, One Money*: European Commission, Luxembourg, 1990.
68 Report of the Inquiry into the Supervision of the Bank of Credit and Commerce International (Bingham Report), 1992.
69 The Cees Maas Report of the Expert Group on the Changeover to the Single Currency, Luxembourg, 10 May 1995.
70 'One Currency for Europe: Green Paper on the Practical Arrangements for the Introduction of the Single Currency', Luxembourg, 31 May 1995.
71 Report of the Board of Banking Supervision into the Circumstances of the Collapse of Barings. HMSO, July 1995.

Among the most useful of official periodical publications are the following: *Bank of England Quarterly Bulletins* (*BEQB*); monthly reports of the Deutsche Bundesbank; those of the various banks of the US Federal Reserve System and the annual reports of the Bank for International Settlements. The International Monetary Fund and World Bank provide an indispensable, authoritative and exhaustive source of information both quantitative and qualitative. In addition, the European

Commission publishes a stream of reports and reviews on monetary and financial issues.

Illustrative of a number of books giving annotated collections and summaries of official and unofficial reports and statistics are:

Capie, F. and Webber, A., (1984) *Monetary Statistics of the UK, 1870–1983.* (London).

Gregory, T. E. (1929). *Select Statutes, Documents and Reports Relating to British Banking, 1832–1928* (Cambridge).

Shaw, W. A. (1896). *Select Tracts and Documents Illustrative of English Monetary History, 1626–1730* (London).

Tawney, R. H. and Power, E. (1924). *Tudor Economic Documents* (London).

Thirsk, J. and Cooper, J. P. (1972). *Seventeenth Century Economic Documents* (Oxford).

There are welcome signs that the relative scarcity of publications on monetary history, to which attention was drawn in the Preface, is at last being addressed by the appearance of a number of recent books and journals. Typical of the latter is the *Financial History Review*, first published in April 1994.

Index

Rome, economy: Augustus to
Aurelian, 93–9; Constantine
onwards, 105–11; Diocletian,
99–105; Graeco-Roman monetary
expansion, 108–11; inflation,
94–104, 107, 110–11; taxation,
94–5, 96, 103–4, 106
Roosevelt, President Franklin D.,
510–11
Rose, George, 323, 334
Rostow, W.W., 599, 607
Rothschild family, 308, 347–8, 352,
484, 558–9
Rotterdam Bank, 552
Rottier brothers, 242
Royal Bank of Scotland, 275–6, 277,
411
Royal Exchange, foundation, 232
Royal Mint, 37, 206; and Tealby
find, 141; contracts out copper
coinage, 293–4; extension, under
Elizabeth I, 205; finds copper
coinage undignified, 208, 244;
location of, 146–7; new mint 1810,
294; Trial of the Pyx, 145–6; recent
statistics, 659–660
RTGS, 661
Rueff Report, 564

savings institutions: Britain, 332–9,
410–11; Europe, 333; Germany,
570–1; Japan, 583; Scotland,
333–4, 337; Singapore, 628; US,
425, 533–4
savings ratio, 408–10, 578, 670
sceattas, 122–3
Schacht, Hjalmar, 504, 574, 575
Schaaffenhausen Bank, 566, 568
Scotland, monetary/banking
development, 271–8, 306, 321; Ayr
Bank, failure, 277–8; Bank of
Scotland, 238, 271, 272–5;
banknote issue, 276–7, 308, 315,
316; branch banking, 276; City of
Glasgow Bank, failure, 319;
currency, 271, 275; Darien
Company, 272–4; English
branches, 321, 411; money supply,
278–9; origin of the overdraft,
275–6; other banks, 276–7; Royal
Bank of Scotland, 275–6; savings
banks, 333–4, 337; union with
England, 208, 271, 274–5, 308
Scott, Sir Walter, 308
Securities Exchange Commission,
US, 433, 512
share transactions, Rome, 92; USA,
'on margin', 509
Shaw–McKinnon thesis, 616–19
Shay's Rebellion 1786, 466
shilling (testoon), first actual coin,
191
Ship Bank (Aberystwyth), 288
Ship Bank (Glasgow), 276
ship money, 210–11
silver coinage, Britain: debasement
under Henry VIII, 199–200; Offa's
penny, 123–7; predominates, 122,
207; recoinage 1696, 244–7;
shortages/substitutes, 19th C.,
294–6; Tudor/Stuart
denominations, 207–8
silver/gold relationship, see
bimetallism
silver mines, Bohemia, 459; Laurion,
69–70; Mount Pangaeus, 84;
Potosi, 187–9; Spain, 93; Tyrol,
179; USA, 494–5
silver movement, US, 495–6, 515
SIMEX, 664–6
Singapore, currency and banking,
625–9, 664–6
Single European Act 1987, 448
single currency, 454, 658, 662–3
Sinking Fund, 269
slaves: role in Greek economy, 68–9;
trading, 264
small and medium-sized enterprises
(SMEs), investment funds for, 379,
403–4, 614–15, 624
Smiles, Samuel, 326
Smith, Adam, 17, 231–2, 238, 279,
281, 463, 549, 555, 599, 629
Smith, Sidney, 298–9
Smith's Bank, 286
Smithsonian Agreement of 1971, 521